RECONSTRUCTING GENDER

TITLES OF RELATED INTEREST FROM MAYFIELD:

Susan Frank Ballentine and Jessica Barksdale Inclán, *Diverse Voices of Women*

Virginia Cyrus, *Experiencing Race, Class, and Gender in the United States*, 2nd edition

Jo Freeman, *Women: A Feminist Perspective*, 5th edition

Amy Kesselman, Lily D. McNair, and Nancy Schniedewind, *Women: Images and Realities: A Multicultural Anthology*

Hilary M. Lips, *Sex and Gender: An Introduction*, 3rd edition, and *Women, Men, and Power*

Sheila Ruth, *Issues in Feminism: An Introduction to Women's Studies*, 3rd edition

Virginia Sapiro, *Women in American Society: An Introduction to Women's Studies*, 3rd edition

Julia T. Wood, editor, *Gendered Relationships*

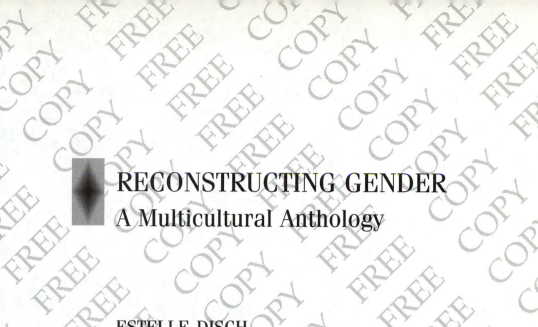

RECONSTRUCTING GENDER
A Multicultural Anthology

ESTELLE DISCH
University of Massachusetts Boston

MAYFIELD PUBLISHING COMPANY
Mountain View, Califorina
London • Toronto

Library of Congress Cataloging-in-Publication Data
Reconstructing gender : a multicultural anthology / [edited by]
   Estelle Disch.
         p.   cm.
      Includes index.
      ISBN 1–55934-579-9
      1. Sex role. 2. Masculinity (Psychology) 3. Femininity
(Psychology) 4. Women—Psychology. 5. Socialization. I. Disch,
Estelle.
   HQ1075.R43   1996
   305.3—dc20   96-17516
                                                                                  CIP

Manufactured in the United States of America
10 9 8 7 6 5 4 3 2 1

Mayfield Publishing Company
1280 Villa Street
Mountain View, California 94041

Sponsoring editor, Serina Beauparlant; production, Publication Services; copyeditor,
Katherine Coyle; art director, Jeanne M. Schreiber; text designers, Linda M.
Robertson and Dorothy Evans; cover design, Donna Davis; manufacturing manager,
Randy Hurst. The text was set in 10/12 Book Antiqua by Publication Services and
printed on 45# Ecolocote by Malloy Lithographing, Inc.

Cover image: Luz Inéz Mercier/Praxis International Art

 This book is printed on acid-free, recycled paper.

Contents

Preface

Afew years ago, in my undergraduate Sociology of Gender course,[1] I asked the class to sit in small groups and identify gender-related problems that each student was currently facing and that were not too personal to discuss in the class. I then asked the students to assess to what extent their problems were private troubles, that is, specific to themselves as individuals, or public issues, reflective of wider issues in the social order and experienced by many people.[2] When the groups reported back, two men responded, "We were raised never to hit girls, and now with the women's movement, we want to know whether or not that's OK." Their question was serious, and the class exploded. Many women in the room became very upset and started yelling at the two men. (I later learned that at least a third of the women in the room had been raped.) I was caught off guard and realized that the course was not designed to effectively address the various issues embedded in the men's question. I did not have nearly enough material on men's socialization and behavior. I was particularly concerned about providing students with enough information to help them begin to make sense of the high rates of men's violence toward women and toward each other.

In my search for better materials about men's socialization, I found a growing literature on men's studies to accompany the already huge literature on women's studies and the sociology of gender. But my favorite articles were scattered in a wide range of sources. Although some excellent anthologies are available about and by women and men separately,[3] no one volume appropriate for use in a social science course gives substantial attention to both genders. Two excellent anthologies are available on race, class, and gender, but the articles do not consistently address gender.[4] Thus, this book is designed to meet the needs of faculty who want to teach about both women and men from a multicultural perspective but want to use one anthology instead of two. I define *multicultural* broadly to include the perspectives and experiences of a wide range of people within the context of power and inequality.

The creation of this book has been made possible by the explosion of work by and about people of color, people of various ethnicities, gay men, lesbians, bisexuals, transgendered people, people with disabilities, and working-class people. Many of the readings included here are ones that colleagues and I have used in classrooms with success. By success, I mean that many students have become engaged with the material in various ways: becoming excited or angered by the ideas expressed, talking with friends and family about the material, making sense of their own experience in relation to the authors' experiences, feeling excited to learn more about a particular issue, or becoming politically involved in response to what they are learning. I teach in a way that encourages interaction among students,[5] and I am particularly committed to using articles that stimulate discussion. I have also included some recent articles not yet tried in the classroom because they address important issues that are just now receiving increased attention, such as transgender issues and new work in men's studies (on men of color, men with disabilities, and men in families). I welcome readers' feedback about what works in classrooms and what doesn't.

This book also emerges, in part, from questions and concerns that I've experienced in my own life, especially my own experience growing up in a sexist, racist, anti-Semitic, white, economically privileged, Protestant family. With three older brothers and a sports-oriented father who was a physician, I often felt like I was immersed in a male club. This club demanded rigid gender expectations of my brothers; my least-athletic brother was brutally teased and called a sissy because of his lack of athletic ability, his pain while watching my father and my other brothers shoot ducks, his interest in music, his ability to cry, and his chubby body. I watched my father rage when my aunt bought that particular brother a pink shirt. My survival strategy in this system was to attempt to fit into the male club. By about age seven I had learned to shoot frogs with a .22 rifle, to clean fish, to brace myself against the pain I felt watching a duck thrash in the water after being shot, to enjoy watching baseball games (or to pretend that I did), and to be otherwise tough and strong.

I also learned about racist and anti-Semitic attitudes in my family. I can remember my grandmother expressing disapproval that my best friend was Jewish and my father telling me an anti-Semitic "joke" that I repeated to my best friend, who didn't find it funny; unfortunately, we had no skills at age ten or so to discuss what was wrong with the "joke." And I can remember my father complaining about the presence of Black baseball players, actors, and newscasters on TV—"That man's got a white man's job. . . ." Luckily, my mother provided a contrast to my father's views. She did not participate in his racist and anti-Semitic discussions, spoke freely about her poverty-stricken origins, and left me with the opportunity to question his values.

I am impressed to this day at the contradictions embedded in what my father expected of boys and men. On the one hand, he seemed at his happiest in the all-male hunting and fishing cultures in which he spent as much free time as he could. When groups of men went hunting, they slept in close quarters, spent days together hunting in tiny gunning boats or hiding in duck blinds, cooked elaborate meals at the end of the day, and kept house— all with no women present. (I begged to go on these trips but was barred.) On the other hand, his homophobia was always there, levying disrespect at any boy or man who might be "too feminine," who might acknowledge his love for a man, or who might choose to make a life with men doing much of what my father, his friends, and my brothers did on hunting trips.

Another personal interest that informs my selections for this anthology is my knowledge about male violence and sexual abuse toward boys, girls, women, and men. I continue to be baffled at our inability to effectively prevent that abuse. I am not so much shocked by the facts (I have accepted them after years of awareness), but by the entrenched system of violence and domination that teaches new generations of people, especially men, how to be violent and oppressive. For the past twelve years, I have worked with survivors of sexual abuse committed by health care and mental health care providers and clergy; I have been struck by the fact that the vast majority of offenders—against both men and women—are men.[6] Although offenses of this type are brutally damaging when perpetrated by members of either gender, the overwhelming imbalance toward male perpetrators has led me to wonder what has caused so many of them to be so exploitative or violent. I am reminded of a very disturbing photo essay of men who had attended a residential religious school in which male clergy physically and sexually abused many of the boys. One of the men shown tells of the abuse he suffered as a child and reports that when he learned that his younger brother was about to be put in the same school, he killed his brother to save him from the abuse.[7] It appears that the only way he had learned to resolve brutal situations was to be brutal himself.

I am also informed here by twenty-five years of working collectively with others: ten years working with white, almost exclusively heterosexual women and men in alternative mental health centers; ten years in a feminist therapy collective where a group of white, heterosexual women and lesbians learned to work closely together; and in working groups at the University of Massachusetts Boston, where faculty, students, and staff built a multicultural, broad-based coalition to win the passage of a diversity requirement for undergraduate students.[8] I have learned that diverse women and men can work together using decision-making processes in which conflict is discussed, compromises are negotiated, and leadership and rewards are shared. If people are committed to communicating, then differences of gender, race, culture, class, sexual orientation, disability, and age can be addressed and dealt with in order to accomplish common goals.

I am also concerned in this anthology with the entrenchment of privilege. I have observed how much time and attention it has taken me to unravel my own prejudices and become aware of my privileges, and I wonder how we will ever construct a humane social order when it is so difficult for those with privilege to see how caught we are in its cushioned web. Even with an education that communicated democratic values, a mother who worked full time and talked extensively about growing up poor, an older brother who mentored me into liberal/radical views, and a feminist movement and support system that has especially supported my antiracist and multicultural activism, I still find it difficult to stay fully conscious of some of the oppressive attitudes I have learned. Although I have analyzed enough of my socialization to feel fully capable of working on my attitudes and to apologize for any lingering insensitivities, I believe that I will be working on this for the rest of my life. I hope the readings that follow will help those with more privilege become clear about what that means for them, that those with less privilege will find inspiration for empowerment, and that both groups will find ways to work toward a more egalitarian social order—one in which all people will have an opportunity to work with others in shared ways, in which real community can evolve from positions of equal respect, and in which all people enjoy basic human rights free of poverty, violence, preventable illness, and discrimination.

Many people have helped with this book. Serina Beauparlant, my editor at Mayfield, approached this project with enthusiasm and support throughout its birth and development. Becky Thompson of Wesleyan University convinced me that I should do the book and provided ongoing support, feedback, creative suggestions, and editing as it evolved; and our ongoing discussions about racism and teaching over the years have contributed to my thinking in many ways. The following reviewers made helpful, constructive suggestions: Tom Gershick, Illinois State University; Sandra Gill, Gettysburg College; C. Lee Harrington, Miami University; Elizabeth Higginbotham, University of Memphis; Jody Miller, University of Southern California; Patricia Murphy, State University of New York–Geneseo; Jodi O'Brien, Seattle University; Christy M. Ponticelli, University of South Florida; Don Sabo, D'Youville College; Jennifer Turpin, University of San Francisco; Christine L. Williams, University of Texas–Austin; and Anna Zajicek, University of Arkansas. Mary Jane Treacy of Simmons College and Gerry Gomez of the University of Massachusetts Boston offered me access to their extensive libraries of books on gender, sexual orientation, and sexuality. Tim Buckley at the University of Massachusetts Boston shared his experience and the reading materials from his course, Men in America. Other friends, family, and colleagues provided direct or indirect suggestions for readings or other support: Edith Benveniste, Larry Blum, Gilda Bruckman and Laura Zimmerman of New Words Bookstore, Elly Bulkin, Connie Chan, Charlotte Corbett, Bob Disch, Cynthia Enloe, dian fitzpatrick, Anne Foxx, Susan Gore, Jean Hardisty, Carol Henry, Kathleen Kelley, Esther Kingston-Mann, Cal Larson, Elaine Morse, Federico, Naïma, and Layla Muchnik, Craig Norberg-Bohm, Denise Patmon, Norma Schultz, Tim Sieber, James Williams, and Vivian Zamel. Laura Cohen provided invaluable research assistance. Julie Wildhaber, April Wells-Hayes, Pamela Trainer, Brian Pecko, Jeanne Schreiber, and Jon Silvers at Mayfield Publishing kept the project moving smoothly and on schedule. The staff at Publication Services—Jan Fisher, Robyn Stone, Dorothy Evans, Katherine Coyle, and Lisa Satterthwaite—provided excellent copyediting and other support. My compañera and intellectual colleague, Rita Arditti, talked with me extensively about the book as it evolved, helping me to clarify my thoughts and lending me numerous relevant books from her library on feminist and multicultural studies. Finally, thanks go to my best teachers—the terrific students at the University of Massachusetts Boston, who frequently challenge and always engage me.

NOTES

1. This was a course at the University of Massachusetts Boston, a public urban university with about 12,000 students, all of whom commute.

2. The class had read an excerpt from C. Wright Mills, *The Sociological Imagination* (NY: Oxford University Press, 1959), pp. 5–9 in which Mills discusses private troubles and public issues.

3. Anthologies regarding women (or primarily women) are Margaret L. Andersen and Patricia Hill Collins, eds., *Race, Class, and Gender: An Anthology*, 2nd ed. (Belmont, CA: Wadsworth Publishing Company, 1995); Jo Freeman, ed., *Women: A Feminist Perspective*, 5th ed. (Mountain View, CA: Mayfield, 1995); Laurel Richardson and Verta Taylor, eds., *Feminist Frontiers III* (New York: McGraw-Hill, 1993).

   Anthologies regarding men (or primarily men): Franklin Abbott, ed., *Boyhood, Growing Up Male: A Multicultural Anthology* (Freedom, CA: The Crossing Press, 1993); Harry Brod, ed., *The Making of Masculinities: The New Men's Studies* (Boston: Allen & Unwin, 1978); Michael S. Kimmel and Michael A. Messner, eds., *Men's Lives* 3rd ed. (Boston: Allyn & Bacon, 1995); Ronald F. Levant and William S. Pollack, eds., *A New Psychology of Men* (New York: Basic Books, 1995).

   A recent anthology designed for composition courses that does foreground gender and that includes material about both women and men, is Karin Bergstrom Costello, ed., *Gendered Voices: Readings from the American Experience* (New York: Harcourt Brace, 1996).

4. Virginia Cyrus, ed., *Experiencing Race, Class, and Gender in the United States* (Mountain View, CA: Mayfield, 1993); Paula S. Rothenberg, ed., *Race, Class, and Gender in the United States*, 3rd ed. (New York: St. Martin's Press, 1995).

5. This teaching method is described in Becky Thompson and Estelle Disch, "Feminist, Anti-Racist, Anti-Oppression Teaching: Two White Women's Experience," in *Radical Teacher*, 41, Spring 1992: 4–10.

6. In a study of survivors of sexual professional abuse, in which I am the principal investigator, 88 percent of the women and 94 percent of the men were abused by men.

7. Photo essay by E. Jane Mundy, "Wounded Boys, Courageous Men," displayed at the Linkup Conference, Chicago, September 1–4, 1995.

8. I have documented this work in an essay entitled, "The Politics of Curricular Change: Establishing a Diversity Requirement at the University of Massachusetts at Boston," in Becky W. Thompson and Sangeeta Tyagi, eds., *Beyond a Dream Deferred: Multicultural Education and the Politics of Excellence* (Minneapolis: University of Minnesota Press, 1993), pp. 195–213.

About the Contributors

Paula Gunn Allen is Professor of English at UCLA. She was awarded the Native American Prize for Literature in 1990. That same year her anthology of short stories, *Spider Woman's Granddaughters,* was awarded the American Book Award, sponsored by the Before Columbus Foundation, and the Susan Koppleman Award. A major Native American poet, writer, and scholar, she's published seven volumes of poetry, a novel, a collection of essays, and two anthologies. Her prose and poetry appear widely in anthologies, journals, and scholarly publications.

Robert L. Allen is a teacher, writer, and community activist who is deeply interested in men's issues. Since 1986 he has worked with the Oakland Men's Project, a community education organization that conducts work-shops dealing with male violence, sexism, racism, and homophobia. At the University of California at Berkeley, he teaches African American and Ethnic Studies and a new course called "Men of Color." Senior Editor of *The Black Scholar* journal, Allen is also coeditor of a recent book titled *Brotherman: The Odyssey of Black Men in America.* He is the father of a son, Casey, who is a junior-college student studying horticulture.

Gloria Anzaldúa writes fiction and nonfiction, including social theory, with intentional reference to her multiple identities—Chicana, *tejana* (Indian), les-bian, feminist, and poet. She has taught and lectured at many institutions, including the University of Texas, San Francisco State, and Vermont College. The selections here are from *Borderlands/La Frontera: The New Mestiza* (1987). She is the editor of *Making Face, Making Soul/Haciendo Caras* (1990) and coed-itor (with Cherrié Moraga) of *This Bridge Called My Back* (1981).

Rita Arditti is an Argentine Sephardic Jew living and working in the United States since 1965. She is on the faculty of the Union Institute, a nonresidential Ph.D. program for adult learners interested in doing interdisciplinary work. Her academic background is in biology. She has been living with breast can-cer for twenty-two years and is one of the founders of the Women's Community Cancer Project (WCCP) in Cambridge, MA. For information about the Project, write to WCCP, c/o the Women's Center, 46 Pleasant Street, Cambridge, MA, 02139.

Ruth Atkin is a middle class, Ashkenazi Jewish feminist activist born in the Midwest. She has been involved in progressive Jewish publishing since 1979 and is a founding and current editor of *Gesher's* successor, *Bridges: A Journal for Jewish Feminists and Our Friends.* On weekdays Ruth works as a medical social worker in an outpatient clinic serving veterans.

xvii

Byllye Y. Avery is founder and executive Director of the National Black Women's Health Project in Atlanta, Georgia.

Tommi Avicolli has adopted his mother's maiden name and is now using the name Tommi Avicolli Mecca. He is a working-class, Southern Italian American, queer writer, activist, and performer living in San Francisco. He has recently written and performed *Il Disgraziato* (the shameful one), a play about coming out gay.

Evelyn L. Barbee is a Black feminist nurse anthropologist who was educated at Teachers College, Columbia University and at the University of Washington. Her writings are published in anthropology and nursing journals. Her current research interests are cultural strategies used by women of color to deal with dysphoria, and violence against women of color. She is currently at the School of Nursing at Boston College.

Edward Broadbent is President of the International Centre for Human Rights and Democratic Development in Montreal. From 1975 until 1989, he was the federated leader of Canada's New Democratic Party. In 1978 he was elected vice-president of Socialist International and was particularly involved in efforts to bring peace to Central America. Before entering active politics, he was Professor of Political Science at York University, Toronto.

Harry Brod is assistant professor in the Philosphy Department at the University of Delaware. He is editor of *The Making of Masculinities: The New Men's Studies, A Mensch Among Men: Explorations in Jewish Masculinity,* and most recently (with Michael Kaufman), *Theorizing Masculinities.* He is author of *Hegel's Philosophy of Politics.* He is a spokesperson for the National Organization for Men Against Sexism. Born in Berlin as a child of temporary (i.e., died prematurely) Holocaust survivors, he grew up in New York City and currently lives in Philadelphia with his family.

Connie Chan was born in Hong Kong, moved to Hawaii as a child, and now lives in Boston, Massachusetts. Bilingual and bicultural in her upbringing, she learned to experience the world with a dual perspective. Currently she is co-director of the Institute for Asian American Studies and associate professor of human services at the University of Massachusetts Boston. She continues to work within Asian American communities to provide access for culturally-appropriate health services.

Joan C. Chrisler is associate professor of psychology at Connecticut College. She earned her doctorate in experimental psychology at Yeshiva University while working nights as a waitress and serving as a shop steward in the hotel and restaurant workers union. Dr. Chrisler has published extensively on the psychology of women and women's health issues, and is particularly known for her work on weight and eating behavior and on psychosocial aspects of the menstrual cycle. She is co-editor of three books: *Lectures on the*

Psychology of Women, Variations on a Theme: Diversity and the Psychology of Women, and *New Directions in Feminist Psychology.*

Judith Ortiz Cofer grew up in Puerto Rico and New Jersey. She is the author of *The Line of the Sun,* a novel, *Silent Dancing,* a collection of essays and poetry, *Terms of Survival* and *Reaching for the Mainland,* two books of poetry, and *The Latin Deli: Prose and Poetry.* Her work has appeared in *Glamour, The Georgia Review, Kenyon Review* and other journals. She has been anthologized in *The Best American Essays, The Norton Book of Women's Lives, The Pushcart Prize,* and the *O. Henry Prize Stories.* She has received fellowships from the National Endowment for the Arts and the Witter Bynner Foundation for Poetry. She is an associate professor of English and creative writing at the University of Georgia. Her most recent book is a collection of short stories, *An Island Like You: Stories of the Barrio,* Orchard Books (New York, 1995).

Patricia Hill Collins received B.A. and Ph.D. degrees from Brandeis University and an M. A. T. degree from Harvard University. While her specialties in sociology include such diverse areas as sociology of knowledge, organizational theory, social stratification, and work and occupations, her research and scholarship have dealt primarily with issues of gender, race, and social class, specifically relating to African American women. Her first book, *Black Feminist Thought: Knowledge, Consciousness, and the Politics of Empowerment,* published in 1990, has won many awards, including the C. Wright Mills Award. Her second book, *Race, Class, and Gender: An Anthology* (edited with Margaret Andersen) is widely used in undergraduate classrooms throughout the United States.

David Deitcher is a gay rights activist and member of ACT UP (AIDS Coalition to Unleash Power). He edited a book on the gay rights movement entitled *The Question of Equality* (Scribner, 1995) to accompany the TV documentary series of the same name.

Edward Donnerstein is professor of communication and psychology at the University of California, Santa Barbara. A social psychologist, he received his Ph.D. in psychology in 1972. Prior to assuming his position at the University of California in 1986, he taught at the University of Wisconsin and held visiting positions at the University of Lethbridge and at Beijing University, China. He has served on the editorial boards of a number of academic journals in both psychology and communication. His major research interests are in mass-media violence, in particular, sexual violence, as well as mass media policy. He has published over 125 scientific articles in these general areas. His most recent books include *The Question of Pornography: Research Findings and Policy Implications,* with Daniel Linz and Steven Penrod, and *Big World, Small Screen: The Role of Television in American Society.*

Diane Dujon teaches welfare organizing and is an administrator at the College of Public and Community Service of the University of Massachusetts Boston. She is co-founder of Advocacy for Resources for Modern Survival, a Boston welfare-rights group.

Gerald Early is the director of the Department of African-American Studies at Washington University in St. Louis. He has written a book on Countee Cullen and edited *Speech and Power,* an anthology of African-American essays. He is also the author of *Tuxedo Junction,* a collection of essays on American culture, and *The Culture of Bruising: Essays on Prizefighting.* He is the recipient of a Whiting Writers' Award and a General Electric Foundation Award. He is a native of Philadelphia and is the father of two girls (near women) who are not Christians (much to his amusement), not jazz lovers (much to his dismay), and not likely to be professors (much to his relief).

Anne Finger is a writer of fiction and nonfiction whose work grapples most often with issues of disability and gender. She has published three books: a novel, *Bone Truth* (Coffee House Press), an autobiographical essay, *Past Due: A Story of Disability, Pregnancy, and Birth* (Seal Press), and a short story collection, *Basic Skills.*

Ben Fong-Torres is a journalist in the San Francisco Bay area. His most recent book is *The Rice Room: Growing Up Chinese-American.*

Clyde W. Franklin II is professor of sociology at the Ohio State University. His research focuses largely on black masculinity. His numerous publications include *The Changing Definition of Masculinity* and *Men and Society.*

Adriane Fugh-Berman, M.D., is on the board of the National Women's Health Network. She practices general medicine in Washington, D.C.

Rus Ervin Funk, currently 30 years old, wrote *Stopping Rape* when he was 28 because "there wasn't anything talking to men about what men can do to become involved in working against men's sexual violence." He has been involved in nonviolent direct action and community organizing for nearly fifteen years, now covering all kinds of issues: rape and sexism, racism, homophobia, peace and justice, and children's rights. Currently, he works in Baltimore at the Sexual Abuse Treatment Center where he works with sex offenders, and does community organizing. He also provides consultation to communities around the world on the issues described above, and was invited to Bosnia in 1993 to train Red Cross and UN personnel on working with male rape survivors and male significant others of the women who were being mass raped there. He lives in Washington, D.C., with his cat, Delta. He just completed a book of poetry, *On a Sojourn,* and another book, *Speaking of Justice.*

Kathleen Gerson is a professor of sociology at New York University, where she helped found the Women's and Gender Studies Program and currently directs the undergraduate program in sociology. Her most recent book, *No Man's Land: Men's Changing Commitments to Family and Work* (Basic Books, 1993), examines the transformation of men's lives in the wake of the gender revolution at home and at work. She is also the author of *Hard Choices: How Women Decide about Work, Career, and Motherhood* (University of California Press, 1985), which investigates how women choose between work and family commitments. She lives in Park Slope, Brooklyn with her husband, John Mollenkopf, and their teenage daughter, Emily.

J. William Gibson teaches sociology at California State Univeristy, Long Beach. He is the author of two books, *The Perfect War: Technowar in Vietnam* (1986) and *Warrior Dreams: Paramilitary Culture in Post-Vietnam America* (1994); he is co-editor of *Making War/Making Peace: Social Foundations of Violent Conflict* (1989).

David Frederick Gordon is an associate professor and chair of the Sociology Department at State University of New York, Geneseo. After he was treated for testicular cancer, he found that there was very little sociological research on the survivors of this disease. He decided that being both a sociologist interested in the self as well as a survivor put him in an unique position to conduct such a study. As a result of his research, he has gained a greater appreciation for the importance of gender and has gained some valuable insights into his own experiences with the disease and its aftermath.

Judy Gradford works with Transition House, a Cambridge, Massachusetts, battered-women's shelter. She is co-founder of Advocacy for Resources for Modern Survival, a Boston welfare-rights group.

Stan Gray worked as an assembler at Westinghouse in Hamilton, Ontario, Canada from 1973–1984, where he was the union health and safety representative and the shop steward. From 1984–1990, he was the director of a province-wide health and safety clinic sponsored by a number of unions. The clinic diagnosed industrial diseases and organized workers around job hazards such as asbestos, PCBs, and sexual harassment. Stan is currently living in Hamilton and works as an independent advocate for workers and unions on issues of health and safety, human rights, and workers' compensation.

Deborah Gregory is a contributing writer for *Essence* magazine. Her work has also appeared in *Vibe* magazine and *Entertainment Weekly*. She is biracial, single, 39 years old, lives in New York City, and grew up in the foster care system.

Theresa Halsey (Standing Rock Sioux) is a long-time community activist, mostly focusing on educational issues. She is currently director of the Title V American Indian Education Program with Boulder Valley (Colorado) School District.

Craig G. Harris is a journalist, poet, and fiction writer whose work has been published in *In the Life: A Black Gay Anthology, Gay Life,* and numerous other publications.

Christy Haubegger, a Mexican-American native of Houston, attended the University of Texas at Austin and received a B.A. in philosophy. She attended Stanford Law School and was president of her class. Frustrated with the lack of positive media portrayal of Latinas in the United States, she put her law degree under her bed to pursue the entrepreneurial venture of creating a magazine for women like herself. *Essence* magazine and Alegre Enterprises, of which Haubegger is the chief executive officer, formed a new joint venture, Latina Publications, to publish *Latina* magazine, the first bilingual lifestyle magazine for Latinas in the United States. The magazine is scheduled to make its debut on newsstands in May of 1996. Ms. Haubegger is single and lives in Manhattan.

Laura Hershey was a poster child for the Muscular Dystrophy Telethon, and today is a disability rights leader and poet . She educates and agitates whenever possible to promote the rights of people with disabilities. Her efforts have earned a Watson Fellowship, a Colorado College honorary degree, a World Institute on Disability Fellowship, and several trips to jail for acts of civil disobedience. Hershey's multi-media presentations with music, poetry, and video address the ways the disability rights movement has the potential to challenge, expand, and transform political action in the United States.

bell hooks is a writer and lecturer who speaks on issues of race, class, and gender. She teaches at City University of New York Graduate Center. Her books include *Ain't I a Woman, Feminist Theory,* and *Talking Back.* Her column, "Sisters of the Yam," appears monthly in Z magazine.

Nan D. Hunter is associate professor of law at Brooklyn Law School. She is a former lawyer for the American Civil Liberties Union, where she was a founding director of Projects on Lesbian and Gay Rights and AIDS. She is co-editor of *AIDS Agenda: Emerging Issues in Civil Rights* and co-author of *The Rights of Lesbians and Gay Men.*

Patricia Jacobs is a columnist for the *New York Post.*

M. Annette Jaimes has changed her name to Mariana Jaimes-Guerrero. She is an enrolled Juañeno/Yaqui and has been a writer and researcher for Women of All Red Nations (WARN), supporter of Indigenous Women's Network, and a board member of the American Indian Anti-Defamation Council. A former instructor with the Center for Studies of Ethnicity and Race in America at the Univeristy of Colorado, she was instrumental in developing the American Indian Studies Program on that campus. In addition to her many published articles on indigenous people, she is editor and contributor of *The State of Native North America* (South End Press), which was awarded a Gustavus Myers International Human Rights Award, and is author of *Native Womanism: Blueprint for a Global Revolution* (South End Press). Jaimes-Guerrero recently established the Center for Indigenous Global Studies.

Melanie Kay/Kantrowitz was born in 1945 in Brooklyn, NY and has worked in social change movements since the sixties. A graduate of the City College of New York, she earned her Ph.D. in Comparative Literature at the University of California at Berkeley. A writer, activist, and teacher, she lives in New York City where she is director of Jews for Racial and Economic Justice. She is author of *My Jewish Face & Other Stories,* co-editor of *The Tribe of Dina: A Jewish Woman's Anthology,* and former editor and publisher of *Sinister Wisdom,* a lesbian/feminist journal.

Leonard Kriegel, author of the novel *Quitting Time* and of a collection of essays, *Falling,* was a professor of English and director of the Center for Worker Education at the City University of New York.

Tracy Lai, a third-generation Chinese-American, was deeply involved in the Asian Pacific Student Movement at Brown University, the University of California at Berkeley, and the University of Washington. The essay in this volume evolved out of that political work and ongoing community organizing and dialogue. She is grateful to all the inspiring sisters who encouraged her to write and to speak out.

Daniel Linz is professor of communication and director of the Program in Law and Society at the University of California–Santa Barbara.

Marilyn Little earned a Ph.D. at the University of Minnesota and is currently at the Centre for Ecology and Spirituality in Ontario, Canada. A medical geographer by specialization, her research is primarily concerned with the political ecology of malnutrition. A recent publication is "Charity Versus Justice: The New World Order and the Old Problem of World Hunger," in *Eliminating Hunger in Africa* (eds. Newman and Griffith).

Audre Lorde, who passed away in 1992, grew up in the West Indian community of Harlem in the 1930s, the daughter of immigrants from Grenada. She attended Hunter College (later becoming professor of English there), ventured to the American expatriate community in Mexico, and participated in the Greenwich Village scene of the early 1950s. She is a major figure in the lesbian and feminist movements. Among her works are *Sister Outsider, Zami: A New Spelling of My Name, Uses of the Erotic, Chosen Poems Old and New, The Black Unicorn,* and *From a Land Where Other People Live.*

Barbara Macdonald is an Anglo European lesbian feminist theorist and lecturer. *Look Me in the Eye: Old Women, Aging, and Ageism* (Spinsters Ink, 1983), has recently appeared in an expanded edition and has been translated into Japanese. Her work is much more political than the essay in this volume suggests.

Nathan McCall grew up in Portsmouth, Virginia. He studied journalism at Norfolk State University after serving three years in prison. He reported for the *Virginian Pilot-Ledger Star* and the *Atlanta Journal-Constitution* before moving to *The Washington Post* in 1989.

Michael A. Messner played high school basketball, but then discovered as a college freshman that he was too short to play forward, too slow to play guard, but just the right size to warm the bench as his teammates played. Though today he still shoots some hoops, he spends the majority of his working hours as associate professor in the Department of Sociology and the

Program for the Study of Women and Men in Society at the University of Southern California. Messner is the author of *Power at Play: Sports and the Problem of Masculinity* (1992), co-author of *Sex, Violence, and Power in Sports: Rethinking Masculinity* (1994), and co-editor of *Men's Lives* (1995). He is the father of two young sons.

Roslyn Arlin Mickelson is associate professor sociology and adjunct associate professor of women's studies at the University of North Carolina at Charlotte. Her scholarly interests include the education of homeless children, educational policy, and the political economy of schooling—in particular, the ways that social class, race, and gender intersect and contribute to educational processes and outcomes. Her current research project is a National Science Foundation-supported investigation of business leaders and school reform.

Joan Nestle, 56, is an author, editor, archivist, and teacher. She is co-founder of the Lesbian Herstory Archives. In her writing, she explores the crossroads where desire, memory, and history meet. Her award-winning publications include *A Restricted Country* (Firebrand Books, 1987; Sheba Press, London, 1989; Pandora, London, 1996), *The Persistent Desire: A Femme-Butch Reader* (Alyson Publications, 1992), *Women on Women 1, 2, and 3* (Plume Books, 1990, 1993, 1996), and *Sister and Brother: Lesbians and Gay Men Talk about Their Lives Together* (Harper, San Francisco, 1965; Cassell, London, 1996), co-edited with John Preston. For thirty years, Nestle taught writing in the SEEK Program at Queens College, City University of New York. In different decades, she has called herself different things—queer, gay, lesbian, feminist, socialist. Now she claims them all.

Pat Parker, Black lesbian poet, feminist medical administrator, mother of two daughters, lover of women, softball devotee, and general progressive troublemaker, died of breast cancer on June 17, 1989 at the age of 45. Her 1978 work, *Movement in Black,* has recently been republished by Firebrand Books.

Irene Padavic earned a Ph.D. at Univeristy of Michigan and is associate professor of sociology at Florida State University. Her research focuses on gender and work, economic restructuring, and labor-management relations.

Gayle Pemberton's interest in autobiographical essays stems from her belief that narratives help us understand each other's lives more completely than theory alone. She is an African American woman who grew up in the Middle West during the 1950s and 1960s. Not only family dynamics, but also place and time had an enormous influence on the development of her personality, dreams, politics, and sexuality. She writes, "It is through the lens of my history that I reach out to people from different and similar backgrounds. I am successful if my writing reminds a reader of his or her own life—or the common bonds of humanity and kinship we all share."

Phil Petrie is a freelance writer in New Jersey.

Suzanne Pharr is a social and economic justice organizer and writer from the South. She is the author of *Homophobia: A Weapon of Sexism* and *Liberation Politics in the Time of The Right.*

Roberta Praeger is a long-time Cambridge, Massachusetts, activist who has worked on housing, welfare, and women's issues.

Minnie Bruce Pratt was born in 1946 in Selma, Alabama. She received her academic education at the University of Alabama in Tuscaloosa and at the University of North Carolina at Chapel Hill. Her actual education occurred through grassroots organizing with women in the army-base town of Fayetteville, North Carolina and through teaching at historically Black universities. With Elly Bulkin and Barbara Smith, she co-authored *Yours In Struggle: Three Feminist Perspectives On Anti-Semitism and Racism* (Firebrand Books). She has published three books of poetry, *The Sound of One Fork* (Night Heron press), *We Say We Love Each Other* (Spinsters/Aunt Lute and Firebrand Books), and *Crime Against Nature* (Firebrand Books); a book of essays, *Rebellion: Essays 1980–1991* (Firebrand), and a book of prose stories *S/He* (Firebrand, 1995). Pratt lives in the New York City area and teaches Women's Studies, Lesbian/Gay Studies, and Creative Writing as part of the Graduate Faculty of The Union Institute, a nonresidential alternative university.

Barbara Reskin is professor of sociology at Ohio State University. In addition to teaching jobs at the Universities of California, Illinois, Michigan, and Indiana, she has had about two dozen clerical jobs, including switchboard operator, freight-bill typist, and "girl Friday." She stayed sane by being active in the civil rights and feminist movements. Nowadays she spends most of her time teaching and doing research on gender, race, and ethnic inequality in the workplace. Her most recent book is *Women and Men at Work* (with Irene Padavic); her most recent classes are Social Stratification, and Gender and Work.

Adrienne Rich, the daughter of a Jewish father and a non-Jewish mother, is a poet and non-fiction writer and an activist. She worked for eight years in New Jewish Agenda, a national organization for progressive Jews, and was a founding editor of *Bridges: A Journal for Jewish Feminists and Our Friends.* Her most recent books are *What Is Found There: Notebooks on Poetry and Politics,* and *Dark Fields of the Republic: Poems 1991-1995.* She lives in California.

Luis J. Rodríguez, the son of Mexican immigrants, grew up in Watts and East Los Angeles. He began writing in his early teens, and eventually won national recognition as a poet, journalist, and critic. He is currently working as a peacemaker among inner-city gangs and runs Tia Chucha Press, which publishes emerging, socially conscious poets. He lives in Chicago.

Lillian B. Rubin lives in San Francisco, where she is a practicing psychotherapist and Senior Research Fellow at the Institute for the Study of Social

Change at the Univeristy of California at Berkeley. As did many women of her generation, Dr. Rubin devoted her early adult years to raising her children. In 1963, at the age of 39, she entered the University of California at Berkeley as a freshman, and emerged eight years later with a Ph.D. in sociology and post-doctoral training in clinical psychology. She has published eight books, including *Worlds of Pain: Life in the Working-Class* (1976); *Intimate Strangers: Men & Women Together* (1983); *Erotic Wars: What Happened to the Sexual Revolution?* (1990); *Families on the Fault Line: America's Working Class Speaks About the Family, The Economy, Race and Ethnicity* (1994); and *Fall Down Seven Times, Get Up Eight* (1996).

Don Sabo is professor of social sciences at D'Youville College, Buffalo, New York. He writes and speaks widely about gender relations, particularly in relation to sport and health. He has, with Michael Messner, co-edited *Sport, Men and the Gender Order* and co-authored *Sex, Violence and Power in Sports: Rethinking Masculinity.* He has co-edited with David Frederick Gordon, *Men's Health and Illness: Gender, Power, and the Body.*

Myra Pollack Sadker was professor of education and dean of the School of Education at American University until 1995. *David Miller Sadker* is currently professor of education and director of the Master of Arts in Teaching Program at American University. They have co-authored five books, including *Teachers, Schools, and Society* (McGraw-Hill) and *Failing at Fairness: How Our Schools Cheat Girls* (Touchstone Press, 1995). More than fifty of their articles have appeared in *Phi Delta Kappan, Harvard Educational Review, Educational Leadership,* and other professional journals. Their research interests have focused on foundations of education, educational equity, teacher preparation and curriculum. They have conducted teaching and equity workshops for principals, teachers, and professors in over forty states and overseas.

Elayne Saltzberg Daniels is a Psychology Fellow at the Yale University School of Medicine, where, among other activities, she works at the Yale Psychiatric Institute with women who have eating disorders. She earned her doctorate in clinical psychology at Rhode Island University and her master's degree at Connecticut College. She has recently completed a research project on the impact of breast cancer surgery on women's body image and sexual functioning, and she has published several articles on body image, eating disorders, and women's pursuit of beauty.

Christopher Scanlan is director of writing programs at The Poynter Institute for Media Studies in St. Petersburg, FL, where he teaches professional and student journalists and edits *Best Newspaper Writing,* an annual collection of prize-winning journalism. For twenty years, he was an award-winning journalist for Knight-Ridder Newspapers, the *St. Petersburg Times,* and the *Providence Journal.* His short stories, articles, and essays have appeared in *Redbook, The Washington Post Magazine,* and numerous other magazines and textbooks.

Tatiana Schreiber is a freelance writer, independent radio producer, and former editor of the Resist foundation newsletter, where this article first appeared. Her most recent project is the radio series "Other Colors: Stories of Women Immigrants," which explores the meanings of home, family, work, and community from the perspective of recent women immigrants to the United States. She is interested in exploring the relationships between sexual diversity, ethnic/racial diversity, and diversity in the natural world, believing that all of these pluralisms must be valued and sustained.

Mab Segrest is a white lesbian writer and organizer who still lives in Durham, North Carolina, with her partner of eighteen years, their daughter (who is now nine), three cats, a poodle, and Elizabeth (their seventy-five-year-old Goddess Mother and resident Crone). Mab's second book, *Memoir of a Race Traitor* (South End 1994), chronicles her anti-Klan work. She first spoke publicly about her anti-Klan work in the speech at Spellman College printed in this volume.

Paul B. Seidman was born in 1960 in Hollywood, California but was raised in West Buxton, Maine, and Staten Island, New York. He has lived his adult years in Portland, Maine, as an activist against sexual violence, as a writer, and as a grandson.

Sonia Shah is an editor/publisher in the South End Press collective. Her recent writing has appeared in *Ms.* magazine, *Z* magazine, and *Sojourner: A Woman's Forum*. She is currently editing an anthology on Asian American feminism.

Ruth Sidel is professor of sociology at Hunter College. She has long been concerned about the well-being of women, children, and families in the United States and in other countries. Her most recent book is *Keeping Women and Children Last: America's War on the Poor* (Penguin).

Stephen Samuel Smith is assistant professor of political science at Winthrop University in Rock Hill, South Carolina. His interests include the politics of education, urban political economy, social movements, and program evaluation. Prior to completing his Ph.D., he spent fifteen years doing factory work and labor organizing.

Brent Staples is assistant metropolitan editor of the *New York Times*.

Dottie Stevens is a Boston-area welfare-rights and poor people's activist, and a co-founder of Advocacy for Resources for Modern Survival, a Boston welfare-rights group.

John Stoltenberg is the author of *Refusing to Be a Man: Essays on Sex and Justice* (Meridian, 1990), *The End of Manhood: A Book for Men of Conscience* (Plume, 1994), and *What Makes Pornography "Sexy"?* (Milkweed Editions, 1994). He is a frequent speaker and workshop leader, and he is executive editor of *On the Issues: The Progressive Woman's Quarterly*. He was born in

Minneapolis in 1944 to working-class parents—his mother is German, and his father is Norwegian. He grew up queer, and he has lived with the writer Andrea Dworkin since 1974.

Deborah Tannen, a native of New York City, received her Ph.D. in linguistics from the University of California at Berkeley. Tannen is University Professor and professor of linguistics at Georgetown University in Washington, D.C. She is best known as the author of *You Just Don't Understand: Women and Men in Conversation.* Her fifteenth and most recent book is *Talking From 9 to 5: Women and Men in the Workplace: Language, Sex, and Power.* She has written and edited a number of academic books as well. In addition to her research and publications in linguistics, Deborah Tannen also writes short stories, poems, and plays. Her first plays, *An Act of Devotion* and *Sisters,* draw on her East European Jewish background.

Becky Thompson teaches African American studies and American studies at Wesleyan University. She came of age as an anti-racist white feminist at the University of California, Santa Cruz and through lessons learned in multiracial feminist organizing in Boston in the 1980s. She is the author of *A Hunger So Wide and So Deep: American Women Speak Out on Eating Problems* (University of Minnesota, 1994); and co-editor, with Sangeeta Tyagi, of *Names We Call Home: Autobiography on Racial Identity* (Routledge, 1996) and *Beyond a Dream Deferred: Multicultural Education and the Politics of Excellence* (University of Minnesota, 1993).

Barrie Thorne, a feminist sociologist who now teaches at the University of California, Berkeley, began studying children when she became a mother. Her ethnographic research on kids' gender relations is reported in full in her 1993 book, *Gender Play: Girls and Boys in School.* Barrie Thorne has also co-edited books on feminism and families (*Rethinking the Family: Some Feminist Questions*) and on gender and language (*Language, Gender and Society*).

Barbara Trees is the first female shop steward in her carpenters' union local and the founder and leader of New York Tradeswomen. She was an organizer of the 1990 hearings on racism and sexism in the construction industry before the New York City Commission on Civil Rights.

Helen Zia, a journalist and former assistant editor of *Ms.* magazine, was a participant in a recent Center for Women Policy Studies Seminar on Hate Crimes and Gender-Bias Crimes.

RECONSTRUCTING GENDER

General Introduction

. . . the system of patriarchy. . . seems to have nearly run its course—it no longer serves the needs of men or women and in its inextricable linkage to militarism, hierarchy, and racism it threatens the very existence of life on earth.

GERDA LERNER[1]

As a Black lesbian feminist comfortable with the many different ingredients of my identity, and a woman committed to racial and sexual freedom from oppression, I find I am constantly being encouraged to pluck out some one aspect of myself and present this as a meaningful whole, eclipsing or denying the other parts of self. But this is a destructive and fragmenting way to live.

AUDRE LORDE[2]

No one is simply a man or a woman. Each of us embodies intersecting statuses and identities, empowered and disempowered, including physical and demographic traits, chosen and unchosen. In any discussion of gender, serious students of the social order need to be prepared to ask, Which men? Which women? If students of gender studies choose to be conscious of the complexity of human life, much of the literature on human nature and gender should be read carefully, and any generalizations should be made with extreme caution. Sometimes findings about men are generalized as findings about people in general. Sometimes data from racially mixed populations are combined and analyzed as a whole, leaving out the details and differences between groups; sometimes an author states briefly that there are no differences between groups, meaning no statistically significant differences, and proceeds with the analysis. Sometimes the "deviant cases" are excluded from analysis for lack of a large enough subsample. In any of these cases, the voices of the few are obscured by those of the many. Unless we focus on the few alongside the many, we not only lose the voices of the few, but we also lose any meaningful understanding of the relationship between the few and the many, particularly in terms of power, privilege, disempowerment, and empowerment.

This collection of readings focuses on power, addressing the conditions under which the gender system intersects with other factors to create various kinds of power and powerlessness. The readings also address how people empower themselves, both personally and collectively. This book is grounded in several important intellectual perspectives that support the acquisition of inclusive knowledge as a prerequisite to empowerment. These perspectives are based on the assumption that we need to understand the complexity of human experience in order to develop effective strategies for humane, inclusive social change.

1

The Personal Is Political—Using a Sociological Imagination

An important sociological knowledge-seeker, C. Wright Mills, argued in 1959 that it is possible to understand human lives only if we can understand the connections between those lives and the social and historical contexts in which they are lived. He further argues that people need to understand the sources of their problems in order to fully understand why their lives are difficult. Thus, he encourages people to distinguish between problems that affect only themselves and perhaps a few others from those problems experienced by large numbers of people and that have their cause in social structures beyond particular individuals or families. He refers to the former as "private troubles" and to the latter as "public issues." He urges people to develop a "sociological imagination" so as to place themselves in social context and identify how public issues affect them at the personal level, arguing that people need to know the source of their problems in order to make sense of their lives.[3] Understanding the source of one's problems opens the possibility to shift the blame off of oneself and onto the social order, when appropriate. It also opens the possibility for working with others to change aspects of the social order that create problems for many individuals. Thus, mental health and effective resistance to oppressive social structures depend on the possession of a sociological imagination.

The second wave of the feminist movement in the United States, which started in the mid-1960s, incorporated a sociological imagination when it adopted the phrase "the personal is political." Arguing that larger political realities were felt at the personal level, women were encouraged to look beyond themselves for the sources of their problems in order to feel less alone and less to blame for the difficulties they faced. Analysis of the real sources of problems allowed women both to understand their personal situations better and to devise individual and collective means of resistance. In many situations, women have used the link between the political and the personal to help each other understand sexism as it is played out in the political structure, the community, the workplace, schools, families, and bedrooms. In response to this awareness, women have established a national network of services for women, such as shelters for battered women, rape crisis centers, and health centers, and have worked for empowering legal changes.[4]

The authors in this book possess a sociological imagination—they are aware of crucial aspects of the historical contexts in which they live and write, and they are conscious that oppressed people are not alone, not to blame, and not crazy for feeling as they do. Most of the material in this book was written in the 1980s and 1990s in the United States. This period of history has seen growing scholarship and activism among women, especially women of color, as well as increased writing by pro-feminist men, especially those working for changes in men's usual roles.[5] During this period, other groups of men also became increasingly public about their various disenchantments with either their own roles or those of women. A men's rights movement emerged to protest the kinds of power its members perceived women to have. A Christian men's movement emerged calling for men to take back the power they had lost as women began to develop more public power. A "mythopoetic" men's movement began to hold men-only retreats at which primarily white, middle-class men attempt to contact their "essential masculinity," while basically ignoring women and feminism. And the Million Man March provided an empowering experience for many Black men, highlighted some of the tensions and conflicts over men's roles and responsibilities in the Black community, and elicited a range of responses from Black women and men.[6] This period also saw conflict among white women, including those who object to feminism and those who critique what mainstream feminism has stood for.[7]

The writings in this book also emerge in a virulent political era in which attacks on feminists, people of color, poor people, Jewish people, and gay men and lesbians have been and continue to be common.[8] Threats to affirmative action, Social Security, Medicare, Medicaid, and reproductive rights are real, along with cuts to welfare, education, and other social services. However, in spite of being under attack for the past fifteen years, writers and activists continue to describe the complexity of gender issues and to engage in progressive social change. How all this will evolve is unpredictable, but I am heartened by this clarity of thought and continuing struggle for justice in an era of hate crimes, backlash, and economic conservatism. People committed to democracy and pluralism will especially need the knowledge that inclusive scholarship provides, both now and in the future, as people formerly silenced make themselves heard and suffer the anger and violence of those who would prefer them to be invisible or at least silent. For example, as the U.S. population has become more multicultural and less white, white supremacist and militia activity has increased. As gay, lesbian, bisexual, and transgendered people have increasingly refused to be labeled and closeted, more resistance to freedom of sexual and affectional expression has been mounted. And as the wealth in the United States has been moving increasingly into the hands of a small proportion of very rich people, women on welfare have been scapegoated as a significant cause of the federal deficit, even though welfare costs constitute only 1 percent of the federal budget.

Dissident Voices

Hearing from a wide range of men and women across many disciplines is crucial. Thus, this book centers on the work in sociology; women's studies; men's studies; African American studies; multicultural studies; gay, lesbian, bisexual, transgender, and queer studies; disability studies; studies of aging; and American studies, that has welcomed the voices and experiences of previously silenced people into scholarly discourse. The expansion of work by people in these fields has provided a rich, exciting base of new information that continues to grow. This book includes research, essays, and autobiographical material from this literature.[9]

By including men's studies in this book, I do not mean to imply that the situations of men are equivalent to those of women. Although women are almost all oppressed in one way or another by some men and by patriarchal structures, the reverse is not true. Thus, while men might suffer from detrimental aspects of male socialization such as participation in war, premature death, increased exposure to violence, and higher rates of suicide, it is generally not women who control the outcome of men's lives. Male-dominated institutions and individual powerful men control both women and less-empowered men. And powerful men reap great benefits from our male-dominant structure even if they do tend to die younger than women and suffer other difficulties related to being male.

Many of the writers in men's studies are dissatisfied with male-dominated society, having personally experienced the painful aspects of male socialization. This perspective puts these writers in a good position to analyze masculinities from within. Their voices are dissident within the ranks of powerful men, and many would not be particularly welcome in many board rooms, locker rooms, or faculty meetings. They are outsiders as they critique the bastions of hegemonic masculinity—the dominant, white, heterosexual, patriarchal, privileged masculinity that still controls many aspects of people's lives. Hegemonic masculinity, which promotes the tough, take-charge, don't-feel, image of men, frequently dominates the socialization process in spite of increasing efforts to develop other masculinities and femininities.[10]

An examination of masculinity in male-dominated society is a crucial aspect of both women's studies and men's studies, especially if we try to understand how to work toward a social order in which there is less violence. A look at the literature on men abused as children, for example, makes clear that many men who grow up to abuse others were themselves abused as children.[11] An understanding of adult male abusers leads us to examine how children are socialized, and helps us to understand the process by which baby boys frequently grow into violent or controlling men. Many of the men included in this book critique the gender system and are committed to working to end male-dominated society.

It is useful to mention some potential conflicts between women's studies and men's studies. One basic question concerns the extent to which men can effectively criticize a system in which they have experienced various amounts of privilege. Another question is the issue of crossover—can men effectively study women or women effectively study men?[12] The study of women by men raises the larger question of whether it is possible for someone from a more empowered group to study, effectively understand, and analyze the experiences of people from a less empowered group. Certainly there is a long history of "scholarship" by men distorting or ignoring the lives of women and by white people distorting or ignoring the lives of people of color. A third area of conflict is the use of the term *feminist* when applied to men. Both sides of this question have passionate proponents, including those who claim that the term "feminist man" is an inherent contradiction and others who claim that it isn't.[13] Finally, the limited resources in academia are an issue. The development of gender studies and men's studies poses a potential threat to women's studies on some campuses, just as multicultural studies poses a threat to Black studies in some situations. These threats include both possible cutbacks in resources and the potential of these studies being placed in a larger program controlled by someone from another discipline. Harry Brod addresses some of these issues in relation to men's studies in Part VII and concludes that men's studies is necessary but that resources for the development of this relatively new field should not come from women's studies.

Intersecting Identities

Another recent effort at truth-seeking is the attention now paid to the complex combination of identities held by each individual.[14] The readings included here address the concerns of Patricia Hill Collins, Audre Lorde, Gloria Anzaldúa, James Baldwin, W. E. B. Du Bois, Susanne Pharr, and others who ask us to acknowledge such complexities. Sociologist W. E. B. Du Bois, writing in 1903, called for awareness of what he named the "double-consciousness" of African Americans—the awareness that they can't simply be Americans, working toward whatever goals they might have; rather, they are simultaneously forced to deal with racism, seeing themselves through the eyes of hateful others. Thus, Du Bois says, African American men and women can never experience themselves as simply men or women because they are constantly hated or pitied.[15]

The importance of acknowledging multiple aspects of identity is also powerfully stated by Patricia Hill Collins, who addresses the complex combination of oppression and privilege held by each individual. She argues that individuals can simultaneously be members of both privileged and oppressed groups, citing the example of white women who are "penalized by their gender but privileged by their race."[16] Collins also argues that there is a matrix of domination, compelling us to look at the intersecting aspects of oppression in individuals and groups. She names race, class, and gender as the three axes of oppression that typically characterize Black women's experiences, and she lists other axes of oppression as well that may or may not affect particular individuals such as sexual orientation, religion, and age. Collins further argues that people experience domination at several levels, including personal biography, group-community interaction, and social institutions.[17] The readings in this volume have been chosen to reflect experience in and analysis of oppression, privilege, or both at all three levels, as well as reflecting people's empowerment struggles at these various levels.

Naming and Owning Privilege

This book is also grounded in the tradition of scholars and activists who struggle to bring privilege into focus.[18] In her well-known essay, Peggy McIntosh names her professional white privilege and heterosexual privilege and discusses how difficult it was to hold onto her awareness of her privileges—ideas about how she was privileged kept slipping away unless she wrote them down.[19] Sociologist Michael S. Kimmel tells about his difficulty in naming and owning his race and gender. Before he attended a seminar on feminist theory in which race and gender were discussed, when he looked in the mirror Kimmel saw ". . . a human being . . . universally generalizable . . . the generic person." As a middle-class white man, he had difficulty identifying how gender and race had affected his experience.[20] Anti-violence and anti-racist activist Paul Kivel, in a recent guide for white people who want to work for racial justice, provides a "White Benefits Checklist" that addresses the intersections of class and race. He also provides a checklist of the "Costs of Racism for White People."[21]

As Patricia Hill Collins argues for a matrix of domination, we might also conceive of a matrix of privilege. Assuming that most people and groups possess some degree of privilege, however limited, we can frequently examine oppression and privilege together. We can identify where privilege lies and analyze how it smoothes the way for those who possess it and simultaneously makes life more difficult for those who don't. The issue here, however, is not simply to identify privilege. Rather, as Audre Lorde said, we should make it available for wider use. Thus, a white person who opposes racism might use his or her contacts with groups of white people as opportunities to educate them about racism. A man who opposes sexism might use his contacts with other men to educate them about sexism.

Privilege is a difficult concept for many of those who have it because it is frequently unnamed in wider U.S. society. In a social order whose mainstream values include individual achievement and competition, many people with privilege are supported to assume that they deserve the "luck" or "normalcy" they experience, whereas those who lack privilege are encouraged to blame themselves.[22] Thus, an able-bodied person might experience the ability to walk up a flight of stairs as simply a normal thing to do, rather than seeing the expectation that all people walk as part of a system that treats stair-climbing as normal and thus fails to build ramps for those on wheels. A white person might assume that white is "normal," might feel lucky to be white, and fail to see that the alleged superiority of whiteness is a piece of a racist system that keeps people of color from moving freely in the social order. A person born wealthy is likely to be taught that he or she deserves the wealth, rather than to be taught how wealth is related to poverty in U.S. society. Although people with less privilege are usually astute analysts of how privilege works, those who enjoy it are frequently less conscious of its impact.[23] Thus, a challenge for people with privilege, especially for those with substantial privilege, is to become aware of the nuances of privilege and to learn how to use it in ways that raise consciousness about oppression and promote fairness.

Another challenge for those with privilege is to identify some of the liabilities that accompany privilege and to use that awareness to work toward changing the system. For example, many white professional men lead highly stressful, dissatisfying lives, with restricted access to feelings and a limited capacity for intimacy. Writer Mark Gerzon, a white professional man, convincingly criticizes the roles and role models available to men like himself and calls for new roles to replace them. After describing what he believes are archetypical roles for men, he asks men to reject these roles in exchange for more democratic and humane ones. Instead of frontiersmen, he wants men to be healers—of both people and the earth; instead of breadwinners, men should be companions; instead of soldiers, mediators; instead of experts, colleagues; and instead of lords, nurturers. Gerzon's work emerged from his dissatisfaction with being male in spite of his race and class privilege.[24]

White people who are not conscious of their white privilege spend their lives in fraudulent disillusion, knowing at some unconscious level that they do not deserve and did not earn the skin-color privilege they enjoy. Many temporarily able-bodied people are thrown into deep shock when they become disabled because they have structured their lives in ways that avoided people with disabilities. They therefore have no framework in which to combine personhood and disability and have suddenly become something that they despise. I have heard many of my students, especially male students, say that they'd rather be dead than physically disabled.

The Reconstruction of Knowledge

Based on the kinds of truth-telling identified thus far—the importance of a sociological imagination and the need to hear marginalized voices, acknowledge intersecting identities, and name privilege—numerous scholars have called for the reconstruction of knowledge.[25] Philosopher Elizabeth Minnich, for example, argues convincingly that four basic errors in knowledge need to be corrected as we move toward more inclusive knowing.[26] The first error is overgeneralization based on information gathered from small sectors of the population throughout history—primarily empowered male writers and the people they chose to acknowledge in their writing. Philosopher Harry Brod argues assertively that the study of men *as* men, in all the nuances of their experiences with masculinity, is crucial to the study of human beings. He asserts that to generalize from male experience to human experience not only distorts what human experience is, but also distorts what is specifically male.[27] Historian Gerda Lerner calls for a restructuring of thought and for an analysis that acknowledges that half the people in the world are women. She states that all generalizations about human beings need to acknowledge this fact.[28] The selections in this book should help readers challenge inaccurate generalizations about men and women and develop new, more limited ones.

A second error in knowledge identified by Elizabeth Minnich is circular reasoning, which justifies traditional knowledge based on the standards embedded in that knowledge. In sociology, for example, for many years certain topics were not studied at all, particularly women's experiences. Students, especially women students, who couldn't relate to the material presented were seen as inadequate. Ultimately, women sociologists began studying gender, and the field of sociology was forced to become more inclusive. Joyce Ladner, for example, in *Tomorrow's Tomorrow*, not only studied Black adolescent girls but refused to accept the standard sociological definition of their lives as "deviant." Rather, she identified some of the ways in which her respondents found empowerment in an economically limited, racist context.[29] Ladner studied and redefined a population that usually had no direct voice in the sociological literature.

The third knowledge error identified by Minnich is our attachment to mystified concepts. When we let go of these concepts, new avenues for research and new questions open up. Masculinity and femininity are two mystified concepts that are frequently used but seldom accurately defined in everyday discourse. Yet as we examine the literature in women's studies and men's studies, for example, we find that many men and women do not conform to the dominant Anglo ideals of femininity and masculinity. Many men, for instance, do not fit the strong, tough, take-charge mode, do not enjoy fighting, and would like more freedom to express their feelings. And, in fact, many men do express themselves openly.[30] Tommi Avicolli (Part II), Phil Petrie (Part IV), Don Sabo (Part V), and Paul Seidman (Part X) all provide examples of men breaking ranks with the masculine norms presented in mainstream U.S. culture. Many women also do not fit the stereotypical visions of women presented in mainstream culture, especially in the media. Christy Haubegger (Part III), bell hooks (Part VII), Melanie Kaye/Kantrowitz (Part X), and Byllye Avery (Part XI), among others, provide examples of women who refuse narrow and limited ideas about femininity.

Gender itself is a mystified concept for the many people who see it as biologically determined. Recent scholars in gender studies argue convincingly, however, that there is nothing necessary or predictable about gender. Rather, gender is socially constructed in various ways in various contexts. Sociologist Judith Lorber, in her recent book *Paradoxes of Gender*, encourages us to "challenge the validity, permanence, and necessity of gender."[31]

Heterosexuality is another mystified concept related to masculinity and femininity that has proven hard to even question. So "normal" is heterosexuality that it is difficult to imagine a world without this expectation.[32] The "sissy" and "lezzie" insults levied at boys and girls who do not conform to heterosexist expectations have a lot to teach us about how charged and compelling the heterosexual mandate is. In spite of the fashion trend toward androgynous clothing in the mainstream media, individuals who choose to express themselves through androgynous presentations risk ridicule and ostracism in many circles. Some of the ridicule stems from standards of masculinity and femininity; some of it relates directly to homophobia.[33] Those who love someone of the same sex know at deeply painful levels the costs of breaking with the heterosexual ideal. This ideal is also tightly bound up with the requirement to match gender with sex. For example, an ironic twist of fate occurred in a tragic atrocity; the man who massacred thirteen women in Montreal because they were studying engineering spared one of the women present because he perceived her to be a man.[34]

Many new questions emerge if we examine the heterosexual ideal: What would life be like without the insults and labels aimed at boys who are gentle, at girls who are athletes, at women who study engineering, or at men who study nursing? What explains the discomfort of the majority of us who want or need people to fit into gender categories? How does this affect the lives of girls, boys, men, and women who express love for someone of the same sex or live their lives in the gender to which they have not been assigned? How does it affect the social order when bisexual women and men who could choose to relate sexually/affectionally to members of the opposite gender choose to do so with the same gender instead? We cannot begin to address these questions without careful attention to the heterosexual ideal and its accompanying homophobia. I often ask myself how gender roles might look without homophobia. Would there even be gender roles as we know them?

Finally, the fourth knowledge error identified by Minnich is our inability, without new knowledge systems, to discard or correct prior ones. If, however, we can embrace new models of knowledge, we can discard the old ones. Charles Lemert's edited volume, *Social Theory: The Multicultural and Classic Readings*, provides an excellent example of this. By expanding the definition of who is considered a social theorist, Lemert allows new voices to enter sociological discourse, and invites readers to consider a wide range of contemporary thinkers not usually included in texts on sociological theory.[35] Ronald Takaki's *A Different Mirror: A History of Multicultural America* provides another very good example of a new knowledge system. Takaki focuses on the lives of ordinary people, including those in various racial and ethnic groups, rather than on the lives of politicians and other famous people. He examines class and gender within the groups he studies.[36]

Empowerment—Challenging the Patriarchal System

The need for inclusive knowledge has broad implications for empowerment at the interpersonal, community, and policy levels. Without inclusive knowledge, we cannot develop comprehensive empowerment strategies or inclusive social policy. Without seeing the complexity of human experience and the complexity of human oppression, we cannot begin to address the real needs of human beings caught in systematically oppressive social structures. Marilyn Frye makes this point effectively and graphically with the metaphor of the bird cage in her essay "Oppression."[37] She argues that when someone is caged, or oppressed, it is crucial to examine all the bars of the cage to get a full understanding of the inability to escape; close, myopic examination of just one bar will not give a full understanding of why the person is trapped. For example, if we look at gender discrimination on the job, we might wonder why women can't just overcome the prejudice and discrimination they experience and get on with their lives, even if they make less money, are passed over for promotion, and can support their families only marginally. But if we simultaneously look at other factors, such as sexual harassment within the workplace, racism, fatphobia, heterosexism, ableism, and violence against women and children, we will come to a clearer understanding of how certain people and groups are caught in a web that they often can't escape; barriers, the bars of the cage, are erected everywhere they turn.

Another metaphor that is useful in making sense of oppression and privilege in order to frame social change is the idea of being tied down. If a person is tied by one oppression rope, say, sexism, it's likely that she or he has some movement, is able to see how the knots are tied, and may be able to maneuver to untie the knot, slide under the rope, or move in and out of the rope at different times, depending on the context. If a rope is light, she or he might even break it. But if someone is tied by several ropes, such that she or he cannot move enough to clearly see the sizes and quality of the ropes or the configurations of the knots, there is little possibility for escape. If we imagine that each oppression is a different rope and that the power of oppressions might vary, creating light ropes and heavy ones, a person could be tied down by an almost infinite combination of ropes of different sizes and strengths. And occasionally there will be people tied by no ropes at all at various moments, such as wealthy, white, Anglo-Saxon, Protestant, heterosexual, married, able-bodied, muscular, normal-weight, physically attractive, tall (but not too tall) men in their middle years who are in good health and have not been in psychotherapy.

The presence or absence of ropes is a public, not a private, matter. The vast majority of people do not tie themselves down; they are born with these limitations due to the structure of the socioeconomic system into which they are born. German theorist Max Weber called this system of possibilities "life chances," referring to the array of opportunities, however limited or plentiful, with which a person is born.[38] Although we live in an alleged democracy that offers the potential for upward mobility for anyone, the probability of that happening is severely limited, especially for those born under multiple ropes. Equal access to wealth and other privileges is not structurally guaranteed, even for white, able-bodied men; and many people in the middle class are currently experiencing downward mobility.[39] There is no systematic training for untying or breaking the ropes of oppression. Those held by fewer ropes are usually not encouraged to share their privilege by helping others to escape their ropes. Those tied down often learn survival, resilience, resistance, and liberation skills from their families, cultures, and communities but are offered little systematic support from the wider social order. Instead, those tied by many ropes are likely to attend poor schools in which race, class, gender, disability, and sexual orientation interact to produce high rates of failure or marginal functioning.

The oppressive social structure surrounding many people sets in place some probabilities for success or failure. It is important to acknowledge, however, how groups and individuals blocked from success in the privileged, wealthy centers of power find ways to empower themselves, solve problems, and survive against very difficult odds. They do, at times, escape from multiple ropes. For example, some people from highly dysfunctional families have grown up to establish healthy relationships for themselves. The strength and resilience found in poor communities, especially in communities of color, also portray empowerment within otherwise very trying circumstances.[40]. Many of the readings in this book report on resilience and personal agency in response to various oppressions.

A look at the web of ropes that surrounds us or the structure of the cages we are in can help us understand how our lives are limited and how to develop institutional, community, and individual strategies for empowerment. An understanding of multiple oppressions helps us see how people can resist oppression at both individual and collective levels and helps us understand why people don't usually escape from multiple ropes. This understanding is especially important in a patriarchal social order in which virtually every woman is tied down by some variety of gender oppression.

Patriarchy, defined in various ways by various theorists, has as its core male control of women at multiple levels simultaneously. Feminist historian Gerda Lerner names an array of ways in which women are socialized, indoctrinated, and coerced into cooperation with patriarchal systems; for example, women are prevented from fully participating in such empowering activities as education (including learning women's history), politics, and the use of economic resources. Lerner names several dynamics particular to women that make this cooperation especially difficult to resist or subvert: women have internalized the idea of their own inferiority; historically, wives and daughters have lived under male domain where they exchange submission for protection and unpaid labor for economic maintenance; women with substantial class privilege have a more difficult time seeing themselves as deprived and subordinated, thus making it especially hard for women of different classes to work together; and women are separated by their differences in sexual expression and activities.[41] When we add race, age, and ability differences to these other divisions, the likelihood of women uniting against patriarchy becomes even less probable.

In spite of these extremely powerful structures that conspire to limit the roles and options of both genders and render those who are multiply oppressed close to powerless at times, there is a long history of resistance to patriarchy.[42] Although we probably cannot expect a unified revolt against patriarchy, people are fighting back in various ways and struggling to change the systems that support inequality. Many of the writers in this book have struggled for empowerment of one sort or another and provide hopeful exceptions to this grim picture. The pages that follow contain examples of people finding their voices, telling unpopular truths, taking charge of their own needs, offering concrete advice for improving the lives of women and men, and organizing for change. Don Sabo, for example, critiques male sports culture (Part V); Christy Haubegger embraces her round body (Part III); Stan Gray fights to include women as equals in his factory (Part VIII); Robert Allen works to prevent male violence (Part XI); and Byllye Avery describes the evolution of the National Black Women's Health Project (Part XI).

I define power broadly to include a range of personal and collective actions. At a personal level, empowerment includes the ability to name and assert one's identity in all its complexity, including the naming of one's privilege and oppression. Related to this is the refusal to accept someone else's definition of who one is. Possessing sociological imagination is another form of personal power; this allows us to know where we fit historically in the world, to know what our options are likely to be, and to know how to determine whether our pain stems from a private trouble or from a public issue felt at the personal level. A sociological imagination contributes to the ability to challenge dominant ideas and to develop a healthy skepticism about how the world works. Based on informed analyses of what is wrong with the social order, people can use the power of knowledge to determine what kinds of social changes to work toward. Finally, people can empower themselves by taking political action, both individually and collectively.

Empowerment develops in stages. The first stage is awareness that something is not right. In order to conceptualize what's wrong, people need inclusive knowledge to develop a case for what feminist writer Elizabeth Janeway calls "disbelief," a piece of which is the refusal to accept the definition of oneself that is put forward by those with more power.[43] Janeway argues that in order to mistrust or disbelieve the messages of those in power, validation from others is necessary. Speaking of women, she argues, "the frightening experience of doubting society's directives and then doubting one's right to doubt them is still very recent."[44] Thus, if one's mistrust of the system is not solid, the presence of other disbelievers is likely to strengthen one's position. The role of Black churches in validating this mistrust has been well documented; congregants name how the racist power structure perpetuates itself, and they support each other to work to lessen its onslaught.[45] Women's consciousness-raising groups have also served this purpose.[46]

Once people are convinced that something is wrong or unfair in their lives, they can consider taking steps toward making it right at several levels. At the individual level, people can practice personal acts of passive resistance, direct confrontation, or other actions such as telling the truth about how they really feel; challenging someone who said something hurtful or insulting; leaving an abusive relationship; insisting on not always being in a particular role in a relationship; avoiding contact with people whose attitudes are disrespectful, including refusing to frequent certain places; and making a public statement. On a collective level, people can resist oppressive arrangements by joining forces. This might happen in small or large ways, including movements for social change in communities, institutions, legislative bodies, other governmental structures, and international forums. All of these levels of resistance to oppressive structures and relationships are necessary if we are to create, in Gerda Lerner's words, ". . . a world free of dominance and hierarchy, a world that is truly human."[47]

This book begins with a chapter called Social Contexts of Gender, in which the authors explore gender expression in various racial, ethnic, and class contexts; the complexity of identity and oppression become obvious here. Part II, Gender Socialization, explores aspects of both childhood and adult socialization. Part III, Embodiment, examines the pressures to look "typically" female or male, which in many cases means white, muscular, slim, and young. Eating disorders are addressed here as well.

Parts IV, V, and VI deal with interpersonal relationships. Part IV, Communication, examines a wide range of communication challenges between men and women, across racial, cultural, class, and sexual-orientation differences, in dyads, in communities, and in public. Part V, Sexuality, looks at various aspects of sexuality, including butch-femme relationships in the fifties, the challenge of non-exploitative heterosexual relationships, sexuality issues for people with disabilities, and the sexual objectification of Black women. Part VI, Families, explores the division of labor within the household, structural barriers to men's involvement in their children's lives, various kinds of families, and how gender affects people's lives within families. Parts VII and VIII, Education and Work, discuss these two major institutions that affect the livelihoods of men and women. Part IX, Health and Illness, documents ways that gender appears to affect health, including cultural contexts of health difficulties. Part X, Violence, looks at the devastation caused by gender-related violence, particularly that committed by men. Part XI, A World That Is Truly Human, concludes the book with some perspectives on empowerment and social change, including empowerment experiences and policy recommendations at the individual, community, national, and global levels.

NOTES

1. Gerda Lerner, *The Creation of Patriarchy*, (New York: Oxford, 1986), pp. 228–29.
2. Audre Lorde, "Age, Race, Class, and Sex: Women Defining Difference." in *Sister Outsider*. (Freedom, CA: Crossing Press, 1984) p. 120.
3. C. Wright Mills, *The Sociological Imagination*, (New York: Oxford University Press, 1959).
4. For a review of legal changes and challenges ahead, see Jo Freeman, "The Revolution for Women in Law and Public Policy," in Jo Freeman, ed., *Woman: A Feminist Perspective*, 5th ed. (Mountain View, CA: Mayfield, 1995), pp. 365–404.
5. For a summary of the development of the contemporary women's movement, including a review of women's activism from the 19th century to the present, see Margaret Andersen, *Thinking About Women: Sociological Perspectives on Sex and Gender*, 3rd Ed., (New York: Macmillan, 1993), pp. 277–85. For a representative look at the scholarship of pro-feminist men, see Michael S. Kimmel and Michael A. Messner, eds., *Men's Lives*, 3rd ed., (Boston: Allyn & Bacon, 1995).
6. For a critique of the mythopoetic men's movement, see Michael S. Kimmel and Michael Kaufman, "The New Men's Movement: Retreat and Regression with America's Weekend Warriors," *Feminist Issues*, fall 1993, pp. 3–21. For a look inside Promise Keepers, one of the large evangelical men's organizations, from the perspective of a feminist woman observer, see Donna Minkowitz, "In the Name of the Father" *Ms.*, November/December 1995, pp. 64–71. For a discussion of the Million Man March and the O. J. Simpson case, see Henry Louis Gates, Jr., "Thirteen Ways of Looking at a Black Man," *The New Yorker*, October 23, 1995, p. 56ff. For a presentation of various men's movement positions not represented in this book, see Robert Bly, *Iron John* (New York: Random House, 1990); Stephen B. Boyd, *The Men We Long to Be: Beyond Domination to a New Christian Understanding of Manhood* (New York: HarperCollins, 1995); Warren Farrell, *The Myth of Male Power: Why Men Are the Disposable Sex* (New York: Berkley Books, 1993); Sam Keen, *Fire in the Belly: On Being a Man* (New York: Bantam, 1991); Keith Thompson, ed., *To Be a Man: In Search of the Deep Masculine* (New York: Putnam, 1991).
7. For objections to feminism, see writings by Beverly LaHaye (Concerned Women for America) and Phyllis Schlafly; for critiques of mainstream feminism, see Camille Paglia, *Sexual Personae: Art and Decadence from Nefertiti to Emily Dickinson* (London: Penguin, 1990); Christina Sommers, *Who Stole Feminism?* (New York: Simon & Schuster, 1994); Katie Roiphe, *The Morning After: Sex, Fear, and Feminism* (London: H. Hamilton, 1994).
8. For ongoing lists of bias-related murders, assaults, arson attacks, bombings, threats, cross burnings, harassment, intimidation, and vandalism, see *Klanwatch Intelligence Report*, published by the Southern Poverty Law Center, Montgomery, AL. For reports on right-wing political activity in general, see *The Public Eye*, published by Political Research Associates, Somerville, MA. For examples of anti-abortion violence, see *Ms.*, May/June 1995.
9. For anthologies with substantial attention to race, class, and gender, see Margaret L. Andersen and Patricia Hill Collins, eds., *Race, Class, and Gender: An Anthology*, 2nd ed. (Belmont, CA: Wadsworth, 1995); Laurel Richardson and Verta Taylor, eds., *Feminist Frontiers III* (New York: McGraw-Hill, 1993); Michael S. Kimmel and Michael A. Messner, eds., *Men's Lives*; Karin Bergstrom Costello, *Gendered Voices: Readings from the American Experience*, (New York: Harcourt Brace, 1996).

   For an extensive bibliography on the sociology of women and women's studies, see Margaret L. Andersen, *Thinking about Women*, pp. 353–87. For an extensive bibliography on the sociology of gender, with references to other disciplines as well, see Claire M. Renzetti and Daniel J. Curran, *Women, Men, and Society* (Boston: Allyn & Bacon, 1995), pp. 525–85. For an ongoing update of the literature on disability, see the *Disability Studies Quarterly,* published in the Department of Sociology at Brandeis University, Waltham, MA. For books and journal articles related to African American men, see Don Belton, ed., *Speak My Name: Black Men on Masculinity and the American Dream* (Boston: Beacon Press, 1995); Richard G. Majors and Jacob U. Gordon, eds., *The American Black Male: His Present Status and His Future* (Chicago: Nelson-Hall Publishers, 1994), pp. 317–47, and Herb Boyd and Robert L. Allen, eds., *Brotherman: The Odyssey of Black Men in America—An Anthology* (New York: Ballantine, 1995). For references to gay, lesbian, bisexual, and queer studies, see Henry Abelove, Michele Aina Barale, and David M. Halperin, eds., *The Lesbian and Gay Studies Reader* (New York: Routledge, 1993); Christie Balka and Andy Rose, eds., *Twice Blessed: On Being Lesbian or Gay and Jewish* (Boston: Beacon Press, 1989); Monica Dorenkamp and Richard Henke, *Negotiating Lesbian and Gay Subjects* (New York: Routledge, 1995); Thomas Geller, ed., *Bisexuality: A Reader and Sourcebook* (Ojai, CA: Times Change Press, 1990); Kobena Mercer, *Welcome to the Jungle: New Positions in Black Cultural Studies* (New York: Routledge, 1994); Michael Warner, ed., *Fear of a Queer Planet* (Minneapolis: University of Minnesota Press, 1993). For information on gender, aging and other intersections, see especially Eleanor Palo Stoller and Rose Campbell Gibson, eds., *Worlds of Difference: Inequality in the Aging Experience* (Thousand Oaks, CA: Pine Forge, 1994); and James S. Jackson, Linda M. Chatters, and Robert Joseph Taylor, eds., *Aging in Black America* (Newbury Park, CA: Sage, 1993).

10. For a discussion of hegemonic masculinity, see R. W. Connell, *Gender and Power* (Palo Alto: Stanford University Press, 1987) and Sharon R. Bird, "Welcome to the Men's Club: Homosociality and the Maintenance of Hegemonic Masculinity," *Gender & Society* 10(2), April 1996: 120–32.

11. John C. Gonsiorek, Walter H. Bera, and Donald LeTourneau, *Male Sexual Abuse: A Trilogy of Intervention Strategies.* (Thousand Oaks, CA: Sage, 1994) pp. 52–55; Mic Hunter, *Abused Boys: The Neglected Victims of Sexual Abuse.* (Lexington, MA: Lexington Books, 1990); Mike Lew, *Victims No Longer: Men Recovering from Incest and Other Child Sexual Abuse.* (New York: Nevraumont, 1988); For a look at men and women who do not repeat destructive patterns from their families, see Steven J. Wolin and Sybil Wolin, *The Resilient Self: How Survivors of Troubled Families Rise above Adversity* (New York: Villard Books, 1994).

12. For examples of recent crossover research, see Todd W. Crosset, *Outsiders in the Clubhouse: The World of Women's Professional Golf* (Albany: State University of New York Press, 1995); the late Elliot Liebow, *Tell Them Who I Am: The Lives of Homeless Women* (New York: Penguin, 1993); Lillian Rubin, *Families on the Fault Line* (New York: Harper, 1994); Kathleen Gerson, *No Man's Land: Men's Changing Commitments to Family and Work* (New York: Basic Books, 1993); and Christine L. Williams, *Still a Man's World: Men Who Do "Women's Work"* (Berkeley: University of California Press, 1995); Ronald Takaki, *A Different Mirror: A History of Multicultural America* (Boston: Little, Brown, 1993).

13. See Renate Duelli Klein, "The 'Men-Problem' in Women's Studies: The Expert, the Ignoramus and the Poor Dear" *Women's Studies International Forum,* 6(4), pp. 413–21, 1983; Michael Awkward, "A Black Man's Place(s) in Black Feminist Criticism," in Marcellus Blount and George P. Cunningham, eds., *Representing Black Men* (New York: Routledge, 1996), pp. 3–26.

14. Gloria Anzaldúa, *Borderlands/La Frontera: The New Mestiza* (San Francisco: Spinsters/Aunt Lute, 1987); Gloria Anzaldúa, ed., *Making Face, Making Soul/ Haciendo Caras: Creative and Critical Perspectives by Women of Color* (San Francisco: Aunt Lute, 1987); Patricia Hill Collins, *Black Feminist Thought: Knowledge,*

Consciousness, and the Politics of Empowerment (New York: Routledge, 1990); Audre Lorde, *Sister Outsider* (Freedom, CA: Crossing Press, 1984); Audre Lorde, *A Burst of Light* (Ithaca, NY: Firebrand Books, 1988); Cherríe Moraga and Gloria Anzaldúa, eds., *This Bridge Called My Back: Writings by Radical Women of Color* (Watertown, MA: Persephone Press, 1981); Rebecca Walker, ed., *To Be Real: Telling the Truth and Changing the Face of Feminism* (New York: Anchor Books, 1995). See also W. E. B. Du Bois, *The Souls of Black Folk* (New York: Penguin, 1989).

15. Du Bois, *Souls,* p. 5.

16. Collins, *Black Feminist Thought,* p. 225.

17. Collins, *Black Feminist Thought,* p. 227.

18. See for example Elly Bulkin, Minnie Bruce-Pratt, and Barbara Smith, *Yours in Struggle: Three Perspectives on Anti-semitism and Racism* (Ithaca, NY: Firebrand Books, 1984); Judith Katz, *White Awareness: Handbook for Anti-Racist Trainings* (Norman, OK: Oklahoma University Press, 1978); Peggy McIntosh, "White Privilege and Male Privilege: A Personal Account of Coming to See Correspondences through Work in Women's Studies," in Margaret L. Andersen and Patricia Hill Collins, *Race, Class, and Gender.* pp. 76–87; Ruth Frankenberg, *White Women, Race Matters: The Social Construction of Whiteness* (Minneapolis: University of Minnesota Press, 1993).

19. McIntosh, "White Privilege."

20. Michael S. Kimmel, "Invisible Masculinity," *Society,* 30(6), September/October 1993: 29–30.

21. Paul Kivel, *Uprooting Racism: How White People Can Work for Racial Justice* (Philadelphia: New Society Publishers, 1996), pp. 30–32 and 37–39.

22. For a critique of competition, see Alfie Kohn, *No Contest: The Case Against Competition* (Boston: Houghton Mifflin, 1986).

23. In the 1970s, I had difficulty teaching the concept of social class to students at an elite private college, whereas the working class and poor students I taught at a nearby public college grasped this concept with ease. For a discussion of people with less power as astute observers of those with more power, see Jean Baker Miller, *Toward a New Psychology of Women* (Boston: Beacon Press, 1977).

24. Mark Gerzon, *A Choice of Heroes: The Changing Face of American Manhood* (Boston: Houghton Mifflin, 1992), pp. 235–262.

25. Harry Brod, ed., *The Making of Masculinities: The New Men's Studies* (Boston: Allen & Unwin, 1987); Sandra Harding, *The Science Question in Feminism* (Ithaca, NY: Cornell University Press, 1986); bell hooks, *Feminist Theory from Margin to Center* (Boston: South End Press, 1984); Evelyn Fox Keller, *Reflections on Gender and Science* (New Haven, CT: Yale University Press, 1985); Michael S. Kimmel and Michael A. Messner, eds., *Men's Lives;* Gerda Lerner, *The Creation of Patriarchy;* Elizabeth Kamarck Minnich, *Transforming Knowledge* (Philadelphia, PA: Temple University Press, 1990); Joseph H. Pleck and Jack Sawyer, eds., *Men and Masculinity* (Englewood Cliffs, NJ: Prentice Hall, 1974); Ronald Takaki, *A Different Mirror: A History of Multicultural America* (Boston: Little, Brown, 1993).

26. Minnich, *Transforming Knowledge,* pp. 185–87.

27. Harry Brod, "Scholarly Studies of Men: The New Field is an Essential Complement to Women's Studies," *The Chronicle of Higher Education,* March 1990. Reprinted in Karin Bergstrom Costello, ed., *Gendered Voices: Readings from the American Experience* (New York: Harcourt Brace, 1996),pp. 333–36.

28. Gerda Lerner, *The Creation of Patriarchy,* p. 220.

29. For some early work on gender by women sociologists, see Jessie Bernard, *Women, Wives, Mothers: Values and Options* (Chicago: Aldine, 1975); Joyce Ladner,

Tomorrow's Tomorrow (Garden City, NY: Doubleday, 1995); Marcia Millman and Rosabeth Moss Kanter, eds., *Another Voice* (Garden City, NY: Doubleday, 1975); Alice Rossi, ed., *Essays on Sex Equality* (Chicago: University of Chicago Press, 1970); Alice Rossi, ed., *The Feminist Papers* (New York: Columbia University Press, 1973); Anne Oakley, *The Sociology of Housework* (London: Mertin Robertson, 1974).

30. For a discussion of research on this issue, see Joseph H. Pleck, "The Gender Role Strain Paradigm: An Update" in Ronald F. Levant and William S. Pollack, eds., *A New Psychology of Men* (New York: Basic Books, 1995) pp. 11–32.

31. Judith Lorber, *Paradoxes of Gender* (New Haven: Yale University Press, 1994), p. 5.

32. Suzanne Pharr, *Homophobia: A Weapon of Sexism* (Chardon Press, 1988); Adrienne Rich, "Compulsory Heterosexuality and Lesbian Existence," *Signs,* 5 (Summer 1980) pp. 631–60.

33. Jennifer Reid Maxcy Myhre talks about reactions she receives as a woman with a crew cut: " 'Daddy, is that a boy or a girl?' I hear the six-year-old girl whisper the question as I pass by. I smile at her; she articulates aloud what the adults around her are thinking. Her question does not offend me in the way that the 'What are you, some kinda monk?' from the burly man in the fast food restaurant, or the 'Hey, is that a fag?' shouted at me from behind as I walk hand-in-hand with a man down the street, offends me." "One Bad Hair Day Too Many or the Hairstory of an Androgynous Young Feminist," in Barbara Findlen, ed., *Listen Up: Voices From the Next Feminist Generation* (Seattle, WA: Seal Press, 1995), p. 132.

    I am reminded also of a talk I heard by the former director of a lobbying group for women's issues in Massachusetts. She reported that it was highly unacceptable for women to wear slacks in the Massachusetts State House if they expected to have any influence. She herself had decided to make the concession of wearing skirts and dresses in order to be more effective in her work.

34. Minnie Bruce Pratt, *S/HE.* (Ithaca, NY: Firebrand Books, 1995), p. 186.

35. Charles Lemert, *Social Theory: The Multicultural and Classic Readings,* (Boulder, CO: Westview Press, 1993). Lemert includes Audre Lorde, Gloria Anzaldúa, Cornell West, and Virginia Woolf, among many others.

36. Takaki, *A Different Mirror.*

37. Marilyn Frye, "Oppression," in *The Politics of Reality: Essays in Feminist Theory* (Freedom, CA: The Crossing Press, 1983), pp. 1–16.

38. Max Weber, "Class, Status, Party," in S. M. Miller, ed. *Max Weber: Selections from His Work* (New York: Crowell, 1963), p. 43.

39. See Katherine S. Newman, *Falling From Grace: The Experience of Downward Mobility in the American Middle Class* (New York: Free Press, 1988) and *Declining Fortunes: The Withering of the American Dream* (New York: Basic Books, 1993).

40. For discussions of individual survival after painful childhoods, see Linda T. Sanford, *Strong at the Broken Places: Overcoming the Trauma of Childhood Abuse* (New York: Random House, 1990) and Stephen J. Wolin and Sybil Wolin, *The Resilient Self: How Survivors of Troubled Families Rise above Adversity* (New York: Villard Books, 1994).

    For a review of past and current literature on strategies for coping with poverty and racism, as well as some new qualitative data documenting creative responses to poverty among single African American women on AFDC, see Robin L. Jarrett, "Living Poor: Family Life among Single Parent, African-American Women," in *Social Problems,* 41(1), February 1994: 30-49.

41. Gerda Lerner, *The Creation of Patriarchy,* pp. 217–19.

42. Sandra Morgen and Ann Bookman, "Rethinking Women and Politics: An

Introductory Essay," in Ann Bookman and Sandra Morgen, eds. *Women and the Politics of Empowerment.* (Philadelphia: Temple University Press, 1988), p. 4.

43. Elizabeth Janeway, *The Powers of the Weak,* (New York: Knopf, 1980), p. 167.

44. Elizabeth Janeway, *The Powers of the Weak,* p. 168.

45. James Blackwell, *The Black Community: Diversity and Unity.* (NY: HarperCollins, 1991).

46. Hester Eisenstein, *Contemporary Feminist Thought* (Boston: G. K. Hall, 1983). Cited in Margaret Andersen, *Thinking about Women,* p. 328.

47. Gerda Lerner, *The Creation of Patriarchy,* p. 229.

PART I
Social Contexts of Gender

The experience for many Black males results in the gradual recognition that they, indeed, are destined to be excluded from mainstream society, and that their situation is futile.

CLYDE FRANKLIN[1]

We are triply oppressed: as Asian Americans, as Asian American women, and as Asian American women workers. Racism has been and continues to be a primary force in shaping our oppression . . . .

TRACY LAI[2]

The gender system is socially constructed. Religious, political, educational, communications, and occupational institutions, along with the family, create and enforce expectations for how women and men should behave in all known societies. Although the gender rules vary from one cultural setting to another, all have such rules, and most of these rules are rooted in patriarchy—the control or dominance of women by men, and the control of less-empowered men by men with more power. Within these institutions, people are systematically socialized to become women or men via complex processes of learning and are frequently bombarded with gender rules from many sources simultaneously, such as home, school, the media, religious institutions, and leisure activities.

Although individuals can break or stretch the rules without changing the structures surrounding human lives, individual change will not have much impact on the structures. For example, many individual women are committed to holding jobs requiring high levels of responsibility and competence but are blocked from promotion for such reasons as sexism, racism, ageism, and homophobia. Men who want to be involved in their children's lives often find it difficult. For some, the need to hold more than one job in order to make ends meet severely limits their time at home. Professional men are often pressured into spending long, inflexible hours at the office. Men who are unemployed and might have more time to spend with their children frequently find their inability to provide economic support to their families humiliating, especially when their children ask for things. And men who do find the time to get involved are often met with disbelief and disapproval from health care and educational systems accustomed to dealing only with mothers. Thus, even when individuals are motivated to stretch the boundaries of gender, social structures often impede them.

How we express our maleness or femaleness varies widely from one social context to another. Sociologists, anthropologists, biologists, and others argue convincingly that it is not reproductive biology alone that determines how a person develops. Rather, there is an interaction between one's genetic, biological

19

makeup, usually referred to as *sex,* and the expectations for male and female behavior in the social contexts in which a person lives, usually referred to as *gender.*[3] Expectations for what constitutes femininity and masculinity are frequently affected by race, class, culture, and other factors. The freedom to be the kind of woman or man a person might like to be is greatly curtailed by sexism, poverty, racism, homophobia, and other cultural constraints and expectations. Thus in order to understand people's identities and opportunities, we need to understand what they've lived through in the past, the historical times and the circumstances in which they are currently living, the possibilities open to them as men or women, the privilege or oppression that they experience, and the possibilities for empowerment that they encounter.

Part I presents six authors' perspectives on factors that impact the lives of people in their various groups. The first five present aspects of the realities of people who are dealing with intersecting oppressions and whose voices are frequently marginalized. We learn about some of the painful realities surrounding the lives of Black men, Latina lesbians, Native American women, Jewish women, and Asian American women and men in the United States today. The sixth author looks at contexts of gender through the institution of men's sports, examining how race and class intersect to produce different experiences in sports for white men and men of color (primarily Black).

Sociologist Clyde Franklin's work emerges from men's studies that call for the study of men as men. Insisting that the term "men" is much too general, he asks, Which men? He then proceeds to describe a range of brutal realities that have circumscribed the lives of Black men in the United States, historically and currently, limiting their ability to be men as defined by the wider society. Instead, he outlines a range of Black masculinities that are not well matched to the hegemonic masculinity expected of middle- and upper-class white men because of black men's blocked access to opportunities. Franklin makes a powerful statement against racism and poverty, and against the violence that so many black families face. He also strongly advocates the acceptance of Black men into the wider society.

Gloria Anzaldúa's excerpt describes her experience as a Chicana lesbian writer who grew up poor in the part of the United States that once belonged to Mexico. She interweaves issues of history, identity, and politics, addressing the challenge of "belonging" within a colonized, sexist, heterosexist society. Writer Paula Gunn Allen then looks at the brutal context in which Native American women are attempting to build empowered lives and concludes that the historical attacks on Native American people and culture make this extremely difficult. Writers Ruth Atkin and Adrienne Rich examine the relationship between anti-Semitism, sexism, and racism, looking at what young Jewish women have experienced on some college campuses. Their essay was written in response to increasing anti-Semitic incidents and addresses internalized anti-Semitism as well.

Next, Tracy Lai names some of the historically oppressive events and laws surrounding the presence of Asians in the United States, and she discusses the specific situation of Asian women, citing stereotyping, exploitation of Asian women as workers, and the difficulty of working for feminist change as crucial aspects of the experiences of Asian American women.

Finally, Michael A. Messner compares the experiences of white men and men of color (primarily Black men) within men's sports. He identifies ways in which masculinity changes over time, how the structure of competitive sports interferes with men's ability to be intimate, and how class and race intersect to determine different experiences for athletes of color and white athletes. This article provides a bridge to the next section of the book—gender socialization.

The authors in Part I identify intersecting oppressions in various combinations and encourage us to think in more complex ways about what ties people down and what provides unearned privilege. By implication and overt recommendation, many of these writers ask for a more democratic and humane world in which a plurality of experiences are acknowledged and respected.

NOTES

1. Clyde Franklin, "Ain't I a Man? The Efficacy of Black Masculinities for Men's Studies," in Richard G. Majors and Jacob U. Gordon, *The American Black Male: His Present Status and His Future* (Chicago: Nelson Hall Publishers, 1994), p. 275.
2. Tracy Lai, "Asian Women: Not for Sale," in Margaret Andersen and Patricia Hill Collins, eds., *Race, Class, and Gender: An Anthology* (Wadsworth, 1995), p. 186.
3. For more about this issue, see Margaret Andersen, *Thinking about Women: Sociological Perspectives on Sex and Gender,* 3rd ed., (New York: Macmillan, 1993) chapter 2, pp. 21–51; Marion Lowe and Ruth Hubbard, eds., *Woman's Nature* (New York: Pergamon Press, 1983); Anne Fausto-Sterling, *Myths of Gender* (New York: Basic Books, 1985); Ruth Hubbard, M. S. Henifin, and B. Fried, eds., *Women Look at Biology Looking at Women* (Cambridge, MA: Schenckman, 1979).

1

AIN'T I A MAN?
The Efficacy of Black Masculinities for Men's Studies in the 1990s

CLYDE W. FRANKLIN, II

Michael Kimmel and Michael Messner (1989) asked a very simple question and yet a very complicated one, in the introduction to their edited work *Men's Lives.* They query, "But what does it mean to examine 'men as men?'" "Most courses in a college curriculum are about men, aren't they?" Kimmel and Messner continue. Still, because such courses seem only to deal with men in their public roles, Kimmel and Messner conclude that "rarely, if ever, are men understood through the prism of gender." Catherine Stimpson (1987), founding editor of *Signs: Journal of Women in Culture and Society,* was confronted with this reality when she wrote the foreword to philosopher Harry Brod's edited volume *The Making of Masculinities* (1987). Stimpson said about the volume, "It's dogged, imaginative scholarship, sticking to its task, in rewriting that deceptively simple word 'man.'" Brod (1987, 39), in an initial attempt to make a case for men's studies, proposed a general theory of men's studies as an academic field, gave illustrative examples of men's studies research endeavors, and compared and contrasted several political perspectives on men's studies. The underlying and persistent theme of Brod's arguments was, "while seemingly about men, traditional scholarship's treatment of generic man as the human norm in fact systematically excludes from consideration what is unique to men qua men." Precluded from traditional scholarship about men, according to Brod, is "the study of masculinity as a *specific male* experience, rather than a universal paradigm for human experience" (p. 40).

But . . . "Ain't I a Man?"—Including Black Men

But what "man" is being studied? It is 1992, and 140 years since Sojourner Truth stood before the second annual convention of the women's rights movement in Akron, Ohio, in 1852 (hooks 1981, 160). In an impassioned plea for Black women's rights, she spoke of the fact that (white) men in the audience were talking about helping (white) women into carriages and over ditches and making sure they had the best places. Yet, Sojourner Truth felt, "Well, children, whar dar is so much racket dar must be something out o' kilter. But what's all dis here talkin' about?" Baring her breast, she asked, "Ain't I a woman? Look at me! Look at my arm! I have plowed and planted, and gathered into barns and no man could hold me—and ain't I a woman? I could work as hard as any man and bear de lash as well . . . and ain't I a woman . . . ?"

What Sojourner Truth does, according to bell hooks, unlike most white women's rights advocates, is refer to her own personal life experience as evidence of women's ability to function as parent; to be the work equal of men; to undergo persecution, physical abuse, rape, torture; and to not only survive but emerge triumphant (hooks 1981, 160).

In 1981, bell hooks repeated Sojourner Truth's cry in her volume *Ain't I a Woman: Black Women and Feminism,* because 129 years later America still had not responded to Black women. The popular Black singer James Brown croons, "It's a Man's World" . . . but is it a Black man's world? Are Black males "men" in America? After all, the concept "man" is socially constructed and for that reason, the question must be raised, *"Are Black males "men" in America?"* Let us explore briefly this question.

Early Black Masculinity in America: In the Beginning

Uprooted from their culture, land, and loved ones, the twenty Black slaves who were brought to Jamestown, Virginia, in 1619 had no idea what awaited them. They could not have imagined that they would be separated from their fellow tribespersons, placed with Blacks from different tribes who spoke different languages, auctioned off like cattle, and beaten and killed culturally and physically. It was during this time period that Black males and white males began to construct masculine identities for Black males. These social constructions have connoted many things over the decades, but all too often they did not signify "man" in the early beginning. This was so because Black males had to live within a social system imposed by planta-tion owners. Yet slave men often attempted to be providers by supplement-ing their meager food supplied by plantation owners by hunting and trapping game. This, however, was not the hegemonic definition of mas-culinity in early America. Black males were not human, and thus it was impossible for them to be masculine.

Characteristics of the Black Male Sex Role: In the Beginning

Characteristics of the Black male sex role constructed and assigned to male slaves were varied. Kitano (1985) notes that the status of Blacks initially was clearly undefined. In the seventeenth century, Blacks were indentured ser-vants with rights to freedom after fulfilling contractual obligations (pp. 104–5). But, Kitano feels, because Blacks were easily identifiable, a racial caste system evolved. This system has been said to be the single most impor-tant experience for the Black person in the United States. It was a system that classified people into human/subhuman, master/servant, adult/child, owner/owned—and meant, essentially, the degradation of a human being to the status of property (p. 106). What did this mean for the Black male's sex role? It meant development of several dimensions of the Black male sex role, some of which are discussed below.

Dimensions of the Black Male Sex Role

The Black man as property. Central to the treatment of the Black male in early America was the notion that he was "property." Actually, not only was he property, but also those persons closest to him were "property." This is a crit-ical point that we will return to later. Succinctly, in the beginning, one critical dimension of Black masculinity—what it means to be a man—was "you were property, owned, could be bought, sold, bartered, given, or eliminated."

The Black man as submissive. Slave masters quickly perceived a very real problem: slaves did not want to comply with their wishes. As a result, discipline became a central feature of socializing Black male slaves. Generally, slaves had come from extended families, but now they were thrown into diverse African groups. Violence had to be used to make slaves fearful, compliant, and submissive.

The Black male as nonprotective. Being slaves, Black males could not exert any protective control over the lives of family members. Black women were used to breed slaves for slave masters. Families could be destroyed at any time in the slave community. The male slave was taught that his proper role was to assume a nonprotective stance regarding the people he loved most.

The Black male as powerless. In America during slavery, a patriarchal system existed. The male was the head of the home. This was the model Black males saw. But Black male slaves could not be heads of families. They had little voice in running their families, telling their children what they could or could not do, beyond what the slave master wanted. Black male slaves were powerless within their families and in the outside world. Still, Gutman found that marriages occurred and endured. They were legitimized often by rituals such as jumping over a broomstick, and fidelity was expected from both males and females after marriage (Gutman 1976).

The Black male as stud supreme. By now it is probably obvious that the Black male slave role was a contradictory and peculiar one. Black male slaves were considered subhuman and expected to behave only marginally as human. Most of the rights and privileges accorded "men" in America were denied this subhuman male. But, the black male slave *was* expected to be healthy and strong, to work hard, and to be a good breeder. Ironically, the very system that mandated nonbinding, intensive, and frequent sexual relationships between Black males and Black females (for breeding purposes) also defined Black males as hypersexual subhumans. A plethora of sexual myths surrounded the Black male slave. The myths ranged from the unusual enormity of the Black male slave's penis to his spectacular feats and endeavors in the sexual arena. Indeed, the Black male slave *was* an animal—a subhuman who was fit only for working and breeding. The perception of Black male slaves as studs supreme meant that white women had to be protected from the potentially sexually aggressive subhumans. This perception of the Black male slave as stud supreme, along with a resulting paranoia that Black male slaves would rape white women led to numerous lynchings of and other heinous crimes against Black male slaves. The perception of the sexual prowess of Black males persists to this very day. Black families, too, were sexually stereotyped, but, as sociologist Robert Staples notes, it was the Black male who was most sexually demeaned. Staples writes:

> Although the sexual stereotypes apply equally to Black men and women, it is the Black male who has suffered the most because of the white notions of his hypersexuality. Between 1884 and 1900 more than 2,500 Black men were lynched, the majority of whom were accused of

sexual interest in white women. The Black man, it was said, had a larger penis, a great sexual capacity, and an insatiable sexual appetite. These stereotypes depicted Black men as primitive sexual beasts without the white man's love for home and family. (Staples 1986, 58)

In summary, during slavery and for a period afterward, the Black male sex role had the following dimensions: property, submissive, nonprotective, powerless, and stud supreme.

Of all the aforementioned sex-role dimensions, perhaps none was more important to the Black male than society's refusal to extend him "manhood." As John O. Killens concluded in his novel, *And Then We Heard the Thunder,* "The only thing they [white society] will not stand for is for a Black man to be a man. And everything else is worthless if a man can't be a man." But how does one become a man? I submit that becoming a generic man with a particular kind of masculinity is a process of social construction. Becoming a Black man with a particular kind of masculinity is an even more difficult and tedious social construction because of the numerous adaptations that must be made in a racist society.

The Black Male as a Unit of Analysis: Being a Black Man

Understanding Black men means recognizing that in America adult black males have been Black "men" for only about twenty years. In addition, even during this time Black males have not been recognized as "societally approved" men. While there has been gradual recognition of Black males as "men," there has been concomitant understanding of Black men as aberrant and not quite capable of assuming the "masculine role." How else is it possible to explain white society's reluctance to extend male power and privilege to Black men? Could it be that Black men still are perceived as subhuman, animalistic sexual perverts?

Seeing the Black male as an object of study means understanding Black males' diversity. Black males, like males of all races, ethnicities, and nationalities, come in all statures, dispositions, attitudes, sexualities, and so forth. Yet, there is a thread of commonality linking Black men in America. This thread of commonality is the experience of oppression. Even so, hooks (1981) suggests that "enslaved Black men were stripped of the patriarchal status that had characterized their social situation in Africa but they were not stripped of their masculinity" (p. 21).

hooks argues that the white slave owners sought to exploit the masculinity of the African male. Defining masculinity in terms of such attributes as strength, virility, vigor, and physical prowess, hooks contends that young, strong, healthy African males were prime targets. She says:

That white people recognized the masculinity of the Black male is evident by the tasks assigned the majority of Black male slaves. No annals of history record that masses of Black slave men were forced to execute roles traditionally performed exclusively by women. Evidence to the contrary exists, documenting the fact that there were many tasks enslaved African men would not perform because they regarded them as female tasks. . . . If white women and men had really been obsessed by the idea of destroying Black masculinity, they could easily have physically castrated all Black men aboard slave ships or they could have forced Black men to assume feminine attire or perform so-called feminine tasks. (1981, 21)

It is apparent in the above statement that hooks feels maintaining Black male slaves' physical strength, virility, and vigor while not making them perform traditional female roles can be equated with maintaining their masculinity. I take issue with hooks on this point because my perception of masculinity is that it is socially constructed. Black male slaves, by definition, were subhuman nonmen. Certainly, if healthy, vigorous, strong, and virile, they were expected to perform tedious tasks for long hours, sire children, obey the master. But this did not mean preserving Black male slave masculinity—in fact, it meant the opposite. Black male slaves had no gender; they did have a sex—but no gender. In order for the Black male slave to have had a gender, he would have had to be recognized as a human being. To the contrary, numerous myths about the Black male during slavery were constructed and perpetuated—all supporting the idea of Black male slave subhumanity.

In a very real sense, the ambiguity surrounding the Black male sex role today may be due in part to the legacy of a nondefinition of the Black male slave sex role, and continued reluctance to perceive the Black male as a man—at least in the hegemonic sense of the word.

The Truth about Masculinity: A Men's Studies Perspective

Men's studies literature in the 1980s recognized an important fact about masculinity in America. The culturally exalted form of masculinity, the hegemonic model, corresponds to the actual character of a small number of men (Carrigan et al. 1987). As Carrigan, Connell, and Lee elaborate, "There is a distance and a tension between collective ideal and actual lives" (p. 92). Few, if any males' actual lives fit the hegemonic model. Still, a critical division exists between hegemonic masculinity and various subordinated masculinities. There are groups of men who possess power and wealth and who legitimate and reproduce social relationships that generate and sustain the hegemonic model. The way Black males fit into this overall power framework, and how Black males construct their various forms of masculinity, are problematic concerns in men's studies. The processes of constructing Black masculinities are difficult ones. They are difficult because the societal institutions are headed by white males who have vested interests in supporting the hegemonic model. This means, as Carrigan, Connell, and Lee imply, Black males continually are negotiating their masculinities from positions of powerlessness.

The results are obvious—many forms of Black masculinities are seen as falling outside of culturally prescribed masculinities. This is not surprising because America has yet to recognize large numbers of Black males as men/masculine. This is so despite the fact that thousands of Black males keep trying to be men.

Ontological and Epistemological Assumptions Underlying the Study of Black Masculinities

Studying Black masculinities before the late 1960s was a rather static process. Black males had participated in various masculinity constructions; however, those masculinities departing from society's conception of the Black male role were considered anomalies—something out of the ordinary. George W. Carver, Marcus Garvey, Elijah Mohammad, Booker T. Washington, E. Franklin Frazier, W. E. B. Du Bois, Langston Hughes, Paul Robeson, Bayard Rustin, A. Phillip Randolph, all were seen as enigmas, and society was ambivalent toward them. These Black males certainly were different from society's prescribed role for Black males. Thus, society really had no response for them and often treated them awkwardly (Rustin 1971).

Actually, American society's treatment of Black men who depart significantly from societal expectations, but do so in a socially acceptable manner, reflects the inadequacy of using sex role models to study Black men. Men's studies scholars point to the fact that "there is variation in masculinity arising from individual experiences that produces a range of personalities . . . the male role is unduly restrictive because hegemonic masculinity does not reflect the true nature of men" (Carrigan et al. 1987, 78). This may be an especially acute problem when studying the lives of *Black males* who reluctantly were extended the label "man" only during the modern day civil-rights movement in the late 1960s. Ironically, the label "man" was extended only when Black males in sufficient numbers threatened to use a mainstay male trait, violence, to accomplish what cooperation and negotiation had *not* been able to accomplish. Just as ironic was the fact that buttressing the extension of the label was not only threatened violence but also frequent objectification and exploitation of white women. The rationale for this aspect of the revolution, according to bell hooks, was that success means little for Black males if they cannot also possess that human object white patriarchal culture offers to men as the supreme reward for masculine achievement (hooks 1981, 113). About Black men hooks writes:

> In their eagerness to gain access to the bodies of white women, many Black men have shown that they were far more concerned with exerting

masculine privilege than challenging racism. Their behavior is not unlike that of white male patriarchs who, on one hand, claimed to be white supremacists, but who could not forego sexual contact with the women of the very race they claimed to hate. (pp. 113–14)

Quite simply, adult Black males became "men" when they publicly incorporated violence and actively sought sexual liaisons with white women—all with the permission of those powerful white males in charge of maintaining hegemonic definitions of masculinity.

Ontological Assumptions Underlying the Study of Black Masculinities: A Proposal

When Black males became "men" in America it had little to do with accepting a static male sex role; it had much to do with actual and perceived alterations in power relations between the supporters of hegemonic masculinities and subordinated masculinities. For a few brief moments, Black-male-led riots in major American cities, kidnappings, and general racial unrest produced novel and different forms of Black masculinity. Challenges to the traditional power holders actually called into question static definitions of masculinity which had implied that there was something called a "male sex role."

Challenging the power holders meant *freeing Black males to become Black men*. It connoted allowing the construction of Black masculinity. Put simply, "male sex role" did not exist. It is impossible to isolate a "role" that constructs masculinity (Carrigan et al. 1987, 80). There is no reality of a sex role out there that gives us the basis for masculinity: *Masculinities are constructed*. Black masculinities, in particular, are constructed under the cloud of oppression.

For Black males historically it was not a matter of having subordinated masculinities because, as stated repeatedly, Black males were not perceived as "men." To reiterate, through *violence* and *sexism* Black males and white males began to construct masculinities for Black males during the modern-day Black-male-led movement in the late 1960s (Staples 1986, 80). When Black males became Black men through these social constructions, various forms of Black masculinities emerged: traditionally heterosexual masculinity, androgynous Black masculinity, homosexual Black masculinity, and ambisexual Black masculinity. But these social constructions all developed simultaneously with societal conditions that produced the following characteristics of Black males in America in the 1980s:

Suicide [was] the third leading cause of death among Black males ages 18–29.

Black-on-Black homicide [was] the leading cause of death for Black males ages 15–34.

The incidence of drug-related disease for Black males under 35 [was] 12 times higher than for any comparable group.

Black males [had] ten times the incidence of heart attacks and prostate cancer as white males.

From 1950–1985 the life expectancy for white males increased from 63 to 74.6 years, while for Black males it increased only from 59 to 65 years over the same period of time.

Between 1973 and 1986 the real earnings of Black males age 18–29 declined 31%, the percentage of young Black males in the full-time work force fell by 20%, and the number who [had] dropped out of the labor force doubled from 13% to 25%.

From 1973–1987, real earnings of Black males ages 20 to 29 decreased by 27.7%.

In 1987, 31.5% of Black males ages 16–19 were unemployed compared to 16% of white males within the same age group.

Blacks [comprised] 48% of the U.S. prison population, yet [comprised] only 12% of the general population.

Black males [comprised] 89% of the Black prison population.

Of the Black male population in large metropolitan areas, 51% [had] been arrested compared to only 14% of white males.

Eighteen percent of all Black males [had served] time in prison compared to only 3% of white males. (*Ohio's African-American Males,* 1990).

Certainly these are heinous, difficult, and debilitating experiences for Black men in America. Still, they form the bases for new Black masculinities produced by a society that still seems ambivalent about extending male privileges and statuses to Black men. But aren't adult Black males "men"? Don't Black males work at some of the most menial tasks which support this country? Don't Black males overwhelmingly protect America in the armed forces? Despite rejections, don't the majority of Black males continue to believe in the American dream? Aren't Black males "men"? Understanding the processes Black men in America use to construct their masculinities in the face of great odds and obstacles is a major task for academicians interested in men's studies. Key ideas here are the ontological assumptions that Black masculinities *are not biological;* they are *socially constructed within a framework of power relations or dynamics often dominated by powerful white males and subordinated minority males.*

Many Black males in America perceive American society to be permeated with normlessness and incapable of controlling individual behavior. This view of society suggests that there is a perceived lack of socially imposed restrictions on individual needs and desires. From this perspective society does not have sufficient resources for its members and thus, the emergence and persistence of anomie (Farley 1990, 218).

Sociologist Robert K. Merton (1968) feels that anomie results when individuals in a society internalize certain needs and desires through societal inculcation but face structural impediments to the realization of these needs and desires. He proposes several modes of individual adaptation that may be used to construct "ideal" types of Black masculinities.

I submit that Black men, more than others in America, experience anomic situations in society. The experience for many Black males results in the gradual recognition that they, indeed, are destined to be excluded from mainstream society, and that their situation is futile. This is the state of countless Black men in America today. Feelings of futility and internalized desires for success generate modes of individual adaptations that define generally various forms of Black masculinities: (1) conforming Black masculinity, (2) ritualistic Black masculinity, (3) innovative Black masculinity, (4) retreatist Black masculinity, and (5) rebellious Black masculinity.

Conforming Black masculinity. Contrary to some opinions, Black males in America overwhelmingly are conforming in the sense that they continue to accept mainstream society's prescriptions and proscriptions for heterosexual males. They do so despite the fact that, when society teaches men to work hard, set high goals, and strive for success, it does not teach Black men simultaneously that their probability of failure is high because blocked opportunities for Black males are endemic to American society. Historically, this strategy paid off quite well for American society—especially white society—because social dislocation characterizing Black males did not reach catastrophic proportions until the mid-1970s, as noted by William J. Wilson (1987). According to Wilson, the increasing rate of social dislocation has been due more to changes in the social organization of inner-city areas than social psychological sources of nonconformity (p. 3). Succinctly, a large proportion of the Black male population chooses the conforming mode of individual adaptation to American society's dictates.

Ritualistic Black masculinity. Because of certain experiences, another group of Black men comes to realize that American societal goals and their individual goals are not coterminous. That is, regardless of whether they accept or reject the goals, America will decide how successful they will be in life. Such men may gradually develop cynical attitudes about the goals of individual success and realizing the American dream. Frequently, these Black men construct uncanny abilities to "follow the rules," giving little thought to any reasons for doing so. They participate in societal institutions, "playing the game" without purpose or commitment. Black men of this genre appear to be conforming but in actuality are ritualistic in their actions—*performing* without rhyme or reason. In one sense, this form of Black masculinity remains highly functional for American society, since it closely resembles conformity. But in another sense, the individual Black male suffers because he becomes a social zombie, following societal dictates regardless of consequences to himself and those close to him.

Innovative Black masculinity. The most publicized, feared, and reviled Black men in America today are those who have constructed innovative Black masculinity forms. The innovative forms of masculinity constructed may be relatively nonthreatening physically but somewhat socially distasteful to many. For example, it may exaggerate one aspect of traditional masculinity which *can* be achieved in order to receive desired responses. An example that comes to mind is 2 Live Crew's recording, "As Nasty As They Wanna Be." The recording emphasizes sexual explicitness and debases women—two aspects of masculinity most American men are very familiar with. Simultaneously, the recording also achieves the societally desired goal of materialistic success. It is very doubtful that rapping about the contempt held for Black women, Black religion, Black parents, and, in essence, the Black culture would have been used as a means for attaining success in America if blocked opportunities did not characterize these Black men's experiences. It is common to find Black men in such circumstances, and it is becoming increasingly common to see similar consequences of such circumstances.

Strikingly different from the aforementioned relatively mild innovative Black masculine form is a much more lethal form of Black masculinity. It is the type of Black masculinity that responds to blocked opportunities by developing and glorifying heinous means of achieving materialistic success, including Black-on-Black homicide, drug dealing, theft, and various other forms of deviance. This is the form of Black masculinity that has resulted in a growing crisis for Black males in America (Strickland 1989; Tiff 1990). What has to be remembered, however, is that it is not lack of resources or poverty that results in the construction of this form of Black masculinity. Rather, it is the fact that one lacks the ability to fulfill the societal masculine role while being surrounded by those not so disabled, in a society that keeps emphasizing that fulfilling the role should be the goal of every American man.

Retreatist Black masculinity. There is an alarmingly growing number of Black men in America who are constructing and nurturing a kind of Black masculinity signifying withdrawal from American society. These Black men may be characterized by high rates of joblessness, welfare dependency, drug addiction, alcoholism, and homelessness. Essentially, having grown weary of participating in a system that denies them the means for achieving common goals most members of society achieve, these men have opted to leave the system—withdraw.

Rebellious Black Masculinity. By and large Black males in America today do not adopt societal anomie by simultaneously rejecting America's *goals* and *means* of achieving the goals. They may reject one or the other as suggested earlier, but rarely do Black men reject both. If sizeable numbers of Black men were to reject both, it is likely that they would construct rebellious forms of Black masculinity similar to or more intense than what occurred during the late 1960s and early 1970s. The new men's studies could be used by Black men as a framework in which to construct new goals and means more compatible with the interests and welfare of Black men. Similarly, Black masculinities could be integrated with the new men's studies in order to further demystify the lives of men in America. In essence, this is the efficacy of Black masculinities for men's studies and vice versa in the 1990s.

Epistemological Assumptions Underlying the Study of Black Masculinities: A Proposal

William J. Wilson (1987, 18) argues that it is not sufficient to rely solely on census data and other secondary data when studying the recent rise in rates of social dislocation in the underclass. This is especially relevant for studying Black men who have disproportionate rates of Black social dislocation.

Also important for Black men's studies in Wilson's view is that the aforementioned methodologies should be augmented with empirical data on both the ghetto underclass experience and conditions in the broader society that have shaped and continue to shape that experience. This calls for a number of different research strategies ranging from survey to ethnography to historical work.

It is clear that little about Black men in America can be gleaned from sterile statistics alone. Without adequate accompanying explanations, knowledgeable interpretations from informed perspectives, and other methodologies, Black men will remain an enigma in the 1990s. Surely the necessity for understanding the everyday experience of Black men is apparent as an appropriate empirical tool in Black men's studies. Correlational and regression analyses certainly have their places in Black masculinity studies. Alone, however, they are not sufficient substitutes for qualitative methodologies that can produce knowledge with human depth and richness of dimension.

It is also possible, with certain qualitative methodologies, to attenuate the problem of reification in Black men's studies. Black men are viewed in many ways, as we have seen. Depending on one's political persuasion, ethnic affiliation, racial group membership, and sex, Black men's intelligence, power, sexuality, compassion, and other traits will vary. To be sure, this is to be expected. But because Black men are relatively isolated in America, dangerous misconceptions, myths, and unsupported conjectures about them abound. Also, these simply are mental constructions. They are abstractions. Yet, with media bombardment supporting myths, research reports without adequate interpretation, and prevailing racism in America, abstractions or mental constructions related to Black men are converted into real, living beings. This is the danger of acquiring knowledge about Black men using only quantitative methodologies. The knowledge obtained may be socially constructed and then may be responded to as though it is real. During slavery Black men were mentally constructed as subhuman, not quite men, and legacies of this abstraction remain today. This is precisely why there is a need for Black men's studies. Without Black men's studies and an appropriate epistemology, it is indeed possible that in the year 2000, many Black men will still be asking the question "Ain't I a man?"

REFERENCES

Brod, H., ed. 1987. *The Making of Masculinities: The New Men's Studies.* Winchester, MA: Allen and Unwin.
————. 1987. "The Case for Men's Studies." In H. Brod (ed.), *The Making of Masculinities: The New Men's Studies.* Winchester, MA: Allen and Unwin.
Carrigan, T.; B. Connell; and J. Lee. 1987. "Toward A New Sociology of Masculinity." In H. Brod (ed.), *The Making of Masculinities: The New Men's Studies.* Winchester, MA: Allen and Unwin.
Farley, J. E. 1990. *Sociology.* Englewood Cliffs, NJ: Prentice-Hall.
Franklin, C. W., II. 1984. *The Changing Definition of Masculinity.* New York: Plenum.
————. 1988. *Men and Society.* Chicago: Nelson-Hall.
Gutman, H. 1976. *The Black in Slavery and Freedom, 1750–1925.* New York: Pantheon.
hooks, b. 1981. *Ain't I a Woman: Black Women and Feminism.* Boston: South End Press.
————. 1984. *Feminist Theory: From Margin to Center.* Boston: South End Press.
Killens, J. O. 1983. *And Then We Heard the Thunder.* Washington, DC: Howard University Press.
Kimmel, M. S., and M. A. Messner, eds. 1989. *Men's Lives.* New York: Macmillan.
Kitano, H. H. L. 1985. *Race Relations,* 3rd ed. Englewood Cliffs, NJ: Prentice-Hall.
Ladner, J. A. 1972. *Tomorrow's Tomorrow: The Black Woman.* Garden City, NY: Doubleday.
Merton, R. 1968. *Social Theory and Social Structure,* rev. ed. New York: Free Press.
"Ohio's African-American Males: A Call to Action." 1990. *Report of the Governor's Commission on Socially Disadvantaged Black Males.* Vol. 1, *Executive Summary.* Columbus, OH: Office of Black Affairs.
Rustin, B. 1971. *Down the Line.* Chicago: Quadrangle Books.
Staples, R. 1986. *The Black Family: Essays and Studies,* 3rd ed. "Black Masculinity, Hypersexuality, and Sexual Aggression." Belmont City, CA: Wadsworth.
————. 1989. "Masculinity and Race: The Dual Dilemma of Black Men." In M. Kimmel and M. Messner, *Men's Lives.* New York: Macmillan. (Reprinted from *Journal of Social Issues* 34(1).)
Stimpson, C. R. 1987. "Foreword." In H. Brod (ed.), *The Making of Masculinities: The New Men's Studies.* Winchester, MA: Allen and Unwin.
Strickland, W. 1989. "Our Men in Crisis." *Essence,* Nov. 1989, pp. 49–52, 109–15.
Tiff, S. 1990. "Fighting the Failure Syndrome." *Time,* May 21, pp. 83–84.
Wilson, W. J. 1987. *The Truly Disadvantaged: The Inner City, the Underclass and Public Policy.* Chicago: University of Chicago Press.

2

THE NEW MESTIZA

GLORIA ANZALDÚA (1987)

El otro México que acá hemos construido
el espacio es lo que ha sido
territorio nacional.
Esté el esfuerzo de todos nuestros hermanos
y latinoamericanos que han sabido
progressar.

—LOS TIGRES DEL NORTE

"The *Aztecas del norte* . . . compose the largest single tribe or nation of *Anishinabeg (Indians) found in the United States today. . . . Some call themselves Chicanos and see themselves as people whose true homeland is Aztlán (The U.S. Southwest)."*

> Wind tugging at my sleeve
> feet sinking into the sand
> I stand at the edge where earth touches ocean
> where the two overlap
> a gentle coming together
> at other times and places a violent clash.
>
> Across the border in Mexico
>   stark silhouette of houses gutted by waves,
>   cliffs crumbling into the sea,
>   silver waves marbled with spume
>   gashing a hole under the border fence.
>
>   *Miro el mar atacar*
>   *la cerca en* Border Field Park
>   *con sus buchones de agua.*
> an Easter Sunday resurrection
> of the brown blood in my veins.
>
> *Oigo el llorido del mar, el respiro del aire,*
>   my heart surges to the beat of the sea.
>   In the gray haze of the sun
>   the gulls' shrill cry of hunger,
>   the tangy smell of the sea seeping into me.

Excerpt from *Borderlands/La Frontera: The New Mestiza* (San Francisco: Spinsters/Aunt Lute, 1987), pp. 1–8. © 1987 by Gloria Anzaldúa. Reprinted by permission of Aunt Lute Books.

I walk   through the hole in the fence
to the other side.
Under my fingers I feel the gritty wire
rusted by 139 years
of the salty breath of the sea.

Beneath the iron sky
Mexican children kick their soccer ball across,
run after it, entering the U.S.

I press my hand to the steel curtain—
chainlink fence crowned with rolled barbed wire
rippling from the sea where Tijuana touches San Diego
unrolling over mountains
and plains
and deserts,
this "Tortilla Curtain" turning into *el rio Grande*
flowing down to the flatlands
of the Magic Valley of South Texas
its mouth emptying into the Gulf.

1,950 mile-long open wound
dividing a *pueblo*, a culture,
running down the length of my body,
staking fence rods in my flesh,
splits me   splits me
me raja   me raja

This is my home
this thin edge of
barbwire.

But the skin of the earth is seamless.
The sea cannot be fenced,
el mar does not stop at borders.
To show the white man what she thought of his
arrogance.
Yemaya blew that wire fence down.

This land was Mexican once,
was Indian always
and is.
And   will be again.

Yo soy un puente tendido
        del mundo gabacho al del mojado,
lo pasado me estirá pa' `trás
        y lo presente pa' `delante,
Que la Virgen de Guadalupe me cuide
Ay ay ay, soy mexicana de este lado.

The U.S.-Mexican border *es una herida abierta* where the Third World grates against the first and bleeds. And before a scab forms it hemorrhages again, the life-blood of two worlds merging to form a third country—a border culture. Borders are set up to define the places that are safe and unsafe, to distinguish *us* from *them*. A border is a dividing line, a narrow strip along a steep edge. A borderland is a vague and undetermined place created by the emotional residue of an unnatural boundary. It is in a constant state of transition. The prohibited and forbidden are its inhabitants. *Los atravesados* live here: the squint-eyed, the perverse, the queer, the troublesome, the mongrel, the mulatto, the half-breed, the half dead; in short, those who cross over, pass over, or go through the confines of the "normal." Gringos in the U.S. Southwest consider the inhabitants of the borderlands transgressors, aliens— whether they possess documents or not, whether they're Chicanos, Indians, or Blacks. Do not enter, trespassers will be raped, maimed, strangled, gassed, shot. The only "legitimate" inhabitants are those in power, the whites and those who align themselves with whites. Tension grips the inhabitants of the borderlands like a virus. Ambivalence and unrest reside there and death is no stranger.

> In the fields, *la migra.* My aunt saying, "*No corran,* don't run. They'll think you're *del otro lao.*" In the confusion, Pedro ran, terrified of being caught. He couldn't speak English, couldn't tell them he was fifth generation American. *Sin papeles*—he did not carry his birth certificate to work in the fields. *La migra* took him away while we watched. *Se lo llevaron.* He tried to smile when he looked back at us, to raise his fist. But I saw the shame pushing his head down, I saw the terrible weight of shame hunch his shoulders. They deported him to Guadalajara by plane. The furthest he'd ever been to Mexico was Reynosa, a small border town opposite Hidalgo, Texas, not far from McAllen. Pedro walked all the way to the Valley. *Se lo llevaron sin un centavo al pobre. Se vino andando desde Guadalajara.*

During the original peopling of the Americas, the first inhabitants migrated across the Bering Straits and walked south across the continent. The oldest evidence of humankind in the U.S.—the Chicanos' ancient Indian ancestors—was found in Texas and has been dated to 3500 B.C. In the Southwest United States archeologists have found 20,000-year-old campsites of the Indians who migrated through, or permanently occupied, the Southwest, Aztlán—land of the herons, land of whiteness, the Edenic place of origin of the Azteca.

In 1000 B.C., descendants of the original Cochise people migrated into what is now Mexico and Central America and became the direct ancestors of many of the Mexican people. (The Cochise culture of the Southwest is the parent culture of the Aztecs. The Uto-Aztecan languages stemmed from the language of the Cochise people.) The Aztecs (the Nahuatl world for people of Aztlán) left the Southwest in 1168 A.D.

Now let us go.
          Tihueque, tihueque,
Vámonos, vámonos.
          Un pájaro cantò
Con sus ocho tribus salieron
          de la "cueva del origen."
los aztecas siguieron al dios
          Huitzilophochtli.

Huitzilopochtli, the God of War, guided them to the place (that later became Mexico City) where an eagle with a writhing serpent in its beak perched on a cactus. The eagle symbolizes the spirit (as the sun, the father); the serpent symbolizes the soul (as the earth, the mother). Together, they symbolize the struggle between the spiritual/celestial/male and the underworld/earth/feminine. The symbolic sacrifice of the serpent to the "higher" masculine powers indicates that the patriarchal order had already vanquished the feminine and matriarchal order in pre-Columbian America.

At the beginning of the 16th century, the Spaniards and Hernán Cortés invaded Mexico and, with the help of tribes that the Aztecs had subjugated, conquered it. Before the Conquest, there were twenty-five million Indian people in Mexico and the Yucatán. Immediately after the Conquest, the Indian population had been reduced to under seven million. By 1650, only one-and-a-half-million pure-blooded Indians remained. The *mestizos* who were genetically equipped to survive small pox, measles, and typhus (Old World diseases to which the natives had no immunity), founded a new hybrid race and inherited Central and South America. *En 1521 nació una nueva raza, el mestizo, el mexicano* (people of mixed Indian and Spanish blood), a race that had never existed before. Chicanos, Mexican-Americans, are the offspring of those first matings.

Our Spanish, Indian, and *mestizo* ancestors explored and settled parts of the U.S. Southwest as early as the sixteenth century. For every gold-hungry *conquistador* and soul-hungry missionary who came north from Mexico, ten to twenty Indians and *mestizos* went along as porters or in other capacities. For the Indians, this constituted a return to the place of origin, Aztlán, thus making Chicanos originally and secondarily indigenous to the Southwest. Indians and *mestizos* from central Mexico intermarried with North American Indians. The continual intermarriage between Mexican and American Indians and Spaniards formed an even greater *mestizaje.* . . .

In the 1800s, Anglos migrated illegally into Texas, which was then part of Mexico, in greater and greater numbers and gradually drove the *tejanos* (native Texans of Mexican descent) from their lands, committing all manner of atrocities against them. Their illegal invasion forced Mexico to fight a war to keep its Texas territory. The Battle of the Alamo, in which the Mexican forces vanquished the whites, became, for the whites, the symbol of the cowardly and villainous character of the Mexicans. It became (and still is) a symbol that legitimized the white imperialist takeover. With the capture of Santa

Anna later in 1836, Texas became a republic. *Tejanos* lost their land and, overnight, became the foreigners. . . .

In 1846, the U.S. incited Mexico to war. U.S. troops invaded and occupied Mexico, forcing her to give up almost half of her nation, what is now Texas, New Mexico, Arizona, Colorado and California.

With the victory of the U.S. forces over the Mexican in the U.S.-Mexican War, *los norteamericanos* pushed the Texas border down 100 miles, from *el río Nueces* to *el río Grande*. South Texas ceased to be part of the Mexican state of Tamaulipas. Separated from Mexico, the Native Mexican-Texan no longer looked toward Mexico as home; the Southwest became our homeland once more. The border fence that divides the Mexican people was born on February 2, 1848 with the signing of the Treaty of Guadalupe-Hidalgo. It left 100,000 Mexican citizens on this side, annexed by conquest along with the land. The land established by the treaty as belonging to Mexicans was soon swindled away from its owners. The treaty was never honored and restitution, to this day, has never been made.

The justice and benevolence of God
will forbid that . . . Texas should again
become a howling wilderness
trod only by savages, or . . . benighted
by the ignorance and superstition,
the anarchy and rapine of Mexican misrule.
The Anglo-American race are destined
to be forever the proprietors of
this land of promise and fulfillment.
Their laws will govern it,
their learning will enlighten it,
their enterprise will improve it.
Their flocks range its boundless pastures,
for them its fertile lands will yield . . .
luxuriant harvests . . .
The wilderness of Texas has been redeemed
by Anglo-American blood & enterprise.
                              —WILLIAM H. WHARTON

The Gringo, locked into the fiction of white superiority, seized complete political power, stripping Indians and Mexicans of their land while their feet were still rooted in it. *Con el destierro y el exilo fuimos desuñados, destroncados, destripados*—we were jerked out by the roots, truncated, disemboweled, dispossessed, and separated from our identity and our history. Many, under the threat of Anglo terrorism, abandoned homes and ranches and went to Mexico. Some stayed and protested. But as the courts, law enforcement officials, and government officials not only ignored their pleas but penalized them for their efforts, *tejanos* had no other recourse but armed retaliation. . . .

Fear of Going Home: Homophobia

For the lesbian of color, the ultimate rebellion she can make against her native culture is through her sexual behavior. She goes against two moral prohibitions: sexuality and homosexuality. Being lesbian and raised Catholic, indoctrinated as straight, I *made the choice to be queer* (for some it is genetically inherent). It's an interesting path, one that continually slips in and out of the white, the Catholic, the Mexican, the indigenous, the instincts. In and out of my head. It makes for *loquería,* the crazies. It is a path of knowledge—one of knowing (and of learning) the history of oppression of our *raza.* It is a way of balancing, of mitigating duality.

In a New England college where I taught, the presence of a few lesbians threw the more conservative heterosexual students and faculty into a panic. The two lesbian students and we two lesbian instructors met with them to discuss their fears. One of the students said, "I thought homophobia meant fear of going home after a residency."

And I thought, how apt. Fear of going home. And of not being taken in. We're afraid of being abandoned by the mother, the culture, *la Raza,* for being unacceptable, faulty, damaged. Most of us unconsciously believe that if we reveal this unacceptable aspect of the self our mother/culture/race will totally reject us. To avoid rejection, some of us conform to the values of the culture, push the unacceptable parts into the shadows. Which leaves only one fear—that we will be found out and that the Shadow-Beast will break out of its cage. Some of us take another route. We try to make ourselves conscious of the Shadow-Beast, stare at the sexual lust and lust for power and destruction we see on its face, discern among its features the undershadow that the reigning order of heterosexual males project on our Beast. Yet still others of us take it another step: we try to waken the Shadow-Beast inside us. Not many jump at the chance to confront the Shadow-Beast in the mirror without flinching at her lidless serpent eyes, her cold clammy moist hand dragging us underground, fangs bared and hissing. How does one put feathers on this particular serpent? But a few of us have been lucky—on the face of the Shadow-Beast we have seen not lust but tenderness; on its face we have uncovered the lie.

Intimate Terrorism: Life in the Borderlands

The world is not a safe place to live in. We shiver in separate cells in enclosed cities, shoulders hunched, barely keeping the panic below the surface of the skin, daily drinking shock along with our morning coffee, fearing the torches being set to our buildings, the attacks on the streets. Shutting down. Woman does not feel safe when her own culture, and white culture, are critical of her; when the males of all races hunt her as prey.

Alienated from her mother culture, "alien" in the dominant culture, the woman of color does not feel safe within the inner life of her Self. Petrified, she can't respond, her face caught between *los intersticios,* the spaces between the different worlds she inhabits.

The ability to respond is what is meant by responsibility, yet our cultures take away our ability to act—shackle us in the name of protection. Blocked, immobilized, we can't move forward, can't move backwards. That writhing serpent movement, the very movement of life, swifter than lightning, frozen.

We do not engage fully. We do not make full use of our faculties. We abnegate. And there in front of us is the crossroads therefore responsible and to blame (being a victim and transferring the blame on culture, mother, father, ex-lover, friend, absolves me of responsibility), or to feel strong, and, for the most part, in control.

My Chicana identity is grounded in the Indian woman's history of resistance. The Aztec female rites of mourning were rites of defiance protesting the cultural changes which disrupted the equality and balance between female and male, and protesting their demotion to a lesser status, their denigration. Like *la Llorona,* the Indian woman's only means of protest was wailing.

So *mamá, Raza,* how wonderful, *no tener que rendir cuentas a nadie.* I feel perfectly free to rebel and to rail against my culture. I fear no betrayal on my part because, unlike Chicanas and other women of color who grew up white or who have only recently returned to their native cultural roots, I was totally immersed in mine. It wasn't until I went to high school that I "saw" whites. Until I worked on my master's degree I had not gotten within an arm's distance of them. I was totally immersed *en lo mexicano,* a rural, peasant, isolated, *mexicanismo.* To separate from my culture (as from my family) I had to feel competent enough on the outside and secure enough inside to live life on my own. Yet in leaving home I did not lose touch with my origins because *lo mexicano* is in my system. I am a turtle, wherever I go I carry "home" on my back.

Not me sold out my people but they me. So yes, though "home" permeates every sinew and cartilage in my body, I too am afraid of going home. Though I'll defend my race and culture when they are attacked by non-*mexicanos, conosco el malestar de mi cultura.* I abhor some of my culture's ways, how it cripples its women, *como burras,* our strengths used against us, lowly *burras* bearing humility with dignity. The ability to serve, claim the males, is our highest virtue. I abhor how my culture makes *macho* caricatures of its men. No, I do not buy all the myths of the tribe into which I was born. I can understand why the more tinged with Anglo blood, the more adamantly my colored and colorless sisters glorify their colored culture's values—to off-set the extreme devaluation of it by the white culture. It's a legitimate reaction. But I will not glorify those aspects of my culture which have injured me and which have injured me in the name of protecting me.

So, don't give me your tenets and your laws. Don't give me your lukewarm gods. What I want is an accounting with all three cultures—white,

Mexican, Indian. I want the freedom to carve and chisel my own face, to staunch the bleeding with ashes, to fashion my own gods out of my entrails. And if going home is denied me then I will have to stand and claim my space, making a new culture—*una cultura mestiza*—with my own lumber, my own bricks and mortar and my own feminist architecture.

3

ANGRY WOMEN ARE BUILDING
Issues and Struggles Facing American Indian Women Today

PAULA GUNN ALLEN

The central issue that confronts American Indian women throughout the hemisphere is survival, *literal survival,* both on a cultural and biological level. According to the 1980 census, population of American Indians is just over one million. This figure, which is disputed by some American Indians, is probably a fair estimate, and it carries certain implications.

Some researchers put our pre-contact population at more than 45 million, while others put it around 20 million. The U.S. government long put it at 450,000—a comforting if imaginary figure, though at one point it was put around 270,000. If our current population is around one million; if, as some researchers estimate, around 25 percent of Indian women and 10 percent of Indian men in the United States have been sterilized without informed consent; if our average life expectancy is, as the best informed research presently says, 55 years; if our infant mortality rate continues at well above national standards; if our average unemployment for all segments of our population—male, female, young, adult, and middle-aged—is between 60 and 90 percent; if the U.S. government continues its policy of termination, relocation, removal, and assimilation along with the destruction of wilderness, reservation land, and its resources, and severe curtailment of hunting, fishing, timber harvesting and water-use rights—then existing tribes are facing the threat of extinction which for several hundred tribal groups has already become fact in the past five hundred years.

In this nation of more than 200 million, the Indian people constitute less than one-half of one percent of the population. In a nation that offers refuge, sympathy, and billions of dollars in aid from federal and private sources in the form of food to the hungry, medicine to the sick, and comfort to the dying, the indigenous subject population goes hungry, homeless, impoverished, cut out of the American deal, new, old, and in between. Americans are daily made aware of the worldwide slaughter of native peoples such as the Cambodians, the Palestinians, the Armenians, the Jews—who constitute only a few groups faced with genocide in this century. We are horrified by South African apartheid and the removal of millions of indigenous African black natives to what is there called "homelands"—but this is simply a replay of nineteenth-century U.S. government removal of American Indians to reservations. Nor do many even notice the parallel or fight South African apartheid by demanding an end to its counterpart within the border of the United States. The American Indian people are in a situation comparable to the imminent genocide in may parts of the world today. The plight of our people north and south of us is no better; to the south it is considerably worse. Consciously or unconsciously, deliberately, as a matter of national policy, or accidentally as a matter of "fate," *every single government,* right, left, or centrist in the western hemisphere is consciously or subconsciously dedicated to the extinction of those tribal people who live within its borders.

Within this geopolitical charnel house, American Indian women struggle on every front for the survival of our children, our people, our self-respect, our value systems, and our way of life. The past five hundred years testify to our skill at waging this struggle: for all the varied weapons of extinction pointed at our hands, we endure.

We survive war and conquest; we survive colonization, acculturation, assimilation; we survive beating, rape, starvation, mutilation, sterilization, abandonment, neglect, death of our children, our loved ones, destruction of our land, our homes, our past, and our future. We survive, and we do more than just survive. We bond, we care, we fight, we teach, we nurse, we bear, we feed, we earn, we laugh, we love, we hang in there, no matter what.

Of course, some, many of us, just give up. Many are alcoholics, many are addicts. Many abandon children, the old ones. Many commit suicide. Many become violent, go insane. Many go "white" and are never seen or heard from again. But enough hold on to their traditions and their ways so that even after almost five hundred brutal years, we endure. And we even write songs and poems, make paintings and drawing that say "We walk in beauty. Let us continue."

Currently our struggles are on two fronts: physical survival and cultural survival. For women this means fighting alcoholism and drug abuse (our own and that of our husbands, lovers, parents, children);[1] poverty; affluence—a destroyer of people who are not traditionally socialized to deal with large sums of money; rape, incest, battering by Indian men; assaults on fertility and other health matters by the Indian Health Service and the Public

Health Service; high infant mortality due to substandard medical care, nutrition, and health information; poor educational opportunities or education that takes us away from our traditions, language, and communities; suicide, homicide, or similar expressions of self-hatred; lack of economic opportunities; substandard housing; sometimes violent and always virulent racist attitudes and behavior directed against us by an entertainment and education system that wants only one thing from Indians: our silence, our invisibility, and our collective death.

A headline in the *Navajo Times* in the fall of 1979 reported that rape was the number one crime on the Navajo reservation. In a professional mental health journal of the Indian Health Services, Phyllis Old Dog Cross reported that incest and rape are common among Indian women seeking services and that their incidence is increasing. "It is believed that at least 80 percent of the Native Women seen at the regional psychiatric service center (5 state area) have experienced some sort of sexual assault."[2] Among the forms of abuse being suffered by Native American women, Old Dog Cross cites a recent phenomenon, something called "training." This form of gang rape is "a punitive act of a group of males who band together and get even or take revenge on a selected woman."[3]

These and other cases of violence against women are powerful evidence that the status of women within the tribes has suffered grievous decline since contact, and the decline has increased in intensity in recent years. The amount of violence against women, alcoholism, and violence, abuse, and neglect by women against their children and their aged relatives have all increased. These social ills were virtually unheard of among most tribes fifty years ago, popular American opinion to the contrary. As Old Dog Cross remarks:

> Rapid, unstable and irrational change was required of the Indian people if they were to survive. Incredible loss of all that had meaning was the norm. Inhuman treatment, murder, death, and punishment was a typical experience for all the tribal groups and some didn't survive.
>
> The dominant society devoted its efforts to the attempt to change the Indian into a white-Indian. No inhuman pressure to effect this change was overlooked. These pressures included starvation, incarceration, and enforced education. Religious and healing customs were banished.
>
> In spite of the years of oppression, the Indian and the Indian spirit survived. Not, however, without adverse effect. One of the major effects was the loss of cultured values and the concomitant loss of personal identity . . . The Indian was taught to be ashamed of being Indian and to emulate the non-Indian. In short, "white was right." For the Indian male, the only route to be successful, to be good, to be right, and to have an identity was to be as much like the white man as he could.[4]

Often it is said that the increase of violence against women is a result of various sociological facts such as oppression, racism, poverty, hopelessness, emasculation of men, and loss of male self-esteem as their own place within traditional society has been systematically destroyed by increasing urbanization, industrialization, and institutionalization, but seldom do we notice that for the past forty to fifty years, American popular media have depicted American Indian men as bloodthirsty savages devoted to treating women cruelly. While traditional Indian men seldom did any such thing—and in fact among most tribes abuse of women was simply unthinkable, as was abuse of children or the aged—the lie about "usual" male Indian behavior seems to have taken root and now bears its brutal and bitter fruit.

Image casting and image control constitute the central process that American Indian women must come to terms with, for on that control rests our sense of self, our claim to a past and to a future that we define and that we build. Images of Indians in media and education materials profoundly influence how we act, how we relate to the world and to each other, and how we value ourselves. They also determine to a large extent how our men act toward us, toward our children, and toward each other. The popular American media image of Indian people as savages with no conscience, no compassion, and no sense of the value of human life and human dignity was hardly true of the tribes—however true it was of the invaders. But as Adolf Hitler noted a little over fifty years ago, if you tell a lie big enough and often enough, it will be believed. Evidently, while Americans and people all over the world have been led into a deep and unquestioned belief that American Indians are cruel savages, a number of American Indian men have been equally deluded into internalizing that image and acting on it. Media images, literary images, and artistic images, particularly those embedded in popular culture, must be changed before Indian women will see much relief from the violence that destroys so many lives.

To survive culturally, American Indian women must often fight the United States government, the tribal governments, women and men of their tribe or their urban community who are virulently misogynist or who are threatened by attempts to change the images foisted on us over the centuries by whites. The colonizers' revisions of our lives, values, and histories have devastated us at the most critical level of all—that of our minds, our own sense of who we are.

Many women express strong opposition to those who would alter our life supports, steal our tribal lands, colonize our cultures and cultural expressions, and revise our very identities. We must strive to maintain tribal status; we must make certain that the tribes continue to be legally recognized entities, sovereign nations within the larger United States, and we must wage this struggle in many ways—political, educational, literary, artistic, individual, and communal. We are doing all we can: as mothers and grandmothers; as family members and tribal members; as professionals, workers, artists, shamans, leaders, chiefs, speakers, writers, and organizers, we daily demonstrate that we have no intention of disappearing, of being silent, or of quietly acquiescing in our extinction.

NOTES

1. It is likely, say some researchers, that fetal alcohol syndrome, which is serious among many Indian groups, will be so serious among the White Mountain Apache and the Pine Ridge Sioux that if present trends continue, by the year 2000 some people estimate that almost one half of all children born on those reservations will in some way be affected by FAS. (Michael Dorris, Native American Studies, Dartmouth College, private conversation. Dorris has done extensive research into the syndrome as it affects native populations in the United States as well as in New Zealand.)
2. Phyllis Old Dog Cross, "Sexual Abuse, A New Threat to the Native American Woman: An Overview," *Listening Post: A Periodical of the Mental Health Programs of Indian Health Services,* vol. 6, no. 2 (April 1982) p. 18.
3. Old Dog Cross, p. 18.
4. Old Dog Cross, p. 20.

4

"J.A.P."-SLAPPING
The Politics of Scapegoating

RUTH ATKIN AND ADRIENNE RICH

Those who remember World War II may well recall the racist imagery and language levelled at Japanese people. The Japanese, formerly idealized as giving us exquisite art, magical paper toys, flower arranging, swiftly became the "Japs," to be "slapped" by American military force: yellow, toothy torturers with a genetic flair for cruelty, the dastardly bombers of Pearl Harbor: the people who would deserve the genocidal bombings of Hiroshima and Nagasaki. The word "Jap" held its own in the monosyllabic language of "kike," "wop," "spic," "chink," "bitch," "slut,"—short, brutal sounds like the impact of a fist. "Slap That Jap" was a familiar wartime slogan.

These memories of the 1940s are part of the background some of us bring to the recent explosion of "Jewish-American Princess" stereotypes on Eastern college campuses. The Jewish feminist magazine *Lilith* first reported the phenomenon in its Fall 1987 issue (#17); since then, articles have appeared in the *New York Times* and the Jewish press. A column, "No

Originally published in *Gesher*, the feminist newsletter of New Jewish Agenda. January 1988, Vol. 2, Issue 2, pp. 4–5. Reprinted by permission of the authors.

Laughing Matter," by Suzanne Messing, appeared in the feminist paper *New Directions for Women*. On December 9, National Public Radio broadcast a segment on the spread of "J.A.P.-baiting," interviewing Evelyn Torton Beck, Professor of Women's Studies at the University of Maryland and editor of *Nice Jewish Girls: A Lesbian Anthology*.

"J.A.P."-baiting has taken a range of forms: novels by post-World War II American Jewish writers such as Herman Wouk's *Marjorie Morningstar*; the routines of Jewish comedians; negative stereotyping of middle-class Jewish women in greeting cards, jewelry, T-shirts, graffiti; and ritualized verbal assaults on Jewish women on college campuses. The Jewish woman is stereotyped as rich, spoiled, avidly materialistic, and solely out for herself. Most of the negative attributes are, of course, familiar anti-Jewish stereotypes: here they are pushed onto the Jewish woman. *Lilith* reported that at Syracuse University basketball games, the pep band would point at certain women who stood up and chant "JAP, JAP, JAP." On other campuses have appeared such graffiti as: "I tolerate JAPS for sex"; "All JAPS are sluts"; "Solution to the JAP question: when they go for their nose jobs, tie their tubes as well." (This last graffito is packed with implications: the "J.A.P." is trying to assimilate, to pass; Jewish women should be sterilized [as thousands were under Hitler]. It implies a knowledge of Nazi vocabulary and practice that belies the theory of "J.A.P."-baiting as ignorant fun and games.)

A different kind of hostility identifies the "J.A.P." not as a "slut" but as a "frigid" woman, unwilling to "put out" sexually. Messing quotes a greeting card (published by Noble Press, New York): "Why do JAPS close their eyes while having sex? So they can pretend they're shopping." National Public Radio reports a fun-fair booth: "Make Her Prove She's Not a JAP—Make Her Swallow."

"J.A.P." imagery has been acceptable in the Jewish community and continues to be. According to the Chicago *Jewish Sentinel*, the National Federation of Temple Sisterhoods adopted a resolution at their national convention this fall condemning "J.A.P." jokes and images, since what began as an object of sexist humor has now become a tool of the anti-Semite. The resolution called on member sisterhoods to discontinue the sale of "J.A.P. items" in their Judaica shops. But if the sisterhoods had challenged the stereotyping of Jewish women from the first, it might have stood less chance to become the tool of the anti-Semite, and within the Jewish community "JAP items" would not have received the endorsement of the National Federation. The issue is sometimes trivialized as a matter of humor ("we can laugh at ourselves"), or on the grounds that the negative stereotypes contain a "kernel of truth." We need to examine these responses.

The semiotics, or signifying power, of the "J.A.P." stereotype is complex. A clear feminist perception is needed to decipher the scapegoating of the **women** within a historically scapegoated group. Within the Jewish community, scapegoating and negative labelling of Jewish women may reflect tensions over gender roles and conflicts specific to the group. They also reveal how Jews participate in the sexism of the society at large.

"Kaleidoscopic" is Susan Schnur's term (in *Lilith*) for the "JAP theme." Rarely have two forms of social hatred—misogyny and anti-Semitism—been so explicitly joined: the "materialistic, pushy" Jew and the "princess," the selfish, privileged rich woman. Conflate these two identities and you have an easy target in a time when the presence of women on campuses is threatening to men, when jobs after college are at a premium, and any woman can be perceived by any man as a competitor for his future job. In fact, "J.A.P." is a conflation of three hated identities: Jew, woman, and those people who are seen, in a society of vast inequalities and injustice, as having "made it."

But to understand the "J.A.P."-baiting phenomenon fully we need an understanding of how the mechanisms of anti-Jewish thought operate. The "Jewish Mother" stereotype—of a too-assertive, domineering woman, devouring the lives of her children—a leftover of the community-building, survival orientation of immigrant culture, is followed by the "Jewish American Princess." The next generation of epithets directed at Jewish women reflects the assimilation of the daughters into American society. As with any stereotype, a complex social pattern is crudely and simplistically caricatured. Young Jewish women are scapegoated for the material "success" of their parents' (usually their fathers') earning power. Scapegoating young Jewish women fits into the historic cyclical pattern of Jewish oppression, whereby some Jews have been allowed a limited access to power (as tax-collectors, money-lenders, etc.), creating the illusion of Jews overall having power. Every period of toleration of Jews in host countries has been followed by periods of economic and social unrest when ruling interests have withdrawn "protection" and support of Jews, and have encouraged the general population to direct their resentments against Jews. This phase has been brutal in the extreme: Eastern European pogroms; the Nazi camps.

Increasing numbers of people in America today are without basic necessities and comforts. The current atmosphere of growing resentment of material success is fully justified. But its historic precedents, for Jews, are troubling. As the economic situation in the U.S. widens the gap between rich and poor, we need to be on the alert for expressions of anger and frustration which divert attention from the real sources of economic hardship—the prioritizing of death over life, of profit over the basic needs of people. This hardship is shared by many Jews, especially older Jewish women. It is not a coincidence that "J.A.P."-baiting is occurring on college campuses, perceived as places of privilege.

Jews have been perceived, and to a certain extent correctly, as a "successful" minority group in America. Writing in *Lilith*, Francine Klagsbrun asks: "Isn't it odd that the term JAP, referring to a spoiled, self-indulgent woman, should be so widely used at a time when women are working outside their homes in unprecedented numbers, struggling to balance their home lives and their work lives, to give as much of themselves as they can to everybody—their husbands, their kids, their bosses?" In the same issue, Susan Schnur notes that "the characterizations of JAPS and Yuppies are often identical." She sees the label of Yuppies as "neutral or even positive," but many a bitter, long-stored anti-Yuppie joke was heard when Wall Street crashed last October. And it is perhaps not coincidental that the acronym "JAP" fits so neatly into a growing anti-Asian racism that has accompanied the increased perception of Asians as a "successful" minority. Insofar as a fraternity house booth inviting passers-by to "Slap a JAP" echoes the "Slap That Jap: Buy War Bonds" posters of World War II, it legitimizes anti-Semitism, misogyny, and anti-Asian racism simultaneously.

As the U.S. economy wavers, as American national identity itself wavers, anti-Semitism is one time-honored escape from critical thinking and political responsibility. Young Jewish women on college campuses may have received little in their education to help them interpret this double assault—especially since the "JAP" label can be applied to non-Jews as well. Some older Jewish women, too, as articles in both *Lilith* and *New Directions for Women* indicate, have reacted by accepting stereotyping, by suggesting that "We should be able to laugh at ourselves." Both Jewish men and women tell "J.A.P." jokes. But, according to Messing, "No one refers to herself as a JAP." Francine Klagsbrun observes, "When we put down other Jewish women, that is a form of self-hatred."

And yes, we do need to laugh at ourselves. But our humor cannot—for our own health—be founded on self-hatred. When we delight in ourselves as women, delight in ourselves as Jews, we can laugh out of the fullness of recognizing ourselves as necessarily flawed and sometimes ridiculous human beings. Our humor need not come out of the arsenal of those who would deny us our humanity.

NOTE

1. Thanks to *Lilith: The Jewish Women's Magazine,* 250 W. 57th Street, N.Y., N.Y. 10107; *New Directions for Women,* 108 Palisade Ave., Englewood, N.J. 07631; the Chicago *Jewish Sentinel,* 323 S. Franklin St., Rm. 501, Chicago, IL, 60606.

5

ASIAN AMERICAN WOMEN
Not for Sale

TRACY LAI

Asian American women are not for sale. We will not be bought off, materially or otherwise. We say this to the white men who use the mail-order bride catalogues, hoping to buy an obedient Asian wife. But we also say this to anyone who participates in the long history of stereotyping Asian peoples and cultures as inferior and exotic. Stereotypes dehumanize people and turn them into objects to be manipulated.

It is a struggle to be an Asian in America. Historically, Asians have been denied political, economic and social equality in America. The very term "Asian American" carries a political assertion that Asians have been and continue to be a legitimate and integral part of American society. We are not forever foreign with an identity attached only to an Asian country. The Asian American movement has its origins in the social uprising of the 1960s and '70s, inspired by the black liberation movement. Chinese Americans, Japanese Americans, Pilipino[1] Americans and Korean Americans united in recognition of a common history of oppression and common goals of community empowerment and pride. Asian American women played a leading role, drawing from the strength of their Vietnamese sisters in the National Liberation Front. The racist war abroad in Vietnam had its counterpart back home. Asian American communities fought the enemy at home, raising such issues as bilingual-bicultural education, ethnic studies, and low-income housing. Today, that quest for equality and political power continues. And Asian American women continue to be an important part of that struggle. The urgency of this struggle is reflected in the rising incidence of anti-Asian violence. *Pacific Citizen,* newspaper of the Japanese American Citizens League, reported the tragic death in February, 1984, of Ly Yung Cheung, a seamstress in New York's Chinatown. She was pushed into the path of an oncoming subway train and was decapitated. Her attacker, John Cardinale, reportedly shouted, "we're even" and later based his defense on a "psychotic phobia about Orientals."

What makes this struggle even more complicated is the die-hard myth that Asians have made it. We are told we have overcome our oppression, and that therefore we are the model minority. *Model* refers to the cherished dictum of capitalism that "pulling hard on your bootstraps" brings due rewards. The lesson drawn is that if you work hard enough, you will succeed—and if you don't succeed, you must not be working hard enough. High-profile Asian American women such as Connie Chung, a national television newscaster with a six-figure salary, are promoted as examples of Asian American success stories. But such examples, while certainly remarkable, do little to illuminate the actual conditions of the majority of Asian Americans. Such examples conceal the more typical Asian American experience of unemployment, underemployment and struggle to survive.

The model minority myth thus classically scapegoats Asian Americans. It labels us in a way that dismisses the real problems that many do face, while at the same time pitting Asians against other oppressed people of color. The fact that Asian Americans lack political representation, power and community control conveniently disappears. Model minority labelling has also given rise to an insidious cultural hierarchy. The concept of cultural deprivation implies that black, Latino, and American Indian cultures lack the cultural reinforcements that lead to successful achievement in education and career advancement, and hence to higher socioeconomic levels. For example, Asians are claimed to value education more than other minorities and to have special intellectual affinities for math and science. In fact, this is a racist rationale implying the intellectual inferiority of other minorities, while ignoring important historical and class differences in backgrounds. The cultural deprivation and model minority analyses also fail to examine capitalism as an economic system that thrives on exploitation by class, sex and race. The lack of success of other minority groups and women of all races is deliberate and necessary under capitalism. Profits for capitalism come from the low wages justified in sexist and racist terms.

A Multifaceted Community

The forces shaping the experience of Asian American women come out of the historical policies of the U.S. toward Asians. These policies were largely aimed at using and discarding Asians as a temporary, cheap labor pool. Thus, young Asian men were desirable while Asian women were not, especially since women would bear children who could legally claim citizenship rights in the United States. Asian Americans are united by our oppression. The racist claim that all Asians look alike could more accurately be stated, "treat all Asians as if they were alike." We are denied respect for our cultural identities, and in the American eye, Asia and the Pacific merge into a single cultural entity. No matter how many generations we have lived in America, we are assumed to be foreigners. The 1980 Census counted more than 20 separate Asian and Pacific nationalities in the United States. The total number of Asian Americans is approximately 3.7 million, or 1.6 percent of the population, mostly concentrated in the western United States. The largest nationality groups, in decreasing order, are Chinese, Pilipino, Japanese, Asian Indian, Korean, and Vietnamese. Others include Hmong, Laotian, (native) Hawaiian, Samoan, Guamanian, Marshallese, and Micronesian. Each of these nationalities has a unique history and culture. However, common to all has been the history of U.S. intervention. Beginning in the nineteenth century, the U.S. followed Britain's example, forcing China and then Japan to open their doors to trade and immigration. Eventually, the U.S. sought to dominate the Pacific and Asia for trade and military purposes. As a consequence, the U.S. annexed, occupied or otherwise dominated Hawaii, the Micronesian Islands, the Philippines, South Korea, Vietnam, and Kampuchea.

Immigration of Asian and Pacific people has been heavily shaped by the nature of U.S. involvement in their countries. Today, the highest rate of immigration for Asians is from South Korea and the Philippines, two countries that are heavily dominated by U.S. capital and are occupied by strategic U.S. military bases. According to the *Seattle Times* (November 15, 1983), the U.S. maintains 38,882 military personnel in South Korea, 15,123 in the Philippines, 48,496 in Japan, 8,959 in Guam, and 23,214 at sea near Asia. The U.S. military bases have a devastating impact on the local Asian women, one that spills over to Asian American women as American military men bring back stereotypes and expectations of conquest. For instance, U.S. bases generate a huge prostitution business, reinforcing the stereotype that Asian women seek fulfillment through serving men.

Historically, the U.S. has also maintained discriminatory immigration policies explicitly aimed at controlling and eliminating the Asian population in the United States. The first wave of Chinese immigrants arrived in the 1850s, but by 1882, an organized movement of trade unions and opportunistic politicians secured the Chinese Exclusion Act which prohibited immigration of Chinese laborers and their wives. Thus, families were curtailed, wives effectively abandoned in China, and an entire generation of Chinese "bachelors" were trapped in the United States. Violent killings and expulsions followed in the wake of this legislation, such as the 1885–86 expulsions of the Chinese communities from Tacoma and Seattle, Washington. The Chinese were wanted for their labor but they were considered undesirable and unassimilable for settlement. The Chinese and, later, other Asians were accused of stealing white workers' jobs and lowering the standard of living. In fact, Asians performed work that white workers refused to do, and Asians had to be recruited to fill the labor shortage of the westward expansion. Their labor laid the foundation for the industrial and agricultural wealth of the West today.

Japanese, Korean and Pilipino workers followed in successive waves, filling one another's footsteps in low-paying, low-status jobs. In turn, each faced similarly hostile accusations and blame for downturns in the economy. Recruited for the sugar plantations in the 1800s, the Japanese immigrated to Hawaii, and subsequently to the mainland. The anti-Chinese movement reorganized itself as the Asiatic Exclusion League [i]n 1905, dedicated to the preservation of the Caucasian race upon American soil. In 1924 the League successfully passed the National Origins Act which barred immigration of all Asians. Only the Pilipinos remained problematic. Pilipinos were considered nationals, since the U.S. had seized the Philippines during the Spanish-American War of 1898. As nationals, they were exempt from exclusionary immigration laws. After 1924, Pilipinos were a primary source of labor and, as their numbers increased, so did white hostility. In 1929 and 1930, anti-Pilipino riots erupted all along the west coast. The Tydings-McDuffie Act of 1934 ostensibly granted independence to the Philippines but its real purpose was to limit the immigration quota of Pilipinos to 50 per year.

In many ways, these exclusionary laws were aimed at Asian women to prevent the development of families and communities. By keeping Asian women from immigrating, and by passing anti-miscegenation laws, it was hoped that the largely male Asian labor force would eventually die out. A common theme in the anti-Asian propaganda threatened destruction of America through an invasion of the "yellow hordes" or the "yellow peril." Asian American women were described as breeding like rats. This stereotype continues into the present in the form of the "Oriental Beauty" who has extraordinary sexual powers. To raise families and to build communities under such conditions become acts of resistance.

A more recent example of U.S. foreign policy impacting Asian Americans is the resettlement in the United States of 760,854 Southeast Asians between 1975–1985. Over half are Vietnamese; the rest are nearly evenly divided between Laotians and Kampucheans. They are all refugees created by the U.S. imperialist war in Southeast Asia, which raged from the 1950s to 1975. These newer Asian Americans have borne the brunt of the anti-Asian violence, as well as a specifically anti-refugee/anti-Southeast Asian hostility. Refugee women are especially vulnerable to attacks such as robbery, rape and intimidation. The perpetrators seem to believe that these attacks are acceptable, even deserved, because the U.S. lost the war in Vietnam, and war can now be made on its victims/refugees. Refugee women are perceived as likely targets, easier to physically overpower and intimidate. Because refugees are unfamiliar with American behavior, language and laws, it is difficult for them to fight back. At the same time, the pressure to assimilate falls heavily on the women, even as the community's traditional values and roles are fundamentally undermined and their children become strangers to them.

Historically, the tendency has been to reject and exclude Asians from participating fully in American society. Besides the exclusionary immigration laws, in many states, Asians could not be naturalized, vote, own property, or marry persons of other races. Their lives and jobs were restricted in every way. Although most of the discriminatory laws have eventually changed, deep-rooted stereotypes and hostility towards Asians have not. Throughout there has been a clear pattern of violence used to intimidate and eliminate Asians. Asians, like other minorities, have been expendable: their lives have not been valued as highly as white lives. Burned into Asian American consciousness is the violent uprooting of more than 110,000 Japanese who were interned in American concentration camps during World War II. Western Defense Commander General John L. DeWitt declared that "the Japanese race is an enemy race," thus providing the racist rationale that all Japanese on the west coast must locked up as a military necessity.[2] They were marched away at gunpoint and imprisoned behind barbed wire, arbitrarily and illegally stripped of all civil rights. They were stripped of their dignity and pride as a people and of their dreams. Most lost their businesses, homes and possessions, an estimated value of as much as $400 million (Weglyn, p. 276). Japanese American women fiercely resisted these attacks on family and community integrity, and the demoralization and shame. They turned the prisons into homes and transformed the anger into the will to survive. Today, the camps remain a warning that the old anti-Asian hysteria could strike at any time; you are not safe behind the yellow face.

Asian American Women: Dangers Within and Without

We are triply oppressed: as Asian Americans, as Asian American women, and as Asian American women workers. Racism has been and continues to be a primary force in shaping our oppression as women and as workers. The model minority stereotype has ominous overtones when applied to Asian American women. Asian American women are described as being desirable because they are cute (as in doll-like), quiet rather than militant, and unassuming rather than assertive. In a word, non-threatening. This is the image being sold as a commodity on the front page of the *Wall Street Journal*, January 25, 1984, headlined: "American Men Find Asian Brides Fill the Unliberated Bill—Mail-order Firms Help Them Look for the Ideal Women They Didn't Find at Home."

There are about 50 mail-order services in the U.S., carrying names such as "Cherry Blossom" and "Love Overseas." For a fee, men receive photo catalogs of Asian women, primarily from poor families in Malaysia and the Philippines. Descriptions of the women include statements such as "They love to do things to make their husbands happy," and "Most, if not all, are very feminine, loyal, loving—and virgins!" (as quoted in *Pacific Citizen*). The men who use these services are often middle-aged or older, disillusioned and divorced. Many have served in the U.S. military overseas in Asia. They blame previous marriage failures on the women's liberation movement. The mail order services claim to sell unliberated women who will supposedly be satisfied homemakers and be subservient to their husbands. The reality is that this market is a by-product of the U.S. military and economic domination in Asia. The mail order phenomenon is a threat not only to Asian and Asian American women, but to all women. It promotes a degrading view of women's roles and the acceptability of selling women.

The stereotypes also pay off in the form of inflated profits extracted by superexploiting Asian American women workers. Businesses want docile, subservient workers who will not complain, file grievances, or organize unions. Many businesses purposely seek immigrant workers with limited English skills as further insurance against back talk. Asian American women are also stereotyped as having special dexterity and endurance for routine, thus making them fit for assembly work of various types. They are thought to be "loyal, diligent and attentive to detail," again good qualities for subordinates, but certainly not for supervisors. Asian American women continue to be hired mainly in low-profile, low-status, low-paying occupations, such as clerical and service work. Asian American families tend to have multiple wage earners, to support larger, often extended, families, and to live in urban areas with a relatively high cost of living. These factors skew the Asian American family median income upwards. This higher figure has been used to suggest wrongly that Asian American families are as or more successful than white families. Comparisons of median income levels within specific cities (instead of using national averages) reveal that Asian Americans, like other minorities, consistently earn less than whites.

The force of history and the conditions of our lives demand many battles, but Asian American women must also simultaneously wage an inner struggle with feudal and religious cultural baggage. In Asian cultures that have been heavily influenced by Confucianism, women are regarded as secondary to men, existing for their service. The Spanish imposed Catholicism on the Philippines with similar results. While the Asian experience in America has modified some of these ideas, every wave of immigration tends to revive the old cultures. Asian American women must be able to reject negative traditions without feeling like they are rejecting their whole Asian American identity. Assimilation appears to demand this same rejection, but it is from the standpoint of shame and self-hatred. No culture is static, and this struggle to consciously develop and redefine the best in Asian American culture is based on pride and love of our people.

Writers Merle Woo and Kitty Tsui have eloquently articulated this many-fronted struggle, becoming a voice for other Asian American lesbians. As lesbians, they have faced a painful rejection from the Asian American community. In "Letter to Ma," Merle directly addresses homophobia in the community: "If my reaction to being a Yellow Woman is different than yours was, please know that that is not a judgment on you, a criticism or denial of you, your worth" (*Bridge*, p. 146). Merle explains that being a Yellow Feminist does not mean "'separatism,' either by cutting myself off from non-Asians or men . . . it means changing the economic class system and psychological forces (sexism, racism, and homophobia) that really hurt all of us" (p. 142). Kitty describes herself as a warrior who grapples with those same three many-headed demons. In *The Words of a Woman Who Breathes Fire,* she affirms: "I am a woman who loves women,/I am a woman who loves myself" (p. 52). Self-affirmation as a source of boldness and vision becomes a strength for Asian American women, lesbian and straight.

Writers/activists Sasha Hohri, Miya Iwataki and Janice Mirikitani are a few more of the unsung Asian American women continuing the strong tradition of political activism and organizing. Their issues range from redress/reparations for the Japanese interned during World War II to racist violence against Asians and the Rainbow Coalition for political power. They continue in the spirit of earlier Korean and Pilipino women who organized and continue to organize in the U.S. for independence in their homelands. A Japanese American woman, Mitsuye Endo, had partial success in the Supreme Court in 1944, challenging the internment of concededly loyal American citizens (Weglyn, p. 227). More recently, some of the largest labor rallies and significant employer concessions have been won by striking Chinese American garment workers. In 1982, 10,000 Chinese American women garment workers rallied in New York, winning a union contract that addressed their substandard working conditions. In 1986, following the shutdown of P & L Sportswear, 300 Chinese American women garment workers forced the city of Boston and the state of Massachusetts to implement the required retraining.

But while the Chinese American community is celebrating these victories, the women's movement has yet to recognize the significance of this achievement. Asian American women are trying to organize one of the least organized sectors of labor. They are fighting for basic working conditions denied to them precisely because they are Asian American women. Asian American women are often most actively involved in their communities and workplaces because those conditions directly determine their future. If we do not fight our own battles, who will? In *East Wind: Focus on Asian Women*, Sasha Hohri and Sadie Lum analyze Asian American women's oppression as intrinsically linked to class and race issues. We cannot separate ourselves from any one part. Our liberation is linked to that of our communities and ultimately, to that of our whole society. Liberation requires revolution.

As yet, feminism has not provided sufficient analysis and direction to the basic struggle of survival facing Asian Americans in this country. Feminism appears to have a more limited agenda, one concerned primarily with women's oppression. However, women's oppression is irresolvable in a society which is inherently unequal. A capitalist society means that a few will profit while the majority will not. Feminism must deal with the structure of capitalism and its exploitation of people by race and class, as well as the way this exploitation parallels and compounds women's oppression. As feminists broaden their perspective on what issues are of priority to women of all colors, more unity can be forged with Asian American and other sisters of color who are moving ahead, organizing and surviving. We cannot choose to stop struggling. We can only choose how we work together.

NOTES

1. "Pilipino"; Filipino is the anglicized form and symbolizes the colonization and domination of the Philippines by foreign powers such as the United States. In Tagalog, the national language of the Philippines, the word is pronounced with a "p" sound, hence "Pilipino."
2. General DeWitt's statement is part of his February 1942 recommendation to Secretary Stimson on exclusion of the Japanese, as quoted in *Personal Justice Denied*, p. 6.

REFERENCES

"American Men Find Asian Brides Fill the Unliberated Bill," Raymond A. Joseph, *Wall Street Journal*, January 25/84, p. 1, 22.

"Chinese Garment Workers Shake Up New York" August 20/82 and "Chinese Garment Workers Win Retraining in Boston" September 12/86 in *Unity*, Unity Publications: Oakland, California.

East Wind: Politicians and Culture of Asians in the U.S. Focus: Asian Women, V. 2 N. 1, Spring/Summer 1983, Getting Together Publications: Oakland, California.

"JACL Report on Asian Bride Catalogs," *Pacific Citizen*, February 22/85, p. 10–11.

"Letter to Ma," Merle Woo, in *This Bridge Called My Back*, Cherríe Moraga and Gloria Anzaldúa, editors, Persephone Press: Watertown, Massachusetts, 1981.

Personal Justice Denied, Report of the Commission on Wartime Relocation and Internment of Civilians, U.S. Government Printing Office, Washington, D.C., 1982.

Recent Activities Against Citizens and Residents of Asian Descent, U.S. Commission on Civil Rights, Clearinghouse Publication No. 88.

With Silk Wings, Elaine H. Kim with Janice Otani, Asian Women United of California, 1983.

The Words of a Woman Who Breathes Fire, Kitty Tsui, Spinsters, Ink: Argyle, New York, 1983.

Years of Infamy, Michi Weglyn, William Morrow and Co.: New York, New York, 1976.

6

BOYHOOD, ORGANIZED SPORTS, AND THE CONSTRUCTION OF MASCULINITIES

MICHAEL A. MESSNER

The rapid expansion of feminist scholarship in the past two decades has led to fundamental reconceptualizations of the historical and contemporary meanings of organized sport. In the nineteenth and twentieth centuries, modernization and women's continued movement into public life created widespread "fears of social feminization," especially among middle-class men (Hantover, 1978; Kimmel, 1987). One result of these fears was the creation of organized sport as a homosocial sphere in which competition and (often violent) physicality was valued, while "the feminine" was devalued. As a result, organized sport has served to bolster a sagging ideology of male superiority, and has helped to reconstitute masculine hegemony (Bryson, 1987; Hall, 1988; Messner, 1988; Theberge, 1981).

The feminist critique has spawned a number of studies of the ways that women's sport has been marginalized and trivialized in the past (Greendorfer, 1977; Oglesby, 1978; Twin, 1978), in addition to illuminating the continued existence of structural and ideological barriers to gender equality within sport (Birrell, 1987). Only recently, however, have scholars begun to use feminist insights to examine men's experiences in sport (Kidd, 1987; Messner, 1987; Sabo, 1985). This article explores the relationship between the construction of masculine identity and boyhood participation in organized sports.

I view gender identity not as a "thing" that people "have," but rather as a *process of construction* that develops, comes into crisis, and changes as a person interacts with the social world. Through this perspective, it becomes possible to speak of "gendering" identities rather than "masculinity" or "femininity" as relatively fixed identities or statuses.

There is an agency in this construction; people are not passively shaped by their social environment. As recent feminist analyses of the construction of feminine gender identity have pointed out, girls and women are implicated in the construction of their own identities and personalities, both in terms of the ways that they participate in their own subordination and the ways that they

Michael A. Messner, *Journal of Contemporary Ethnography,* Vol. 18, No. 4, January 1990, 416–444.

resist subordination (Benjamin, 1988; Haug, 1987). Yet this self-construction is not a fully conscious process. There are also deeply woven, unconscious motivations, fears, and anxieties at work here. So, too, in the construction of masculinity. Levinson (1978) has argued that masculine identity is neither fully "formed" by the social context, nor is it "caused" by some internal dynamic put into place during infancy. Instead, it is shaped and constructed through the interaction between the internal and the social. The internal gendering identity may set developmental "tasks," may create thresholds of anxiety and ambivalence, yet it is only through a concrete examination of people's interactions with others within social institutions that we can begin to understand both the similarities and differences in the construction of gender identities.

In this study I explore and interpret the meanings that males themselves attribute to their boyhood participation in organized sport. In what ways do males construct masculine identities within the institution of organized sports? In what ways do class and racial differences mediate this relationship and perhaps lead to the construction of different meanings, and perhaps different masculinities? And what are some of the problems and contradictions within these constructions of masculinity?

Description of Research

Between 1983 and 1985, I conducted interviews with 30 male former athletes. Most of the men I interviewed had played the (U.S.) "major sports"—football, basketball, baseball, track. At the time of the interview, each had been retired from playing organized sports for at least five years. Their ages ranged from 21 to 48, with the median, 33; 14 were black, 14 were white, and two were Hispanic; 15 of the 16 black and Hispanic men had come from poor or working-class families, while the majority (9 of 14) of the white men had come from middle-class or professional families. All had at some time in their lives based their identities largely on their roles as athletes and could therefore be said to have had "athletic careers." Twelve had played organized sports through high school, 11 through college, and seven had been professional athletes. Though the sample was not randomly selected, an effort was made to see that the sample had a range of difference in terms of race and social class backgrounds, and that there was some variety in terms of age, types of sports played, and levels of success in athletic careers. Without exception, each man contacted agreed to be interviewed.

The tape-recorded interviews were semi-structured and took from one and one-half to six hours, with most taking about three hours. I asked each man to talk about four broad eras in his life: (1) his earliest experiences with sports in boyhood, (2) his athletic career, (3) retirement or disengagement from the athletic career, and (4) life after the athletic career. In each era, I focused the interview on the meanings of "success and failure," and on the boy's/man's relationships with family, with other males, with women, and with his own body.

In collecting what amounted to life histories of these men, my overarching purpose was to use feminist theories of masculine gender identity to explore how masculinity develops and changes as boys and men interact within the socially constructed world of organized sports. In addition to using the data to move toward some generalizations about the relationship between "masculinity and sport," I was also concerned with sorting out some of the variations among boys, based on class and racial inequalities, that led them to relate differently to athletic careers. I divided my sample into two comparison groups. The first group was made up of 10 men from higher-status backgrounds, primarily white, middle-class, and professional families. The second group was made up of 20 men from lower-status backgrounds, primarily minority, poor, and working-class families.

Boyhood and the Promise of Sports

Zane Grey once said, "All boys love baseball. If they don't they're not real boys" (as cited in Kimmel, 1990). This is, of course, an ideological statement; In fact, some boys do *not* love baseball, or any other sports, for that matter. There are millions of males who at an early age are rejected by, become alienated from, or lose interest in organized sports. Yet all boys are, to a greater or lesser extent, judged according to their ability, or lack or ability, in competitive sports (Eitzen, 1975; Sabo, 1985). In this study I focus on those males who did become athletes—males who eventually poured thousands of hours into the development of specific physical skills. It is in boyhood that we can discover the roots of their commitment to athletic careers.

How did organized sports come to play such a central role in these boy's lives? When asked to recall how and why they initially got into playing sports, many of the men interviewed for this study seemed a bit puzzled: after all, playing sports was "just the thing to do." A 42-year-old black man who had played college basketball put it this way:

> It was just what you did. It's kind of like, you went to school, you played athletics, and if you didn't, there was something wrong with you. It was just like brushing your teeth: it's just what you did. It's part of your existence.

Spending one's time playing sports with other boys seemed as natural as the cycle of the seasons: baseball in the spring and summer, football in the fall, basketball in the winter—and then it was time to get out the old baseball glove and begin again. As a black 35-year-old former professional football star said:

> I'd say when I wasn't in school, 95% of the time was spent in the park playing. It was the only thing to do. It just came as natural.

And a black, 34-year-old professional basketball player explained his early experiences in sports:

> My principal and teacher said, "Now if you work at this you might be pretty damned good." So it was more or less a community thing—everybody in the community said, "Boy, if you work hard and keep your nose clean, you gonna be good." Cause it was natural instinct.

"It was natural instinct." "I was a natural." Several athletes used words such as these to explain their early attraction to sports. But certainly there is nothing "natural" about throwing a ball through a hoop, hitting a ball with a bat, or jumping over hurdles. A boy, for instance, may have amazingly dexterous inborn hand-eye coordination, but this does not predispose him to a career of hitting baseballs any more than it predisposes him to life as a brain surgeon. When one listens closely to what these men said about their early experiences in sports, it becomes clear that their adoption of the self-definition of "natural athlete" was the result of what Connell (1990) has called "a collective practice" that constructs masculinities. The boyhood development of masculine identity and status—truly problematic in a society that offers no official rite of passage into adulthood—results from a process of interaction with people and social institutions. Thus, in discussing early motivations in sports, men commonly talk of the importance of relationships with family members, peers, and the broader community.

Family Influences

Though most of the men in this study spoke of their mothers with love, respect, even reverence, their descriptions of their earliest experiences in sports are stories of an exclusively male world. The existence of older brothers or uncles who served as teachers and athletic role models—as well as sources of competition for attention and status within the family—was very common. An older brother, uncle, or even close friend of the family who was a successful athlete appears to have acted as a sort of standard of achievement against whom to measure oneself. A 34-year-old black man who had been a three-sport star in high school said:

> My uncles—my Uncle Harold went to the Detroit Tigers, played pro ball—all of 'em, everybody played sports, so I wanted to be better than anybody else. I knew that everybody in this town knew them—their names were something. I wanted my name to be just like theirs.

Similarly, a black 41-year-old former professional football player recalled:

> I was the younger of three brothers and everybody played sports, so consequently I was more or less forced into it. 'Cause one

brother was always better than the next brother and then I came
along and had to show them that I was just as good as them. My
oldest brother was an all-city ballplayer, then my other brother
comes along he's all-city and all-state, and then I have to come
along.

For some, attempting to emulate or surpass the athletic accomplishments of older male family members created pressures that were difficult to
deal with. A 33-year-old white man explained that he was a good athlete
during boyhood, but the constant awareness that his two older brothers had
been better made it difficult for him to feel good about himself, or to have
fun in sports:

I had this sort of reputation that I followed from the playgrounds
through grade school, and through high school. I followed these
guys who were all-conference and all-state.

Most of these men, however, saw their relationships with their athletic
older brothers and uncles in a positive light; it was within these relationships
that they gained experience and developed motivations that gave them a
competitive "edge" within their same-aged peer group. As a 33-year-old
black man describes his earliest athletic experiences:

My brothers were role models. I wanted to prove—especially to my
brothers—that I had heart, you know, that I was a man.

When asked, "What did it mean to you to be 'a man' at that age?" he
replied:

Well, it meant that I didn't want to be a so-called scaredy-cat. You
want to hit a guy even though he's bigger than you to show that,
you know, you've got this macho image. I remember that at that
young an age, that feeling was exciting to me. And that carried over,
and as I got older, I got better and I began to look around me and
see, well hey! I'm competitive with these guys, even though I'm
younger, you know? And then of course all the compliments come—
and I began to notice a change, even in my parents—especially in
my father—he was proud of that, and that was very important to
me. He was extremely important . . . he showed me more affection,
now that I think of it.

As this man's words suggest, if men talk of their older brothers and
uncles mostly as role models, teachers, and "names" to emulate, their talk of
their relationships with their fathers is more deeply layered and complex.
Athletic skills and competition for status may often be learned from older
brothers, but it is in boys' relationships with fathers that we find many of the
keys to the emotional salience of sports in the development of masculine
identity.

Relationships with Fathers

The fact that boys' introductions to organized sports are often made by fathers who might otherwise be absent or emotionally distant adds a powerful emotional charge to these early experiences (Osherson, 1986). Although playing organized sports eventually came to feel "natural" for all of the men interviewed in this study, many needed to be "exposed" to sports, or even gently "pushed" by their fathers to become involved in activities like Little League baseball. A white, 33-year-old man explained:

> I still remember it like it was yesterday—Dad and I driving up in his truck, and I had my glove and my hat and all that—and I said, "Dad, I don't want to do it." He says, "What?" I says, "I don't want to do it." I was nervous. That I might fail. And he says, "Don't be silly. Lookit: There's Joey and Petey and all your friends out there." And so Dad says, "You're gonna do it, come on." And in my memory he's never said that about anything else; he just knew I needed a little kick in the pants and I'd do it. And once you're out there and you see all the other kids making errors and stuff, and you know you're better than those guys, you know: Maybe I *do* belong here. As it turned out, Little League was a good experience.

Some who were similarly "pushed" by their fathers were not so successful as the aforementioned man had been in Little League baseball, and thus the experience was not altogether a joyous affair. One 34-year-old white man, for instance, said he "inherited" his interest in sports from his father, who started playing catch with him at the age of four. Once he got into Little League, he felt pressured by his father, one of the coaches, who expected him to be the star of the team:

> I'd go 0-for-four sometimes, strike out three times in a Little League game, and I'd dread the ride home. I'd come home and he'd say, "Go in the bathroom and swing the bat in the mirror for an hour," to get my swing level . . . It didn't help much, though, I'd go out and strike out three or four times again the next game too [laughs ironically].

When asked if he had been concerned with having his father's approval, he responded:

> Failure in his eyes? Yeah, I always thought that he wanted me to get some kind of [athletic] scholarship. I guess I was afraid of him when I was a kid. He didn't hit that much, but he had a rage about him— he'd rage, and that voice would just rattle you.

Similarly, a 24-year-old black man described his awe of his father's physical power and presence, and his sense of inadequacy in attempting to emulate him:

My father had a voice that sounded like rolling thunder. Whether it was intentional on his part or not, I don't know, but my father gave me a sense, an image of him being the most powerful being on earth, and that no matter what I ever did I would never come close to him . . . There were definite feelings of physical inadequacy that I couldn't work around.

It is interesting to note how these feelings of physical inadequacy relative to the father lived on as part of this young man's permanent internalized image. He eventually became a "feared" high school football player and broke school records in weight-lifting, yet,

As I grew older, my mother and friends told me that I had actually grown to be a larger man than my father. Even though in time I required larger clothes than he, which should have been a very concrete indication, neither my brother nor I could ever bring ourselves to say that I was bigger. We simply couldn't conceive of it.

Using sports activities as a means of identifying with and "living up to" the power and status of one's father was not always such a painful and difficult task for the men I interviewed. Most did not describe fathers who "pushed" them to become sports stars. The relationship between their athletic strivings and their identification with their fathers was more subtle. A 48-year-old black man, for instance, explained that he was not pushed into sports by his father, but was aware from an early age of the community status his father had gained through sports. He saw his own athletic accomplishments as a way to connect with and emulate his father:

I wanted to play baseball because my father had been quite a good baseball player in the Negro leagues before baseball was integrated, and so he was kind of a model for me. I remember, quite young, going to a baseball game he was in—this was before the war and all—I remember being in the stands with my mother and seeing him on first base, and being aware of the crowd . . . I was aware of people's confidence in him as a serious baseball player. I don't think my father ever said anything to me like "play sports" . . . [But] I knew he would like it if I did well. His admiration was important . . . he mattered.

Similarly, a 24-year-old white man described his father as a somewhat distant "role model" whose approval mattered:

My father was more of an example . . . he definitely was very much in touch with and still had very fond memories of being an athlete and talked about it, bragged about it. . . . But he really didn't do that much to teach me skills, and he didn't always go to every game I played like some parents. But he approved and that was important, you know. That was important to get his approval. I always knew that playing sports was important to him, so I knew implicitly that it was good and there was definitely a value on it.

First experiences in sports might often come through relationships with brothers or older male relatives, and the early emotional salience of sports was often directly related to a boy's relationship with his father. The sense of commitment that these young boys eventually made to the development of athletic careers is best explained as a process of development of masculine gender identity and status in relation to same-sex peers.

Masculine Identity and Early Commitment to Sports

When many of the men in this study said that during childhood they played sports because "it's just what everybody did," they of course meant that is was just what *boys* did. They were introduced to organized sports by older brothers and fathers, and once involved, found themselves playing within an exclusively male world. Though the separate (an unequal) gendered worlds of boys and girls came to appear as "natural," they were in fact socially constructed. Thorne's observations of children's activities in schools indicated that rather than "naturally" constituting "separate gendered cultures," there is considerable interaction between boys and girls in classrooms and on playgrounds. When adults set up legitimate contact between boys and girls, Thorne observed, this usually results in "relaxed interactions." But when activities in the classroom or on the playground are presented to children as sex-segregated activities and gender is marked by teachers and other adults ("boys line up here, girls over there"), "gender boundaries are heightened, and mixed-sex interaction becomes an explicit arena of risk" (Thorne, 1986; 70). Thus sex-segregated activities such as organized sports as structured by adults, provide the context in which gendered identities and separate "gendered cultures" develop and come to appear natural. For the boys in this study, it became "natural" to equate masculinity with competition, physical strength, and skills. Girls simply did not (could not, it was believed) participate in these activities.

Yet it is not simply the separation of children, by adults, into separate activities that explains why many boys came to feel such strong connection with sports activities, while so few girls did. As I listened to men recall their earliest experiences in organized sports, I heard them talk of insecurity, loneliness, and especially a need to connect with other people as a primary motivation in their early sports strivings. As a 42-year-old white man stated, "The most important thing was just being out there with the rest of the guys—being friends." Another 32-year-old interviewee was born in Mexico and moved to the United States at a fairly young age. He never knew his father, and his mother died when he was only nine years old. Suddenly he felt rootless, and threw himself into sports. His initial motivations, however, do not appear to be based on a need to compete and win:

Actually, what I think sports did for me is it brought me into kind of an instant family. By being on a Little League team, or even just playing with all kinds of different kids in the neighborhood, it brought what I really wanted, which was some kind of closeness. It was just being there, and being friends.

Clearly, what these boys needed and craved was that which was most problematic for them: connection and unity with other people. But why do these young males find *organized sports* such an attractive context in which to establish "a kind of closeness" with others? Comparative observations of young boys' and girls' game-playing behaviors yield important insights into this question. Piaget (1965) and Lever (1976) both observed that girls tend to have more "pragmatic" and "flexible" orientations to the rules of games; they are more prone to make exceptions and innovations in the middle of a game in order to make the game more "fair." Boys, on the other hand, tend to have a more firm, even [in]flexible orientation to the rules of a game; to them, the rules are what protects any fairness. This difference, according to Gilligan (1982), is based on the fact that early developmental experiences have yielded deeply rooted differences between males' and females' developmental tasks, needs, and moral reasoning. Girls, who tend to define themselves primarily through connection with others, experience highly competitive situations (whether in organized sports or in other hierarchical institutions) as threats to relationships, and thus to their identities. For boys, the development of gender identity involves the construction of positional identities, where a sense of self is solidified through separation from others (Chodorow, 1978). Yet feminist psychoanalytic theory has tended to oversimplify the internal lives of men (Lichterman, 1986). Males do appear to develop positional identities, yet despite their fears of intimacy, they also retain a human need for closeness and unity with others. This ambivalence toward intimate relationships is a major thread running through masculine development throughout the life course. Here we can conceptualize what Craib (1987) calls the "elective affinity" between personality and social structure: For the boy who both seeks and fears attachment with others, the rule-bound structure of organized sports can promise to be a safe place in which to seek nonintimate attachment with others within a context that maintains clear boundaries, distance, and separation.

Competitive Structures and Conditional Self-Worth

Young boys may initially find that sports give them the opportunity to experience "some kind of closeness" with others, but the structure of sports and athletic careers often undermines the possibility of boys learning to transcend their fears of intimacy, thus becoming able to develop truly close and intimate relationships with others (Kidd, 1990; Messner, 1987). The sports world is extremely hierarchical, and an incredible amount of importance is placed on winning, on "being number one." For instance, a few years ago I observed a basketball camp put on for boys by a professional basketball coach and his staff. The youngest boys, about eight years old (who could barely reach the basket with their shots) played a brief scrimmage. Afterwards, the coaches lined them up in a row in front of the older boys who were sitting in the grandstands. One by one, the coach would stand behind each boy, put his hand on the boy's head (much in the manner of a priestly benediction), and the older boys in the stands would applaud and cheer, louder or softer, depending on how well or poorly the young boy was judged to have performed. The two or three boys who were clearly the exceptional players looked confident that they would receive the praise they were due. Most of the boys, though, had expressions ranging from puzzlement to thinly disguised terror on their faces as they awaited the judgments of the older boys.

This kind of experience teaches boys that it is not "just being out there with the guys—being friends" that ensures the kind of attention and connection that they crave; it is being *better* than the other guys—*beating* them—that is the key to acceptance. Most of the boys in this study did have some early successes in sports, and thus their ambivalent need for connection with others was met, at least for a time. But the institution of sport tends to encourage the development of what Schafer (1975) has called "conditional self-worth" in boys. As boys become aware that acceptance by others is contingent upon begin good—a "winner"—narrow definitions of success, based upon performance and winning, become increasingly important to them. A 33-year-old black man said that by the time he was in his early teens:

> It was expected of me to do well in all my contests—I mean by my coaches, my peers, and my family. So I in turn expected to do well, and if I didn't do well, then I'd be very disappointed.

The man from Mexico, discussed above, who said that he had sought "some kind of closeness" in his early sports experiences began to notice in his early teens that if he played well, was a *winner,* he would get attention from others:

> It got to the point where I started realizing, noticing that people were always there for me, backing me all the time—sports got to be really fun because I always had some people there backing me. Finally my oldest brother started going to all my games, even though I had never really seen who he was [laughs]—after the game, you know, we never really saw each other, but he was at all my baseball games, and it seemed like we shared a kind of closeness there, but only in those situations. Off the field, when I wasn't in uniform, he was never around.

By high school, he said, he felt "up against the wall." Sports hadn't delivered what he had hoped it would, but he thought if he just tried harder, won one more championship trophy, he would get the attention he truly craved. Despite his efforts, this attention was not forthcoming. And, sadly, the pressures he had put on himself to excel in sports had taken most of the fun out of playing.

For many of the men in this study, throughout boyhood and into adolescence, this conscious striving for successful achievement became the primary means through which they sought connection with other people (Messner, 1987). But it is important to recognize that young males' internalized ambivalences about intimacy do not fully determine the contours and directions of their lives. Masculinity continues to develop through interaction with the social world—and because boys from different backgrounds are interacting with substantially different familial, educational, and other institutions, these differences will lead them to make different choices and define situations in different ways. Next, I examine the differences in the ways that boys from higher- and lower-status families and communities related to organized sports.

Status Differences and Commitments to Sports

In discussing early attractions to sports, the experiences of boys from higher- and lower-status backgrounds are quite similar. Both groups indicate the importance of fathers and older brothers in introducing them to sports. Both groups speak of the joys of receiving attention and acceptance among family and peers for early successes in sports. Note the similarities, for instance, in the following descriptions of boyhood athletic experiences of two men. First, a man born in a white, middle-class family:

> I loved playing sports so much from a very early age because of early exposure. A lot of the sports came easy at an early age, and because they did, and because you were successful at something, I think that you're inclined to strive for that gratification. It's like, if you're good, you like it, because it's instant gratification. I'm doing something that I'm good at and I'm gonna keep doing it.

Second, a black man from a poor family:

> Fortunately I had some athletic ability, and, quite naturally, once you start doing good in whatever it is—I don't care if it's jacks—you show off what you do. That's your ability, that's your blessing, so you show it off as much as you can.

For boys from both groups, early exposure to sports, the discovery that they had some "ability," shortly followed by some sort of family, peer, and community recognition, all eventually led to the commitment of hundreds and thousands of hours of playing, practicing, and dreaming of future stardom. Despite these similarities, there are also some identifiable differences that begin to explain the tendency of males from lower-status backgrounds to develop higher levels of commitment to sports careers. The most clear-cut difference was that while men from higher-status backgrounds are likely to describe their earliest athletic experiences and motivations almost exclusively in terms of immediate family, men from lower-status backgrounds more commonly describe the importance of a broader community context. For instance, a 46-year-old man who grew up in a "poor working class" black family in a small town in Arkansas explained:

> In that community, at the age of third or fourth grade, if you're a male, they expect you to show some kind of inclination, some kind of skill in football or basketball. It was an expected thing, you know? My mom and my dad, they didn't push at all. It was the general environment.

A 48-year-old man describes sports activities as a survival strategy in his poor black community:

> Sports protected me from having to compete in gang stuff, or having to be good with my fists. If you were an athlete and got into the fist world, that was your business, and that was okay—but you didn't have to if you didn't want to. People would generally defer to you, give you your space away from trouble.

A 35-year-old man who grew up in "a poor black ghetto" described his boyhood relationship to sports similarly:

> Where I came from, either you were one of two things: you were in sports or you were out on the streets being a drug addict, or breaking into places. The guys who were in sports, we had it a little easier, because we were accepted by both groups. . . . So it worked out to my advantage, cause I didn't get into a lot of trouble—some trouble, but not alot.

The fact that boys in lower-status communities faced these kinds of realities gave salience to their developing athletic identities. In contrast, sports were important to boys from higher-status backgrounds, yet the middle-class environment seemed more secure, less threatening, and offered far more options. By the time most of these boys got into junior high or high school, many had made conscious decisions to shift their attentions away from athletic careers to educational and (nonathletic) career goals. A 32-year-old white college athletic director told me that he had seen his chance to pursue a pro baseball career as "pissing in the wind," and instead, focused on education. Similarly, a 33-year-old white dentist who was a three-sport star in high school, decided not to play sports in college, so he could focus on getting into dental school. As he put it,

> I think I kind of downgraded the stardom thing. I thought it was
> small potatoes. And sure, that's nice in high school and all that, but
> on a broad scale, I didn't think it amounted to all that much.

This statement offers an important key to understanding the construction of masculine identity within a middle-class context. The status that this boy got through sports had been *very* important to him, yet he could see that "on a broad scale," this sort of status was "small potatoes." This sort of early recognition is more than a result of the oft-noted middle-class tendency to raise "future-oriented" children (Rubin, 1976; Sennett and Cobb, 1973). Perhaps more important, it is that the *kinds* of future orientations developed by boys from higher-status backgrounds are consistent with the middle-class context. These men's descriptions of their boyhoods reveal that they grew up immersed in a wide range of institutional frameworks, of which organized sports was just one. And—importantly—they could see that the status of adult males around them was clearly linked to their positions within various professions, public institutions, and bureaucratic organizations. It was clear that access to this sort of institutional status came through educational achievement, not athletic prowess. A 32-year-old black man who grew up in a professional-class family recalled that he had idolized Wilt Chamberlain and dreamed of being a pro basketball player, yet his father discouraged his athletic strivings:

> He knew I liked the game. I *loved* the game. But basketball was not
> recommended; my dad would say, "That's a stereotyped image for
> black youth. . . . When your basketball is gone and finished, what
> are you gonna do? One day, you might get injured. What are you
> gonna look forward to?" He stressed education.

Similarly, a 32-year-old man who was raised in a white, middle-class family, had found in sports a key means of gaining acceptance and connection in his peer group. Yet he was simultaneously developing an image of himself as a "smart student," and becoming aware of a wide range of non-sports life options:

> My mother was constantly telling me how smart I was, how good I
> was, what a nice person I was, and giving me all sorts of positive
> strokes, and those positive strokes became a self-motivating kind of
> thing. I had this image of myself as smart, and I lived up to that
> image.

It is not that parents of boys in lower-status families did not also encourage their boys to work hard in school. Several reported that their parents "stressed books first, sports second." It's just that the broader social context—education, economy, and community—was more likely to *narrow* lower-status boys' perceptions of real-life options, while boys from higher-status backgrounds faced an expanding world of options. For instance, with a different socioeconomic background, one 35-year-old black man might have become a great musician instead of a star professional football running back. But he did not. When he was a child, he said, he was most interested in music:

> I wanted to be a drummer. But we couldn't afford drums. My dad couldn't go out and buy me a drum set or a guitar even—it was just one of those things; he was just trying to make ends meet.

But he *could* afford, as could so many in his socioeconomic condition, to spend countless hours at the local park, where he was told by the park supervisor

> that I was a natural—not only in gymnastics or baseball—whatever I did, I was a natural. He told me I shouldn't waste this talent, and so I immediately started watching the big guys then.

In retrospect, this man had potential to be a musician or any number of things, but his environment limited his options to sports, and he made the best of it. Even within sports, he, like most boys in the ghetto, was limited:

> We didn't have any tennis courts in the ghetto—we used to have a lot of tennis balls, but not racquets. I wonder today how good I might be in tennis if I had gotten a racquet in my hands at an early age.

It is within this limited structure of opportunity that many lower-status young boys found sports to be *the* place, rather than *a* place, within which to construct masculine identity, status, the relationships. A 36-year-old white man explained that his father left the family when he was very young and his mother faced a very difficult struggle to make ends meet. As his words suggest, the more limited a boy's options, and the more insecure his family situation, the more likely he is to make an early commitment to an athletic career:

> I used to ride my bicycle to Little League practice—if I'd waited for someone to pick me up and take me to the ball park I'd have never played. I'd get to the ball park and all the other kids would have their dad bring them to practice or games. But I'd park my bike to the side and when it was over I'd get on it and go home. Sports was the way for me to move everything to the side—family problems, just all the embarrassments—and think about one thing, and that was sports . . . In the third grade, when the teacher went around the classroom and asked everybody, "What do you want to be when you grow up?" I said, "I want to be a major league baseball player," and everybody laughed their heads off.

This man eventually did enjoy a major league baseball career. Most boys from lower-status backgrounds who make similar early commitments to athletic careers are not so successful. As stated earlier, the career structure of organized sports is highly competitive and hierarchical. In fact, the chances of attaining professional status in sports are approximately 4:100,000 for a white man, 2:100,000 for a black man, and 3:1 million for a Hispanic man in the United States (Leonard and Reyman, 1988). Nevertheless, the immediate rewards (fun, status, attention), along with the constricted (nonsports) structure of opportunity, attract disproportionately large numbers of boys from lower-status backgrounds to athletic careers as their major means of constructing a masculine identity. These are the boys who later, as young men, had to struggle with "conditional self-worth," and, more often than not, occupational dead ends. Boys from higher-status backgrounds, on the other hand, bolstered their boyhood, adolescent, and early adult status through their athletic accomplishments. Their wide range of experiences and life changes led to an early shift away from sports careers as the major basis of identity (Messner, 1989).

Conclusion

The conception of the masculinity-sports relationship developed here begins to illustrate the idea of an "elective affinity" between social structure and personality. Organized sports is a "gendered institution"—an institution constructed by gender relations. As such, its structure and values (rules, formal organization, sex composition, etc.) reflect dominant conceptions of masculinity and femininity. Organized sports is also a "gendering institution"—an institution that helps to construct the current gender order. Part of this construction of gender is accomplished through the "masculinizing" of male bodies and minds.

Yet boys do not come to their first experiences in organized sports as "blank slates," but arrive with already "gendering" identities due to early developmental experiences and previous socialization. I have suggested here that an important thread running through the development of masculine identity is males' ambivalence toward intimate unity with others. Those boys who experience early athletic successes find in the structure of organized sport an affinity with this masculine ambivalence toward intimacy: The rule-bound, competitive, hierarchical world of sport offers boys an attractive means of establishing an emotionally distant (and thus "safe") connection with others. Yet as boys begin to define themselves as "athletes," they learn that in order to be accepted (to have connection) through sports, they must be winners. And in order to be winners, they must construct relationships with others (and with themselves) that are consistent with the competitive and hierarchical values and structure of the sports world. As a result, they often develop a "conditional self-worth" that leads them to construct more instrumental relationships with themselves and others. This ultimately exacerbates their difficulties in constructing intimate relationships with others. In effect, the interaction between the young male's preexisting internalized ambivalence toward intimacy with the competitive hierarchical institution of sport has resulted in the construction of a masculine personality that is characterized by instrumental rationality, goal-orientation, and difficulties with intimate connection and expression (Messner, 1987).

This theoretical line of inquiry invites us not simply to examine how social institutions "socialize" boys, but also to explore the ways that boys' already-gendering identities interact with social institutions (which, like organized sport, are themselves the product of gender relations). This study has also suggested that is it not some singular "masculinity" that is being constructed through athletic careers. It may be correct, from a psychoanalytic perspective, to suggest that all males bring ambivalences toward intimacy to their interactions with the world, but "the world" is a very different place for males from different racial and socioeconomic backgrounds. Because males have substantially different interactions with the world, based on class, race, and other differences and inequalities, we might expect the construction of masculinity to take on different meanings for boys and men from differing backgrounds (Messner, 1989). Indeed, this study has suggested that boys from higher-status backgrounds face a much broader range of options than do their lower-status counterparts. As a result, athletic careers take on different meanings for these boys. Lower-status boys are likely to see athletic careers as *the* institutional context for the construction of their masculine status and identities, while higher-status males make an early shift away from athletic careers toward other institutions (usually education and nonsports careers). A key line of inquiry for future studies might begin by exploring this irony of sports careers: Despite the fact that "the athlete" is currently an example of an exemplary form of masculinity in public ideology, the vast majority of boys who become most committed to athletic careers are never well-rewarded for their efforts. The fact that class and racial dynamics lead boys from higher-status backgrounds, unlike their lower-status counterparts, to move into nonsports careers illustrates how the construction of different kinds of masculinities is a key component of the overall construction of the gender order.

References

Birrell, S. (1987) "The woman athlete's college experience: knowns and unknowns." *J. of Sport and Social Issues* 11:82–96.

Benjamin, J. (1988) *The Bonds of Love: Psychoanalysis, Feminism, and the Problem of Domination.* New York: Pantheon.

Bryson, L. (1987) "Sport and the maintenance of masculine hegemony." Women's Studies International *Forum* 10:349–360.

Chodorow, N. (1978) *The Reproduction of Mothering.* Berkeley: Univ. of California Press.

Connell, R. W. (1990) "An iron man: the body and some contradictions of hegemonic masculinity," in M.A. Messner and D. F. Sabo (eds.) *Sport, Men and the Gender Order: Critical Feminist Perspectives.* Champaign, IL: Human Kinetics.

Craib, I. (1987) "Masculinity and male dominance." *Soc. Rev.* 38:721–743.

Eitzen, D. S. (1975) "Athletics in the status system of male adolescents: a replication of Coleman's *The Adolescent Society.*" *Adolescence* 10:268–276.

Gilligan, C. (1982) *In a Different Voice: Psychological Theory and Women's Development.* Cambridge, MA: Harvard Univ. Press.

Greendorfer, S. L. (1977) "The role of socializing agents in female sport involvement." *Research Q.* 48:304–310.

Hall, M. A. (1988) "The discourse on gender and sport: from femininity to feminism." *Sociology of Sport J.* 5:330–340.

Hantover, J. (1978) "The boy scouts and the validation of masculinity." *J. of Social Issues* 34:184–195.

Haug, F. (1987) *Female Sexualization.* London: Verso.

Kidd, B. (1987) "Sports and masculinity," pp. 250–265 in M. Kaufman (ed.) *Beyond Patriarchy: Essays by Men on Pleasure, Power, and Change.* Toronto: Oxford Univ. Press.

Kidd, B. (1990) "The men's cultural centre: sports and the dynamic of women's oppression/men's repression," in M. A. Messner and D. F. Sabo (eds.) *Sport, Men and the Gender Order: Critical Feminist Perspectives.* Champaign, IL: Human Kinetics.

Kimmel, M. S. (1987) "Men's responses to feminism at the turn of the century." *Gender and Society* 1:261–283.

Kimmel, M. S. (1990) "Baseball and the reconstitution of American masculinity: 1880–1920," in M. A. Messner and D. F. Sabo (eds.) *Sport, Men and the Gender Order: Critical Feminist Perspectives.* Champaign, IL: Human Kinetics.

Leonard, W. M. II and J. M. Reyman (1988) "The odds of attaining professional athlete status: refining the computations." *Sociology of Sport J.* 5.: 162–169.

Lever, J. (1976) "Sex differences in the games children play." *Social Problems* 23:478–487.

Levinson, D. J. et al. (1978) *The Seasons of a Man's Life.* New York: Ballantine.

Lichterman, P. (1986) "Chodorow's psychoanalytic sociology: a project half-completed." *California Sociologist* 9:147–166.

Messner, M. (1987) "The meaning of success: the athletic experience and the development of male identity," pp. 193–210 in H. Brod (ed.) *The Making of Masculinities: The New Men's Studies.* Boston: Allen & Unwin.

Messner, M. (1988) "Sports and male domination: the female athlete as contested ideological terrain." *Sociology of Sport J.* 5:197–211.

Messner, M. (1989) "Masculinities and athletic careers." *Gender and Society* 3:71–88.

Oglesby, C. A. (ed.) (1978) *Women and Sport: From Myth to Reality.* Philadelphia: Lea & Farber.

Osherson, S. (1986) *Finding our Fathers: How a Man's Life is Shaped by His Relationship with His Father.* New York: Fawcett Columbine.

Piaget, J. H. (1965) *The Moral Judgment of the Child.* New York: Free Press.

Rubin, L. B. (1976) *Worlds of Pain: Life in the Working Class Family.* New York: Basic Books.

Sabo, D. (1985) "Sport, patriarchy and male identity: new questions about men and sport." *Arena Rev.* 9:2.

Schafer, W. E. (1975) "Sport and male sex role socialization." *Sport Sociology Bull.* 4:47–54.

Sennett, R. and J. Cobb (1973) *The Hidden Injuries of Class.* New York: Random House.

Theberge, N. (1981) "A critique of critiques: radical and feminist writings on sport." *Social Forces* 60:2.

Thorne, B. (1986) "Girls and boys together . . . but mostly apart: gender arrangements in elementary schools," pp. 167–184 in W. W. Hartup and Z. Rubin (eds.) *Relationships and Development.* Hillsdale, NJ: Lawrence Erlbaum.

Twin, S. L. (ed.) (1978) *Out of the Bleachers: Writings on Women and Sport.* Old Westbury, NY: Feminist Press.

PART II
Gender Socialization

When she was about eighteen, after hearing him go on about the qualities he and his friends sought in a woman, my sister reduced my father to an abashed silence by saying, "I guess I wouldn't have had much of a chance with your group." The number one quality was fair skin—which neither Carolyn nor I had.

GAYLE PEMBERTON[1]

Having been branded a sissy by neighborhood children because I preferred jump rope to baseball, and dolls to playing soldiers, I was often taunted with "hey sissy" or "hey faggot" or "yoo hoo honey" (in a mocking voice) when I left the house.

TOMMI AVICOLLI[2]

The gender system, embedded in other institutions, ensures its continuance through systematic socialization of children, adolescents, and adults. Even though there is substantial variation in how different cultural groups and families within the United States teach their children to be girls or boys, and even though men and women are more alike than they are different, the presence of gender training persists, and the larger institutional structures reinforce it. Sociologist Michael Messner, for example, in a telling account of white male socialization in childhood, describes the day he attended his first little league practice and was told by his father that he threw like a girl. A week later, after careful coaching by his father and intense fear of being thought a sissy, he had learned to throw like a man.[3] In a study of Black and white elementary school children, Jacqueline Jordan Irvine concluded that teachers systematically encouraged Black girls to act submissive, and that, by upper elementary school, both Black and white girls are rendered relatively invisible in classrooms, receiving significantly less attention from teachers than boys of both races receive.[4]

From the time we are born until we die, gender socialization is a constant part of our lives. Although the genes that determine sex come in several combinations (not just two), and although the hormonal makeup and physical characteristics of human beings fall along a continuum defined as masculine at one end and feminine at the other, allowing for many combinations and permutations that define one's biological sex, the social contexts in which infants are assigned a gender do not allow for more than two categories. Based on examination of its genitalia, an infant will be defined as female or male, whatever its chromosomal and hormonal makeup. Within this powerful system of gender assignment, women and men work to define their individual identities. Because gender is a socialized aspect of life rather than a purely genetic/biological one, there is flexibility in how it is expressed.

A commonly cited case of an atypical mix of genetic/biological makeup and gender is that of an identical twin boy who was accidentally castrated in the course of a circumcision at seven months of age. After considering the various options, the parents agreed to reassign the child's gender on the assumption that he could be socialized as a girl and later go through the various hormone treatments and surgeries necessary to make his body appear female. The parents succeeded in raising this genetically male child as a very feminine girl.[5]

In another case of gender reassignment, children in three villages in the Dominican Republic inherited a syndrome that produced ambiguous genitalia at birth that became male genitalia at puberty. Of eighteen children originally raised as girls, sixteen successfully assumed male genders after their penises developed.[6] Thus, the influence of socialization and the potential for resocialization appears to be present beyond the early years. This is clearly illustrated by adults who become transsexuals or transgendered, making a choice to resocialize themselves, to varying degrees, into the gender in which they were not raised. This resocialization process is often accompanied by a new sexual orientation as well.[7] Research literature on adult development suggests that expressions of gender shift throughout the life cycle.[8] Socialization patterns and expectations for male and female behavior also change over time related to the historical context. For example, many middle-class women were needed in factories during World War II but were sent home when men, returning from the war, were given priority in hiring; these women were then encouraged to be housewives and mothers, forced to resocialize themselves to match prior expectations.

Part II looks at selected aspects of gender socialization from the perspectives of marginalized voices, intersecting identities, the reconstruction of knowledge, and empowerment. A recurring theme in the study of gender socialization is the presence of homophobia—overtly expressed against boys and girls who don't fit gender stereotypes and internalized by gay men, lesbians, bisexuals, and transgendered people as fear of ostracism or as self-hatred.

The first three articles in Part II address socialization in childhood. First, Barrie Thorne reports on her observations of girls and boys in racially and ethnically mixed working-class elementary schools. She finds that although boys and girls spend most of their time in sex-segregated play, there are important points of contact that should not be overlooked.

Following Thorne, Chicano poet Luis Rodríguez provides a glimpse of what it is like to grow up in a context where gangs meet the needs of young people and violence is a way of life. Rodríguez first describes a time when he and his brother cross the tracks into a white neighborhood to buy groceries and are attacked by a group of white boys. Badly beaten, Rodríguez's brother is more humiliated over the fact that he cried than he is over the fact that he was beaten up. Then Rodríguez describes his initiation into a gang and his eventual sense of exhaustion with violence and gang life. Tired of "always running," he starts to hang out at a teen center and finds a role model who helps him learn new ways to live. At the end of his book (not included here), Rodríguez makes a passionate plea for changes in the social order that would help poor, urban youth avoid gangs; he links the problem of street violence to a lack of jobs and decent futures, and hopes that his own son, now a member of a gang, will find a positive life for himself.

Next, African American essayist and scholar Gayle Pemberton discusses growing up in a middle-class family in which light skin was valued over dark skin, and in which she had to learn to value her dark-skinned self on her own. She discusses the brutal impact of racism, along with sexism and color bias within both her own family and the Black community, and describes how she developed a positive sense of self in the midst of these pressures.

The next two authors address the pressures of heterosexist definitions of what is normal. Tommi Avicolli shares some of his experiences as a boy who doesn't conform to the athletic, masculine norm for males. As a child and especially as an adolescent, he is viciously teased and beaten for not fitting what his peers demand of boys, and he is unsupported by the adults in his life, who urge him to behave in more masculine ways. Ultimately he finds support and sanity in the gay pride movement. The next article is an excerpt from the book *S/HE* by anti-racist activist and poet Minnie Bruce Pratt. Pratt opens the issue of the intersections of sex, sexuality, and gender, inviting the reader to explore the various combinations and permutations of these categories. She talks of her own socialization and the development of her identity as a feminine lesbian from childhood to midlife, inviting us to reflect on what gender socialization is and why it is so strongly mandated.

These articles, together with Michael Messner's article in Part I, urge us to become more conscious of various aspects of gender socialization and to consider ways to change what limits people of both genders from being fully human in their own right. There are policy implications here regarding how we accept people who don't fit the norms of masculinity and femininity; regarding the separation of boys and girls in childhood activities; regarding the way to help boys to participate in sports *and* learn to be intimate; regarding the disaster of limited economic options for poor and working-class children; and regarding the intersections of racism, elitism, and sexism as they affect people's lives.

NOTES

1. Gayle Pemberton, "Mrs. Brent," in Becky Thompson and Sangeeta Tyagi, eds., *Names We Call Home* (New York: Routledge, 1995).
2. Tommi Avicolli, "He Defies You Still: The Memoirs of a Sissy," in Paula S. Rothenberg, *Race, Class, and Gender in the United States: An Integrated Study* 3rd ed., (New York: St. Martin's Press, 1995), p. 231.
3. Michael A. Messner, "Ah, Ya Throw Like a Girl!," in Michael A. Messner and Donald F. Sabo, *Sex, Violence and Power in Sports: Rethinking Masculinity* (Freedom, CA: Crossing Press, 1994), pp. 28–32. Messner also reports that this way of throwing is

so unnatural and injurious to the shoulder that few pitchers in childhood survive as pitchers into adulthood, having permanently injured their shoulders.

4. Jacqueline Jordan Irvine (1985). "Teacher Communication Patterns as Related to the Race and Sex of the Student," *Journal of Educational Research,* 78(6):338–45. Jacqueline Jordan Irvine (1986). "Teacher-Student Interactions: Effects of Student Race, Sex, and Grade Level," *Journal of Educational Psychology,* 78(1):14–21. Reported in Hilary M. Lips, "Gender-Role Socialization: Lessons in Feminity," in Jo Freeman, ed., *Women: A Feminist Perspective,* 5th ed. (Mountain view, CA: Mayfield, 1995), pp. 128–48.

5. See Margaret Andersen, *Thinking About Women: Sociological Perspectives on Sex and Gender,* 3rd ed. (New York: Macmillan, 1993), pp. 24–26, for a summary of the literature on ambiguous sexual makeup. For example, people with Klinefelter's syndrome have both male and female chromosomal patterns, have small penises and breast enlargement, low levels of testosterone, and confused gender identity.

6. Anne Fausto-Sterling, *Myths of Gender* (New York: Basic Books, 1985), pp. 86–87.

7. For discussions of the experiences of transsexuals and gender benders, see the new *Journal of Gay, Lesbian, and Bisexual Identity.* Also see Paul Hewitt, *A Self-Made Man: The Diary of a Man Born in a Woman's Body* (London: Headline, 1995); Richard Ekins, *Blending Genders: Social Aspects of Cross-Dressing and Sex Changing* (New York: Routledge, 1995). For a critical look at solving gender confusion via transsexual surgery, see Janice Raymond, *The Transsexual Empire: The Making of the She-Male* (Boston: Beacon Press, 1979).

8. Margaret L. Andersen, *Thinking about Women: Sociological Perspectives on Sex and Gender,* 3rd ed. (New York: Macmillan, 1993), p. 44.

7

GIRLS AND BOYS TOGETHER . . . BUT MOSTLY APART
Gender Arrangements in Elementary School

BARRIE THORNE

Throughout the years of elementary school, children's friendships and casual encounters are strongly separated by sex. Sex segregation among children, which starts in preschool and is well established by middle childhood, has been amply documented in studies of children's groups and friendships (e.g., Eder & Hallinan, 1978; Schofield, 1981) and is

From *Relationships and Development,* Willard W. Hartup and Zick Rubin, eds., pp. 167–184. Volume sponsored by the Social Science Research Center. Copyright © 1986 by Lawrence Erlbaum Associates, Inc. Reprinted by permission of Lawrence Erlbaum Associates, Inc.

immediately visible in elementary school settings. When children choose seats in classrooms or the cafeteria, or get into line, they frequently arrange themselves in same-sex clusters. At lunchtime, they talk matter-of-factly about "girls' tables" and "boys' tables." Playgrounds have gendered turfs, with some areas and activities, such as large playing fields and basketball courts, controlled mainly by boys, and others—smaller enclaves like jungle-gym areas and concrete spaces for hopscotch or jump rope—more often controlled by girls. Sex segregation is so common in elementary schools that it is meaningful to speak of separate girls' and boys' worlds.

Studies of gender and children's social relations have mostly followed this "two worlds" model, separately describing and comparing the subcultures of girls and of boys (e.g., Lever, 1976; Maltz & Borker, 1983). In brief summary: Boys tend to interact in larger, more age-heterogeneous groups (Lever, 1976; Waldrop & Halverson, 1975; Eder & Hallinan, 1978). They engage in more rough and tumble play and physical fighting (Maccoby & Jacklin, 1974). Organized sports are both a central activity and a major metaphor in boys' subcultures; they use the language of "teams" even when not engaged in sports, and they often construct interaction in the form of contests. The shifting hierarchies of boys' groups (Savin-Williams, 1976) are evident in their more frequent use of direct command, insults, and challenges (Goodwin, 1980).

Fewer studies have been done of girls' groups (Foot, Chapman, & Smith, 1980; McRobbie & Garber, 1975), and—perhaps because categories for description and analysis have come more from male than female experience—researchers have had difficulty seeing and analyzing girls' social relations. Recent work has begun to correct this skew. In middle childhood, girls' worlds are less public than those of boys; girls more often interact in private places and in smaller groups or friendship pairs (Eder & Hallinan, 1978; Waldrop & Halverson, 1975). Their play is more cooperative and turn-taking (Lever, 1976). Girls have more intense and exclusive friendships, which take shape around keeping and telling secrets, shifting alliances, and indirect ways of expressing disagreement (Goodwin, 1980; Lever, 1976; Maltz & Borker, 1983). Instead of direct commands, girls more often use directives which merge speaker and hearer, e.g., "let's" or "we gotta" (Goodwin, 1980).

Although much can be learned by comparing the social organization and subcultures of boys' and of girls' groups, the separate worlds approach has eclipsed full, contextual understanding of gender and social relations among children. The separate worlds model essentially involves a search for group sex differences, and shares the limitations of individual sex difference research. Differences tend to be exaggerated and similarities ignored, with little theoretical attention to the integration of similarity and difference. Statistical findings of difference are often portrayed as dichotomous, neglecting the considerable individual variation that exists; for example, not all boys fight, and some have intense and exclusive friendships. The sex difference approach tends to abstract gender from its social context, to assume that males and females are qualitatively and permanently different (with differences perhaps unfolding through separate developmental lines). These assumptions mask the possibility that gender arrangements and patterns of similarity and difference may vary by situation, race, social class, region, and subculture.

Sex segregation is far from total, and is a more complex and dynamic process than the portrayal of separate worlds reveals. Erving Goffman (1977) has observed that sex segregation has a "with-then-apart" structure; the sexes segregate periodically, with separate spaces, rituals, and groups, but they also come together and are, in crucial ways, part of the same world. This is certainly true in the social environment of elementary schools. Although girls and boys do interact as boundaried collectivities—an image suggested by the separate worlds approach—there are other occasions when they work or play in relaxed and integrated ways. Gender is less central to the organization and meaning of some situations than others. In short, sex segregation is not static, but is a variable and complicated process.

To gain an understanding of gender which can encompass both the "with" and the "apart" of sex segregation, analysis should start not with the individual, nor with a search for sex differences, but with social relationships. Gender should be conceptualized as a system of relationships rather than as an immutable and dichotomous given. Taking this approach, I have organized my research on gender and children's social relations around questions like the following: How and when does gender enter into group formation? In a given situation, how is gender made more or less salient or infused with particular meanings? By what rituals, processes, and forms of social organization and conflict do "with-then-apart" rhythms get enacted? How are these processes affected by the organization of institutions (e.g., different types of schools, neighborhoods, or summer camps), varied settings (e.g., the constraints and possibilities governing interaction on playgrounds vs. classrooms), and particular encounters?

Methods and Sources of Data

This study is based on two periods of participant observation. In 1976-1977 I observed for 8 months in a largely working-class elementary school in California, a school with 8% Black and 12% Chicana/o students. In 1980 I did fieldwork for 3 months in a Michigan elementary school in similar size (around 400 students), social class, and racial composition. I observed in several classrooms—a kindergarten, a second grade, and a combined fourth-fifth grade—and in school hallways, cafeterias, and playgrounds. I set out to follow the round of the school day as children experience it, recording their interactions with one another, and with adults, in varied settings.

Participant observation involves gaining access to everyday, "naturalistic" settings and taking systematic notes over an extended period of time.

Rather than starting with preset categories for recording, or with fixed hypotheses for testing, participant-observers record detail in ways which maximize opportunities for discovery. Through continuous interaction between observation and analysis, "grounded theory" is developed (Glaser & Strauss, 1967).

The distinctive logic and discipline of this mode of inquiry emerges from: (1) theoretical sampling—being relatively systematic in the choice of where and whom to observe in order to maximize knowledge relevant to categories and analysis which are being developed; and (2) comparing all relevant data on a given point in order to modify emerging propositions to take account of discrepant cases (Katz, 1983). Participant observation is a flexible, open-ended and inductive method, designed to understand behavior within, rather than stripped from, social context. It provides richly detailed information which is anchored in everyday meanings and experience.

Daily Processes of Sex Segregation

Sex segregation should be understood not as a given, but as the result of deliberate activity. The outcome is dramatically visible when there are separate girls' and boys' tables in school lunchrooms, or sex-separated groups on playgrounds. But in the same lunchroom one can also find tables where girls and boys eat and talk together, and in some playground activities the sexes mix. By what processes do girls and boys separate into gender-defined and relatively boundaried collectivities? And in what contexts, and through what processes, do boys and girls interact in less gender-divided ways?

In the school settings I observed, much segregation happened with no mention of gender. Gender was implicit in the contours of friendship, shared interest, and perceived risk which came into play when children chose companions—in their prior planning, invitations, seeking-of-access, saving-of-places, denials of entry, and allowing or protesting of "cuts" by those who violated the rules for lining up. Sometimes children formed mixed-sex groups for play, eating, talking, working on a classroom project, or moving through space. When adults or children explicitly invoked gender—and this was nearly always in ways which separated girls and boys—boundaries were heightened and mixed-sex interaction became an explicit arena of risk.

In the schools I studied, the physical space and curricula were not formally divided by sex, as they have been in the history of elementary schooling (a history evident in separate entrances to old school buildings, where the words "Boys" and "Girls" are permanently etched in concrete). Nevertheless, gender was a visible marker in the adult-organized school day. In both schools, when the public address system sounded, the principal inevitably opened with: "Boys and girls . . . ," and in addressing clusters of children, teachers and aides regularly used gender terms ("Heads down, girls"; "The girls are ready and the boys aren't"). These forms of address made gender visible and salient, conveying an assumption that the sexes are separate social groups.

Teachers and aides sometimes drew upon gender as a basis for sorting children and organizing activities. Gender is an embodied and visual social category which roughly divides the population in half, and the separation of girls and boys permeates the history and lore of schools and playgrounds. In both schools—although through awareness of Title IX, many teachers had changed this practice—one could see separate girls' and boys' lines moving, like caterpillars, through the school halls. In the 4th–5th grade classroom the teacher frequently pitted girls against boys for spelling and math contests. On the playground in the Michigan school, aides regarded the space close to the building as girls' territory, and the playing fields "out there" as boys' territory. They sometimes shooed children of the other sex away from those spaces, especially boys who ventured near the girls' area and seemed to have teasing in mind.

In organizing their activities, both within and apart from the surveillance of adults, children also explicitly invoked gender. During my fieldwork in the Michigan school, I kept daily records of who sat where in the lunchroom. The amount of sex segregation varied: It was least at the first grade tables and almost total among sixth graders. There was also variation from classroom to classroom within a given age, and from day to day. Actions like the following heightened the gender divide:

> In the lunchroom, when the two second grade tables were filling, a high-status boy walked by the inside table, which had a scattering of both boys and girls, and said loudly, "Oooo, too many girls," as he headed for a seat at the far table. The boys at the inside table picked up their trays and moved, and no other boys sat at the inside table, which the pronouncement had effectively made taboo.

In the end, that day (which was not the case every day), girls and boys ate at separate tables.

Eating and walking are not sex-typed activities, yet in forming groups in lunchrooms and hallways children often separated by sex. Sex segregation assumed added dimensions on the playground, where spaces, equipment, and activities were infused with gender meanings. My inventories of activities and groupings on the playground showed similar patterns in both schools: Boys controlled the large fixed spaces designated for team sports (baseball diamonds, grassy fields used for football or soccer); girls more often played closer to the building, doing tricks on the monkey bars (which, for 6th graders, became an area for sitting and talking) and using cement areas for jumprope, hopscotch, and group games like four-square. (Lever, 1976, provides a good analysis of sex-divided play.) Girls and boys most often played together in kickball, and in group (rather than team) games like four-square, dodgeball, and handball. When children used gender to exclude others from play, they often drew upon beliefs connecting boys to some activities and girls to others:

> A first grade boy avidly watched an all-female game of jump rope. When the girls began to shift positions, he recognized a means of access to the play and he offered, "I'll swing it." A girl responded, "No way, you don't know how to do it, to swing it. You gotta be a girl." He left without protest.

Although children sometimes ignored pronouncements about what each sex could or could not do, I never heard them directly challenge such claims.

When children had explicitly defined an activity or a group as gendered, those who crossed the boundary—especially boys who moved into female-marked space—risked being teased. ("Look! Mike's in the girls' line!" "That's a girl over there," a girl said loudly, pointing to a boy sitting at an otherwise all-female table in the lunchroom.") Children, and occasionally adults, used teasing—especially the tease of "liking" someone of the other sex, or of "being" that sex by virtue of being in their midst—to police gender boundaries. Much of the teasing drew upon heterosexual romantic definitions, making cross-sex interaction risky, and increasing social distance between boys and girls.

Relationships between the Sexes

Because I have emphasized the "apart" and ignored the occasions of "with," this analysis of sex segregation falsely implies that there is little contact between girls and boys in daily school life. In fact, relationships between girls and boys—which should be studied as fully as, and in connection with, same-sex relationships—are of several kinds:

1. "Borderwork," or forms of cross-sex interaction which are based upon and reaffirm boundaries and asymmetries between girls' and boys' groups;
2. Interactions which are infused with heterosexual meanings;
3. Occasions where individuals cross gender boundaries to participate in the world of the other sex; and
4. Situations where gender is muted in salience, with girls and boys interacting in more relaxed ways.

Borderwork

In elementary school settings boys' and girls' groups are sometimes spatially set apart. Same-sex groups sometimes claim fixed territories such as the basketball court, the bars, or specific lunchroom tables. However, in the crowded, multifocused, and adult-controlled environment of the school, groups form and disperse at a rapid rate and can never stay totally apart. Contact between girls and boys sometimes lessens sex segregation, but gender-defined groups also come together in ways which emphasize their boundaries.

"Borderwork" refers to interaction across, yet based upon and even strengthening gender boundaries. I have drawn this notion from Fredrik Barth's (1969) analysis of social relations which are maintained across ethnic boundaries without diminishing dichotomized ethnic status.[1] His focus is on more macro, ecological arrangements: mine is on face-to-face behavior. But the insight is similar: Groups may interact in ways which strengthen their borders, and the maintenance of ethnic (or gender) groups can best be understood by examining the boundary that defines the group, "not the cultural stuff that it encloses" (Barth, 1969, p. 15). In elementary schools there are several types of borderwork: contests or games where gender-defined teams compete; cross-sex rituals of chasing and pollution; and group invasions. These interactions are asymmetrical, challenging the separate-but-parallel model of "two worlds."

Contests   Boys and girls are sometimes pitted against each other in classroom competitions and playground games. The 4th–5th grade classroom had a boys' side and a girls' side, an arrangement that reemerged each time the teacher asked children to choose their own desks. Although there was some within-sex shuffling, the result was always a spatial moiety system—boys on the left, girls on the right—with the exception of one girl (the "tomboy" whom I'll describe later), who twice chose a desk with the boys and once with the girls. Drawing upon and reinforcing the children's self-segregation, the teacher often pitted the boys against the girls in spelling and math competitions, events marked by cross-sex antagonism and within-sex solidarity:

> The teacher introduced a math game; she would write addition and subtraction problems on the board, and a member of each team would race to be the first to write the correct answer. She wrote two scorekeeping columns on the board: 'Beastly boys'. . . 'Gossipy Girls.' The boys yelled out, as several girls laughed, 'Noisy girls! Gruesome girls!' The girls sat in a row on top of their desks; sometimes they moved collectively, pushing their hips or whispering 'pass it on.' The boys stood along the wall, some reclining against desks. When members of either group came back victorious from the front of the room, they would do the 'giving five' handslapping ritual with their team members.

On the playground a team of girls occasionally played against a team of boys, usually in kickball or team two-square. Sometimes these games proceeded matter-of-factly, but if gender became the explicit basis of team solidarity, the interaction changed, becoming more antagonistic and unstable:

Two fifth-grade girls against two fifth-grade boys in a team game of two-square. The game proceeded at an even pace until an argument ensued about whether the ball was out or on the line. Karen, who had hit the ball, became annoyed, flashed her middle finger at the other team, and called to a passing girl to join their side. The boys then called out to other boys, and cheered as several arrived to play. 'We got five and you got three!' Jack yelled. The game continued, with the girls yelling, 'Bratty boys! Sissy boys!' and the boys making noises—'weee haw' 'ha-ha-ha'—as they played.

Chasing   Cross-sex chasing dramatically affirms boundaries between girls and boys. The basic elements of chase and elude, capture and rescue (Sutton-Smith, 1971) are found in various kinds of tag with formal rules, and in informal episodes of chasing which punctuate life on playgrounds. These episodes begin with a provocation (taunts like "You can't get me!" or "Slobber monster!," bodily pokes, or the grabbing of possessions). A provocation may be ignored, or responded to by chasing. Chaser and chased may then alternate roles. In an ethnographic study of chase sequences on a school playground, Christine Finnan (1982) observes that chases vary in number of chasers to chased (e.g., one chasing one, or five chasing two); form of provocation (a taunt or a poke); outcome (an episode may end when the chased outdistances the chaser, or with a brief touch, being wrestled to the ground, or the recapturing of a hat or a ball); and in use of space (there may or may not be safety zones).

Like Finnan (1982), and Sluckin (1981), who studied a playground in England, I found that chasing has a gendered structure. Boys frequently chase one another, an activity which often ends in wrestling and mock fights. When girls chase girls, they are usually less physically aggressive; they less often, for example, wrestle one another to the ground.

Cross-sex chasing is set apart by special names—"girls chase the boys"; "boys chase the girls"; "the chase"; "chasers"; "chase and kiss"; "kiss chase" "kissers and chasers"; "kiss or kill"—and by children's animated talk about the activity. The names vary by region and school, but contain both gender and sexual meanings (this form of play is mentioned, but only briefly analyzed, in Finnan, 1982; Sluckin, 1981; Parrott, 1972; and Borman, 1979).

In "boys chase the girls" and "girls chase the boys" (the names most frequently used in both the California and Michigan schools) boys and girls become, by definition, separate teams. Gender terms override individual identities, especially for the other team ("Help, a girl's chasin' me!"; "C'mon Sarah, let's get that boy"; "Tony, help save me from the girls"). Individuals may call for help from, or offer help to, others of their sex. They may also grab someone of their sex and turn them over to the opposing team: Ryan grabbed Billy from behind, wrestling him to the ground. "Hey, girls, get 'im," Ryan called.

Boys more often mix episodes of cross-sex with same-sex chasing. Girls more often have safety zones, places like the girls' restroom or an area by the school wall, where they retreat to rest and talk (sometimes in animated post-mortems) before new episodes of cross-sex chasing begin.

Early in the fall in the Michigan school, where chasing was especially prevalent, I watched a second grade boy teach a kindergarten girl how to chase. He slowly ran backwards, beckoning her to pursue him, as he called, "Help, a girl's after me." In the early grades chasing mixes with fantasy play, e.g., a first-grade boy who played "sea monster," his arms outflung and his voice growling, as he chased a group of girls. By third grade, stylized gestures—exaggerated stalking motions, screams (which only girls do), and karate kicks—accompany scenes of chasing.

Names like "chase and kiss" mark the sexual meanings of cross-sex chasing, a theme I return to later. The threat of kissing—most often girls threatening to kiss boys—is a ritualized form of provocation. Cross-sex chasing among sixth graders involves elaborate patterns of touch and touch avoidance, which adults see as sexual. The principal told the sixth graders in the Michigan school that they were not to play "pom-pom," a complicated chasing game, because it entailed "inappropriate touch."

Rituals of Pollution   Cross-sex chasing is sometimes entwined with rituals of pollution, as in "cooties," where specific individuals or groups are treated as contaminating or carrying "germs." Children have rituals for transferring cooties (usually touching someone else and shouting "You've got cooties!"), for immunization (e.g., writing "CV" for "cootie vaccination" on their arms), and for eliminating cooties (e.g., saying "no gives" or using "cootie catchers" made of folded paper described in Knapp & Knapp, 1976). While girls may give cooties to girls, boys do not generally give cooties to one another (Samuelson, 1980).

In cross-sex play, either girls or boys may be defined as having cooties, which they transfer through chasing and touching. Girls give cooties to boys more often than vice versa. In Michigan, one version of cooties is called "girl stain"; the fourth-graders whom Karkau, 1973, describes, used the phrase "girl touch." "Cootie queens," or "cootie girls" (there are no "kings" or "boys") are female pariahs, the ultimate school untouchables, seen as contaminating not only by virtue of gender, but also through some added stigma such as being overweight or poor.[2] That girls are seen as more polluting than boys is a significant asymmetry, which echoes cross-cultural patterns, although in other cultures female pollution is generally connected to menstruation, and not applied to prepubertal girls.

Invasions   Playground invasions are another asymmetric form of border-work. On a few occasions I saw girls invade and disrupt an all-male game, most memorably a group of tall sixth-grade girls who ran onto the playing field and grabbed a football which was in play. The boys were surprised and frustrated, and, unusual for boys this old, finally tattled to the aide. But in the majority of cases, boys disrupt girls' activities rather than vice versa. Boys grab the ball from girls playing foursquare, stick feet into a jump rope and stop an ongoing game, and dash through the area of the bars, where girls are taking turns performing, sending the rings flying. Sometimes boys ask to join a girls' game and then, after a short period of seemingly earnest play, disrupt the game:

> Two second-grade boys begged to "twirl" the jumprope for a group of second-grade girls who had been jumping for some time. The girls agreed, and the boys began to twirl. Soon, without announcement, the boys changed from "seashells, cockle bells" to "hot peppers" (spinning the rope very fast), and tangled the jumper in the rope. The boys ran away laughing.

Boys disrupt girls' play so often that girls have developed almost ritualized responses: They guard their ongoing play, chase boys away, and tattle to the aides. In a playground cycle which enhances sex segregation, aides who try to spot potential trouble before it occurs sometimes shoo boys away from areas where girls are playing. Aides do not anticipate trouble from girls who seek to join groups of boys, with the exception of girls intent on provoking a chase sequence. And indeed, if they seek access to a boys' game, girls usually play with boys in earnest rather than breaking up the game.

A close look at the organization of borderwork—or boundaried interactions between the sexes—shows that the worlds of boys and girls may be separate but they are not parallel, nor are they equal. The worlds of girls and boys articulate in several asymmetric ways:

1. On the playground, boys control as much as ten times more space than girls, when one adds up the area of large playing fields and compares it with the much smaller areas where girls predominate. Girls, who play closer to the building, are more often watched over and protected by the adult aides.
2. Boys invade all-female games and scenes of play much more than girls invade boys'. This, and boys' greater control of space, correspond with other findings about the organization of gender, and inequality, in our society: compared with men and boys, women and girls take up less space, and their space, and talk, are more often violated and interrupted (Henley, 1977).
3. Although individual boys are occasionally treated as contaminating (e.g., a third grade boy who [to] both boys and girls was "stinky" and "smelled like pee"), girls are more often defined as polluting. This pattern ties to themes that I discuss later: It is more taboo for a boy to play with (as opposed to invade) girls, and girls are more sexually defined than boys.

A look at the boundaries between the separated worlds of girls and boys illuminates within-sex hierarchies of status and control. For example, in the sex-divided seating in the 4th–5th grade classroom, several boys recurringly sat near "female space": their desks were at the gender divide in the classroom, and they were more likely than other boys to sit at a predominantly female table in the lunchroom. These boys—two nonbilingual Chicanos and an over-weight "loner" boy who was afraid of sports—were at the bottom of the male hierarchy. Gender is sometimes used as a metaphor for male hierarchies; the inferior status of boys at the bottom is conveyed by calling them "girls":

> Seven boys and one girl were playing basketball. Two younger boys came over and asked to play. While the girl silently stood, fully accepted in the company of players, one of the older boys disparagingly said to the younger boys, 'You girls can't play.'[3]

In contrast, the girls who more often travel in the boys' world, sitting with groups of boys in the lunchroom or playing basketball, soccer, and baseball with them, are not stigmatized. Some have fairly high status with other girls. The worlds of girls and boys are asymmetrically arranged, and spatial patterns map out interacting forms of inequality.

Heterosexual Meanings

The organization and meanings of gender (the social categories "woman/man," "girl/boy") and of sexuality vary cross-culturally (Ortner & Whitehead, 1981)—and, in our society, across the life course. Harriet Whitehead (1981) observed that in our (Western) gender system, and that of many traditional North American Indian cultures, one's choice of a sexual object, occupation, and one's dress and demeanor are closely associated with gender. However, the "center of gravity" differs in the two gender systems. For Indians, occupational pursuits provide the primary imagery of gender; dress and demeanor are secondary, and sexuality is least important. In our system, at least for adults, the order is reversed: heterosexuality is central to our definitions of "man" and "woman" ("masculinity"/"femininity"), and the relationships that obtain between them, whereas occupation and dress/demeanor are secondary.

Whereas erotic orientation and gender are closely linked in our definitions of adults, we define children as relatively asexual. Activities and dress/demeanor are more important than sexuality in the cultural meanings of "girl" and "boy." Children are less heterosexually defined than adults, and we have nonsexual imagery for relations between girls and boys. However, both children and adults sometimes use heterosexual language— "crushes," "like," "goin' with," "girlfriends," and "boyfriends"—to define cross-sex relationships. This language increases through the years of elementary school; the shift to adolescence consolidates a gender system organized around the institution of heterosexuality.

In everyday life in the schools, heterosexual and romantic meanings infuse some ritualized forms of interaction between groups of boys and girls (e.g., "chase and kiss") and help maintain sex segregation. "Jimmy likes

Beth" or "Beth likes Jimmy" is a major form of teasing, which a child risks in choosing to sit by or walk with someone of the other sex. The structure of teasing, and children's sparse vocabulary for relationships between girls and boys, are evident in the following conversation which I had with a group of third-grade girls in the lunchroom:

> Susan asked me what I was doing, and I said I was observing the things children do and play. Nicole volunteered, 'I like running, boys chase all the girls. See Tim over there? Judy chases him all around the school. She likes him.' Judy, sitting across the table, quickly responded, 'I hate him. I like him for a friend.' 'Tim loves Judy,' Nicole said in a loud, sing-song voice.

In the younger grades, the culture and lore of girls contain more heterosexual romantic themes than that of boys. In Michigan, the first-grade girls often jumped rope to a rhyme which began: "Down in the valley where the green grass grows, there sat Cindy (name of the jumper), as sweet as a rose. She sat, she sat, she sat so sweet. Along came Jason, and kissed her on the cheek . . . first comes love, then comes marriage, then along comes Cindy with a baby carriage . . ." Before a girl took her turn at jumping, the chanters asked her, "Who do you want to be your boyfriend?" The jumper always proffered a name, which was accepted matter-of-factly. In chasing, a girl's kiss carried greater threat than a boy's kiss; "girl touch," when defined as contaminating, had sexual connotations. In short, starting at an early age, girls are more sexually defined than boys.

Through the years of elementary school, and increasing with age, the idiom of heterosexuality helps maintain the gender divide. Cross-sex interactions, especially when children initiate them, are fraught with the risk of being teased about "liking" someone of the other sex. I learned of several close cross-sex friendships, formed and maintained in neighborhoods and church, which went underground during the school day.

By the fifth grade a few children began to affirm, rather than avoid, the charge of having a girlfriend or a boyfriend; they introduced the heterosexual courtship rituals of adolescence:

> In the lunchroom in the Michigan school, as the tables were forming, a high-status fifth-grade boy called out from his seat at the table: 'I want Trish to sit by me.' Trish came over, and almost like a king and queen, they sat at the gender divide—a row of girls down the table on her side, a row of boys on his.

In this situation, which inverted earlier forms, it was not a loss, but a gain in status to publicly choose a companion of the other sex. By affirming his choice, the boy became unteasable (note the familiar asymmetry of heterosexual courtship rituals: the male initiated). This incident signals a temporal shift in arrangements of sex and gender.

Traveling in the World of the Other Sex

Contests, invasions, chasing, and heterosexually-defined encounters are based upon and reaffirm boundaries between girls and boys. In another type of cross-sex interaction, individuals (or sometimes pairs) cross gender boundaries, seeking acceptance in a group of the other sex. Nearly all the cases I saw of this were tomboys—girls who played organized sports and frequently sat with boys in the cafeteria or classroom. If these girls were skilled at activities central in the boys' world, especially games like soccer, baseball, and basketball, they were pretty much accepted as participants.

Being a tomboy is a matter of degree. Some girls seek access to boys' groups but are excluded; other girls limit their "crossing" to specific sports. Only a few—such as the tomboy I mentioned earlier, who chose a seat with the boys in the sex-divided fourth–fifth grade—participate fully in the boys' world. That particular girl was skilled at the various organized sports which boys played in different seasons of the year. She was also adept at physical fighting and at using the forms of arguing, insult, teasing, naming, and sports-talk of the boys' sub-culture. She was the only Black child in her classroom, in a school with only 8% Black students; overall that token status, along with unusual athletic and verbal skills, may have contributed to her ability to move back and forth across the gender divide. Her unique position in the children's world was widely recognized in the school. Several times, the teacher said to me, "She thinks she's a boy."

I observed only one boy in the upper grades (a fourth grader) who regularly played with all-female groups, as opposed to "playing at" girls' games and seeking to disrupt them. He frequently played jumprope and took turns with girls doing tricks on the bars, using the small gestures—for example, a helpful push on the heel of a girl who needed momentum to turn her body around the bar—which mark skillful and earnest participation. Although I never saw him play in other than an earnest spirit, the girls often chased him away from their games, and both girls and boys teased him. The fact that girls seek, and have more access to boys' worlds than vice versa, and the fact that girls who travel with the other sex are less stigmatized for it, are obvious asymmetries, tied to the asymmetries previously discussed.

Relaxed Cross-Sex Interactions

Relationships between boys and girls are not always marked by strong boundaries, heterosexual definitions, or by interacting on the terms and turfs of the other sex. On some occasions girls and boys interact in relatively comfortable ways. Gender is not strongly salient nor explicitly invoked, and girls and boys are not organized into boundaries collectively. These "with" occasions have been neglected by those studying gender and children's relationships, who have emphasized either the model of separate worlds (with little attention to their articulation) or heterosexual forms of contact.

Occasions where boys and girls interact without strain, where gender wanes, rather than waxes in importance, frequently have one or more of the following characteristics:

1. The situations are organized around an absorbing task, such as a group art project or creating a radio show, which encourages cooperation and lessens attention to gender. This pattern accords with other studies finding that cooperative activities reduce group antagonism (e.g., Sherif & Sherif, 1953, who studied divisions between boys in a summer camp; and Aronson et al., 1978, who used cooperative activities to lessen racial divisions in a classroom).
2. Gender is less prominent when children are not responsible for the formation of the group. Mixed-sex play is less frequent in games like football, which require the choosing of teams, and more frequent in games like handball or dodgeball which individuals can join simply by getting into a line or a circle. When adults organize mixed-sex encounters— which they frequently do in the classroom and in physical education periods on the playground—they legitimize cross-sex contact. This removes the risk of being teased for choosing to be with the other sex.
3. There is more extensive and relaxed cross-sex interaction when principles of grouping other than gender are explicitly involved—for example, counting off to form teams for spelling or kickball, dividing lines by hot lunch or cold lunch, or organizing a work group on the basis of interests or reading ability.
4. Girls and boys may interact more readily in less public and crowded settings. Neighborhood play, depending on demography, is more often sex and age integrated than play at school, partly because with fewer numbers, one may have to resort to an array of social categories to find play partners or to constitute a game. And in less crowded environments there are fewer potential witnesses to "make something of it" if girls and boys play together.

Relaxed interactions between girls and boys often depend on adults to set up and legitimize the contact.[4] Perhaps because of this contingency—and the other, distancing patterns which permeate relations between girls and boys—the easeful moments of interaction rarely build to close friendship. Schofield (1981) makes a similar observation about gender and racial barriers to friendship in a junior high school.

Implications for Development

I have located social relations within an essentially spatial framework, emphasizing the organization of children's play, work and other activities within specific settings, and in one type of institution, the school. In contrast, frameworks of child development rely upon temporal metaphors, using images of growth and transformation over time. Taken alone, both spatial and temporal frameworks have shortcomings; fitted together, they may be mutually correcting.

Those interested in gender and development have relied upon conceptualizations of "sex role socialization" and "sex differences." Sexuality and gender, I have argued, are more situated and fluid than these individualist and intrinsic models imply. Sex and gender are differently organized and defined across situations, even within the same institution. This situational variation (e.g., in the extent to which an encounter heightens or lessens gender boundaries, or is infused with sexual meanings) shapes and constrains individual behavior. Features which a developmental perspective might attribute to individuals, and understand as relatively internal attributes unfolding over time, may, in fact, be highly dependent on context. For example, children's avoidance of cross-sex friendship may be attributed to individual gender development in middle-childhood. But attention to varied situations may show that this avoidance is contingent on group size, activity, adult behavior, collective meanings, and the risk of being teased.

A focus on social organization and situation draws attention to children's experiences in the present. This helps correct a model like "sex role socialization" which casts the present under the shadow of the future, or presumed "endpoints" (Speier, 1976). A situated analysis of arrangements of sex and gender among those of different ages may point to crucial disjunctions in the life course. In the fourth and fifth grades, culturally defined heterosexual rituals ("goin' with") begin to suppress the presence and visibility of other types of interaction between girls and boys, such as nonsexualized and comfortable interaction, and traveling in the world of the other sex. As "boyfriend/girlfriend" definitions spread, the fifth-grade tomboy I described had to work to sustain "buddy" relationships with boys. Adult women who were tomboys often speak of early adolescence as a painful time when they were pushed away from participation in boys' activities. Other adult women speak of the loss of intense, even erotic ties with other girls when they entered puberty and the rituals of dating, that is, when they became absorbed into the institution of heterosexuality (Rich, 1980). When Lever (1976) describes best-friend relationships among fifth-grade girls as preparation for dating, she imposes heterosexual ideologies onto a present which should be understood on its own terms.

As heterosexual encounters assume more importance, they may alter relations in same-sex groups. For example, Schofield (1981) reports that for sixth- and seventh-grade children in a middle school, the popularity of girls with other girls was affected by their popularity with boys, while boys' status with other boys did not depend on their relations with girls. This is an asymmetry familiar from the adult world; men's relationships with one another are defined through varied activities (occupations, sports), while relationships among women—and their public status—are more influenced by their connections to individual men.

A full understanding of gender and social relations should encompass cross-sex as well as within-sex interactions. "Borderwork" helps maintain separate, gender-linked subcultures, which, as those interested in development have begun to suggest, may result in different milieux for learning. Daniel Maltz and Ruth Borker (1983) for example, argue that because of different interactions within girls' and boys' groups, the sexes learn different rules for creating and interpreting friendly conversation, rules which carry into adulthood and help account for miscommunication between men and women. Carol Gilligan (1982) fits research on the different worlds of girls and boys into a theory of sex differences in moral development. Girls develop a style of reasoning, she argues, which is more personal and relational; boys develop a style which is more positional, based on separateness. Eleanor Maccoby (1982), also following the insight that because of sex segregation, girls and boys grow up in different environments, suggests implications for gender differentiated prosocial and antisocial behavior.

This separate worlds approach, as I have illustrated, also has limitations. The occasions when the sexes are together should also be studied, and understood as contexts for experience and learning. For example, asymmetries in cross-sex relationships convey a series of messages: that boys are more entitled to space and to the nonreciprocal right of interrupting or invading the activities of the other sex; that girls are more in need of adult protection, and are lower in status, more defined by sexuality, and may even be polluting. Different types of cross-sex interaction—relaxed, boundaried, sexualized, or taking place on the terms of the other sex—provide different contexts for development.

By mapping the array of relationships between and within the sexes, one adds complexity to the overly static and dichotomous imagery of separate worlds. Individual experiences vary, with implications for development. Some children prefer same-sex groupings; some are more likely to cross the gender boundary and participate in the world of the other sex; some children (e.g., girls and boys who frequently play "chase and kiss") invoke heterosexual meanings, while others avoid them.

Finally, after charting the terrain of relationships, one can trace their development over time. For example, age variation in the content and form of borderwork, or of cross and same-sex touch, may be related to differing cognitive, social, emotional, or physical capacities, as well as to age-associated cultural forms. I earlier mentioned temporal shifts in the organization of cross-sex chasing, for mixing with fantasy play in the early grades to more elaborately ritualized and sexualized forms by the sixth grade. There also appear to be temporal changes in same and cross-sex touch. In kindergarten, girls and boys touch one another more freely than in fourth grade, when children avoid relaxed cross-sex touch and instead use pokes, pushes, and other forms of mock violence, even when the touch clearly couches affection. This touch taboo is obviously related to the risk of seeming to *like* someone of the other sex. In fourth grade, same-sex touch begins to signal sexual meanings among boys, as well as between boys and girls. Younger boys touch one another freely in cuddling (arm around shoulder) as well as mock violence ways. By fourth grade, when homophobic taunts like "fag" become more common among boys, cuddling touch begins to disappear for boys, but less so for girls.

Overall, I am calling for more complexity in our conceptualization of gender and of children's social relationships. Our challenge is to retain the temporal sweep, looking at individual and group lives as they unfold over time, while also attending to social structure and context, and to the full variety of experiences in the present.

Acknowledgement

I would like to thank Jane Atkinson, Nancy Chodorow, Arlene Daniels, Peter Lyman, Zick Rubin, Malcolm Spector, Avril Thorne, and Margery Wolf for comments on an earlier version of this paper. Conversations with Zella Luria enriched this work.

NOTES

1. I am grateful to Frederick Erickson for suggesting the relevance of Barth's analysis.
2. Sue Samuelson (1980) reports that in a racially mixed playground in Fresno, California, Mexican-American, but not Anglo children gave cooties. Racial, as well as sexual inequality may be expressed through these forms.
3. This incident was recorded by Margaret Blume, who, for an undergraduate research project in 1982, observed in the California school where I earlier did fieldwork. Her observations and insights enhanced my own, and I would like to thank her for letting me cite this excerpt.
4. Note that in daily school life, depending on the individual and the situation, teachers and aides sometimes lessened, and at other times heightened sex segregation.

REFERENCES

Aronson, F., et al. (1978). *The jigsaw classroom.* Beverly Hills, CA: Sage.

Barth, F. (Ed.). (1969). *Ethnic groups and boundaries.* Boston: Little, Brown.

Borman, K. M. (1979). Children's interactions in playgrounds. *Theory into Practice, 18,* 251–257.

Eder, D., & Hallinan, M. T. (1978). Sex differences in children's friendships. *American Sociological Review, 43,* 237–250.

Finnan, C. R. (1982). The ethnography of children's spontaneous play. In G. Spindler (Ed.), *Doing the ethnography of schooling,* pp.358–80. New York: Holt, Rinehart & Winston.

Foot, H. C., Chapman, A. J., & Smith, J. R. (1980). Introduction. *Friendship and social relations in children* (pp. 1–14). New York: Wiley.

Gilligan, C. (1982). *In a different voice: Psychological theory and women's development.* Cambridge, MA: Harvard University Press.

Glaser, B. G., & Strauss, A. L. (1967). *The discovery of grounded theory.* Chicago: Aldine.

Goffman, E. (1977). The arrangement between the sexes. *Theory and Society, 4,* 301–336.

Goodwin, M. H. (1980). Directive-response sequences in girls' and boys' task activities. In S. McConnell-Ginet, R. Borker, & N. Furman (Eds.). *Women and language in literature and society* (pp. 157–173). New York: Praeger.

Henley, N. (1977). *Body politics: Power, sex, and nonverbal communication.* Englewood Cliffs, NJ: Prentice-Hall.

Karkau, K. (1973). *Sexism in the fourth grade.* Pittsburgh: KNOW, Inc. (pamphlet)

Katz, J. (1983). A theory of qualitative methodology: The social system of analytic fieldwork. In R. M. Emerson (Ed.), *Contemporary field research* (pp. 127–148). Boston: Little, Brown.

Knapp, M., & Knapp, H. (1976). *One potato, two potato: The secret education of American children.* New York: W. W. Norton.

Lever, J. (1976). Sex differences in the games children play. *Social Problems, 23,* 478–487.

Maccoby, E. (1982). *Social groupings in childhood: Their relationship to prosocial and antisocial behavior in boys and girls.* Paper presented at conference on The Development of Prosocial and Antisocial Behavior. Voss, Norway.

Maccoby, E., & Jacklin, C. (1974). *The psychology of sex differences.* CA: Stanford University Press.

Maltz, D. N., & Borker, R. A. (1983). A cultural approach to male-female miscommunication. In J. J. Gumperz (Ed.), *Language and social identity* (pp. 195–216). New York: Cambridge University Press.

McRobbie, A., & Garber, J. (1975). Girls and subcultures. In S. Hall and T. Jefferson (Eds.), *Resistance through rituals* (pp. 209–223). London: Hutchinson.

Ortner, S. B., & Whitehead, H. (1981). *Sexual meanings.* New York: Cambridge University Press.

Parrott, S. (1972). Games children play: Ethnography of a second-grade recess. In J. P. Spradley & D. W. McCurdy (Eds.), *The cultural experience* (pp. 206–219). Chicago: Science Research Associates.

Rich, A. (1980). Compulsory heterosexuality and lesbian existence. *Signs, 5,* 631–660.

Samuelson, S. (1980). The cooties complex. *Western Folklore, 39,* 198–210.

Savin-Williams, R. C. (1976). An ethological study of dominance formation and maintenance in a group of human adolescents. *Child Development, 47,* 972–979.

Schofield, J. W. (1981). Complementary and conflicting identities: Images and interaction in an interracial school. In S. R. Asher & J. M. Gottman (Eds.), *The development of children's friendships* (pp. 53–90). New York: Cambridge University Press.

Sherif, M., & Sherif, C. (1953). *Groups in harmony and tension.* New York: Harper.

Sluckin, A. (1981). *Growing Up in the Playground.* London: Routledge and Kegan Paul.

Speier, M. (1976). The adult ideological viewpoint in studies of childhood. In A. Skolnick (Ed.), *Rethinking Childhood* (pp. 168–186) Boston: Little, Brown.

Sutton-Smith, B. (1971). A syntax for play and games. In R. E. Herron and Brian Sutton-Smith (Eds.), *Child's Play* (pp. 298–307). New York: Wiley.

Waldrop, M. F., & Halverson, C. F. (1975). Intensive and extensive peer behavior: Longitudinal and cross-sectional analyses. *Child Development, 46,* 19–26.

Whitehead, H. The bow and the burden strap: A new look at institutionalized homosexuality in native America. In S.B. Ortner and H. Whitehead (Eds.), *Sexual Meanings* (pp. 80–115). New York: Cambridge University Press.

8

ALWAYS RUNNING

LUIS J. RODRÍGUEZ

One day, my mother asked Rano and me to go to the grocery store. We decided to go across the railroad tracks into South Gate. In those days, South Gate was an Anglo neighborhood, filled with families of workers from the auto plant and other nearby industry. Like Lynwood or Huntington Park, it was forbidden territory for the people of Watts.

My brother insisted we go. I don't know what possessed him, but then I never did. It was useless to argue; he'd force me anyway. He was nine then, I was six. So without ceremony, we started over the tracks, climbing over discarded market carts and tore-up sofas, across Alameda Street, into South Gate: all-white, all-American.

We entered the first small corner grocery store we found. Everything was cool at first. We bought some bread, milk, soup cans and candy. We each walked out with a bag filled with food. We barely got a few feet, though, when five teenagers on bikes approached. We tried not to pay attention and proceeded to our side of the tracks. But the youths pulled up in front of us. While two of them stood nearby on their bikes, three of them jumped off theirs and walked over to us.

"What do we got here?" one of the boys said. "Spics to order—maybe with some beans?"

He pushed me to the ground; the groceries splattered onto the asphalt. I felt melted gum and chips of broken beer bottle on my lips and cheek. Then somebody picked me up and held me while the others seized my brother, tossed his groceries out, and pounded on him. They punched him in the face, in the stomach, then his face again, cutting his lip, causing him to vomit.

I remember the shrill, maddening laughter of one of the kids on a bike, this laughing like a raven's wail, a harsh wind's shriek, a laugh that I would hear in countless beatings thereafter. I watched the others take turns on my brother, this terror of a brother, and he doubled over, had blood and spew on his shirt, and tears down his face. I wanted to do something, but they held me and I just looked on, as every strike against Rano opened me up inside.

They finally let my brother go and he slid to the ground, like a rotten banana squeezed out of its peeling. They threw us back over the tracks. In

---

the sunset I could see the Watts Towers, shimmers of 70,000 pieces of broken bottles, sea shells, ceramic and metal on spiraling points puncturing the heavens, which reflected back the rays of a falling sun. My brother and I then picked ourselves up, saw the teenagers take off, still laughing, still talking about those stupid greasers who dared to cross over to South Gate.

Up until then my brother had never shown any emotion to me other than disdain. He had never asked me anything, unless it was a demand, an expectation, an obligation to be his throwaway boy-doll. But for this once he looked at me, tears welled in his eyes, blood streamed from several cuts—lips and cheeks swollen.

"Swear—you got to swear—you'll never tell anybody how I cried," he said.

I suppose I did promise. It was his one last thing to hang onto, his rep as someone who could take a belt whipping, who could take a beating in the neighborhood and still go back risking more—it was this pathetic plea from the pavement I remember. I must have promised.

The Animal Tribe practically died with the death of one of its last presidents: John Fabela.

17-year-old John—whose girlfriend had just given birth to his infant daughter—succumbed to a shotgun blast in his living room as his younger brother watched from beneath a bed in an adjacent room. About 13 members of the Sons of Soul car club, made up of recent Mexican immigrants living in East L.A., were rounded up by the police.

By then Joaquín López was already in prison for a heroin beef. Many of the older Tribe members were also incarcerated or hard-core *tecatos*.* As the Tribe's influence diminished, Lomas initiated Tribe members into the various sets based on age groupings: the Pequeños, Chicos, the Dukes and the Locos. Lomas was reorganizing and recruiting. No longer could one claim Lomas just by being there. Chicharrón invited me to get in.

"They beat on you for about three minutes—that's all," Chicharrón urged. "You get a busted lip. So what? It's worth it."

So later I decided to go to a party in the Hills, fully aware I would join a Lomas set. Like most barrio parties, it started without any hassle. *Vatos* and *rucas* filled every corner in the small house; some ventured outside, smoking or drinking. The house belonged to Nina, this extremely pretty girl whom everyone respected. Nina's mother shuffled in the kitchen, making tacos from large pots of meat and beans simmering on low flames.

The dudes were polite; dignified. *Señora* this and *Señora* that. You couldn't imagine how much danger hung on their every breath.

As the night wore on, the feel of the place transformed. The air was rife with anticipation. Talk became increasingly louder. Faces peeled into hardness. The music played oldies we all knew by heart, and *gritos* punctuated key

---

* See Glossary, p. 100, for translation of words in Spanish.

verses. Fists smashed against the walls. Just as the food simmered to a boil, the room also bubbled and churned. Weed, pills, and hard liquor passed from hand to hand. Outside, behind the house, a row of dudes shot up heroin. In the glow of the back porch light, they whispered a sea of shorn sentences.

A crew of older, mean-eyed *vatos* arrived and the younger guys stacked behind them. Nina's mother showed concern. She pulled Nina into the kitchen; I could see her talking severely to her daughter.

I didn't know these dudes. They were *veteranos* and looked up to by the homeys. They had just come out of the joint—mostly Tracy, Chino or Youth Training School, known as YTS, a prison for youth offenders. Chicharrón pressed his face close to my ear and told me their names: Ragman, Peaches, Natividad, Topo . . . and the small, muscular one with a mustache down the sides of his mouth was called Puppet.

I then recalled some their reputations: Natividad, for example, had been shot five times and stabbed 40 times—and still lived! Peaches once used a machine gun against some dudes in a shoot-out. And Puppet had been convicted of murder at the age of 16.

"Who wants in?" Puppet later announced to a row of dark, teenaged male faces in front of him. Chicharrón whispered something in Puppet's ear. Puppet casually looked toward me. They designated me the first to get jumped.

Topo walked up to me. He was stout, dark and heavily tattooed. He placed his arm around me and then we marched toward the driveway. Chicharrón managed to yell: "Protect your head."

I assumed when I got to the driveway, a handful of dudes would encircle me, provide me a signal of sorts, and begin the initiation. Instead, without warning, Topo swung a calloused fist at my face. I went down fast. Then an onslaught of steel-tipped shoes and heels rained on my body. I thought I would be able to swing and at least hit one or two—but no way! Then I remembered Chicharrón's admonition. I pulled my arms over my head, covered it the best I could while the kicks seemed to stuff me beneath a parked car.

Finally the barrage stopped. But I didn't know exactly when. I felt hands pull me up. I looked back at everyone standing around the driveway. My right eye was almost closed. My lip felt like it stuck out a mile. My sides ached. But I had done well.

Hands came at me to congratulate. There were pats on the back. Chicharrón embraced me, causing me to wince. I was a Lomas *loco* now. Then a homegirl came up and gave me a big kiss on my inflamed lip; I wished I could have tasted it. Then other homegirls did the same. It didn't seem half-bad, this initiation. Later they invited me to pounce on the other dudes who were also jumped in, but I passed.

As the night wore on, Puppet, Ragman and Nat had the initiates pile into a pickup truck. I was already quite plastered but somehow still standing. Puppet drove the truck toward Sangra. Elation rasped our throats.

"Fuck Sangra," one of the new dudes chimed in, and other voices followed the sentiment.

We came across a cherried-out 1952 DeSoto, with pinstripes and a metal-flake exterior. Puppet pulled the truck up to the side of it. There were four dudes inside drinking and listening to cassette tapes. We didn't know if they were Sangra or what. We followed Ragman as he approached the dudes. One of them emerged from the passenger side. He looked like a nice-enough fellow.

"Hey, we don't want no trouble," he said.

I knew they weren't Sangra. They looked like hard-working recreational lowriders out for a spin. But Ragman wouldn't have it. He punched the dude down. A couple of other guys came out of the car, and they too tried to salvage the night, tried to appeal for calm.

"Listen, man, how about a beer," one of them offered.

Nat grabbed his neck from behind and pulled him to the ground, then beat on him. Ragman looked at the other guys who were clearly scared.

"Who don't like it?" he demanded. "Who don't like it . . . you?"

Ragman hit another guy. By then the dudes in the truck had climbed out and bashed in the car, breaking windows and crunching in metal with tire irons and two-by-fours which had been piled in the back of the truck. One dude tried to run off, but somebody chased him down with a wine bottle and struck him on the head. The dude fell down and I saw the wine bottle keep coming down on him, as if it was supposed to break, but it wouldn't.

The driver of the DeSoto tried to pull out, but somebody threw a brick at his head. For a long time, I observed the beatings as if I were outside of everything, as if a moth of tainted wings floating over the steamed sidewalk. The I felt a hand pull at my arm and I sluggishly turned toward it. Puppet looked squarely into my one opened eye. He had a rusty screwdriver in his other hand.

"Do it, man," he said. Simply that.

I clasped the screwdriver and walked up to the beaten driver in the seat whose head was bleeding. The dude looked at me through glazed eyes, horrified at my presence, at what I held in my hand, at this twisted, swollen face that came at him through the dark. *Do it!* were the last words I recalled before I plunged the screwdriver into flesh and bone, and the sky screamed.

Within a year, the local headlines' business boomed:

"Gang Violence: Teen Wars Bring Death To Two"

"Valley Teen Gangs Flourish"

"Three Wounded By School Intruders"

"Youth, 17, Murdered: Victim Shot In Chest"

"Five Hurt, Two Arrested In Rosemead Party Crash"

"Three Still Held In Gang Deaths"

"San Gabriel Teenager Shot In The Face"

"Rosemead Youth Gunned Down: Murder Said Gang Related"

"Shooting Victim Critical"

"Fired From Car: Four Wounded By Gunshots"

"Rosemead Boy, 17, Shot By Deputy, Dies"

"Deputy Escapes Sniper"

"Slaying Suspect Bound Over To Superior Court"

"Sheriff Moving On Gangs"

Committees, task forces, community centers, born-again storefront churches and behavior guidance counselors proliferated in response. Rosemead's South Side, South San Gabriel and San Gabriel's barrio became targets of programs, monies and studies. Local reporters drove along with law enforcement officers through Lomas and Sangra to get "the feel" of these misaligned and misunderstood communities. Gang members were interviewed and news photographers worked the Hills to depict the poverty—usually of children playing in mud next to rusted cars, trash cans and pregnant mothers peering out of makeshift sheds.

La Casa Community Center served the needs of Sangra; Bienvenidos Community Center and its John Fabela Youth Center covered Lomas; and the Zapopan Center catered to the southside of Rosemead. The centers offered dropout programs, welfare assistance, federal job placements, teen mother day care and places for young people to hang out.

The people who worked at the centers put in 80-hour weeks, covered weekly funerals and had to enter the doors of domestic conflicts armed with nothing but a prayer. Some were ex-gang members who ventured back to help. Or they were the first wave of minority college students who entered institutions of higher learning through special scholarships and economic opportunity grants.

At La Casa and Zapopan, community activists made the payroll. The triumvirate of community centers began to play a leading role in the struggles which emerged out of the Mexican sections here. Besides the gang killings, there was widespread drug use. Police beatings and killings became prominent. And the battles in the schools for decent education intensified. Because the three centers were dealing with similar crises, their staffs often met together to consult on strategy.

By 1970 I felt disjointed, out of balance, tired of just acting and reacting. I wanted to flirt with depth of mind, to learn more about my world. My society. About what to do. I became drawn to the people who came to work at the community centers; they were learned. Full of ideas and concepts; they were, I realized, similar to my father, this former teacher and biologist, who once labeled all the trees and plants in the backyard so we would know their scientific names.

Amid South San Gabriel's hottest summer, the Bienvenidos Community Center hired Chente Ramírez. His credentials included a lifetime in the White Fence barrio in East L.A.—known as the oldest "street gang" in the country. But Chente managed to avoid gang involvement, went to school, worked in industry, helped his father with his trucking business and pretty much took care of his mom, six sisters and a brother while his dad traversed the land in a tractor-trailer rig.

Chente, in his late 20s then, had already gone to a university, been a founding member of the United Mexican American Students (UMAS), helped organize the East L.A. school walkouts of 1968, participated in forming MEChA (Movimiento Estudiantil Chicano de Aztlán) and the Brown Berets. Later still he put together a number of East Los Angeles study groups engaged in revolutionary theory. He was also a martial arts expert.

I had certain yearnings at the time, which a lot of us had, to acquire authority in our own lives in the face of police, joblessness and powerlessness. Las Lomas was our path to that, but I was frustrated because I felt the violence was eating us alive.

Chente impressed me as someone I could learn from. He was calm, but also street enough to go among all those crazy guys and know how to handle himself. He didn't need to act bad to operate. He could be strong, intelligent, and in control. He was the kind of dude who could get the best from the system—education, karate training—without being a snitch or giving in. I wanted to be able to do this too.

I was in my mid-teens and Chente was about twelve years older. I looked up to him, but not as a big brother. He was someone who could influence me without judging me morally or telling me what to do. He was just there. He listened, and when he knew you were wrong, before he would say anything, he would get you to think.

GLOSSARY

Cholo(s)/chola(s); cholillos: A low life. Appropriated by Chicano barrio youth to describe the style and people linked to local gang structures.

Gritos: Referring to the long, deep Mexican soul yells.

Las Lomas: The Hills; a barrio east of Los Angeles on county territory.

Loco(s)/loca(s): The crazies. Another term for barrio youth.

Ruca(s): Barrio woman, literally means "old lady."

Sangra: The barrio surrounding the San Gabriel Mission church.

Señor(a): Mister, missis.

Tecato: Heroin addict.

Vatos: Dudes or guys.

Veteranos: Veterans of barrio street warfare. The African American gang equivalent is "Original Gangster." Among Mexicans, some of these veterans go back two or more generations.

9

MRS. BRENT

GAYLE PEMBERTON

My sister Carolyn and I found Papa's flashlight. In the broad, full sun of a late summer Los Angeles morning in 1956 we trained its beam on the side of the white stucco duplex on Fourth Avenue. Then we marched several times around this home, owned by our grandparents—with its red tile roof and carefully manicured lawn—pointing the beam everywhere and anywhere. There was no flash in the light until we moved to the very end of the backyard, where a screened-in playhouse stood. It was a large, lovely space, shaded by a quartet of evergreen trees and shrubs that identified property borderlines. It was cool and dark, with a high ceiling. Carolyn and I had never really learned to make good use of the playhouse, though. It demanded a kind of play that I assign to the nineteenth century—or to my idea of large, well-to-do English families: an open, unadorned space where the imagination created everything that was necessary for fun. Peter Pan could have appeared to the Lord children in this space; Alice's looking glass might well have been in its corner. Nana, Papa and Mother encouraged us to spend our days there, but we had no toys or playthings during our summers in California. More to the point, play for my sister and me always was grounded in some kind of reality, and the emptiness of the playhouse was simply too much for us.

On this day, we had been cast out of the house seconds after my mother had received a telephone call from my father in Chicago. We knew something was wrong. Long-distance calls were too expensive to make even at night, but we *never* made them during daylight hours. This call had to be weighty and the odds were heavily on the side of awful news. We were dispatched so quickly that I have no recollection of even seeing my mother after she put the receiver down. And there was no call for lunch that day, although meals were a formal part of our lives and we always ate three of them, on schedule.

The flashlight provided no information for our Holmes and Watson probe. The playhouse seemed extra cavernous that day, arrogantly rebuking our labored attempts at play. We were worried and afraid. And we knew we were being protected from something we did not want to be protected from—whatever it was. Carolyn, older than I—and too old for the playhouse—tried

From *Names We Call Home*, B. Thompson & S. Tyagi (eds.), Routledge, 1995. Reprinted by permission of the publisher, Routledge: New York and London.

her best to keep us both calm despite the pall, despite the eerie brightness of the house and of the day as we looked out from the dark, behind the playhouse screens.

Our agitated boredom and concern were finally allayed hours into the afternoon, when Nana came out to tell us that Mrs. Brent, my mother's best friend, had been killed in an automobile accident. For hours my mother had been inconsolable, and following conventional wisdom, my grandparents deemed it a sight children should not see. They could only shelter us from the knowledge for a short time, however. Any longer would have encouraged our own barely suppressed panic.

We learned some details: Mrs. Brent had been thrown from the car; her daughter and husband had been injured, but not gravely. Carolyn and I looked at each other with a mixture of embarrassment and distress. Our search for clues with a flashlight now appeared thoroughly without style, intelligence or sensitivity. We knew how much our mother had treasured her friend. Carolyn knew Mrs. Brent's daughter, Sylvia, but not well. We could not imagine losing our mother; what must Sylvia have felt? And much as we had been screened all day from this awful news, we wished we could have protected our mother from it, just as Sylvia, broken and motherless in some Chicago hospital, would have given everything, I'm sure, to save her mother.

I was seven. Mrs. Brent was the first person I knew who had died. And I witnessed her last meeting with my mother. Carolyn, Mother and I were set to leave the next day for the biennial California summer. Hair-washing routines in black families can be arduous. Having just done mine—which meant washing and pressing and braiding it—my mother went about doing her own, which took much less time as hers is almost completely straight. She had just finished washing it in the bathroom upstairs, when Mrs. Brent appeared at the front door. It was a warm June morning, and the breeze through the screen was promising and comforting. Mrs. Brent stepped in the door and mother, wrapping a towel around her head, smiled and apologized for her state. I was standing there, too, as I chose never to be very far away from my mother. Mrs. Brent said she was only stopping by to say good-bye. She looked up at us and insisted that Mother go about her business. Mrs. Brent was a pretty, fair-skinned woman with black curly hair, whom I adored because she was easy to be around, and other adults weren't. She was pretty, as my mother was, and the two of them together seemed right to me. She said she would call later, and as quickly as she had appeared on the threshold, she was off and away.

For months after the sad day we learned of her death, I was haunted by the image of Mrs. Brent standing there. Why that image of looking down the stairs at her gaze up to us planted itself on my memory in the first place confounded me. But, perhaps by seven, I already knew melodrama, and all the scene lacked as it occurred was a soundtrack with appropriate foreboding music, to indicate that something significant, or tragic, was going to happen.

Now, so many years later, the import of what came to be my last sight of Mrs. Brent is charged with emotions tied to my racial, sexual and class identities.

How and when the specter of race penetrates the consciousness of a black American cannot be gauged, of course. Frequently, in literature, our heroes—at five or six—discover their blackness in one daunting moment at school, or in a crowd, or from an evil adult. The children, spurned, are never the same after these revelations. Their ingenuous children's songs are replaced by those of experience and sad wisdom—their black selves invariably assaulted by the implicit or explicit repugnance that has accompanied the news. Famous fictional and autobiographical moments like this abound—in James Weldon Johnson's *The Autobiography of an Ex-coloured Man*; in Zora Neale Hurston's *Their Eyes Were Watching God*; in the first chapter of W. E. B. Du Bois's *The Souls of Black Folk*; in Langston Hughes's short story, "One Christmas Eve"—and in many, many others. However, chances are these memories and fictional creations are only partially correct, and that for most black people, the elements that lead to a discovery of one's racial self are rarely bound into one portentous moment or crystallized into one dramatic scene. It is the repetition of the elements—so often all negative—that gives the illusion of one, titanic moment. And while I can recall any number of attacks on my blackness in childhood, my understanding of what being black meant, and of what my status in life would probably be, was as much a result of unpleasant incidents as it consisted of more tender ones, like my memory of Mrs. Brent the few times I saw her.

My most basic—and problematic—understanding of my racial being involved color. Long before there were genetic counselors, there was folklore. A considerable amount of it had (and still has) to do with the outward manifestation of one's black blood, be it a smidgen or a full dose. Perhaps some black people have residual memories from cradle days, when sage adult relatives, family friends, or hospital nurses, bent down to their baby faces and looked carefully at the backs of their ears in order to pronounce, with stentorian assurance, what color they would grow up to be. This was a *eureka* moment, savored by no one save the folk detective. As the back of the ear is almost never lighter than the rest of the body, when it is darker than the newborn's face—given our culture's worship of the fair—the news is bad. Hair texture, eye color, size of lips and nose all come under great scrutiny. My mother still wonders where the point on my baby nose went. I say, "It filled out."

In our unfinished passage from slavery to freedom we American blacks have managed, collectively, to resist many things. That resistance caused us to develop music of supreme beauty, irony, anger, humor and reverence. Our laughter cascades over a spectrum that begins with the deadly serious and ends there, but that includes the zany and ribald along the way. Our speech is endlessly inventive, understated, mocking. But inwardly, the resistance always has been harder. The weight of white supremacy has taken its toll, and legions of black Americans have learned to hate themselves with a zeal reserved, we thought, only for those who hated us.

The range of color in my family went from the very fair, "passable" to very, very dark. My mother's father was the lightest of the ten children in his family, as fair as all but the whitest white people. His older brother, Frank, was very dark, and I remember seeing him a few times during other California visits. He would take my hands and play with the skin over my knuckles. I often wondered what it all meant, but I was sure there was some color logic involved. I was more fascinated with the fact that in the heat of California he would wear a black suit, and long, white underwear, the legs of which would show when he sat down. It was all very confusing since the only long underwear I had ever seen was on cartoon clotheslines. Uncle Frank was a kind old man, though, a World War I veteran, who had survived syphilis to live well into his eighties. He had never married—probably because of the syphilis. And like half of his married brothers and sisters who remained childless, probably because of what blackness in the United States meant to them, he had no children.

Uncle Frank was a living presence to me for a brief time, but it was in photographs that the power of color politics exerted itself. It was quite clear that lighter skin was in predominance in the pictures. But, as I also noticed, color was gendered. In a 1938 photograph, taken at a formal Christmas dance of my father's social club, a line of fifty men stand behind their seated ladies, fewer than five of whom are brown-skinned, although a good three-quarters of the men are of darker skin. In other kinds of group photographs—of people at picnics and parties, high school clubs and college Greek societies—the message was that *successful* women, those with some kind of power, or with men on their arms, or who were queens of this or that, were always fair. When she was about eighteen, after hearing him go on about the qualities he and his friends sought in a woman, my sister reduced my father to an abashed silence by saying, "I guess I wouldn't have had much of a chance with your group." The number one quality was fair skin— which neither Carolyn nor I had.

I remembered relatives saying that it didn't really matter what a man looked like—white or black—to get ahead. They would commiserate with each other over their brown girl children, sighing when they didn't "get the color" or at least "the hair." In the world of middle-class, northern Negroes to which I was born, the message was loud and clear. For me, the photographs—these chronicles of fifty years of family life—constituted a photographic montage with the soundtrack of reprised adult conversations, all forecasting my place as a brown black woman. I might aspire to be great— and there were certainly great brown black women held up to me as epitomes of possibility, steely-eyed founders of institutions and teachers of enormous power and depth, artists of great range and skill—but I would never be a woman in the way the light-skinned ones were.

It took many years for me to learn to luxuriate in my circumstances, to recognize that I did not want to be seen, as light-skinned women so frequently were, as objects of class, family and male competitiveness. But at seven, I loved Mrs. Brent precisely because she was what I could not be. And if I thought her easy to be around, it was as much attributable to her kindness as it was to my appreciation of light-skinned being. Quite simply, she was my first crush.

———————

How and whether black people can protect each other and themselves from the physical, psychological and emotional effects of racism are matters of politics, opinion and custom. By this I mean that in its largest sense, we have not been able to do it with much success at all. Black men and women have suffered and died trying to protect each other and their children from assaults by whites. Black children, too, have wondered how they might protect their parents from the tedium of underpaid and thankless work or from the insult of no work. The inequities of race continue. Not long ago, I wanted to protect a black maid from the practiced, supervisory gaze of her white six-year-old charge who rode in the grocery basket she was pushing in a Memphis supermarket. I wished I were in a time warp, but I was not; it was 1993. And small as our futile search for clues to life and death with a flashlight was in the great continuum, my grandparents wanted to protect Carolyn and me from my mother's agony, and her from our inquisitiveness when Mrs. Brent died.

It is difficult enough for adults to try to protect a child from all sorts of dangerous and paltry things, not to mention the rude realities of racism. Poverty, ignorance, habit and hunger—and all that they spawn—make such protection impossible for a large proportion of black people. For the rest, the difficulties reside in technique and strategy. Time, circumstance and the everlasting racism are the opponents. There are those parents who never have tried, who have been philosophically against postponing the lessons. Symbolically they throw their children into the pool of racism, and yell "sink or swim." They reason that it is better to do the tossing themselves, than leave it up to fate and strangers in a place—like at school or in a store—before their children have developed reflexes and resources for survival.

These parents are matched by their philosophical opposites, who try to rise above the racial vilification the world directs at their children. They put as good a face as they can on the meanness of the world and rightfully and righteously tell their children that racism is primarily a white problem. I suspect a few more black nationalists are created by the first technique, and optimists by the second, but in the grand scheme of things, the point is moot.

What I knew because my parents loved me very much was what many children know: all the love in the world cannot protect us against sadness or evil. My parents could not keep from me the reality of racism. What I also learned was that all the love in the world could not protect a black person from the inanities of chauvinism and bias within the group. And the zero sum game I played with myself for years meant that the quality of affection I had for someone like Mrs. Brent, would necessarily diminish the love I had for myself. I did not know how to like the fair-skinned others and affirm myself, too.

I became a dreamer, a blood sister of Walter Mitty, a watcher, a large, large-breasted adolescent girl whose fantasies were solo voyages both to far-away places and to the abyss of her own heart. Academic achievement became the ideal displacement. Smart, I could aspire to the genderless category the world creates for bright white women and powerful brown black ones. Smart, I could be funny and make people laugh. Smart, I also could be a "drum majorette for justice," for myself and others, beating the odds and the racial stereotypes through academic glory.

The nineteen-sixties were an appropriate time for all of this, too. From the vantage points of my *de facto* segregated junior and senior high schools, the future to me actually seemed to hold promise—a far more palpable and buoyant promise than that implied in the canned optimism of "diamonds in the rough" graduation speeches. The election of John F. Kennedy to the White House was part of it. He looked different, he certainly sounded different—there was none of Ike's standard midwestern in that seemingly Kennedy-exclusive Massachusetts accent. We were going toward the future with a young man leading us.

In 1960, the roughest days of the Civil Rights Movement were still ahead. But, in Birmingham, Little Rock, New Orleans, Prince Edward County, Virginia and a host of other places the foaming-at-the-mouth resistance of whites to desegregation exposed their counterfeit southern gentility for the whole world to see. What assurance we had when we sang the "God is on our side" line from *We Shall Overcome,* even though it hurt to be so constantly reminded that we were despised! What a time to be growing up.

There's something about adolescence that even shots heard round the world can't shake. Yell "Fire!" and a significant proportion of teenagers will make sure their hair is right before heading for the egress. None of my unsubstantiated optimism about the future could possibly alter my creed of self-loathing. I was frumpy. I hated my body. The clothes my family could afford did nothing for it, and my taste did less. I carried large black purses; I hid behind glasses. And after major surgery to reconstruct my left knee after a fall down steel and concrete stairs at school, I half-believed, half-wished that I might walk with a limp for the rest of my life. With such an attitude, I could finally have used the Los Angeles playhouse; I was a gold mine of bathetic scenarios. In this way, I must have been like at least fifty percent of all adolescents, and eighty percent of all adolescents who become academics.

In 1962 Nana and Papa came to live with us in Kansas City. My father, who had grown up without his father, showed no hesitation in welcoming them into our home—he liked my grandparents and they liked him. It would mean a little more food and mortgage money, and he believed in the sanctity of the family. The idea of placing ambulatory and sound parents in a nursing home was obscene to him, plain and simple.

I had seen little of Nana and Papa since my little girl California summers, and I looked forward to being with them, too. But I could not know that by being complete my family would become generationally divided. My parents were closer in age to Nana and Papa than they were to their own, somewhat late children. The dominant relationships in the house became those of people born in the 1880s and in the first decade of the 1900s. There was little these four adults—middle class blacks with Victorian sensibilities—could say to guide their nuclear age progeny through the turbulent sixties, other than to reiterate their own Victorian sensibilities. Sex meant disease or pregnancy (they held equal weight). Acceptable pleasure was food.

My parents, especially my father, encouraged my scholarly bent—as he had my sister's. By 1962 she was in college. For many years I thought he encouraged us because he wanted to make sure we would become financially independent through reliable careers—like teaching. His mother had been treated badly by her husband, and she divorced him, striking out into the world with two children, little education and only one marketable skill: to clean. I'll give her this: she made the most of it, becoming a high priestess of clean. Daddy did not want his daughters to meet with a similar fate. But now, I know it went further than that—to the marrow of race and gender. If all the desirable women were fair—or if brown, necessarily very cute—then our independence was important not as an immunity from worthless or dependent men: it was the key to our survival as women alone. My father never once asked me if I was lonely, if I felt bad about being at home every Friday and Saturday night, or, during my years in college, if I had ever gone out on a date. What's more, I would have been shocked if he had asked, so convinced was I of the legitimacy of his aesthetic of life and love. My mother once allowed that perhaps I was too forthright in my opinions to be thought desirable by men. I was about seventeen then, and convinced that if one had to play dumb to be a woman, I would rather be the genderless thing I was. Maybe she had played dumb, but she was fair, so what difference did it make?

My tenuous self-regard was enhanced when I spent a year as an exchange student in the United Kingdom. The relationship between race and gender did not disappear; it merely became defined differently. I could see—as writers and critics had seen for years—that England's social fabric depended upon various charades, paramount being the predominance and preponderance of single-sex schools. Coeducation was only very slowly coming about, and then in what they called "secondary modern" schools for those not destined for a university education. The grammar and boarding schools remained for either boys or girls exclusively.

I was a curiosity: an American, a black at the day grammar school I attended. The school had only recently admitted the daughter of a Pakistani family to what we would call the third grade. This concession was deemed worthwhile and brave by the community, despite the fact that the population of Pakistanis was growing at an enormous clip in Bradford. Mocked by

T. S. Eliot in *The Waste Land,* the "Bradford millionaires" were changing their hue. It only made sense that their children would attend the best schools.

We wore uniforms to school for half the year. It made such great sense not to worry over clothes every day. More important for the British—and another charade category—uniforms leveled the playing field a bit. The scholarship girls, who befriended me and who naturally were my friends, could not be distinguished immediately from their more affluent school-mates. And unless one hung around the senior prefect's room, or watched the wealthier girls being picked up in Jaguars and Bentleys at the end of the day, there was no telling who was what. Some of the well-to-do even rode busses.

In England, the great lesson I learned was that while I wrestled with my female identity via its racial implications, I watched my white British girl-friends sort theirs out in terms of class. My blackness was classed, of course; the black bourgeois world that created my parents prided itself on being the opposite of the putatively sexually licentious black lower classes. What else is any middle class for? But the colonized are not colonizers, and class was as palpable a reality in England as color was among black people. On the other hand, rocket science is not required to explain the non-existent differ-ence between an upper class black and a lower class one in the minds of racist white Americans.

I watched my schoolmates act out scenarios as old as their fading empire. The rich ones, who smoked and who sought to have about them a smart and knowing air—like Diana Rigg as Mrs. Peel on the British televi-sion hit of that season, *The Avengers*—were relaxed about sex. They could afford to be. If their A-level examinations failed to guarantee them a spot in some university, they had alternatives. I envision them now, permanent denizens of some Merchant and Ivory film, traipsing regularly out to the guest cottage of a country home to have trysts with earnest and ardent, but clumsy public school lovers.

The middle class and scholarship girls ran the gamut from the cloistered, to the fast, to those whose boyfriends of several years, it was understood, would become their husbands in a few years more. Some of these girls were religious non-conformists as they were still called—non-Church of England Protestants. And while many of them were con-sidered "outsiders," these more actively Christian girls were quite com-fortable with their identities. As far as I could see, their transgressions never threatened their class identities, as when a good friend of mine left school and was next seen as a waitress in Keswick, in the Lake District. She had shattered her chances to go to a university. The reason seemed clear to me and others, and her actions were consistent with her class and gender according to the adult custodians of the status quo: she feared she might not do well on her examinations. There might well have been panic among the mostly sympathetic had she run off with a hod-carrier or a lord.

I left England reluctantly; I had become comfortable in my genderless, foreigner role. The prospect of going home merely intensified my sense of being an outsider in the land where I was born—more of a witness than a participant in life.

World and campus politics of the late nineteen-sixties were enough to unravel even the most poised and self-confident young people. At the precise moment when white colleges and universities began to open their doors to significant numbers of young black men and women, the Black Power Movement appeared with its impromptu nationalistic idioms, railing against the liberal integrationist sensibility supporting the black students' admission. On campuses with more than ten black students, this group would create prescriptions about what constituted appropriate black identity. I understood it. Students now took the opportunity to vent publicly the rage, frustration and anger that had been suppressed for so many years. But I could only partially enter into the deal, as the Civil Rights and Black Power Movements had quite openly cosigned women to roles of helpmates at best, sexual vessels at worst. Within the context of black power campus politics, there was little room for me to mature beyond my very real alienation or my sophomoric certainty that the alienation would last forever.

I was still smart, though, and funny. Late at night I would make popcorn with my friend Karen, who was of Italian and Irish extraction. I transferred after two years, but I will always remember her with fondness because she believed we both suffered from the same malady. "Ace," she would say—the only nickname I've ever had that I liked—"Men look at our faces and they see that we're serious." Somehow that made the moment fine, because we wanted to be serious as much as—or even more than—we wanted men. She was attractive, but she was also smart, funny and tough. The last I heard she had married a much older man.

I walked a campus tightrope, spending most of my time with white female friends, going to black campus meetings and helping plan programs. But I cloistered myself from the sexual identity politics of black power—and that may have been the first self-affirming thing I'd done in years. Living in England had taught me enough to know that racial reasoning alone was inadequate to the task of explaining oppression. It was an early lesson in the limits of identity politics. I was content not to be fair, or cute, if brown. I may have been a pariah to those who looked upon my association with white students as the cardinal sin. But I preferred my apostasy over their deprecation and shunning of my female being. Of the two kisses I received in all my college years, the one from a woman was the best, but I was sure—as she was—that we did it only because we were castoffs who coincidentally had a particular urge at the same time.

Boston, according to the attitudes of millions of white and black people, is supposed to be a lousy town for black people. Perhaps it is because Boston is so self-consciously white—in its Irish, Italian and WASP forms. The Irish are routinely singled out for their racism. But, Boston is more than Irish. Boston's religious character, the diverse Roman Catholics, and the dominant Congregational and Unitarian Protestants also reinforce white ethnic identities. Driving to the North End to buy some of the truly splendid ricotta and mozzarella cheeses one can find there my friend Kathy—blue-eyed and fair—said she was made to feel decidedly out of place as she entered the Italian cheese store.

I moved to the Boston area in 1969, and discovered that I liked it. I always ask people "compared to what?" when they speak of its racial climate. Could one seriously say that Chicago, or Detroit, or New York, or Washington, or Los Angeles, or Houston, or the oft-cited Atlanta, are really better places to be black? Perhaps they are because there are more blacks in those cities. But, having lived in several of them, I don't think so. El Dorado for black people hasn't yet been found. However, most people inside and out of Boston believe the press about it and conform. I never made a habit of going to Fenway Park, at that. But Boston was a fine place for me. I was in graduate school at Harvard. I could see what centuries of white, patrician success had wrought. Some people—professors included—made it a point to suggest that the university had gone to exceptional lengths to bring me and other blacks there. I allowed as how that was very good; we were worth it. Those blacks who say affirmative action makes them feel inferior because they can never, ever *really* know if they're good enough have always appeared to me to be foolish. They should relax and look around them to see that pure merit is a very difficult category to define. Does a high grade on a law school entrance examination ensure a brilliant student and great future lawyer? No. Are these white peers so unremittingly, without exception, fabulous? No. One's worth is intangible and incalculable on a scale of caprice.

In graduate school, I realized that some of my professors and classmates would never accept me on equal terms, and that others would. There are many more interesting exercises in life than trying to change the attitudes of people hardened not against one's self—they can't *see* that—but against one's color. And graduate study had enough pre-existing hoops for me to jump through already without my creating more.

I navigated through Harvard's waters by staying well away from my fellow graduate students in English and the black graduate contingent on campus. My independence, no matter what had brought it about, was complete. My only group association was with students and co-resident advisors at Radcliffe's North House, where I spent the lion's share of my residential graduate years. I've been told by a male friend that people looked upon my role as house mother at the small dormitory at 60 Walker Street as that of mammy. The free three squares a day in the House cafeterias had stimulated my tendency toward fat—and mammies are supposed to be fat—but his observation merely reaffirmed why I was independent. From the outside people would never understand the affirming, non-stereotypical relationships a group of women can develop among themselves. My charges were all of two or three years younger than I, so in honor of that wide chasm in age, they called me "Mother." And because my life at Radcliffe provided the longest and most cohesive residential life I'd had since puberty, I looked upon it more as an undergraduate life than as a graduate one. I feel no attachment to my two true undergraduate institutions; I will forever be devoted to Radcliffe.

Moreover, my journey through graduate school at Radcliffe resembled an undergraduate's journey. I revelled in the lives of my housemates: a group of nine women perceived to be bluestockings because they insisted on a single-sex dorm when the Harvard and Radcliffe houses were becoming coeducational. And they supported me in my life. We all were thought to be apolitical in a time when one was as likely to see the North Vietnamese flag hanging out of a dormitory window as the Stars and Stripes. We spent large chunks of time in the house kitchen, making and eating sweets. There was a regular presence of various males—half of them enamored, futilely, with one house resident or another, the other half hanging on tenaciously and barely to sleep-over status. Their visibility kept another label, that of lesbian, away from the house, although the two of us living there had no idea we were.

"Ace, men look at our faces and they see that we're serious." The black men in my life were homosexuals who liked me because I was serious, and funny. Maurice was one of my oldest friends. We said hello in our seventh grade classroom and I said goodbye to him two weeks before he died of AIDS, at the age of forty-five. He was as important to me as anyone in my life. We loved each other very much; we laughed hard, fought often but not seriously, and found comfort in silence together. I did not ask him more than he would tell me about his private life. He followed in like fashion, all the while accepting as a given the reality of my sexual existence and passion, when I did not know how to express it. And, perhaps because he was gay, he understood very, very well that gender and sexuality are inextricable components of racial identity. Our last fight, which was serious, and fraught with unnamed and unexamined ire, was in part due to his indignation and fear that I had given up on life. Maurice was wrong about me and life, but the fight did nothing to alter him in my memory: he was, quite simply, grand.

Remembering a year abroad, graduate school life, and Maurice establishes the link between my childhood sense—inchoate, but still sound—that my racial identity was inextricably tied to my being a girl—and my young adult acceptance of myself as foremost an independent traveler on the slippery slopes of racial, gender and sexual politics. Long since past the idea of playing dumb, I realized I wasn't particularly interested in men. From the outside it seemed that all heterosexual relations were ultimately predicated upon the management of his ego. There were exceptions, of course, but they were just exceptions to me. It was easy, then, to settle into a private life that revolved around family, and a few close friends.

As a black, female English professor—a rare bird in the academic land-scape—I was what I had always been: the fulfillment or lack thereof of white expectations of what a black person is. I was simultaneously a stereotype and an original at any given moment. As a woman in the academy, I was like my interest in black writing or my white female colleagues, undervalued and rarely rewarded. And as a romantic without an object, I was in good company.

———

Nothing remains of the house my grandparents owned in Los Angeles except photographs. It was in the path of the Santa Monica Freeway. I am sure that if I could see the playhouse now, I would marvel at its small size—just as the vast football field behind our home in the Chicago pro-jects somehow turned into a standard-sized alley when I visited it as an adult. I don't know what happened to Mrs. Brent's daughter or husband, or if this memory of her would resurrect in them feelings of happiness or dismay. I do know that the fitful attempt that Carolyn and I made to find the secret of our mother's sadness, with a flashlight, on white stucco, on a bright, smogless Los Angeles day in 1956, stayed with me for almost forty years. Seeking knowledge in broad daylight, with a hand-carried light (Papa called it a *torch*) is an appropriate metaphor for my attempt—and I believe that of my sister, too—to find out what being black is supposed to mean.

We went to the playhouse and tried to improvise something, in spite of the fact that we had not satisfactorily done it before. Excluded from the main drama in the house, we tried to figure out how to star in our own, to choose ways of pleasing ourselves, if we couldn't please anyone else. In the tacit belief of our family that women should be light-skinned, being brown meant that we had already lost some race that we didn't even know was being run. Improvising the self, then, became both a necessity and a choice. Going through life holding a light up to all the surfaces revealed not only the flaws and pretenses, but the hidden beauty, too. Living in a society where surfaces stand for all, I quickly learned that I would be judged by mine. It made the urge to reach the heart of things urgent, and I learned to distrust all narrowly prescribed ways of being either black, or a woman, or both. Life literally became a quest, not for the Grail—how boring to find it—but for more days to improvise a self.

My memory of Mrs. Brent is significant to me because I understand that not being able to look like her, I was released to make myself. Throughout the years since her death, I rarely look anyone in the eye who is leaving for more than a short, local trip. I absolutely refuse to wave or look down from a set of stairs at anyone who is walking out of the door. For almost forty years, I have averted my eyes at partings at airports, train stations and curbs. For almost forty years I thought that was my only legacy from Mrs. Brent.

10

HE DEFIES YOU STILL
The Memoirs of a Sissy

TOMMI AVICOLLI

You're just a faggot
No history faces you this morning
A faggot's dreams are scarlet
Bad blood bled from words that scarred[1]

Scene One

A homeroom in a Catholic high school in South Philadelphia. The boy sits quietly in the first aisle, third desk, reading a book. He does not look up, not even for a moment. He is hoping no one will remember he is sitting there. He wishes he were invisible. The teacher is not yet in the classroom so the other boys are talking and laughing loudly.

Suddenly, a voice from beside him:

"Hey, you're a faggot, ain't you?"

The boy does not answer. He goes on reading his book, or rather pretending he is reading his book. It is impossible to actually read the book now.

"Hey, I'm talking to you!"

The boy still does not look up. He is so scared his heart is thumping madly; it feels like it is leaping out of his chest and into his throat. But he can't look up.

"Faggot, I'm talking to you!"

To look up is to meet the eyes of the tormentor.

Suddenly, a sharpened pencil point is thrust into the boy's arm. He jolts, shaking off the pencil, aware that there is blood seeping from the wound.

"What did you do that for?" he asks timidly.

"Cause I hate faggots," the other boy says, laughing. Some other boys begin to laugh, too. A symphony of laughter. The boy feels as if he's going to cry. But he must not cry. Must not cry. So he holds back the tears and tries to read the book again. He must read the book. Read the book.

When the teacher arrives a few minutes later, the class quiets down. The boy does not tell the teacher what has happened. He spits on the wound to clean it, dabbing it with a tissue until the bleeding stops. For weeks he fears some dreadful infection from the lead in the pencil point.

From *Radical Teacher*, 24, 1985, pp. 4–5. Reprinted with permission.

Scene Two

The boy is walking home from school. A group of boys (two, maybe three, he is not certain) grab him from behind, drag him into an alley and beat him up. When he gets home, he races up to his room, refusing dinner ("I don't feel well," he tells his mother through the locked door) and spends the night alone in the dark wishing he would die. . . .

These are not fictitious accounts—I *was* that boy. Having been branded a sissy by neighborhood children because I preferred jump rope to baseball and dolls to playing soldiers, I was often taunted with "hey sissy" or "hey faggot" or "yoo hoo honey" (in a mocking voice) when I left the house.

To avoid harassment, I spent many summers alone in my room. I went out on rainy days when the street was empty.

I came to like being alone. I didn't need anyone, I told myself over and over again. I was an island. Contact with others meant pain. Alone, I was protected. I began writing poems, then short stories. There was no reason to go outside anymore. I had a world of my own.

In the schoolyard today
they'll single you out
Their laughter will leave your ears ringing
like the church bells
which once awed you. . . .[2]

School was one of the more painful experiences of my youth. The neighborhood bullies could be avoided. The taunts of the children living in those endless repetitive row houses could be evaded by staying in my room. But school was something I had to face day after day for some two hundred mornings a year.

I had few friends in school. I was a pariah. Some kids would talk to me, but few wanted to be known as my close friend. Afraid of labels. If I was a sissy, then he had to be a sissy, too. I was condemned to loneliness.

Fortunately, a new boy moved into our neighborhood and befriended me; he wasn't afraid of the labels. He protected me when the other guys threatened to beat me up. He walked me home from school; he broke through the terrible loneliness. We were in third or fourth grade at the time.

We spent a summer or two together. Then his parents sent him to camp and I was once again confined to my room.

Scene Three

High school lunchroom. The boy sits at a table near the back of the room. Without warning, his lunch bag is grabbed and tossed to another table. Someone opens it and confiscates a package of Tastykakes; another boy takes the sandwich. The empty bag is tossed back to the boy who stares at it, dumbfounded. He should be used to this; it has happened before.

Someone screams, "faggot," laughing. There is always laughter. It does not annoy him anymore.

There is no teacher nearby. There is never a teacher around. And what would he say if there were? Could he report the crime? He would be jumped after school if he did. Besides, it would be his word against theirs. Teachers never noticed anything. They never heard the taunts. Never heard the word, "faggot." They were the great deaf mutes, pillars of indifference; a sissy's pain was not relevant to history and geography and god made me to love honor and obey him, amen.

Scene Four

High school Religion class. Someone has a copy of *Playboy*. Father N. is not in the room yet; he's late, as usual. Someone taps the boy roughly on the shoulder. He turns. A finger points to the centerfold model, pink fleshy body, thin and sleek. Almost painted. Not real. The other asks, mocking voice, "Hey, does she turn you on? Look at those tits!"

The boy smiles, nodding meekly; turns away.

The other jabs him harder on the shoulder, "Hey, whatsamatter, don't you like girls?"

Laughter. Thousands of mouths; unbearable din of laughter. In the Arena: thumbs down. Don't spare the queer.

"Wanna suck my dick? Huh? That turn you on, faggot!"

The laughter seems to go on forever . . .

Behind you, the sound of their laughter
echoes a million times
in a soundless place
They watch you walk/sit/stand/breathe. . . .[3]

What did being a sissy really mean? It was a way of walking (from the hips rather than the shoulders); it was a way of talking (often with a lisp or in a high-pitched voice); it was a way of relating to others (gently, not wanting to fight, or hurt anyone's feelings). It was being intelligent ("an egghead" they called it sometimes); getting good grades. It means not being interested in sports, not playing football in the street after school; not discussing teams and scores and playoffs. And it involved not showing fervent interest in girls, not talking about scoring with tits or *Playboy* centerfolds. Not concealing naked women in your history book; or porno books in your locker.

On the other hand, anyone could be a "faggot." It was a catch-all. If you did something that didn't conform to what was the acceptable behavior of the group, then you risked being called a faggot. If you didn't get along with the "in" crowd, you were a faggot. It was the most commonly used put-down. It kept guys in line. They became angry when somebody called them a faggot. More fights started over someone calling someone else a faggot than anything else. The word had power. It toppled the male ego, shattered his delicate facade, violated the image he projected. He was tough. Without feeling. Faggot cut through all this. It made him vulnerable. Feminine. And feminine was the worst thing he could possibly be. Girls were fine for fucking, but no boy in his right mind wanted to be like them. A boy was the opposite of a girl. He was not feminine. He was not feeling. He was not weak.

Just look at the gym teacher who growled like a dog; or the priest with the black belt who threw kids against the wall in rage when they didn't know their Latin. They were men, they got respect.

But not the physics teacher who preached pacifism during lectures on the nature of atoms. Everybody knew what he was—and why he believed in the anti-war movement.

My parents only knew that the neighborhood kids called me names. They begged me to act more like the other boys. My brothers were ashamed of me. They never said it, but I knew. Just as I knew that my parents were embarrassed by my behavior.

At times, they tried to get me to act differently. Once my father lectured me on how to walk right. I'm still not clear on what that means. Not from the hips, I guess, don't "swish" like faggots do.

A nun in elementary school told my mother at Open House that there was "something wrong with me." I had draped my sweater over my shoulders like a girl, she said. I was a smart kid, but I should know better than to wear my sweater like a girl!

My mother stood there, mute. I wanted her to say something, to chastise the nun; to defend me. But how could she? This was a nun talking—representative of Jesus, protector of all that was good and decent.

An uncle once told me I should start "acting like a boy" instead of like a girl. Everybody seemed ashamed of me. And I guess I was ashamed of myself, too. It was hard not to be.

Scene Five

> Priest: Do you like girls, Mark?
> Mark: Uh-huh.
> Priest: I mean *really* like them?
> Mark: Yeah—they're okay.
> Priest: There's a role they play in your salvation. Do you understand it, Mark?
> Mark: Yeah.
> Priest: You've got to like girls. Even if you should decide to enter the seminary, it's important to keep in mind God's plan for a man and a woman. . . .[4]

Catholicism of course condemned homosexuality. Effeminacy was tolerated as long as the effeminate person did not admit to being gay. Thus, priests could be effeminate because they weren't gay.

As a sissy, I could count on no support from the church. A male's sole purpose in life was to father children—souls for the church to save. The only hope a homosexual had of attaining salvation was by remaining totally celibate. Don't even think of touching another boy. To think of a sin was a sin. And to sin was to put a mark upon the soul. Sin—if it was a serious offense against god—led to hell. There was no way around it. If you sinned, you were doomed.

Realizing I was gay was not an easy task. Although I knew I was attracted to boys by the time I was about eleven, I didn't connect this attraction to homosexuality. I was not queer. Not I. I was merely appreciating a boy's good looks, his fine features, his proportions. It didn't seem to matter that I didn't appreciate a girl's looks in the same way. There was no twitching in my thighs when I gazed upon a beautiful girl. But I wasn't queer.

I resisted that label—queer—for the longest time. Even when everything pointed to it, I refused to see it. I was certainly not queer. Not I.

We sat through endless English classes, and History courses about the wars between men who were not allowed to love each other. No gay history was ever taught. No history faces you this morning. You're just a faggot. Homosexuals had never contributed to the human race. God destroyed the queers in Sodom and Gomorrah.

We learned about Michelangelo, Oscar Wilde, Gertrude Stein—but never that they were queer. They were not queer. Walt Whitman, the "father of American poetry," was not queer. No one was queer. I was alone, totally unique. One of a kind. Were there others like me somewhere? Another planet, perhaps?

In school, they never talked of the queers. They did not exist. The only hint we got of this other species was in religion class. And even then it was clouded in mystery—never spelled out. It was sin. Like masturbation. Like looking at *Playboy* and getting a hard-on. A sin.

Once a progressive priest in senior year religion class actually mentioned homosexuals—he said the word—but was into Erich Fromm, into homosexuals as pathetic and sick. Fixated at some early stage; penis, anal, whatever. Only heterosexuals passed on to the nirvana of sexual development.

No other images from the halls of the Catholic high school except those the other boys knew: swishy faggot sucking cock in an alley somewhere, grabbing asses in the bathroom. Never mentioning how much straight boys craved blow jobs, it was part of the secret.

It was all a secret. You were not supposed to talk about the queers. Whisper maybe. Laugh about them, yes. But don't be open, honest; don't try to understand. Don't cite their accomplishments. No history faces you this morning. You're just a faggot   faggot   no history   just a faggot

Epilogue

The boy marching down the Parkway. Hundreds of queers. Signs proclaiming gay pride. Speakers. Tables with literature from gay groups. A miracle, he is thinking. Tears are coming loose now. Someone hugs him.

You could not control
the sissy in me
nor could you exorcise him
nor electrocute him
You declared him illegal illegitimate
insane and immature
But he defies you still.[5]

NOTES

1. From the poem "Faggot" by Tommi Avicolli, published in *GPU News*, Sept. 1979.
2. Ibid.
3. Ibid.
4. From the play *Judgment of the Roaches* by Tommi Avicolli, produced in Philadelphia at the Gay Community Center, the Painted Bride Arts Center and the University of Pennsylvania; aired over WXPN-FM, in four parts; and presented at the Lesbian/Gay Conference in Norfolk, VA, July, 1980.
5. From the poem "Sissy Poem," published in *Magic Doesn't Live Here Anymore* (Philadelphia: Spruce Street Press, 1976).

11

GENDER QUIZ, LUNCH, PROFITS

MINNIE BRUCE PRATT

quiz, n. [? suggested by L. *quis,* who, which, what, *quid,* how, why, wherefore]. 1. [Rare], a queer or eccentric person. 2. a practical joke; hoax. 3. a questioning, especially an informal oral or written examination to test one's knowledge.

WEBSTER'S NEW WORLD DICTIONARY OF THE AMERICAN LANGUAGE

In 1975, when I first fell in love with another woman, and knew that was what I was doing, I was married to a man, had been for almost ten years, and I had two small sons. Everyone was shocked at the turn I was taking in my life, including me. Everyone—from the male lawyer who handled the divorce to my handful of lesbian friends—wanted to know: Had I ever had these feelings before? When had I realized I was "different"? When had I started to "change"? And the state of North Carolina, where I was living, certainly wanted to know: Did I understand that I could not be both a mother— a good woman—and also a lesbian—a perverted woman?

To answer their questions and my own, I did what perhaps every person who identifies as lesbian or gay does when we come out to ourselves. I looked back at my own life for the clues of memory to use as I struggled through a maze of questions: I didn't feel "different," but was I? (From who?) Had I changed? (From what?) Was I heterosexual in adolescence only to become lesbian in my late twenties? Was I lesbian always but coerced into heterosexuality? Was I a less authentic lesbian than my friends who had "always known" that they were sexually and affectionally attracted to other women? What kind of woman was a lesbian woman? Was I a "real" woman?

What I found at the center of my exploration was my first friendship, when I was five and she was five, with a white girl who had lived next door to me, a tomboy. I had not talked to her since our high school graduation in our small Alabama town, but I knew from my mother that she had never married. I wondered at how intensely I remembered her. Then one evening, as I read my poetry in a Birmingham bookstore, she walked in, looking grown and fine in her cowboy boots, white shirt open at the collar, tailored slacks—looking like the butch dyke she had turned out to be. She was someone who had known me since I was small, but she was as shocked as everyone else that I had grown up to be a lesbian too.

When I found her, I found other questions that required me to turn back and look yet again: How was it possible that coming from the woman-hating, race-baiting, church town of our childhood, we had both grown up to live as lesbians? Why was she the first person I felt passionately about outside my family—someone who was not only a lesbian, but a butch lesbian? How had we recognized each other then, with no language for who we were? What mark had we each left on the other? And who *were* we to each other, at five years old? Were we "butch" and "femme"? Were we "boy" and "girl"? Why was I invisible in her memories, a "girl" but not a "lesbian"?

I turned and looked back again at the two of us, those two girls. I saw the kite string slack in my hand, the kite falling and crumpling, and how she reached out and pulled me forward into the wind with it. I said to her, "But after we were little, I never saw you. You were always playing with the boys. I was afraid of the boys." And she said, "But what you didn't know was that I was afraid of the girls." All through high school she fell miserably in love with straight girls who were aggressively femme, but at the senior prom she dated the captain of the football team. I sat sedate, awkward, and alone, in a strapless pink prom dress, full of anticipated power but unable to sail into a room of dancers who, like me, desired and despised the power of women.

Twenty years later these questions unwound before me: Was my femme style—the tilt of my head, my way of asking questions, the tone of my voice—related to my sexual desire? To my notion of myself as a woman? What did maleness and femaleness have to do with the identities of butch and femme we had grown up into? What did the gestures of masculinity and femininity have to do with us as women?

————————

The next time I came home she arranged another reunion, a dinner with queer folks from our high school years. That night there were five, all of us white, a friendship network as segregated as our education, our never even getting to meet the Black students in the school on the other side of town. We hadn't known much about many of the lives hidden in our town, and now we gathered, ready to find out: Me and the woman who was my first friend, almost my first memory. And my best girlfriend from high school, who'd also grown up to be a lesbian and a mother. My first boyfriend, who'd turned out to be a gay man so sweet I remembered why I wanted to be his girl. And another gay man who still lived in our hometown. We gossiped about who we'd had crushes on, who we held hands with on the sly, who flirted back.

The list of people became staggeringly long, far beyond my idea of who might have been "lesbian" or "gay" in my tiny town of about two thousand. There was the girl classmate, long since married, who'd graduated and then had an affair with a woman gym teacher. And the girl classmate who had gone from one woman lover to another until her front door got broken down in the middle of the night. And the married Sunday School teacher whose daughter, later married, had had an affair with a girlfriend, who years later had had an affair with the teacher-mother. There were the boys who either did it with each other or watched the fucking that went on between them in a church, in a parsonage, with the preacher's son. There was the gay man who opened his door one night to find an envelope on his doorstep stuffed with photographs of a married male acquaintance, and a pleading invitation.

We told stories about taking the compulsory heterosexual quiz in high school, with its two ways to answer, its two ways to turn: straight or gay, heterosexual or queer. One choice would lead us out of the maze into adulthood, the other directly to hell. But it seemed that the public tally of our choices had almost no relation to our hidden lives, to whose hand was on whose ass, to the dream we buried, dead center, in our heart. The institution of heterosexuality certainly existed, but its daily practice—at least in my hometown in the deep South—suddenly seemed no more sturdy than the wedding pictures of man and wife printed on flimsy yellow paper in the local weekly.

Yet law and custom had usually been strong enough to make our public lives match the picture. The boundaries of heterosexuality strengthened other institutions—including those of race and class—whose limits were also unacknowledged. In the town newspaper I saw photographs of the sheriff and his deputies by the courthouse, pouring confiscated whiskey into the street gutters until the town reeked of moonshine. But there were no pic- tures of my girlfriend inside her house, on her hands and knees in the kitchen with a mother almost broken by poverty. No picture of her father jailed for trying to buy their way out by selling bootleg liquor. When my white father died in the county nursing home, the paper printed one version of his life, from semi-pro baseball to the lumber mill. No mention of him drinking the bootleg whiskey, no mention of his racist theories on who was taking over the world. The Black woman who raised me died across the hall from him in the home. There was nothing in the paper to say she had lived or died, or how many children she had mothered, nothing of her daughters or her grandchildren.

When I was engaged to be married to a man, the local paper published an announcement and a picture of me, groomed and womanly, ready to be a wife. Of those of us gathered at out queer reunion, there was no public record in our town—no note in the weekly chat column from Greenpond or Six Mile—of those we had loved faithfully for five years, ten years, the chil- dren we had familied. But in our bodies we knew that our way had not led to a dead end, a blank wall, a blank piece of paper. We had walked through into our own lives.

The last time I went home, I introduced my new love to my first girl- friend, and watched them greet each other warmly. After years of loving butch lesbians, I had taken as my mate a woman so stone in her masculinity that she could, and did, sometimes pass as a queer man. I had no language to talk about her or us together. I had to learn to say that I had fallen in love with a woman so *transgendered,* with such perceived contradictions between her birth sex and her gender expression, that someone at one end of a city block could call her "Ma'am" and someone at the other end would call her "Sir." I was learning that I was more complicated than I'd had any idea. I was beginning to pull the thread of who I was out of the tangle of words: *woman* and *lesbian, femme* and *female.*

That night I looked back at my first friend, a girl scalded by her mother's shame. The threats of walk-like-a-lady, of don't-be-so-loud-and-angry. (And hate yourself enough to almost go crazy.) I looked back at myself, the child flirting in photographs with angled head, sidelong glance. The child given an impossible choice by her teachers: Be smart or be a girl, be a girl or be strong. (And hate yourself enough to almost leave your body.) The two of us had sat at playtime in the dirt, barefoot, battling furiously hand-to-hand in the desire to defeat the other. How had we survived to meet again? Survived to grow up to be women for whom the word *woman* did not adequately describe the twists and turns our bodies, our lives, took through sex and gender?

No one had turned to us and held out a handful of questions: How many ways are there to have the *sex* of girl, boy, man, woman? How many ways are there to have *gender*—from masculine to androgynous to feminine? Is there a connection between the *sexualities* of lesbian, bisexual, heterosexual, between desire and liberation? No one told us: The path divides, and divides again, in many directions. No one asked: How many ways can the *body's sex* vary by chromosomes, hormones, genitals? How many ways can *gender expression* multiply—between home and work, at the computer and when you kiss someone, in your dreams and when you walk down the street? No one asked us: What is your dream of who you want to be?

————

In 1975, when I first fell in love with another woman, and knew that was what I wanted, I had just begun to call myself a feminist. I was learning how many traps the female body could be caught in—sexual assault and rape, beatings in the home, our thoughts turned back in shame on our bodies. I learned how women's bodies could be used to reproduce children without our consent, to produce someone else's "pleasure" at our expense. Most importantly, I began to be able to explain many of the events of my own life that had been unintelligible to me.

I was able to recall and find a pattern in certain acts that had made no sense—like a sexually suggestive comment from a male co-worker—and acts that I hadn't understood as significant—such as the fact that a male job interviewer questioned me on my childcare arrangements. For the first time in my life, I understood myself as *woman*, the "opposite sex," a group of people subject to discrimination and oppression—and capable of resistance. I was able to locate my body and my life in the maze of history and power.

The oppression of women was a revelation to me; the liberation of women was my freedom. There was tremendous exhilaration in being part of a liberation movement, in gathering together with other women to explore how to get to freedom. In consciousness-raising circles, political action groups, cultural events, literary collectives—in all kinds of women's groups and spaces, we identified the ways oppression had fenced in our lives.

And we read the theories of women who had ideas about how to end the oppression of women as a sex. I found a few writers who examined the relation of capitalist economic development to women's oppression. But most of the theory available to me was ahistorical and monocultural. It emphasized that the solution was to eliminate differences between *women* and *men*. Some proposed abolishing distinctions in biological functioning—as in Shulamith Firestone's suggestion for artificial wombs to erase female biological functions that she believed were the basis of male and female, and of inequality. Others felt that the answer was to end modes of gender expression, patterns of femininity and masculinity. Carolyn Heilbrun advocated androgyny, the elimination of the polarities of "gender roles" that she considered the cause of power differences between men and women. Andrea Dworkin campaigned to alter the practice of sexual intercourse, to get rid of sexual images and acts she believed would perpetuate maleness and femaleness, and therefore domination and submission.

I found these theories persuasive. Maybe eliminating sex differences or transcending gender expression would end *woman* as a place of oppression. But, in fact, the theories didn't explain some important aspects of oppression against me as a woman in my daily life. I'd been pregnant with two children and given birth to them. The way the doctors treated me only made me ask, "If there were artificial wombs, whose hands would administer the technology, and for whose profits?" And those two children had been two boys, each of whom had possessed, by the time he was two or three, his own unique blend of masculine and feminine. Was it possible to train them into androgyny? Was this the skill they needed to take action against unjust power in the world? As for intercourse, this was where I had experienced the most pleasure in my relationship with a man; my husband had tried carefully to please me. I would have had more pleasure if my sexual play had not been damaged by fear about pregnancy—and by shame about what I could want as a woman. But my husband's penis was not dominating my life. Instead, I was concerned about the power of white men who interviewed me for possible jobs at large institutions, and then protected their economic position by never hiring me.

———————

And, when I stood up to face the public opponents of my liberation as a woman, I got little help from the theories I was reading. When I debated right-wing women in my community in North Carolina, as they lambasted the Equal Rights Amendment, their tactics were based on baiting the women's movement precisely on the issue of elimination of sex and gender differences. They accused: Equal rights means unisex bathrooms. Equal rights means homosexual marriages. They meant: If you challenge gender boundaries, you will make women more vulnerable to abuse by eliminating gender protection. They meant: If you challenge gender boundaries, you will have men and women adopting the behavior of the opposite sex and getting pleasure from it.

I didn't know how to answer their raging remarks, accusations which were echoed throughout the United States as part of a concerted antifeminist campaign. Some of the first slogans I'd learned in the women's movement were "Biology is not destiny" and "Women are made, not born." I'd read feminist theory that analyzed how jobs and household chores and emotions were divided up between men and women according to sex. But I—and the primarily white middle-to-upper-class reform women's movement that backed the E.R.A.—did not have an analysis of sex, gender expression, and sexuality that was complex enough to respond to these right-wing attacks.

We could have said, in these debates, that the answer to violence against women was not the illusion of protection by limiting women's activity, but a movement in which women learned to fight back, with allies, to protect ourselves, and to move through the whole world safely. We could have answered that the split between *man* and *woman* was designed to keep one sex up and one sex down in an economic system where profiteers make money off a war between the sexes. We could have answered that *woman* was not the opposite of *man,* and that liberation meant crossing all arbitrary gender boundaries, to place ourselves anywhere we chose on the continuum of maleness and femaleness, in any aspect of our lives.

In some more private spaces within women's liberation, we did advance these arguments. But in hostile public space it was controversial to propose even the slightest changes in "normal" male and female behaviors. *That* was to question the foundation of "civilization." The reform wing of the women's movement was profoundly ambivalent about taking on lesbian and transgender issues publicly. It dealt with issues of race and class reluctantly and inconsistently, when at all. A victory for these reformers meant only a fractional expansion of the old public boundaries on what was acceptable behavior for "womanhood," on who was a "respectable" woman.

Some of these reformists accepted limits on what constituted womanhood because of uncritical allegiances to their own class and race positions. For others, this was a strategic decision; they believed a political definition of woman that deemphasized difference would secure more territory for more women in a hostile world. They hoped to establish a bulwark, and then a place that could be built on for greater liberation. In fact, the exclusion of women who blurred the edges of what was considered legitimate as *woman*— because of race or class or sexuality or gender presentation—made women's space smaller and more dangerous, made this aspect of the women's movement weaker and more limited in foundation.

In the end, I moved away from reform politics into cultural and political actions that embraced the complexities of *woman.* The group of women I began to work with was, at first, predominantly white, both working class and middle class, and lesbian. But we had been deeply influenced by the Black civil rights and liberation movements. We saw the freedom of all women as linked inextricably to the elimination of racism. In addition, we learned from the political and theoretical work of feminists and lesbians of color who showed us how to question—and place in an economic and historical context—the many categories of "difference," including those of race, sex, class, and sexuality.

But even as we traced how women's liberation could be extended through these connections, these untanglings and re-braidings, we still had not fully explored sex and gender. There were unanswered questions, and questions that were never raised, about "manhood" and "womanhood." We carried with us many of the negative assumptions and values that the larger culture had assigned to *woman, feminine, man, masculine*—ideas that served to limit women's behaviors and to prevent examination of how "masculinity" and "femininity" are not the basis of sex, race, and class oppression.

Often a lesbian considered "too butch" was assumed to be, at least in part, a male chauvinist. She might get thrown out of her lesbian collective for this, or refused admittance to a lesbian bar. Frequently a lesbian who was "too femme" was perceived as a woman who had not liberated her mind or her body. In ordinary arguments with a lesbian friend or lover, she could be dismissed—as I sometimes was—with, "You act just like a heterosexual woman." Yet during this same time, lesbians who were butch, femme, and all gender expressions in between were trying to decipher which of our behaviors still did reflect oppressive patterns learned in a woman-hating culture. These struggles were present in 1982, in New York City, when an alliance of women with a range of sexualities had planned "The Scholar and the Feminist" annual conference as a way to examine the complex intersections of pleasure and danger in women's sexuality and gender expression. They were condemned as "sexual deviants" and "sluts" by a group of women organizing against pornography, who identified themselves as "real feminists."

At about this time, I was teaching women's studies at a state university near Washington, D.C. One day in the classroom, we were discussing lesbian life in general, and butch/femme in particular. I was dressed casually, but in femme style. The white woman to my left was a muscular, big woman, with short hair and a black leather jacket; she drove a Harley to school every day. She said forcefully, "Butch and femme don't exist anymore." It was a moment typical, in many ways, of the lesbian-feminist space I lived inside during the 1980s. As women and as lesbians we wanted to step outside traps set for us as people sexed as *woman,* to evade negative values gendered to us. We didn't want to be women as defined by the larger culture, so we had to get rid of femininity. We didn't want to be oppressed by men, so we had to get rid of masculinity. And we wanted to end enforced desire, so we had to get rid of heterosexuality.

For some lesbians, one way out of these traps was to choose androgyny, or to practice a sexuality of "mutuality and equality"—an attempt to eliminate the variations of "man" and "woman" we saw in each other every day. Another way was to explain hostility toward "masculine" lesbians and "feminine" lesbians as arising from homophobia, rather than from prejudices about what kind of gender expression was appropriate for "respectable" women and "liberated" women. One answer for many was to deny the deep fear in the larger culture, and therefore within ourselves, about sex and gender fluidity.

The fear can take different forms. The classified sections of gay and lesbian newspapers still run personal ads that say "No butches, no drugs"—a statement equating gender defiance in a woman with self-destruction, a lesbian version of a gay man's "straight-appearing, no femmes" ad. Discussions of sexuality may exclude butch/butch and femme/femme pairings as too homoerotically queer. Some of us who talk of ourselves as butch or femme may reject identification with people like us who live at the extremes of gender. A coolly sophisticated lesbian at a dance may say, "I'm a femme, but I'm not like *her*,"—dismissing the woman she sees as "going too far" in her femininity.

We know, from being alive in the United States in the twentieth century, that there are severe punishments dealt to those who cross sex and gender boundaries, and terrible penalties visited on women who claim their womanhood independently. This is really no surprise, though, since the institutions of power are based, at least in part, on controlling difference—by sex, gender, and sexuality. No wonder we may feel there is safety in moderation, in assimilation, in a "normal" expression of sex and gender. But *moderation* means "to keep within bounds." Inside whose boundaries are we living?

And despite the punishments for boundary crossing, we continue to live, daily, with all our contradictory differences. Here I still stand, unmistakably "feminine" in style, and "womanly" in personal experience—and unacceptably "masculine" in political interests and in my dedication to writing a poetry that stretches beyond the woman's domain of home. Here I am, assigned a "female" sex on my birth certificate, but not considered womanly enough—because I am a lesbian—to retain custody of the children I delivered from my woman's body. As a white girl raised in a segregated culture, I was expected to be "ladylike"—sexually repressed but acquiescent to white men of my class—while other, darker women were damned as "promiscuous" so their bodies could be seized and exploited. I've worked outside the home for at least part of my living since I was a teenager—a fact deemed masculine by some. But my occupation now is that of teacher, work suitably feminine for a woman as long as I don't tell my students I'm a lesbian—a sexuality thought too aggressive and "masculine" to fit with my "femininity."

I am definitively lesbian to myself, but not in a way recognizable to a heterosexual world that assumes lesbians to be "mannish." Unless I announce myself to be lesbian, which I do often—in my classroom, at poetry readings, to curious taxi drivers—I am usually assumed to be straight. But unless I "butch up" my style, sometimes I am suspect inside my lesbian world as too feminine to be lesbian. And both inside and outside lesbian space, there is another assumption held by some: No "real" lesbian would be attracted to as much masculinity as I prefer in my lesbian lover.

How can I reconcile the contradictions of sex and gender, in my experience and my politics, in my body? We are all offered a chance to escape this puzzle at one time or another. We are offered the True or False correct answer. We are handed the questionnaire to fill out. But the boxes that we check, *M* or *F,* the categories *male* and *female,* do not contain the complexity of sex and gender for any of us.

The stories that follow are part of a new theory about that complexity which is appearing at the intersections: between the feminism of U.S. women's liberation; the writings of women of color nationally and internationally; the queer ideas of lesbian, gay, and bisexual liberation; and the emerging thought of transgender liberation—a movement that embraces drag queens and kings, transsexuals, cross-dressers, he-shes and she-males, intersexed people, transgenderists, and people of ambiguous, androgynous, or contradictory sex and gender. These intersections make clear that every aspect of a person's gender expression and sex will not be consistently either masculine or feminine, man or woman. I find many layers of my own experience in this theory, and I find an exhilaration at the connections between myself and others as I see, with increasing clarity, how gender oppression and liberation affect everyone, how my struggle as a woman and a lesbian overlaps and joins with the struggles of other gender and sexually oppressed people. A friend of mine has said of this exhilaration: "It's like being released from a cage I didn't know I was in."

This is a theory that explores the infinities, the fluidities of sex and gender. The African-American woman eating sushi at the next table may be a woman lovely in her bones, gestures, tone of voice, but this does not mean that her genitals are female. If the handsome Filipino man in the upstairs apartment is straight-appearing, this does not mean his erotic preference is the "opposite sex." The white woman next to you at the doctor's office may have been born male, and have a complex history of hormones and surgery. Or she may have been born female and have a different but equally complex history of hormones and surgery. The person on the subway who you perceive as a white man in a business suit may have been born female, may consider herself a butch lesbian, or may identify himself as a gay man. The *M* and the *F* on the questionnaire are useless.

Now here I stand, far from where I was born, from the small segregated hospital in Alabama where a nurse checked *F* and *W* on my birth certificate. Far from my first tomboy girlfriend and the ways we played together, splashing barefoot in rainwater. Far from who I was as a wife and mother, almost twenty years ago, when I began to question the destiny I had been assigned as a woman. I have lived my life at the intersection of great waves of social change in the United States in the twentieth century: the Black civil rights and liberation movements, the women's liberation movement, the lesbian/gay/bisexual liberation movement, the transgender liberation movement. The theory developed by each has complicated our questions about the categories of race, sex, gender, sexuality, and class. And these theories have advanced our ability to struggle against oppressions that are imposed and justified using these categories. But we can not move theory into action unless we can find it in the eccentric and wandering ways of our daily life. I have written the stories that follow to give theory flesh and breath.

Lunch

I am sitting in on lunch at the deli where you are meeting with a new acquaintance, and I am struggling with my pronouns. She is a big woman, over six feet, with a pulled-back ponytail and a sweet face. She is a woman with a spouse of fifteen years and four children and a life that started out as male and is now being lived as female. "At least," she says, "I am more that than I am a man." The inadequacy of the words. The duality of pronouns. She is talking to me about you, a narration of a moment on the phone with you, "So I said to *him* . . ."

This is not a man passing on the street who sees you as a man, arm in arm with me, a woman. This is not a lesbian who watches us dancing at a party, and sees you as either a butch lesbian or a woman trying to be a man, and me as femme or deluded. This is someone who lives in a world where gender and sex are fluid. Not an academic exercise, but what she tells the kids about who she was as their father. The shock to me of *you* sitting here as *him*, at this ordinary formica table, though of course that is the pronoun that suits your masculine spirit, short hair, oxford shirt, men's slacks. The word spoken about you not in hostility or misperception, but because, for you both, that is how flexible gender is.

Meeting you for the first time over curried chicken and *masala dosa*, she is socially appropriate to refer to you as *him*. Meanwhile, you are saying that you are a woman and transgendered, that your masculinity is a range of gender expression that should be available to all women, as femininity should be to men. You insist that you are *him* and also *her*. When I enter the conversation, I call you both by your given names to be respectful. The either/or pronouns suddenly are the jaws of a steel trap snapping shut on infinities that exist where body, self, sex, gender, the world, and lunch intersect.

The fluorescent light brightens in the little deli, as if a cloud has shifted from the sun. Your words become sharper and more distinct, someone turning up the volume on a radio. I see and hear the bothness, the severalness of this moment, a chaotic heightening of sense very akin to my first look at who really lives under the rigid grid of *black* and *white*. In a long-ago meeting of first-grade parents, every person was a woman of color except me, except some of them were almost as light-skinned as me, sitting there worrying about their children like me, and like the women who were darker-skinned than us. Then later, in the city, I met proper Black ladies walking home, gloved and hatted, from church. Their profiles, lips pursed, were exactly those of my aunts. And even later I learned how the laws of race and property had been laid over us, the bodies of some white men had lain on us, reproducing *white* and *black*, producing *owner* and *owned*, to divide our lives.

Over the clatter of the lunch-time rush, she says that she did "the femme thing" for a while to prove she was a woman, but now she believes in not denying her past. In the past I have denied I was a woman. The pronoun *she* was a trap set by others to catch me. I watch her talk, cheeks flushed pink, eyes gleaming silver and green. I imagine wrapping womanhood around me like a length of shimmering metallic cloth. She looks at me frequently as she talks, careful to divide her attention between you and me. How my aunts talked to me as a little girl, curly-headed and new in my mother's arms. No words from them to me without sex or gender.

———————

Suddenly I see you and me and her on the edge of town, a place out of my view when I was growing up, like the Quarters or the Milltown, but this is another kind of gathering. It is a world of those the world casts out, calls freaks, the women-men of the sideshow at the circus, seen as tawdry, pitiful, hidden, wasted, walking their path of reeking sawdust between the tents. Except the people there have lovers, marriages, children, poor-paying jobs. They have marigolds in pots, they play the harmonica, they write books. You live there, and now I live there too, with those who know they are both *man* and *woman*, those who have transmuted one to the other, those who insist they are neither. Outside the pegged tents people stand and peer in at us, no words for us, though just by stepping over the ropes they could join us. I could cross back into that staring crowd and be without question a woman amusing herself, Sunday afternoon at the carnival. But I would rather stay here and talk to you in this in-between place, sitting with a friend, our food spread out, savory, spicy, on the table before us.

Profits

On the first anniversary of the Montreal massacre, I tell my feminist theory class about the moment when a man with a rifle entered an engineering class at that university. He divided the students up, men to one wall, women to the other. When he had decided who was male and who was female, he shot the women, killing fourteen of them. Later he said he wanted the women dead because they were feminists and were taking jobs away from men. I say that there is no record of how many, if any, of the women considered them-selves feminists. Perhaps they were just women who wanted to work in a job designated *male* in this century, on this continent. I say crossing gender boundaries as women does not automatically make us feminists, but the consequences of doing so may, if we live.

———————

During the discussion, a student raises her hand. At a women's music festival last summer, she had met a survivor of the massacre. The woman had lived because the male terrorist had perceived her as male, and put her in the group with the men. Although my student, who herself looks like a teenage boy, doesn't recount how the woman felt watching the other women die, her face is blotched and etched with anguish. I imagine that room: The woman facing a man so sure he knows who is *man* and who is *woman*. His illusion of omniscience spares her, allows her to become an engineer, and then she spends years trying to find work. She gets turned down for jobs as "too masculine" if she is seen as woman, "too effeminate" if seen as man. To the students I say there is no gender boundary that can make us into either one or the other. There is no method, including violence, that can enforce complete conformity to "man," to "woman." I say we know that this man hated women, that he meant to kill women, but what we do not know is how many ways of being human have been hidden in the word *woman*. We don't yet know how large is this *other* that has been made the opposite of the narrow rod of *man*. We don't know who was male or female in that Montreal room, how many genders lived or died. I say that *here* we are trying to end a war on women in which we all get caught in the crossfire.

In this basement classroom, the steam pipes crisscross the ceiling and drip on our heads. Other students on campus bait those who take this women's studies course—the men are called feminine, the women masculine, the men queer, the women dykes. They are seen as crossing sex and gender boundaries simply because they question them. Today we all jump at noises in the hall, imagining that the one we fear stands in the doorway. Perhaps an unknown man, perhaps someone from our family with a cold, murderous stare. The ones who believe the lie that there are only men and women, and that the first should rule the last. The ones who believe we should keep separate, sheep and goats, until judgment day. It is 3:30 P.M., the end of today's class. I assign readings on the origin of the family, private property, women, and the State. I say, "Next time we will talk about gender stratification and corporate profit."

PART III
Embodiment

I didn't see myself as fat. I didn't see myself. I wasn't there. I get so sad about that because I missed so much.

"Martha"[1]

In time, I learned to smother the rage I felt at so often being taken for a criminal. No to do so would surely have led to madness . . . .

Brent Staples[2]

One afternoon they all decided to go skinny dipping . . . . They hassled me until I finally stripped and jumped in the water. It was about the worst experience of my life. First off, the other guys had better bodies than I did. My stomach stuck out, . . . and I had no shoulders or chest, and of course, no biceps . . . . [Then] an ex-girlfriend of mine swam by with the man she was living with at the time and made a comment about how I won the 'funniest-shape-of-the-day award' . . . .

"Larry"[3]

Our relationships to our bodies and our decisions about how we present ourselves to the world are heavily influenced by the historical and cultural contexts in which we live. These contexts are determined to a large extent by the media in U.S. society. A brief look at the history of clothing and fashion or at the history of women in sports, for example, shows changes in ideal female body image over time. Laced corsets, once very popular, are now used by few women. Sports such as track and field, once considered unacceptable for women, are now acceptable for women athletes, although female athletes are much more easily accepted if they appear to be feminine. Many of the dominant messages about bodies are tied to images of gender, race, and class, mandating different expectations for various women and men.[4]

Physical appearance is often an obsession for people in U.S. society, especially for people privileged enough to have the time and money to attend to their bodies. The pressure to look "right" can be internalized as profound self-disapproval. It drives many people to spend long hours exercising and preening and many years dieting. Even for people who would be considered attractive within their own communities, the dominant culture's obsession with youth, muscles, whiteness, blondness, and thinness can undermine positive attitudes for many.[5] With rare exceptions, most of us will look seriously "wrong" at some point if we have the privilege of growing old. People whose bodies don't match dominant images of what is defined as normal suffer immense discrimination, especially on the basis of skin color, weight, looks, or disability.[6]

Sports-oriented culture intensifies the pressure for a perfect body. Sports themselves are also a problem for many athletes because sports are highly competitive, few participants are able to make a career of sports (see Messner, Part I), sports injuries occur frequently, sexism pervades sports, and sports support heterosexism and homophobia. Homophobia is ever-present; male athletes are pressured to nurture their homophobia as they express their athletic masculinity in homoerotic contexts, and female athletes are pressured to be feminine, lest they look too much like men and challenge the division of the world into male and female.[7]

Objectification pervades our understanding of gender. People are frequently seen not for who they are, but for what they represent to both themselves and observers. People may become beauty objects, sex objects, racial objects, athletic objects, unattractive objects, or disabled objects. The media feed this process by providing distorted messages about how people should look, what makes people happy, and how people spend their time: middle-class, white housewives excited over laundry detergent or toothpaste, white men buying cars and selling life insurance, Black men with muscular bodies playing sports, and so on. Few women believe they have acceptable bodies, and the media nurture this insecurity and self-hatred, pounding away at the expectation of perfection, leading people to see themselves as imperfect objects. Even men are now seeking plastic surgery in increasing numbers to mask the effects of aging or to lengthen or enlarge their penises.[8]

According to a recent television documentary, of 40,000 female applicants to a modeling agency, only four were selected as acceptable.[9] Despite the impossibility of ever looking like a model for the vast majority of women, the media message is so powerful that many women wish they did; many will have face-lifts, get breast implants, or go on extreme diets in quest of the perfect body, in spite of the health risks involved. According to a recent study by sociologists Diana Dull and Candace West, plastic surgery is a heavily gendered process. The plastic surgeons they interviewed readily supported plastic surgery to enhance a woman's appearance, but they did not support it to enhance a man's appearance.[10]

The authors in this chapter address various aspects of embodiment. First, Elayne A. Saltzberg and Joan C. Chrisler summarize the activities women engage in to pursue the perfect body, and they discuss the effects of race, class, and disability on the image of the perfect woman. Then Deborah Gregory and Patricia Jacobs provide us a glimpse of life with one of the so-called perfect bodies, looking at racism in the modeling industry.

Next, sociologist Becky Thompson presents data from a qualitative study of women with eating problems and argues that obsession with thinness and the dominant ideals of feminine beauty are not necessarily the sources of bulimia, anorexia, and binging. Rather, the women she interviewed used food for comfort in response to various sorts of trauma, including sexual abuse, racism, heterosexism, and poverty. Thompson encourages us to reassess the assumption that eating disorders relate only to the ideal of thinness, and to work toward a world in which girls and women are free of trauma and discrimination.

The next four articles discuss the implications of having a body that lies outside the mainstream definition of acceptable or beautiful. Brent Staples describes how being a tall Black man carries a power of its own—the power to intimidate others even though he has no interest in doing that. He describes strategies he has devised in response to these racist reactions, including dealing with his rage and whistling classical music when he takes walks after dark; he assumes, apparently correctly, that the public doesn't expect a typical mugger to whistle Vivaldi. Next, Leonard Kriegel describes his battle against polio, which he waged with his upper-body muscles. His way of being a man was to work out obsessively; he now looks back with some regret at the damage he appears to have done to his arms. He ties masculinity directly to his way of coping with the aftermath of polio.

Next, Barbara Macdonald shares what it's like to have an aging body—grappling with adjusting to a body that seems unfamiliar to her as she faces the inevitability of growing old and eventually dying. This chapter concludes with an essay by Christy Haubegger, in which she challenges white, mainstream definitions of beauty and embraces her round, Latina body.

The authors in this chapter argue either directly or indirectly for a different world in which people are seen for who they are, not for what their bodies represent, and in which people own their bodies, free from negative judgments.

NOTES

1. Quoted in Becky W. Thompson, "'A Way Outa No Way': Eating Problems among African-American, Latina and White Women," *Gender & Society,* 6(4) December 1992: 546–561.

2. Brent Staples, "Just Walk on By: A Black Man Ponders His Power to Alter Public Space," in Laurel Richardson and Verta Taylor, *Feminist Frontiers II: Rethinking Sex, Gender, and Society* (New York: Random House, 1989), p. 403.

3. "Larry" interviewed by Barry Glassner, in "Men and Muscles," *Bodies: Why We Look the Way We Do (And How We Feel about It)* (New York: Putnam, 1988). Reprinted in *Men's Lives,* 3rd ed., quote, pp. 254–255; article, pp. 252–261.

4. On the history of fashion and clothing, see Saltzberg and Chrisler, this chapter. For a discussion of clothing and identity, see Mary Ellen Roach-Higgins, Joanne B. Eichner, and Kim K. P. Johnson, eds., *Dress and Identity* (New York: Fairchild Publishers, 1995). For a history of women in sports, see Susan K. Cahn, *Coming On Strong: Gender and Sexuality in Twentieth-Century Women's Sport* (Cambridge, MA: Harvard University Press, 1994). For perspectives on the influence of the media on gender, see Gail Dines and Jean M. Humez, eds., *Gender, Race and Class in Media: A Text-Reader* (Thousand Oaks, CA: Sage, 1995).

5. For an interesting discussion of the use of blue contact lenses by people with brown eyes, including women of color, see Susan Bordo, " 'Material Girl'—The Effacements of Postmodern Culture," in *Unbearable Weight: Feminism, Western Culture and the Body* (Berkeley, CA: University of California Press, 1993), pp. 245–259.

6. For discussions of the impact of looks, obesity, and various kinds of disabilities on employment and other aspects of life, see Susan E. Browne, Debra Connors, and Nanci Stern, eds., *With the Power of Each Breath* (Pittsburgh: Cleis Press, 1985); Lisa Schoenfielder and Barbara Wieser, eds., *Shadow on a Tightrope* (Iowa City: Aunt Lute, 1983); Irving Kenneth Zola, *Missing Pieces: A Chronicle of Living with a Disability* (Philadelphia: Temple University Press, 1982); Gwyneth Matthews, *Voices from the Shadows: Women with Disabilities Speak Out* (Toronto: Women's Educational Press, 1983); Lucy Grealy, *Autobiography of a Face* (Boston: Houghton Mifflin, 1994).

7. For research and critical analysis of gender and sports, see Greta Cohen, ed., *Women in Sports: Issues and Controversies* (Newbury Park, CA: Sage, 1993); Susan K. Cahn, *Coming on Strong*; Michael A. Messner, *Power at Play: Sports and the Problem of Masculinity* (Boston: Beacon Press, 1992); Michael A. Messner and Donald F. Sabo, *Sex, Violence and Power in Sport: Rethinking Masculinity* (Freedom, CA: Crossing Press, 1994).

8. Dale Koppel, "About Face: The Focus on Appearance is Becoming a Male Obsession," *Your Health, The Boston Globe*, April 23, 1995, pp. 10, 23, 26. An ad in *The Boston Globe* announced plastic surgery for "male enhancement" May 1995.

9. *The Famine Within*, Public Broadcasting System, winter 1995.

10. Diana Dull and Candace West, "Accounting for Cosmetic Surgery: The Accomplishment of Gender," *Social Problems*, 38(1) February 1991: 54–70.

12

BEAUTY IS THE BEAST

Psychological Effects of the Pursuit of the Perfect Female Body

ELAYNE A. SALTZBERG AND JOAN C. CHRISLER

A mbrose Bierce (1958) once wrote, "To men a man is but a mind. Who cares what face he carries or what he wears? But woman's body is the woman." Despite the societal changes achieved since Bierce's time, his statement remains true. Since the height of the feminist movement in the early 1970s, women have spent more money than ever before on products and treatments designed to make them beautiful. Cosmetic sales have increased annually to reach $18 billion in 1987 ("Ignoring the economy . . . ,"

From *Women: A Feminist Perspective*, Jo Freeman, ed. Copyright © 1995 by Mayfield Publishing Company. Reprinted by permission. The authors thank Jo Freeman, Sue Wilkinson, and Paulette Leonard for their helpful comments on an earlier version of this paper and Barbara Weber for locating the business and industry statistics.

1989), sales of women's clothing averaged $103 billion per month in 1990 (personal communication, U.S. Bureau of Economic Analysis, 1992), dieting has become a $30-billion-per-year industry (Stoffel, 1989), and women spent $1.2 billion on cosmetic surgery in 1990 (personal communication, American Society of Plastic and Reconstructive Surgeons, 1992). The importance of beauty has apparently increased even as women are reaching for personal freedoms and economic rights undreamed of by our grandmothers. The emphasis on beauty may be a way to hold onto a feminine image while shedding feminine roles.

Attractiveness is prerequisite for femininity but not for masculinity (Freedman, 1986). The word *beauty* always refers to the female body. Attractive male bodies are described as "handsome," a word derived from "hand" that refers as much to action as appearance (Freedman, 1986). Qualities of achievement and strength accompany the term *handsome;* such attributes are rarely employed in the description of attractive women and certainly do not accompany the term *beauty,* which refers only to a decorative quality. Men are instrumental; women are ornamental.

Beauty is a most elusive commodity. Ideas of what is beautiful vary across cultures and change over time (Fallon, 1990). Beauty cannot be quantified or objectively measured; it is the result of the judgments of others. The concept is difficult to define, as it is equated with different, sometimes contradictory, ideas. When people are asked to define beauty, they tend to mention abstract, personal qualities rather than external, quantifiable ones (Freedman, 1986; Hatfield & Sprecher, 1986). The beholder's perceptions and cognitions influence the degree of attractiveness at least as much as do the qualities of the beheld.

Because beauty is an ideal, an absolute, such as truth and goodness, the pursuit of it does not require justification (Herman & Polivy, 1983). An ideal, by definition, can be met by only a minority of those who strive for it. If too many women are able to meet the beauty standards of a particular time and place, then those standards must change in order to maintain their extraordinary nature. The value of beauty standards depends on their being special and unusual and is one of the reasons why the ideal changes over time. When images of beauty change, female bodies are expected to change, too. Different aspects of the female body and varying images of each body part are modified to meet the constantly fluctuating ideal (Freedman, 1986). The ideal is always that which is most difficult to achieve and most unnatural in a given time period. Because these ideals are nearly impossible to achieve, failure and disappointment are inevitable (Freedman, 1988).

Although people have been decorating their bodies since prehistoric times, the Chinese may have been the first to develop the concept that the female body can and should be altered from its natural state. The practice of foot binding clearly illustrates the objectification of parts of the female body as well as the demands placed on women to conform to beauty ideals. The custom called for the binding of the feet of five-year-old girls so that as they grew, their toes became permanently twisted under their arches and would actually shrink in size. The big toe remained untouched. The more tightly bound the feet, the more petite they became and the more attractive they were considered to be (Freedman, 1986; Hatfield & Sprecher, 1986; Lakoff & Scherr, 1984). The painful custom of foot binding finally ended in the twentieth century after women had endured over one thousand years of torture for beauty's sake (Brain, 1979).

In the sixteenth century, European women bound themselves into corsets of whalebone and hardened canvas. A piece of metal or wood ran down the front to flatten the breasts and abdomen. This garment made it impossible to bend at the waist and difficult to breathe. A farthingale, which was typically worn over the corset, held women's skirts out from their bodies. It consisted of bent wood held together with tapes and made such simple activities as sitting nearly impossible. Queen Catherine of France introduced waist binding with a tortuous invention consisting of iron bands that minimized the size of the waist to the ideal measurement of thirteen inches (Baker, 1984). In the seventeenth century, the waist was still laced, but breasts were once again stylish, and fashions were designed to enhance them. Ample breasts, hips, and buttocks became the beauty ideal, perhaps paralleling a generally warmer attitude toward family life (Rosenblatt & Stencel, 1982). A white pallor was also popular at that time, probably as an indication that the woman was so affluent that she did not need to work outdoors, where the sun might darken her skin. Ceruse, a white lead-based paint now known to be toxic, was used to accentuate the pallor.

Tight corsets came back into vogue in Europe and North America in the mid-nineteenth century, and many women were willing to run the risk of developing serious health problems in order to wear them. The tight lacing often led to pulmonary disease and internal organ damage. American women disregarded the advice of their physicians, who spoke against the use of corsets because of their potential to displace internal organs. Fainting, or "the vapors," was the result of wearing such tightly laced clothing that normal breathing became impossible. Even the clergy sermonized against corsets; miscarriages were known to result in pregnant women who insisted on lacing themselves up too tightly. In the late nineteenth century, the beauty ideal required a tiny waist and full hips and bustline. Paradoxically, women would go on diets to gain weight while, at the same time, trying to achieve a smaller waistline. Some women were reported to have had their lower ribs removed so that their waists could be more tightly laced (Brain, 1979).

In the twentieth century, the ideal female body has changed several times, and American women have struggled to change along with it. In the 1920s, the ideal had slender legs and hips, small breasts, and bobbed hair and was physically and socially active. Women removed the stuffing from their bodices and bound their breasts[1] to appear young and boyish. In the 1940s and 1950s, the ideal returned to the hourglass shape. Marilyn Monroe was considered the epitome of the voluptuous and fleshy yet naive and childlike ideal. In the 1960s, the ideal had a youthful, thin, lean body and long, straight hair. American women dieted relentlessly in an attempt to emulate the tall, thin, teenage model Twiggy, who personified the 1960s' beauty ideal. Even pregnant women were on diets in response to their doctors' orders not to gain more than twenty pounds, advice physicians later rejected as unsafe (Fallon, 1990). Menopausal women begged their physicians to prescribe hormone replacement therapy, which was rumored to prevent wrinkles and keep the body youthful, and were willing to run any health risk to preserve their appearance (Chrisler, Torrey, & Matthes, 1989). In the 1970s, a thin, tan, sensuous look was "in." The 1980s' beauty ideal remained slim but required a more muscular, toned, and physically fit body. In recent decades the beauty ideal has combined such opposite traits as erotic sophistication with naive innocence, delicate grace with muscular athleticism (Freedman, 1988), and thin bodies with large breasts. The pressure to cope with such conflicting demands and to keep up with the continual changes in the ideal female body is highly stressful (Freedman, 1988) and has resulted in a large majority of American women with negative body images (Dworkin & Kerr, 1987; Rosen, Saltzberg, & Srebnik, 1989). Women's insecurity about their looks has made it easy to convince them that small breasts are a "disease" that require surgical intervention. The sophisticated woman of the 1990s who is willing to accept the significant health risks of breast implants in order to mold her body to fit the beauty ideal has not progressed far beyond her sisters who bound their feet and waists.

The value of beauty depends in part on the high costs of achieving it. Such costs may be physical, temporal, economic, or psychological. Physical costs include the pain of ancient beauty rituals such as foot binding, tattooing, and nose and ear piercing as well as more modern rituals such as wearing pointy-toed, high-heeled shoes, tight jeans, and sleeping with one's hair in curlers. Side effects of beauty rituals have often been disastrous for women's health. Tattooing and ear piercing with unsanitary instruments have lead to serious, sometimes fatal, infections. Many women have been poisoned by toxic chemicals in cosmetics (e.g., ceruse, arsenic, benzene, and petroleum) and have died from the use of unsafe diet products such as rainbow pills and liquid protein (Schwartz, 1986). The beauty-related disorders anorexia nervosa and bulimia have multiple negative health effects, and side effects of plastic surgery include hemorrhages, scars, and nerve damage. Silicone implants have resulted in breast cancer, autoimmune disease, and the formation of thick scar tissue.

Physical costs of dieting include a constant feeling of hunger that leads to emotional changes, such as irritability; in cases of very low caloric intake, dieters can experience difficulty concentrating, confusion, and even reduced cognitive capacity. The only growing group of smokers in the United States are young women, many of whom report that they smoke to curb their appetites (Sorensen & Pechacek, 1987). High heels cause lower back pain and lead to a variety of podiatric disorders. Furthermore, fashion trends have increased women's vulnerability in a variety of ways; long hair and dangling earrings have gotten caught in machinery and entangled in clothing and led to injury. High heels and tight skirts prevent women from running from danger. The *New York Times* fashion reporter Bernardine Morris was alarmed to see in Pierre Cardin's 1988 summer fashion show tight wraps that prevented the models from moving their arms (Morris, 1988).

Attaining the beauty ideal requires a lot of money. Expensive cosmetics (e.g., makeup, moisturizers, and hair dyes and straighteners) are among the most popular and are thought to be the most effective, even though their ingredients cost the same (and sometimes are the same) as those in less expensive products (Lakoff & Scherr, 1984). Health spas have become fashionable again as vacation spots for the rich and famous, and everyone wants to wear expensive clothing with designer labels. Plastic surgery has become so accepted and so common that, although it's quite expensive, surgeons advertise their services on television. Surgery is currently performed that can reduce the size of lips, ear lobes, noses, buttocks, thighs, abdomens, and breasts; rebuild a face; remove wrinkles; and add "padding" to almost any body part. Not surprisingly, most plastic surgery patients are women (Hamburger, 1988).

Beauty rituals are time-consuming activities. Jokes about how long women take to get ready for a date are based on the additional tasks women do when getting dressed. It takes time to pluck eyebrows, shave legs, manicure nails, apply makeup, and arrange hair. Women's clothing is more complicated than men's, and many more accessories are used. Although all women know that the "transformation from female to feminine is artificial" (Chapkis, 1986, p. 5), we conspire to hide the amount of time and effort it takes, perhaps out of fear that other women don't need as much time as we do to appear beautiful. A lot of work goes into looking like a "natural" beauty, but that work is not acknowledged by popular culture, and the tools of the trade are kept out of view. Men's grooming rituals are fewer, take less time, and need not be hidden away. Scenes of men shaving have often been seen on television and in movies and have even been painted by Norman Rockwell. Wendy Chapkis (1986) challenges her readers to "imagine a similar cultural celebration of a woman plucking her eyebrows, shaving her armpits, or waxing her upper lip" (p. 6). Such a scene would be shocking and would remove the aura of mystery that surrounds beautiful women.

Psychological effects of the pursuit of the perfect female body include unhappiness, confusion, misery, and insecurity. Women often believe that if only they had perfect looks, their lives would be perfectly happy; they blame their unhappiness on their bodies. American women have the most negative body image of any culture studied by the Kinsey Institute (Faludi, 1991). Dissatisfaction with their bodies is very common among adolescent girls

(Adams & Crossman, 1978; Clifford, 1971; Freedman, 1984), and older women believe that the only way to remain attractive is to prevent the development of any signs of aging. Obsessive concern about body shape and weight have become so common among American women of all ages that they now constitute the norm (Rodin, Silberstein, & Striegel-Moore, 1985). The majority of women in the United States are dieting at any given time. For them, being female means feeling fat and inadequate and living with chronic low self-esteem (Rodin, et al., 1985). Ask any woman what she would like to change about her body and she'll answer immediately. Ask her what she likes about her body and she'll have difficulty responding.

Those women who do succeed in matching the ideal thinness expected by modern beauty standards usually do so by exercising frenetically and compulsively, implementing severely restrictive and nutritionally deficient diets, developing bizarre eating habits, and using continuous self-degradation and self-denial. Dieting has become a "cultural requirement" for women (Herman & Polivy, 1983) because the ideal female body has become progressively thinner at the same time that the average female body has become progressively heavier. This cultural requirement remains in place despite the fact that physiology works against weight loss to such an extent that 98 percent of diets fail (Chrisler, 1989; Fitzgerald, 1981). In fact, it is more likely for someone to fully recover from cancer than for an obese person to lose a significant amount of weight and maintain that loss for five years (Brownell, 1982). Yet a recent study (Davies & Furnham, 1986) found that young women rate borderline anorexic bodies as very attractive. Thus, even the thinnest women find it nearly impossible to meet and maintain the beauty ideal.

The social pressure for thinness can be directly linked to the increasing incidence of anorexia nervosa and bulimia among women (Brumberg, 1988; Caskey, 1986). There are presently at least one million Americans with anorexia nervosa, and 95 percent of them are women. Between sixty thousand and 150,000 of them will die as a result of their obsession (Schwartz, 1986). Although cases of anorexia nervosa have been reported in the medical literature for hundreds of years (Bell, 1985), it was considered to be a rare disorder until the 1970s. Today's anorexics are also thinner than they were in the past (Brumberg, 1988). It is estimated that at least seven million American women will experience symptoms of bulimia at some point in their lives (Hatfield & Sprecher, 1986). A recent study (Hall & Cohn, 1988) found that 25 to 33 percent of female first-year college students were using vomiting after meals as a method of weight control. An accurate estimate of the number of women who are caught in the binge-purge cycle is difficult because women with bulimia are generally secretive about their behavior and the physical signs of bulimia are not nearly are obvious as those of anorexia nervosa.

Exercise has become for many women another manifestation of their body dissatisfaction. Studies have found that most men who exercise regularly do so to build body mass and to increase cardiovascular fitness; most women who exercise do so to lose weight and to change the shape of their bodies in order to increase their attractiveness (Garner, Rockert, Olmstead, Johnson, & Coscina, 1985; Saltzberg, 1990). Exercise has lost its status as a pleasurable activity and become yet another way for women to manipulate their bodies, another vehicle for narcissistic self-torture. Reports of the number of women exercising compulsively are increasing and may become as widespread as compulsive calorie counting and the compulsive eating habits of anorexics and bulimics.

Beauty ideals are created and maintained by society's elite. Racism, class prejudice, and rejection of the disabled are clearly reflected (Chapkis, 1986) in current American beauty standards. For example, women from lower socioeconomic groups typically weigh more than women in higher socio-economic groups (Moore, Stunkard, & Srole, 1962); they are thus excluded by popular agreement from being considered beautiful. The high costs of chic clothing, cosmetics, tanning salons, skin and hair treatments, weight loss programs, and plastic surgery prevent most American women from access to the tools necessary to approach the ideal. Furthermore, the beauty standard idealizes Caucasian features and devalues those of other races (Lewis, 1977; Miller, 1969). In recent years, Asian American and African-American women have sought facial surgery in order to come closer to the beauty ideal (Faludi, 1991), and psychotherapists have noted increased reports from their black women clients of guilt, shame, anger, and resentment about skin color, hair texture, facial features, and body size and shape (Greene, 1992; Neal & Wilson, 1989; Okazawa-Rey, Robinson, & Ward, 1987). Obviously, women with visible disabilities will never be judged to have achieved "perfection." Whoopi Goldberg's routine about the black teenager who wrapped a towel around her head to pretend it was long, blonde hair and Alice Walker's (1990) essay about her psychological adjustment after the eye injury that resulted in the development of "hideous" scar tissue provide poignant examples of the pain women experience when they cannot meet beauty standards.

The inordinate emphasis on women's external selves makes it difficult for us to appreciate our own internal selves (Kano, 1985). The constant struggle to meet the beauty ideal leads to high stress and chronic anxiety. Failure to meet the beauty ideal leads to feelings of frustration, low self-worth, and inadequacy in women whose sense of self is based on their physical appearance. The intensity of the drive to increase attractiveness may also contribute to the high rate of depression among women.[2]

Insecurity is common even among beautiful women, and studies show that they are as likely as their plain sisters to be unhappy about their looks (Freedman, 1988). Beautiful women are all too aware of the fleeting nature of their beauty; the effects of aging must be constantly monitored, and these women worry that the beauty ideal they've tried so hard to match may change without warning. When such women lose their beauty due to illness or accidents, they often become depressed and are likely to have difficulty functioning in society and to believe that their entire identity has been threatened.

Given the high costs of striving to be beautiful, why do women attempt it? Attractiveness greatly affects first impressions and later interpersonal relationships. In a classic study titled "What Is Beautiful Is Good," psychologists Kenneth Dion, Ellen Berscheid, and Elaine Walster Hatfield (1972) asked college students to rate photographs of strangers on a variety of personal characteristics. Those who were judged to be attractive were also more likely to be rated intelligent, kind, happy, flexible, interesting, confident, sexy, assertive, strong, outgoing, friendly, poised, modest, candid, and successful than those judged unattractive. Teachers rate attractive children more highly on a variety of positive characteristics including IQ and sociability, and attractive babies are cuddled and kissed more often than unattractive babies (Berscheid & Walster, 1974). Attractive people receive more lenient punishment for social transgressions (Dion, 1972; Landy & Aronson, 1969), and attractive women are more often sought out in social situations (Walster, Aronson, Abrahams, & Rottman, 1966; Reis, Nezlek, & Wheeler, 1980).

Furthermore, because unattractive people are more harshly punished for social transgressions and are less often sought after social partners, failure to work toward the beauty ideal can result in real consequences. Television newswoman Christine Craft made the news herself when she was fired for being too old and too unattractive. Street harassers put women "in their place" by commenting loudly on their beauty or lack of it. Beauty norms limit the opportunities of women who can't or won't meet them. Obese women, for example, have experienced discrimination in a number of instances including hiring and promotion (Larkin & Pines, 1979; Rothblum, Miller, & Gorbutt, 1988) and college admissions (Canning & Mayer, 1966). Obese people even have a harder time finding a place to live; Lambros Karris (1977) found that landlords are less likely to rent to obese people. Even physicians view their obese patients negatively (Maddox & Liederman, 1969).

There is considerable evidence that women's attractiveness is judged more harshly than men's. Christine Craft was fired, yet David Brinkley and Willard Scott continue to work on major television news shows; their abilities are not thought to be affected by age or attractiveness. Several studies (Adams & Huston, 1975; Berman, O'Nan, & Floyd, 1981; Deutsch, Zalenski, & Clark, 1986; Wernick & Manaster, 1984) that asked participants to rate the attractiveness of photographs of people of varying ages found that although attractiveness ratings of both men and women decline with age, the rate of decline for women was greater. In one study (Deutsch, Zalenski, & Clark, 1986), participants were asked to rate the photographs for femininity and masculinity as well as attractiveness. The researchers found that both the attractiveness and femininity ratings of the female photographs diminished with age; the masculinity ratings were unaffected by the age or attractiveness of the photographs. Women are acutely aware of the double standard of attractiveness. At all ages women are more concerned than men about weight and physical appearance and have lower appearance self-esteem; women who define themselves as feminine are the most concerned about their appearance and have the lowest self-esteem (Pliner, Chaiken, & Flett, 1990). In fact, women are so concerned about their body size that they typically overestimate it. Women who overestimate their size feel worse about themselves, whereas men's self-esteem is unrelated to their body size estimates (Thompson, 1986). In a review of research on the stigma of obesity, Esther Rothblum (1992) concluded that the dieting industry, combined with Western attitudes toward weight and attractiveness, causes more pain and problems for women than for men.

Thus, the emphasis on beauty has political as well as psychological consequences for women, as it results in oppression and disempowerment. It is important for women to examine the effects that the pursuit of the perfect female body has had on their lives, challenge their beliefs, and take a stand against continued enslavement to the elusive beauty ideal. Women would then be able to live life more freely and experience the world more genuinely. Each woman must decide for herself what beauty really is and the extent to which she is willing to go to look attractive. Only a more diverse view of beauty and a widespread rebellion against fashion extremes will save us from further physical and psychological tolls.

Imagine an American society where the quality and meaning of life for women are not dependent on the silence of bodily shame. Imagine a society where bodies are decorated for fun and to express creativity rather than for self-control and self-worth. Imagine what would happen if the world's women released and liberated all of the energy that had been absorbed in the beautification process. The result might be the positive, affirming, healthy version of a nuclear explosion!

REFERENCES

Adams, Gerald R., & Crossman, Sharyn M. (1978). *Physical attractiveness: A cultural imperative.* New York: Libra.

Adams, Gerald R., & Huston, Ted L. (1975). Social perception of middle-aged persons varying in physical attractiveness. *Developmental Psychology, 11,* 657–58.

Baker, Nancy C. (1984). *The beauty trap: Exploring woman's greatest obsession.* New York: Franklin Watts.

Bell, Rudolph M. (1985). *Holy anorexia.* Chicago: University of Chicago Press.

Berman, Phyllis W., O'Nan, Barbara A., & Floyd, Wayne. (1981). The double standard of aging and the social situation: Judgments of attractiveness of the middle-aged woman. *Sex Roles, 7,* 87–96.

Berscheid, Ellen, & Walster, Elaine. (1974). Physical attractiveness. *Advances in Experimental Social Psychology, 7,* 158–215.

Bierce, Ambrose. (1958). *The devil's dictionary.* New York: Dover.

Brain, R. (1979). *The decorated body.* New York: Harper & Row.

Brownell, Kelly. (1982). Obesity: Understanding and treating a serious, prevalent, and refractory disorder. *Journal of Consulting and Clinical Psychology, 55,* 889–97.

Brumberg, Joan J. (1988). *Fasting girls.* Cambridge, MA: Harvard University Press.

Canning, H., & Mayer, J. (1966). Obesity: An influence on high school performance. *Journal of Clinical Nutrition, 20,* 352–54.

Caskey, Noelle. (1986). Interpreting anorexia nervosa. In Susan R. Suleiman (Ed.), *The female body in western culture* (pp. 175–89). Cambridge, MA: Harvard University Press.

Chapkis, Wendy. (1986). *Beauty secrets: Women and the politics of appearance.* Boston: South End Press.

Chrisler, Joan C. (1989). Should feminist therapists do weight loss counseling? *Women & Therapy, 8*(3), 31–37.

Chrisler, Joan C. , Torrey, Jane W., & Matthes, Michelle. (1989, June). *Brittle bones and sagging breasts, loss of femininity and loss of sanity: The media describe the menopause.* Paper presented at the meeting of the Society for Menstrual Cycle Research, Salt Lake City, UT.

Clifford, Edward. (1971). Body satisfaction in adolescence. *Perceptual and Motor Skills, 33,* 119–25.

Davies, Elizabeth, & Furnham, Adrian. (1986). The dieting and body shape concerns of adolescent females. *Child Psychology and Psychiatry, 27,* 417–28.

Deutsch, Francine M., Zalenski, Carla M., & Clark, Mary E. (1986). Is there a double standard of aging? *Journal of Applied Social Psychology, 16,* 771–85.

Dion, Kenneth K. (1972). Physical attractiveness and evaluation of children's transgressions. *Journal of Personality and Social Psychology, 24,* 285–90.

Dion, Kenneth, Berscheid, Ellen, & Walster [Hatfield], Elaine. (1972). What is beautiful is good. *Journal of Personality and Social Psychology, 24,* 285–90.

Dworkin, Sari H., & Kerr, Barbara A. (1987). Comparison of interventions for women experiencing body image problems. *Journal of Consulting and Clinical Psychology, 34,* 136–40.

Fallon, April. (1990). Culture in the mirror: Sociocultural determinants of body image. In Thomas Cash & Thomas Pruzinsky (Eds.), *Body images: Development, deviance, and change* (pp. 80–109). New York: Guilford Press.

Faludi, Susan. (1991). *Backlash: The undeclared war against American women.* New York: Crown Publishers.

Fitzgerald, Faith T. (1981). The problem of obesity. *Annual Review of Medicine, 32,* 221–31.

Freedman, Rita. (1984). Reflections on beauty as it relates to health in adolescent females. In Sharon Golub (Ed.), *Health care of the female adolescent* (pp. 29–45). New York: Haworth Press.

Freedman, Rita. (1986). *Beauty bound.* Lexington, MA: D. C. Heath.

Freedman, Rita. (1988). *Bodylove: Learning to like our looks—and ourselves.* New York: Harper & Row.

Garner, David M., Rockert, Wendy, Olmstead, Marion P., Johnson, C., & Coscina, D. V. (1985). Psychoeducational principles in the treatment of bulimia and anorexia nervosa. In David M. Garner & Paul E. Garfinkel (Eds.), *Handbook of psychotherapy for anorexia nervosa and bulimia* (pp. 513–62). New York: Guilford.

Greene, Beverly. (1992). Still here: A perspective on psychotherapy with African American women. In Joan C. Chrisler & Doris Howard (Eds.), *New directions in feminist psychology: Practice, theory, and research* (pp. 13–25). New York: Springer.

Hall, L., & Cohn, L. (1988). *Bulimia: A guide to recovery.* Carlsbad, CA: Gurze Books.

Hamburger, A. C. (1988, May). Beauty Quest. *Psychology Today, 22,* 28–32.

Hatfield, Elaine, & Sprecher, Susan. (1986). *Mirror, mirror: The importance of looks in everyday life.* Albany: State University of New York Press.

Herman, Peter, & Polivy, Janet. (1983). *Breaking the diet habit.* New York: Basic Books.

Ignoring the economy, cosmetic firms look to growth. (1989, July 13). *Standard and Poor's Industry Surveys, 1,* 37–38.

Kano, Susan. (1985). *Making peace with food: A step-by-step guide to freedom from diet/weight conflict.* Danbury, CT: Amity.

Karris, Lambros. (1977). Prejudice against obese renters. *Journal of Social Psychology, 101,* 159–60.

Lakoff, Robin T., & Scherr, Raquel L. (1984). *Face value: The politics of beauty.* Boston: Routledge & Kegan Paul.

Landy, David, & Aronson, Elliot. (1969). The influence of the character of the criminal and his victim on the decisions of simulated jurors. *Journal of Experimental Social Psychology, 5,* 141–52.

Larkin, Judith, & Pines, Harvey. (1979). No fat person need apply. *Sociology of Work and Occupations, 6,* 312–27.

Lewis, Diane K. (1977). A response to inequality: Black women, racism, and sexism. *Signs, 3*(2), 339–61.

Maddox, G., & Liederman, V. (1969). Overweight as a social disability with medical implications. *Journal of Medical Education, 44,* 214–20.

Miller, E. (1969). Body image, physical beauty, and color among Jamaican adolescents. *Social and Economic Studies, 18*(1), 72–89.

Moore, M. E., Stunkard, Albert, & Srole, L. (1962). Obesity, social class, and mental illness. *Journal of the American Medical Association, 181,* 138–42.

Morris, Bernardine. (1988, July 26). Paris couture: Opulence lights a serious mood. *New York Times,* p. B8.

Neal, Angela, & Wilson, Midge. (1989). The role of skin color and features in the black community: Implications for black women and therapy. *Clinical Psychology Review, 9,* 323–33.

Okazawa-Rey, Margo, Robinson, Tracy, & Ward, Janie V. (1987). Black women and the politics of skin color and hair. *Women & Therapy, 6*(1/2), 89–102.

Pliner, Patricia, Chaiken, Shelly, & Flett, Gordon L. (1990). Gender differences in concern with body weight and physical appearance over the life span. *Personality and Social Psychology Bulletin, 16,* 263–73.

Reis, Harry T., Nezlek, John, & Wheeler, Ladd. (1980). Physical attractiveness in social interaction. *Journal of Personality and Social Psychology, 38,* 604–17.

Rodin, Judith, Silberstein, Lisa, & Striegel-Moore, Ruth. (1985). Women and weight: A normative discontent. In Theo B. Sonderegger (Ed.), *Nebraska symposium on motivation: Psychology and gender* (pp. 267–307). Lincoln: University of Nebraska Press.

Rosen, James C., Saltzberg, Elayne A., & Srebnik, Debra. (1989). Cognitive behavior therapy for negative body image. *Behavior Therapy, 20,* 393–404.

Rosenblatt, J., & Stencel, S. (1982). *Weight control: A natural obsession.* Washington, DC: Congressional Quarterly.

Rothblum, Esther D. (1992). The stigma of women's weight: Social and economic realities. *Feminism & Psychology, 2*(1), 61–73.

Rothblum, Esther D., Miller, Carol, & Gorbutt, Barbara. (1988). Stereotypes of obese female job applicants. *International Journal of Eating Disorders, 7,* 277–83.

Saltzberg, Elayne A. (1990). *Exercise participation and its correlates to body awareness and self-esteem.* Unpublished master's thesis, Connecticut College, New London, CT.

Schwartz, Hillel. (1986). *Never satisfied: A cultural history of diets, fantasies, and fat.* New York: Free Press.

Sorensen, Gloria, & Pechacek, Terry F. (1987). Attitudes toward smoking cessation among men and women. *Journal of Behavioral Medicine, 10,* 129–38.

Stoffel, Jennifer. (1989, November 26). What's new in weight control: A market mushrooms as motivations change. *New York Times,* p. C17.

Thompson, J. Kevin. (1986, April). Larger than life. *Psychology Today,* pp. 41–44.

Walker, Alice. (1990). Beauty: When the other dancer is the self. In Evelyn C. White (Ed.), *The black women's health book: Speaking for ourselves* (pp. 280–87). Seattle: Seal Press.

Walster, Elaine, Aronsen, Vera, Abrahams, Darcy, & Rottman, Leon. (1966). Importance of physical attractiveness in dating behavior. *Journal of Personality and Social Psychology, 4,* 508–16.

Wernick, Mark, & Manaster, Guy J. (1984). Age and the perception of age and attractiveness. *Gerontologist, 24,* 408–14.

Williams, Juanita H. (1985). *Psychology of women: Behavior in a biosocial context.* New York: Norton.

NOTES

1. Bras were originally designed to hide breasts.
2. Statistics indicate that women are far more likely than men to be diagnosed as depressed. The ratio is at least 3 : 1 (Williams, 1985).

13

THE UGLY SIDE OF THE MODELING BUSINESS

DEBORAH GREGORY AND PATRICIA JACOBS

On a chilly afternoon last winter, the atmosphere inside Club USA— one of New York City's hottest nightspots—matched the outdoor temperature, but for a different reason: America's Black supermodels were in revolt. The Black Girls Coalition (BGC), a consortium of fashion models formed in 1988 by supermodel Iman and former model Bethann Hardison (now owner of the modeling agency Bethann Management Co., Inc.) to aid the homeless, had chosen this site for a press conference to speak out on an issue that's been hidden beneath the glamour and glitter of the profession: namely, racism within the fashion and modeling business.

About 20 strong, almost all of BGC's members were in attendance— among them Karen Alexander, Cynthia Bailey, Tyra Banks, Kersti Bowser, Naomi Campbell, Peggy Dillard, Iman, Coco Mitchell, Gail O'Neill, Beverly Peele, Phina, Karla Otis, Akure Wall, Veronica Webb, Roshumba Williams and the designated leader, Bethann Hardison.

Also present were more than 100 members of the press representing Black and White American and European publications, who got an earful from the Black beauties gathered to expose the industry's ugly side.

From *Essence,* September 1993. Reprinted by permission of Deborah Gregory.

Accustomed to being seen and not heard, the models—who for the most part were stripped of their ready-to-work glamour-girl makeup—nonetheless took their turn at the podium and spoke candidly about the everyday injustices that exist within their "workplace."

Among the specific grievances addressed: the gross underrepresentation of African-Americans in fashion advertising (television commercials, billboards, magazines, catalogs, in-store promotions), designer shows and even the editorial pages of consumer magazines. "People don't realize there are hundreds of jobs related to the fashion industry, from being a makeup artist to scouting locations for a photo shoot," said a Black fashion editor at a women's magazine. "But you can practically count on both hands the number of Blacks who have any of these jobs in what's become a very closed arena." This is despite the fact that collectively African-Americans spend over $16 *billion* on clothing annually, according to the Consumer Expenditure Survey, and will represent approximately 13 percent of the total population by the year 2000, according to the U.S. Census Bureau.

What Price Beauty?

As "soldiers" at the forefront of the style wars, the models also expressed outrage at other more subtle but unmistakable signs of racism that exist in their field: everything from the lack of Black behind-the-scenes fashion personnel—art directors, editors, designers, photographers—to being controlled around the clock right down to how they wear their locks, or indeed, told whether or not they can even wear "locks." Many, instead, are forced to wear wigs, falls and weaves.

"In more than ten years as a model," explained Coco Mitchell, "I've always had to look like what other people wanted me to look like, never how I wanted to." Most of the models admitted to being under pressure to have flowing hair that emulates that of the White models. Two have refused to give in to such pressure, however: Roshumba Williams and British-born Phina both wear their hair natural and closely cropped. Phina, in fact, stepped on these shores wearing her hair in spiky twists. "I wear my hair like this because I want to—not because I am militant, as I am so often told," she explains. "I think it's really sad that time and time again I'm asked to adhere to a certain look or value that is justifiable only to certain people." Adds Roshumba, "I'm constantly arriving at a photographer's studio and being told that I have to wear a wig." Roshumba, though, is one of the few Black models who still gets a lot of work while sporting her short natural.

The grievances of the Black models were dramatically supported in a groundbreaking study conducted by the City of New York's Department of Consumer Affairs in 1991. The report, titled "Invisible People," looked at how often Blacks and other ethnic groups were used in magazine and catalog advertising—and the findings were shocking. A paltry 3.4 percent of all consumer-magazine advertisements depicted African-Americans—despite the fact that we comprise approximately 11.3 percent of the readership of all consumer magazines and 12.5 percent of the U.S. population.

In addition to its study, New York City's Department of Consumer Affairs conducted a special survey of repeat advertisers in 634 issues of general-circulation magazines and found that some of the most prolific fashion advertisers rarely, if ever, depict Blacks (or Asian-Americans) in their ads. And when they do, it is usually as stereotypes, not consumers. The companies included Calvin Klein (out of 148 ad insertions reviewed, none depicted "identifiable minorities"), Perry Ellis, Giorgio Armani, Gucci and Guess? by Georges Marciano. In the case of Calvin Klein, one of his ad campaigns in particular—which features White rapper Marky Mark and White model Kate Moss profiling in low-slung, oversize jeans—doesn't exactly have the rap-music community singing "Hip-hop hooray." After all, it was the Black rappers who created—and still perpetuate—the urbanized, flavorized look, yet no major advertising campaigns have come their way.

When asked about the Marky Mark advertising campaign, Calvin Klein asserted that "it wasn't about Marky Mark being a White or Black rapper, but more about his body than his music. He had been wearing the underwear in his concerts and the ads were capitalizing on something he started." Marky Mark's latest contract with Klein is triple the amount of the first—and Klein's sales are up about 30 percent.

One of the reasons that the gross inequity in fashion advertisements persists, says Consumer Affairs Commissioner Mark Green, is that the Department of Consumer Affairs has no legal jurisdiction to require that ads reflect the racial makeup of magazine readership in America. There are also no laws on the books that require advertisers to "fill quotas," although according to a survey of 470 marketing and media executives conducted by *Advertising Age,* the trade publication for the advertising industry, 54.8 percent agreed that there were too few Blacks in print ads, period.

The Effect on Self-Esteem

There can be no doubt that the exclusion of Blacks from ads has had a negative impact, especially on our youths, who often feel little connection to the larger society. According to Marilyn Kern-Foxworth, a journalism professor at Texas A&M University and the author of an upcoming book on Blacks in advertising, "There's been a drastic erosion of self-esteem with young African-Americans—and it's partially because the images they see of themselves are either negative, offensive or not there." Adds Michele Wallace, author of the book *Invisibility Blues: From Pop to Theory* (Routledge, 1990), "Not seeing our images reproduced—in particular in ads that constitute such a visible medium in our society—suggests to our children that we have no power, that having power is inconceivable."

Other areas of inequity, the models say, are fashion shows and even fashion layouts in magazines—and most notably fashion-magazine covers, on which Black models are rarely seen. For example, supermodel Tyra Banks, who has appeared on 17 magazine covers in Europe, has graced only two in the United States (including the June 1993 issue of this magazine). During the press conference for *Sports Illustrated*'s venerable swimsuit issue last winter, Banks, who was the only Black model featured in the issue, noted that *Sports Illustrated* has never had a Black or Asian model on the cover of the swimsuit issue in its nearly 30 years of publishing the special issue.

As for designer shows, at the fall–winter 1993 collections that took place in March in New York City, fewer Black models were seen on the runways than in any recent season gone by. (Coincidentally, many Black supermodels were seen for the first time in years either without weaves or with drastically shorter weaves—including Naomi Campbell and Beverly Peele.) Calvin Klein's collection, for example, featured only one model of color, Aya Thorgren, who is also one of the three models to appear in Revlon's ColorStyle ads. White designer Jennifer George, however, bucked the current grunge trend and tomboy, waiflike wave of innocent White models by using almost all Black models to show her collection.

One Black model who can afford to take a more militant position and turn down jobs from designers she considers racist is supermodel Naomi Campbell. "What I've started to do with certain designers who simply say they don't want Black girls—not individual models—is not do their shows and not wear their clothes, even in editorials [magazine fashion layouts that feature the clothes of a particular designer]," Campbell said at the BGC press conference. "I don't see why we [Black models] should make their clothes look good and then not be represented by them in any way." Campbell, however, one of the most popular and highest-paid models of any color in the industry, is still in demand, even when she turns down work. This is a claim few other Black models can make, and it limits their ability to take controversial stands.

On the Good Side

It would be unfair and inaccurate to suggest that there has been *no* progress for Blacks in the fashion industry during the last few years. Witness, for instance, the spanking-new Armani Exchange (AX) billboards and fashion ads profiling the cool beauty of Marvin Gaye's daughter, Nona Gaye. Or the new Ralph Lauren Safari fragrance campaign with Tyra Banks (one of the first high-profile designer-fragrance campaigns depicting a Black model in recent history) resplendent in florals amid colonial African chic. Or Liz Claiborne Jewelry ads (also with Tyra). Fernando Sanchez's lingerie ads feature sultry Kara Young, and Roshumba Williams is on the pages of the Tweeds catalogs and in the Robert Lee Morris jewelry ads for Saks Fifth Avenue. On the downside, however, none of these manufacturers advertises in any of the Black publications.

The beauty industry, which has been somewhat better than the fashion industry in recognizing the financial clout of Black women, made history when some of the biggest cosmetics firms all launched major advertising campaigns featuring products for Black women: Maybelline (Shades of You), Cover Girl and Revlon (ColorStyle). Even better: Both Revlon and Cover Girl awarded Black supermodels Veronica Webb and Lana Ogilvie, respectively, exclusive contracts to advertise their products—a lucrative domain previously reserved for such White supermodels as Christy Turlington and Linda Evangelista.

In the final analysis, what it all comes down to is power—the power to change the things we can, and the power to choose what we will change. We can choose the clothes, accessories and beauty products we buy, for instance. And we can write letters to fashion and beauty manufacturers if those products or publications don't reflect our image.

Unfortunately, when approached by New York City's Department of Consumer Affairs following its study on the lack of people of color in print advertising, not one magazine or non-Black ad agency or advertiser would agree to sign a general pledge to depict people of color more accurately on their pages and in their advertisements. "We can only hope that our new appeal to advertisers will encourage them to act in their own economic interest as well as in the public interest by including more people of color in their product promotions," stated Commissioner Mark Green. "Ad agencies can exert considerable influence on the selection of models used in ads, but advertisers pay the bills and ultimately call the shots." And as Bethann Hardison points out, "It's a rare White person who helps people of color forge ahead. We have to raise their consciousness and appeal to their humanity."

The Black male model Alvin Clayton-Fernandes does not order from those mail-order catalogs that never or seldom use Black male models. Civil-rights attorney Flo Kennedy believes in the power of the boycott: "If Blacks aren't represented in a particular clothing company's advertisements, don't buy from them," she says simply.

Ultimately, as consumers we can decide where to spend our fashion dollars. Now, more than ever, there are African-American designers manufacturing style that's available at retail or in catalogs or can be custom-made. From hip-hop gear to glamour gowns, African-American designers, such as Cross Colours, Byron Lars, Tracy Reese for Magaschoni, Shaka King and Ahneva Ahneva in California, are at the forefront of our style.

Only when "buying Black" becomes a regular part of our economic lifestyle will mainstream style setters get the message and recognize that racism is not only out of fashion in the beauty business but also will not be tolerated by all those people of color who help keep the bottom line black in a multi-billion-dollar clothing industry.

14

"A WAY OUTA NO WAY"
Eating Problems among African-American, Latina, and White Women

BECKY W. THOMPSON

Bulimia, anorexia, binging, and extensive dieting are among the many health issues women have been confronting in the last 20 years. Until recently, however, there has been almost no research about eating problems among African-American, Latina, Asian-American, or Native American women, working-class women, or lesbians.[1] In fact, according to the normative epidemiological portrait, eating problems are largely a white, middle- and upper-class heterosexual phenomenon. Further, while feminist research has documented how eating problems are fueled by sexism, there has been almost no attention to how other systems of oppression may also be implicated in the development of eating problems.

In this article, I reevaluate the portrayal of eating problems as issues of appearance based in the "culture of thinness." I propose that eating problems begin as ways women cope with various traumas including sexual abuse, racism, classism, sexism, heterosexism, and poverty. Showing the interface between these traumas and the onset of eating problems explains why women may use eating to numb pain and cope with violations to their bodies. This theoretical shift also permits an understanding of the economic, political, social, educational, and cultural resources that women need to change their relationship to food and their bodies.

Existing Research on Eating Problems

There are three theoretical models used to explain the epidemiology, etiology, and treatment of eating problems. The biomedical model offers important scientific research about possible physiological causes of eating problems and the physiological dangers of purging and starvation (Copeland 1985; Spack 1985). However, this model adopts medical treatment

From *Gender & Society*, Vol. 6, No. 4, December 1992, 546–561. Copyright © 1992 Sociologists for Women in Society. Reprinted by permission of the author.

strategies that may disempower and traumatize women (Garner 1985; Orbach 1985). In addition, this model ignores many social, historical, and cultural factors that influence women's eating patterns. The psychological model identifies eating problem as "multidimensional disorders" that are influenced by biological, psychological, and cultural factors (Garfinkel and Garner 1982). While useful in its exploration of effective therapeutic treatments, this model, like the biomedical one, tends to neglect women of color, lesbians, and working-class women.

The third model, offered by feminists, asserts that eating problems are gendered. This model explains why the vast majority of people with eating problems are women, how gender socialization and sexism may relate to eating problems, and how masculine models of psychological development have shaped theoretical interpretations. Feminists offer the culture of thinness model as a key reason why eating problems predominate among women. According to this model, thinness is a culturally, socially, and economically enforced requirement for female beauty. This imperative makes women vulnerable to cycles of dieting, weight loss, and subsequent weight gain, which may lead to anorexia and bulimia (Chernin 1981; Orbach 1978, 1985; Smead 1984).

Feminists have rescued eating problems from the realm of individual psychopathology by showing how the difficulties are rooted in systematic and pervasive attempts to control women's body sizes and appetites. However, researchers have yet to give significant attention to how race, class, and sexuality influence women's understanding of their bodies and appetites. The handful of epidemiological studies that include African-American women and Latinas casts doubt on the accuracy of the normative epidemiological portrait. The studies suggest that this portrait reflects which particular populations of women have been studied rather than actual prevalence (Andersen and Hay 1985; Gray, Ford, and Kelly 1987; Hsu 1987; Nevo 1985; Silber 1986).

More important, this research shows that bias in research has consequences for women of color. Tomas Silber (1986) asserts that many well-trained professionals have either misdiagnosed or delayed their diagnoses of eating problems among African-American and Latina women due to stereotypical thinking that these problems are restricted to white women. As a consequence, when African-American women or Latinas are diagnosed, their eating problems tend to be more severe due to extended processes of starvation prior to intervention. In her autobiographical account of her eating problems, Retha Powers (1989), an African-American woman, describes being told not to worry about her eating problems since "fat is more acceptable in the Black community" (p. 78). Stereotypical perceptions held by her peers and teachers of the "maternal Black woman" and the "persistent mammy-brickhouse Black woman image" (p. 134) made it difficult for Powers to find people who took her problems with food seriously.

Recent work by African-American women reveals that eating problems often relate to women's struggles against a "simultaneity of oppression" (Clarke 1982; Naylor 1985; White 1991). Byllye Avery (1990), the founder of the National Black Women's Health Project, links the origins of eating problems among African-American women to the daily stress of being undervalued and overburdened at home and at work. In Evelyn C. White's (1990) anthology, *The Black Woman's Health Book: Speaking for Ourselves,* Georgiana Arnold (1990) links her eating problems partly to racism and racial isolation during childhood.

Recent feminist research also identifies factors that are related to eating problems among lesbians (Brown 1987; Dworkin 1989; Iazzetto 1989; Schoenfielder and Wieser 1983). In her clinical work, Brown (1987) found that lesbians who have internalized a high degree of homophobia are more likely to accept negative attitudes about fat than are lesbians who have examined their internalized homophobia. Autobiographical accounts by lesbians have also indicated that secrecy about eating problems among lesbians partly reflects their fear of being associated with a stigmatized illness ("What's Important" 1988).

Attention to African-American women, Latinas, and lesbians paves the way for further research that explores the possible interface between facing multiple oppressions and the development of eating problems. In this way, this study is part of a larger feminist and sociological research agenda that seeks to understand how race, class, gender, nationality, and sexuality inform women's experiences and influence theory production.

Methodology

I conducted 18 life history interviews and administered lengthy questionnaires to explore eating problems among African-American, Latina, and white women. I employed a snowball sample, a method in which potential respondents often first learn about the study from people who have already participated. This method was well suited for the study since it enabled women to get information about me and the interview process from people they already knew. Typically, I had much contact with the respondents prior to the interview. This was particularly important given the secrecy associated with this topic (Russell 1986; Silberstein, Striegel-Moore, and Rodin 1987), the necessity of women of color and lesbians to be discriminating about how their lives are studied, and the fact that I was conducting across-race research.

To create analytical notes and conceptual categories from the data, I adopted Glaser and Strauss's (1967) technique of theoretical sampling, which directs the researcher to collect, analyze, and test hypotheses during the sampling process (rather than imposing theoretical categories onto the data). After completing each interview transcription, I gave a copy to each woman who wanted one. After reading their interviews, some of the women clarified or made additions to the interview text.

Demographics of the Women in the Study

The 18 women I interviewed included 5 African-American women, 5 Latinas, and 8 white women. Of these women, 12 are lesbian and 6 are heterosexual. Five women are Jewish, 8 are Catholic, and 5 are Protestant. Three women grew up outside of the United States. The women represented a range of class backgrounds (both in terms of origin and current class status) and ranged in age from 19 to 46 years old (with a median age of 33.5 years).

The majority of the women reported having had a combination of eating problems (at least two of the following: bulimia, compulsive eating, anorexia, and/or extensive dieting). In addition, the particular types of eating problems often changed during a woman's life span. (For example, a woman might have been bulimic during adolescence and anorexic as an adult.) Among women, 28 percent had been bulimic, 17 percent had been bulimic and anorexic, and 5 percent had been anorexic. All of the women who had been anorexic or bulimic also had a history of compulsive eating and extensive dieting. Of the women, 50 percent were compulsive eaters and dieters (39 percent) or compulsive eaters (11 percent) but had not been bulimic or anorexic.

Two-thirds of the women have had eating problems for more than half of their lives, a finding that contradicts the stereotype of eating problems as transitory. The weight fluctuation among the women varied from 16 to 160 pounds, with an average fluctuation of 74 pounds. This drastic weight change illustrates the degree to which the women adjusted to major changes in body size at least once during their lives as they lost, gained, and lost weight again. The average age of onset was 11 years old, meaning that most of the women developed eating problems prior to puberty. Almost all of the women (88 percent) consider themselves as still having a problem with eating, although the majority believe they are well on the way to recovery.

The Interface of Trauma and Eating Problems

One of the most striking findings in this study was the range of traumas the women associated with the origins of their eating problems, including racism, sexual abuse, poverty, sexism, emotional or physical abuse, heterosexism, class injuries, and acculturation.[2] The particular constellation of eating problems among the women did not vary with race, class, sexuality, or nationality. Women from various race and class backgrounds attributed the origins of their eating problems to sexual abuse, sexism, and emotional and/or physical abuse. Among some of the African-American and Latina women, eating problems were also associated with poverty, racism, and class injuries. Heterosexism was a key factor in the onset of bulimia, compulsive eating, and extensive dieting among some of the lesbians. These oppressions are not the same nor are the injuries caused by them. And certainly, there are a variety of potentially harmful ways that women respond to oppression (such as using drugs, becoming a workaholic, or committing suicide). However, for all these women, eating was a way of coping with trauma.

Sexual Abuse

Sexual abuse was the most common trauma that the women related to the origins of their eating problems. Until recently, there has been virtually no research exploring the possible relationship between these two phenomena. Since the mid-1980s, however, researchers have begun identifying connections between the two, a task that is part of a larger feminist critique of traditional psychoanalytic symptomatology (DeSalvo 1989; Herman 1981; Masson 1984). Results of a number of incidence studies indicate that between one-third and two-thirds of women who have eating problems have been abused (Oppenheimer et al. 1985; Root and Fallon 1988). In addition, a growing number of therapists and researchers have offered interpretations of the meaning and impact of eating problems for survivors of sexual abuse (Bass and Davis 1988; Goldfarb 1987; Iazzetto 1989; Swink and Leveille 1986). Kearney-Cooke (1988) identifies dieting and binging as common ways in which women cope with frequent psychological consequences of sexual abuse (such as body image disturbances, distrust of people and one's own experiences, and confusion about one's feelings). Root and Fallon (1989) specify ways that victimized women cope with assaults by binging and purging: bulimia serves many functions, including anesthetizing the negative feelings associated with victimization. Iazzetto's innovative study (1989), based on in-depth interviews and art therapy sessions, examines how a woman's relationship to her body changes as a consequence of sexual abuse. Iazzetto discovered that the process of leaving the body (through progressive phases of numbing, dissociating and denying) that often occurs during sexual abuse parallels the process of leaving the body made possible through binging.

Among the women I interviewed, 61 percent were survivors of sexual abuse (11 of the 18 women), most of whom made connections between sexual abuse and the beginning of their eating problems. Binging was the most common method of coping identified by the survivors. Binging helped women "numb out" or anesthetize their feelings. Eating sedated, alleviated anxiety, and combated loneliness. Food was something that they could trust and was accessible whenever they needed it. Antonia (a pseudonym) is an Italian-American woman who was first sexually abused by a male relative when she was four years old. Retrospectively, she knows that binging was a way she coped with the abuse. When the abuse began, and for many years subsequently, Antonia often woke up during the middle of the night with anxiety attacks or nightmares and would go straight to the kitchen cupboards to get food. Binging helped her block painful feelings because it put her back to sleep.

Like other women in the study who began binging when they were very young, Antonia was not always fully conscious as she binged. She described eating during the night as "sleep walking. It was mostly desperate—like I had to have it." Describing why she ate after waking up with nightmares, Antonia said, "What else do you do? If you don't have any coping mechanisms, you eat." She said that binging made her "disappear," which made her feel protected. Like Antonia, most of the women were sexually abused before puberty; four of them before they were five years old. Given their youth, food was the most accessible and socially acceptable drug available to them. Because all of the women endured the psychological consequences alone, it is logical that they coped with tactics they could do alone as well.

One reason Antonia binged (rather than dieted) to cope with sexual abuse is that she saw little reason to try to be the small size girls were supposed to be. Growing up as one of the only Italian Americans in what she described as a "very WASP town," Antonia felt that everything from her weight and size to having dark hair on her upper lip were physical characteristics she was supposed to hide. From a young age she knew she "never embodied the essence of the good girl. I don't like her. I have never acted like her. I can't be her. I sort of gave up." For Antonia, her body was the physical entity that signified her outsider status. When the sexual abuse occurred, Antonia felt she had lost her body. In her mind, the body she lived in after the abuse was not really hers. By the time Antonia was 11, her mother put her on diet pills. Antonia began to eat behind closed doors as she continued to cope with the psychological consequences of sexual abuse and feeling like a cultural outsider.

Extensive dieting and bulimia were also ways in which women responded to sexual abuse. Some women thought that the men had abused them because of their weight. They believed that if they were smaller, they might not have been abused. For example when Elsa, an Argentine woman, was sexually abused at the age of 11, she thought her chubby size was the reason the man was abusing her. Elsa said, "I had this notion that these old perverts liked these plump girls. You heard adults say this too. Sex and flesh being associated." Looking back on her childhood, Elsa believes she made fat the enemy partly due to the shame and guilt she felt about the incest. Her belief that fat was the source of her problems was also supported by her socialization. Raised by strict German governesses in an upper-class family, Elsa was taught that a woman's weight was a primary criterion for judging her worth. Her mother "was socially conscious of walking into places with a fat daughter and maybe people staring at her." Her father often referred to

Elsa's body as "shot to hell." When asked to describe how she felt about her body when growing up, Elsa described being completely alienated from her body. She explained,

> Remember in school when they talk about the difference between body and soul? I always felt like my soul was skinny. My soul was free. My soul sort of flew. I was tied down by this big bag of rocks that was my body. I had to drag it around. It did pretty much what it wanted and I had a lot of trouble controlling it. It kept me from doing all the things that I dreamed of.

As is true for many women who have been abused, the split that Elsa described between her body and soul was an attempt to protect herself from the pain she believed her body caused her. In her mind, her fat body was what had "bashed in her dreams." Dieting became her solution, but, as is true for many women in the study, this strategy soon led to cycles of binging and weight fluctuation.

Ruthie, a Puerto Rican woman who was sexually abused from 12 until 16 years of age, described bulimia as a way she responded to sexual abuse. As a child, Ruthie liked her body. Like many Puerto Rican women of her mother's generation, Ruthie's mother did not want skinny children, interpreting that as a sign that they were sick or being fed improperly. Despite her mother's attempts to make her gain weight, Ruthie remained thin through puberty. When a male relative began sexually abusing her, Ruthie's sense of her body changed dramatically. Although she weighed only 100 pounds, she began to feel fat and thought her size was causing the abuse. She had seen a movie on television about Romans who made themselves throw up and so she began doing it, in hopes that she could look like the "little kid" she was before the abuse began. Her symbolic attempt to protect herself by purging stands in stark contrast to the psychoanalytic explanation of eating problems as an "abnormal" repudiation of sexuality. In fact, her actions and those of many other survivors indicate a girl's logical attempt to protect herself (including her sexuality) by being a size and shape that does not seem as vulnerable to sexual assault.

These women's experiences suggest many reasons why women develop eating problems as a consequence of sexual abuse. Most of the survivors "forgot" the sexual abuse after its onset and were unable to retrieve the abuse memories until many years later. With these gaps in memory, frequently they did not know why they felt ashamed, fearful, or depressed. When sexual abuse memories resurfaced in dreams, they often woke feeling upset but could not remember what they had dreamed. These free-floating, unexplained feelings left the women feeling out of control and confused. Binging or focusing on maintaining a new diet were ways women distracted or appeased themselves, in turn, helping them regain a sense of control. As they grew older, they became more conscious of the consequences of these actions. Becoming angry at themselves for binging or promising themselves they would not purge again was a way to direct feelings of shame and self-hate that often accompanied the trauma.

Integral to this occurrence was a transference process in which the women displaced onto their bodies painful feelings and memories that actually derived from or were directed toward the persons who caused the abuse. Dieting became a method of trying to change the parts of their bodies they hated, a strategy that at least initially brought success as they lost weight. Purging was a way women tried to reject the body size they thought was responsible for the abuse. Throwing up in order to lose the weight they thought was making them vulnerable to the abuse was a way to try to find the body they had lost when the abuse began.

Poverty

Like sexual abuse, poverty is another injury that may make women vulnerable to eating problems. One woman I interviewed attributed her eating problems directly to the stress caused by poverty. Yolanda is a Black Cape Verdean mother who began eating compulsively when she was 27 years old. After leaving an abusive husband in her early 20s, Yolanda was forced to go on welfare. As a single mother with small children and few financial resources, she tried to support herself and her children on $539 a month. Yolanda began binging in the evenings after putting her children to bed. Eating was something she could do alone. It would calm her, help her deal with loneliness, and make her feel safe. Food was an accessible commodity that was cheap. She ate three boxes of macaroni and cheese when nothing else was available. As a single mother with little money, Yolanda felt as if her body was the only thing she had left. As she described it,

> I am here, [in my body] 'cause there is no where else for me to go,
> Where am I going to go? This is all I got . . . that probably con-
> tributes to putting on so much weight cause staying in your body, in
> your home, in yourself, you don't go out. You aren't around other
> people . . . . You hide and as long as you hide you don't have to face
> . . . nobody can see you eat. You are safe.

When she was eating, Yolanda felt a momentary reprieve from her worries. Binging not only became a logical solution because it was cheap and easy but also because she had grown up amid positive messages about eating. In her family, eating was a celebrated and joyful act. However, in adulthood, eating became a double-edged sword. While comforting her, binging also led to weight gain. During the three years Yolanda was on welfare, she gained seventy pounds.

Yolanda's story captures how poverty can be a precipitating factor in eating problems and highlights the value of understanding how class inequalities may shape women's eating problems. As a single mother, her financial constraints mirrored those of most female heads of households. The dual hazards of a race- and sex-stratified labor market further limited her options (Higginbotham 1986). In an article about Black women's health, Byllye Avery (1990) quotes a Black woman's explanation about why she eats compulsively. The woman told Avery,

> I work for General Electric making batteries, and, I know it's killing me. My old man is an alcoholic. My kid's got babies. Things are not well with me. And one thing I know I can do when I come home is cook me a pot of food and sit down in front of the TV and eat it. And you can't take that away from me until you're ready to give me something in its place. (p. 7)

Like Yolanda, this woman identifies eating compulsively as a quick, accessible, and immediately satisfying way of coping with the daily stress caused by conditions she could not control. Connections between poverty and eating problems also show the limits of portraying eating problems as maladies of upper-class adolescent women.

The fact that many women use food to anesthetize themselves, rather than other drugs (even when they gained access to alcohol, marijuana, and other illegal drugs), is partly a function of gender socialization and the competing demands that women face. One of the physiological consequences of binge eating is a numbed state similar to that experienced by drinking. Troubles and tensions are covered over as a consequence of the body's defensive response to massive food intake. When food is eaten in that way, it effectively works like a drug with immediate and predictable effects. Yolanda said she binged late at night rather than getting drunk because she could still get up in the morning, get her children ready for school, and be clearheaded for the college classes she attended. By binging, she avoided the hangover or sickness that results from alcohol or illegal drugs. In this way, food was her drug of choice since it was possible for her to eat while she continued to care for her children, drive, cook, and study. Binging is also less expensive than drinking, a factor that is especially significant for poor women. Another woman I interviewed said that when her compulsive eating was at its height, she ate breakfast after rising in the morning, stopped for a snack on her way to work, ate lunch at three different cafeterias, and snacked at her desk throughout the afternoon. Yet even when her eating had become constant, she was still able to remain employed. While her patterns of eating no doubt slowed her productivity, being drunk may have slowed her to a dead stop.

Heterosexism

The life history interviews also uncovered new connections between heterosexism and eating problems. One of the most important recent feminist contributions has been identifying compulsory heterosexuality as an institution which truncates opportunities for heterosexual and lesbian women (Rich 1986). All of the women interviewed for this study, both lesbian and heterosexual, were taught that heterosexuality was compulsory, although the versions of this enforcement were shaped by race and class. Expectations about heterosexuality were partly taught through messages that girls learned about eating and their bodies. In some homes, boys were given more food than girls, especially as teenagers, based on the rationale that girls need to be thin to attract boys. As the girls approached puberty, many were told to stop being athletic, begin wearing dresses, and watch their weight. For the women who weighed more than was considered acceptable, threats about their need to diet were laced with admonitions that being fat would ensure becoming an "old maid."

While compulsory heterosexuality influenced all of the women's emerging sense of their bodies and eating patterns, the women who linked heterosexism directly to the beginning of their eating problems were those who knew they were lesbians when very young and actively resisted heterosexual norms. One working-class Jewish woman, Martha, began compulsively eating when she was 11 years old, the same year she started getting clues of her lesbian identity. In junior high school, as many of her female peers began dating boys, Martha began fantasizing about girls, which made her feel utterly alone. Confused and ashamed about her fantasies, Martha came home every day from school and binged. Binging was a way she drugged herself so that being alone was tolerable. Describing binging, she said, "It was the only thing I knew. I was looking for a comfort." Like many women, Martha binged because it softened painful feelings. Binging sedated her, lessened her anxiety, and induced sleep.

Martha's story also reveals ways that trauma can influence women's experience of their bodies. Like many other women, Martha had no sense of herself as connected to her body. When I asked Martha whether she saw herself as fat when she was growing up she said, "I didn't see myself as fat. I didn't see myself. I wasn't there. I get so sad about that because I missed so much." In the literature on eating problems, *body image* is the term that is typically used to describe a woman's experience of her body. This term connotes the act of imagining one's physical appearance. Typically, women with eating problems are assumed to have difficulties with their body image. However, the term body image does not adequately capture the complexity and range of bodily responses to trauma experienced by the women. Exposure to trauma did much more than distort the women's visual image of themselves. These traumas often jeopardized their capacity to consider themselves as having bodies at all.

Given the limited connotations of the term body image, I use the term *body consciousness* as a more useful way to understand the range of bodily responses to trauma.[3] By body consciousness I mean the ability to reside comfortably in one's body (to see oneself as embodied) and to consider one's body as connected to oneself. The disruptions to their body consciousness that the women described included leaving their bodies, making a split between their body and mind, experiencing being "in" their bodies as painful, feeling unable to control what went in and out of their bodies, hiding in one part of their bodies, or simply not seeing themselves as having bodies. Binging, dieting, or purging were common ways women responded to disruptions to their body consciousness.

Racism and Class Injuries

For some of the Latinas and African-American women, racism coupled with the stress resulting from class mobility related to the onset of their eating problems. Joselyn, an African-American woman, remembered her white grandmother telling her she would never be as pretty as her cousins because they were lighter skinned. Her grandmother often humiliated Joselyn in front of others, as she made fun of Joselyn's body while she was naked and told her she was fat. As a young child, Joselyn began to think that although she could not change her skin color, she could at least try to be thin. When Joselyn was young, her grandmother was the only family member who objected to Joselyn's weight. However, her father also began encouraging his wife and daughter to be thin as the family's class standing began to change. When the family was working class, serving big meals, having chubby children, and keeping plenty of food in the house was a sign the family was doing well. But, as the family became mobile, Joselyn's father began insisting that Joselyn be thin. She remembered, "When my father's business began to bloom and my father was interacting more with white businessmen and seeing how they did business, suddenly thin became important. If you were a truly well-to-do family, then your family was slim and elegant."

As Joselyn's grandmother used Joselyn's body as territory for enforcing her own racism and prejudice about size, Joselyn's father used her body as the territory through which he channeled the demands he faced in the white-dominated business world. However, as Joselyn was pressured to diet, her father still served her large portions and bought treats for her and the neighborhood children. These contradictory messages made her feel confused about her body. As was true for many women in this study, Joselyn was told she was fat beginning when she was very young even though she was not overweight. And, like most of the women, Joselyn was put on diet pills and diets before even reaching puberty, beginning the cycles of dieting, compulsive eating, and bulimia.

The confusion about body size expectations that Joselyn associated with changes in class paralleled one Puerto Rican woman's association between her eating problems and the stress of assimilation as her family's class standing moved from poverty to working class. When Vera was very young, she was so thin that her mother took her to a doctor who prescribed appetite stimulants. However, by the time Vera was eight years old, her mother began trying to shame Vera into dieting. Looking back on it, Vera attributed her mother's change of heart to competition among extended family members that centered on "being white, being successful, being middle class, . . . and it was always, 'Ay Bendito. She is so fat. What happened?'"

The fact that some of the African-American and Latina women associated the ambivalent messages about food and eating to their family's class mobility and/or the demands of assimilation while none of the eight white women expressed this (including those whose class was stable and changing) suggests that the added dimension of racism was connected to the imperative to be thin. In fact, the class expectations that their parents experienced exacerbated standards about weight that they inflicted on their daughters.

Eating Problems as Survival Strategies

Feminist Theoretical Shifts

My research permits a reevaluation of many assumptions about eating problems. First, this work challenges the theoretical reliance on the culture-of-thinness model. Although all of the women I interviewed were manipulated and hurt by this imperative at some point in their lives, it is not the primary source of their problems. Even in the instances in which a culture of thinness was a precipitating factor in anorexia, bulimia, or binging, this influence occurred in concert with other oppressions.

Attributing the etiology of eating problems primarily to a woman's striving to attain a certain beauty ideal is also problematic because it labels a common way that women cope with pain as essentially appearance-based disorders. One blatant example of sexism is the notion that women's foremost worry is about their appearance. By focusing on the emphasis on slenderness, the eating problems literature falls into the same trap of assuming that the problems reflect women's "obsession" with appearance. Some women were raised in families and communities in which thinness was not considered a criterion for beauty. Yet, they still developed eating problems. Other women were taught that women should be thin, but their eating problems were not primarily in reaction to this imperative. Their eating strategies began as logical solutions to problems rather than problems themselves as they tried to cope with a variety of traumas.

Establishing links between eating problems and a range of oppressions invites a rethinking of both the groups of women who have been excluded from research and those whose lives have been the basis of theory formation. The construction of bulimia and anorexia as appearance-based disorders is rooted in a notion of femininity in which white middle- and upper-class women are portrayed as frivolous, obsessed with their bodies, and overly accepting of narrow gender roles. This portrayal fuels women's tremendous shame and guilt about eating problems—as signs of self-centered vanity. This construction of white middle- and upper-class women is intimately linked to the portrayal of working-class white women and women of color as their opposite: as somehow exempt from accepting the dominant standards of beauty or as one step away from being hungry and therefore not susceptible to eating problems. Identifying that women may binge to cope with poverty contrasts the notion that eating problems are class bound. Attending to the intricacies of race, class, sexuality, and gender pushes us to rethink the demeaning construction of middle-class femininity and establishes bulimia and anorexia as serious responses to injustices.

Understanding the link between eating problems and trauma also suggests much about treatment and prevention. Ultimately, their prevention depends not simply on individual healing but also on changing the social conditions that underlie their etiology. As Bernice Johnson Reagon sings in Sweet Honey in the Rock's song "Oughta Be a Woman," "A way outa no way is too much to ask/too much of a task for any one woman" (Reagon 1980).[4] Making it possible for women to have healthy relationships with their bodies and eating is a comprehensive task. Beginning steps in this direction include ensuring that (1) girls can grow up without being sexually abused, (2) parents have adequate resources to raise their children, (3) children of color grow up free of racism, and (4) young lesbians have the chance to see their reflection in their teachers and community leaders. Ultimately, the prevention of eating problems depends on women's access to economic, cultural, racial, political, social, and sexual justice.

NOTES

Author's Note: The research for this study was partially supported by an American Association of University Women Fellowship in Women's Studies. An earlier version of this article was presented at the New England Women's Studies Association Meeting in 1990 in Kingston, Rhode Island. I am grateful to Margaret Andersen, Liz Bennett, Lynn Davidman, Mary Gilfus, Evelynn Hammonds, and two anonymous reviewers for their comprehensive and perceptive comments on earlier versions of this article. Reprint Requests: Becky Wangsgaard Thompson, American Studies Program, Wesleyan University, Middletown, CT, 06459 (860)685-3568.

1. I use the term *eating problems* as an umbrella term for one or more of the following: anorexia, bulimia, extensive dieting, or binging. I avoid using the term *eating disorder* because it categorizes the problems as individual pathologies, which deflects attention away from the social inequalities underlying them (Brown 1985). However, by using the term *problem* I do not wish to imply blame. In fact, throughout, I argue that the eating strategies that women develop begin as logical solutions to problems, not problems themselves.

2. By trauma I mean a violating experience that has long-term emotional, physical, and/or spiritual consequences that may have immediate or delayed effects. One reason the term *trauma* is useful conceptually is its association with the diagnostic label Post Traumatic Stress Disorder (PTSD) (American Psychological Association 1987). PTSD is one of the few clinical diagnostic categories that recognizes social problems (such as war or the Holocaust) as responsible for the symptoms identified (Trimble 1985). This concept adapts well to the feminist assertion that a woman's symptoms cannot be understood as solely individual, considered out-

side of her social context, or prevented without significant changes in social conditions.

3. One reason the term *consciousness* is applicable is its intellectual history as an entity that is shaped by social context and social structures (Delphy 1984; Marx 1964). This link aptly applies to how the women described their bodies because their perceptions of themselves as embodied (or not embodied) directly relate to their material conditions (living situations, financial resources, and access to social and political power).

4. Copyright © 1980. Used by permission of Songtalk Publishing.

REFERENCES

American Psychological Association. 1987. *Diagnostic and statistical manual of mental disorders.* 3rd ed. rev., Washington, DC: American Psychological Association.

Andersen, Arnold, and Andy Hay. 1985. Racial and socioeconomic influences in anorexia nervosa and bulimia. *International Journal of Eating Disorders* 4:479–87.

Arnold, Georgiana. 1990. Coming home: One Black woman's journey to health and fitness. In *The Black women's health book: Speaking for ourselves,* edited by Evelyn C. White. Seattle, WA: Seal Press.

Avery, Byllye Y. 1990. Breathing life into ourselves: The evolution of the National Black Women's Health Project. In *The Black women's health book: Speaking for ourselves,* edited by Evelyn C. White. Seattle, WA: Seal Press.

Bass, Ellen, and Laura Davis. 1988. *The courage to heal: A guide for women survivors of child sexual abuse.* New York: Harper & Row.

Brown, Laura S. 1985. Women, weight and power: Feminist theoretical and therapeutic issues. *Women and Therapy* 4:61–71.

———. 1987. Lesbians, weight and eating: New analyses and perspectives. In *Lesbian psychologies,* edited by the Boston Lesbian Psychologies Collective. Champaign: University of Illinois Press.

Chernin, Kim. 1981. *The obsession: Reflections on the tyranny of slenderness.* New York: Harper & Row.

Clarke, Cheryl. 1982. *Narratives.* New Brunswick, NJ: Sister Books.

Copeland, Paul M. 1985. Neuroendocrine aspects of eating disorders. In *Theory and treatment of anorexia nervosa and bulimia: Biomedical sociocultural and psychological perspectives,* edited by Steven Wiley Emmett. New York: Brunner/Mazel.

Delphy, Christine. 1984. *Close to home: A materialist analysis of women's oppression.* Amherst: University of Massachusetts Press.

DeSalvo, Louise. 1989, *Virginia Woolf: The impact of childhood sexual abuse on her life and work.* Boston, MA: Beacon.

Dworkin, Sari H. 1989. Not in man's image: Lesbians and the cultural oppression of body image. In *Loving boldly: Issues facing lesbians,* edited by Ester D. Rothblum and Ellen Cole. New York: Harrington Park Press.

Garfinkel, Paul E., and David M. Garner. 1982. *Anorexia nervosa: A multidimensional perspective.* New York: Brunner/Mazel.

Gamer, David. 1985. Iatrogenesis in anorexia nervosa and bulimia nervosa. *International Journal of Eating Disorders* 4:701–26.

Glaser, Barney G., and Anselm L. Strauss. 1967. *The discovery of grounded theory: Strategies for qualitative research.* New York: Aldine DeGruyter.

Goldfarb, Lori. 1987. Sexual abuse antecedent to anorexia nervosa, bulimia and compulsive overeating: Three case reports. *International Journal of Eating Disorders* 6:675–80.

Gray, James, Kathryn Ford, and Lily M. Kelly. 1987. The prevalence of bulimia in a Black college population. *International Journal of Eating Disorders* 6:733-40.

Herman, Judith. 1981. *Father-daughter incest.* Cambridge, MA: Harvard University Press.

Higginbotham, Elizabeth. 1986. We were never on a pedestal: Women of color continue to struggle with poverty, racism and sexism. In *For crying out loud,* edited by Rochelle Lefkowitz and Ann Withorn. Boston, MA: Pilgrim Press.

Hsu, George. 1987. Are eating disorders becoming more common in Blacks? *International Journal of Eating Disorders* 6:113–24.

Iazzetto, Demetria. 1989. When the body is not an easy place to be: Women's sexual abuse and eating problems. Ph.D. diss., Union for Experimenting Colleges and Universities, Cincinnati, Ohio.

Kearney-Cooke, Ann. 1988. Group treatment of sexual abuse among women with eating disorders. *Women and Therapy* 7:5–21.

Marx, Karl. 1964. *The economic and philosophic manuscripts of 1844.* New York: International.

Masson, Jeffrey. 1984. *The assault on the truth: Freud's suppression of the seduction theory.* New York: Farrar, Strauss & Giroux.

Naylor, Gloria. 1985. *Linden Hills.* New York: Ticknor & Fields.

Nevo, Shoshana. 1985. Bulimic symptoms: Prevalence and ethnic differences among college women. *International Journal of Eating Disorders* 4:151–68.

Oppenheimer, R., K. Howells, R. L. Palmer, and D. A. Chaloner. 1985. Adverse sexual experience in childhood and clinical eating disorders: A preliminary description. *Journal of Psychiatric Research* 19:357–61.

Orbach, Susie. 1978. *Fat is a feminist issue.* New York: Paddington.

———. 1985. Accepting the symptom: A feminist psychoanalytic treatment of anorexia nervosa. In *Handbook of psychotherapy for anorexia nervosa and bulimia,* edited by David M. Garner and Paul E. Garfinkel. New York: Guilford.

Powers, Retha. 1989. Fat is a Black women's issue. *Essence,* Oct., 75, 78, 134, 136.

Reagon, Bernice Johnson. 1980. Oughta be a woman. On Sweet Honey in the Rock's album, *Good News.* Music by Bernice Johnson Reagon; lyrics by June Jordan. Washington, DC: Songtalk.

Rich, Adrienne. 1986. Compulsory heterosexuality and lesbian existence. In *Blood, bread and poetry.* New York: Norton.

Root, Maria P. P., and Patricia Fallon. 1988. The incidence of victimization experiences in a bulimic sample. *Journal of Interpersonal Violence* 3:161–73.

———. 1989. Treating the victimized bulimic: The functions of binge-purge behavior. *Journal of Interpersonal Violence* 4:90–100.

Russell, Diana E. 1986. *The secret trauma: Incest in the lives of girls and women.* New York: Basic Books.

Schoenfielder, Lisa, and Barbara Wieser, eds. 1983. *Shadow on a tightrope: Writings by women about fat liberation.* Iowa City, IA: Aunt Lute Book Co.

Silber, Tomas. 1986. Anorexia nervosa in Blacks and Hispanics. *International Journal of Eating Disorders* 5:121–28.

Silberstein, Lisa, Ruth Striegel-Moore, and Judith Rodin. 1987. Feeling fat: A woman's shame. In *The role of shame in symptom formation,* edited by Helen Block Lewis. Hillsdale, NJ: Lawrence Erlbaum.

Smead, Valerie. 1984. Eating behaviors which may lead to and perpetuate anorexia nervosa, bulimarexia, and bulimia. *Women and Therapy* 3:37–49.

Spack, Norman. 1985. Medical complications of anorexia nervosa and bulimia. In *Theory and treatment of anorexia nervosa and bulimia: Biomedical sociocultural and psychological perspectives,* edited by Steven Wiley Emmett. New York: Brunner/Mazel.

Swink, Kathy, and Antoinette E. Leveille. 1986. From victim to survivor: A new look at the issues and recovery process for adult incest survivors. *Women and Therapy* 5:119–43.

Trimble, Michael. 1985. Post-traumatic stress disorder: History of a concept. In *Trauma and its wake: The study and treatment of post-traumatic stress disorder,* edited by C. R. Figley. New York: Brunner/Mazel.

What's important is what you look like. 1988. *Gay Community News,* July, 24–30.

White, Evelyn C., ed. 1990. *The Black women's health book: Speaking for ourselves.* Seattle, WA: Seal Press.

———. 1991. Unhealthy appetites. *Essence,* Sept., 28, 30.

15

JUST WALK ON BY
A Black Man Ponders His Power
to Alter Public Space

BRENT STAPLES

My first victim was a woman—white, well dressed, probably in her early twenties. I came upon her late one evening on a deserted street in Hyde Park, a relatively affluent neighborhood in an otherwise mean, impoverished section of Chicago. As I swung onto the avenue behind her, there seemed to be a discreet, uninflammatory distance between us. Not so. She cast back a worried glance. To her, the youngish black man—a broad six feet two inches with a beard and billowing hair, both hands shoved into the pockets of a bulky military jacket—seemed menacingly close. After a few more quick glimpses, she picked up her pace and was soon running in earnest. Within seconds she disappeared into a cross street.

That was more than a decade ago. I was 22 years old, a graduate student newly arrived at the University of Chicago. It was in the echo of that terrified woman's footfalls that I first began to know the unwieldy inheritance I'd come into—the ability to alter public space in ugly ways. It was clear that she thought herself the quarry of a mugger, a rapist, or worse. Suffering a bout of insomnia, however, I was stalking sleep, not defenseless wayfarers. As a softy who is scarcely able to take a knife to a raw chicken—let along to hold it to a person's throat—I was surprised, embarrassed, and dismayed all at once. Her flight made me feel like an accomplice in tyranny. It also made it clear that I was indistinguishable from the muggers who occasionally seeped into the area from the surrounding ghetto. That first encounter, and those that followed, signified that a vast, unnerving gulf lay

From *Ms.* Magazine, September 1986. Reprinted by permission of the author.

between nighttime pedestrians—particularly women—and me. And I soon gathered that being perceived as dangerous is a hazard in itself. I only needed to turn a corner into a dicey situation, or crowd some frightened, armed person in a foyer somewhere, or make an errant move after being pulled over by a policeman. Where fear and weapons meet—and they often do in urban America—there is always the possibility of death.

In that first year, my first away from my hometown, I was to become thoroughly familiar with the language of fear. At dark, shadowy intersections in Chicago, I could cross in front of a car stopped at a traffic light and elicit the *thunk, thunk, thunk, thunk* of the driver—black, white, male, female—hammering down the door locks. On less traveled streets after dark, I grew accustomed to but never comfortable with people who crossed to the other side of the street rather than pass me. Then there were the standard unpleasantries with police, doormen, bouncers, cab drivers, and others whose business it is to screen out troublesome individuals *before* there is any nastiness.

I moved to New York nearly two years ago and I have remained an avid night walker. In central Manhattan, the near-constant crowd cover minimizes tense one-on-one street encounters. Elsewhere—visiting friends in SoHo, where sidewalks are narrow and tightly spaced buildings shut out the sky—things can get very taut indeed.

Black men have a firm place in New York mugging literature. Norman Podhoretz in his famed (or infamous) 1963 essay, "My Negro Problem— And Ours," recalls growing up in terror of black males; they "were tougher than we were, more ruthless," he writes—and as an adult on the Upper West Side of Manhattan, he continues, he cannot constrain his nervousness when he meets black men on certain streets. Similarly, a decade later, the essayist and novelist Edward Hoagland extols a New York where once "Negro bitterness bore down mainly on other Negroes." Where some see mere panhandlers, Hoagland sees "a mugger who is clearly screwing up his nerve to do more than just *ask* for money." But Hoagland has "the New Yorker's quick-hunch posture for broken-field maneuvering," and the bad guy swerves away.

I often witness that "hunch posture," from women after dark on the warrenlike streets of Brooklyn where I live. They seem to set their faces on neutral and, with their purse straps strung across their chests bandolier style, they forge ahead as though bracing themselves against being tackled. I understand, of course, that the danger they perceive is not a hallucination. Women are particularly vulnerable to street violence, and young black males are drastically overrepresented among the perpetrators of that violence. Yet these truths are no solace against the kind of alienation that comes of being ever the suspect, against being set apart, a fearsome entity with whom pedestrians avoid making eye contact.

It is not altogether clear to me how I reached the ripe old age of 22 without being conscious of the lethality nighttime pedestrians attributed to me.

Perhaps it was because in Chester, Pennsylvania, the small, angry industrial town where I came of age in the 1960s, I was scarcely noticeable against a backdrop of gang warfare, street knifings, and murders. I grew up one of the good boys, had perhaps a half-dozen fist fights. In retrospect, my shyness of combat has clear sources.

Many things go into the making of a young thug. One of those things is the consummation of the male romance with the power to intimidate. An infant discovers that random flailings send the baby bottle flying out of the crib and crashing to the floor. Delighted, the joyful babe repeats those motions again and again, seeking to duplicate the feat. Just so, I recall the points at which some of my boyhood friends were finally seduced by the perception of themselves as tough guys. When a mark cowered and surrendered his money without resistance, myth and reality merged—and paid off. It is, after all, only manly to embrace the power to frighten and intimidate. We, as men, are not supposed to give an inch of our lane on the highway; we are to seize the fighter's edge in work and in play and even in love; we are to be valiant in the face of hostile forces.

Unfortunately, poor and powerless young men seem to take all this nonsense literally. As a boy, I saw countless tough guys locked away; I have since buried several, too. They were babies, really—a teenage cousin, a brother of 22, a childhood friend in his mid-twenties—all gone down in episodes of bravado played out in the streets. I came to doubt the virtues of intimidation early on. I chose, perhaps even unconsciously, to remain a shadow—timid, but a survivor.

The fearsomeness mistakenly attributed to me in public places often has a perilous flavor. The most frightening of these confusions occurred in the late 1970s and early 1980s when I worked as a journalist in Chicago. One day, rushing into the office of a magazine I was writing for with a deadline story in hand, I was mistaken for a burglar. The office manager called security and, with an ad hoc posse, pursued me through the labyrinthine halls, nearly to my editor's door. I had no way of proving who I was. I could only move briskly toward the company of someone who knew me.

Another time I was on assignment for a local paper and killing time before an interview. I entered a jewelry store on the city's affluent Near North Side. The proprietor excused herself and returned with an enormous red Doberman pinscher straining at the end of a leash. She stood, the dog extended toward me, silent to my questions, her eyes bulging nearly out of her head. I took a cursory look around, nodded, and bade her good night. Relatively speaking, however, I never fared as badly as another black male journalist. He went to nearby Waukegan, Illinois, a couple of summers ago to work on a story about a murderer who was born there. Mistaking the reporter for the killer, police hauled him from his car at gunpoint and but for his press credentials would have tried to book him. Such episodes are not uncommon. Black men trade tales like this all the time.

In "My Negro Problem—And Ours," Podhoretz writes that the hatred he feels for blacks makes itself known to him through a variety of avenues—one being his discomfort with that "special brand of paranoid touchiness" to which he says blacks are prone. No doubt he is speaking here of black men. In time, I learned to smother the rage I felt at so often being taken for a criminal. Not to do so would surely have led to madness—via that special "paranoid touchiness" that so annoyed Podhoretz at the time he wrote the essay.

I began to take precautions to make myself less threatening. I move about with care, particularly late in the evening. I give a wide berth to nervous people on the subway platforms during the wee hours, particularly when I have exchanged business clothes for jeans. If I happen to be entering a building behind some people who appear skittish, I may walk by, letting them clear the lobby before I return, so as not to seem to be following them. I have been calm and extremely congenial on those rare occasions when I've been pulled over by the police.

And on late-evening constitutionals along streets less traveled by, I employ what has proved to be an excellent tension-reducing measure: I whistle melodies from Beethoven and Vivaldi and the more popular classical composers. Even steely New Yorkers hunching toward nighttime destinations seem to relax, and occasionally they even join in the tune. Virtually everybody seems to sense that a mugger wouldn't be warbling bright, sunny selections from Vivaldi's *Four Seasons.* It is my equivalent of the cowbell that hikers wear when they know they are in bear country.

16

TAKING IT

LEONARD KRIEGEL

In 1944, at the age of eleven, I had polio. I spent the next two years of my life in an orthopedic hospital, appropriately called a reconstruction home. By 1946, when I returned to my native Bronx, polio had reconstructed me to the point that I walked very haltingly on steel braces and crutches.

But polio also taught me that, if I were to survive, I would have to become a man—and become a man quickly. "Be a man!" my immigrant father urged, by which he meant "become an American." For, in 1946, this country had very specific expectations about how a man faced adversity. Endurance, courage, determination, stoicism—these might right the balance with fate.

"I couldn't take it, and I took it," says the wheelchair-doomed poolroom entrepreneur William Einhorn in Saul Bellow's *The Adventures of Augie March*. "And I *can't* take it, yet I do take it." In 1953, when I first read these words, I knew that Einhorn spoke for me—as he spoke for scores of other men who had confronted the legacy of a maiming disease by risking whatever they possessed of substance in a country that believed that such risks were a man's wagers against his fate.

How one faced adversity was, like most of American life, in part a question of gender. Simply put, a woman endured, but a man fought back. You were better off struggling against the effects of polio as a man than as a woman, for polio was a disease that one confronted by being tough, aggressive, decisive, by assuming that all limitations could be overcome, beaten, conquered. In short, by being "a man." Even the vocabulary of rehabilitation was masculine. One "beat" polio by outmuscling the disease. At the age of eighteen, I felt that I was "a better man" than my friends because I had "overcome a handicap." And I had, in the process, showed that I could "take it." In the world of American men, to take it was a sign that you were among the elect. An assumption my "normal" friends shared. "You're lucky," my closest friend said to me during an intensely painful crisis in his own life. "You had polio." He meant it. We both believed it.

Obviously, I wasn't lucky. By nineteen, I was already beginning to understand—slowly, painfully, but inexorably—that disease is never "conquered" or "overcome." Still, I looked upon resistance to polio as the essence of my manhood. As an American, I was self-reliant. I could create my own possibilities from life. And so I walked mile after mile on braces and crutches. I did hundreds of push-ups every day to build my arms, chest, and shoulders. I lifted weights to the point that I would collapse, exhausted but strengthened, on the floor. And through it all, my desire to create a "normal" life for myself was transformed into a desire to become the man my disease had decreed I should be.

I took my heroes where I found them—a strange, disparate company of men: Hemingway, whom I would write of years later as "my nurse"; Peter Reiser, whom I dreamed of replacing in Ebbets Field's pastures and whose penchant for crashing into outfield walls fused in my mind with my own war against the virus; Franklin Delano Roosevelt, who had scornfully faced polio with aristocratic disdain and patrician distance (a historian acquaintance recently disabused me of that myth, a myth perpetrated, let me add, by almost all of Roosevelt's biographers); Henry Fonda and Gary Cooper, in whose resolute Anglo-Saxon faces Hollywood blended the simplicity, strength and courage a man needed if he was going to survive as a man; any number of boxers in whom heart, discipline and training combined to stave off defeats the boy's limitations made inevitable. These were the "manly" images I conjured up as I walked those miles of Bronx streets, as I did those relentless push-ups, as I moved up and down one subway staircase after another by turning each concrete step into a personal insult. And they were still the images when, fifteen years later, married, the father of two sons of my own, a Fulbright professor in the Netherlands, I would grab hold of vertical poles in a train in The Hague and swing my brace-bound body across the dead space between platform and carriage, filled with self-congratulatory vanity as amazement spread over the features of the Dutch conductor.

It is easy to dismiss such images as adolescent. Undoubtedly they were. But they helped remind me, time and time again, of how men handled their diseases and their pain. Of course, I realized even then that it was not the idea of manhood alone that had helped me fashion a life out of polio. I might write of Hemingway as "my nurse," but it was an immigrant Jewish mother—already transformed into a cliché by scores of male Jewish writers—who serviced my crippled body's needs and who fed me love, patience and care even as I fed her the rhetoric of my rage.

But it was the need to prove myself an American man—tough, resilient, independent, able to take it—that pulled me through the war with the virus. I have, of course, been reminded again and again of the price extracted for such ideas about manhood. And I am willing to admit that my sons may be better off in a country in which "manhood" will mean little more than, say, the name for an after-shave lotion. It is forty years since my war with the virus began. At fifty-one, even an American man knows that mortality is the only legacy and defeat the only guarantee. At fifty-one, my legs still encased in braces and crutches still beneath my shoulders, my elbows are increasingly arthritic from all those streets walked and weights lifted and stairs climbed. At fifty-one, my shoulders burn with pain from all those push-ups done so relentlessly. And at fifty-one, pain merely bores—and hurts.

Still, I remain an American man. If I know where I'm going, I know, too, where I have been. Best of all, I know the price I have paid. A man endures his diseases until he recognizes in them his vanity. He can't take it, but he takes it. Once, I relished my ability to take it. Now I find myself wishing that taking it were easier. In such quiet surrenders do we American men call it quits with our diseases.

17

DO YOU REMEMBER ME?

BARBARA MACDONALD

I am less than five feet high and except that I may have shrunk a quarter of an inch or so in the past few years, I have viewed the world from this height for sixty-five years. I have taken up some space in the world; I weigh about a hundred and forty pounds and my body is what my mother used to call dumpy. My mother didn't like her body and so of course didn't like mine. My mother was not always rational and her judgment was further impaired because she was a recluse, but the "dumpy" was her word, and just as I have had to keep the body, somehow I have had to keep the word—thirty-eight-inch bust, no neck, no waistline, fat, hips—that's dumpy.

My hair is grey, white at the temples, with only a little of the red cast of earlier years showing through. My face is wrinkled and deeply lined. Straight lines have formed on the upper lip as though I had spent many years with my mouth pursed. This has always puzzled me and I wonder what years those were and why I can't remember them. My face has deep lines that extend from each side of the nose down the face past the corners of my mouth. My forehead is wide and the lines across my forehead and between my eyes are there to testify that I was often puzzled and bewildered for long periods of time about what was taking place in my life. My cheekbones are high and become more noticeably so as my face is drawn further and further down. My chin is small for such a large head and below the chin the skin hangs in a loose vertical fold from my chin all the way down to my neck where it meets a horizontal scar. The surgeon who made the scar said that the joints of my neck were worn out from looking up so many years. For all kinds of reasons, I seldom look up to anyone or anything anymore.

My eyes are blue and my gaze is usually steady and direct. But I look away when I am struggling with some nameless shame, trying to disclaim parts of myself. My voice is low and my speech sometimes clipped and rapid if I am uncomfortable; otherwise I have a pleasant voice. I like the sound of it from in here where I am. When I was younger, some people, lovers mostly, enjoyed my singing, but I no longer have the same control of my voice and sing only occasionally now when I am alone.

In *Look Me in the Eye*, by Barbara Macdonald with Cynthia Rich. San Francisco: Spinsters, Ink: 1983. Available from Spinsters Ink, 32 East First Street #330, Duluth, MN 55802. Reprinted by permission. Summer 1979.

My hands are large and the backs of my hands begin to show the brown spots of aging. Sometimes lately, holding my arms up reading in bed or lying with my arms clasped around my lover's neck, I see my own arms with the skin hanging loosely from my own forearm and cannot believe that the arm I see is really my own. It seems disconnected from me; it is someone else's, it is the arm of an old woman. It is the arm of such old women as I myself have seen, sitting on benches in the sun with their hands folded in their laps; old women I have turned away from. I wonder now, how and when these arms I see came to be my own—arms I cannot turn away from. . . .

The truth is I like growing old. Oh, it isn't that I don't feel at moments the sharp irrevocable knowledge that I have finally grown old. That is evident every time I stand in front of the bathroom mirror and brush my teeth. I may begin as I often do, wondering if those teeth that are so much a part of myself, teeth I've clenched in anger all my life, felt with my own tongue with a feeling of possession, as a cat licks her paw lovingly just because it is hers—wondering, will these teeth always be mine? Will they stay with me loyally and die with me, or will they desert me before the Time comes? But I grow dreamy brushing my teeth and find myself, unaware, planning as I always have when I brush my teeth—that single-handed crossing I plan to make. From East to West, a last stop in the Canaries and then the trade winds. What will be the best time of year? What boat? How much sail? I go over again the list of supplies, uninterrupted until some morning twinge in my left shoulder reminds me with uncompromising regret that I will never make that single-handed crossing—probably. That I have waited too long. That there is no turning back.

But I always say probably. Probably I'll never make that single-handed crossing. Probably, I've waited too long. Probably, I can't turn back now. But I leave room now, at sixty-five, for the unexpected. That was not always true of me. I used to feel I was in a kind of linear race with life and time. There were no probablies; it was a now or never time of my life. There were landmarks placed by other generations and I had to arrive on time or fail in the whole race. If I didn't pass—if the sixth grade went on to the seventh without me, I would be one year behind for the rest of my life. If I graduated from high school in 1928, I had to graduate from college in 1932. When I didn't graduate from college until 1951, it took me twenty years to realize the preceding twenty years weren't lost. But now I begin to see that I may get to have the whole thing and that no experience longed for is really going to be missed.

"I like growing old." I say it to myself with surprise. I had not thought that it could be like this. There are days of excitement when I feel almost a kind of high with the changes I feel taking place in my body, even though I know the inevitable course my body is taking will lead to debilitation and death. I say to myself frequently in wonder, "This is my body doing this thing." I cannot stop it, I don't even know what it is doing, I wouldn't know how to direct it; my own body is going through a process that only my body knows about. I never grew old before; never died before. I don't really know how it's done, I wouldn't know where to begin, and God knows, I certainly wouldn't know when to begin—for no time would be right. And then I realize, lesbian or straight, I belong to all the women who carried my cells for generations and my body remembers how for each generation this matter of ending is done.

Cynthia tells me now about being a young girl, watching and enjoying what her body was doing in preparation for her life. Seeing her breasts develop, watching the cleft disappear behind a cushion of dark pubic hair, discovering her own body making a bright red stain, feeling herself and seeing herself in the process of becoming.

When I was young, I watched this process with dread, seeing my breasts grow larger and larger and my hips widen. I was never able to say, "This is my body doing this wonderful unknown thing." I felt fear with every visible change, I felt more exposed, more vulnerable to attack. My swelling breasts, my widening hips, my growing pubic hair and finally the visible bleeding wound, all were acts of violence against my person, and could only bring me further acts of violence. I never knew in all the years of living in my woman's body that other women had found any pleasure in that early body experience, until Cynthia told me. But now, after a lifetime of living, my body has taken over again. I have this second chance to feel my body living out its own plan, to watch it daily change in the direction of its destiny. . . .

I wanted a different body when I was young. I have lived in this body for sixty-five years. "It is a good body, it is mine."

I wanted another mother and another beginning when I was young. I wanted a mother who liked herself, who liked her body and so would like mine. "My mother did not like herself and she did not like me; that is part of the definition of who she was and of who I am. She was my mother."

When I was fifty-two, my lover left me after fourteen years of living our lives together. I wanted her to return. I waited for many years and she did not come back. "I am the woman whose lover did not return."

I was lonely for years of my life and I wandered in search of a lover. "I am a person who loves again. I am a woman come home."

So often we think we know how an experience is going to end so we don't risk the pain of seeing it through to the end. We think we know the outcome so we think there is no need to experience it, as though to anticipate an ending were the same as living the ending out. We drop the old and take up the new—drop an idea and take up a new one—drop the middle-aged and old and start concentrating on the young, always thinking somehow it's going to turn out better with a new start. I have never had a child, but sometimes I see a young woman beginning to feel the urge to have a child at about the same time she feels some disappointment at how her own life is turning out. And soon the young mother feels further disappointment when her own mother withdraws her loving investment in her daughter to pour it into her grandchild. I see how all are devalued, the grandmother devalued by society, devalued by her own self, the daughter devalued by her mother, and the granddaughter, valued not for who she is but for who she may become, racing for the landmarks, as I once did.

We never really know the beginning or the middle, until we have lived out an ending and lived on beyond it.

Of course, this time, for me, I am not going to live beyond this ending. The strangeness of that idea comes to me at the most unexpected moments and always with surprise and shock; sometimes I am immobilized by it. Standing before the mirror in the morning, I feel that my scalp is tight. I see that the skin hangs beneath my jaw, beneath my arm; my breasts are pulled low against my body; loose skin hangs from my hips, and below my stomach a new horizontal crease is forming over which the skin will hang like the hem of a skirt turned under. A hem not to be "let down," as once my skirts were, because I was "shooting up," but a widening hem to "take up" on an old garment that has been stretched. Then I see that my body is being drawn into the earth—muscle, tendon, tissue and skin is being drawn down by the earth's pull back to the loam. She is pulling me back to herself; she is taking back what is hers.

Cynthia loves bulbs. She digs around in the earth every fall, looking for the rich loamy mold of decayed leaves and vegetation, and sometimes as she takes a sack of bone meal and works it into the damp earth, I think, "Why not mine? Why not?"

I think a lot about being drawn into the earth. I have the knowledge that one day I will fall and the earth will take back what is hers. I have no choice, yet I choose it. Maybe I won't buy that boat and that list of supplies; maybe I will. Maybe I will be able to write about my life; maybe I won't. But uncertainty will not always be there, for this is like no other experience I have ever had—I can count on it. I've never had anything before that I could really count on. My life has been filled with uncertainties, some were not of my making and many were: promises I made myself I did not keep, promises I made others I did not keep, hopes I could not fulfill, shame carried like a weight heavier by the years, at my failure, at my lack of clear purpose. But this time I can rely on myself, for life will keep her promise to me. I can trust her. She isn't going to confuse me with a multitude of other choices and beckon me down other roads with vague promises. She will give me finally only one choice, one road, one sense of possibility. And in exchange for the multitude of choices she no longer offers, she gives me, at last, certainty. Nor do I have to worry this time that I will fail myself, fail to pull it off. This time, for sure I am going to make that single-handed crossing.

18

I'M NOT FAT, I'M LATINA

CHRISTY HAUBEGGER

I recently read a newspaper article that reported that nearly 40 percent of Hispanic and African-American women are overweight. At least I'm in good company. Because according to even the most generous height and weight charts at the doctor's office, I'm a good 25 pounds overweight. And I'm still looking for the panty-hose chart that has me on it (according to Hanes, I don't exist). But I'm happy to report that in the Latino community, my community, I fit right in.

Latinas in this country live in two worlds. People who don't know us may think we're fat. At home, we're called *bien cuidadas* (well cared for).

I love to go dancing at Cesar's Latin Palace here in the Mission District of San Francisco. At this hot all-night salsa club, it's the curvier bodies like mine that turn heads. I'm the one on the dance floor all night while some of my thinner friends spend more time waiting along the walls. Come to think of it, I wouldn't trade my body for any of theirs.

But I didn't always feel this way. I remember being in high school and noticing that none of the magazines showed models in bathing suits with bodies like mine. Handsome movie heroes were never hoping to find a chubby damsel in distress. The fact that I had plenty of attention from Latino boys wasn't enough. Real self-esteem cannot come from male attention alone.

My turning point came a few years later. When I was in college, I made a trip to Mexico, and I brought back much more than sterling-silver bargains and colorful blankets.

I remember hiking through the awesome ruins of the Maya and the Aztecs, civilizations that created pyramids as large as the ones in Egypt. I loved walking through temple doorways whose clearance was only two inches above my head, and I realized that I must be a direct descendant of those ancient priestesses for whom those doorways had originally been built.

For the first time in my life, I was in a place where people like me were the beautiful ones. And I began to accept, and even like, the body that I have.

I know that medical experts say that Latinas are twice as likely as the rest of the population to be overweight. And yes, I know about the health problems that often accompany severe weight problems. But most of us are not in the danger zone; we're just bien cuidadas. Even the researchers who found

From *Essence*, December 1994. Reprinted by permission of the author.

that nearly 40 percent of us are overweight noted that there is a greater "cultural acceptance" of being overweight within Hispanic communities. But the article also commented on the cultural-acceptance factor as if it were something unfortunate, because it keeps Hispanic women from becoming healthier. I'm not so convinced that we're the ones with the problem.

If the medical experts were to try and get to the root of this so-called problem, they would probably find that it's part genetics, part enchiladas. Whether we're Cuban-American, Mexican-American, Puerto Rican or Dominican, food is a central part of Hispanic culture. While our food varies from fried plaintains to tamales, what doesn't change is its role in our lives. You feed people you care for, and so if you're well cared for, *bien cuidada,* you have been fed well.

I remember when I used to be envious of a Latina friend of mine who had always been on the skinny side. When I confided this to her a while ago, she laughed. It turns out that when she was growing up, she had always wanted to look more like me. She had trouble getting dates with Latinos in high school, the same boys that I dated. When she was little, the other kids in the neighborhood had even given her a cruel nickname: *la seca,* "the dry one." I'm glad I never had any of those problems.

Our community has always been accepting of us well-cared-for women. So why don't we feel beautiful? You only have to flip through a magazine or watch a movie to realize that beautiful for most of this country still means tall, blond and underfed. But now we know it's the magazines that are wrong. I, for one, am going to do what I can to make sure that *mis hijas,* my daughters, won't feel the way I did.

PART IV
Communication

The first thing you do is to forget that i'm Black.
Second, you must never forget that i'm Black.

PAT PARKER[1]

The whole goddam business of what you're calling intimacy bugs the hell out
of me. I never know what you women mean when you talk about it. Karen
complains that I don't talk to her, but it's not talk she wants, it's some other
damn thing, only I don't know what the hell it is.

MAN INTERVIEWED BY LILLIAN RUBIN[2]

Telling the truth about one's experience is one task of communicating with
others. The other task, frequently more challenging than the first, is listening
carefully, empathizing, and trying to understand without being defensive or
interrupting. Most people have a sense of how difficult this can be. A growing literature, especially related to counseling and psychotherapy, focuses on
basic communication skills, such as listening, and on multicultural communication skills, which include acknowledging how the various intersections
of gender, race, class, ethnicity, disability, sexual orientation, and age affect
communication. The task of becoming multiculturally competent takes time
and effort, and it is necessary for all groups since most people are intimately
familiar with only their own culture.[3]

Communication patterns reflect power relationships. Those who have
more power control what is communicated, including what gets media
attention; they especially control the extent to which people with less
power are listened to and seen for who they are without prejudice.
Theories of the limited images of women in the media examine, among
other things, the absence of women in positions of power in the communications industries, and the capitalist system that sells products and avoids
offending potential consumers with more realistic images.[4] Studies of face-
to-face male-female communication document how power affects these
relationships as well.[5]

Literature from men's studies addresses the challenge of men's friendships with each other, identifying various aspects of male-male communication that facilitate or impede close friendships. Even when differences like
race and class are not present and power between the people involved is relatively equal, difficulty sharing feelings, heavy competition for success, and
fear of admitting dependency or vulnerability combine with homophobia to
keep men apart.[6]

Finally, communication is difficult because the array of prejudices we
learn in childhood frequently follows us into adulthood, often uncon-

sciously. As children, we learn attitudes in situations in which we have little or no control, and we frequently live in families in which communication is far from ideal.[7] Until schools and communities routinely work to help people appreciate diversity, acknowledge differences of power and privilege, listen to each other, and learn peaceful methods of dispute resolution, we are on our own as individuals to improve communication across differences.

This chapter opens with two authors who address multicultural communication. In a poem by the late Pat Parker entitled "For the white person who wants to know how to be my friend," the poet asks white people to simultaneously hold conscious her racial self and the self she has in common with all people. This challenge is one of the more difficult tasks of communication across combinations of differences since it requires the ability to hold two or more seemingly contradictory realities conscious at the same time. Although Parker doesn't explicitly address gender, I have included her poem because the complexity of her advice applies to people trying to communicate across gender, as well as other, differences.

Next is an essay by Judith Ortiz Cofer, who identifies gender-based communication styles among Puerto Rican women. She illustrates the difference between Anglo and Puerto Rican styles of dress, explaining the various messages embedded in each presentation of self and the frequent misunderstandings that result. She also describes being treated as a sex object because she is Latina.

The next two pieces deal with miscommunication. The first is an excerpt from Deborah Tannen's study of male-female communication, *You Just Don't Understand: Women and Men in Conversation.* Tannen addresses what she calls asymmetries—women and men talking at cross-purposes. She uses examples from female-female and male-male conversations, as well as cross-gender conversations in various relationships. Readers are encouraged to decide whether her analyses of communication styles apply to various cultural groups, since the race and ethnicity of the speakers are unclear in this excerpt. Tannen's piece is followed by a selection that focuses on communication within a heterosexual Black couple. In response to learning that the delivery of their first child will not be covered by their health insurance, Phil Petrie withdraws into his music and does not discuss the dilemma. His wife, on the other hand, wants to talk. He writes about the intense pressure he feels to be a good provider—pressure that is heightened by racism and other issues related to being an African American man.

The next article is about an interracial, same-sex friendship. African American journalist Nathan McCall, in an excerpt from his autobiography, describes his first friendship with a white man, in which he discovers that both he and Danny, who is Jewish, share a similar critique of white, macho, corporate culture. He describes the process of becoming friends with Danny when they are both living in the South, and he reflects on the sad state of Black-white relations in the United States.

Next is an essay by activist Suzanne Pharr, in which she addresses the challenge of communicating across class and sexual-orientation differences in a rural southern town where she organized against the use of Agent Orange. A lesbian from working-class, rural origins, Pharr urges that people take the time necessary to communicate across deeply felt differences that frequently have the potential for violence. In the political activism she describes, class differences created an unbridgeable chasm.

This Part concludes with excerpts from an essay in which M. Annette Jaimes and Theresa Halsey describe women's activism in various aspects of the Native American struggle for survival. They see this struggle for survival as the most important issue for American Indian nations, and they critique white feminists for failing to understand its crucial role. They believe that this lack of common ground makes it very difficult for Native American women and white feminists to work together.

The authors in this Part speak of things often unspoken and suggest directions for change in order to create better communication and a more humane world.

NOTES

1. Pat Parker, "For the white person who wants to know how to be my friend" from *Movement in Black*. Reprinted in Gloria Anzaldúa, ed., *Making Face, Making Soul: Haciendo Caras* (San Francisco: Aunt Lute, 1990), p. 297.
2. Lillian B. Rubin, *Intimate Strangers: Men and Women Together* (New York: Harper & Row, 1983), p. 66.
3. See for example Joseph G. Ponterotto, et al., eds. *Handbook of Multicultural Counseling* (Thousand Oaks: Sage, 1995); Larra A. Samovar and Richard E. Porter, eds., *Intercultural Communication: A Reader* (Belmont, CA: Wadsworth, 1991). For a report of how different ethnic groups in the United States see each other, including the stereotypes their members hold about each other, see "Taking America's Pulse: Summary Report of the National Conference Survey On Inter-Group Relations," (New York: The National Conference of Christians and Jews, 1994).
4. For a summary of these theoretical perspectives, see Margaret L. Andersen, *Thinking About Women: Sociological Perspectives on Sex and Gender,* 3rd ed., (New York: Macmillan, 1993), pp. 54–62.
5. See, for example: Nancy Henley, *Body Politics: Power, Sex and Nonverbal Communication* (Englewood Cliffs, NJ: Prentice-Hall, 1977); Deborah Tannen, *You Just Don't Understand: Women and Men in Conversation* (New York: Morrow, 1990), plus much of her other work; Lillian Rubin, *Intimate Strangers*.
6. Michael S. Kimmel and Michael A. Messner, eds., *Men's Lives,* 3rd ed., (Boston: Allyn & Bacon, 1995), p. 323; Gregory K. Lehne, "Homophobia among Men: Supporting and Defining the Male Role," in *Men's Lives,* pp. 325–336.
7. In my years as a teacher and psychotherapist, I have met only a small proportion of people who would like to continue using the communication patterns of the adults in the households in which they grew up; more frequently, they experienced successful communication with siblings—enjoying the relative equality of power that allowed for more open communication.

19

FOR THE WHITE PERSON WHO WANTS TO KNOW HOW TO BE MY FRIEND

PAT PARKER

The first thing you do is to forget that i'm black.
Second, you must never forget that i'm black.

You should be able to dig Aretha,
but don't play her every time i come over.
And if you decide to play Beethoven—don't tell me
his life story. They make us take music appreciation too.

Eat soul food if you like it, but don't expect me
to locate your restaurants
or cook it for you.

And if some Black person insults you,
mugs you, rapes your sister, rapes you,
rips your house or is just being an ass—
please, do not apologize to me
for wanting to do them bodily harm.
It makes me wonder if you're foolish.

And even if you really believe Blacks are better lovers than
whites—don't tell me. I start thinking of charging stud fees.

In other words—if you really want to be my friend—*don't*
make a labor of it. I'm lazy. Remember.

20

THE MYTH OF THE LATIN WOMAN
I Just Met a Girl Named María

JUDITH ORTIZ COFER

On a bus trip to London from Oxford University where I was earning some graduate credits one summer, a young man, obviously fresh from a pub, spotted me and as if struck by inspiration went down on his knees in the aisle. With both hands over his heart he broke into an Irish tenor's rendition of "María" from *West Side Story*. My politely amused fellow passengers gave his lovely voice the round of gentle applause it deserved. Though I was not quite as amused, I managed my version of an English smile: no show of teeth, no extreme contortions of the facial muscles—I was at this time of my life practicing reserve and cool. Oh, that British control, how I coveted it. But María had followed me to London, reminding me of a prime fact of my life: you can leave the Island, master the English language, and travel as far as you can, but if you are a Latina, especially one like me who so obviously belongs to Rita Moreno's gene pool, the Island travels with you.

This is sometimes a very good thing—it may win you that extra minute of someone's attention. But with some people, the same things can make *you* an island—not so much a tropical paradise as an Alcatraz, a place nobody wants to visit. As a Puerto Rican girl growing up in the United States and wanting like most children to "belong," I resented the stereotype that my Hispanic appearance called forth from many people I met.

Our family lived in a large urban center in New Jersey during the sixties, where life was designed as a microcosm of my parents' casas on the island. We spoke in Spanish, we ate Puerto Rican food bought at the bodega, and we practiced strict Catholicism complete with Saturday confession and Sunday mass at a church where our parents were accommodated into a one-hour Spanish mass slot, performed by a Chinese priest trained as a missionary for Latin America.

As a girl I was kept under strict surveillance, since virtue and modesty were, by cultural equation, the same as family honor. As a teenager I was instructed on how to behave as a proper señorita. But it was a conflicting message girls got, since the Puerto Rican mothers also encouraged their daughters to look and act like women and to dress in clothes our Anglo friends and their mothers found too "mature" for our age. It was, and is, cultural, yet I often felt humiliated when I appeared at an American friend's party wearing a dress more suitable to a semiformal than to a playroom birthday celebration. At Puerto Rican festivities, neither the music nor the colors we wore could be too loud. I still experience a vague sense of letdown when I'm invited to a "party" and it turns out to be a marathon conversation in hushed tones rather than a fiesta with salsa, laughter and dancing—the kind of celebration I remember from my childhood.

I remember Career Day in our high school, when teachers told us to come dressed as if for a job interview. It quickly became obvious that to the barrio girls, "dressing up" sometimes meant wearing ornate jewelry and clothing that would be more appropriate (by mainstream standards) for the company Christmas party than as daily office attire. That morning I had agonized in front of my closet, trying to figure out what a "career girl" would wear because, essentially, except for Marlo Thomas on TV, I had no models on which to base my decision. I knew how to dress for school: at the Catholic school I attended we all wore uniforms; I knew how to dress for Sunday mass, and I knew what dresses to wear for parties at my relatives' homes. Though I do not recall the precise details of my Career Day outfit, it must have been a composite of the above choices. But I remember a comment my friend (an Italian-American) made in later years that coalesced my impressions of that day. She said that at the business school she was attending the Puerto Rican girls always stood out for wearing "everything at once." She meant, of course, too much jewelry, too many accessories. On that day at school, we were simply made the negative models by the nuns who were themselves not credible fashion experts to any of us. But it was painfully obvious to me that to the others, in their tailored skirts and silk blouses, we must have seemed "hopeless" and "vulgar." Though I now know that most adolescents feel out of step much of the time, I also know that for the Puerto Rican girls of my generation that sense was intensified. The way our teachers and classmates looked at us that day in school was just a taste of the culture clash that awaited us in the real world, where prospective employers and men on the street would often misinterpret our tight skirts and jingling bracelets as a come-on.

Mixed cultural signals have perpetuated certain stereotypes—for example, that of the Hispanic woman as the "Hot Tamale" or sexual firebrand. It is a one-dimensional view that the media have found easy to promote. In their special vocabulary, advertisers have designated "sizzling" and "smoldering" as the adjectives of choice for describing not only the foods but also the women of Latin America. From conversations in my house I recall hearing about the harassment that Puerto Rican women endured in factories where the "boss men" talked to them as if sexual innuendo was all they understood and, worse, often gave them the choice of submitting to advances or being fired.

It is custom, however, not chromosomes, that leads us to choose scarlet over pale pink. As young girls, we were influenced in our decisions about clothes and colors by the women—older sisters and mothers who had grown up on a tropical island where the natural environment was a riot of primary colors, where showing your skin was one way to keep cool as well as to look sexy. Most important of all, on the island, women perhaps felt freer to dress and move more provocatively, since, in most cases, they were protected by the traditions, mores, and laws of a Spanish/Catholic system of morality and machismo whose main rule was: *You may look at my sister, but if you touch her I will kill you.* The extended family and church structure could provide a young woman with a circle of safety in her small pueblo on the island; if a man "wronged" a girl, everyone would close in to save her family honor.

This is what I have gleaned from my discussions as an adult with older Puerto Rican women. They have told me about dressing in their best party clothes on Saturday nights and going to the town's plaza to promenade with their girlfriends in front of the boys they liked. The males were thus given an opportunity to admire the women and to express their admiration in the form of *piropos:* erotically charged street poems they composed on the spot. I have been subjected to a few piropos while visiting the Island, and they can be outrageous, although custom dictates that they must never cross into obscenity. This ritual, as I understand it, also entails a show of studied indifference on the woman's part; if she is "decent," she must not acknowledge the man's impassioned words. So I do understand how things can be lost in translation. When a Puerto Rican girl dressed in her idea of what is attractive meets a man from the mainstream culture who has been trained to react to certain types of clothing as a sexual signal, a clash is likely to take place. The line I first heard based on this aspect of the myth happened when the boy who took me to my first formal dance leaned over to plant a sloppy overeager kiss painfully on my mouth, and when I didn't respond with sufficient passion said in a resentful tone: "I thought you Latin girls were supposed to mature early"—my first instance of being thought of as a fruit or vegetable—I was supposed to *ripen,* not just grow into womanhood like other girls.

It is surprising to some of my professional friends that some people, including those who should know better, still put others "in their place." Though rarer, these incidents are still commonplace in my life. It happened to me most recently during a stay at a very classy metropolitan hotel favored by young professional couples for their weddings. Late one evening after the theater, as I walked toward my room with my new colleague (a woman with whom I was coordinating an arts program), a middle-aged man in a tuxedo, a young girl in satin and lace on his arm, stepped directly into our path. With his champagne glass extended toward me, he exclaimed, "Evita!"

Our way blocked, my companion and I listened as the man half-recited, half-bellowed "Don't Cry for Me, Argentina." When he finished, the young girl said: "How about a round of applause for my daddy?" We complied, hoping this would bring the silly spectacle to a close. I was becoming aware that our little group was attracting the attention of the other guests. "Daddy" must have perceived this too, and he once more barred the way as we tried to walk past him. He began to shout-sing a ditty to the tune of "La Bamba"— except the lyrics were about a girl named María whose exploits all rhymed with her name and gonorrhea. The girl kept saying "Oh, Daddy" and look-ing at me with pleading eyes. She wanted me to laugh along with the others. My companion and I stood silently waiting for the man to end his offensive song. When he finished, I looked not at him but at his daughter. I advised her calmly never to ask her father what he had done in the army. Then I walked between them and to my room. My friend complimented me on my cool handling of the situation. I confessed to her that I really had wanted to push the jerk into the swimming pool. I knew that this same man—probably a corporate executive, well educated, even worldly by most standards— would not have been likely to regale a white woman with a dirty song in public. He would perhaps have checked his impulse by assuming that she could be somebody's wife or mother, or at least *somebody* who might take offense. But to him, I was just an Evita or a María: merely a character in his cartoon-populated universe.

Because of my education and my proficiency with the English language, I have acquired many mechanisms for dealing with the anger I experience. This was not true for my parents, nor is it true for the many Latin women working at menial jobs who must put up with stereotypes about our ethnic group such as: "They make good domestics." This is another facet of the myth of the Latin women in the United States. Its origin is simple to deduce. Work as domestics, waitressing, and factory jobs are all that's available to women with little English and few skills. The myth of the Hispanic menial has been sustained by the same media phenomenon that made "Mammy" from *Gone with the Wind* America's idea of the black woman for generations; María, the housemaid or counter girl, is now indelibly etched into the national psyche. The big and the little screens have presented us with the picture of the funny Hispanic maid, mispronouncing words and cooking up a spicy storm in a shiny California kitchen.

This media-engendered image of the Latina in the United States has been documented by feminist Hispanic scholars, who claim that such por-trayals are partially responsible for the denial of opportunities for upward mobility among Latinas in the professions. I have a Chicana friend working on a Ph.D. in philosophy at a major university. She says her doctor still shakes his head in puzzled amazement at all the "big words" she uses. Since I do not wear my diplomas around my neck for all to see, I too have on occa-sion been sent to that "kitchen," where some think I obviously belong.

One such incident that has stayed with me, though I recognize it as a minor offense, happened on the day of my first public poetry reading. It took place in Miami in a boat-restaurant where we were having lunch before the event. I was nervous and excited as I walked in with my notebook in hand. An older woman motioned me to her table. Thinking (foolish me) that she wanted me to autograph a copy of my brand new slender volume of verse, I went over. She ordered a cup of coffee from me, assuming that I was the waitress. Easy enough to mistake my poems for menus, I suppose. I know that it wasn't an intentional act of cruelty, yet of all the good things that happened that day, I remember that scene most clearly, because it reminded me of what I had to overcome before anyone would take me seriously. In retrospect I understand that my anger gave my reading fire, that I have almost always taken doubts in my abilities as a challenge—and that the result is, most times, a feeling of satisfaction at having won a convert when I see the cold, appraising eyes warm to my words, the body language change, the smile that indicates that I have opened some avenue for communication. That day I read to that woman and her lowered eyes told me that she was embarrassed at her little faux pas, and when I willed her to look up to me, it was my victory, and she graciously allowed me to punish her with my full attention. We shook hands at the end of the reading, and I never saw her again. She has probably forgotten the whole thing but maybe not.

Yet I am one of the lucky ones. My parents made it possible for me to acquire a stronger footing in the mainstream culture by giving me the chance at an education. And books and art have saved me from the harsher forms of ethnic and racial prejudice that many of my Hispanic *compañeras* have had to endure. I travel a lot around the United States, reading from my books of poetry and my novel, and the reception I most often receive is one of positive interest by people who want to know more about my culture. There are, however, thousands of Latinas without the privilege of an education or the entrée into society that I have. For them life is a struggle against the misconceptions perpetuated by the myth of the Latina as whore, domestic, or criminal. We cannot change this by legislating the way people look at us. The transformation, as I see it, has to occur at a much more individual level. My personal goal in my public life is to try to replace the old pervasive stereotypes and myths about Latinas with a much more interesting set of realities. Every time I give a reading, I hope the stories I tell, the dreams and fears I examine in my work, can achieve some universal truth which will get my audience past the particulars of my skin color, my accent, or my clothes.

I once wrote a poem in which I called us Latinas "God's brown daughters." This poem is really a prayer of sorts, offered upward, but also, through the human-to-human channel of art, outward. It is a prayer for communication, and for respect. In it, Latin women pray "in Spanish to an Anglo God/with a Jewish heritage," and they are "fervently hoping/that if not omnipotent,/at least He be bilingual."

21

YOU JUST DON'T UNDERSTAND

DEBORAH TANNEN

Intimacy is key in a world of connection where individuals negotiate complex networks of friendship, minimize differences, try to reach consensus, and avoid the appearance of superiority, which would highlight differences. In a world of status, *independence* is key, because a primary means of establishing status is to tell others what to do, and taking orders is a marker of low status. Though all humans need both intimacy and independence, women tend to focus on the first and men on the second. It is as if their lifeblood ran in different directions.

These differences can give women and men differing views of the same situation, as they did in the case of a couple I will call Linda and Josh. When Josh's old high-school chum called him at work and announced he'd be in town on business the following month, Josh invited him to stay for the weekend. That evening he informed Linda that they were going to have a houseguest, and that he and his chum would go out together the first night to shoot the breeze like old times. Linda was upset. She was going to be away on business the week before, and the Friday night when Josh would be out with his chum would be her first night home. But what upset her the most was that Josh had made these plans on his own and informed her of them, rather than discussing them with her before extending the invitation.

Linda would never make plans, for a weekend or an evening, without first checking with Josh. She can't understand why he doesn't show her the same courtesy and consideration that she shows him. But when she protests, Josh says, "I can't say to my friend, 'I have to ask my wife for permission'!"

To Josh, checking with his wife means seeking permission, which implies that he is not independent, not free to act on his own. It would make him feel like a child or an underling. To Linda, checking with her husband has nothing to do with permission. She assumes that spouses discuss their plans with each other because their lives are intertwined, so the actions of one have consequences for the other. Not only does Linda not mind telling someone, "I have to check with Josh"; quite the contrary——she likes it. It makes her feel good to know and show that she is involved with someone, that her life is bound up with someone else's.

Linda and Josh both felt more upset by this incident, and others like it, than seemed warranted, because it cut to the core of their primary concerns. Linda was hurt because she sensed a failure of closeness in their relationship: He didn't care about her as much as she cared about him. And he was hurt because he felt she was trying to control him and limit his freedom.

A similar conflict exists between Louise and Howie, another couple, about spending money. Louise would never buy anything costing more than a hundred dollars without discussing it with Howie, but he goes out and buys whatever he wants and feels they can afford, like a table saw or a new power mower. Louise is disturbed, not because she disapproves of the purchases, but because she feels he is acting as if she were not in the picture.

Many women feel it is natural to consult with their partners at every turn, while many men automatically make more decisions without consulting their partners. This may reflect a broad difference in conceptions of decision making. Women expect decisions to be discussed first and made by consensus. They appreciate the discussion itself as evidence of involvement and communication. But many men feel oppressed by lengthy discussions about what they see as minor decisions, and they feel hemmed in if they can't just act without talking first. When women try to initiate a freewheeling discussion by asking, "What do you think?" men often think they are being asked to decide. . . .

Asymmetries: Women and Men Talking at Cross-Purposes

Eve had a lump removed from her breast. Shortly after the operation, talking to her sister, she said that she found it upsetting to have been cut into, and that looking at the stitches was distressing because they left a seam that had changed the contour of her breast. Her sister said, "I know. When I had my operation I felt the same way." Eve made the same observation to her friend Karen, who said, "I know. It's like your body has been violated." But when she told her husband, Mark, how she felt, he said, "You can have plastic surgery to cover up the scar and restore the shape of your breast."

Eve had been comforted by her sister and her friend, but she was not comforted by Mark's comment. Quite the contrary, it upset her more. Not only didn't she hear what she wanted, that he understood her feelings, but, far worse, she felt he was asking her to undergo more surgery just when she was telling him how much this operation had upset her. "I'm not having any more surgery!" she protested. "I'm sorry you don't like the way it looks." Mark was hurt and puzzled. "I don't care," he protested. "It doesn't bother me at all." She asked, "Then why are you telling me to have plastic surgery?" He answered, "Because you were saying *you* were upset about the way it looked."

Eve felt like a heel: Mark had been wonderfully supportive and concerned throughout her surgery. How could she snap at him because of what he said —"just words"—when what he had done was unassailable? And yet she had perceived in his words metamessages that cut to the core of their relationship. It was self-evident to him that his comment was a reaction to her complaint, but she heard it as an independent complaint of his. He thought he was reassuring her that she needn't feel bad about her scar because there was something she could *do* about it. She heard his suggestion that she do something about the scar as evidence that *he* was bothered by it. Furthermore, whereas she wanted reassurance that it was normal to feel bad in her situation, his telling her that the problem could easily be fixed implied she had no right to feel bad about it.

Eve wanted the gift of understanding, but Mark gave her the gift of advice. He was taking the role of problem solver, whereas she simply wanted confirmation for her feelings.

A similar misunderstanding arose between a husband and wife following a car accident in which she had been seriously injured. Because she hated being in the hospital, the wife asked to come home early. But once home, she suffered pain from having to move around more. Her husband said, "Why didn't you stay in the hospital where you would have been more comfortable?" This hurt her because it seemed to imply that he did not want her home. She didn't think of his suggestion that she should have stayed in the hospital as a response to her complaints about the pain she was suffering; she thought of it as an independent expression of his preference not to have her at home.

"They're My Troubles—Not Yours"

If women are often frustrated because men do not respond to their troubles by offering matching troubles, men are often frustrated because women do. Some men not only take no comfort in such a response, they take offense. For example, a woman told me that when her companion talks about a personal concern—for example, his feelings about growing older—she responds, "I know how you feel; I feel the same way." To her surprise and chagrin, he gets annoyed; he feels she is trying to take something away from him by denying the uniqueness of his experience.

A similar miscommunication was responsible for the following interchange, which began as a conversation and ended as an argument:

> He: I'm really tired. I didn't sleep well last night.
> She: I didn't sleep well either. I never do.
> He: Why are you trying to belittle me?
> She: I'm not! I'm just trying to show that I understand!

This woman was not only hurt by her husband's reaction; she was mystified by it. How could he think she was belittling him? By "belittle me," he meant "belittle my experience." He was filtering her attempts to establish connection through his concern with preserving independence and avoiding being put down.

"I'll Fix it For You"

Women and men are both often frustrated by the other's way of responding to their expression of troubles. And they are further hurt by the other's frustration. If women resent men's tendency to offer solutions to problems, men complain about women's refusal to take action to solve the problems they complain about. Since many men see themselves as problem solvers, a complaint or a trouble is a challenge to their ability to think of a solution, just as a woman presenting a broken bicycle or stalling car poses a challenge to their ingenuity in fixing it. But whereas many women appreciate help in fixing mechanical equipment, few are inclined to appreciate help in "fixing" emotional troubles. . . .

Trying to solve a problem or fix a trouble focuses on the message level of talk. But for most women who habitually report problems at work or in friendships, the message is not the main point of complaining. It's the metamessage that counts: Telling about a problem is a bid for an expression of understanding ("I know how you feel") or a similar complaint ("I felt the same way when something similar happened to me"). In other words, troubles talk is intended to reinforce rapport by sending the metamessage "We're the same; you're not alone." Women are frustrated when they not only don't get this reinforcement but, quite the opposite, feel distanced by the advice, which seems to send the metamessage "We're not the same. You have the problems; I have the solutions."

Furthermore, mutual understanding is symmetrical, and this symmetry contributes to a sense of community. But giving advice is asymmetrical. It frames the advice giver as more knowledgeable, more reasonable, more in control—in a word, one-up. And this contributes to the distancing effect. . . .

Matching Troubles

The very different way that women respond to the telling of troubles is dramatized in a short story, "New Haven," by Alice Mattison. Eleanor tells Patsy that she has fallen in love with a married man. Patsy responds by first displaying understanding and then offering a matching revelation about a similar experience:

"Well," says Patsy. "I know how you feel."
"You do?"

"In a way, I do. Well, I should tell you. I've been sleeping with a married man for two years."

Patsy then tells Eleanor about her affair and how she feels about it. After they discuss Patsy's affair, however, Patsy says:

"But you were telling me about this man and I cut you off. I'm sorry. See? I'm getting self-centered."
"It's OK." But she is pleased again.

The conversation then returns to Eleanor's incipient affair. Thus Patsy responds first by confirming Eleanor's feelings and matching her experience, reinforcing their similarity, and then by encouraging Eleanor to tell more. Within the frame of Patsy's similar predicament, the potential asymmetry inherent in revealing personal problems is avoided, and the friendship is brought into balance.

What made Eleanor's conversation with Patsy so pleasing to Eleanor was that they shared a sense of how to talk about troubles, and this reinforced their friendship. Though Eleanor raised the matter of her affair, she did not elaborate on it until Patsy pressed her to do so. In another story by the same author, "The Knitting," a woman named Beth is staying with her sister in order to visit her sister's daughter Stephanie in a psychiatric hospital. While there, Beth receives a disturbing telephone call from her boyfriend, Alec. Having been thus reminded of her troubles, she wants to talk about them, but she refrains, because her sister doesn't ask. She feels required, instead, to focus on her sister's problem, the reason for her visit:

She'd like to talk about her muted half-quarrels with Alec of the last weeks, but her sister does not ask about the phone call. Then Beth thinks they should talk about Stephanie.

The women in these stories are balancing a delicate system by which troubles talk is used to confirm their feelings and create a sense of community.

When women confront men's ways of talking to them, they judge them by the standards of women's conversational styles. Women show concern by following up someone else's statement of trouble by questioning her about it. When men change the subject, women think they are showing a lack of sympathy—a failure of intimacy. But the failure to ask probing questions could just as well be a way of respecting the other's need for independence. When Eleanor tells Patsy that she is in love with Peter, Patsy asks, "Are you sleeping with him?" This exploration of Eleanor's topic could well strike many men—and some women—as intrusive, though Eleanor takes it as a show of interest that nourishes their friendship.

Women tend to show understanding of another woman's feelings. When men try to reassure women by telling them that their situation is not so bleak, the women hear their feelings being belittled or discounted. Again, they encounter a failure of intimacy just when they were bidding to reinforce it. Trying to trigger a symmetrical communication, they end up in an asymmetrical one.

22

REAL MEN DON'T CRY . . . AND OTHER "UNCOOL" MYTHS

PHIL W. PETRIE

Things were not going well. Do they ever for young couples struggling to understand each other, raise a family, pay the mortgage and at least keep the Joneses in sight? I had wanted to comfort my pregnant wife, soothe her with words that would temper the harshness of our reality. The baby was due in two months and my employer had just informed me that I didn't have hospitalization coverage for childbirth. I was frustrated and wanted to scream, lay my head in my wife's lap and cry. I needed to be soothed as well as she. She wanted to talk about our predicament, needed to talk it out. So did I, but I couldn't. I felt that I had failed her. Guilt stood at my side. But how could she know any of that, since all I did was to turn on the stereo system—my electronic security blanket—and listen to Miles Davis. I was cool. Her words shot through the space of "All Blues." "You're a cold SOB," she hissed.

She's being emotional again, I thought, *Just like a woman.* I, on the other hand, was controlling the situation because I was cool—which in reality was only a few degrees away from being cold. Wasn't that what she really wanted from me as head of the household—control? Wasn't Freud correct when he proclaimed that our anatomy was our destiny (that is, our genitals determine our behavior)? In spite of her protestations that we had to talk, there was nothing in my upbringing that negated for me the power of coolness. I knew by the example of my elders that men controlled themselves and women did not.

In Mt. Olive, the Baptist church of my youth, it was expected that the "sisters" would "carry on" at church services. And they did. Moved by

From *Essence,* November 1982. Reprinted by permission of the author.

something that the preacher had said or by the mystery of a song, they would leap from their seats, run, scream, hurtle down the aisles. Transformed. Private feeling was suddenly public spectacle. Ushers came. White-gloved hands brushed away the tears. The men of the church, the elders, sat glued to their seats. I watched, instructed by this example of male control. I watched in silence but wished that I could know the electric transformation that moved those souls to dance.

"The larger culture creates expectations for males," says Dr. Walter Tardy, a psychiatrist in New York City. "In spite of the Women's Liberation Movement, men still live in a very macho culture and role play. Women tend to display their feelings more."

One of the roles men play is that of the rational being devoid of strong emotions. Profound feelings, it is thought, will interfere with the male task, whether that means making it at the nine-to-five or making it at war. Objective decisions must be made without distracting emotions, which women are thought to be prone to—even by some other women. For many persons, "being a man" is synonymous with being emotionless—cool.

One need not be told this. Like air, it seems to be a pervasive part of the male atmosphere. If one missed it at church (as I did not), one might pick it up at the barbershop or the playground—places where the elements of the culture are passed on without the benefit of critical examination.

> Didn't Wimpy Sheppard tell me at Tom Simon's Barbershop that only babies, women and sissies cried? A man, he said, ain't supposed to cry. That's why my father, at the death of his mother, slipped out to the backyard away from his family to sit among the chickens and wail. How could I explain to my wife—to myself—that I couldn't rest my head in her lap and weep? I had to protect my masculinity. Asking me to cry, to drop my cool, was asking me to redefine my life.

Says Margo Williams, a widow residing in San Diego, California, with her two children, "If you can't let down to your mate, friend or what have you, then you have to ask yourself what the relationship is all about—is it worth being involved with? For me, it's not about my man being strong and hard. I want him to be a human being—warm, sensitive and willing to share his life with me."

What if he balks? Williams is asked. "If the relationship is a serious one, I would urge him to let us try to work through the problems," she says. "I would want to establish a relationship wherein we could express to each other our needs and wants—even express our dislikes. We have to establish an honest relationship."

Dr. Tardy cautions that "there are degrees of honesty. Do you tell the truth all of the time, or is a white lie something appropriate? One can only be just so honest. The truth may set you free, but some truths should be withheld because they can hurt more than they help. But even if you don't tell it all, you must tell *something*. Communication is the key."

Therein lies the danger of being cool and playing roles. In doing this, one reveals a persona rather than a person, plays a part rather than being part of the relationship. Communication, by its root definition, means "sharing, making something common between people." It is this fear of sharing— giving up something—that drives some men into being noncommunicative except in the area of sex.

Robert Staples, a sociologist, states in his book *Black Masculinity* (Black Scholar Press) that when Black men "have been unable to achieve status in the workplace, they have exercised the privilege of their manliness and attempted to achieve it [power] in the bedroom. Feeling a constant need to affirm their masculinity, tenderness and compassion are eschewed as signs of weakness, which leaves them vulnerable to the ever-feared possibility of female domination."

It could be argued that in today's climate of women's liberation, all men are on the defensive because of the developing assertiveness of women. No doubt some men—if not many—use sex as a controlling force. "But," says Wilbur Suesberry, a pediatrician practicing in Compton, California, "I don't believe that sex is racially restrictive. Black sexuality is a myth started and supported by whites and perpetuated by Blacks. Men find it difficult to express their inner feelings but they must find a way to do it. If you have things pent up inside of you and they do not come out in a healthy way, then they exit in an unhealthy way. Sex as an outlet for your emotions is not good. To communicate you can't sulk or take to the bed, you must talk." Talk? Yes, talk is a more precise method of communicating than sex, intuition or an "understanding."

> "The birth is due in two months," she persisted. "What are we going to do?" Annoyed, not at her but at the apparent futility of the situation, I turned up the record player and went deeper into myself. Didn't she *understand* me well enough to know that I would do something? Hadn't I always? Couldn't she look at me and see that I was worried too? Didn't she *trust* me well enough to know that I would do something? All of those questions might have been eliminated with my telling her simply and directly what my feelings really were. How could she really know them unless she were a mind reader, just as I didn't know what she felt? Screaming and crying isn't quite the same thing as communicating effectively. I pulled her to me, caressed her.

Hugging and kissing are not substitutes for words, for language. Talking to each other allows us to bring order to the disruption and confusion engendered by silence. *Talk to me*, Little Willie John used to sing, *talk to me in your own sweet gentle way.*

This simple verbal act is made all the more difficult for men (and women, for that matter) if we don't know (or won't admit) what our feelings really are. We can't talk about things if we can't conceptualize them. Communication is more than mouthing words or rapping. I see it as defining an aspect of one's life by framing that aspect into words and then sharing it with someone. It is not only a problem for lovers; it also bedevils fathers and sons, mothers and daughters. It is problematic because it drives you within. The first act of communication is with your self—"the private self," Dr. Tardy calls it. This journey within involves both introspection and openness.

Yet what I face within myself—if indeed I face it—may never be completely shared with anyone. An insistence that I communicate *all* of my feelings is asking too much. We men are now being urged not only to redefine our roles and relationships with our mates and society but also to become vulnerable by revealing our private selves to another public, although it may be a public of only one. The degree to which I can do this—express *some* of my feelings—is determined by the self-awareness I have of myself and the trust I have for my spouse.

I closet my feelings out of self-protection and fear of the unknown. Women in their newfound drive for liberation have the example of men to direct them. It seems that all women are asking for is some of the prerogatives once claimed by men only. But what is to be the model for me? White men? I think not. Granted they are the movers and shakers within this society, but the madness of the world that they have created does not make them legitimate role models. Yet for many Black women the term *man* is synonymous with *white man*. I resent being asked to pattern myself after a man whose reality—full of avarice and destruction—is so antithetical to mine. I hold on to my cool.

For Black men, being cool is not just an attitude; it becomes a political stance, a metaphor for power. To give that up is, in effect, to render oneself powerless—to lose control. For Black men, who control so little, to lose this cool is to lose a weapon in their arsenal for survival. Do Black women know that?

> "Maybe you could call somebody [white?] who can help," she suggested, determined to get a word out of me. And if I can't find someone white to help us with my problems, I thought, then I can fold up and cry to you. Ugh. Is this what you ask of me: to imitate white men or act like women (that is, take control or cry)? What brave new world are you asking me to enter into by dropping my cool, discarding my role as leader, drowning my strength with tears? It is a scenario that no other group of men in history has ever played. Yet you ask me, the most politically weak person within the society, to lead the way to this new world. How can you ask me that, baby? And if I go, will you cast me aside as being weak? You

scream about a man who is strong enough to cry, strong enough to admit weaknesses, and at the same time you want a "take-charge" person, a man who won't let anyone run over him. Caught between such confusion, I turn to the ball game, to the television, to the silence within myself. Love is withheld. Restrained. Tentative.

"I think that our generation is too tentative," says Lee Atkins, a publishing-company sales representative living in Chicago. "Those of us born in the 1940's and before were given too many caveats. Black men or boys were told not to do this and not to do that. Avoid the police. Stay out of trouble. All of this was done to protect us in an extremely racist and hostile society. In effect, we were being told: behave or you will be destroyed." That made us cautious and we are now paying the price for all that caution. As men we find that we are too careful, too private, not open and not willing to explore. We find it difficult to open up even to those we care about the most.

"Those kids born in the 1950's and 1960's," Atkins continues, "were born into a world where the expectations for the Black male were more positive. A whole set of new possibilities was suddenly available. Sexually, things were more permissive, and in the do-your-own-thing attitude of the 1960's and 1970's Black men were actually encouraged to be more unconventional, to open up."

This has led to young Black men who are more candid about their feelings, more carefree in their attitudes. "I would be surprised," says Dr. Tardy, "if these young adults weren't more open in their dealings with each other. The drawback may be that they don't want to establish the permanent relations that were expected in the past. I can imagine that many young women will say that the young men today aren't 'serious' or are too much into themselves. That's the legacy of hanging loose."

Whether we are young or old, one thing is certain: we men cannot expect to go through a lifetime in silence, repressing our feelings, denying our emotions, without being run down by frustrations, failed opportunities and unfulfilled promises. And why would we do this? Is it because of the protrusion dangling between our legs? Is it because we hold on to a fixed role in a changing world? Or is it because of our fear of losing an imagined power? Perhaps the answer is all of the above. If so, we must rush to get rid of these contrived ghosts. In the real world our women are calling to us. How long will they keep it up before they give up? Or as writer Amiri Baraka asks, "How long till the logic of our lives runs us down?"

She stood before me pleading, belly swollen with my seed. She wasn't asking for much, just that I talk to her. She was richly human and was demanding that I be nothing less, saying that I couldn't be a man until I showed that I was human—warm, tender, compassionate, feeling, and able to express that feeling. It was difficult, but with a guide so dedicated to my good health I began the journey from within to without that day. We found the money for the hospital. But more important, I found that I could talk to her about me, could share my life in trust with her. I write this as a souvenir of remembrance—a gift for her.

23

DANNY

NATHAN McCALL

Sitting at my desk, working, I noticed a tall, lanky white dude walk into the newsroom and head toward my row. He was casually dressed: a silly-looking stingy-brimmed straw hat on his curly head, a lightweight mustard-colored zip-up jacket, paddy-boy slacks, and a pair of those shoes construction workers wear. No sport coat or tie. He was dressed so casual I assumed he'd come in for a story interview. Then he walked straight over to the aisle where I sat, plopped a notepad down on the empty desk behind me, and took a seat. I thought, *Just what I need. Another cracker near me.*

I stood up to go to the supply cabinet. Before I could leave, the new guy sprang from his seat, extended his hand, and said, "Hi. I'm Danny. Danny Baum." He was three inches from my face, smiling like there was something funny. I shook his hand. "I'm Nathan." And I walked away.

Later, I saw Danny walking across the newsroom. He had a goofy demeanor—long strides, arms swinging wild—like a northern Gomer Pyle or Mr. Green Jeans on *Captain Kangaroo*. A white woman reporter who sat near me leaned over to another white reporter, pointed at Danny, and whispered, "That's the new guy. Do you know what he did? He moved into a *black* neighborhood. Everybody's talking about it. *Somebody's* got to talk to him." Apparently unaware that I overheard, they burst out laughing, as if this new guy—this crazy northerner—had done the stupidest thing in the world. I looked at them a minute and thought to myself, *Uh-huh. These are the same pseudo-liberal crackers who will get up in your face and swear they're not racist and they don't see color. Yet they thought it was hilarious that a white guy was so color-blind that he'd moved into a black neighborhood.* I decided that the next time a white person told me he didn't see color, I was gonna call him a liar to his face. Let him know that he can't insult my intelligence and get away with it.

After I finished going off on white people in my head, I turned my thoughts back to this Danny guy. What kind of a person *was* he to move into a black neighborhood? Was it a mistake on his part or did he do that intentionally?

Newsroom gossip held that he had come to the *Atlanta Journal-Constitution* from *The Wall Street Journal*. Normally, that's considered a step down professionally. *The Wall Street Journal* is, after all, one of the top newspapers in the country. When asked why he left the *Journal* to come to Atlanta, Danny had told someone, "The people at *The Wall Street Journal* were too stuffy and pretentious. I decided I'd get a real job with real people who would let me chase fire engines and write about it."

In the following weeks, I watched him closely to see what he was about. It didn't take long to see that there was something different about this cat. Other people in the newsroom, blacks and whites, recognized it, too. I found him to be different in a pleasant way. Whenever he said something to me, there was a straightforwardness, a childlike honesty, that I didn't get from most other white people. With him, I didn't feel the hesitancy I felt from other whites or the racial baggage getting in the way. And he'd ask me the damnedest things out of the blue. One day, he slid his swivel chair back near mine and asked, "Why aren't black reporters more aggressive around here, Nate?"

It was the kind of thing I knew a lot of whites around there wondered about but were afraid to ask for fear of sounding racist or for fear of revealing that they were, in fact, racist. But Danny didn't seem to care. I concluded it must have been because he was secure in his mind that he wasn't racist, and he had nothing to hide. He was simply curious. He didn't know, so he did what any intelligent person should have done: He asked rather than assume. I respected that about him and found that, in spite of myself, there was something about this dude I really liked.

Since we sat so close to each other, we began rapping a lot at our desks. I learned Danny had done his own examination of the white mainstream and reached some of the same conclusions as me: that it was totally fucked up, that they needed to scratch all the rules governing the macho corporate game and go back to drawing stickmen on cave walls because that's about how far they'd come in human development. By the time he came to *The Atlanta Journal-Constitution*, Danny had decided that he was no longer going to play the game by their silly rules. He didn't brownnose the bosses or try to join the white folks' privileged insiders' club in the newsroom. He didn't try to get in with all the *right* people to gain an edge. In fact, he held management in contempt and talked about them as much as I did.

When Hosea Williams led a march in Forsythe County to protest the racism and open hostility to blacks who moved there, Danny took part in the march, even though our bosses had ordered reporters to stay out of it for the sake of objectivity. When he did that, I concluded that this dude was *truly* wild.

———————

One day, Danny slid his seat near mine and said, "Nate, how about coming over to my place for dinner this weekend?"

"Lemme see what I've got planned," I said, "and I'll get back to you on that." I didn't have anything planned. I said that to buy time to think about it. Thinking about it, even *considering* spending my free weekend time at a white person's house, was a major leap for me. Had it been anyone else I wouldn't have had to think about it at all. I'd have declined without blinking an eye. But I considered it with Danny and decided, *What the hell. I'll give it a try.* Besides, I wanted to see just where he lived and ask him why he had moved into a black neighborhood.

I went to Danny's place that weekend. He definitely lived in the 'hood. He'd rented a detached house in a working-class neighborhood in Hosea Williams's council district. Danny was dating another reporter at the paper, Meg Knox, who lived in Savannah and worked for the paper's bureau there, several hours from Atlanta. She seemed just as laid-back and cool as Danny. We ate, then went into his living room, sat down, talked, and drank beer. It was the most comfortable I'd ever felt around white people. I didn't feel like Danny and Meg were judging me by their standards all the time. They didn't try to pretend there were no differences between us, like everybody else I knew. They celebrated our differences, and we joked about contrasts in the way blacks and whites talked, cooked, dressed, danced, and did everything else.

At some point, Danny told me he'd moved into this black neighborhood because he could get the best deal for his money there. "I like this house. It has a porch and a yard. The neighbors are friendly. . . . Actually, I'm thinking about buying it."

We talked about our tastes in white music and black music. I told them how I'd learned about white music—about the time I stole those tapes out of some white person's car. Danny played a tape for me and explained why a particular white artist I'd asked about was currently so popular. The singer was Bruce Springsteen, and the tape was *Born in the U.S.A.*

We talked a lot about race. I guess it helped that Danny was Jewish. Danny told me that he'd had his share of brushes with racism, and it didn't sit well with him. He asked me about Louis Farrakhan, whom he said frightened Jews with his statement that Hitler was a great man. "Nate," he asked, "why does Farrakhan hate Jews?"

I said, "I don't agree with everything Farrakhan says, but I don't think he hates Jews. I think he's widely misunderstood and his comments are often taken out of context. He's simply pro-black. A lot of white people assume that if you're pro-black then you must be anti-white. . . .You have to listen closely to what Farrakhan says to understand where he's coming from."

He asked to borrow a tape of Farrakhan so that he could hear it for himself.

We talked about a lot of other things. I was surprised to learn that he had actually read books written by black people: James Baldwin, Richard Wright, Ralph Ellison. It amazed me that a white person would do that when it wasn't required of him. He seemed equally as surprised to learn that one of my favorite authors was the Jewish writer Chaim Potok.

I left Danny's place late that night surprised that time had passed so quickly and shocked that I had actually spent a weekend evening—voluntarily—with whites and had a grand time. In return, I invited Meg and Danny over to my place for dinner. They met Debbie and our small children. It was one of those evenings when the differences between Debbie and me seemed to vanish, a night when there were no arguments about in-laws and money problems. After we put the children to bed, the four of us sat on the front porch and laughed and talked for hours. It was the first time I'd had any white people over to my house.

———

After a while, I found that I looked forward to talking with Danny. We grew closer and, in jest, gave each other silly nicknames. I started calling him "Danny Boy," and he called me "Nate McMann." He'd walk into the newsroom, look at me, and say, "Nate McMann, how ya doin', bro." I'd say, "Fine, Danny Boy, just fine."

At some point during the two years he lived in Atlanta, somebody broke into Danny's house. I felt strange about that. On its face, it supported the stereotype of crime-ridden black neighborhoods. I wondered if it would conjure up racial stereotypes and send him running for cover, as it would many pretentious liberal whites I'd seen. But Danny treated it like any break-in. It didn't seem to matter to him whether the burglar was black or white. He stayed right in the neighborhood until he left Atlanta. More than anything else, that told me that this cat was for real.

———

When Danny found out that I had a bike, he suggested we get together and go riding one Saturday morning. I agreed, and we were on. He pulled up to my place the following Saturday driving an old green station wagon he'd bought from a colleague. We threw the bikes in and he drove deep into the country. We picked a turnoff spot, parked the car alongside the road, and unloaded the bikes. We rode for hours and talked about everything. I asked him tough questions about whites. He asked me tough questions about blacks. He'd offer his theory on a matter, then wait for my response. I respected his sincerity—so much so that I even confided in him that I'd been to prison. I hadn't told anyone else at the paper about my prison past, not even other blacks.

The country road was deserted, except for an occasional passing pickup truck. After a long period of silence, Danny came at me with another question. "You're pretty angry inside, aren't you, Nate McMann?"

"Naw, Danny Boy, I'm not angry. I'm fuckin' furious."

Danny frowned. "God, Nate, you think about race all the time. Give it a rest, man. It ain't healthy."

I told Danny I didn't have a choice in the matter. "You can sit around and intellectualize about race when you want to, and when you get tired of it you can set it aside and go surfing or hang gliding and forget about it. But I can't. Race affects every facet of my life, man. I can't get past race because white folks won't let me get past it. They remind me of it everywhere I go. Every time I step in an elevator and a white woman bunches up in the corner like she thinks I wanna rape her, I'm forced to think about it. Every time I walk into stores, the suspicious looks in white shopkeepers' eyes make me think about it. Every time I walk past whites sitting in their cars, I hear the door locks clicking and I think about it. I can't get away from it, man. I stay so mad all the time because I'm forced to spend so much time and energy reacting to race. I hate it. It wearies me. But there's no escape, man. No escape."

When I finished talking, I felt like I had preached a sermon. I didn't realize I had so much frustration bottled up until I let it out on Danny. At first, I wondered why I had told him so much of what was going on inside my head. Then I realized that despite all I'd said in the past about not caring what white folks thought, I cared a lot. In fact, I had spent my whole life reacting to what they thought. The notion that one of them cared, really cared, about what I thought moved me. Danny was the first white person I met whom I actually saw trying hard to understand. It meant a lot to me that he tried because he wanted to and not because he had to. By the same token, he helped me see the world through white eyes and helped me better understand the fear and ignorance behind prejudice.

I learned something else from Danny that hadn't been clear to me before. I learned how little even the most highly educated white folks really know about blacks. He was very well educated and yet he struggled to understand some of the most basic things about black life in America. He struggled because in school he hadn't been taught diddly about blacks. Even though he saw us every day and interacted with us, we were puzzles to him. That showed me that the education system in this country has failed white people more than it's failed anybody else. It has crippled them and limited their humanity. They're the ones who need to know the most about everybody because they're the ones running the country. They've been taught so little about anybody other than white people that they can't understand, even when they try.

During one of our bike rides, we stopped and sat down on the side of a grassy mound to take a break from the scorching sun. About a hundred yards behind us, there was a huge white house sitting on a large tract of land. We were sitting there, talking and tossing pebbles onto the street, when a white man crept up behind us. "Hi," he said.

We both said hello. I expected the man to tell us to get the hell off his grass. Instead, he said something that startled me. "You guys look hot. I've got a full-sized swimming pool in my backyard if you want to take a swim."

Initially, his words didn't register with me. In my mind, there was something wrong with that picture. After all, this *was* Deep South Georgia and we *were* in some country town. I'd come out there half expecting to encounter hillbillies with gun racks in the windows of their pickup trucks. Now this cat was inviting us—a black and a white—to take a dip in his swimming pool?

Danny looked at me and I said, "No thanks. We're about to leave."

The man was almost insistent. "Really, I don't mind. Help yourselves and cool off if you want."

"No, we've got to leave."

The man smiled warmly and said, "O.K. If you change your mind, feel free to come on over."

"Thanks."

We got up and rode off. Later, I reflected on what that might have been about. I think the white man was moved by the picture of a white guy and a black dude sitting on the side of the road, rapping. I could be wrong, but I think the sight of us warmed his heart and he wanted to take part in our interracial communion for reasons of his own. Danny and I never discussed it, but I never forgot it, because gestures like that were so rare in my experience.

———————

Danny told me sometime in 1987 that he and Meg planned to go to Africa to travel and work as freelance writers for a while. Initially, I felt envious that he, a white guy, would get the chance to go to my homeland, which I'd never been to as an adult. I told him how I felt: "See, you white motherfuckas get to do everything in the world you wanna do."

He insisted, "Nate, there's nothing stopping you from doing what you want to do in life. You can go to Africa, too."

That started a running debate. "No, I can't, Danny. You don't understand. You white boys can take off from work anytime and hitchhike across the country or spend a coupla years hoboing in Europe. Then, when you get ready to resume your career, the white establishment will welcome you back with open arms. But if I tried to do some shit like that, Mr. Charlie's gonna wanna know where I been and why there's a gap on my résumé. He's gonna want me to give an account of any time that was not spent slaving for him."

I had no frame of reference for Danny's opinion. All I knew was that every black person I had ever met had lived life aware of the limitations imposed by race, and that those who had tried to do what they truly wanted were met with intense opposition. I felt it was easy for Danny to think there were no ceilings because he hadn't known any.

Danny didn't win me over on that issue before leaving Atlanta, but he dropped a piece of advice on me that changed my thinking about something else. He said, "Look, Nate McMann, you may not believe this, but there are several white people in the newsroom who are *really* good people. You should give them a chance before writing them off as racists. Get to know some of them. You might be pleasantly surprised."

Later, I thought about what he had said. I thought about those whites who had tried to be friendly and the semi-meaningful talks I'd had with some of them in the newsroom: Among them was a political reporter who seemed sincere and two editors I had grown to like. *Maybe,* I thought, *I should open up more and be receptive to the fact that there are some good whites in the world.*

Somehow, just thinking that thought made me feel better. I realized that I needed to know that there might be other white people like Danny and Meg, and that there was some reason for hope in this deeply disturbed nation of ours.

Danny and Meg just left for Africa. Of all the white people I know, they are among the very few I can call friends. It's sad, this gulf between blacks and whites. We're so afraid of each other. . . .

January 10, 1987

24

RURAL ORGANIZING
Building Community across Difference

SUZANNE PHARR

I n 1993, Wanda and Brenda Henson purchased land to create a women's education center and retreat in Ovett, Mississippi. When the townspeople came upon a newsletter that, among other things, indicated that lesbians were involved, there was a highly emotional reaction to this perceived threat to the local community. After organizing by some preachers and local officials, two town meetings, relentless media coverage, intervention by Janet Reno, and supportive responses from lesbians and gay men nationally, the situation in Ovett today can be described as an emotionally charged, potentially violent standoff.

The complicated conflict that has unfolded between the women of Sister Spirit and the townspeople of Ovett, Mississippi, has been much on my

Reprinted by permission of *Sojourner: The Women's Forum,* June 1994, and the author.

mind for some months now. I have been fearful that someone would be killed: a member of Sister Spirit, a townsperson, or a visitor arriving to observe the situation. With trepidation, I have watched the widespread media coverage help keep emotions intense and people stratified.

The conflict has been depicted as between diametrically opposed groups, with little middle ground: the dykes against the bigots. I've been wishing, however, that I could see more of the middle ground. I know it's there, because I'm standing on a little piece of it. As a lesbian, I have strong identification with the women of Sister Spirit, and as a woman from a low-income rural Southern family, I identify with the working-class people who make up Ovett. They are both my people.

I have a vested interest in these groups learning how to make community together, for if they and others like them cannot, how then can lesbians such as myself live openly with and among our rural families and friends? If we cannot do rural organizing around lesbian and gay issues, then rural lesbians and gay men are left with limited options: leaving our roots to live in cities; living fearful invisible lives in our rural communities; or with visibility, becoming marginalized, isolated, and endangered. Not one of these options holds the promise of wholeness or freedom. We are compelled to do rural organizing because we cannot accept freedoms restricted by geography—or by race or gender or class or any other boundary our society uses for exclusion.

Ovett, then, becomes for us an opening to talk about rural issues, about how to create social change in all of our communities, without exception.

It's difficult for me to talk about rural life without first talking about the antirural attitudes that are prevalent in this country. Urban dwellers, particularly within the lesbian and gay movement, are pretty consistently disrespectful of rural people, especially Southerners. Our first clue is in the language that describes rural places as "hinterlands," "boondocks," "the sticks," "back side of nowhere," and the people as "rednecks," "clods," "bubbas," and "bigots." For a movement that touts "difference" as positive, this level of prejudice and ignorance is appalling. Articles in the lesbian and gay press, as well as the mainstream press, about Sister Spirit have been filled with these antirural attitudes.

It is remarkable to me that someone writing from the chaos and deterioration of our major cities would assume a position of condescension toward rural people. We all have our troubles in this country, no matter where we live. I believe, however, that antirural attitudes are based in class prejudice. The rural United States, outside of resort and retirement communities, is mostly working class and often low income. Because of isolation and an inadequate tax base due to low population density and income, rural areas are often characterized by limited services. We must remember that lack of access and economic standing do not equal ignorance or stupidity or bigotry. Culture simply gets shaped along different lines, with different values. Both urban and rural life offer positive and negative values.

The first rule of rural organizing (as it is for all other groups) is that it needs to be done by the people affected, not others imposing their vision and will. Since resources in rural areas are often limited, this organizing should be supported but not driven by urban people. To achieve this partnership, we all have to get over our bad attitudes: urban disrespect and rural resentment of outsiders.

I believe that the basis of all of our organizing has to be building relationships. This belief runs counter to the notion that we are in a war and a shoot-out is required as we line up along strictly marked and separated sides. In Ovett, community has to be built if Sister Spirit is to stay on their land and thrive; otherwise, there will have to be a shoot-out of one kind or another (guns, lawsuits, increasing harassment), and there will be death or flight or the restricted and tortuous life of two armed camps. It is through building relationships that we achieve transformation.

One day, when I was being particularly angry at the people of Ovett (having very little information about them and forgetting that they were my people), I began thinking about my own rural background. I remembered my first sixteen years of lesbian invisibility, how terrified I was of losing my family and community relationships, and how I lost their authenticity anyway because I cut so much of myself off from them. I thought about how everybody lost: I lost part of my humanity, and they lost a chance to develop theirs through knowing me. The road to coming out publicly was long and slow. Building relationships based on authenticity (our whole and true selves) is slow work. Now, 25 years later, I have deep, loving relationships with my large rural Georgia family, people very much like the townspeople of Ovett. Yet, here I was in 1994, judging the people of Ovett harshly because they couldn't do overnight what it took me, as a lesbian, sixteen years to do: to overcome my fear, my misunderstanding, my lack of information and support, and my homophobia. I had to stop myself and say, "Isn't it a bit much to ask the local people to do immediate change?" Yes, far more information is out there now to help them (and young lesbians and gay men), but who is delivering that information and how?

Relationships are not built on abstractions but on human interactions: they have to have a human face. Part of our work is to figure out how to put a human face on what for most people is the *idea* of homosexuality, to transform it through genuine relationships with lesbians and gay men.

In rural communities (and elsewhere), whether we are just becoming public about being lesbian or gay or are moving in from the outside, we are usually entering the community for the first time. It is, in a sense, someone else's community, because we have not had a presence there as who we are in this part of ourselves. Consequently, we have to be thoughtful about how we enter. We have to ask if immediate confrontation gives the best result; i.e., does it open up the most space for living freely, for creating the most productive dialogue?

In the early '70s, I spent four years on a women's farm in a thinly populated rural farming area in the mountains of northwest Arkansas. Our household ranged from five to twelve women and children, plus dogs, cats, goats, and countless visitors who were part of the great lesbian migration back and forth across the country at that time. Our farm was both isolated and exposed, and we could not survive there without strong relationships with our neighbors.

We built those relationships slowly in numerous ways. The first was by introducing ourselves to our neighbors and to those who lived in the small town and by constantly asking for advice. We hung out where the local people did—at stores, the lumber mill, restaurants—and had long conversations about ourselves and about the area. We purchased goods and services from people who lived around us. When people drove by and stopped on the dirt road by our house to chat, we stopped whatever we were doing and talked. We went to community events such as basketball games and estate sales and church fundraisers. People became interested in our successes and disasters and our stubborn hard work. They thought we were strange but good hearted and often amusing.

Our sexual orientation was not directly announced to the community at large but lived openly and talked about to some privately. While trying to live as openly as possible, we also tried to respect the community's customs. For example, almost every urban lesbian who arrived at our door to visit wanted to 1) take off her shirt and "be free" and 2) let her dog off its leash to "be free." We did not permit either. This was not a simple nor an easy decision. We understood that bare breasts had become symbolic of women's freedom (if men can bare theirs . . .) and that urban women had dreams and fantasies of some isolated place where they and their dogs could run free. We lived among farming people, however, and the dogs, untrained in farm behavior, threatened both our animals and the animals of our neighbors. As for the bare breasts, we decided that this was not the issue that we would choose as the focus for our struggle for freedom. There were many more compelling issues, and besides, we wanted to choose them for ourselves as long-term residents rather than having them pressed upon us by someone who was merely passing through.

This work was not always easy or successful. One of the local teachers at Kingston (town of 300, now notorious because of Whitewater) was fired for being a lesbian because she was seen hanging out with us. Generally, though, the community came to terms with us as we did with them. The greatest dissension and conflict came not from our being lesbians or part of the perceived back-to-the-land hippie lifestyle but from our political work that threatened their economic lives. The major chemical companies were bringing back defoliants from Vietnam and selling them to local farmers to clear their mountain land of trees and brush. These defoliants (now called Agent Orange) contained dioxin and were already causing concern about their effect on the community's health. We were documenting stillbirths, deformities, cancer, and other ill effects and vigorously and publicly opposing the use of 24-D and 245-T, the chemicals used. It was this work that brought rage from farmers because they felt hurt economically when they could not use this new technology to clear previously impossible-to-reach pastureland.

The lessons we learned then remain true now in this time when lesbians and gay men are under massive attack from the Right. All of the polls show that when people personally know lesbians and gay men, they often overcome their homophobia. It is the lack of knowledge that creates the climate for prejudice and bigotry.

I am struck by the fact that those who made trouble for my friends and me in northwest Arkansas for being a lesbian teacher or for fighting Dow Chemical and the policies of the Vietnam era are the same ones making trouble in Ovett. They are rural people entrenched in the literal interpretation of the Bible, unfamiliar with lesbians and gay men, and, most importantly, struggling for economic survival in an economy that is discarding them. The difference is that they are now bolstered by national organizations that provide support and money and who pump out strategic misinformation so fast that people live in a state of heightened confusion. Another major difference is that twenty years ago we had time to deal with our differences and to do it on the community level. Today, a fast, ever-circling media shapes public opinion so rapidly that we are impeded in doing the slow, face-to-face work that must take place in community.

Putting a human face on homosexuality addresses one part of the issue. The Right's primary success, however, comes from being able to scapegoat effectively lesbians and gay men as contributing to economic ills, just as they have scapegoated African Americans and Jews. Their major success has come from linking civil rights to "minority status," which supposedly provides "special rights" such as affirmative action and quotas. In the historic rhetoric of anti-Semitism, the Right argues falsely that lesbians and gay men, though small in numbers, are wealthier than "average" citizens and control institutions such as the media secretly, from behind the scenes. Then, with a leap into the rhetoric of racism, they argue that if lesbians and gay men achieve civil rights enforcement, through "affirmative action and quotas," we will indeed take away jobs from deserving heterosexuals and destroy the small piece of the pie now allotted to low-income people. Clearly, building community will take more than getting people to recognize our humanity as lesbians and gay men; it is also necessary for all of us to learn how to make connections with people around issues of economic injustice. Those were the conversations we failed to hold in northwest Arkansas while we were busy breaking new ground around lesbian and gay issues.

The places where those economic justice connections can be made in rural areas are most obvious in the arena where direct services and community organizing meet: food banks, housing construction (such as Habitat for

Humanity), battered women's organizations, youth organizing (especially through community sports), senior centers and meals-on-wheels, and environmental cleanup. These are some of the places where lesbians and gay men belong, a visible presence working for economic and social justice and talking about our lives.

What I have learned from rural organizing is virtually the same as what I've learned from urban organizing: we must build lasting authentic relationships across many boundaries—race, gender, class, sexual identity, physical disability, and so on—but of all of these, the most difficult for U.S. citizens as a whole is class. It is here that we do not make full connections, that we have not built alliances and coalitions. And it is this refusal to deal with economic injustice that will trip us up over and over again and prevent our dream of creating a multiracial, multi-issue movement for justice. We cannot separate ourselves from rural communities or communities of color or working-class communities or any other where economic injustice has had an extraordinary impact. To do so takes the heart out of our work for social justice, and without that center, it will not hold; we will always be working on the fringe of true and lasting social change.

25

AMERICAN INDIAN WOMEN
At the Center of Indigenous Resistance in Contemporary North America

M. ANNETTE JAIMES WITH THERESA HALSEY

A people is not defeated until the hearts of its women are on the ground.
TRADITIONAL CHEYENNE SAYING

The United States has not shown me the terms of my Surrender.
MARIE LEGO, PIT RIVER NATION, 1970

The two brief quotations forming the epigraph of this chapter were selected to represent a constant pattern of reality within Native North American life from the earliest times. This is that women have always formed the backbone of indigenous nations on this continent. Contrary to

From *The State of Native America: Genocide, Colonization, and Resistance,* M. Annette Jaimes, ed., 1992. Reprinted with permission of the publisher, South End Press.

those images of meekness, docility, and subordination to males with which we women typically have been portrayed by the dominant culture's books and movies, anthropology, and political ideologues of both rightist and leftist persuasions, it is women who have formed the very core of indigenous resistance to genocide and colonization since the first moment of conflict between Indians and invaders. In contemporary terms, this heritage has informed and guided generations of native women such as the elder Marie Lego, who provided crucial leadership to the Pit River Nation's land claims struggle in northern California during the 1970s.[1]

In Washington state, women such as Janet McCloud (Tulalip) and Ramona Bennett (Puyallup) had already assumed leading roles in the fishing rights struggles of the '60s, efforts which, probably more than any other phenomena, set in motion the "hard-line" Indian liberation movements of the modern day. These were not political organizing campaigns of the ballot and petition sort. Rather, they were, and continue to be, conflicts involving the disappearance of entire peoples. As Bennett has explained the nature of the fishing rights confrontations:

> At this time, our people were fighting to preserve their last treaty right— the right to fish. We lost our land base. There was no game in the area . . . We're dependent not just economically but culturally on the right to fish. Fishing is part of our art forms and religion and diet, and the entire culture is based around it. And so when we talk about [Euroamerica's] ripping off the right to fish, we're talking about cultural genocide.[2]

The fish-ins . . . were initially pursued within a framework of "civil disobedience" and "principled nonviolence," which went nowhere other than to incur massive official and quasi-official violence in response. "They [the police] came right on the reservation with a force of three hundred people," Bennett recounts. "They gassed us, they clubbed people around, they laid $125,000 bail on us. At that time I was a member of the Puyallup Tribal Council, and I was spokesman for the camp [of local fishing rights activists]. And I told them what our policy was: that we were there to protect our Indian fishermen. And because I used a voice-gun, I'm being charged with inciting a riot. I'm faced with an eight year sentence."[3] It was an elder Nisqually woman who pushed the fishing rights movement in western Washington to adopt the policy of armed self-defense which ultimately proved successful (the struggle in eastern Washington took a somewhat different course to the same position and results):

> Finally, one of the boys went down to the river to fish, and his mother went up on the bank. And she said: "This boy is nineteen years old and we've been fighting on this river for as many years as he's been alive. And no one is going to pound my son around, no one is going to arrest

him. No one is going to touch my son or I'm going to shoot them. " And she had a rifle . . . Then we had an armed camp in the city of Tacoma.[4]

The same sort of dynamic was involved in South Dakota during the early 1970s, when elder Oglala Lakota women such as Ellen Moves Camp and Gladys Bissonette assumed the leadership in establishing what was called the Oglala Sioux Civil Rights Organization (OSCRO) on the Pine Ridge Reservation. According to Bissonette, "Every time us women gathered to protest or demonstrate, they [federal authorities] always aimed machine guns at us women and children."[5] In response, she became a major advocate of armed self-defense at the reservation hamlet of Wounded Knee in 1973, remained within the defensive perimeter for the entire 71 days the U.S. government besieged the Indians inside, and became a primary negotiator for what was called the "Independent Oglala Nation."[6] Both women remained quite visible in the Oglala resistance to U.S. domination despite a virtual counterinsurgency war waged by the government on Pine Ridge during the three years following Wounded Knee.[7]

At Big Mountain, in the former "Navajo-Hopi Joint Use Area" in Arizona, where the federal government is even now attempting to forcibly relocate more than 10,000 traditional Diné (Navajos) in order to open the way for corporate exploitation of the rich coal reserves underlying their land, it is again elder women who have stood at the forefront of resistance, refusing to leave the homes of their ancestors. One of them, Pauline Whitesinger, was the first to physically confront government personnel attempting to fence off her land. Another, Katherine Smith, was the first to do so with a rifle.[8] Such women have constituted a literal physical barrier blocking consummation of the government's relocation/mining effort for more than a decade.[9] Many similar stories, all of them accruing from the past quarter-century, might be told in order to demonstrate the extent to which women have galvanized and centered contemporary native resistance.

The costs of such uncompromising (and uncompromised) activism have often been high. To quote Ada Deer, who, along with Lucille Chapman, became an essential spokesperson for the Menominee restoration movement in Wisconsin during the late 1960s and early '70s: "I wanted to get involved. People said I was too young, too naïve—you can't fight the system. I dropped out of law school. That was the price I had to pay to be involved."[10] Gladys Bissonette lost a son, Pedro, and a daughter, Jeanette, murdered by federal surrogates on Pine Ridge in the aftermath of Wounded Knee.[11] Other native women, such as American Indian Movement (AIM) members Tina Trudell and Anna Mae Pictou Aquash, have paid with their own and sometimes their children's lives for their prominent defiance of their colonizers.[12] Yet, it stands as a testament to the strength of American Indian women that such grim sacrifices have served, not to deter them from standing up for the rights of native people, but as an inspiration to do so. Mohawk activist and scholar Shirley Hill Witt recalls the burial of Aquash after her execution-style murder on Pine Ridge:

> Some women had driven from Pine Ridge the night before—a very dangerous act—"to do what needed to be done." Young women dug the grave. A ceremonial tipi was set up . . . A woman seven months pregnant gathered sage and cedar to be burned in the tipi. Young AIM members were pallbearers: they laid her on pine boughs while spiritual leaders spoke the sacred words and performed the ancient duties. People brought presents for Anna Mae to take with her to the spirit world. They also brought presents for her two sisters to carry back to Nova Scotia with them to give to her orphaned daughters . . . The executioners of Anna Mae did not snuff out a meddlesome woman. They exalted a Brave Hearted Woman for all time.[13]

The motivations of indigenous women in undertaking such risks are unequivocal. As Maria Sanchez, a leading member of the Northern Cheyenne resistance to corporate "development" of their reservation puts it: "I am the mother of nine children. My concern is for their future, for their children, and for future generations. As a woman, I draw strength from the traditional spiritual people . . . from my nation. The oil and gas companies are building a huge gas chamber for the Northern Cheyennes."[14] Pauline Whitesinger has stated, "I think there is no way we can survive if we are moved to some other land away from ours. We are just going to waste away. People tell me to move, but I've got no place to go. I am not moving anywhere, that is certain."[15] Roberta Blackgoat, another leader of the Big Mountain resistance, concurs: "If this land dies, the people die with it. We are a nation. We will fight anyone who tries to push us off our land."[16] All across North America, the message from native women is the same.[17] The explicitly nationalist content of indigenous women's activism has been addressed by Lorelei DeCora Means, a Minneconjou Lakota AIM member and one of the founders of Women of All Red Nations (WARN):

> We are *American Indian* women, in that order. We are oppressed, first and foremost, as American Indians, as peoples colonized by the United States of America, *not* as women. As Indians, we can never forget that. Our survival, the survival of every one of us—man, woman and child—*as Indians* depends on it. Decolonization is the agenda, the whole agenda, and until it is accomplished, it is the *only* agenda that counts for American Indians. It will take every one of us—every single one of us—to get the job done. We haven't got the time, energy or resources for anything else while our lands are being destroyed and our children are dying of avoidable diseases and malnutrition. So we tend to view those who come to us wanting to form alliances on the basis of "new" and "different" or "broader" and "more important" issues to be a little less than friends, especially

since most of them come from the Euroamerican population which ben-efits most directly from our ongoing colonization.[18]

As Janet McCloud sees it:

Most of these "progressive" non-Indian ideas like "class struggle" would at the present time divert us into participating as "equals" in our own colonization. Or, like "women's liberation," would divide us among ourselves in such a way as to leave us colonized in the name of "gender equity." Some of us can 't help but think maybe a lot of these "better ideas" offered by non-Indians claiming to be our "allies" are intended to accomplish exactly these sorts of diversion and disunity within our movement. So, let me toss out a different sort of "progres-sion" to all you marxists and socialists and feminists out there. *You* join *us* in liberating *our* land and lives. Lose the privilege *you* acquire at *our* expense by occupying *our* land. Make *that* your first priority for as long as it takes to make it happen. *Then* we'll join you in fixing up whatever's left of the class and gender problems in your society, and our own, if need be. *But,* if you're not willing to do that, then don't presume to tell *us* how we should go about our liberation, what priorities and values we should have. Since you're standing on our land, we've got to view you as just another oppressor trying to hang on to what's ours. And that doesn't leave us a whole lot to talk about, now does it?[19]

The Road Ahead

Interestingly, women of other nonwhite sectors of the North American pop-ulation have shared many native women's criticisms of the Euroamerican feminist phenomenon. African American women in particular have been outspoken in this regard. As Gloria Joseph argues:

The White women's movement has had its own explicit forms of racism in the way it has given high priority to certain aspects of struggles and neglected others . . . because of the inherently racist assumptions and per-spectives brought to bear in the first articulations by the White women's movement . . . The Black movement scorns feminism partially on the basis of misinformation, and partially due to a valid perception of the White middle class nature of the movement. An additional reason is due to the myopic ways that white feminists have generalized their sexual-political analysis and have confirmed their racism in the forms their fem-inism has assumed.[20]

The "self-righteous indignation" and defensiveness that Joseph discerns as experienced by most Euroamerican feminists when confronted with such critiques is elsewhere explained by bell hooks as a response resting in the vested interest of those who feel it:

> [F]eminist emphasis on "common oppression" in the United States was less a strategy for politicization than an appropriation by conservative and liberal women of a radical political vocabulary that masked the extent to which they shaped the movement so that it addressed and promoted their class interests . . . White women who dominate feminist discourse, who for the most part make and articulate feminist theory, have little or no understanding of white supremacy as a racial politic, of the psychological impact of class, of their [own] political status within a racist, sexist, capitalist state."[21]

"I was struck," hooks says in her book, *Ain't I A Woman*, "by the fact that the ideology of feminism, with its emphasis on transforming and changing the social structure of the U.S., in no way resembled the reality of American feminism. Largely because [white] feminists themselves, as they attempted to take feminism beyond the realm of radical rhetoric into the sphere of American life, revealed that they remained imprisoned in the very structures they hoped to change. Consequently, the sisterhood we all talked about has not become a reality."[22] It is time to "talk back" to white feminists, hooks argues, "spoiling their celebration, their 'sisterhood,' their 'togetherness.'"[23] This must be done because in adhering to feminism in its present form:

> We learn to look to those empowered by the very systems of domination that wound and hurt us for some understanding of who we are that will be liberating and we never find that. It is necessary for [women of color] to do the work ourselves if we want to know more about our experience, if we want to see that experience from perspectives not shaped by domination.[24]

Asian American women, Chicanas, and Latinas have agreed in substantial part with such assessments.[25] Women of color in general tend not to favor the notion of a "politics" which would divide and weaken their communities by defining "male energy" as "the enemy." It is not for nothing that no community of color in North America has ever produced a counterpart to white feminism's SCUM (Society for Cutting Up Men). Women's liberation, in the view of most "minority" women in the United States and Canada, cannot occur in any context other than the wider liberation, from Euroamerican colonial domination, of the peoples of which women of color are a part. Our sense of priorities is therefore radically—and irrevocably—different from those espoused by the "mainstream" women's movement.

Within this alienation from feminism lies the potential for the sorts of alliances which may in the end prove most truly beneficial to American Indian people. By forging links to organizations composed of other women of color, founded not merely to fight gender oppression, but also to struggle against racial and cultural oppression, native women can prove instrumental in creating an alternative movement of women in North America, one which is mutually respectful of the rights, needs, cultural particularities, and historical divergences of each sector of its membership, and which is therefore free of the adherence to white supremacist hegemony previously marring feminist thinking and practice. Any such movement of women—including those Euroamerican women who see its thrust as corresponding to their own values and interests as human beings—cannot help but be of crucial importance within the liberation struggles waged by peoples of color to dismantle the apparatus of Eurocentric power in every area of the continent. The greater the extent to which these struggles succeed, the closer the core agenda of Native North America—recovery of land and resources, reassertion of self-determining forms of government, and reconstitution of traditional social relations within our nations—will come to realization.

NOTES

1. For further information on Marie Lego and the context of her struggle, see Jaimes, M. Annette, "The Pit River Indian Land Claims Dispute in Northern California," *Journal of Ethnic Studies*, Vol. 4, No. 4, Winter 1987.

2. Quoted in Katz, Jane B., *I Am the Fire of Time: The Voices of Native American Women*, E. P. Dutton Publisher, New York 1977, p. 146.

3. Quoted in ibid., p. 147. Bennett was eventually acquitted after being shot, while seven months pregnant, and wounded by white vigilantes.

4. Ibid.

5. Quoted in ibid., p. 141.

6. The best account of the roles of Gladys Bissonette and Ellen Moves Camp during the siege may be found in Editors, *Voices from Wounded Knee, 1973*, Akwesasne *Notes*, Mohawk Nation via Rooseveltown, NY, 1974.

7. Churchill, Ward, and Tim Van der Wall. *The COINTELPRO Papers: Documents on the FBI's Secret Wars Against Dissent in the United States*, South End Press, Boston, 1990, pp. 231–302. Also see Matthiessen, Peter, *In the Spirit of Crazy Horse*, Viking Press, New York (2nd edition) 1991.

8. Kammer, Jerry, *The Second Long Walk: The Navajo-Hopi Land Dispute*, University of New Mexico Press, Albuquerque, 1980, pp. 1–2, 209.

9. For further information on Big Mountain, see Parlow, Anita, *Cry, Sacred Land: Big Mountain, USA*, Christic Institute, Washington. D.C., 1988.

10. Quoted in Katz. op. cit., p. 151. For further background on Ada Deer, see her autobiography (Deer, Ada, with R. E. Simon, Jr., *Speaking Out*, Children's Press, Chicago, 1970).

11. On the murders of Pedro and Jeanette Bissonette, see Churchill, Ward, and Jim Vander Wall, *Agents of Repression: The FBI's Secret Wars Against the Black Panther Party and the American Indian Movement*, South End Press, Boston, 1988, pp. 187, 200–3.

12. Concerning the murders of Tina Manning Trudell, her three children (Ricarda Star, age five; Sunshine Karma, three; and Eli Changing Sun, one), and her mother, Leah Hicks Manning, see ibid., pp. 361–4. On Aquash, see Brand,

Johanna, *The Life and Death of Anna Mae Aquash,* James Lorimax Publishers, Toronto, 1978.

13. Hill Witt, Shirley, "The Brave-Hearted Women: The Struggle at Wounded Knee," *Akwesasne Notes,* Vol. 8, No. 2, 1976, p. 16.

14. Quoted in Katz, op. cit., pp. 145–6.

15. Quoted in Kammer, op. cit., p. 18.

16. From a talk delivered during International Women's Week, the University of Colorado at Boulder, April 1984 (tape on file).

17. Such sentiments are hardly unique to the United States. For articulation by Canadian Indian women, see Silman, Janet, *Enough is Enough: Aboriginal Women Speak Out,* The Women's Press, Toronto, 1987.

18. From a talk delivered during International Women's Week, the University of Colorado at Boulder, April 1985 (tape on file).

19. From a talk delivered during International Women's Week, University of Colorado at Boulder, April 1984 (tape on file).

20. Joseph, Gloria I., and Jill Lewis, *Common Differences: Conflicts in Black and White Feminist Perspectives,* South End Press, Boston, 1981, pp. 4–6.

21. hooks, bell, *Feminist Theory: From Margin to Center,* South End Press, Boston, 1984, pp. 4–8.

22. hooks, bell, *Ain't I A Woman: Black Women and Feminism,* South End Press, Boston, 1981, p. 190.

23. hooks, bell, *Talking Back: Thinking Feminist, Thinking Black,* South End Press, Boston, 1989, p. 149.

24. Ibid., pp. 150–1.

25. For a sample of these perspectives, see Moraga, Cherríe, and Gloria Anzaldúa, eds., *This Bridge Called My Back: Writings by Radical Women of Color,* Kitchen Table Press, New York, 1983.

PART V
Sexuality

. . . all Black women are affected by the widespread controlling image that African-American women are sexually promiscuous, potential prostitutes.

PATRICIA HILL COLLINS[1]

Dating becomes a sport in itself, and "scoring," or having sex with little or no emotional involvement, is a mark of masculine achievement.

DON SABO[2]

Human sexuality encompasses a wide range of behaviors and identities in spite of what mainstream socialization would have us believe. The expectation that traditionally feminine, heterosexual women and traditionally masculine, heterosexual men will have sex only with each other and by mutual agreement is challenged by many people who do not conform to the dominant norms. It is also challenged by the rates of abusive sexual exploitation perpetrated by the more powerful on the less powerful, most frequently by men against women and children. The AIDS epidemic has also added a highly volatile variable to people's sexual expression since unsafe sex can carry a death risk. The threat of AIDS has also changed sexual practices by forcing people to discuss sexual practices more openly.

The combinations and permutations of biological sex, gender, and sexual orientation are many. A person could be, for example, genetically and biologically male, heterosexual, and "feminine" (whatever *feminine* means in his context). When we acknowledge that one's genetic/biological makeup is the only aspect of sexuality that is immutable, options for the expression of gender and sexuality can become part of the discussion about who people are or want to be. For example, some gay men take on a very masculine identity in adulthood, effectively distancing themselves from the "feminine" boys now considered pathological by the American Psychiatric Association.[3]

Psychologist Carla Golden, in a study of undergraduates at an elite women's college in the Northeast, found that students' sexual identities did not necessarily match their sexual behavior. For example, some women who identified themselves as heterosexual were exclusively involved sexually with women; some who had never had a same-sex sexual experience nevertheless identified themselves as bisexual because they perceived in themselves the potential for same-sex attraction and sexual activity. Golden also interviewed women who identified themselves as "political lesbians" whose sexual behavior was exclusively heterosexual. Golden concludes that the congruence between sexual feelings, behavior, and identity is often lacking, and she urges people to acknowledge the complex expressions of sexuality and sexual identity that result.[4]

Apart from examining the complex ways in which people define and express their sexuality, passionate debates abound in the field of sexuality. The origins of sexual orientations have been the subject of much research, as scholars explore the extent to which genetic predispositions or cultural influences might cause people to become heterosexual, gay, lesbian, or bisexual. Heated debate ensues about whether violent and degrading pornography should continue to be legal in the United States. Others argue for or against butch-femme roles in lesbian and gay communities. Still others debate the pros and cons of sadomasochistic sexual practices. And the sexual oppression and objectification of people of color is also a theme in this literature.[5]

The authors in this chapter address several sexuality issues, including the freedom to be sexual in a wider range of ways, the elimination of sexual objectification, the freedom of people with disabilities to be sexual and reproduce, freedom from racism and poverty, and respectful, responsive sexual relating free of violence.

The first selection in this chapter is an essay by John Stoltenberg, in which he raises theoretical questions about the sexual nature of human beings and argues for a separation of sex from gender; he believes people should just "have sex" without all the roles, labels, and burdens that surround what sex is and with whom it can be had. Implicit in his essay is the assumption that people should be free to choose their sexuality without the constraints of socialization or the imposition of sexual activity or abuse by others. Although he is describing an ideal world, he also makes some concrete suggestions to men about how to engage in more respectful, intimate sexual activity without objectifying their partners.

Next, Don Sabo takes us into the men's locker room and discusses some of the myths and painful realities of male heterosexuality that Stoltenberg would like to see changed. He addresses the abuse of women, sex as a competitive performance, and the challenge of intimacy, using his own experience as a former athlete.

In the next essay, Patricia Hill Collins examines pornography, prostitution, and rape in the context of race, class, and gender oppression, providing data about, and analysis of, the sexual exploitation of African American women.

In the next selection, Joan Nestle discusses butch-femme relations in the working-class lesbian community of the 1950s, challenging stereotypes of what the butch-femme labels really mean. She argues that women in these roles were not simply imitating heterosexual relationships but were instead finding ways to express strength, power, and intimacy. Behind the images, there were complex human beings whose real lives were often made invisible.

Finally, Anne Finger documents some of the ways in which sexuality and reproductive rights are completely denied to women and men with disabilities. She asks for the basic right to be sexual and to bear children, when desired.

The authors in this chapter would like to see a world that is free of sexual exploitation and in which people are free to choose to be sexual in any nonexploitative ways they choose.

NOTES:

1. Patricia Hill Collins, "The Sexual Politics of Black Womanhood," in *Black Feminist Thought* (New York: Routledge, 1991), p. 174.
2. Don Sabo, "The Myth of the Sexual Athlete," in Michael A. Messner and Donald F. Sabo, *Sex, Violence & Power in Sports* (Freedom, CA: Crossing Press, 1994), p. 38.
3. For an interesting discussion of the process by which the American Psychiatric Association removed homosexuality from the pathology list and simultaneously added "gender identity disorder of childhood," see Eve Kosofsky Sedgwick, "How to Bring Your Kids Up Gay," *Tendencies* (Durham: Duke University Press, 1993), pp. 154–164.
4. Carla Golden, "Diversity and Variability in Women's Sexual Identities," in the Boston Lesbian Psychologies Collective, eds., *Lesbian Psychologies: Explorations and Challenges* (Chicago: University of Illinois Press, 1987), pp. 19–34.
5. For discussions of causes of sexual orientation, see Alan P. Bell and Martin S. Weinberg, *Homosexualities: A Study of Human Diversity* (South Melbourne, Victoria: Macmillan, 1978); Martin S. Weinberg, *Dual Attraction: Understanding Bisexuality* (New York: Oxford University Press, 1994); and Jan Clausen, *Why Are People Gay or Straight?* (New York: Chelsea House, 1996). For a discussion of class and pornography, see Laura Kipnis, "(Male) Desire and (Female) Disgust: Reading *Hustler*," in Lawrence Grossberg, Cary Nelson, and Paula Treichler, *Cultural Studies* (New York: Routledge, 1992), pp. 373–391. For a presentation of the anti-pornography position in the feminist pornography debate, see Dorchen Leidholdt and Janice G. Raymond, eds., *The Sexual Liberals and the Attack on Feminism* (New York: Pergamon Press, 1990); Laura Lederer and Richard Delgado, eds., *The Price We Pay: The Case against Racist Speech, Hate Propaganda, and Pornography* (New York: Hill and Wang, 1995). For a discussion of the feminist position in support of pornography, see Lisa Duggan and Nan D. Hunter, eds., *Sex Wars: Sexual Dissent and Political Culture* (New York: Routledge, 1995). For an example from Queer studies of the role of racism in gay pornographic videos, see Richard Fung, "Looking for My Penis: The Eroticized Asian in Gay Video Porn," in Bad Object-Choices, ed., *How Do I Look? Queer Film and Video* (Seattle: Bay Press, 1991). For a discussion of butch-femme roles in the lesbian community, see Joan Nestle, "Butch-Femme Relationships: Sexual Courage In The 1950s," in *A Restricted Country* (Ithaca, New York: Firebrand, 1987) pp. 100–109. For a discussion of sadomasochism, see Robin Ruth Linden, et al., eds., *Against Sadomasochism: A Radical Feminist Analysis* (San Francisco: Frog in the Well, 1982); Pat Califia, *Sapphistry: The Book of Lesbian Sexuality* (Tallahassee, FL: Naiad Press, 1980).

26

HOW MEN HAVE (A) SEX

JOHN STOLTENBERG

An address to college students

In the human species, how many sexes are there?
Answer A: *There are two sexes.*
Answer B: *There are three sexes.*
Answer C: *There are four sexes.*
Answer D: *There are seven sexes.*
Answer E: *There are as many sexes as there are people.*

I'd like to take you, in an imaginary way, to look at a different world, somewhere else in the universe, a place inhabited by a life form that very much resembles us. But these creatures grow up with a peculiar knowledge. They know that they have been born in an infinite variety. They know, for instance, that in their genetic material they are born with hundreds of different chromosome formations at the point in each cell that we would say determines their "sex." These creatures don't just come in XX or XY; they also come in XXY and XYY and XXX plus a long list of "mosaic" variations in which some cells in a creature's body have one combination and other cells have another. Some of these creatures are born with chromosomes that aren't even quite X or Y because a little bit of one chromosome goes and gets joined to another. There are hundreds of different combinations, and though all are not fertile, quite a number of them are. The creatures in this world enjoy their individuality; they delight in the fact that they are not divisible into distinct categories. So when another newborn arrives with an esoterically rare chromosomal formation, there is a little celebration: "Aha," they say, "another sign that we are each unique."

These creatures also live with the knowledge that they are born with a vast range of genital formations. Between their legs are tissue structures that vary along a continuum, from clitorises with a vulva through all possible combinations and gradations to penises with a scrotal sac. These creatures live with an understanding that their genitals all developed prenatally from exactly the same little nub of embryonic tissue called a genital tubercle, which grew and developed under the influence of varying amounts of the hormone androgen. These creatures honor and respect everyone's natural-born genitalia—including what we would describe as a microphallus or a clitoris several inches long. What these creatures find amazing and precious is that because everyone's genitals stem from the same embryonic tissue, the nerves inside all their genitals got wired very much alike, so these nerves of touch just go crazy upon contact in a way that resonates completely between them. "My gosh," they think, "you must feel something in your genital tubercle that intensely resembles what I'm feeling in my genital tubercle." Well, they don't exactly *think* that in so many words; they're actually quite heavy into their feelings at that point; but they do feel very connected—throughout all their wondrous variety.

I could go on. I could tell you about the variety of hormones that course through their bodies in countless different patterns and proportions, both before birth and throughout their lives—the hormones that we call "sex hormones" but that they call "individuality inducers." I could tell you how these creatures think about reproduction: For part of their lives, some of them are quite capable of gestation, delivery, and lactation; and for part of their lives, some of them are quite capable of insemination; and for part or all of their lives, some of them are not capable of any of those things—so these creatures conclude that it would be silly to lock anyone into a lifelong category based on a capability variable that may or may not be utilized and that in any case changes over each lifetime in a fairly uncertain and idiosyncratic way. These creatures are not oblivious to reproduction; but nor do they spend their lives constructing a self-definition around their variable reproductive capacities. They don't have to, because what is truly unique about these creatures is that they are capable of having a sense of personal identity without struggling to fit into a group identity based on how they were born. These creatures are quite happy, actually. They don't worry about sorting *other* creatures into categories, so they don't have to worry about whether they are measuring up to some category they themselves are supposed to belong to.

These creatures, of course, have sex. Rolling and rollicking and robust sex, and sweaty and slippery and sticky sex, and trembling and quaking and tumultuous sex, and tender and tingling and transcendent sex. They have sex fingers to fingers. They have sex belly to belly. They have sex genital tubercle to genital tubercle. They *have* sex. They do not have *a* sex. In their erotic lives, they are not required to act out their status in a category system—because there *is* no category system. There are no sexes to belong to, so sex between creatures is free to be between genuine individuals—not representatives of a category. They have sex. They do not have a sex. Imagine life like that.

Perhaps you have guessed the point of this science fiction: Anatomically, each creature in the imaginary world I have been describing could be an identical twin of every human being on earth. These creatures, in fact, *are us*—in every way except socially and politically. The way they are born is the way we are born. And we are not born belonging to one or the other of two

sexes. We are born into a physiological continuum on which there is no discrete and definite point that you can call "male" and no discrete and definite
point that you can call "female." If you look at all the variables in nature that
are said to determine human "sex," you can't possibly find one that will
unequivocally split the species into two. Each of the so-called criteria of
sexedness is itself a continuum—including chromosomal variables, genital
and gonadal variations, reproductive capacities, endocrinological proportions, and any other criterion you could think of. Any or all of these different variables may line up in any number of ways, and all of the variables
may vary independently of one another.[1]

What does all this mean? It means, first of all, a logical dilemma: Either
human "male" and human "female" actually exist in nature as fixed and discrete entities and you can credibly base an entire social and political system
on those absolute natural categories, or else the variety of human sexedness
is infinite. As Andrea Dworkin wrote in 1974:

> The discovery is, of course, that "man" and "woman" are fictions, cari-
> catures, cultural constructs. As models they are reductive, totalitarian,
> inappropriate to human becoming. As roles they are static, demeaning
> to the female, dead-ended for male and female both.[2]

The conclusion is inescapable:

> We are, clearly, a multisexed species which has its sexuality spread along
> a vast continuum where the elements called male and female are not dis-
> crete.[3]

"We are . . . a multisexed species." I first read those words a little over ten
years ago—and that liberating recognition saved my life.

All the time I was growing up, I knew that there was something really
problematical in my relationship to manhood. Inside, deep inside, I never
believed I was fully male—I never believed I was growing up enough of a
man. I believed that someplace out there, in other men, there was something
that was genuine authentic all-American manhood—the real stuff—but I
didn't have it: not enough of it to convince *me* anyway, even if I managed to
be fairly convincing to those around me. I felt like an impostor, like a fake. I
agonized a lot about not feeling male enough, and I had no idea then how
much I was not alone.

Then I read those words—those words that suggested to me for the first
time that the notion of manhood is a cultural delusion, a baseless belief, a false
front, a house of cards. It's not true. The category I was trying so desperately
to belong to, to be a member of in good standing—it doesn't exist. Poof. Now
you see it, now you don't. Now you're terrified you're not really part of it;
now you're free, you don't have to worry anymore. However removed you
feel inside from "authentic manhood," it doesn't matter. What matters is the
center inside yourself—and how you live, and how you treat people, and
what you can contribute as you pass through life on this earth, and how hon-

estly you love, and how carefully you make choices. Those are the things that really matter. Not whether you're a real man. There's no such thing.

The idea of the male sex is like the idea of an Aryan race. The Nazis believed in the idea of an Aryan race—they believed that the Aryan race really exists, physically, in nature—and they put a great deal of effort into making it real. The Nazis believed that from the blond hair and blue eyes occurring naturally in the human species, they could construe the existence of a separate *race*—a distinct category of human beings that was unambiguously rooted in the natural order of things. But traits do not a race make; traits only make traits. For the idea to be real that these physical traits comprised a race, the race had to be socially constructed. The Nazis inferiorized and exterminated those they defined as "non-Aryan." With that, the notion of an Aryan race began to seem to come true. That's how there could be a political entity known as an Aryan race, and that's how there could be for some people a personal, subjective sense that they belonged to it. This happened through hate and force, through violence and victimization, through treating millions of people as things, then exterminating them. The belief system shared by people who believed they were all Aryan could not exist apart from that force and violence. The force and violence created a racial class system, *and* it created those people's membership in the race considered "superior." The force and violence served their class interests in large part because it created and maintained the class itself. But the idea of an Aryan race could never become metaphysically true, despite all the violence unleashed to create it, because there simply *is* no Aryan race. There is only the idea of it—and the consequences of trying to make it seem real. The male sex is very like that.

Penises and ejaculate and prostate glands occur in nature, but the notion that these anatomical traits comprise a sex—a discrete class, separate and distinct, metaphysically divisible from some other sex, *the* "other sex"—is simply that: a notion, an idea. The penises exist; the male sex does not. The male sex is socially constructed. It is a political entity that flourishes only through acts of force and sexual terrorism. Apart from the global inferiorization and subordination of those who are defined as "nonmale," the idea of personal membership in the male sex class would have no recognizable meaning. It would make no sense. No one could be a member of it and no one would think they *should* be a member of it. There would be no male sex to belong to. That doesn't mean there wouldn't still be penises and ejaculate and prostate glands and such. It simply means that the center of our selfhood would not be required to reside inside an utterly fictitious category—a category that only seems real to the extent that those outside it are put down.

We live in a world divided absolutely into two sexes, even though nothing about human nature warrants that division. We are sorted into one category or another at birth based solely on a visual inspection of our groins, and the only question that's asked is whether there's enough elongated tissue around your urethra so you can pee standing up. The presence or absence of a long-enough penis is the primary criterion for separating who's to grow up male from who's to grow up female. And among all the ironies in that utterly whimsical and arbitrary selection process is the fact that *anyone* can pee both sitting down and standing up.

Male sexual identity is the conviction or belief, held by most people born with penises, that they are male and not female, that they belong to the male sex. In a society predicated on the notion that there are two "opposite" and "complementary" sexes, this idea not only makes sense, it *becomes* sense; the very idea of a male sexual identity produces sensation, produces the meaning of sensation, becomes the meaning of how one's body feels. The sense and the sensing of a male sexual identity is at once mental and physical, at once public and personal. Most people born with a penis between their legs grow up aspiring to feel and act unambiguously male, longing to belong to the sex that is male and daring not to belong to the sex that is not, and feeling this urgency for a visceral and constant verification of their male sexual identity—for a fleshy connection to manhood—as the driving force of their life. The drive does not originate in the anatomy. The sensations derive from the idea. The idea gives the feelings social meaning; the idea determines which sensations shall be sought.

People born with penises must strive to make the idea of male sexual identity personally real by doing certain deeds, actions that are valued and chosen because they produce the desired feeling of belonging to a sex that is male and not female. Male sexual identity is experienced only in sensation and action, in feeling and doing, in eroticism and ethics. The feeling of belonging to a male sex encompasses both sensations that are explicitly "sexual" and those that are not ordinarily regarded as such. And there is a tacit social value system according to which certain acts are chosen because they make an individual's sexedness feel real and certain other acts are eschewed because they numb it. That value system is the ethics of male sexual identity—and it may well be the social origin of all injustice.

Each person experiences the idea of sexual identity as more or less real, more or less certain, more or less true, depending on two very personal phenomena: one's feelings and one's acts. For many people, for instance, the act of fucking makes their sexual identity feel more real than it does at other times, and they can predict from experience that this feeling of greater certainty will last for at least a while after each time they fuck. Fucking is not the only such act, and not only so-called sex acts can result in feelings of certainty about sexual identity; but the act of fucking happens to be a very good example of the correlation between *doing* a specific act in a specific way and *sensing* the specificity of the sexual identity to which one aspires. A person can decide to do certain acts and not others just because some acts will have the payoff of a feeling of greater certainty about sexual identity and others will give the feedback of a feeling of less. The transient reality of one's sexual identity, a person can know, is always a function of what one does and how one's acts make one feel. The feeling and the act must conjoin for the idea of the sexual identity to come true. We all keep longing for surety of our sexedness that we can feel; we all keep striving through our actions to make the idea real.

In human nature, eroticism is not differentiated between "male" and "female" in any clear-cut way. There is too much of a continuum, too great a resemblance. From all that we know, the penis and the clitoris are identically "wired" to receive and retransmit sensations from throughout the body, and the congestion of blood within the lower torso during sexual excitation makes all bodies sensate in a remarkably similar manner. Simply put, we all share all the nerve and blood-vessel layouts that are associated with sexual arousal. Who can say, for instance, that the penis would not experience sensations the way that a clitoris does if this were not a world in which the penis is supposed to be hell-bent on penetration? By the time most men make it through puberty, they believe that erotic sensation is supposed to *begin* in their penis; that if engorgement has not begun there, then nothing else in their body will heat up either. There is a massive interior dissociation from sensations that do not explicitly remind a man that his penis is still there. And not only there as sensate, but *functional and operational*.

So much of most men's sexuality is tied up with gender-actualizing—with feeling like a real man—that they can scarcely recall an erotic sensation that had no gender-specific cultural meaning. As most men age, they learn to cancel out and deny erotic sensations that are not specifically linked to what they think a real man is supposed to feel. An erotic sensation unintentionally experienced in a receptive, communing mode—instead of in an aggressive and controlling and violative mode, for instance—can shut down sensory systems in an instant. An erotic sensation unintentionally linked to the "wrong" sex of another person can similarly mean sudden numbness. Acculturated male sexuality has a built-in fail-safe: Either its political context reifies manhood or the experience cannot be felt as sensual. Either the act creates his sexedness or it does not compute as a sex act. So he tenses up, pumps up, steels himself against the dread that he be found not male enough. And his dread is not stupid; for he sees what happens to people when they are treated as nonmales.

My point is that sexuality does not *have* a gender; it *creates* a gender. It creates for those who adapt to it in narrow and specified ways the confirmation for the individual of belonging to the idea of one sex or the other. So-called male sexuality is a learned connection between specific physical sensations and the idea of a male sexual identity. To achieve this male sexual identity requires that an individual *identify with* the class of males—that is, accept as one's own the values and interests of the class. A fully realized male sexual identity also requires *nonidentification with* that which is perceived to be nonmale, or female. A male must not identify with females; he must not associate with females in feeling, interest, or action. His identity as a member of the sex class men absolutely depends on the extent to which he repudiates the values and interests of the sex class "women."

I think somewhere inside us all, we have always known something about the relativity of gender. Somewhere inside us all, we know that our bodies harbor deep resemblances, that we are wired inside to respond in a profound harmony to the resonance of eroticism inside the body of someone near us. Physiologically, we are far more alike than different. The tissue structures that have become labial and clitoral or scrotal and penile have not forgotten their common ancestry. Their sensations are of the same source. The nerve networks and interlock of capillaries throughout our pelvises electrify and engorge as if plugged in together and pumping as one. That's what we feel when we feel one another's feelings. That's what can happen during sex that is mutual, equal, reciprocal, profoundly communing.

So why is it that some of us with penises think it's sexy to pressure someone into having sex against their will? Some of us actually get harder the harder the person resists. Some of us with penises actually believe that some of us without penises want to be raped. And why is it that some of us with penises think it's sexy to treat other people as objects, as things to be bought and sold, impersonal bodies to be possessed and consumed for our sexual pleasure? Why is it that some of us with penises are aroused by sex tinged with rape, and sex commoditized by pornography? Why do so many of us with penises want such antisexual sex?

There's a reason, of course. We have to make a lie seem real. It's a very big lie. We each have to do our part. Otherwise the lie will look like the lie that it is. Imagine the enormity of what we each must do to keep the lie alive in each of us. Imagine the awesome challenge we face to make the lie a social fact. It's a lifetime mission for each of us born with a penis: to have sex in such a way that the male sex will seem real—and so that we'll feel like a real part of it.

We all grow up knowing exactly what kind of sex that is. It's the kind of sex you can have when you pressure or bully someone else into it. So it's a kind of sex that makes your will more important than theirs. That kind of sex helps the lie a lot. That kind of sex makes you feel like someone important and it turns the other person into someone unimportant. That kind of sex makes you feel real, not like a fake. It's a kind of sex men have in order to feel like a real man.

There's also the kind of sex you can have when you force someone and hurt someone and cause someone suffering and humiliation. Violence and hostility in sex help the lie a lot too. Real men are aggressive in sex. Real men get cruel in sex. Real men use their penises like weapons in sex. Real men leave bruises. Real men think it's a turn-on to threaten harm. A brutish push can make an erection feel really hard. That kind of sex helps the lie a lot. That kind of sex makes you feel like someone who is powerful and it turns the other person into someone powerless. That kind of sex makes you feel dangerous and in control—like you're fighting a war with an enemy and if you're mean enough you'll win but if you let up you'll loose your manhood. It's a kind of sex men have *in order to have* a manhood.

There's also the kind of sex you can have when you pay your money into a profit system that grows rich displaying and exploiting the bodies and body parts of people without penises for the sexual entertainment of people with. Pay your money and watch. Pay your money and imagine. Pay your money and get real turned on. Pay your money and jerk off. That kind of sex helps the lie a lot. It helps support an industry committed to making people with penises believe that people without are sluts who just want to be ravished and reviled—an industry dedicated to maintaining a sex-class system in which men believe themselves sex machines and men believe women are mindless fuck tubes. That kind of sex helps the lie a lot. It's like buying Krugerrands as a vote of confidence for white supremacy in South Africa.

And there's one more thing: That kind of sex makes the lie indelible— burns it onto your retinas right adjacent to your brain—makes you remember it and makes your body respond to it and so it makes you believe that the lie is in fact true: You really are a real man. That slavish and submissive creature there spreading her legs is really not. You and that creature have nothing in common. That creature is an alien inanimate thing, but your penis is completely real and alive. Now you can come. Thank god almighty—you have a sex at last.

Now, I believe there are many who are sick at heart over what I have been describing. There are many who were born with penises who want to stop collaborating in the sex-class system that needs us to need these kinds of sex. I believe some of you want to stop living out the big lie, and you want to know how. Some of you long to touch truthfully. Some of you want sexual relationships in your life that are about intimacy and joy, ecstasy and equality—not antagonism and alienation. So what I have to say next I have to say to you.

When you use sex to have a sex, the sex you have is likely to make you feel crummy about yourself. But when you have sex in which you are not struggling with your partner in order to act out "real manhood," the sex you have is more likely to bring you close.

This means several specific things:

1. *Consent is absolutely essential.* If both you and your partner have not freely given your informed consent to the sex you are about to have, you can be quite certain that the sex you go ahead and have will make you strangers to each other. How do you know if there's consent? You ask. You ask again if you're sensing any doubt. Consent to do one thing isn't consent to do another. So you keep communicating, in clear words. And you don't take anything for granted.
2. *Mutuality is absolutely essential.* Sex is not something you do *to* someone. Sex is not a one-way transitive verb, with a subject, you, and an object, the body you're with. Sex that is mutual is not about doing and being done to; it's about being-with and feeling-with. You have to

really be there to experience what is happening between and within the two of you—between every part of you and within both your whole bodies. It's a matter of paying attention—as if you are paying attention to someone who matters.

3. *Respect is absolutely essential.* In the sex that you have, treat your partner like a real person who, like you, has real feelings—feelings that matter as much as your own. You may or may not love—but you must always respect. You must respect the integrity of your partner's body. It is not yours for the taking. It belongs to someone real. And you do not get ownership of your partner's body just because you are having sex—or just because you have had sex.

For those who are closer to the beginning of your sex lives than to the middle or the end, many things are still changing for you about how you have sex, with whom, why or why not, what you like or dislike, what kind of sex you want to have more of. In the next few years, you are going to discover and decide a lot. I say "discover" because no one can tell you what you're going to find out about yourself in relation to sex—and I say "decide" because virtually without knowing it you are going to be laying down habits and patterns that will probably stay with you for the rest of your life. You're at a point in your sexual history that you will never be at again. You don't know what you don't know yet. And yet you are making choices whose consequences for your particular sexuality will be sealed years from now.

I speak to you as someone who is closer to the middle of my sexual history. As I look back, I see that I made many choices that I didn't know I was making. And as I look at men who are near my age, I see that what has happened to many of them is that their sex lives are stuck in deep ruts that began as tiny fissures when they were young. So I want to conclude by identifying what I believe are three of the most important decisions about your sexuality that you can make when you are at the beginning of your sexual history. However difficult these choices may seem to you now, I promise you they will only get more difficult as you grow older. I realize that what I'm about to give is some quite unsolicited nuts-and-bolts advice. But perhaps it will spare you, later on in your lives, some of the obsessions and emptiness that have claimed the sexual histories of many men just a generation before you. Perhaps it will not help, I don't know; but I hope very much that it will.

First, you can start choosing now not to let your sexuality be manipulated by the pornography industry. I've heard many unhappy men talk about how they are so hooked on pornography and obsessed with it that they are virtually incapable of a human erotic contact. And I have heard even more men talk about how, when they do have sex with someone, the pornography gets in the way, like a mental obstacle, like a barrier preventing a full experience of what's really happening between them and their partner. The sexuality that the pornography industry needs you to have is not about communicating and caring; it's about "pornographizing" people—objectifying and conquering them, not being with them as a person. You do not have to buy into it.

Second, you can start choosing now not to let drugs and alcohol numb you through your sex life. Too many men, as they age, become incapable of having sex with a clear head. But you need your head clear—to make clear choices, to send clear messages, to read clearly what's coming in on a clear channel between you and your partner. Sex is no time for your awareness to sign off. And another thing: Beware of relying on drugs or alcohol to give you "permission" to have sex, or to trick your body into feeling something that it's not, or so you won't have to take responsibility for what you're feeling or for the sex that you're about to have. If you can't take sober responsibility for your part in a sexual encounter, you probably shouldn't be having it—and you certainly shouldn't be zonked out of your mind *in order* to have it.

Third, you can start choosing now not to fixate on fucking—especially if you'd really rather have sex in other, noncoital ways. Sometimes men have coital sex— penetration and thrusting then ejaculating inside someone— not because they particularly feel like it but because they feel they *should* feel like it: It's expected that if you're the man, you fuck. And if you don't fuck, you're not a man. The corollary of this cultural imperative is that if two people don't have intercourse, they have not had real sex. That's baloney, of course, but the message comes down hard, especially inside men's heads: Fucking is *the* sex act, the act in which you act out what sex is supposed to be—and what sex you're supposed to be.

Like others born with a penis, I was born into a sex-class system that requires my collaboration every day, even in how I have sex. Nobody told me, when I was younger, that I could have noncoital sex and that it would be fine. Actually, much better than fine. Nobody told me about an incredible range of other erotic possibilities for mutual lovemaking—including rubbing body to body, then coming body to body; including multiple, nonejaculatory orgasms; including the feeling you get when even the tiniest place where you and your partner touch becomes like a window through which great tidal storms of passion ebb and flow, back and forth. Nobody told me about the sex you can have when you stop working at having a sex. My body told me, finally. And I began to trust what my body was telling me more than the lie I was supposed to make real.

I invite you too to resist the lie. I invite you too to become an erotic traitor to male supremacy.

NOTES

1. My source for the foregoing information about so-called sex determinants in the human species is a series of interviews I conducted with the sexologist Dr. John Money in Baltimore, Maryland, in 1979 for an article I wrote called "The Multisex Theorem," which was published in a shortened version as "Future Genders" in *Omni* magazine, May 1980, pp. 67–73ff.
2. Dworkin, Andrea. *Woman Hating* (New York: Dutton, 1974), p. 174.
3. Dworkin, *Woman Hating,* p. 183.

27

THE MYTH OF THE SEXUAL ATHLETE

DON SABO

The phrase "sexual athlete" commonly refers to male heterosexual virtuosity in the bedroom. Images of potency, agility, technical expertise, and an ability to attract and satisfy women come to mind. In contrast, the few former athletes who have seriously written on the subject, like Dave Meggyesy and Jim Bouton, and films such as *Raging Bull* and *North Dallas Forty*, depict the male athlete as sexually uptight, fixated on early adolescent sexual antics and exploitative of women. The former image of athletic virility, however, remains fixed within the popular imagination. Partly for this reason, little has been said about the *real* connections between sports and male sexuality.

Locker-Room Sex Talk

Organized sports were as much a part of my growing up as Cheerios, television, and homework. My sexuality unfolded within the all-male social world of sports where sex was always a major focus. I remember, for example, when as prepubertal boys I and my friends pretended to be shopping for baseball cards so we could sneak peeks at *Playboy* and *Swank* magazines at the newsstand. After practices, we would talk endlessly about "boobs" and what it must feel like to kiss and neck. Later, in junior high, we teased one another in the locker room about "jerking off" or being virgins, and there were endless interrogations about "how far" everybody was getting with their girlfriends.

Eventually, boyish anticipation spilled into *real* sexual relationships with girls, which, to my delight and confusion, turned out to be a lot more complex than I ever imagined. While sex (kissing, necking, and petting) got more exciting, it also got more difficult to figure out and talk about. Inside, all the boys, like myself, needed to love and be loved. We were awkwardly reaching out for intimacy. Yet we were telling one another to "catch feels," be cool, connect with girls but don't allow yourself to depend on them. When I was a high-school junior, the gang in the weight room once accused me of being wrapped around my girlfriend's finger. Nothing could be further from the

From *Sex, Violence & Power in Sports: Rethinking Masculinity*, Michael A. Messner and Donald F. Sabo, 1994, pp. 36–41. Reprinted by permission of Crossing Press.

truth, I assured them, and to prove it I broke up with her. I felt miserable about this at the time, and I still feel bad about it.

Within the college jock subculture, men's public protests against intimacy sometimes became exaggerated and ugly. I remember two teammates, drunk and rowdy, ripping girls' blouses off at a party and crawling on their bellies across the dance floor to look up skirts. Then there were the late Sunday morning breakfasts in the dorm. We jocks would usually all sit at one table listening to one braggart or another describe his sexual exploits of the night before. Though a lot of us were turned off by such boasting, ego-boosting tactics, we never openly criticized it. Stories of raunchy, or even abusive sex, real or fabricated, were also assumed to "win points." A junior fullback claimed to have defecated on a girl's chest after she passed out during intercourse. There were also some laughing reports of "gang-bangs."

When sexual relationships were "serious," that is, tempered by love and commitment, the unspoken rule was silence. Rarely did we young men share our feeling about women, our uncertainty about sexual performance, or our disdain for the crudeness and insensitivity of some of our teammates. I now see the tragic irony in this: we could talk about casual sex and about using, trivializing, or debasing women, but frank discussions about sexuality that unfolded within a loving relationship were taboo. Within the locker room subculture, sex and love were seldom allowed to mix. There was a terrible split between our inner needs and outer appearances, between our desire for love from women and our feigned indifference toward them.

Sex as a Sport

Organized sports provide a social setting in which gender (i.e., masculinity and femininity) learning melds with sexual learning. Our sense of "female-ness" or "maleness" influences the ways we see ourselves as sexual beings. Indeed, as we develop, sexual identity emerges as an extension of an already formed gender identity, and sexual behavior tends to conform to cultural norms. To be manly in sports, traditionally, means to be competitive, successful, dominating, aggressive, stoical, goal-directed, and physically strong. Many athletes accept this definition of masculinity and apply it in their relationships with women. Dating becomes a sport in itself, and "scoring," or having sex with little or no emotional involvement, is a mark of masculine achievement. Sexual relationships are games in which women are seen as opponents, and his scoring means her defeat. Too often, women are pawns in men's quests for status within the male pecking order. For many of us jocks, sexual relationships are about man as a hunter and woman as prey.

Why is this? What transforms us from boys who depend on women to men who misunderstand, alienate ourselves from, and sometimes mistreat women? One part of the problem is the expectation that we are supposed to act as though we want to be alone, like the cowboy who always rides off into the sunset alone. In sports, there is only one "most valuable player" on the team.

Too often this prevents male athletes from understanding women and their life experiences. Though women's voices may reach men's ears from the sidelines and grandstands, they remain distant and garbled by the clamor of male competition. In sports, communication gaps between the sexes are due in part to women's historical exclusion, from refusal to allow girls to play along with boys, and coaching practices which quarantine boys from the "feminizing" taint of female influence. One result of this isolation is that sexual myths flourish. Boys end up learning about girls and female sexuality from other males, and the information that gets transmitted within the male network is often inaccurate and downright sexist. As boys, we lacked a vocabulary of intimacy, which would have enabled us to better share sexual experiences with others. The locker-room language that filled our adolescent heads did not exactly foster insights into the true nature of women's sexuality—or our own, for that matter.

Performance and Patriarchy

Traditional gender learning and locker-room sexual myths can also shape men's lovemaking behavior. Taught to be "achievement machines," many athletes organize their energies and perceptions around a performance ethic that influences sexual relations. Men apply their goal-directedness and pre-occupation with performance to their lovemaking. In the movie *Joe*, a sexually liberated woman tells her hard-hat lover that "making love isn't like running a fifty-yard dash."

Making intercourse the chief goal of sex limits men's ability to enjoy other aspects of sexual experience. It also creates problems for both men and their partners. Since coitus requires an erection, men pressure themselves to get and maintain erections. If erections do not occur, or men ejaculate too quickly, their self-esteem as lovers and men can be impaired. In fact, sex therapists tell us that men's preoccupation and anxieties about erectile potency and performance can cause the very sexual dysfunctions they fear.

It is important to emphasize that not only jocks swallow this limiting model of male sexuality. Sports are not the only social setting that promotes androcentrism and eroticism without emotional intimacy. Consider how male sexuality is developed in fraternities, motorcycle gangs, the armed forces, urban gangs, pornography, corporate advertising, MTV, magazines like *Playboy* or *Penthouse*, and the movies—to name but a few examples. These are not random and unrelated sources of traditional masculine values. They all originate in patriarchy.

Sexual relations between men and women in Western societies have been conducted under the panoply of patriarchal power. The sexual values that derive from patriarchy emphasize male dominance and the purely physical dimensions of the sex act while reducing women to delectable but expendable objects. An alternative conception of human sexuality, however, is also gaining ascendancy within the culture. Flowing out of women's experiences and based on egalitarian values, it seeks to integrate eroticism with love and commitment. It is deeply critical of the social forces that reduce women (and men) to sex objects, depersonalize relationships, and turn human sexuality into an advertising gimmick or commodity to be purchased. This is the sexual ethos proffered by the women's movement.

Today's young athletes don't seem as hooked as their predecessors on the hypermasculine image traditional sports have provided. Perhaps this is because alternative forms of masculinity and sexuality have begun to enter the locker-room subculture. More girls are playing sports than ever before, and coeducational athletic experiences are more common. As more women enter the traditionally male settings of sports, business, factories, and government, men are finding it more difficult to perceive women in only one dimension. Perhaps we are becoming better able to see them as fellow human beings and, in the process, we are beginning to search for alternative modes of being men.

What Do Men Really Want (or Need)?

Most of us do not really know what it is we want from our sexual lives. Men seem torn between yearning for excitement and longing for love and intimacy. On one side, we feel titillated by the glitter of corporate advertising. Eroticism jolts our minds and bodies. We're sporadically attracted by the simple hedonism of the so-called sexual revolution and the sometimes slick, sometimes sleazy veil of pornography, soft and hard. Many of us fantasize about pursuing eroticism without commitment; some actually live the fantasy. Yet more men are recently becoming aware of genuine needs for intimate relationships. We are beginning to recognize that being independent, always on the make and emotionally controlled, is not meeting our needs. Furthermore, traditional masculine behavior is certainly not meeting women's expectations or satisfying their emotional needs. More and more men are starting to wonder if sexuality can be a vehicle for expressing and experiencing love.

In our culture many men are suffering from sexual schizophrenia. Their minds lead them toward eroticism while their hearts pull them toward emotional intimacy. What they think they want rarely coincides with what they need. Perhaps the uneasiness and the ambivalence that permeate male sexuality are due to this root fact: the traditional certainties that men have used to define their manhood and sexuality no longer fit the realities of their lives. Until equality between the sexes becomes more of a social reality, no new model of a more humane sexuality will take hold.

As for me, I am still exploring and redefining my sexuality. Although I don't have all the answers yet, I do have direction. I am listening more closely to women's voices, turning my head away from the sexist legacy of the locker room and pursuing a profeminist vision of sexuality. I feel good to have stopped pretending that I enjoy being alone. I never did like feeling alone.

28

THE SEXUAL POLITICS OF BLACK WOMANHOOD

PATRICIA HILL COLLINS

Even I found it almost impossible to let her say what had happened to her as she perceived it . . . And why? Because once you strip away the lie that rape is pleasant, that children are not permanently damaged by sexual pain, that violence done to them is washed away by fear, silence, and time, you are left with the positive horror of the lives of thousands of children . . . who have been sexually abused and who have never been permitted their own language to tell about it.

ALICE WALKER 1988, 57

In *The Color Purple* Alice Walker creates the character of Celie, a Black adolescent girl who is sexually abused by her stepfather. By writing letters to God and forming supportive relationships with other Black women, Celie finds her own voice, and her voice enables her to transcend the fear and silence of her childhood. By creating Celie and giving her the language to tell of her sexual abuse, Walker adds Celie's voice to muted yet growing discussions of the sexual politics of Black womanhood in Black feminist thought. Black feminists have investigated how rape as a specific form of sexual violence is embedded in a system of interlocking race, gender, and class oppression (Davis 1978, 1981, 1989; Hall 1983). Reproductive rights issues such as access to information on sexuality and birth control, the struggles for abortion rights, and patterns of forced sterilization have also gar-

From *Black Feminist Thought: Knowledge, Consciousness, and the Politics of Empowerment,* by Patricia Hill Collins, 1991. Reprinted by permission of the publisher, Routledge: New York and London.

nered attention (Davis 1981). Black lesbian feminists have vigorously challenged the basic assumptions and mechanisms of control underlying compulsory heterosexuality and have investigated homophobia's impact on African-American women (Clarke 1983; Shockley 1983; Barbara Smith 1983; Lorde 1984).

But when it comes to other important issues concerning the sexual politics of Black womanhood, like Alice Walker, Black feminists have found it almost impossible to say what has happened to Black women. In the flood of scholarly and popular writing about Black heterosexual relationships, analyses of domestic violence against African-American women—especially those that link this form of sexual violence to existing gender ideology concerning Black masculinity and Black femininity—remain rare. Theoretical work explaining patterns of Black women's inclusions in the burgeoning international pornography industry has been similarly neglected. Perhaps the most curious omission has been the virtual silence of the Black feminist community concerning the participation of far too many Black women in prostitution. Ironically, while the image of African-American women as prostitutes has been aggressively challenged, the reality of African-American women who work as prostitutes remains unexplored.

These patterns of inclusion and neglect in Black feminist thought merit investigation. Examining the links between sexuality and power in a system of interlocking race, gender, and class oppression should reveal how important controlling Black women's sexuality has been to the effective operation of domination overall. The words of Angela Davis, Audre Lorde, Barbara Smith, and Alice Walker provide a promising foundation for a comprehensive Black feminist analysis. But Black feminist analyses of sexual politics must go beyond chronicling how sexuality has been used to oppress. Equally important is the need to reconceptualize sexuality with an eye toward empowering African-American women.

A Working Definition of Sexual Politics

Sexual politics examines the links between sexuality and power. In defining sexuality it is important to distinguish among sexuality and the related terms, *sex* and *gender* (Vance 1984; Andersen 1988). Sex is a biological category attached to the body—humans are born female or male. In contrast, gender is socially constructed. The sex/gender system consists of marking the categories of biological sex with socially constructed gender meanings of masculinity and femininity. Just as sex/gender systems vary from relatively egalitarian systems to sex/gender hierarchies, ideologies of sexuality attached to particular sex/gender systems exhibit diversity. Sexuality is socially constructed through the sex/gender system on both the personal level of individual consciousness and interpersonal relationships and the social structural level of social institutions (Foucault 1980). This multilevel sex/gender system reflects the needs of a given historical moment such that social constructions of sexuality change in tandem with changing social conditions.

African-American women inhabit a sex/gender hierarchy in which inequalities of race and social class have been sexualized. Privileged groups define their alleged sexual practices as the mythical norm and label sexual practices and groups who diverge from this norm as deviant and threatening (Lorde 1984; Vance 1984). Maintaining the mythical norm of the financially independent, white middle-class family organized around a monogamous heterosexual couple requires stigmatizing African-American families as being deviant, and a primary source of this assumed deviancy stems from allegations about black sexuality. This sex/gender hierarchy not only operates on the social structural level but is potentially replicated within each individual. Differences in sexuality thus take on more meaning than just benign sexual variation. Each individual becomes a powerful conduit for social relations of domination whereby individual anxieties, fears, and doubts about sexuality can be annexed by larger systems of oppression (Hoch 1979; Foucault 1980, 99).

According to Cheryl Clarke, African-Americans have been profoundly affected by this sex/gender hierarchy:

> Like all Americans, black Americans live in a sexually repressive culture. And we have made all manner of compromise regarding our sexuality in order to live here. We have expended much energy trying to debunk the racist mythology which says our sexuality is depraved. Unfortunately, many of us have overcompensated and assimilated . . . . Like everyone else in America who is ambivalent in these respects, black folk have to live with the contradictions of this limited sexual system by repressing or closeting any other sexual/erotic urges, feelings, or desires. (Clarke 1983, 199)

Embedded in Clarke's statement is the theme of self-censorship inherent when a hierarchy of any kind invades interpersonal relationships among individuals and the actual consciousness of individuals themselves. Sexuality and power as domination become intertwined.

In her ground-breaking essay, "Uses of the Erotic: The Erotic as Power," Black feminist poet Audre Lorde explores this fundamental link between sexuality and power:

> There are many kinds of power, used and unused, acknowledged or otherwise. The erotic is a resource within each of us that lies in a deeply female and spiritual plane, firmly rooted in the power of our unexpressed or unrecognized feeling. In order to perpetuate itself, every oppression must corrupt or distort those various sources of power within the culture of the oppressed that can provide energy

for change. For women, this has meant a suppression of the erotic as a considered source of power and information in our lives. (Lorde 1984, 53)

For Lorde sexuality is a component of the larger construct of the erotic as a source of power in women. Lorde's notion is one of power as energy, as something people possess which must be annexed in order for larger systems of oppression to function.[1]

Sexuality becomes a domain of restriction and repression when this energy is tied to the larger system of race, class, and gender oppression. But Lorde's words also signal the potential for black women's empowerment by showing sexuality and the erotic to be a domain of exploration, pleasure, and human agency. From a Black feminist standpoint sexuality encompasses the both/and nature of human existence, the potential for a sexuality that simultaneously oppresses and empowers.

One key issue for Black feminist thought is the need to examine the processes by which power as domination on the social structural level—namely, institutional structures of racism, sexism, and social class privilege—annexes this basic power of the erotic on the personal level—that is, the construct of power as energy, for its own ends.

Black Women and the Sex/Gender Hierarchy

The social construction of Black women's sexuality is embedded in this larger, overarching sex/gender hierarchy designed to harness power as energy to the exigencies of power as race, gender, and social class domination . . . . Pornography, prostitution, and rape as a specific tool of sexual violence have . . . been key to the sexual politics of Black womanhood. Together they form three essential and interrelated components of the sex/gender hierarchy framing Black women's sexuality.

Pornography and Black Women's Bodies

For centuries the black woman has served as the primary pornographic "outlet" for white men in Europe and America. We need only think of the black women used as breeders, raped for the pleasure and profit of their owners. We need only think of the license the "master" of the slave women enjoyed. But, most telling of all, we need only study the old slave societies of the South to note the sadistic treatment—at the hands of white "gentlemen"—of "beautiful young quadroons and octoroons" who became increasingly (and were deliberately bred to become) indistinguishable from white women, and were the more highly prized as slave mistresses because of this. (Walker 1981, 42)

Alice Walker's description of the rape of enslaved African women for the "pleasure and profit of their owners" encapsulates several elements of contemporary pornography. First, Black women were used as sex objects for the pleasure of white men. This objectification of African-American women parallels the portrayal of women in pornography as sex objects whose sexuality is available for men (McNall 1983). Exploiting Black women as breeders objectified them as less than human because only animals can be bred against their will. In contemporary pornography women are objectified through being portrayed as pieces of meat, as sexual animals awaiting conquest. Second, African-American women were raped, a form of sexual violence. Violence is typically an implicit or explicit theme in pornography. Moreover, the rape of Black women linked sexuality and violence, another characteristic feature of pornography (Eisenstein 1983). Third, rape and other forms of sexual violence act to strip victims of their will to resist and make them passive and submissive to the will of the rapist. Female passivity, the fact that women have things done to them, is a theme repeated over and over in contemporary pornography (McNall 1983). Fourth, the profitability of Black women's sexual exploitation for white "gentlemen" parallels pornography's financially lucrative benefits for pornographers (Eisenstein 1983). Finally, the actual breeding of "quadroons and octoroons" not only reinforces the themes of Black women's passivity, objectification, and malleability to male control but reveals pornography's grounding in racism and sexism. The fates of both Black and white women were intertwined in this breeding process. The ideal African-American woman as a pornographic object was indistinguishable from white women and thus approximated the images of beauty, asexuality, and chastity forced on white women. But inside was a highly sexual whore, a "slave mistress" ready to cater to her owner's pleasure.[2]

Contemporary pornography consists of a series of icons or representations that focus the viewer's attention on the relationship between the portrayed individual and the general qualities ascribed to that class of individuals. Pornographic images are iconographic in that they represent realities in a manner determined by the historical position of the observers, their relationship to their own time, and to the history of the conventions which they employ (Gilman 1985). The treatment of Black women's bodies in nineteenth-century Europe and the United States may be the foundation upon which contemporary pornography as the representation of women's objectification, domination, and control is based. Icons about the sexuality of Black women's bodies emerged in these contexts. Moreover, as race/gender-specific representations, these icons have implications for the treatment of both African-American and white women in contemporary pornography.

I suggest that African-American women were not included in pornography as an afterthought but instead form a key pillar on which contemporary pornography itself rests. As Alice Walker points out, "the more ancient roots of modern pornography are to be found in the almost always pornographic treatment of black women who, from the moment they entered slavery . . . were subjected to rape as the 'logical' convergence of sex and violence. Conquest, in short " (1981, 42).

One key feature about the treatment of Black women in the nineteenth century was how their bodies were objects of display. In the antebellum American South white men did not have to look at pornographic pictures of women because they could become voyeurs of Black women on the auction block. A chilling example of this objectification of the Black female body is provided by the exhibition, in early nineteenth-century Europe, of Sarah Bartmann, the so-called Hottentot Venus. Her display formed one of the original icons for Black female sexuality. An African woman, Sarah Bartmann was often exhibited at fashionable parties in Paris, generally wearing little clothing, to provide entertainment. To her audience she represented deviant sexuality. At the time European audiences thought that Africans had deviant sexual practices and searched for physiological differences, such as enlarged penises and malformed female genitalia, as indications of this deviant sexuality. Sarah Bartmann's exhibition stimulated these racist and sexist beliefs. After her death in 1815, she was dissected. Her genitalia and buttocks remain on display in Paris (Gilman 1985).

Sander Gilman explains the impact that Sarah Bartmann's exhibition had on Victorian audiences:

> It is important to note that Sarah Bartmann was exhibited not to show her genitalia—but rather to present another anomaly which the European audience . . . found riveting. This was the steatopygia, or protruding buttocks, the other physical characteristic of the Hottentot female which captured the eye of early European travelers . . . . The figure of Sarah Bartmann was reduced to her sexual parts. The audience which had paid to see her buttocks and had fantasized about the uniqueness of her genitalia when she was alive could, after her death and dissection, examine both. (1985, 213)

In this passage Gilman unwittingly describes how Bartmann was used as a pornographic object similar to how women are represented in contemporary pornography. She was reduced to her sexual parts, and these parts came to represent a dominant icon applied to Black women throughout the nineteenth century. Moreover, the fact that Sarah Bartmann was both African and a woman underscores the importance of gender in maintaining notions of racial purity. In this case Bartmann symbolized Blacks as a "race." Thus the creation of the icon applied to Black women demonstrates that notions of gender, race, and sexuality were linked in overarching structures of political domination and economic exploitation.

The process illustrated by the pornographic treatment of the bodies of enslaved African women and of women like Sarah Bartmann has developed into a full-scale industry encompassing all women objectified differently by racial/ethnic category. Contemporary portrayals of Black women in pornography represent the continuation of the historical treatment of their actual bodies. African-American women are usually depicted in a situation of bondage and slavery, typically in a submissive posture, and often with two white men. As Bell observes, "this setting reminds us of all the trappings of slavery: chains, whips, neck braces, wrist clasps" (1987, 59). White women and women of color have different pornographic images applied to them. The image of Black women in pornography is almost consistently one featuring them breaking from chains. The image of Asian women in pornography is almost consistently one of being tortured (Bell 1987, 161).

The pornographic treatment of Black women's bodies challenges the prevailing feminist assumption that since pornography primarily affects white women, racism has been grafted onto pornography. African-American women's experiences suggest that Black women were not added into a pre-existing pornography, but rather that pornography itself must be reconceptualized as an example of the interlocking nature of race, gender, and class oppression. At the heart of both racism and sexism are notions of biological determinism claiming that people of African descent and women possess immutable biological characteristics marking their inferiority to elite white men (Gould 1981; Fausto-Sterling 1989; Halpin 1989). In pornography these racist and sexist beliefs are sexualized. Moreover, for African-American women pornography has not been timeless and universal but was tied to Black women's experiences with the European colonization of Africa and with American slavery. Pornography emerged within a specific system of social class relationships.

This linking of views of the body, social constructions of race and gender, and conceptualizations of sexuality that inform Black women's treatment as pornographic objects promises to have significant implications for how we assess contemporary pornography. Moreover, examining how pornography has been central to the race, gender, and class oppression of African-American women offers new routes for understanding the dynamics of power as domination.

Investigating racial patterns in pornography offers one route for such an analysis. Black women have often claimed that images of white women's sexuality were intertwined with the controlling image of the sexually denigrated black woman: "In the United States, the fear and fascination of female sexuality was projected onto black women; the passionless lady arose in symbiosis with the primitively sexual slave" (Hall 1983, 333). Comparable linkages exist in pornography (Gardner 1980). Alice Walker provides a fictional account of a Black man's growing awareness of the different ways that African-American and white women are objectified in pornography: "What he has refused to see—because to see it would reveal yet another area in which he is unable to protect or defend black women—is that where white women are depicted in pornography as 'objects,' black women are depicted as animals. Where white women are depicted as human bodies if not beings, black women are depicted as shit" (Walker 1981, 52).

Walker's distinction between "objects" and "animals" is crucial in untangling gender, race, and class dynamics in pornography. Within the mind/body, culture/nature, male/female oppositional dichotomies in Western social thought, objects occupy an uncertain interim position. As objects white women become creations of culture—in this case,the mind of white men—using the materials of nature—in this case, uncontrolled female sexuality. In contrast, as animals Black women receive no such redeeming dose of culture and remain open to the type of exploitation visited on nature overall. Race becomes the distinguishing feature in determining the type of objectification women will encounter. Whiteness as symbolic of both civilization and culture is used to separate objects from animals.

The alleged superiority of men to women is not the only hierarchical relationship that has been linked to the putative superiority of the mind to the body. Certain "races" of people have been defined as being more body-like, more animallike, and less godlike than others (Spelman 1982, 52). Race and gender oppression may both revolve around the same axis of disdain for the body; both portray the sexuality of subordinate groups as animalistic and therefore deviant. Biological notions of race and gender prevalent in the early nineteenth century which fostered the animalistic icon of Black female sexuality were joined by the appearance of a racist biology incorporating the concept of degeneracy (Foucault 1980). Africans and women were both perceived as embodied entities, and Blacks were seen as degenerate. Fear of and disdain for the body thus formed a key element in both sexist and racist thinking (Spelman 1982).

While the sexual and racial dimensions of being treated like an animal are important, the economic foundation underlying this treatment is critical. Animals can be economically exploited, worked, sold, killed, and consumed. As "mules," African-American women become susceptible to such treatment. The political economy of pornography also merits careful attention. Pornography is pivotal in mediating contradictions in changing societies (McNall 1983). It is no accident that racist biology, religious justifications for slavery and women's subordination, and other explanations for nineteenth-century racism and sexism arose during a period of profound political and economic change. Symbolic means of domination become particularly important in mediating contradictions in changing political economies. The exhibition of Sarah Bartmann and Black women on the auction block were not benign intellectual exercises—these practices defended real material and political interests. Current transformations in international capitalism require similar ideological justifications. Where does pornography fit in these current transformations? This question awaits a comprehensive Afrocentric feminist analysis.

Publicly exhibiting Black women may have been central to objectifying Black women as animals and to creating the icon of Black women as animals. Yi-Fu Tuan (1984) offers an innovative argument about similarities in efforts to control nature—especially plant life—the domestication of animals, and the domination of certain groups of humans. Tuan suggests that displaying humans alongside animals implies that such humans are more like monkeys and bears than they are like "normal" people. This same juxtaposition leads spectators to view the captive animals in a special way. Animals acquire definitions of being like humans, only more openly carnal and sexual, an aspect of animals that forms a major source of attraction for visitors to modern zoos. In discussing the popularity of monkeys in zoos, Tuan notes: "some visitors are especially attracted by the easy sexual behavior of the monkeys. Voyeurism is forbidden except when applied to subhumans" (1984, 82). Tuan's analysis suggests that the public display of Sarah Bartmann and of the countless enslaved African women on the auction blocks of the antebellum American South—especially in proximity to animals—fostered their image as animalistic.

This linking of Black women as animals is evident in nineteenth-century scientific literature. The equation of women, Blacks, and animals is revealed in the following description of an African woman published in an 1878 anthropology text:

> She had a way of pouting her lips exactly like what we have
> observed in the orangutan. Her movements had something abrupt
> and fantastical about them, reminding one of those of the ape. Her
> ear was like that of many apes . . . . These are animal characters. I
> have never seen a human head more like an ape than that of this
> woman. (Halpin 1989, 287)

In a climate such as this, it is not surprising that one prominent European physician even stated that Black women's "animallike sexual appetite went so far as to lead black women to copulate with apes" (Gilman 1985, 212).

The treatment of all women in contemporary pornography has strong ties to the portrayal of Black women as animals. In pornography women become nonpeople and are often represented as the sum of their fragmented body parts. Scott McNall observes:

> This fragmentation of women relates to the predominance of rear-
> entry position photographs . . . . All of these kinds of photographs
> reduce the woman to her reproductive system, and, furthermore,
> make her open, willing, and available—not in control . . . . The other
> thing rear-entry position photographs tell us about women is that
> they are animals. They are animals because they are the same as
> dogs—bitches in heat who can't control themselves. (McNall 1983,
> 197–98)

This linking of animals and white women within pornography becomes feasible when grounded in the earlier denigration of Black women as animals.

Developing a comprehensive analysis of the race, gender, and class dynamics of pornography offers possibilities for change. Those Black feminist intellectuals investigating sexual politics imply that the situation is much more complicated than that advanced by some prominent white feminists (see, e.g., Dworkin 1981) in which "men oppress women" because they are men. Such approaches implicitly assume biologically deterministic views of sex, gender, and sexuality and offer few possibilities for change. In contrast, Afrocentric feminist analyses routinely provide for human agency and its corresponding empowerment and for the responsiveness of social structures to human action. In the short story "Coming Apart," Alice Walker describes one Black man's growing realization that his enjoyment of pornography, whether of white women as "objects" or Black women as "animals," degraded him:

> He begins to feel sick. For he realizes that he has bought some of the advertisements about women, black and white. And further, inevitably, he has bought the advertisements about himself. In pornography the black man is portrayed as being capable of fucking anything . . . even a piece of shit. He is defined solely by the size, readiness and unselectivity of his cock. (Walker 1981, 52)

Walker conceptualizes pornography as a race/gender system that entraps everyone. But by exploring an African-American *man's* struggle for a self-defined standpoint on pornography, Walker suggests that a changed consciousness is essential to social change. If a Black man can understand how pornography affects him, then other groups enmeshed in the same system are equally capable of similar shifts in consciousness and action.

Prostitution and the Commodification of Sexuality

In *To Be Young, Gifted and Black,* Lorraine Hansberry creates three characters: a young domestic worker, a chic, professional, middle-aged woman, and a mother in her thirties. Each speaks a variant of the following:

> In these streets out there, any little white boy from Long Island or Westchester sees me and leans out of his car and yells—"Hey there, *hot chocolate*! Say there, Jezebel! Hey you—'Hundred Dollar Misunderstanding'! YOU! Bet you know where there's a good time tonight . . . . " Follow me sometimes and see if I lie. I can be coming from eight hours on an assembly line or fourteen hours in Mrs. Halsey's kitchen. I can be all filled up that day with three hundred years of rage so that my eyes are flashing and my flesh is trembling—and the white boys in the streets, they look at me and think of sex. They look at me and that's *all* they think . . . . Baby, you could be Jesus in drag—but if you're brown they're sure you're selling! (Hansberry 1969, 98)

Like the characters in Hansberry's fiction, all Black women are affected by the widespread controlling image that African-American women are sexually promiscuous, potential prostitutes. The pervasiveness of this image is vividly recounted in Black activist lawyer Pauli Murray's description of an incident she experienced while defending two women from Spanish Harlem who had been arrested as prostitutes: "The first witness, a white man from New Jersey, testified on the details of the sexual transaction and his payment of money. When asked to identify the woman with whom he had engaged in sexual intercourse, he unhesitatingly pointed directly at me, seated beside my two clients at the defense table!" (Murray 1987, 274). Murray's clients were still convicted.

The creation of Jezebel, the image of the sexually denigrated Black woman, has been vital in sustaining a system of interlocking race, gender, and class oppression. Exploring how the image of the African-American woman as prostitute has been used by each system of oppression illustrates how sexuality links the three systems. But Black women's treatment also demonstrates how manipulating sexuality has been essential to the political economy of domination within each system and across all three.

Yi-Fu Tuan (1984) suggests that power as domination involves reducing humans to animate nature in order to exploit them economically or to treat them condescendingly as pets. Domination may be either cruel and exploitative with no affection or may be exploitative yet coexist with affection. The former produces the victim—in this case, the Black woman as "mule" whose labor has been exploited. In contrast, the combination of dominance and affection produces the pet, the individual who is subordinate but whose survival depends on the whims of the more powerful. The "beautiful young quadroons and octoroons" described by Alice Walker were bred to be pets—enslaved black mistresses whose existence required that they retain the affection of their owners. The treatment afforded these women illustrates a process that affects all African-American women: their portrayal as actual or potential victims and pets of elite white males.[3]

African-American women simultaneously embody the coexistence of the victim and the pet, with survival often linked to the ability to be appropriately subordinate as victims or pets. Black women's experiences as unpaid and paid workers demonstrate the harsh lives victims are forced to lead. While the life of the victim is difficult, pets experience a distinctive form of exploitation. Zora Neale Hurston's 1943 essay, "The 'Pet' Negro System," speaks contemptuously of this ostensibly benign situation that combines domination with affection. Written in a Black oratorical style, Hurston notes, "Brother and Sisters, I take my text this morning from the Book of Dixie . . . . Now it says here, 'And every white man shall be allowed to pet himself a Negro. Yea, he shall take a Black man unto himself to pet and cherish, and this same Negro shall be perfect in his sight'" (Walker 1979a, 156). Pets are treated as exceptions and live with the constant threat that they will no longer be "perfect in his sight," that their owners will tire of them and relegate them to the unenviable role of victim.

Prostitution represents the fusion of exploitation for an economic purpose—namely, the commodification of Black women's sexuality—with the demeaning treatment afforded pets. Sex becomes commodified not merely in the sense that it can be purchased—the dimension of economic exploitation—but also in the sense that one is dealing with a totally alienated being who is separated from and who does not control her body: the dimension of power as domination (McNall 1983). Commodified sex can then be appropriated by the powerful. When the "white boys from Long Island" look at Black women and *all* they think about is sex, they believe that they can appropriate Black women's bodies. When they yell "Bet you know where there's a good time tonight," they expect commodified sex with Black women as "animals" to be better than sex with white women as "objects." Both pornography and prostitution commodify sexuality and imply to the "white boys" that all African-American women can be bought.

Prostitution under European and American capitalism thus exists within a complex web of political and economic relationships whereby sexuality is conceptualized along intersecting axes of race and gender. Gilman's (1985) analysis of the exhibition of Sarah Bartmann as the "Hottentot Venus" suggests another intriguing connection between race, gender, and sexuality in nineteenth-century Europe—the linking of the icon of the Black woman with the icon of the white prostitute. While the Hottentot woman stood for the essence of Africans as a race, the white prostitute symbolized the sexualized woman. The prostitute represented the embodiment of sexuality and all that European society associated with it: disease as well as passion. As Gilman points out, "it is this uncleanliness, this disease, which forms the final link between two images of women, the black and the prostitute. Just as the genitalia of the Hottentot were perceived as parallel to the diseased genitalia of the prostitute, so too the power of the idea of corruption links both images" (1985, 237). These connections between the icons of Black women and white prostitutes demonstrate how race, gender, and the social class structure of the European political economy interlock.

In the American antebellum South both of these images were fused in the forced prostitution of enslaved African women. The prostitution of Black women allowed white women to be the opposite: Black "whores" make white "virgins" possible. This race/gender nexus fostered a situation whereby white men could then differentiate between the sexualized woman-as-body who is dominated and "screwed" and the asexual woman-as-pure-spirit who is idealized and brought home to mother (Hoch 1979, 70). The sexually denigrated woman, whether she was made a victim through her rape or a pet through her seduction, could be used as the yardstick against which the cult of true womanhood was measured. Moreover, this entire situation was profitable.

Rape and Sexual Violence

Force was important in creating African-American women's centrality to American images of the sexualized woman and in shaping their experiences with both pornography and prostitution. Black women did not willingly submit to their exhibition on southern auction blocks—they were forced to do so. Enslaved African women could not choose whether to work—they were beaten and often killed if they refused. Black domestics who resisted the sexual advances of their employers often found themselves looking for work where none was to be found. Both the reality and the threat of violence have acted as a form of social control for African-American women.

Rape has been one fundamental tool of sexual violence directed against African-American women. Challenging the pervasiveness of Black women's rape and sexual extortion by white men has long formed a prominent theme in Black women's writings. Autobiographies such as Maya Angelou's *I Know Why the Caged Bird Sings* (1970) and Harriet Jacobs's "The Perils of a Slave Woman's Life" (1860/1987) from *Incidents in the Life of a Slave Girl* record examples of actual and threatened sexual assault. The effects of rape on African-American women is a prominent theme in Black women's fiction. Gayl Jones's *Corregidora* (1975) and Rosa Guy's *A Measure of Time* (1983) both explore interracial rape of Black women. Toni Morrison's *The Bluest Eye* (1970), Alice Walker's *The Color Purple* (1982), and Gloria Naylor's *The Women of Brewster Place* (1980) all examine rape within African-American families and communities. Elizabeth Clark-Lewis's (1985) study of domestic workers found that mothers, aunts, and community othermothers warned young Black women about the threat of rape. One respondent in Clark-Lewis's study, an 87-year-old North Carolina Black domestic worker, remembers, "nobody was sent out before you was told to be careful of the white man or his sons" (Clark-Lewis 1985, 15).

Rape and other acts of overt violence that Black women have experienced, such as physical assault during slavery, domestic abuse, incest, and sexual extortion, accompany Black women's subordination in a system of race, class, and gender oppression. These violent acts are the visible dimensions of a more generalized, routinized system of oppression. Violence against Black women tends to be legitimated and therefore condoned while the same acts visited on other groups may remain nonlegitimated and nonexcusable. Certain forms of violence may garner the backing and control of the state while others remain uncontrolled (Edwards 1987). Specific acts of sexual violence visited on African-American women reflect a broader process by which violence is socially constructed in a race- and gender-specific manner. Thus Black women, Black men, and white women experience distinctive forms of sexual violence. As Angela Davis points out, "It would be a mistake to regard the institutionalized pattern of rape during slavery as an expression of white man's sexual urges . . . . Rape was a weapon of domination, a weapon of repression, whose covert goal was to extinguish slave women's will to resist, and in the process, to demoralize their men" (1981, 23).

Angela Davis's work (1978, 1981, 1989) illustrates this effort to conceptualize sexual violence against African-American women as part of a system of interlocking race, gender, and class oppression. Davis suggests that sexual violence has been central to the economic and political subordination of African-Americans overall. But while Black men and women were both victims of sexual violence, the specific forms they encountered were gender specific.

Depicting African-American men as sexually charged beasts who desired white women created the myth of the Black rapist.[4] Lynching emerged as the specific form of sexual violence visited on Black men, with the myth of the Black rapist as its ideological justification. The significance of this myth is that it "has been methodically conjured up when recurrent waves of violence and terror against the Black community required a convincing explanation" (Davis 1978, 25). Black women experienced a parallel form of race- and gender-specific sexual violence. Treating African-American women as pornographic objects and portraying them as sexualized animals, as prostitutes, created the controlling image of Jezebel. Rape became the specific act of sexual violence forced on Black women, with the myth of the Black prostitute as its ideological justification.

Lynching and rape, two race/gender-specific forms of sexual violence, merged with their ideological justifications of the rapist and prostitute in order to provide an effective system of social control over African-Americans. Davis asserts that the controlling image of Black men as rapists has always "strengthened its inseparable companion: the image of the Black woman as chronically promiscuous. And with good reason, for once the notion is accepted that Black men harbor irresistible, animal-like sexual urges, the entire race is invested with bestiality" (1978, 27). A race of "animals" can be treated as such—as victims or pets. "The mythical rapist implies the mythical whore—and a race of rapists and whores deserves punishment and nothing more" (Davis 1978, 28).

Some suggestive generalizations exist concerning the connection between the social constructions of the rapist and the prostitute and the tenets of racist biology. Tuan (1984) notes that humans practice certain biological procedures on plants and animals to ensure their suitability as pets. For animals the goal of domestication is manageability and control, a state that can be accomplished through selective breeding or, for some male animals, by castration. A similar process may have affected the historical treatment of African-Americans. Since dominant groups have generally refrained from trying to breed humans in the same way that they breed animals, the pervasiveness of rape and lynching suggests that these practices may have contributed to mechanisms of population control. While not widespread, in some slave settings selective breeding and, if that failed, rape were used to produce slaves of a certain genetic heritage. In an 1858 slave narrative, James Roberts recounts the plantation of Maryland planter Calvin Smith, a man who kept 50–60 "head of women" for reproductive purposes. Only whites were permitted access to these women in order to ensure that 20–25 racially mixed children were born annually. Roberts also tells of a second planter who competed with Smith in breeding mulattos, a group that at that time brought higher prices, the "same as men strive to raise the most stock of any kind, cows, sheep, horses, etc." (Weisbord 1975, 27). For Black men, lynching was frequently accompanied by castration. Again, the parallels to techniques used to domesticate animals, or at least serve as a warning to those Black men who remained alive, is striking.

Black women continue to deal with this legacy of the sexual violence visited on African-Americans generally and with our history as collective rape victims. One effect lies in the treatment of rape victims. Such women are twice victimized, first by the actual rape, in this case the collective rape under slavery. But they are victimized again by family members, community residents, and social institutions such as criminal justice systems which somehow believe that rape victims are responsible for their own victimization. Even though current statistics indicate that Black women are more likely to be victimized than white women, Black women are less likely to report their rapes, less likely to have their cases come to trial, less likely to have their trials result in convictions, and, most disturbing, less likely to seek counseling and other support services. Existing evidence suggests that African-American women are aware of their lack of protection and that they resist rapists more than other groups (Bart and O'Brien 1985).

Another significant effect of this legacy of sexual violence concerns Black women's absence from antirape movements. Angela Davis argues, "if black women are conspicuously absent from the ranks of the anti-rape movement today, it is, in large part, their way of protesting the movement's posture of indifference toward the frame-up rape charge as an incitement to racist aggression" (1978, 25). But this absence fosters Black women's silence concerning a troubling issue: the fact that most Black women are raped by Black men. While the historical legacy of the triad of pornography, prostitution, and the institutionalized rape of Black women may have created the larger social context within which all African-Americans reside, the unfortunate current reality is that many Black men have internalized the controlling images of the sex/gender hierarchy and condone either Black women's rape by other Black men or their own behavior as rapists. Far too many African-American women live with the untenable position of putting up with abusive Black men in defense of an elusive Black unity.

The historical legacy of Black women's treatment in pornography, prostitution, and rape forms the institutional backdrop for a range of interpersonal relationships that Black women currently have with Black men, whites, and one another. Without principled coalitions with other groups, African-American women may not be able to effect lasting change on the social structural level of social institutions. But the first step to forming such coalitions is examining exactly how these institutions harness power as energy for their own use by invading both relationships among individuals and individual consciousness itself. Thus, understanding the contemporary dynamics of the sexual politics of Black womanhood in order to empower African-American women requires investigating how social structural factors infuse the private domain of Black women's relationships.

NOTES

1. French philosopher Michel Foucault makes a similar point: "I believe that the political significance of the problem of sex is due to the fact that sex is located at the point of intersection of the discipline of the body and the control of the population" (1980, 125). The erotic is something felt, a power that is embodied. Controlling sexuality harnesses that power for the needs of larger, hierarchical systems by controlling the body and hence the population.

2. Offering a similar argument about the relationship between race and masculinity, Paul Hoch (1979) suggests that the ideal white man is a hero who upholds honor. But inside lurks a "Black beast" of violence and sexuality, traits that the white hero deflects onto men of color.

3. Any group can be made into pets. Consider Tuan's (1984) discussion of the role that young Black boys played as exotic ornaments for wealthy white women in the 1500s to the early 1800s in England. Unlike other male servants, the boys were favorite attendants of noble ladies and gained entry into their mistresses' drawing rooms, bedchambers, and theater boxes. Boys were often given fancy collars with padlocks to wear. "As they did with their pet dogs and monkeys, the ladies grew genuinely fond of their black boys" (p. 142).

4. See Hoch's (1979) discussion of the roots of the white hero, black beast myth in Eurocentric thought. Hoch contends that white masculinity is based on the interracial competition for women. To become a "man," the white, godlike hero must prove himself victorious over the dark "beast" and win possession of the "white goddess." Through numerous examples Hoch suggests that this explanatory myth underlies Western myth, poetry, and literature. One example describing how Black men were depicted during the witch hunts is revealing. Hoch notes, "the Devil was often depicted as a lascivious black male with cloven hoofs, a tail, and a huge penis capable of super-masculine exertion—an archetypal leering "black beast from below" (1979, 44).

REFERENCES

Andersen, Margaret. 1988. *Thinking about Women: Sociological Perspectives on Sex and Gender.* 2d ed. New York: Macmillan.

Angelou, Maya. 1969. *I Know Why the Caged Bird Sings.* New York: Bantam.

Bart, Pauline B., and Patricia H. O'Brien. 1985. "Ethnicity and Rape Avoidance: Jews, White Catholics and Blacks." In *Stopping Rape: Successful Survival Strategies,* edited by Pauline B. Bart and Patricia H. O'Brien, 70–92. New York: Pergamon Press.

Bell, Laurie, ed. 1987. *Good Girls/Bad Girls: Feminists and Sex Trade Workers Face to Face.* Toronto: Seal Press.

Clarke, Cheryl. 1983. "The Failure to Transform: Homophobia in the Black Community." In *Home Girls: A Black Feminist Anthology,* edited by Barbara Smith, 197–208. New York: Kitchen Table Press.

Clark-Lewis, Elizabeth. 1985. *"This Work Had a 'End'" The Transition from Live-In to Day Work.* Southern Women: The Intersection of Race, Class and Gender. Working Paper #2. Memphis, TN: Center for Research on Women, Memphis State University.

Davis, Angela Y. 1978. "Rape, Racism and the Capitalist Setting." *Black Scholar* 9(7): 24–30.

———. 1981. *Women, Race and Class.* New York: Random House.

———. 1989. *Women, Culture, and Politics.* New York: Random House.

Dworkin, Andrea. 1981. *Pornography: Men Possessing Women.* New York: Perigee.

Edwards, Ann. 1987. "Male Violence in Feminist Theory: An Analysis of the Changing Conceptions of Sex/Gender Violence and Male Dominance." In *Women, Violence and Social Control,* edited by Jalna Hanmer and Mary Maynard, 13–29. Atlantic Highlands, NJ: Humanities Press.

Eisenstein, Hester. 1983. *Contemporary Feminist Thought.* Boston: G. K. Hall.

Fausto-Sterling, Anne. 1989. "Life in the XY Corral." *Women's Studies International Forum* 12(3): 319–31.

Foucalt, Michel. 1980. *Power/Knowledge:Selected Interviews and Other Writings 1972–1977,* edited by Colin Gordon. New York: Pantheon.

Gardner, Tracey A. 1980. "Racism and Pornography in the Women's Movement." In *Take Back the Night: Women on Pornography,* edited by Laura Lederer, 105–14. New York: William Morrow.

Gilman, Sander L. 1985. "Black Bodies, White Bodies: Toward an Iconography of Female Sexuality in Late Nineteenth-Century Art, Medicine and Literature." *Critical Inquiry* 12(1): 205–43.

Gould, Stephen Jay. 1981. *The Mismeasure of Man.* New York: W. W. Norton.

Guy, Rosa. 1983. *A Measure of Time.* New York: Bantam.

Hall, Jacqueline Dowd. 1983. "The Mind that Burns in Each Body: Women, Rape, and Racial Violence." In *Powers of Desire: The Politics of Sexuality,* edited by Ann Snitow, Christine Stansell, and Sharon Thompson, 329–49. New York: Monthly Review Press.

Halpin, Zuleyma Tang. 1989."Scientific Objectivity and the Concept of 'The Other.'" *Women's Studies International Forum* 12(3): 285–94.

Hansberry, Lorraine. 1969. *To Be Young, Gifted and Black.* New York: Signet.

Hoch, Paul. 1979. *White Hero Black Beast: Racism, Sexism and the Mask of Masculinity.* London: Pluto Press.

Jacobs, Harriet. [1860] 1987. "The Perils of a Slave Woman's Life." In *Invented Lives: Narratives of Black Women 1860–1960,* edited by Mary Helen Washington, 16–67. Garden City, NY: Anchor.

Jones, Gayl. 1975. *Corregidora.* New York: Bantam.

Lorde, Audre. 1984. Sister Outsider. Trumansberg, NY: The Crossing Press.

McNall, Scott G. 1983. "Pornography: The Structure of Domination and the Mode of Reproduction." In *Current Perspectives in Social Theory, Volume 4,* edited by Scott McNall, 181–203. Greenwich, CT: JAI Press.

Morrison, Toni. 1970. *The Bluest Eye.* New York: Pocket Books.

Murray, Pauli. 1987. *Song in a Weary Throat: An American Pilgrimage.* New York: Harper & Row.

Naylor, Gloria. 1980. *The Women of Brewster Place.* New York: Penguin.

Shockley, Ann Allen. 1983. "The Black Lesbian in American Literature: An Overview." In *Home Girls: A Black Feminist Anthology,* edited by Barbara Smith, 83–93. New York: Kitchen Table Press.

Smith, Barbara. 1983. "Introduction." In *Home Girls: A Black Feminist Anthology,* edited by Barbara Smith, xix–lvi. New York: Kitchen Table Press.

Spelman, Elizabeth V. 1982. "Theories of Race and Gender: The Erasure of Black Women." *Quest* 5(4): 36–62.

Tuan, Yi-Fu. 1984. *Dominance and Affection: The Making of Pets.* New Haven, CT: Yale University Press.

Vance, Carole S. 1984. "Pleasure and Danger: Toward a Politics of Sexuality." In *Pleasure and Danger: Exploring Female Sexuality,* edited by Carole S. Vance, 1–27. Boston: Routledge & Kegan Paul.

Walker, Alice, ed. 1979. *I Love Myself When I Am Laughing, And Then Again When I Am Looking Mean and Impressive: A Zora Neal Hurston Reader.* Old Westbury, NY: Feminist Press.

Walker, Alice. 1981. "Coming Apart." In *You Can't Keep a Good Woman Down,* 41–53. New York: Harcourt Brace Jovanovich.

——— 1982. *The Color Purple.* New York: Washington Square Press.

Weisbord, Robert G. 1975. *Genocide? Birth Control and the Black American.* Westport, CT: Greenwood Press.

29

BUTCH-FEMME RELATIONSHIPS
Sexual Courage in the 1950s

JOAN NESTLE

For many years now, I have been trying to figure out how to explain the special nature of butch-femme relationships to Lesbian-feminists who consider butch-femme a reproduction of heterosexual models. My own roots lie deep in the earth of this Lesbian custom, and what follows is one Lesbian's understanding of her own experience.

In the late 1950s I walked the streets looking so butch that straight teenagers called me a bulldyke; however, when I went to the Sea Colony, a working-class Lesbian bar in Greenwich Village, looking for my friends and sometimes for a lover, I was a femme, a woman who loved and wanted to nurture the butch strength in other women. I am now forty years old (1981). Although I have been a Lesbian for over twenty years and I embrace feminism as a world view, I can spot a butch thirty feet away and still feel the thrill of her power. Contrary to belief, this power is not bought at the expense of the femme's identity. Butch-femme relationships, as I experienced them, were complex erotic statements, not phony heterosexual replicas. They were filled with a deeply Lesbian language of stance, dress, gesture, loving, courage, and autonomy. None of the butch women I was with, and this included a passing woman, ever presented themselves to me as men; they did announce themselves as tabooed women who were willing to identify their passion for other women by wearing clothes that symbolized the taking of responsibility. Part of this responsibility was sexual expertise. In the 1950s this courage to feel comfortable with arousing another woman became a political act.

Butch-femme was an erotic partnership serving both as a conspicuous flag of rebellion and as an intimate exploration of women's sexuality. It was not an accident that butch-femme couples suffered the most street abuse and provoked more assimilated or closeted Lesbians to plead with them not to be so obvious. An excerpt from a letter by Lorraine Hansberry, published in the *Ladder*[1] in 1957, shows the political implications of the butch-femme statement. The letter is a plea for discretion because, I believe, of the erotic clarity of the butch-femme visual image.

> Someday I expect the "discrete" lesbian will not turn her head on the streets at the sight of the "butch" strolling hand in hand with her friend in their trousers and definitive haircuts. But for the moment it still disturbs. It creates an impossible area for discussion with one's most enlightened (to use a hopeful term) heterosexual friends.[2]

A critic of this essay has suggested that what was really the problem here was that "many other Lesbians at that time felt the adoption of culturally defined roles by the butch-femme was not a true picture of the majority of Lesbians. They found these socialized roles a limiting reality and therefore did not wish to have the butch-femme viewpoint applied or expressed as their own."[3]

My sense of the time says this was not the reason. The butch-femme couple embarrassed other Lesbians (and still does) because they made Lesbians culturally visible, a terrifying act for the 1950s. Hansberry's language—the words *discrete* and *definitive*—is the key, for it speaks of what some wanted to keep hidden: the clearly sexual implications of the two women together. The *Ladder* advocated a "mode of behavior and dress acceptable to society," and it was this policy Hansberry was praising. The desire for passing, combined with the radical work of survival that the *Ladder* was undertaking, was a paradox created by the America of the fifties. The writing in the *Ladder* was bringing to the surface years of pain, opening a door on an intensely private experience, giving a voice to an "obscene" population in a decade of McCarthy witch hunts. To survive meant to take a public stance of societal cleanliness. But in the pages of the journal itself, all dimensions of Lesbian life were explored including butch-femme relationships. The *Ladder* brought off a unique balancing act for the 1950s. It gave nourishment to a secret and subversive life while it flew the flag of assimilation.

However, it was not the rejection by our own that taught the most powerful lesson about sex, gender, and class that butch-femme represented, but the anger we provoked on the streets. Since at times femmes dressed similarly to their butch lovers, the aping of heterosexual roles was not always visually apparent, yet the sight of us was enraging. My understanding of why we angered straight spectators so is not that they saw us modeling ourselves after them, but just the opposite: we were a symbol of women's erotic autonomy, a sexual accomplishment that did not include them. The physical attacks were a direct attempt to break into this self-sufficient erotic partnership. The most frequently shouted taunt was, "Which one of you is the man?" This was not a reflection of our Lesbian experience as much as it was a testimony to the lack of erotic categories in straight culture. In the fifties, when we walked in the Village holding hands, we knew we were courting violence, but we also knew the political implications of how we were courting each other and chose not to sacrifice our need to their anger.[4]

The irony of social change has made a radical, sexual political statement of the 1950s appear today as a reactionary, nonfeminist experience. This is one reason I feel I must write about the old times—not to romanticize butch-femme relationships but to salvage a period of Lesbian culture that I know to be important, a time that has been too easily dismissed as the decade of self-hatred.

Two summers ago in Kansas at the National Women's Studies Association Conference, a slide show was presented to the Lesbian caucus in which a series of myths about Lesbians was entertainingly debunked. The show was to be used in straight sex-education classrooms. One of the slides was a comic representation of the "myth" of butch-femme relationships with voiceover something like: "In the past, Lesbians copied heterosexual styles, calling themselves butch and femme, but they no longer do so." I waited until the end to make my statement, but I sat there feeling that we were so anxious to clean up our lives for heterosexual acceptance that we were ready to force our own people into a denial of some deep parts of their lives. I know what a butch or femme woman would feel seeing this slide show, and I realized that the price for social or superficial feminist acceptance was too high. If we deny the subject of butch-femme relationships, we deny the women who lived them, and still do.

Because of the complexity and authenticity of the butch-femme experience, I think we must take another look at the term *role-playing,* used primarily to summarize this way of loving. I do not think the term serves a purpose either as a label for or as a description of the experience. As a femme, I did what was natural for me, what I felt right. I did not learn a part; I perfected a way of loving. The artificial labels stood waiting for us as we discovered our sexualities.

We labeled ourselves as part of our cultural ritual, and the language reflected our time in history, but the words which seem so one-dimensional now stood for complex sexual and emotional exchanges. Women who were new to the life and entered bars have reported they were asked: "Well, what are you—butch or femme?" Many fled rather than answer the question. The real questions behind this discourse were, "Are you sexual?" and "Are you safe?" When one moved beyond the opening gambits, a whole range of sexuality was possible. Butch and femme covered a wide variety of sexual responses. We joked about being a butchy femme or a femmy butch or feeling kiki (going both ways). We joked about a reversal of expectations: "Get a butch home and she turns over on her back." We had a code language for a courageous world for which many paid dearly. It is hard to re-create for the 1980s what Lesbian sexual play meant in the 1950s, but I think it is essential for Lesbian-feminists to understand, without shame, this part of their erotic heritage. I also think the erotic for us, as a colonized people, is part of our social struggle to survive and change the world.

A year ago some friends of mine were discussing their experiences in talking about butch-femme relationships to a women's studies class. Both had been gay since the 1950s and were active in the early gay liberation struggles. "I tried to explain the complex nature of butch sexuality, its balance of strength and delicacy," Madeline said. "The commitment to please each other was totally different from that in heterosexual relationships in which the woman existed to please the man."

As she spoke, I realized that not only was there the erotic statement made by the two women together, but there was and still is a butch sexuality and a femme sexuality, not a woman-acting-like-a-man or a woman-acting-like-a-woman sexuality, but a developed Lesbian-specific sexuality that has a historical setting and a cultural function. For instance, as a femme I enjoyed strong, fierce love-making; deep, strong givings and takings; erotic play challenges; calculated teasings that called forth the butch-femme encounter. But the essential pleasure was that we were two women, not masqueraders. When a woman said, "Give it to me baby!" as I strained to take more of her hand inside of me, I never heard the voice of a man or of socially conditioned roles. I heard the call of a woman world-traveler, a brave woman, whose hands challenged every denial laid on woman's life.

For me, the erotic essence of the butch-femme relationship was the external difference of women's textures and the bond of knowledgeable caring. I loved my lover for how she stood as well as for what she did. Dress was a part of it: the erotic signal of her hair at the nape of her neck, touching the shirt collar; how she held a cigarette; the symbolic pinky ring flashing as she waved her hand. I know this sounds superficial, but all these gestures were a style of self-presentation that made erotic competence a political statement in the 1950s. A deep partnership could be formed with as many shared tasks as there are now and with an encouragement of the style which made the woman I loved feel most comfortable. In bed, the erotic implications of the total relationship only became clearer. My hand and lips did what felt comfortable for me to do. I did not limit my sexual responses because I was a femme. I went down on my lovers to catch them in my mouth and to celebrate their strength, their caring for me. Deeper than the sexual positioning was the overwhelming love I felt for their courage, the bravery of their erotic independence.

As a way of ignoring what butch-femme meant and means, feminism is often viewed as the validating starting point of healthy Lesbian culture. I believe, however, that many pre-Stonewall Lesbians were feminists, but the primary way this feminism—this autonomy of sexual and social identities— was expressed, was precisely in the form of sexual adventuring that now appears so oppressive. If butch-femme represented an erotically autonomous world, it also symbolized many other forms of independence. Most of the women I knew in the Sea Colony were working women who either had never married or who had left their husbands and were thus responsible for their own economic survival. Family connections had been severed, or the families were poorer than the women themselves. These were women who knew they were going to work for the rest of their Lesbian days to support themselves and the homes they chose to create. They were hair-dressers, taxi drivers, telephone operators who were also butch-femme women. Their feminism was not an articulated theory; it was a lived set of options based on erotic choices.

We Lesbians from the fifties made a mistake in the early seventies: we allowed our lives to be trivialized and reinterpreted by feminists who did not share our culture. The slogan "Lesbianism is the practice and feminism is the theory" was a good rallying cry, but it cheated our history. The early writings need to be reexamined to see why so many of us dedicated our-selves to understanding the homophobia of straight feminists rather than the life-realities of Lesbian women "who were not feminists" (an empty phrase which comes too easily to the lips). Why did we expect and need Lesbians of earlier generations and differing backgrounds to call their struggle by our name? I am afraid of the answer because I shared both worlds and know how respectable feminism made me feel, how less dirty, less ugly, less butch and femme. But the pain and anger at hearing so much of my past judged unacceptable have begun to surface. I believe that Lesbians are a people, that we live as all people do, affected by the eco-nomic and social forces of our times. As a people, we have struggled to pre-serve our people's ways, the culture of women loving women. In some sense, Lesbians have always opposed the patriarchy; in the past, perhaps most when we looked most like men.

As you can tell by now, this essay is an attempt to shake up our pre-vailing judgments. We disowned the near-past too quickly, and since it was a quiet past—the women in the Sea Colony did not write books—it would be easy not to hear it. Many women have said to me, "I could never have come out when you did." But I am a Lesbian of the fifties, and that world created me. I sit bemused at Lesbian conferences, wondering at the acade-mic course listings, and I know I would have been totally intimidated by the respectability of some parts of our current Lesbian world. When Monique Wittig said at the Modern Language Association Conference several years ago, "I am not a woman, I am a Lesbian," there was a gasp from the audi-ence, but the statement made sense to me. Of course I am a woman, but I belong to another geography as well, and the two worlds are complicated and unique.

The more I think of the implications of the butch-femme world, the more I understand some of my discomfort with the customs of the late 1970s. Once, when the Lesbian Herstory Archives presented a slide show on pre-1970 Lesbian images, I asked the women how many would feel comfortable using the word *Lesbian* alone without the adjunct *feminism.* I was curious about the power of the hyphenated word when so few women have an understanding of the Lesbian 1950s. Several of the women could not accept the word *Lesbian* alone, and yet it stood for women who did stand alone.

I suggest that the term *Lesbian-feminist* is a butch-femme relationship, as it has been judged, not as it was, with *Lesbian* bearing the emotional weight the butch does in modern judgment and *feminist* becoming the emotional equivalent of the stereotyped femme, the image that can stand the light of day. Lesbianism was theory in a different historical setting. We sat in bars and talked about our lives; we held hands in the streets and talked about the challenge of knowing what we were not permitted to do and how to go beyond that; we took on police harassment and became families for each other. Many of us were active in political change struggles, fed by the energy of our hidden butch-femme lives which even our most liberal-left friends could not tolerate. Articulated feminism added another layer of analysis and understanding, a profound one, one that felt so good and made such wonderful allies that for me it was a gateway to another world—until I realized I was saying *radical feminist* when I could not say *Lesbian.*

My butch-femme days have gifted me with sensitivities I can never disown. They make me wonder why there is such a consuming interest in the butch-femme lives of upper-class women, usually the more removed literary figures, while real-life, working butch and femme women are seen as imitative and culturally backward. Vita Sackville-West, Jane Heap, Missy, Gertrude Stein, and Radclyffe Hall are all figures who shine with audacious self-presentation, and yet the reality of passing women, usually a working-class Lesbian's method of survival, has provoked very little academic Lesbian-feminist interest.

Grassroots Lesbian history research projects are beginning to change this, however. The San Francisco Lesbian and Gay Men's History Research Project has created a slide show called ". . . And She Also Chewed Tobacco," which discusses passing women in San Francisco at the turn of the century. The Buffalo Lesbian Oral History Project (Madeline Davis and Liz Kennedy) is focusing on the lives of pre-1970 working-class Lesbians.[5] The Lesbian Herstory Archives of New York has a slide show in progress called "Lesbian Courage, Pre-1970," and there are groups in Boston, Washington, D.C., and Philadelphia attempting to be more inclusive of the Lesbian experience.

Because I quickly got the message in my first Lesbian-feminist CR group that such topics as butch-femme relationships and the use of dildoes were lower class, I was forced to understand that sexual style is a rich mixture of class, history, and personal integrity. My butch-femme sensibility also incorporated the wisdom of freaks. When we broke gender lines in the 1950s, we fell off the biologically charted maps. One day many years ago, as I was walking through Central Park, a group of cheerful straight people walked past me and said, "What shall we feed it?" The *it* has never left my consciousness. A butch woman in her fifties reminisced the other day about when she was stoned in Washington Square Park for wearing men's clothes. These searing experiences of marginality because of sexual style inform my feminism.

Butch-femme women made Lesbians visible in a terrifyingly clear way in a historical period when there was no Movement protection for them. Their appearance spoke of erotic independence, and they often provoked rage and censure both from their own community and straight society. Now it is time to stop judging and begin asking questions, to begin listening. Listening not only to words which may be the wrong ones for the 1980s, but also gestures, sadnesses in the eyes, gleams of victories, movements of hands, stories told with self-dismissal yet stubbornness. There is a silence among us, the voices of the 1950s, and this silence will continue until some of us are ready to listen. If we do, we may begin to understand how our Lesbian people survived and created an erotic heritage.

NOTES

Author Note: It took me forty years to write this essay. The following women helped make it possible: Frances Taylor, Naomi Holoch, Eleanor Batchelder, Paula Grant, and Judith Schwarz, as well as the *Heresies 12* collective, especially Paula Webster, who said "do it" for years. Most deeply I thank Deborah Edel, my butchy Lesbian-feminist former lover who never thought I was a freak.

1. The *Ladder,* published from 1956 to 1972, was the most sustaining Lesbian cultural creation of this period. As a street femme living on the Lower East Side, I desperately searched newspaper stands and drugstore racks for this small slim journal with a Lesbian on its cover. A complete set is now available at the Lesbian Herstory Archives in New York.

2. The *Ladder,* No. 1, May 1957, p. 28.

3. Letter from Sandy DeSando, August 1980.

4. An article in *Journal of Homosexuality* (Summer 1980), "Sexual Preference or Personal Styles? Why Lesbians are Disliked" by Mary Reige Laner and Roy H. Laner, documented the anger and rejection of 511 straight college students toward Lesbians who were clearly defined as butch-femme. These results led the Laners to celebrate the withering away of butch-femme styles and to advocate androgyny as the safest road to heterosexual acceptance, a new plea for passing. This is the liberal voice turned conservative, the frightened voice that warns Blacks not to be too Black, Jews not to be too Jewish, and Lesbians not to be too Lesbian. Ironically, this advice can become the basis for a truly destructive kind of role-playing, a self-denial of natural style so the oppressor will not wake up to the different one in his or her midst.

5. To be published under the title, *Boots of Leather, Slippers of Gold.*

30

FORBIDDEN FRUIT

ANNE FINGER

Before she became a paraplegic, Los Angeles resident DeVonna Cervantes liked to dye her pubic hair "fun colours"—turquoise, purple, jet black. After DeVonna became disabled, a beautician friend of hers came to the rehabilitation unit and, as a Christmas present, dyed DeVonna's pubic hair a hot pink.

But there's no such thing as "private parts" in a rehab hospital. Soon the staff, who'd seen her dye job when they were catheterizing her, sent the staff psychiatrist around to see her. Cervantes says that he told her: "I know it is very hard to accept that you have lost your sexuality but you don't need to draw attention to it this way." Cervantes spent the remainder of the 50-minute session arguing with him, and, in perhaps the only true medical miracle I've ever heard of, convinced him that he was wrong—that this was normal behaviour for her.

Cervantes' story not only illustrates woeful ignorance on the part of a "medical expert"; equating genital sensation with sexuality. But it shows clearly a disabled woman's determination to define her own sexuality.

Sadly, it's not just medical experts who are guilty of ignoring the reproductive and sexual rights and needs of people with disabilities. The movements for sexual and reproductive freedom have paid little attention to disability issues. And the abortion rights movement has sometimes crudely exploited fears about "defective fetuses" as a reason to keep abortion legal.

Because the initial focus of the women's movement was set by women who were overwhelmingly non-disabled (as well as young, white, and middle-class), the agenda of reproductive rights has tended to focus on the right to abortion as the central issue. Yet for disabled women, the right to bear and rear children is more at risk. Zoe Washburn, in her poem "Hannah," grieves the child she wanted to have and the abortion she was coerced into: ". . . so she went to the doctor, and let him suck Hannah out with a vacuum cleaner. . . . The family stroked her hair when she cried and cried because her belly was empty and Hannah was not only dead, but never born. They looked at her strange crippled-up body and thought to themselves, thank God that's over."

From *New Internationalist,* July 1992, pp. 8–10. Copyright © by New Internationalist. Reprinted by permission. Anne Finger teaches English literature at Wayne State University, Detroit, US. In her book *Past Due* (Women's Press, 1990) she describes her experience of childbirth as a disabled woman.

Yet the disability rights movement has certainly not put sexual rights at the forefront of its agenda. Sexuality is often the source of our deepest oppression; it is also often the source of our deepest pain. It's easier for us to talk about—and formulate strategies for changing—discrimination in employment, education, and housing than to talk about our exclusion from sexuality and reproduction. Also, although it is changing, the disability rights movement in the U.S. has tended to focus its energies on lobbying legislators and creating an image of "the able disabled."

Barbara Waxman and I once published an article in *Disability Rag* about the U.S. Supreme Court's decision that states could outlaw "unnatural" sex acts, pointing out the effect it could have on disabled people—especially those who were unable to have "standard" intercourse. The *Rag* then received a letter asking how "the handicapped" could ever be expected to be accepted as "normal" when we espoused such disgusting ideas.

Because reproduction is seen as a "women's issue," it is often relegated to the back burner. Yet it is crucial that the disability-rights movement starts to deal with it. Perhaps the most chilling situation exists in China where a number of provinces ban marriages between people with developmental and other disabilities unless the parties have been sterilized. In Gansu Province more than 5,000 people have been sterilized since 1988. Officials in Szechuan province stated: "Couples who have serious hereditary diseases including psychosis, mental deficiency and deformity must not be allowed to bear children." When disabled women are found to be pregnant, they are sometimes subjected to forced abortions. But despite widespread criticism of China's population policies, there was almost no public outcry following these revelations.

Even in the absence of outright bans on reproduction, the attitude that disabled people should not have children is common. Disabled women and men are still sometimes subject to forced and coerced sterilizations—including hysterectomies performed without medical justification but to prevent the "bother" of menstruation. Los Angeles newscaster Bree Walker has a genetically transmitted disability, ectrodactyly, which results in fused bones in her hands and feet. Pregnant with her second child, last year, she found her pregnancy the subject of a call-in radio show. Broadcaster Jane Norris informed listeners in a shocked and mournful tone of voice that Bree's child had a 50-percent chance of being born with the same disability. "Is it fair to bring a child into the world knowing there's two strikes against it at birth . . . ? Is it socially responsible?" When a caller objected that it was no one else's business, Norris argued, "It's everybody's business." And many callers agreed with Norris's viewpoint. One horrified caller said, "It's not just her hands—it's her feet, too. She has to [dramatic pause] wear orthopaedic shoes."

The attitude that disabled people should not have children is certainly linked with the notion that we should not even be sexual. Yet, as with society's silence about the sexuality of children, this attitude exists alongside widespread sexual abuse. Some authorities estimate that people with disabilities are twice as likely to be victims of rape and other forms of sexual abuse as the general population. While the story of rape and sexual abuse of disabled people must be told and while we must find ways to end it, the current focus on sexual exploitation of disabled people can itself become oppressive.

As Barbara Faye Waxman, the former Disability Project Director for Los Angeles Planned Parenthood states, "The message for disabled kids is that their sexuality will be realized through their sexual victimization . . . . I don't see an idea that good things can happen, like pleasure, intimacy, like a greater understanding of ourselves, a love of our bodies." Waxman sees a "double whammy" effect for disabled people, for whom there are few, if any, positive models of sexuality, and virtually no social expectation that they will become sexual beings.

The attitude that we are and should be asexual seems to exist across a broad range of cultures. Ralf Hotchkiss, famous for developing wheelchairs in Third World countries, has travelled widely in Latin America and Asia. He says that while attitudes vary "from culture to culture, from subculture to subculture," he sees nearly everywhere he travels, "extreme irritation [on the part of disabled people] at the stereotypical assumptions that people . . . make about their sexuality, their lack of it." He also noted: "In Latin American countries once they hear I'm married, the next question is always, 'How old are your kids?'"

Some of these prejudices are enshrined in law. In the U.S., "marital disincentives" remain a significant barrier. To explain this Byzantine system briefly: benefits (including government-funded health care) are greatly reduced and sometimes even eliminated when a disabled person marries. Tom Fambro writes of his own difficulties with the system: "I am a 46-year-old black man with cerebral palsy. A number of years ago I met a young lady who was sexually attracted to me (a real miracle)." Fambro learned, however, that he would lose his income support and, most crucially, his medical benefits, if he married. "People told us that we should just live together . . . but because both of us were born-again Christians that was unthinkable . . . . The Social Security Administration has the idea that disabled people are not to fall in love, get married, have sex or have a life of our own. Instead, we are to be sexual eunuchs. They are full of shit."

Institutions—whether traditional hospital or euphemistically named "homes," "schools," or newer community-care facilities—often out-and-out forbid sexual contact for their residents. Or they may outlaw gay and lesbian relationships, while allowing heterosexual ones. Disabled lesbians and gays may also find that their sexual orientation is presumed to occur by default. Restriction of access to sexual information occurs on both a legal and a social plane. The U.S. Library of Congress, a primary source of material for blind and other print-handicapped people, was instructed by Congress in 1985 to no longer make *Playboy* available in braille or on tape. And relay services, which provide telecommunication between deaf and hearing people, have sometimes refused to translate sexually explicit speech. In her poem "Seeing," blind poet Mary McGinnis writes of a woman being watched by sighted men while bathing nude:

. . . the guys sitting at the edge of the pond
looked at her, but she couldn't see them . . .
and whose skin, hair, shirts and belts
would remain unknown to her
because she couldn't go up to them and
say, now fair is fair, let me touch the places
on your bodies you try to hide,
it's my turn—don't draw back or sit on
your hands, let me count your rings, your
scars,
the hairs coming from your nose . . . .

I have quoted poets several times in this piece; many disability-rights activists now see that while we need changes in laws and policies, the formation of culture is a key part of winning our freedom. Disabled writers and artists are shaping work that is often powerful in both its rage and its affirmation. In Cheryl Marie Wade's "side and belly," she writes:

He is wilty muscle sack and sharp bones fitting my gnarlypaws.
I am soft cellulite and green eyes of middle-age memory. We are
side and belly trading dreams and fantasies of able-bodied
former and not real selves: high-heel booted dancers making love
from black rooftops and naked dim doorways . . . .
. . . Contradictions in the starry night of wars within and being
not quite whole together and whole. Together in sighs we say yes
broken and fire and yes singing.

PART VI
Families

I believe I have as much right in raising a child as she does, but I found a lot of reverse discrimination. . . . Like pediatricians: they speak to my wife, they won't speak to me. . . . The same thing with the nursery school. I went out on all the interviews. They looked at me like, "What're you doing here?"

"ERNIE"[1]

Raising Black children—female and male—in the mouth of a racist, sexist, suicidal dragon is perilous and chancy. . . . I wish to raise a Black man who will recognize that the legitimate objects of his hostility are not women, but the particulars of a structure that programs him to fear and despise women as well as his own Black self.

AUDRE LORDE[2]

The structures of families reflect gender expectations within particular cultures, and cultures themselves are shaped by surrounding social forces, such as sexism, poverty, and homophobia. Attention to changing gender expectations within families is on many people's minds, even in mainstream U.S. society. People in the women's and men's movements have been talking about this issue for decades, but today people from all walks of life are addressing this issue. Even the National Conference of Catholic Bishops has recently urged married couples to move beyond gender stereotypes and develop more equality in marriages through shared decision making, shared household duties when both spouses are employed, fathers who are actively engaged in their children's lives, and the expression of feelings by both spouses.[3]

In 1992, 57.8 percent of married women were in the labor force. The task of balancing paid work and family work now affects women across the economic spectrum; it is no longer a challenge only for poor and working-class women, who have always been in the work force. In 1990, for example, 68 percent of women college graduates with a child under one year of age were in the labor force. In 1992, the husband worked outside the home and the wife did unpaid work at home in only 18 percent of families.[4] However, women who work outside the home are most likely to be responsible for arranging child care, and they continue to do most of the housework, working what is frequently referred to as the "second shift" or the "double day."[5]

Family life requires complex negotiations and compromises that are often hidden from view. For example, in a family studied by Arlie Hochschild and Anne Machung, the wife gave up her ideal of a marriage in which household tasks and child care would be shared; she redefined what her husband was willing to do as acceptable, in order to keep the marriage together. He was unwilling to take on much responsibility at home and would have preferred that she work part time so she could handle the work at home with less conflict. Committed to her career, she did not want to work part time. The image of the happy professional mother, her child in one hand and a briefcase in the other, is seldom what it appears to be, even for professional women with enough money to hire people to help at home.[6]

The stress and turmoil that poverty imposes on families is well documented.[7] The risk of becoming homeless is a pernicious presence for poor families. Many families that are able to escape homelessness function at the margins of the social order, living in crowded conditions and working, at times, in the informal economy—outside the realm of W-2 forms, benefits, and any protection from exploitation by employers.[8] The negative effects of humiliating, illness-inducing work are often brought home in the form of exhaustion, drunkenness, and violence.[9] In response to the conditions of poor families, especially single mothers with children, professor of education Valerie Polakow asks, ". . . where are our commitments to the existential futures of children as we approach the twenty-first century?" Clearly, the structure of the economy is wreaking havoc in many families, though, as Pokalow argues, homelessness and poverty are often pathologized—victims of poverty are labeled and blamed for their own conditions. Rather, society should focus on the economic structure as the source of blame and potential solutions.[10] Later in this book, the situations of poor families are addressed in more depth. See the article by Diane Dujon, Judy Gradford, and Dottie Stevens in Part VIII, and see the article by Roberta Praeger in Part XI.

The readings in this section open with an excerpt from Lillian Rubin's recent study of white, Black, Latino, and Asian working-class families. This excerpt focuses on struggles over household and family responsibilities when both spouses work outside the home. For many couples, the battle over household chores adds stress to an already tense economic situation. Rubin reports differences across groups, finding that Black couples have the most egalitarian arrangements of any couples she studied.

In the next reading, based on a qualitative study, sociologist Kathleen Gerson explores the parenting experience of primarily white, middle- and working-class men. She reports on the experience of a group of "involved fathers" (13 percent of her respondents), documenting their joys and frustrations at trying to be involved in their children's lives, in a social order that provides little support for such involvement. The interaction between the wider economic and social structure and these men's individual lives is very clear; even men who want to be involved with their children are blocked from doing so by the economic necessity to work long hours and by the social pressures against involved fatherhood.

Keeping a family intact in the face of oppression and stress is a huge task. The late African American poet and activist Audre Lorde, writing when her children were teenagers, talks about raising Black children in a racist context that teaches Black boys, in particular, to hate both women and themselves. The essay was written at a time when Lorde, a lesbian, was barred from bringing her son to a women-only event. Next, Christopher Scanlan shares his experience as a father at the edge of his patience with his two daughters, and middle-class African American writer Gerald Early addresses the challenge of raising a daughter with a learning disability in a racist social order.

Finally, Nan D. Hunter describes the almost insurmountable difficulties Karen Thompson and Sharon Kowalski faced in keeping their relationship intact after Sharon was very seriously injured in an automobile accident. The absence of legal sanctions for committed gay and lesbian relationships, combined with homophobia in Kowalski's family, prevented the couple from seeing each other for three and a half years. Hunter concludes her essay with a list of other legal decisions that affect various kinds of families.

The authors in this chapter give voice to many of the challenging aspects of family life today. Embedded in their stories and research are implications for changes in personal relations and policy, including sharing household and child-rearing tasks; support for fathers' involvement in family life; sensitive treatment of children with disabilities; talking rather than yelling; the elimination of racism; the development of jobs that pay enough to keep families going; and the legitimation of various kinds of families.

NOTES

1. Quoted in Kathleen Gerson, *No Man's Land: Men's Changing Commitments to Family and Work* (New York: Basic Books, 1993), p. 249.
2. Audre Lorde, "Man Child: A Black Lesbian Feminist's Response," *Sister Outsider* (Freedom, CA: Crossing Press, 1984), p. 74.
3. National Conference of Catholic Bishops, *Follow the Way of Love* (Washington, DC: United States Catholic Conference, 1994), pp. 20–21.
4. All data in this paragraph are from Barbara Reskin and Irene Padavic, *Women and Men at Work* (Thousand Oaks, CA: Pine Forge Press, 1994), pp. 143–144.
5. Ibid., pp. 149–153. See also Arlie Russell Hochschild with Anne Machung, *The Second Shift: Working Parents and the Revolution at Home* (New York: Avon Books, 1990).
6. Hochschild and Machung, *The Second Shift.*
7. Elliot Liebow, *Tell Them Who I Am: The Lives of Homeless Women* (New York: Penguin, 1993); Valerie Polakow, *Lives on the Edge: Single Mothers and Their Children in the Other America* (Chicago: University of Chicago Press, 1994); Doug A. Timmer, Stanley D. Eitzen, and Kathryn D. Talley, *Paths to Homelessness: Extreme Poverty and the Urban Housing Crisis* (Boulder, Colorado: Westview Press, 1994).
8. See, for example, "Patchworking: Households in the Economy," in Nazli Kibria, *Family Tightrope: The Changing Lives of Vietnamese Americans* (Princeton: Princeton University Press, 1993), pp. 73–107.
9. See, for example, Sue Doro, "The Father Poem," in Janet Zandy, ed., *Calling Home: Working-Class Women's Writings: An Anthology* (New Brunswick: Rutgers University Press, 1990), pp. 132–138.
10. Polakow, *Lives on the Edge,* p. 3.

31

THE TRANSFORMATION OF FAMILY LIFE

LILLIAN B. RUBIN

"I know my wife works all day, just like I do," says Gary Braunswig, a twenty-nine-year-old white drill press operator, "but it's not the same. She doesn't *have* to do it. I mean, she *has* to because we need the money, but it's different. It's not really her job to have to be working; it's mine." He stops, irritated with himself because he can't find exactly the words he wants, and asks, "Know what I mean? I'm not saying it right; I mean, it's the man who's supposed to support his family, so I've got to be responsible for that, not her. And that makes one damn big difference."

"I mean, women complain all the time about how hard they work with the house and the kids and all. I'm not saying it's not hard, but that's her responsibility, just like the finances are mine."

"But she's now sharing that burden with you, isn't she?" I remark.

"Yeah, and I do my share around the house, only she doesn't see it that way. Maybe if you add it all up, I don't do as much as she does, but then she doesn't bring in as much money as I do. And she doesn't always have to be looking for overtime to make an extra buck. I got no complaints about that, so how come she's always complaining about me? I mean, she helps me out financially, and I help her out with the kids and stuff. What's wrong with that? It seems pretty equal to me."

Cast that way, his formulation seems reasonable: They're each responsible for one part of family life; they each help out with the other. But the abstract formula doesn't square with the lived reality. For him, helping her adds relatively little to the burden of household tasks he *must* do each day. A recent study by University of Wisconsin researchers, for example, found that in families where both wife and husband work full-time, the women average over twenty-six hours a week in household labor, while the men do about ten.[1] That's because there's nothing in the family system to force him to accountability or responsibility on a daily basis. He may "help her out with the kids and stuff" one day and be too busy or preoccupied the next.

But for Gary's wife, Irene, helping him means an extra eight hours every working day. Consequently, she wants something more consistent from him than a helping hand with a particular task when he has the time, desire, or

---

feels guilty enough. "Sure, he helps me out," she says, her words tinged with resentment. "He'll give the kids a bath or help with the dishes. But only when I ask him. He doesn't have to *ask* me to go to work every day, does he? Why should I have to ask him?"

"Why should I have to ask him?"—words that suggest a radically different consciousness from the working-class women I met twenty years ago. Then, they counted their blessings. "He's a steady worker; he doesn't drink; he doesn't hit me," they told me by way of explaining why they had "no right to complain."[2] True, these words were reminders to themselves that life could be worse, that they shouldn't take these things for granted— reminders that didn't wholly work to obscure their discontent with other aspects of the marriage. But they were nevertheless meaningful statements of value that put a brake on the kinds of demands they felt they could make of their men, whether about the unequal division of household tasks or about the emotional content of their lives together.

Now, the same women who reminded themselves to be thankful two decades ago speak openly about their dissatisfaction with the role divisions in the family. Some husbands, especially the younger ones, greet their wives' demands sympathetically. "I try to do as much as I can for Sue, and when I can't, I feel bad about it," says twenty-nine-year-old Don Dominguez, a Latino father of three children, who is a construction worker.

Others are more ambivalent. "I don't know, as long as she's got a job, too, I guess it's right that I should help out in the house. But that doesn't mean I've got to like it," says twenty-eight-year-old Joe Kempinski, a white warehouse worker with two children.

Some men are hostile, insisting that their wives' complaints are unreasonable, unjust, and oppressive. "I'm damn tired of women griping all the time; it's nothing but nags and complaints," Ralph Danesen, a thirty-six-year-old white factory worker and the father of three children, says indignantly. "It's enough! You'd think they're the only ones who've got it hard. What about me? I'm not living in a bed of roses either."

"Christ, what does a guy have to do to keep a wife quiet these days? What does she want? It's not like I don't do anything to help her out, but it's never enough."

In the past there was a clear understanding about the obligations and entitlements each partner took on when they married. He was obliged to work outside the home; she would take care of life inside. He was entitled to her ministrations, she to his financial support. But this neat division of labor with its clear-cut separation of rights and obligations no longer works. Now, women feel obliged to hold up their share of the family economy—a partnership men welcome. In return, women believe they're entitled to their husband's full participation in domestic labor. And here is the rub. For while men enjoy the fruits of their wives' paid work outside the home, they have been slow to accept the reciprocal responsibilities—that is, to become real partners in the work inside the home.

The women, exhausted from doing two days' work in one, angry at the need to assume obligations without corresponding entitlements, push their men in ways unknown before. The men, battered by economic uncertainty and by the escalating demands of their wives, feel embattled and victimized on two fronts—one outside the home, the other inside. Consequently, when their wives seem not to see the family work they do, when they don't acknowledge and credit it, when they fail to appreciate them, the men feel violated and betrayed. "You come home and you want to be appreciated a little. But it doesn't work that way, leastwise not here anymore," complains Gary Braunswig, his angry words at odds with the sadness in his eyes. "There's no peace, I guess that's the real problem; there's no peace anywhere anymore."

The women often understand what motivates their husbands' sense of victimization and even speak sympathetically about it at times. But to understand and sympathize is not to condone, especially when they feel equally assaulted on both the home and the economic fronts. "I know I complain a lot, but I really don't ask for that much. I just want him to help out a little more," explains Ralph Danesen's wife, Helen, a thirty-five-year-old office worker. "It isn't like I'm asking him to cook the meals or anything like that. I know he can't do that, and I don't expect him to. But every time I try to talk to him, you know, to ask him if I couldn't get a little more help around here, there's a fight."

One of the ways the men excuse their behavior toward family work is by insisting that their responsibility as breadwinner burdens them in ways that are alien to their wives. "The plant's laying off people left and right; it could be me tomorrow. Then what'll we do? Isn't it enough I got to worry about that? I'm the one who's got all the worries; she doesn't. How come that doesn't count?" demands Bob Duckworth, a twenty-nine-year-old factory worker.

But, in fact, the women don't take second place to their men in worrying about what will happen to the family if the husband loses his job. True, the burden of finding another one that will pay the bills isn't theirs—not a trivial difference. But the other side of this truth is that women are stuck with the reality that the financial welfare of the family is out of their control, that they're helpless to do anything to prevent its economic collapse or to rectify it should it happen. "He thinks I've got it easy because it's not my job to support the family," says Bob's wife, Ruthanne. "But sometimes I think it's worse for me. I worry all the time that he's going to get laid off, just like he does. But I can't do anything about it. And if I try to talk to him about it, you know, like maybe make a plan in case it happens, he won't even listen. How does he think *that* makes me feel? It's my life, too, and I can't even talk to him about it."

Not surprisingly, there are generational differences in what fuels the conflict around the division of labor in these families. For the older couples—those who grew up in a different time, whose marriages started with another set of ground rules—the struggle is not simply around how much men do or about whether they take responsibility for the daily tasks of

living without being pushed, prodded, and reminded. That's the overt manifestation of the discord, the trigger that starts the fight. But the noise of the
explosion when it comes serves to conceal the more fundamental issue
underlying the dissension: legitimacy. What does she have a *right* to expect?
"What do I know about doing stuff around the house?" asks Frank Moreno,
a forty-eight-year-old foreman in a warehouse. "I wasn't brought up like
that. My pop, he never did one damn thing, and my mother never complained. It was her job; she did it and kept quiet. Besides, I work my ass off
every day. Isn't that enough?"

For the younger couples, those under forty, the problem is somewhat
different. The men may complain about the expectation that they'll participate more fully in the care and feeding of the family, but talk to them about
it quietly and they'll usually admit that it's not really unfair, given that their
wives also work outside the home. In these homes, the issue between husband and wife isn't only who does what. That's there, and it's a source of
more or less conflict, depending upon what the men actually do and how
forceful their wives are in their demands. But in most of these families
there's at least a verbal consensus that men *ought* to participate in the tasks
of daily life. Which raises the next and perhaps more difficult issue in contest between them: Who feels responsible for getting the tasks done? Who
regards them as a duty, and for whom are they an option? On this, tradition
rules.

Even in families where husbands now share many of the tasks, their
wives still bear full responsibility for the organization of family life. A man
may help cook the meal these days, but a woman is most likely to be the one
who has planned it. He may take the children to child care, but she virtually
always has had to arrange it. It's she also who is accountable for the emotional life of the family, for monitoring the emotional temperature of its
members and making the necessary corrections. It's this need to be responsible for it all that often feels as burdensome as the tasks themselves. "It's not
just doing all the stuff that needs doing," explains Maria Jankowicz, a white
twenty-eight-year-old assembler in an electronics factory. "It's worrying all
the time about everything and always having to arrange everything, you
know what I mean. It's like I run the whole show. If I don't stay on top of it
all, things fall apart because nobody else is going to do it. The kids can't and
Nick, well, forget it," she concludes angrily.

If, regardless of age, life stage, or verbal consensus, women usually still
carry the greatest share of the household burdens, why is it important to
notice that younger men grant legitimacy to their wives' demands and older
men generally do not? Because men who believe their wives have a right to
expect their participation tend to suffer guilt and discomfort when they
don't live up to those expectations. And no one lives comfortably with guilt.
"I know I don't always help enough, and I feel bad about it, you know, guilty
sometimes," explains Bob Beardsley, a thirty-year-old white machine operator, his eyes registering the discomfort he feels as he speaks.

"Does it change anything when you feel guilty?" I ask.

A small smile flits across his face, and he says, "Sometimes. I try to do a little more, but then I get busy with something and forget that she needs me to help out. My wife says I don't pay attention, that's why I forget. But I don't know. Seems like I've just got my mind on other things."

It's possible, of course, that the men who speak of guilt and rights are only trying to impress me by mouthing the politically correct words. But even if true, they display a sensitivity to the issue that's missing from the men who don't speak those words. For words are more than just words. They embody ideas; they are the symbols that give meaning to our thoughts; they shape our consciousness. New ideas come to us on the wings of words. It's words that bring those ideas to life, that allow us to see possibilities unrecognized before we gave them words. Indeed, without words, there is no conscious thought, no possibility for the kind of self-reflection that lights the path of change.[3]

True, there's often a long way between word and deed. But the man who feels guilty when he disappoints his wife's expectations has a different consciousness than the one who doesn't—a difference that usually makes for at least some small change in his behavior. Although the emergence of this changing male consciousness is visible in all the racial groups in this study, there also are differences among them that are worthy of comment.

Virtually all the men do some work inside the family—tending the children, washing dishes, running the vacuum, going to the market. And they generally also remain responsible for those tasks that have always been traditionally male—mowing the lawn, shoveling the snow, fixing the car, cleaning the garage, doing repairs around the house. Among the white families in this study, 16 percent of the men share the family work relatively equally, almost always those who live in families where they and their wives work different shifts or where the men are unemployed. "What choice do I have?" asks Don Bartlett, a thirty-year-old white handyman who works days while his wife is on the swing shift. "I'm the only one here, so I do what's got to be done."

Asian and Latino men of all ages, however, tend to operate more often on the old male model, even when they work different shifts or are unemployed, a finding that puzzled me at first. Why, I wondered, did I find only two Asian men and one Latino who are real partners in the work of the family? Aren't these men subject to the same social and personal pressures others experience?

The answer is both yes and no. The pressures are there but, depending upon where they live, there's more or less support for resisting them. The Latino and Asian men who live in ethnic neighborhoods—settings where they are embedded in an intergenerational community and where the language and culture of the home country is kept alive by a steady stream of new immigrants—find strong support for clinging to the old ways. Therefore, change comes much more slowly in those families. The men who live outside the ethnic quarter are freer from the mandates and constraints of these often tight-knit communities, and therefore are more responsive to the winds of change in the larger society.

These distinctions notwithstanding, it's clear that Asian and Latino men generally participate least in the work of the household and are the least likely to believe they have much responsibility there beyond bringing home a paycheck. "Taking care of the house and kids is my wife's job, that's all," says Joe Gomez flatly.

"A Chinese man mopping a floor? I've never seen it yet," says Amy Lee angrily. Her husband, Dennis, trying to make a joke of the conflict with his wife, says with a smile, "In Chinese families men don't do floors and windows. I help with the dishes sometimes if she needs me to or," he laughs, "if she screams loud enough. The rest, well, it's pretty much her job."

The commonly held stereotype about black men abandoning women and children, however, doesn't square with the families in this study. In fact, black men are the most likely to be real participants in the daily life of the family and are more intimately involved in raising their children than any of the others. True, the men's family work load doesn't always match their wives', and the women are articulate in their complaints about this. Nevertheless, compared to their white, Asian, or Latino counterparts, the black families look like models of egalitarianism.

Nearly three-quarters of the men in the African-American families in this study do a substantial amount of the cooking, cleaning, and child care, sometimes even more than their wives. All explain it by saying one version or another of: "I just figure it's my job, too." Which simply says what is, without explaining how it came to be that way.

To understand that, we have to look at family histories that tell the story of generations of African-American women who could find work and men who could not, and to the family culture that grew from this difficult and painful reality. "My mother worked six days a week cleaning other people's houses, and my father was an ordinary laborer, when he could find work, which wasn't very often," explains thirty-two-year-old Troy Payne, a black waiter and father of two children. "So he was home a lot more than she was, and he'd do what he had to do around the house. The kids all had to do their share, too. It seemed only fair, I guess."

Difficult as the conflict around the division of labor is, it's only one of the many issues that have become flash points in family life since mother went to work. Most important, perhaps, is the question: Who will care for the children? For the lack of decent, affordable facilities for the care of the children creates unbearable problems and tensions for these working-class families.

It's hardly news that child care is an enormous headache and expense for all two-job families. In many professional middle-class families, where the child-care bill can be $1,500–2,000 a month, it competes with the mortgage payment as the biggest single monthly expenditure. Problematic as this may be, however, these families are the lucky ones when compared to working-class families, many of whom don't earn much more than the cost of child care in these upper middle-class families. Even the families in this study at the highest end of the earnings scale, those who earn $42,000 a year, can't dream of such costly arrangements.

For most working-class families, therefore, child care often is patched together in ways that leave parents anxious and children in jeopardy. "Care for the little ones, that's a real big problem," says Beverly Waldov, a thirty-year-old white mother of three children, the youngest two, products of a second marriage, under three years old. "My oldest girl is nine, so she's not such a problem. I hate the idea of her being a latchkey kid, but what can I do? We don't even have the money to put the little ones in one of those good day-care places, so I don't have any choice with her. She's just *got* to be able to take care of herself after school," she says, her words a contest between anxiety and hope.

"We have a kind of complicated arrangement for the little kids. Two days a week, my mom takes care of them. We pay her, but at least I don't have to worry when they're with her; I know it's fine. But she works the rest of the time, so the other days we take them to this woman's house. It's the best we can afford, but it's not great because she keeps too many kids, and I know they don't get good attention. Especially the little one; she's just a baby, you know." She pauses and looks away, anguished. "She's so clingy when I bring her home; she can't let go of me, like nobody's paid her any mind all day. But it's not like I have a choice. We barely make it now; if I stop working, we'd be in real trouble."

Even such makeshift solutions don't work for many families. Some speak of being unable to afford day care at all. "We couldn't pay our bills if we had to pay for somebody to take care of the kids."

Some say they're unwilling to leave the children in the care of strangers. "I just don't believe someone else should be raising our kids, that's all."

Some have tried a variety of child-care arrangements, only to have them fail in a moment of need. "We tried a whole bunch of things, and maybe they work for a little while," says Faye Ensey, a black twenty-eight-year-old office worker. "But what happens when your kid gets sick? Or when the baby sitter's kids get sick? I lost two jobs in a row because my kids kept getting sick and I couldn't go to work. Or else I couldn't take my little one to the baby sitter because her kids were sick. They finally fired me for absenteeism. I didn't really blame them, but it felt terrible anyway. It's such a hassle, I sometimes think I'd be glad to just stay home. But we can't afford for me not to work, so we had to figure out something else."

For such families, that "something else" is the decision to take jobs on different shifts—a decision made by one-fifth of the families in this study. With one working days and the other on swing or graveyard, one parent is home with the children at all times. "We were getting along okay before Daryl junior was born, because Shona, my daughter, was getting on. You know, she didn't need somebody with her all the time, so we could both work days," explains Daryl Adams, a black thirty-year-old postal clerk with a ten-year-old daughter and a nine-month-old son. "I used to work the early shift—seven to three—so I'd get home a little bit after she got here. It worked out okay. But then this here big surprise came along." He stops, smiles down fondly at his young son and runs his hand over his nearly bald head.

"Now between the two of us working, we don't make enough money to pay for child care and have anything left over, so this is the only way we can manage. Besides, both of us, Alesha and me, we think it's better for one of us to be here, not just for the baby, for my daughter, too. She's growing up and, you know, I think maybe they need even more watching than when they were younger. She's coming to the time when she could get into all kinds of trouble if we're not here to put the brakes on."

But the cost such arrangements exact on a marriage can be very high. When I asked these husbands and wives when they have time to talk, more often than not I got a look of annoyance at a question that, on its face, seemed stupid to them. "Talk? How can we talk when we hardly see each other?" "Talk? What's that?" "Talk? Ha, that's a joke."

Mostly, conversation is limited to the logistics that take place at shift-changing time when children and chores are handed off from one to the other. With children dancing around underfoot, the incoming parent gets a quick summary of the day's or night's events, a list of reminders about things to be done, perhaps about what's cooking in the pot on the stove. "Sometimes when I'm coming home and it's been a hard day, I think: Wouldn't it be wonderful if I could just sit down with Leon for half an hour and we could have a quiet beer together?" thirty-one-year-old Emma Guerrero, a Latina baker, says wistfully.

But it's not to be. If the arriving spouse gets home early enough, there may be an hour when both are there together. But with the pressures of the workday fresh for one and awaiting the other, and with children clamoring for parental attention, this isn't a promising moment for any serious conversation. "I usually get home about forty-five minutes or so before my wife has to leave for work," says Ralph Jo, a thirty-six-year-old Asian repairman whose children, ages three and five, are the product of a second marriage. "So we try to take a few minutes just to make contact. But it's hard with the kids and all. Most days the whole time gets spent with taking care of business—you know, who did what, what the kids need, what's for supper, what bill collector was hassling her while I was gone—all the damn garbage of living. It makes me nuts."

Most of the time even this brief hour isn't available. Then the ritual changing of the guard takes only a few minutes—a quick peck on the cheek in greeting, a few words, and it's over. "It's like we pass each other. He comes in; I go out; that's it."

Some of the luckier couples work different shifts on the same days, so they're home together on weekends. But even in these families there's so little time for normal family life that there's hardly any room for anyone or anything outside. "There's so much to do when I get home that there's no time for anything but the chores and the kids," says Daryl's wife, Alesha Adams. "I never get to see anybody or do anything else anymore and, even so, I'm always feeling upset and guilty because there's not enough time for them. Daryl leaves a few minutes after I get home, and the rest of the night is like a blur—Shona's homework, getting the kids fed and down for the night, cleaning up, getting everything ready for tomorrow. I don't know; there's always something I'm running around doing. I sometimes feel like— What do you call them?—one of those whirling dervishes, rushing around all the time and never getting everything done.

"Then on the weekends, you sort of want to make things nice for the kids—and for us, too. It's the only time we're here together, like a real family, so we always eat with the kids. And we try to take them someplace nice one of the days, like to the park or something. But sometimes we're too tired, or there's too many other catch-up things you have to do. I don't even get to see my sister anymore. She's been working weekends for the last year or so, and I'm too busy week nights, so there's no time.

"I don't mean to complain; we're lucky in a lot of ways. We've got two great kids, and we're a pretty good team, Daryl and me. But I worry sometimes. When you live on this kind of schedule, communication's not so good."

For those whose days off don't match, the problems of sustaining both the couple relationship and family life are magnified enormously. "The last two years have been hell for us," says thirty-five-year-old Tina Mulvaney, a white mother of two teenagers. "My son got into bad company and had some trouble, so Mike and I decided one of us had to be home. But we can't make it without my check, so I can't quit.

"Mike drives a cab and I work in a hospital, so we figured one of us could transfer to nights. We talked it over and decided it would be best if I was here during the day and he was here at night. He controls the kids, especially my son, better than I do. When he lays down the law, they listen." She interrupts her narrative to reflect on the difficulty of raising children. "You know, when they were little, I used to think about how much easier it would be when they got older. But now I see it's not true; that's when you really have to begin to worry about them. This is when they need someone to be here all the time to make sure they stay out of trouble."

She stops again, this time fighting tears, then takes up where she left off. "So now Mike works days and I work graveyard. I hate it, but it's the only answer; at least this way somebody's here all the time. I get home about 8:30 in the morning. The kids and Mike are gone. It's the best time of the day because it's the only time I have a little quiet here. I clean up the house a little, do the shopping and the laundry and whatever, then I go to sleep for a couple of hours until the kids come home from school.

"Mike gets home at five; we eat; then he takes over for the night, and I go back to sleep for another couple of hours. I try to get up by 9 so we can all have a little time together, but I'm so tired that I don't make it a lot of times. And by 10, he's sleeping because he has to be up by 6 in the morning.

So if I don't get up, we hardly see each other at all. Mike's here on weekends, but I'm not. Right now I have Tuesday and Wednesday off. I keep hoping for a Monday–Friday shift, but it's what everybody wants, and I don't have the seniority yet. It's hard, very hard; there's no time to live or anything," she concludes with a listless sigh.

NOTES

1. James Sweet, Larry Bumpass, and Vaugn Call, *National Survey of Families and Households* (Madison, Wisc.: Center for Demography and Ecology, University of Wisconsin, 1988). This study featured a probability sample of 5,518 households and included couples with and without children. See also Joseph Pleck, *Working Wives/Working Husbands* (Beverly Hills: Sage Publications, 1985), who summarizes time-budget studies; and Iona Mara-Drita, "The Effects of Power, Ideology, and Experience on Men's Participation in Housework," unpublished paper (1993), whose analysis of Sweet, Bumpass, and Call's data shows that when housework and employment hours are added together, a woman's work week totals 69 hours, compared to 52 hours for a man.
2. Rubin, *Worlds of Pain*, p. 93.
3. See Daniel Stern, *The Interpersonal World of the Infant* (New York: Basic Books, 1985), who argues that a child's capacity for self-reflection coincides with the development of language.

32

DILEMMAS OF INVOLVED FATHERHOOD

KATHLEEN GERSON

Work's a necessity, but the things that really matter are spending time with my family. If I didn't have a family, I don't know what I would have turned to. That's why I say you're rich in a lot of ways other than money. I look at my daughter and think, "My family is everything."

—CARL, A THIRTY-FOUR-YEAR-OLD UTILITIES WORKER

Social disapproval and economic inequality put full-time domesticity out of reach for almost all men. Yet most also found that economic necessity and employer intransigence made anything less than full-time work an equally distant possibility. Few employers offered the option of part-time work, especially in male-dominated fields. Arthur, a married sanitation worker planning for fatherhood, complained:

> If it was feasible, I would love to spend more time with my child. That would be more important to me than working. I'd love to be able to work twenty-five hours a week or four days a week and have three days off to spend with the family, but most jobs aren't going to accommodate you that way.

Yet, even if part-time work were available, involved fathers still needed the earnings that only full-time and overtime work could offer. Lou, the sewage worker who worked the night shift in order to spend days with his young daughter, could not accept lower wages or fewer benefits:

> If I knew that financially everything would be set, I'd stay home. I'd like to stay more with my daughter. It's a lot of fun to be with a very nice three-year-old girl. But if I work less, I would equate it to less money and then I wouldn't be taking care of my family. If it meant less work and the same or more money, I'd say, "Sure!" I'd be dumb if I didn't.

Dean, the driver for a city department of parks, agreed that his economic obligations could not take a backseat to his nurturing ones:

> It always comes down to the same thing: I would like to have more time to spend with my children, but if I didn't have money, what's the sense of having time off? If I could work part-time and make enough money, that would be fine and dandy.

Since involved fathers tried to nurture as well as support their children, they made an especially hard choice between money and time. Like many mothers, they had to add caretaking onto full-time workplace responsibilities, but employers are generally reluctant to recognize male (or female) parental responsibility as a legitimate right or need.[1] Worse yet, paternal leaves are rarely considered a legitimate option for men even if they formally exist. Involved fathers wished to take time off for parenting, but like most men they were reluctant to do so for fear of imperiling their careers.[2] And even though most employers allow health-related leaves with impunity, they have not been so flexible when it comes to the job of parenting. Workers receive the message that illness is unavoidable, but parenting is voluntary— an indication of a lack of job commitment. Our current corporate culture thus makes parenting hazardous to anyone's career, and choosing a "daddy track" can be just as dangerous as the much-publicized "mommy track." Juan, a financial analyst, knew he could not pull back from his job for more than a few days or a week without jeopardizing his job security. To parental leave,

> I'd say yes, but realistically no. It would be a problem because it's very difficult for me to tell my boss that I have to leave at such a time. I have deadlines to meet. If I leave the office for two or three months, my job is in jeopardy.

Because employers did not offer flexible options for structuring work on a daily basis or over the course of a career, some involved fathers looked to self-employment or home-based work for more flexibility and control. Craig, the ex-dancer currently working in an office, hoped he would be able to integrate work and parenting by working at home:

> I would like to find myself in the situation where I'm not locked into a nine-to-five schedule. Ultimately, I hope I'm doing consulting on my own at home, which means time close to the family. So that in the middle of my own workday, at the house, I'm available. I can just put my work aside and play Daddy.

Most could not even entertain this option. They had to fit parenting in around the edges of their work lives.[3]

Domestic arrangements also impede full equality. Child rearing remains an undervalued, isolating, and largely invisible accomplishment for *all* parents. This has fueled women's flight from domesticity and also dampened men's motivation to choose it. Russell, the legal-aid attorney and father of two, recognized that child rearing was less valued than employment:

> I think I would feel somewhat meaningless to not be engaged in any form of productive work—although certainly raising children is productive work. But I couldn't be responsible for that on a full-time basis. While I love my guys, I don't think I could be around them all the time.

Child rearing can be invisible as well as undervalued. Unlike the size of a paycheck or the title one holds at work, there are few socially recognized rewards for the time a parent devotes to raising a child or the results it produces. This made only the most dedicated, like Hank, willing to consider full-time parenting:

> Nobody will know the time and the effort I put in the family. They will look down on it. I would devote time, hours, and nobody will be happy with it except me because I'll know what I was trying for.

The forces pulling women out of the home are stronger than the forces pulling men into it. Since the social value of public pursuits outstrips the power and prestige of private ones, men are likely to resist full-time domesticity even as women move toward full-time employment. This process is similar to the one pulling women into male-dominated occupations while leaving men less inclined to enter female-dominated ones. In addition, just as women in male-dominated occupations face prejudice and discrimination, fathers who become equal or primary parents are stigmatized—treated as "tokens" in a female-dominated world.[4] Roger shied away from the pervasive questioning about his life as a custodial parent:

> I think I've become somewhat more introverted than I used to be— because I get tired of explaining my situation at home. . . . The thing

that blows all the kids' minds—they're all living with Mommy and my kids are living with Daddy.

In the face of such disincentives, most involved fathers rejected staying home for the same reasons many women do and more. Female breadwinning and male homemaking did not seem acceptable even when they made economic sense. Robin, a stockbroker, rejected domesticity precisely because his poor work prospects left him in no state to bear the additional stigma of becoming a househusband. Although he was making a lot less money than his wife was, he felt too "demoralized" to consider staying home. "I'm not secure enough, I guess, to stay home and be a househusband."

Of course, involved fathers actively resisted the discrimination they encountered. They asserted their nurturing competence and insisted on being taken as seriously as female parents are. The prevailing skepticism about men's parental abilities, however, made this an uphill battle. Ernie complained:

> I believe I have as much right in raising the child as she does, but I found a lot of reverse discrimination—people assuming that the mother takes care of the child. It's a lot of stereotyping, a lot that's taken for granted. Like pediatricians: they speak to my wife; they won't speak to me. I say, "Hey, I take care of her, too." They look at me like I'm invisible. The same thing with the nursery school. I went out on all the interviews. They looked at me like, "What're *you* doing here?"

Economic, social, and ideological arrangements thus made involved fatherhood difficult. The lack of workplace and domestic supports diluted and suppressed the potential for involvement even among the most motivated men. In the absence of these hurdles, fathers who wished to be involved might have participated far more than they actually did. They might, in fact, have made choices that now remain open to a rapidly diminishing number of women. Ernie wished he had options that only full-time mothers enjoy:

> I'm not the type that has career aspirations and is very goal-oriented. If I didn't have to work, I wouldn't. But I would volunteer. I would work in a nursery school. I would do a lot more volunteer work with my daughter's school. I would love to go on trips like the mothers who don't work, be more active in the P.T.A. I would love that. But I can't.

As the supports for homemaking mothers erode, supports for equal and primary fathers have not emerged to offset the growing imbalance between children's needs and families' resources. Fathers have had to depend on paid help, relatives, and already overburdened wives even when they did not wish to do so.

These obstacles not only left mothers giving up more. They also made involved fathers appear heroic about *whatever* they did. Comparisons with other men could be used to ward off complaints and resist further change. Ernie maintained:

> Sometimes she didn't think I did enough. I couldn't stand that because I thought I was doing too much. I really felt I was doing more than I should, whatever that means. I told her to go talk to some of her friends and see what their husbands are doing.

Nurturing fathers faced deeply rooted barriers to full equality in parenting. Social arrangements at work and in the home dampened even willing men's ability to share equally. The truncated range of choices open to most of these men limited the options of their wives, ex-wives, and partners as well. We can only guess how many mothers' helpers would become equal parents if these obstacles did not exist or, better yet, were replaced by positive supports for involved fatherhood.

Benefiting from the Loss of Privilege: Incentives for Change

If full equality remained beyond the reach of most involved fathers, they nevertheless moved a notable distance toward it. They were not simply forced to make concessions; nor were they just being altruistic. They also perceived offsetting, if unheralded, benefits. After all, parenting can be its own reward—offering intrinsic pleasures and a powerful sense of accomplishment. Rick explained:

> I have an extremely close relationship with my kids, and that makes me feel good. The fact that they're both doing very well in school—I know that at least a little bit of that comes from having been with them when they were young. So there's all those interactions in seeing them on their way to being healthy and vibrant kids.

These feelings took on added significance when other avenues for building self-esteem were blocked. Todd, the aspiring actor who became a construction worker, hoped his talents could be channeled toward his daughter instead of his job:

> If there's any Creator at all up there, She or It or They're going to ask for some sort of accounting at the end. They're going to be pleased if they gave you a certain amount of gifts and you were able to do something with them. I'd still like to be a part of something more meaningful than putting in a new fire hydrant—I guess through my influence on this little one's life.

If children offered a source of pride for those whose workplace aspirations had not been met, this was not just a concern for passing on genes or the family name. Contributions of time and emotions counted more. Carl, who chose utility repair work so that he could care for his daughter after school, saw his "investment" reflected in her talents and achievements:

> I've had a lot of compliments on her, and I take them as a compliment also. It's something that became part of you—teaching them different things, helping them grow up. They'll do something, and it's like seeing a reflection of you.

As work opportunities stall in an age of stagnant economic growth, parenting offers men another avenue for developing self-esteem. But economically successful fathers also reaped benefits from involvement because it balanced lives that would otherwise have been more narrowly focused on paid work. For Charles, the attorney with a young son, caretaking provided a legitimate reason for limiting the demands of work: "I'm working a little less hard, taking on fewer responsibilities. . . . But I think it's great. I don't need all the other shit."

Children also provided the hope of permanence in an age of divorce. Even happily married fathers came to see their children as the bedrock of stability in a shaky world, the one bond that could not be severed or assailed. Having been reared by a single mother, Juan viewed his children rather than his wife as the best chance for enduring emotional ties: "What if one day my wife and I get sick of each other after so many years? So I would like to have children."

Involved fatherhood also provided emotional supports by creating a bond between husbands and wives. Married men were less likely to feel rejected by their wives and excluded from the new relationships that form with the birth of a child. Timothy, the worker at a city dump, could not understand why less involved fathers complained of being rejected when a new baby arrived:

> They have these books about how fathers are supposed to go through blues because the wife is giving her attention to the child. Is this some kind of maniac that wrote this? I take care of him just as much as she does.

Sharing the load of caring for a newborn also seemed to decrease the chances that a mother would feel overwhelmed and alone during a critical, and trying, turning point in a marriage.[5] Carlos hoped that sharing the caretaking would help him avoid the hostility that he felt unequal arrangements would generate:

> I think it's a great burden to have one parent do all the caretaking. It would burn out that person, and they're not going to be able to respond to you. Then I would start feeling resentment towards her and possibly the child. So the only way I could see avoiding that is by sharing the responsibility.

Since involved fathers believed that a satisfying relationship depended on both partners being able to meet their needs, thwarting a partner's dreams by refusing to participate seemed to be a Pyrrhic victory. The costs of *not* sharing appeared greater than the costs of sharing. Carl was pleased to escape his parents' pattern:

> My parents are the old school. He never really touched a dish. I like what I'm doing better. The older way, I feel the woman will think, "I never really had an opportunity to do things." She will become resentful later on. Where my wife can't say nothing because she's had her freedom, she's worked, she's not stayed in the kitchen bare-foot and pregnant, and I did what I had to do. I feel in the long run it pays off. The other way, maybe she would have left.

Involved fatherhood thus offered two ways of coping with the risks of marriage in an era of divorce. It provided another source of emotional suste-nance in the event that the marital bond did not survive. And it offered a way to build less rancorous relationships by reducing wives' resentment. Indeed, there is growing evidence that egalitarian relationships do provide benefits to husbands and wives. In one report, wives whose husbands participate in domestic duties showed lower rates of depression than those with husbands who don't, while another found that the more housework a husband does, the lower are the chances that his wife has considered divorce.[6]

Emotional gratification and marital peace were not the only payoffs. In agreeing to share the domestic load, men can also share the economic load. Their wives' income lessens the pressure to work long hours and take on sec-ond jobs. Wesley was pleased to exchange extra hours at work for domestic sharing:

> If Cindy wants to be home, she can stay home. But that would probably mean I would have to either get myself another job or work overtime on the job I have. I would do it. She knows that. But she doesn't want me to. We spend more time with each other this way.

Involved fathers also believed their children would benefit in both the short and long runs—perceptions that research on both married and divorced fathers supports.[7] Larry observed:

> Having spent a lot of time with both of us, she's not really depen-dent on either one of us. Mommy's like daddy; daddy's like mommy. At times I *am* her mother. It's good to switch roles. She don't run to mommy or run to daddy. She runs to both of us.

They hoped their example would help their daughters and sons develop a flexible approach to building their own lives. Ernie decided his involve-ment created a better domestic environment for his daughter:

> The sharing—it's a good role model for her. She sees me cook. I'm
> trying to teach her baking, and I think it's nice my daughter is learn-
> ing baking from her father. So I'm hoping she sees that it's split and
> not that just the wife does this and the man does that.

He also hoped his participation would give his daughter a sense of self-
reliance, agreeing with a growing group of psychologists who argue that
girls no less than boys need their fathers. Both sexes identify in varying
degrees with both parents, and girls look to fathers as well as mothers to
provide models for living:[8]

> Raising my child, that is my priority—seeing that she's raised well
> in the sense of preparing her to face the world, trying to get her
> exposed as much as possible, so she may find out what she likes to
> pursue. I hope she has a career. I hope she finds something she
> really likes and works for it.

These men concluded that their domestic arrangements would also benefit their sons, echoing recent research showing that sons of involved fathers
are likely to show a more developed capacity for empathy.[9] Wesley thus concluded that his two sons "feel close to the two of us. Maybe when they get
married, they'll share in the house."

Just as these fathers created families that differed from the households in
which they were reared, so their children will take the lessons of their childhood into unknown futures. Involved fathers' belief in the advantages of
domestic sharing cannot guarantee a similar response in their children, but
it can and did strengthen their own resolve to create a more egalitarian
household. As more fathers become involved, their growing numbers
should prompt wider social acceptance of egalitarian households, bolstering
the option to make such choices.

Ultimately, however, men's movement toward domestic equality will
depend on their ability to overcome the obstacles to change and their desire
to resist the social pressures to conform. Equal fathers were willing and able
to defy social expectations, to overcome social constraints, and to reject the
pathways of the past. There is good reason to believe that their outlooks and
choices reflect a simmering mood among many American men, who long for
more work flexibility and fewer work demands. There is even reason to
believe many would be willing to relinquish some earnings in exchange for
spending more time with their families. A *Time* survey found that 56 percent
of a random sample of men said they would forfeit up to one-fourth of their
salaries "to have more family and personal time," and 45 percent "said they
would probably refuse a promotion that involved sacrificing hours with
their families."[10] Carl reflects this mood:

> It's amazing how many people don't understand the way I feel. I
> would prefer to be home than work overtime, where they would kill

to get it. They say, "What are you, rich?" No, but you only need a certain amount of money to live. God forbid you walk down the street and get struck by a car, or whatever, and it's over. I don't want to say, "Why didn't I spend more time with my family?" It's not going to happen to me. You can control it.

By focusing on the advantages and discounting the drawbacks of their choices, men are able to overcome some of the social and ideological barriers to equal parenting. In adding up the sacrifices and the gains, Larry spoke for the group: "I've given some things up, sure, but the changes in my lifestyle are eighty or ninety percent in the positive."

Though few in number, equal fathers demonstrate that men can discover or acquire nurturing skills and find pleasure in using them. Those men who did find support for being an equal father made contingent choices just like those who did not. In both instances, different circumstances could easily have produced different outcomes. It is not surprising that Rick found his rare and unexpected path to be a matter of chance:

I have very conservative attitudes in many respects. The fact that we got married and had children was very conservative. The fact that within those parameters, we shared, co-shared, work and family— that was not conservative. We've never discussed it, but I feel that the outcome is built much more on chance. I may not have always felt that way, but my own experiences confirmed it.

Chance, however, is just another way of saying that his choice was based on unusual and unexpected opportunities. Given how rare are the supports for involved fathering and how pervasive the obstacles, its rise is even more significant than its limited nature. For the potential of the many men who wish to be more involved to be realized, however, the unusual circumstances that now prompt only a small fraction of men to become equal parents must become real for a much larger group.

NOTES

1. See Lawson, Carol. 1991. "Baby Beckons: Why Is Daddy at Work?" *New York Times* (May 16): C1, C8. The Family Leave Act that finally became law in 1993 is an important first step, but much more will be needed for men to feel able to choose equal parenting.
2. Joseph H. Pleck. 1983. "Husbands' Paid Work and Family Roles: Current Research Trends," *Research in the Interweave of Social Roles: Jobs and Families* 3:251–333.
3. Barbara J. Risman and Maxine P. Atkinson. 1990. "Gender in Intimate Relationships: Toward a Dialectical Structural Theory." Paper presented at the National Council on Family Relations Theory, Construction, and Research Methodology Workshop (November), Seattle, Washington. According to Risman and Atkinson: "No matter how involved 'new feminist' fathers become in child-care, they . . . are expected to work harder and are constrained from leaving less than optimal jobs because of their economic responsibilities. When they do care

for their children after work, they are praised highly by friends, family members, and wives as wonderful, modern, 'involved' fathers" (pp. 15–16).

4. Hal Strauss. 1989. "Freaks of Nature." *American Health* (January-February): 70–71; Rosabeth M. Kanter. 1977. *Men and Women of the Corporation.* New York: Basic Books; Bryan E. Robinson. 1986. "Men Caring for the Young: A Profile." In *Men's Changing Roles in the Family,* pp. 151–61. Edited by Robert A. Lewis and Marvin B. Sussman. New York: Haworth Press. Men who become primary parents face barriers similar to those faced by the first female managers, who had to cope with being "tokens." Strauss discusses the stigmatization and social isolation of househusbands. Kanter analyzes how the first female managers were tokens in the corporation. Robinson, 1986, reports that male caregivers who work in nursery schools and day-care programs also faced discrimination and stigma from employers, co-workers, and even parents.

5. See Alice A. Rossi. 1960. "Transition to Parenthood." *Journal of Marriage and the Family* 30: 26–39.

6. Joan Huber and Glenna Spitze. 1983. *Sex Stratification: Children, Housework, and Jobs.* New York: Academic Press; Catherine E. Ross, John Mirowsky, and Joan Huber. 1983. "Dividing Work, Sharing Work, and In-Between: Marriage Patterns and Depression." *American Sociological Review* 48 (6) (December): 809–23; See also Michael E. Lamb, Joseph H. Pleck, and James A. Levine. 1987. "Effects of Increased Paternal Involvement on Fathers and Mothers." In *Reassessing Fatherhood: New Observations on Fathers and the Modern Family,* pp. 103–25. Edited by Charlie Lewis and Margaret O'Brien. Newberry Park, CA: Sage Publications; Arlie R. Hochschild with Anne Machung. 1989. *The Second Shift: Working Parents and the Revolution at Home.* New York: Viking.

7. See Frank F. Furstenberg, Jr., S. Phillip Morgan, and Paul D. Allison. 1987. "Paternal Participation and Children's Well-Being After Marital Dissolution." *American Sociological Review* 52(5):695–701; Shirley M. H. Hanson. 1986. "Father/Child Relationships: Beyond *Kramer vs. Kramer.*" In *Men's Changing Roles in the Family,* pp. 135–50. Edited by Robert A. Lewis and Marvin B. Sussman. New York: Haworth Press; Michael E. Lamb, ed. 1976 *The Role of the Father in Child Development.* New York: Wiley; J. W. Santrock and R. A. Warshak. 1979. "Father Custody and Social Development in Boys and Girls." *Journal of Social Issues* 32: 112–25; J. W. Santrock, R. A. Warshak, and G. L. Elliot. 1982. "Social Development and Parent-Child Interaction in Father-Custody and Stepmother Families." In *Nontraditional Families: Parenting and Child Development,* pp. 289–314. Edited by Michael E. Lamb. Hillside, NJ: Lawrence Erlbaum.

8. Victoria Secunda. 1992. *Women and Their Fathers: The Sexual and Romantic Impact of the First Man in Your Life.* New York: Delacorte Press.

9. Daniel Goleman. 1990. "Surprising Findings about the Development of Empathy in Children." *New York Times* (July 10): C1.

10. Reported in Judith Stacey. 1991. "Backwards toward the Post-Modern Family." In *America at Century's End,* pp. 17–34. Edited by Alan Wolfe. Berkeley and Los Angeles: University of California Press. See also Phyllis Moen and Donna I. Dempster-McClain. 1987. "Employed Parents: Role Strain, Work Time, and Preferences for Working Less." *Journal of Marriage and the Family* 49 (3): 579–90; Eli Chinoy. 1955. *Automobile Workers and the American Dream.* New York: Random House. If Chinoy found that automobile workers in the 1950s dreamed about retiring, inheriting wealth, or opening their own businesses as an alternative to dead-end factory jobs, then the decline of well-paying, secure manufacturing jobs over the last decade has given this dream of independence through self-employment new life.

33

MAN CHILD
A Black Lesbian Feminist's Response

AUDRE LORDE

This article is not a theoretical discussion of Lesbian Mothers and their Sons, nor a how-to article. It is an attempt to scrutinize and share some pieces of that common history belonging to my son and to me. I have two children: a fifteen-and-a-half-year-old daughter Beth, and a four-teen-year-old son Jonathan. This is the way it was/is with me and Jonathan, and I leave the theory to another time and person. This is one woman's telling.

I have no golden message about the raising of sons for other lesbian mothers, no secret to transpose your questions into certain light. I have my own ways of rewording those same questions, hoping we will all come to speak those questions and pieces of our lives we need to share. We are women making contact within ourselves and with each other across the restrictions of a printed page, bent upon the use of our own/one another's knowledges.

The truest direction comes from inside. I give the most strength to my children by being willing to look within myself, and by being honest with them about what I find there, without expecting a response beyond their years. In this way they begin to learn to look beyond their own fears.

All our children are outriders for a queendom not yet assured.

My adolescent son's growing sexuality is a conscious dynamic between Jonathan and me. It would be presumptuous of me to discuss Jonathan's sexuality here, except to state my belief that whomever he chooses to explore this area with, his choices will be nonoppressive, joyful, and deeply felt from within, places of growth.

One of the difficulties in writing this piece has been temporal; this is the summer when Jonathan is becoming a man, physically. And our sons must become men—such men as we hope our daughters, born and unborn, will be pleased to live among. Our sons will not grow into women. Their way is more difficult than that of our daughters, for they must move away from us, without us. Hopefully, our sons have what they have learned from us, and a howness to forge it into their own image.

Our daughters have us, for measure or rebellion or outline or dream; but the sons of lesbians have to make their own definitions of self as men. This

From *Sister Outside* by Audre Lorde, 1984, pp. 72–80. Reprinted by permission of Crossing Press.

is both power and vulnerability. The sons of lesbians have the advantage of our blueprints for survival, but they must take what we know and transpose it into their own maleness. May the goddess be kind to my son, Jonathan.

Recently I have met young Black men about whom I am pleased to say that their future and their visions, as well as their concerns within the present, intersect more closely with Jonathan's than do my own. I have shared vision with these men as well as temporal strategies for our survivals and I appreciate the spaces in which we could sit down together. Some of these men I met at the First Annual Conference of Third World Lesbians and Gays held in Washington, D.C. in October, 1979. I have met others in different places and do not know how they identify themselves sexually. Some of these men are raising families alone. Some have adopted sons. They are Black men who dream and who act and who own their feelings, questioning. It is heartening to know our sons do not step out alone.

When Jonathan makes me angriest, I always say he is bringing out the testosterone in me. What I mean is that he is representing some piece of myself as a woman that I am reluctant to acknowledge or explore. For instance, what does "acting like a man" mean? For me, what I reject? For Jonathan, what he is trying to redefine?

Raising Black children—female and male—in the mouth of a racist, sexist, suicidal dragon is perilous and chancy. If they cannot love and resist at the same time, they will probably not survive. And in order to survive they must let go. This is what mothers teach—love, survival—that is, self-definition and letting go. For each of these, the ability to feel strongly and to recognize those feelings is central: how to feel love, how to neither discount fear nor be overwhelmed by it, how to enjoy feeling deeply.

I wish to raise a Black man who will not be destroyed by, nor settle for, those corruptions called *power* by the white fathers who mean his destruction as surely as they mean mine. I wish to raise a Black man who will recognize that the legitimate objects of his hostility are not women, but the particulars of a structure that programs him to fear and despise women as well as his own Black self.

For me, this task begins with teaching my son that I do not exist to do his feeling for him.

Men who are afraid to feel must keep women around to do their feeling for them while dismissing us for the same supposedly "inferior" capacity to feel deeply. But in this way also, men deny themselves their own essential humanity, becoming trapped in dependency and fear.

As a Black woman committed to a liveable future, and as a mother loving and raising a boy who will become a man, I must examine all my possibilities of being within such a destructive system.

Jonathan was three and one half when Frances, my lover, and I met; he was seven when we all began to live together permanently. From the start, Frances' and my insistence that there be no secrets in our household about the fact that we were lesbians has been the source of problems and strengths

for both children. In the beginning, this insistence grew out of the knowledge, on both parts, that whatever was hidden out of fear could always be
used either against the children or ourselves—one imperfect but useful argument for honesty. The knowledge of fear can help make us free.

> for the embattled
> there is no place
> that cannot be
> home
> nor is.[1]

For survival, Black children in America must be raised to be warriors.
For survival, they must also be raised to recognize the enemy's many faces.
Black children of lesbian couples have an advantage because they learn, very
early, that oppression comes in many different forms, none of which have
anything to do with their own worth.

To help give me perspective, I remember that for years, in the name-
calling at school, boys shouted at Jonathan not—"your mother's a lesbian"—
but rather—"your mother's a nigger."

When Jonathan was eight years old and in the third grade we moved,
and he went to a new school where his life was hellish as a new boy on the
block. He did not like to play rough games. He did not like to fight. He did
not like to stone dogs. And all this marked him early on as an easy target.

When he came in crying one afternoon, I heard from Beth how the corner bullies were making Jonathan wipe their shoes on the way home whenever Beth wasn't there to fight them off. And when I heard that the
ringleader was a little boy in Jonathan's class his own size, an interesting and
very disturbing thing happened to me.

My fury at my own long-ago impotence, and my present pain at his suffering, made me start to forget all that I knew about violence and fear, and
blaming the victim, I started to hiss at the weeping child. "The next time you
come in here crying . . . ," and I suddenly caught myself in horror.

This is the way we allow the destruction of our sons to begin—in the
name of protection and to ease our own pain. *My* son get beaten up? I was
about to demand that he buy that first lesson in the corruption of power, that
might makes right. I could hear myself beginning to perpetuate the age-old
distortions about what strength and bravery really are.

And no, Jonathan didn't have to fight if he didn't want to, but somehow
he did have to feel better about not fighting. An old horror rolled over me of
being the fat kid who ran away, terrified of getting her glasses broken.

About that time a very wise woman said to me, "Have you ever told
Jonathan that once you used to be afraid, too?"

The idea seemed far-out to me at the time, but the next time he came in
crying and sweaty from having run away again, I could see that he felt
shamed at having failed me, or some image he and I had created in his head

of mother/woman. This image of woman being able to handle it all was bolstered by the fact that he lived in a household with three strong women, his lesbian parents and his forthright older sister. At home, for Jonathan, power was clearly female.

And because our society teaches us to think in an either/or mode—kill or be killed, dominate or be dominated—this meant that he must either surpass or be lacking. I could see the implications of this line of thought. Consider the two western classic myth/models of mother/son relationships: Jocasta/Oedipus, the son who fucks his mother, and Clytemnestra/Orestes, the son who kills his mother.

It all felt connected to me.

I sat down on the hallway steps and took Jonathan on my lap and wiped his tears. "Did I ever tell you about how I used to be afraid when I was your age?"

I will never forget the look on that little boy's face as I told him the tale of my glasses and my after-school fights. It was a look of relief and total disbelief, all rolled into one.

It is as hard for our children to believe that we are not omnipotent as it is for us to know it, as parents. But that knowledge is necessary as the first step in the reassessment of power as something other than might, age, privilege, or the lack of fear. It is an important step for a boy, whose societal destruction begins when he is forced to believe that he can only be strong if he doesn't feel, or if he wins.

I thought about all this one year later when Beth and Jonathan, ten and nine, were asked by an interviewer how they thought they had been affected by being children of a feminist.

Jonathan said that he didn't think there was too much in feminism for boys, although it certainly was good to be able to cry if he felt like it and not to have to play football if he didn't want to. I think of this sometimes now when I see him practicing for his Brown Belt in Tae Kwon Do.

The strongest lesson I can teach my son is the same lesson I teach my daughter: how to be who he wishes to be for himself. And the best way I can do this is to be who I am and hope that he will learn from this not how to be me, which is not possible, but how to be himself. And this means how to move to that voice from within himself, rather than to those raucous, persuasive, or threatening voices from outside, pressuring him to be what the world wants him to be.

And that is hard enough.

Jonathan is learning to find within himself some of the different faces of courage and strength, whatever he chooses to call them. Two years ago, when Jonathan was twelve and in the seventh grade, one of his friends at school who had been to the house persisted in calling Frances "the maid." When Jonathan corrected him, the boy then referred to her as "the cleaning woman." Finally Jonathan said, simply, "Frances is not the cleaning woman, she's my mother's lover." Interestingly enough, it is the teachers at this school who still have not recovered from his openness.

Frances and I were considering attending a Lesbian/Feminist conference this summer, when we were notified that no boys over ten were allowed. This presented logistic as well as philosophical problems for us, and we sent the following letter:

> Sisters:
>
> Ten years as an interracial lesbian couple has taught us both the dangers of an oversimplified approach to the nature and solutions of any oppression, as well as the danger inherent in an incomplete vision.
>
> Our thirteen-year-old son represents as much hope for our future world as does our fifteen-year-old daughter, and we are not willing to abandon him to the killing streets of New York City while we journey west to help form a Lesbian-Feminist vision of the future world in which we can all survive and flourish. I hope we can continue this dialogue in the near future, as I feel it is important to our vision and our survival.

The question of separatism is by no means simple. I am thankful that one of my children is male, since that helps to keep me honest. Every line I write shrieks there are no easy solutions.

I grew up in largely female environments, and I know how crucial that has been to my own development. I feel the want and need often for the society of women, exclusively. I recognize that our own spaces are essential for developing and recharging.

As a Black woman, I find it necessary to withdraw into all-Black groups at times for exactly the same reasons—differences in stages of development and differences in levels of interaction. Frequently, when speaking with men and white women, I am reminded of how difficult and time-consuming it is to have to reinvent the pencil every time you want to send a message.

But this does not mean that my responsibility for my son's education stops at age ten, any more than it does for my daughter's. However, for each of them, that responsibility does grow less and less as they become more woman and man.

Both Beth and Jonathan need to know what they can share and what they cannot, how they are joined and how they are not. And Frances and I, as grown women and lesbians coming more and more into our power, need to relearn the experience that difference does not have to be threatening.

When I envision the future, I think of the world I crave for my daughters and my sons. It is thinking for survival of the species—thinking for life.

Most likely there will always be women who move with women, women who live with men, men who choose men. I work for a time when women with women, women with men, men with men, all share the work of a world that does not barter bread or self for obedience, nor beauty, nor love. And in that world we will raise our children free to choose how best to fulfill themselves. For we are jointly responsible for the care and raising of the young, since *that* they be raised is a function, ultimately, of the species.

Within that tripartite pattern of relating/existence, the raising of the young will be the joint responsibility of all adults who choose to be associated with children. Obviously, the children raised within each of these three relationships will be different, lending a special savor to that eternal inquiry into how best can we live our lives.

Jonathan was three and a half when Frances and I met. He is now fourteen years old. I feel the living perspective that having lesbian parents has brought to Jonathan is a valuable addition to his human sensitivity.

Jonathan has had the advantage of growing up within a nonsexist relationship, one in which this society's pseudo-natural assumptions of ruler/ruled are being challenged. And this is not only because Frances and I are lesbians, for unfortunately there are some lesbians who are still locked into patriarchal patterns of unequal power relationships.

These assumptions of power relationships are being questioned because Frances and I, often painfully and with varying degrees of success, attempt to evaluate and measure over and over again our feelings concerning power, our own and others'. And we explore with care those areas concerning how it is used and expressed between us and between us and the children, openly and otherwise. A good part of our biweekly family meetings are devoted to this exploration.

As parents, Frances and I have given Jonathan our love, our openness, and our dreams to help form his visions. Most importantly, as the son of lesbians, he has had an invaluable model—not only of a relationship—but of relating.

Jonathan is fourteen now. In talking over this paper with him and asking his permission to share some pieces of his life, I asked Jonathan what he felt were the strongest negative and the strongest positive aspects for him in having grown up with lesbian parents.

He said the strongest benefit he felt he had gained was that he knew a lot more about people than most other kids his age that he knew, and that he did not have a lot of the hang-ups that some other boys did about men and women.

And the most negative aspect he felt, Jonathan said, was the ridicule he got from some kids with straight parents.

"You mean, from your peers?" I said.

"Oh no," he answered promptly. "My peers know better. I mean other kids."

NOTES

1. From "School Note" in *The Black Unicorn* (W. W. Norton and Company, New York, 1978), p. 55.

34

IT'S LATE AT NIGHT, AND I'M SCREAMING AT MY KIDS AGAIN
A Father Confronts His Rage

CHRISTOPHER SCANLAN

Yelling at the top of my lungs at three little girls lying still and terrified in their beds. Like a referee in a lopsided boxing match, my wife is trying to pull me away, but I am in the grip of a fury I am unwilling to relinquish. "And if you don't get to sleep right now," I shout, "there are going to be consequences you're not going to like."

With that vague but ominous threat, I slam the door so hard that I hear plaster falling behind the walls and throw myself on my own bed, out of breath, pulse jackhammering in my temples, throat bruised and burning, a growing tide of remorse and revulsion rising within. From the children's room, howls descend into sobs and then sniffling whimpers as my wife murmurs a lullaby of explanations. "Daddy loves you very much," I hear Kathy tell them, a bedtime story in which I appear as a monster whose true, kinder side is obscured by fatigue and worry. "He's just tired, and he wants you to go to sleep. No, you're right, he shouldn't lose his temper, but sometimes parents get upset, and they do things they shouldn't."

All my life, I have struggled with anger and its manifestations in fits of temper.

In college, I once punched a kitchen cabinet in anger, and while I no longer recall what I was so frustrated about, I have never forgotten how, for months afterward, I couldn't shake hands without wincing. But it was only after I became a parent—we have a 7-year-old and two 5-year-old fraternal twins—that my rages grew worse and more frequent.

I have never hit my wife, but I have punched walls during arguments with her.

I love my kids, but I have left my handprint, a faint blush, on the back of their thighs when I've spanked them. I have seen them recoil from me in terror.

At the office, I'm friendly, easygoing, generally considered a nice guy. It's only at home that I display this vein-popping, larynx-scraping rage. It's not just that I never show this secret, ugly side of my personality to others; I don't even seem to feel it in any other spheres of my life. Why must loved ones bear the brunt of anger?

Originally published in *The Boston Globe Magazine,* March 5, 1995, pp. 14, 16, 19ff. Reprinted by permission of the author.

It's 6:15 a.m. Two of the kids are slurping their way, with a solemn determination, through their Ripple Crisps and Cheerios. The laggard remains in bed, curled in her comforter, thumb planted firmly in her mouth.

"I'm counting to three," I call up from the landing.

Silence.

"One."

The whiny protest is muffled by the blanket and the finger.

"Don't count!"

"You're going to miss the bus. You can't be late. Two."

Nothing.

"If I get to three, no *Scooby Doo* tonight." Denying them this inane cartoon, their latest favorite, has proven a potent threat, and from the howl it sparks I know I have hit a nerve. She doesn't move. Inside my head, some unseen force is unleashed and my anger spews forth, like a race car's fiery exhaust. "That's it," I roar, my anger all out of proportion to the offense. "THREE-EEEE."

With that, the recalcitrant child is howling, her twin joins in, while the eldest begins berating me. The peaceful breakfast is now a war zone.

I didn't want to believe that anything was wrong. I shrugged off my wife's complaints that I had become the out-of-control parent her father had been. "I don't want my kids to have a father they're afraid of," she said, after one of my outbursts.

Wait a minute, I countered. The kids know I love them. Didn't I always apologize after my anger had spent itself? Wasn't I unstinting with hugs and kisses? "Maybe you should talk to somebody about it," she said, but I rebuffed that gentle hint. Everybody loses his temper sometimes. People get angry. Kids can drive you crazy. It's not as if I beat my wife or kids.

Kathy began clipping the occasional newspaper article about anger and pinning it to the refrigerator door. Eventually, she told me flat-out that she wouldn't tolerate any more verbal abuse. Her ultimatum, along with a particularly awful late-night screaming assault on the kids that left me ashamed and, most of all, afraid, finally broke through the wall of denial. I still resisted the idea of professional help. Instead, I did what I always do when I'm trying to get hold of something elusive: I wrote about it. Two years ago, I sat down in front of my computer and began what became a series of meditations. I called it my Temper Log.

I didn't write in it every day, or every week, not even every month. But a pattern emerged from the sporadic entries. I was then working as a newspaper reporter in Washington, D.C. I constantly felt under the gun of deadlines at work, worries about supporting a family of five on a single paycheck, and the incessant demands of the children.

I seemed to lose it most often early in the morning, in the rush to get sleepy children to school, or at the end of a long day and a deadening ride home on the Metro, I was usually tired, hungry, overwhelmed by the frustrations that studded my workday, beset by the responsibilities of a family.

Half of me wanted to be Superdad; the other half wanted to left alone. And for the first time, I had someone I could yell at without immediate consequences; someone who wouldn't fire me, or hang up and give the story I was after to a competitor, someone who loved me so much that she took this crap that she shouldn't have to take.

From my Temper Log:

> Tuesday night shortly before midnight.
> The last two days I have lost my temper with the children as I got ready for work and tried to get them up. Today I got so furious with Michaela when she wouldn't put on her OshKosh jumper, I picked her up and dropped her on the bed against the bunched-up comforter. This is how 'normal' people wind up on the child-abuse hot line, accused of mistreating their children. I am sick at heart for acting this way. I love my children so much, and I don't want them to remember bad things about me, the way I remember Daddy breaking the rosary that night in the kitchen.

I am no more than 9, and I am standing just outside our family kitchen. My father has come home drunk again. He is in his mid-40s (about the age I am today). By now, he has had three strokes, land mines in his brain that he seems to shrug off, like his hangovers, but which in a year will kill him. He has lost his job selling paper products, which he detested, and has had no luck finding another. He and my mother begin arguing in the kitchen. Somehow, he has gotten hold of her rosary beads. I hear his anger, her protests, and then, suddenly, they are struggling over the black necklace. (Has he found her at the kitchen table, praying for him? I can imagine his rage. "If your God is so good, why are the sheriffs coming to the door about the bills I can't pay? Why am I broke? Why can't I find a job? Why am I so sick? Why, dammit? Why?") Out of control now, he tears the rosary apart. I can still hear the beads dancing like marbles on the linoleum.

I don't want to make this another one of those "it's all my parent's fault" stories, the convenient apologia of the adult child of an alcoholic. Like me, my father was the product—and victim—of his own upbringing: the only child born to a mother who had numerous miscarriages and a second-generation Irish-American father from Charlestown who squandered several fortunes and ended up, along with his memories, in a furnished room in the YMCA.

While my own memories of my father are fragmentary, my mother's stories describe a vibrant, winning man, rich with an aura of promise that became deadened by alcohol and the burden of supporting a large family on a salesman's uncertain salary. No wonder he was angry.

Whatever psychic wounds my father's death caused when I was 10 seem to have frozen over my recollection of him. I have few conscious memories: Those I have are starkly etched scenes of drunkenness, grief, and rage that left me with a reservoir of unresolved anger. This limitless supply feeds the frustrations of my own life, as do my templates of parental behavior that I, the loyal son, can reenact with my own children. For many years I thought that I hated the dimly remembered stranger who was my father. I believed that I hated him for dying before I could learn who he was, for scaring me when he was drunk, but now I realize that I hate him only because he left me before I could say, "I love you."

From my Temper Log:

> I told Caitlin that I am trying to control my temper because I don't want to frighten her and Lianna and Michaela. Last night, she angered me because she didn't want to go to bed, but I tried to put myself in her shoes and realized she was worried because Mommy wasn't home yet. So I lay down with her until she fell asleep.
>
> It's a balancing act, I see now, between my needs and theirs. Sometimes mine will have to take precedence. And sometimes, like last night, when Caitlin just wasn't ready to sleep because she was afraid, I have to let the anger go and focus on what they need.

They read like confessions, these recitations of my outbursts, and the act of setting them down, however painful, has helped me. I've also gotten better, with my wife's help, at recognizing the flash points. Like an early-warning system, she can detect the first signs of a blowup—the edge in my voice, my impatience with the bedtime-delaying antics of the children—and steer me clear. I've finally begun to take her advice to just walk away, shut the door, go for a walk, without feeling guilty. Unlike, or perhaps because of, my father, I rarely drink. I talk about my temper with the kids. They know Daddy has a problem and he's working on it. I'd like to be able to say that I never lose my temper anymore, but I can't. Kids are constantly testing you, and often, I know now, they can inspire deserved anger.

The night my father broke my mother's rosary, my younger brother and I lay crying in our beds. The door opened, and light spilled in. In the placid cruelty of what passes for reason in a drunk's mind, he told us, "Don't worry, boys, your mother and I are getting a divorce," which of course sent our wails even higher. There have been moments when I have remembered that scene, and the memory has checked me from saying something equally terrible to the children huddled in their beds.

Even then, I knew that he was terrified of something, and now I see that my worst anger seems to come when I am most deeply afraid—about work, about money, about whether I will amount to anything or if I will die as he did, bitter and unfulfilled. I don't want my children to remember me the way I remember my father, as this looming, frightened man.

"At every corner," the poet Robert Lowell wrote, "I meet my father, my age, still alive." The other morning, the barber who cuts my hair stood behind me with an oval mirror to show off his handiwork. I found myself looking at the same bald spot on the back of my head that I used to stare at from the back seat of our family Ford, my father at the wheel. There are mornings when I wake up afraid and wonder: How many mornings was he afraid? How many nights was he squeezed to the breaking point? I meet my father now in the dark of my children's bedroom, hearing in my shouts the echoes of his rage, the legacy of anger passed from father to son. As our children have grown from cribs to their own beds, I have begun to hear myself in their outbursts: temper tantrums from the oldest, impulsive slaps from the youngest. Rivers of rage run from one generation to another, and it may be impossible to staunch the flow. But I have to keep trying. One breakfast, one bedtime, one day at a time.

35

"GOD BE GRACIOUS TO THE WINNERS"

GERALD EARLY

It was not uncommon in the early days of Linnet's schooling, before Ida and I understood or even knew of her learning disability, for me to make speeches, give impassioned lectures to her about her repeated failures in school. In retrospect, these speeches must have convinced her that I was either a theatrical lunatic or an arrogant race man. The only time, with perhaps one or two exceptions, I ever talked about race in my household, made a point of race pride or racial identification, was during these lectures. I am sure that it was all a reflection of my own insecurity, my own anxiety about the white world in which I found myself living, in which I found her being educated. I was not only embarrassed *for* her, but for a long time I was probably embarrassed *by* Linnet. At night, in our bedroom, when Linnet was asleep (or at least we thought she was asleep; one wonders how many of these conversations she actually may have overheard), I would sometimes go into nearly uncontrollable rages with Ida:

"Linnet wants pity from her white teachers. She has to be stronger than that. I can't stand that. I can't stand the idea of accepting pity from anyone. It shows you're weak. I especially cannot stand accepting pity from a white person, for being dumb," I would say angrily to Ida.

"I cannot understand how a person who can be as kind as you can be," Ida would respond, "goes off the deep end about this. You sound like a crazy man whenever we talk about Linnet's schooling. First, you say you don't care what she does in school, that school is unimportant. Then, you talk about her not being strong enough, that she seeks the pity and comfort of the white teachers in her school, plays upon her weaknesses so that they will feel sorry for her. You want her to hold school in the utter disdain that you do, yet you also want her to do well, because, to your mind, that's the best way to hold school in disdain."

"You cannot show yourself as weak, especially if you're black, especially in front of whites. I can't stand the idea of anyone, especially a white person, feeling sorry for me. Linnet must adopt the same attitude. All they see in her is a dumb, black kid," I would shout.

"You're crazy," Ida would say, exasperated.

"Why? Because I don't want to have a weak kid, because I want her to have pride for herself, for her—"

"Don't say 'race,' because this has nothing to do with race. It's deeper and more personal than that with you. It has to do with your own childhood, your own rearing. There is something puritanical and harsh in you. You value endurance and forbearing above anything else. Race pride? Are you kidding? You're suffering from race inferiority, from the John Henry syndrome, from the 'I gotta show the white folks I'm better than they are' blues. I don't want my child infected with your nuttiness."

"John Henry syndrome? Well, what's wrong with that? There could be worse models than that."

"Not really," Ida would say, rolling over in bed, turning out her lamp and pulling the covers up. "You see what happened to him. You keep acting like that, I don't expect you to live too long. When are you going to learn that nobody has to prove anything to anybody out here? When are you going to learn that character is not built on stoicism and certainly not on bitterness?"

It would do very little if I were to tell Linnet now that I am deeply ashamed of the shame I felt then, some of which was rooted in my reaction to her. On another level, though, it was not directly attached to her. I felt a shame for myself, my blackness, that manifested itself as a kind of perverse strength, or a bitter determination to prove myself. I think shame often winds up being expressed in people as odd forms of strength or excessive pride. My mother was a strong woman who felt great skepticism, utter disdain, about the idea of needing other people, of having other people, whether black or white, think that they ever had done or ever could do anything for her. I am sure that this insistent independence found its source in some well of shame. But, in her situation, this probably made her a more effective parent by giving her a sense of more control over a decidedly precarious life. Having inherited something of that pride, it has made me, in my very different situation, many times, a lesser parent, less understanding, less patient, less forgiving of myself or anyone else. What was a nobility in my mother expresses itself often in me as a neurosis. For a long time, I wanted Linnet to have this same strength, which meant that she had to have the shame that was the source of the strength. I could not understand that she was as different from me as I was from my mother.

But it has been the years of Linnet's schooling, very difficult years for us all, that have made me aware of one inescapable yet largely unnoticed fact: namely, that fatherhood, my own obsession with relation, was not a role at all but rather a mask or, even more accurately put, a series of masks. I could be, I discovered, by turns stern, loving, wise, silly, youthful, aged, racial, universal, indulgent, strict, with a remarkably easy and often cunning detachment that led me to the question of not whether I loved my children but what sort of love there is between a parent and a child, at last. And for her part, I wonder now what Linnet must have thought, then, and what she thinks now, of these masks, dropped and put in place so adeptly, whether she sees her father not quite as a human being, but rather as a series of personifications of adult moods, of various ways that an adult, spurred by guilt, by annoyance, by condescension, by loneliness, deals with the prerogatives of power and love.

"Are you glad you had me?" Linnet asked once.

"I cannot live without you," I respond with sincere heartfelt expression, with real thanksgiving for this loving child; it is for both of us, however, a cunningly manipulative evasion.

———————

My demeanor as a parent perfectly mimicked my mother's. She was neither sympathetic nor affectionate when I was a boy. Whenever I would cry, she would always tell me to hush, that crying never solved anything. Whenever she combed my hair, I wanted very much to cry because it hurt a great deal. She said I was, as the black folk put it, "tender-headed," and would simply grab my head and tell me to "be still." Then she would relentlessly grease and brush my hair until it felt as if it were on fire. I suppose this small act, this duty I am sure she found to be a headache, had something to do with the pressure she was under in rearing three children by herself, with the peculiar social stress of rearing a boy in a way that he might be able to function in the society with some sense of confidence, with the constraint of having no money. "So much of what we as black people are," wrote actor Sidney Poitier, "has to do directly with the fact that our forefathers were not able to pass on the good life to us." My mother certainly knew that she could not pass on any sort of good life to me. "You have to be a man," she would say, "and learn to take care of yourself in this world." And my response to Linnet, its lack of empathy, of tenderness, may very well have been my own fear of being unable—insecure, tenuously positioned professional that I was then—to pass the good life on to Linnet, and wanting to make sure, as my mother did, that if I could not, she might be able to find it herself. I cannot be soft because it will make her soft, I thought, and soft black children cannot survive in this world. I do not know if this is true, but it was (and is) for me an undying truism.

36

SEXUAL DISSENT AND THE FAMILY
The Sharon Kowalski Case

NAN D. HUNTER

"No connection between family, marriage, or procreation on the one hand and homosexual activity on the other has been demonstrated."

SUPREME COURT, BOWERS V. HARDWICK, 1986

"Sharon Kowalski is the child of a divorce between her consanguineous family and her family of affinity, the petitioner Karen Thompson. . . . That Sharon's family of affinity has not enjoyed societal recognition in the past is unfortunate."

MINNESOTA STATE DISTRICT COURT
IN RE: GUARDIANSHIP OF SHARON KOWALSKI, WARD, 1991

In the effort to end second-class citizenship for lesbian and gay Americans, no obstacle has proved tougher to surmount than the cluster of issues surrounding "the family." The concept of family functions as a giant cultural screen. Projected onto it, contests over race, gender, sexuality and a range of other "domestic" issues from crime to taxes constantly create and recreate a newly identified zone of social combat, the politics of the family. Activists of all persuasions eagerly seek to enter the discursive field, ever ready to debate and discuss: Who counts as a family? Which "family values" are the authentic ones? Is there a place in the family for queers? As battles are won and lost in this cultural war, progressives and conservatives agree on at least one thing—the family is highly politicized terrain.

For lesbians and gays, these debates have dramatic real-life consequences, probably more so than with any other legal issue. Relationship questions touch almost every person's life at some point, in a way that military issues, for example, do not. Further, the unequal treatment is blatant, *de jure* and universal, as compared with the employment arena, where discrimination may be more subtle and variable. No state allows a lesbian or gay couple to marry. No state recognizes (although a number of counties and cities do) domestic partnership systems under which unmarried couples (gay or straight) can become eligible for certain benefits usually available only to spouses. The fundamental inequity is that, barring mental incompetence or consanguinity, virtually any straight couple has the option to marry and thus establish a next-of-kin relationship that the state will enforce. No

---

From the October 7, 1991 issue of *The Nation*. Reprinted with permission.

lesbian or gay couple can. Under the law, two women or two men are forever strangers, regardless of their relationship.

One result is that every lesbian or gay man's nightmare is to be cut off from one's primary other, physically incapacitated, stranded, unable to make contact, without legal recourse. It is a nightmare that could not happen to a married couple. But it did happen to two Minnesota women, Sharon Kowalski and Karen Thompson, in a remarkable case that threaded its way through the courts for seven years.

Sharon Kowalski, notwithstanding the Minnesota State District Court's characterization of her as a "child of divorce," is an adult with both a committed life partner and parents who bitterly refuse to acknowledge either her lesbianism or her lover. Kowalski is a former physical education teacher and amateur athlete, whose Minnesota women's high school shot-put record still stands. In 1983, she was living with her lover, Thompson, in the home they had jointly purchased in St. Cloud. Both women were deeply closeted; they exchanged rings with each other but told virtually no one of their relationship. That November, Kowalski suffered devastating injuries in a car accident, which left her unable to speak or walk, with arms deformed and with major brain damage, including seriously impaired short-term memory.

After the accident, both Thompson and Kowalski's father petitioned to be appointed Sharon's guardian; initially, an agreement was entered that the father would become guardian on the condition that Thompson retain equal rights to visit and consult with doctors. By the summer of 1985, after growing hostilities, the father refused to continue the arrangement, and persuaded a local court that Thompson's visits caused Kowalski to feel depressed. One doctor hired by the father wrote a letter stating that Kowalski was in danger of sexual abuse. Within twenty-four hours after being named sole guardian, the father cut off all contact between Thompson and Kowalski, including mail. By this time, Kowalski had been moved to a nursing home near the small town where she grew up in the Iron Range, a rural mining area in northern Minnesota.

Surely one reason the Kowalski case is so compelling is that, for millions of parents, learning that one's son is gay or daughter is lesbian would be *their* worst nightmare. That is all the more true in small-town America, among people who are religiously observant and whose expectations for a daughter are primarily marriage and motherhood. "The good Lord put us here for reproduction, not that kind of way," Donald Kowalski told the *Los Angeles Times* in 1988. "It's just not a normal life style. The Bible will tell you that." Karen Thompson, he told other reporters, was "an animal" and was lying about his daughter's life."I've never seen anything that would make me believe" that his daughter is lesbian, he said to *The New York Times* in 1989. How much less painful it must be to explain a lesbian daughter's life as seduction, rather than to experience it as betrayal.

In 1988, Thompson's stubborn struggle to "bring Sharon home" entered a new stage. A different judge, sitting in Duluth, ordered Kowalski moved to a new facility for medical evaluation. Soon thereafter, based on staff recommendations from the second nursing facility, the court ordered that Thompson be allowed to visit. The two women saw each other again in the spring of 1989, after three and a half years of forced separation. Kowalski, who can communicate by typing on a special keyboard, said that she wanted to live in "St. Cloud with Karen."

In May 1990, citing a heart condition for which he had been hospitalized, Donald Kowalski resigned as his daughter's guardian. This resignation set the stage for Thompson to file a renewed petition for appointment as guardian, which she did. But in an April 1991 ruling, Minnesota State District Court Judge Robert Campbell selected as guardian Karen Tomberlin—a friend of both Kowalski and her parents, who supported Tomberlin's request. On the surface, the court sought balance. The judge characterized the Kowalski parents and Karen Thompson as the "two wings" of Sharon Kowalski's family. He repeatedly asserted that both must have ample access to visitation with Kowalski. He described Tomberlin as a neutral third party who would not exclude either side. But the biggest single reason behind the decision, the one that he characterized as "instrumental," seemed to be the judge's anger at Thompson for ever telling Kowalski's parents (in a private letter), and then the world at large, that she and Kowalski were lovers.

The court condemned Thompson's revelation of her own relationship as the "outing" of Sharon Kowalski. Thompson did write the letter to Kowalski's parents without telling Kowalski (who was at the time just emerging from a three-month coma after the accident) and did build on her own an active political organization around the case, composed chiefly of disability and lesbian and gay rights groups. Of course, for most of that period, she could not have consulted Kowalski because the two were cut off from each other.

In truth, though, the judge's concern seemed to be more for the outing of Kowalski's parents. He describes the Kowalskis as "outraged and hurt by the public invasion of Sharon's privacy and their privacy," and he blames this outing for the bitterness between Thompson and the parents. Had Thompson simply kept this to herself, the court implies, none of these nasty facts would ever have had to be discussed. The cost, of course, would have been the forfeiture of Thompson's relationship with her lover.

An openly stated preference for ignorance over knowledge is remarkable in a judicial opinion. One imagines the judge silently cursing Thompson for her arrogance in claiming the role of spouse, and for her insistence on shattering the polite fiction of two gym teachers living and buying a house together as just good friends. Women, especially, aren't supposed to be so stubborn or uppity. One can sense the court's empathetic response of shared embarrassment with the parents, of the desire not to be told and thus not to be forced to speak on this subject.

The final chapter in the Kowalski case vindicated Karen Thompson's long struggle. The Minnesota Court of Appeals granted Thompson's guardianship petition in December, 1991, reversing the trial judge on every point.

The conflict in the Kowalski case illustrates one of the prime contradictions underlying all the cases seeking legal protection for lesbian and gay couples. This culture is deeply invested with a notion of the ideal family as not only a zone of privacy and a structure of authority (preferably male in the conservative view) but also as a barrier against sexuality unlicensed by the state. Even many leftists and progressives, who actively contest male authority and at least some of the assumptions behind privacy, are queasy about constructing a family politics with queerness on the inside rather than the outside.

When such sexuality is culturally recognized *within* family bounds, "the family" ceases to function as an enforcer of sexual norms. That is why the moms and dads in groups like P-FLAG, an organization primarily of parents supportive of their lesbian and gay children, make such emotionally powerful spokespersons for the cause of civil rights. Parents who welcome sexual dissenters within the family undermine the notion that such dissent is intrinsically antithetical to deep human connection.

The theme of cultural anxiety about forms of sexuality not bounded and controlled by the family runs through a series of recent judicial decisions. In each case, the threat to norms did not come from an assault on the prerogatives of family by libertarian outsiders, a prospect often cited by the right wing to trigger social anxieties. Instead, each court faced the dilemma of how to repress, at least in the law, the anomaly of unsanctioned sexuality within the family.

In a stunning decision in 1989, the Supreme Court ruled in *Michael H. v. Gerald D.* that a biological father had no constitutionally protected right to a relationship with his daughter, despite both paternity (which was not disputed) and a psychological bond that the two had formed. Instead, the Court upheld the rule that because the child's mother—who had had an affair with the child's biological father—was married to another man, the girl would be presumed to be the husband's child. It was more important, the Court declared, to protect the "unitary family," that is, the marriage, than to subject anyone to "embarrassment" by letting the child and her father continue to see each other. The Court ruled that a state could properly force the termination of that bond rather than "disrupt an otherwise harmonious and apparently exclusive marital relationship." We are not bound, the Court said, to protect what it repeatedly described as "adulterous fathers."

In *Hodgson v. Minnesota,* the Supreme Court upheld a Minnesota requirement that a pregnant teenager had to notify both of her parents—even if they were divorced or if there was a threat of violence from her family—prior to obtaining an abortion, so long as she had the alternative option to petition a court. The decision was read primarily as an abortion decision and a ruling on the extent of privacy protection that will be accorded a minor who decides to have an abortion. But the case was also, at its core, about sex in the family and specifically about whether parents could rely on the state for assistance in learning whether a daughter is sexually active.

In two very similar cases in 1991, appellate courts in New York and California ruled that a lesbian partner who had coparented a child with the biological mother for some years had no standing to seek visitation after the couple split up. Both courts acknowledged that the best interests of the child would be served by allowing a parental relationship to continue, but both also ruled that the law would not recognize what the New York court called "a biological stranger." Such a person could be a parent only if there had been a marriage or an adoption.

Indeed, perhaps the most important point in either decision was the footnote in the California ruling that invited lesbian and gay couples to adopt children jointly: "We see nothing in these [statutory] provisions that would preclude a child from being jointly adopted by someone of the same sex as the natural parent." This opens the door for many more such adoptions, at least in California, which is one of six states where lesbian- or gay-couple adoption has occurred, although rarely. The New York court made no such overture.

The effort to legalize gay marriage will almost certainly emerge as a major issue in the next decade. Lawsuits seeking a right to marry have been filed in the District of Columbia and Hawaii, and activists in other states are contemplating litigation. In 1989, the Conference of Delegates of the State Bar of California endorsed an amendment of that state's law to permit lesbian and gay couples to marry.

The law's changes to protect sexual dissent within the family will occur at different speeds in different places, which might not be so bad. Family law has always been a province primarily of state rather than federal regulation, and often has varied from state to state; grounds for divorce, for example, used to differ dramatically depending on geography. What seems likely to occur in the next wave of family cases is the same kind of variability in the legal definition of the family itself. Those very discrepancies may help to denaturalize concepts like "marriage" and "parent," and to expose the utter contingency of the sexual conventions that, in part, construct the family.

PART VII
Education

While race differences in educational attainment have virtually disappeared, and women attain slightly more education than men, both minorities and women remain "less equal" than men—that is, on average they earn less income than white males with comparable educational credentials.

ROSLYN MICKELSON AND STEPHEN SMITH[1]

"Why are women's brains smaller than men's?" asked a surgeon of a group of male medical students in the doctor's lounge . . . . "Because they're missing logic!"

ADRIENNE FUGH-BERMAN[2]

There is substantial agreement in the United States that equal opportunity is something worth providing to our citizens and that the education system is the central institution that should prepare people for equal opportunity.[3] Even in the face of tension and competition between various racial and ethnic groups, the value of an adequate education for all is shared by nearly everyone. For example, in a recent survey conducted by the National Conference of Christians and Jews, about 90 percent of the 3,000 Asian, Black, Latino, and white respondents said they would be willing to work with members of other racial or ethnic groups, even those with whom they felt the least in common, in order to "help schools teach kids what they really need to learn to succeed."[4]

In spite of programs designed to create equal opportunity through the education system, research demonstrates that race, class, and gender continue to affect students' experiences and educational outcomes. Jonathan Kozol, for example, describes how race and poverty intersect in brutally impoverished schools in several U.S. cities.[5] A report entitled *How Schools Shortchange Girls,* commissioned by the American Association of University Women Educational Foundation, documents how gender, race, and class affect educational achievement. Some of the data suggest that class is the most important of these three variables.[6] Bernice Sandler, director of the Project on the Status and Education of Women at the Association of American Colleges and Universities, discovered that men in college were given both overt and subtle support, whereas women were undermined in both overt and subtle ways. Studying interaction in classrooms, Sandler found frequent cases of disparaging remarks about women, such as sexist jokes, made by male professors, and she found subtle differences in treatment of male and female students, such as calling on men more frequently than women, by faculty of both genders.[7] Sadker and Sadker observed that boys receive more attention than girls at the elementary and secondary levels.[8]

Other educators have documented ways that subtle and overt stereotypes are reinforced in the curriculum, and many have worked toward changing it.

For example, substantial attention has been given to gendered images in children's books, and now attention is focusing on the intersections of gender with other factors.[9] Other scholars are examining the success or failure of the testing system for various groups. For example, in a recent finding that helps explain why bright Black students do not perform as well as expected on tests, Claude Steele, a social psychologist at Stanford University, identified what he calls "stereotype vulnerability"—the tendency for group members to perform badly when they think their performance is a reflection of their group. Concerned that even highly qualified Black students tend to earn increasingly lower grades as they progressed through college, Steele set out to identify the cause. He found that when Black Stanford University undergraduates were given a difficult verbal test, those who were told that it was a "genuine test of your verbal abilities and limitations" received lower scores than the white students also being tested. But when another group of Black students taking the same test was told that it was designed to study "psychological factors involved in solving verbal problems," they performed as well as the white students. Steele repeated this experiment in various places and formats, documenting that stereotype vulnerability also affected women when they were told that a given math test showed "gender differences." It even affected white men who were told that Asians tended to outperform whites on a difficult math test.[10]

The context of test-taking is just one aspect of the hidden curriculum— the myriad messages, subtle and obvious, that affect students' attitudes and performance, apart from course content. For example, in an ethnographic study of Black and white women on two college campuses, anthropologists Dorothy Holland and Margaret Eisenhart found that peer culture eroded career plans for many women in both groups as romance became more important than their studies.[11]

The truth-seeking traditions outlined in the introduction to this book have led to voluminous literature designed to eliminate the invisibility of many groups in the curriculum at the university level. Simultaneously, the numbers of white women and of women and men of color in various academic ranks show that in the upper echelons, the proportion of white males in positions of authority remains very high.[12]

This chapter begins with an article by Roslyn Arlin Mickelson and Stephen Samuel Smith that presents a history of compensatory education in the United States. The authors discuss equality, equal opportunity, and educational outcomes, arguing that changes in education alone cannot bring about equality when good jobs are lacking and discrimination occurs in the workplace.

Next, David Sadker and the late Myra Sadker, in their study of gender in elementary schools, present some of the liabilities boys face in school. Although their overall conclusion is that girls fare worse than boys in schools, they document areas in which boys are especially vulnerable.

The next three articles address the challenges of surviving in higher education. First, sociologist Ruth Sidel reports on the climate for women students, students of color, Jewish students, and gay students on college campuses. Citing incidents from many campuses of racism, sexism, homo-phobia, sexual harassment, rape of women, and anti-Semitism, Sidel presents upsetting findings that reflect tensions in the wider social order. Next, writer and professor bell hooks shares some of her experience as a Black graduate student in racist and sexist English departments. Then physician Adriane Fugh-Berman describes her sexist experiences in medical school.

Finally, sociologist Harry Brod defends the establishment of men's stud-ies in higher education. The sexist and racist professors described by hooks and Fugh-Berman could benefit from the curriculum changes Brod advo-cates. Brod's work and the argument to establish men's studies emerge after years of groundbreaking work in women's studies, Black studies, and ethnic studies.[13] Although Brod acknowledges that men's studies is a relatively new field that should not be given resources at the expense of women's stud-ies, he argues that it should be included in the curriculum because it con-tributes to the reconstruction of knowledge.

The messages in this chapter echo many that have been heard through-out this book so far: people need validation of their varied experiences; knowledge is incomplete without a broad range of voices and perspectives; and discrimination greatly interferes with people's abilities to move freely in the world and achieve their goals. Some of these themes are heard again in Part VIII in the context of paid work and unemployment.

NOTES

1. Roslyn Arlin Mickelson and Stephen Samuel Smith, "Education and the Struggle against Race, Class, and Gender Inequality," in Berch Berberoglu, ed., *Critical Perspectives in Sociology: A Reader* (Dubuque, IA: Kendall-Hunt, 1991). (See also reading number 37 in this book.)

2. Adrienne Fugh-Berman, "Tales Out of Medical School," *The Nation,* January 20, 1992: 54.

3. Mickelson and Smith, "Education and the Struggle."

4. "Taking America's Pulse: A Summary Report of The National Conference Survey On Inter-Group Relations," New York: paper from The National Conference of Christians and Jews, (1994), p. 11.

5. Jonathan Kozol, *Savage Inequalities* (New York: Crown, 1991).

6. American Association of University Women Educational Foundation, *How Schools Shortchange Girls* (New York: Marlowe & Company, 1995).

7. Bernice Resnick Sandler, "The Classroom Climate: Still a Chilly One for Women," in Carol Lasser, ed., *Educating Men and Women Together: Coeducation in a Changing World* (Urbana: University of Illinois Press in conjunction with Oberlin College: 1987). Reprinted in Karin Bergstrom Costello, *Gendered Voices: Readings from the American Experience* (New York: Harcourt Brace, 1996) pp. 359–68. Sandler does not discuss the intersections of gender with other factors.

8. Myra Sadker and David Sadker, *Failing at Fairness: How Our Schools Cheat Girls* (New York: Simon & Schuster, 1994).

9. For a recent look at gendered images in children's books and references to prior work in this area, see Roger Clark, Rachel Lennon, and Leanna Morris, "Of

Caldecotts and Kings: Gendered Images in Recent American Children's Books by Black and Non-Black Illustrators," *Gender & Society,* 7(2) June 1993: 227–45.

10. See Claude Steele and Joshua Aronson, "Stereotype Threat and the Intellectual Test Performance of African Americans," *Journal of Personality and Social Psychology,* 69(5) Fall 1995: 797ff. For a discussion of bias, especially gender bias, in standardized college entrance tests (PSAT and SAT), see Myra Sadker and David Sadker, "Test Drive," in *Failing at Fairness.*

11. Dorothy C. Holland and Margaret A. Eisenhart, *Educated in Romance: Women, Achievement, and College Culture* (Chicago: University of Chicago Press, 1990).

12. For a look at the numbers of women at various levels of academia, including students and faculty, see Margaret L. Andersen, *Thinking about Women: Sociological Perspectives on Sex and Gender, 3rd ed.,* (New York: Macmillan, 1993) p. 64. Andersen draws on data from Charles J. Andersen, Deborah J. Carter, and Andrew Malizio, 1989–90 *Fact Book on Higher Education* (New York: Macmillan, 1989).

13. For a history of the establishment of ethnic studies programs during the past twenty-five years, see Evelyn Hu DeHart, "Rethinking America: The Practice and Politics of Multiculturalism in Higher Education," in Becky W. Thompson and Sangeeta Tyagi, eds., *Beyond a Dream Deferred: Multicultural Education and the Politics of Excellence* (Minneapolis: University of Minnesota Press, 1993) pp. 3–17.

37

EDUCATION AND THE STRUGGLE AGAINST RACE, CLASS, AND GENDER INEQUALITY

ROSLYN ARLIN MICKELSON AND STEPHEN SAMUEL SMITH

Introduction

For the past 35 years, policy makers have claimed that federal education policies seek, among other things, to further equality among the races, between the sexes, and, to a much lesser extent, among social classes.[1] In this respect, educational policy makers have shared one of the assumptions that has long been part of the putative dominant ideology: a "good education" is *the* meal ticket. It will unlock the door to economic opportunity and thus enable disadvantaged groups or individuals to improve their lot dramatically. According to the dominant ideology, the United States is basically a

From *Critical Perspectives in Sociology,* Berch Bergeroglu, ed., 1991. Reprinted by permission of Kendall/Hunt Publishing Company.

meritocracy in which hard work and individual effort are rewarded, especially in financial terms. Related to this central belief are a series of culturally enshrined misconceptions about poverty and wealth. The central one is that poverty and wealth are the result of individual inadequacies or strengths rather than the results of the distributive mechanisms of the capitalist economy. A second misconception is the belief that everyone is the master of her or his own fate.[2] The dominant ideology assumes that American society is open and competitive, a place where an individual's status depends on talent and motivation, not inherited position. To compete, everyone must have access to education free of the fetters of family background or ascriptive factors like gender and race.[3] Since the middle of this century the reform policies of the federal government have been designed, at least officially, to enhance individuals' opportunities to acquire education.

We begin this essay by discussing the major educational doctrines and policies of the past 35 years that claim to have been aimed at promoting equality through greater equality of educational opportunity. This discussion includes the success and failures of programs such as school desegregation, compensatory education, Title IX, and job training. We then focus on the barriers such programs face in actually promoting equality. Here our point is that inequality is so deeply rooted in the structure and operation of the U.S. political economy that, at best, educational reforms can play only a limited role in ameliorating such inequality. Considerable evidence indicates that the educational system helps legitimate, if not actually reproduce, significant aspects of social inequality.

First, let us distinguish among equality, equality of opportunity, and equality of educational opportunity. The term *equality* has been the subject of extensive scholarly and political debate, much of which is beyond the scope of this essay. Most Americans reject equality of life conditions as a goal, because it would require a fundamental transformation of our basic economic and political institutions, a scenario most are unwilling to accept.[4] In the words of one observer, "So long as we live in a democratic capitalist society—that is, so long as we maintain the formal promise of political and social equality while encouraging the practice of economic inequality—we need the idea of equal opportunity to bridge that otherwise unacceptable contradiction."[5] The distinction between equality of opportunity and equality of outcome is important. Through this country's history, equality has most typically been understood in the former way. Rather than a call for the equal distribution of money, property, or many other social goods, the concern over equality has been with equal opportunity in pursuit of these goods. As Ralph Waldo Emerson put it: "The genius of our country has worked out our true policy—opportunity. Opportunity of civil rights, of education, of personal power, and not less of wealth; doors wide open."[6] To use a current metaphor: If life is a game, the playing field must be level; if life is a race, the starting line must be in the same place for everyone. For the playing field to be level, many believe education is crucial, giving individuals the wherewithal to compete in the allegedly meritocratic system. Thus equality of opportunity hinges on equality of educational opportunity.[7]

The Spotty Record of Federal Educational Reforms

In the past 35 years a series of educational reforms initiated at the national level has been introduced into local school systems. All of the reforms aimed to move education closer to the ideal of equality of educational opportunity. Here we discuss several of these reforms and how the evolution of the concept of equality of educational opportunity, spurred on by the Coleman Report, shaped many of these reforms during the past two decades. Given the importance of race and racism in American social history, many of the federal education policies during this period attempted to redress the most egregious forms of inequality based on race.

School Desegregation

Although American society has long claimed to be based on freedom, justice, and equality of opportunity, the history of race relations has long suggested the opposite. Perhaps the most influential early discussion of this disparity was Gunnar Myrdal's *An American Dilemma,* published in 1944, which vividly exposed the contradictions between the ethos of freedom, justice, equality of opportunity, and the actual experiences of African Americans in the United States.[8] Segregated schools presented observers like Myrdal with direct evidence of the shallowness of American claims to equality for all.

The school desegregation movement, whose first phase culminated in the 1954 *Brown* decision outlawing de jure segregation in schools, was the first orchestrated attempt in U.S. history to directly address inequality of educational opportunity.[9] The links among desegregation, equality of educational opportunity, and the larger issue of equality of opportunity are very clear from the history of the desegregation movement. The NAACP strategically chose school segregation to be the camel's nose under the tent of Jim Crow society.[10] That one of the nation's foremost civil rights organizations saw the attack on segregated schools as the opening salvo in the battle against societywide inequality indicates the pivotal role of education in the American belief system in promoting equality of opportunity.

Has desegregation succeeded? This is really two questions: First, have desegregation efforts integrated public schools? Second, have desegregation efforts enhanced students' educational opportunities? Since 1954 progress toward integrated education has been limited at best. As Hochschild notes, racial isolation has only diminished; it has not gone away. In 1968, 77 percent of African American students were in schools with student bodies composed of predominantly nonwhite youths. By 1984, 64 percent of African Americans were in such schools. Moreover, 70.5 percent of Hispanic students attend predominantly minority schools.[11] Furthermore, integrated schools are often resegregated at the classroom level by tracking or ability grouping. Since 1954 racial isolation has declined everywhere but the Northeast. Ironically, today the greatest degree of racial segregation occurs in the Northeast and the least is in the South.[12] The answer to the first question, then, is that desegregation policies have had only a limited effect on overall school integration.

Has desegregation helped to equalize educational outcomes nationwide? As Hochschild points out, a better question might be which desegregation programs under which circumstances accomplish which goals.[13] Where desegregation has succeeded, its effects have been for the most part positive.[14] Evidence from desegregation research suggests that, overall, minority and majority children benefit academically and socially from well-run programs. The city in which we live, Charlotte, North Carolina, is an example of one such success story.[15] Despite these limited but positive outcomes, in the last decade of the twentieth century, most American children attend schools segregated by race, ethnicity, and class. Consequently, 35 years of official federal interventions aimed at achieving equality of educational opportunity through school desegregation have not achieved that goal; children from different race and class backgrounds continue to receive significantly segregated and largely unequal educations.[16]

The Coleman Report

Based largely on the massive data introduced in the 1954 *Brown* desegregation case, which showed that resources in black and white schools were grossly unequal, Congress mandated in 1964 a national study of the "lack of availability of equality of educational opportunity for individuals due to race, color, religious, or national origin in public schools." The authors of the study, James Coleman and his associates, expected to find glaring disparities in educational resources available to African American and white students and that these differences would explain the substantial achievement differences between white and minority students.[17]

Instead, the Coleman Report, released in 1966, produced some very unexpected findings. The researchers found that 12 years after *Brown*, most Americans still attended segregated schools but that the characteristics of black and white schools (such as facilities, books, labs, teacher experience, and expenditures) were surprisingly similar. Apparently, segregated Southern districts upgraded black educational facilities in the wake of the *Brown* decisions. More importantly, Coleman and his colleagues found that school resources had relatively little to do with variations in students' school performance. Instead, they found that family background influenced school achievement more than any other factor, including school characteristics.[18]

The effects of the last finding were dramatic. It deflected attention from how schools operate and instead focused public policy upon poor and minority children and their families as the ultimate sources of unequal school outcomes. Numerous observers concluded that schools were not primarily to blame for black-white educational differences, overlooking another Coleman Report finding that could implicate schools in inequality of educational outcomes. The overlooked finding showed that African American and white achievement differences increased with every year of schooling. That is, the achievement gap between black and white first graders was much smaller than the gap between twelfth graders. This finding suggests that at best schools reinforce the disadvantages of race and class and at worst are themselves a major source of educational inequality.

Although published a quarter of a century ago, the Coleman Report remains one of the most important and controversial pieces of social research ever completed. One of its many lasting results was a redefinition of the concept of equality of educational opportunity because it made clear that greater inputs into schools were not associated with greater student achievement. No longer were financial inputs a satisfactory measure of equality of opportunity. Only to the extent that academic outcomes of achievement (how well a student performs in school) and attainment (how many years of education a student acquires) are equal can claims be advanced about the putative extent of equality of educational opportunity.[19]

Compensatory Education

A second lasting outcome of the Coleman Report was widespread support for compensatory education. Policy makers interpreted the finding that family background explains more of the variance in students' achievement than any other factor as evidence of "cultural deprivation" among poor and minority families. This notion was consistent with Oscar Lewis' then-popular thesis on the culture of poverty.[20] Such an interpretation of the Coleman Report gave impetus to an education movement to compensate for the alleged cultural deficiencies of non-middle-class, nonwhite families so that when so-called disadvantaged children came to school they could compete without the handicap of their background.

Compensatory education refers to the many programs that began with the passage of the Elementary and Secondary Education Act in 1965. These programs target children who are both poor and underachieving and provide them with developmental preschool or a variety of individualized programs in math, reading, and language arts once they are in elementary school. The following are included under the compensatory education rubric:

- Early childhood education such as Head Start
- Follow Through, where Head Start children, now in elementary school, continue to receive special programs
- Bilingual education
- Chapter 1 (formerly called Title I), which provides language arts and math programs plus food, medicine, and clothing to needy children in primary schools

- Guidance and counseling in secondary schools
- Higher education programs designed to identify potential college students in high schools and special admissions, transition, and retention programs for qualified students going to college[21]

Compensatory education has a controversial history. Initially, critics from the left charged that the underlying premise of compensatory education, that poor and minority families were deficient relative to middle-class white families, was racist and elitist. Compensatory education's most famous critic on the right was Arthur Jensen. His 1969 article on IQ and scholastic achievement argued that compensatory education was a waste of time and money because the lower African American achievement scores indicated that blacks were less intelligent than whites.[22] This criticism of compensatory education miscast the debate over poverty and education into one about race and education because it ignored the fact that many compensatory education students were white and most African American children at the time did not participate in the programs.

Despite attacks like Jensen's and an initial absence of evidence that the programs accomplished any of their goals, the compensatory education movement survived the past 20 years. Recent research has begun to demonstrate both the cognitive and social benefits from compensatory education,[23] although the achievement gaps between minority and white and between working- and middle-class children remain. No doubt this is true in part because today only 18 percent of income-eligible students participate in the most famous and successful program, Head Start.[24] While the recent evidence regarding the effects of these programs continues to be positive, we must conclude that compensatory education, like integrated education, has not brought about equality of school outcomes.

Human Capital Theory and Job Training Programs

The notion that "good" education is *the* meal ticket has received theoretical exposition in human capital theory, which views education as a capital investment in human beings. Theodore Schultz, a University of Chicago economist, originally put forth this theory. He argued that "earnings, especially those of minority groups, reflect . . . inadequate investment in their health and education."[25] The social policies developed to remedy shortages in human capital among minority and working-class youth included job training programs like the Comprehensive Education and Training Act (CETA) and its successor, the Job Training and Partnership Act (JTPA). A central problem with both programs is that graduates have few if any jobs once the training is over.[26] The failure of both programs to eradicate inequality stems from the faulty premise that individual, not structural, factors are at the heart of poverty. The poor often have a great deal of skills and education. What they lack is available, well-paying jobs in which to invest their skills.[27] We elaborate on this crucial point later in this article.

These criticisms apply as well to more-conventional high school vocational education programs. Vocational students tend to be disproportionately working class and minority, and the courses are highly segregated by gender. Vocational education classes in high school and community colleges are frequently tailored to local businesses' labor force requirements. Too often they train students in obsolete, narrow skills that are virtually useless once the student graduates from the educational program. Much of the recent corporate interest in school reform stems from the results of these processes.[28] The track record of job training programs (CETA and JTPA) and secondary school vocational education programs indicate human capital-based educational reforms do not, and cannot, narrow race, class, and gender differences in equality of educational opportunity in this society.

Title IX

Title IX is the primary federal law prohibiting sex discrimination in education. It states, "No person in the United States shall, on the basis of sex, be excluded from participation in, be denied benefit of, or be subjected to discrimination under any program or activity receiving Federal financial assistance." Until its passage in 1972, gender inequality in educational opportunity received minimal legislative attention. Title IX covers admissions quotas by sex, different courses, and athletic programs. It requires [that] existing school programs be examined for gender-based discrimination and mandates equal treatment of all students in courses, financial aid, counseling services, and employment.[29]

Although Title IX was passed in 1972, it lacked implementing regulations until 1975. Nor was it ever accompanied by substantial federal or state financial assistance. Title IX was potentially damaged in February 1984, when the Supreme Court ruled in *Grove City College* v. *Bell* that coverage of Title IX was limited to programs and activities, rather than entire institutions, receiving federal money.[30] The effects of this ruling remain unclear.[31]

Sexism in education persists despite laws prohibiting it. Even though female achievement and attainment levels are comparable to those of males, many sexist practices remain an integral part of schooling at all levels. For example, curricular materials from kindergarten to college reveal a preponderance of male characters. In addition, male and female characters usually reflect traditional gender roles and behaviors. Although the gap is narrowing, women who graduate from high school are frequently less well prepared in college-level math and science than men are and consequently cannot enroll in math, science, engineering, or computer science courses in the same frequencies as men.[32] Vocational education at the high school and college level remains highly sex segregated. Administrators are overwhelmingly male although most teachers are female. Women in academia face barriers to promotion and continue to earn less than their male colleagues.[33]

Recent civil rights legislation fails to address any of these problems. Like the laws and policies aimed at eliminating race differences in school processes and outcomes, those aiming to eliminate gender differences in educational opportunities have, at best, only narrowed differences. Educational opportunity in the United States remains highly unequal for people of different gender, race, ethnic, and class backgrounds.

Equality of Educational Opportunity and Equality of Income

The educational reforms intended to lessen inequality were designed primarily to give all students access to better playgrounds, computers, books, teachers, and athletic facilities. Greater equality in the distribution of these resources was seen as a means to better equip minorities, women, and to a lesser extent, working-class whites to improve their chances in life once they become adults. Equality of educational opportunity, as noted earlier, was viewed as a means of promoting equality of opportunity.

Whatever increase in the equality of educational opportunity has resulted from the reforms discussed earlier, it has not led to a significantly greater equality of life-chances, at least as measured by income, one of the most telling and broadest gauges of equality in the United States. Much of a person's social standing depends on income because in a capitalist society income is related to all other forms of inequality. Although this measure does not address the social class basis of inequality, income is one useful and clear measure of inequality in this society.[34] In addition, the disjunction between the greater equality of educational opportunity and lack of a corresponding increase in the equality of incomes can be explained by the nature of the U.S. political economy. The main cause of income inequality is the structure and operation of U.S. capitalism, which have scarcely been affected by the educational reforms discussed earlier.

Several years after the publication of the landmark Coleman Report, Jencks and his associates reanalyzed the data on which it was based to explore the conventional wisdom that a "good education" was how disadvantaged individuals and groups could improve their economic situation. Their findings were published in a now famous book, *Inequality* (1972). Among its conclusions was the following:

> The evidence suggests that equalizing educational opportunity
> [achievement and attainment] would do very little to make adults
> more equal . . . . The experience of the past 25 years suggests that
> even fairly substantial reductions in the range of educational attain-
> ments do not appreciably reduce economic inequality among adults.[35]

Almost 20 years of educational reforms have elapsed since those remarks were made. Sadly, the evidence in support of that conclusion is stronger now than it was in 1972. Current statistics on educational and income attainment show that race and gender differences in educational achievement continue to narrow and differences in attainment have all but disappeared.[36] Nevertheless, race and gender differences in income remain stable over time (see Figures 1 and 2).

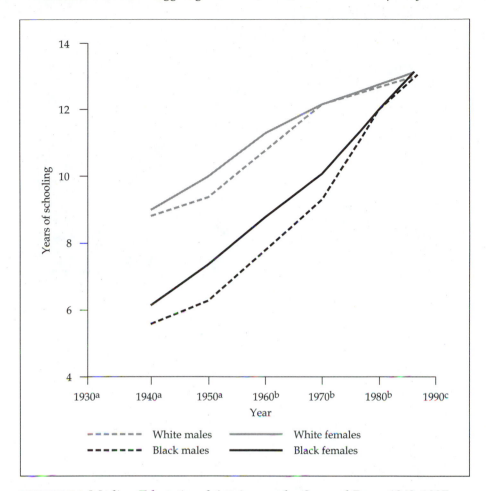

FIGURE 7.1 Median Educational Attainment by Sex and Race, 1940–1987

[a]*Source: Series H395-406 Historical Statistics of U.S. Colonial Times to 1957. U.S. Dept. of Commerce. Bureau of the Census. Washington, DC: U.S. Government Printing Office.*
[b]*Source: U.S. Census of Population 1960, 1970, 1980; Current Population Reports Series P-20 N. 403, U.S. Dept. of Commerce. Bureau of the Census. Washington, DC: U.S. Government Printing Office.*
[c]*Source: Current Population Reports Series P-20 N. 428. U.S. Dept. of Commerce. Bureau of the Census. Washington, DC: U.S.Government Printing Office.*

While race differences in educational attainment have virtually disappeared, and women attain slightly more education than men, both minorities and women remain "less equal" than men—that is, on average they earn significantly less income than white males with comparable educational credentials (see Figure 2). Equality of educational opportunity, indicated by years of attainment, simply has not produced anything resembling equality of income.

The greater equality of educational opportunity has not led to a corresponding increase in the equality of incomes because educational reforms do

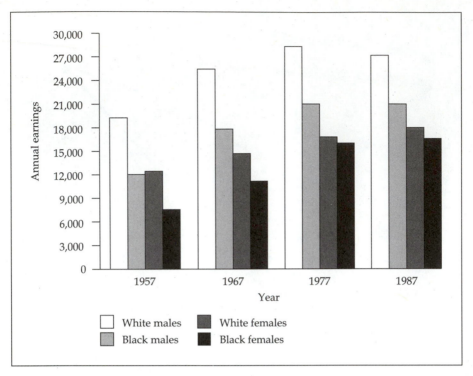

FIGURE 7.2 Median Individual Earnings by Sex and Race, 1957–1987, in 1987 Constant Dollars

Source. Current Population Series P-60 N. 162. U.S. Dept. of Commerce. Bureau of the Census. Washington, DC: U.S. Government Printing Office.

not create more good-paying jobs, affect sex-segregated and racially segmented occupational structures, or limit the mobility of capital either between regions of the country or between the United States and other countries. For example, no matter how good an education white working-class or minority youth may receive, it does nothing to alter the fact that thousands of relatively good-paying manufacturing jobs have left Northern inner cities for Northern suburbs, the Sunbelt, or foreign countries.[37] Perhaps service jobs are left in the wake of such capital flight or have been created in its place, but they pay less than manufacturing jobs. An economy in which McDonald's employs more people than USX Corporation (the former industrial giant U.S. Steel Corporation) is one in which the economic opportunities for minority and working-class youth are limited. Without changes in the structure and operation of the capitalist economy, educational reforms may enable some members of disadvantaged groups to improve their situation, but they cannot markedly improve the social and economic position of these groups in their entirety. This is the primary reason that educational reforms do little to affect the gross social inequalities that inspired them in the first place.

Beyond Attainment: The Persistence of Educational Inequality

Educational reforms have not led to greater equality for several additional reasons. Many aspects of school processes and curricular content are deeply connected to race, class, and gender inequality. But gross measures of educational outputs, such as median years of schooling completed, mask these indicators of inequality. The data in Figure 1 indicate that today African Americans as a group have attained essentially as much education as have whites as a group; the same is true for women compared to men. But aggregate data like these obscure gross differences in attainment within race and gender groups. These within-group differences are primarily linked to class and region. For example, in the 1980s children of black farmers averaged 8.65 years of educational attainment; children of black professionals averaged 13.97 years of schooling.[38] Similar differences by class exist for whites. Within-group differences demonstrate the extent to which educational opportunity remains inequitable. Despite significant within-group differences, the comparable median levels of educational attainment by race and gender can illustrate our theoretical point regarding the structural inability of increases in education to reduce income inequality. Were we to compare income by race and by gender for different levels of educational attainment, our argument would be even stronger. For any level of educational attainment, blacks earn less than whites with comparable levels of education and women earn less than men with similar credentials. Furthermore, the disparities in returns to education increase as levels of educational attainment increase.[39]

Another example of persistent inequality of educational opportunity is credential inflation. Even though women, minorities, and members of the working class now obtain higher levels of education than they did before, the most privileged in society gain even higher levels of education. At the same time, the educational requirements for the best jobs (those with the highest salaries, benefits, agreeable working conditions, autonomy, responsibility) are growing so that only those with the most education from the best schools are eligible for the best jobs. Because the more privileged are almost always in a better position to gain these desirable educational credentials, members of the working class, women, and minorities are still at a competitive disadvantage. Due to credential inflation, previous educational requirements for good jobs, now within the reach of many dispossessed groups, are inadequate and insufficient in today's labor market.[40]

Although gaps in educational attainment between males and females and between minorities and whites have narrowed (see Figure 1), not all educational experiences are alike. Four years of public high school in Beverly Hills are quite different from four years in an inner-city school.[41] Dreeben and Gamoran examined race differences in learning to read among first-grade children in the Chicago area. They concluded that the explanation for why nonblacks learned more than blacks rests, in part, in features of teacher instructional practices, which differ by school. Black children in their sample who attended minority schools were provided with less time in basal instruction—the core activity of primary school reading—and covered fewer new vocabulary words than did black and white children in either integrated or all white schools. The authors concluded, "Blacks learned less than nonblacks . . . mainly because of the instructional inadequacies prevailing in all-black schools."[42]

One additional aspect of these differences is what sociologists of education call the hidden curriculum, which refers to two separate but related processes. The first is that the content and process of education differ for children according to their race, gender, and class. The second is that these differences help reproduce the inequalities based on race, gender, and class that characterize U.S. society.

One aspect of the hidden curriculum is the formal curriculum's ideological content. Anyon's work on U.S. history texts demonstrates that children from more privileged backgrounds are more likely to be exposed to rich, sophisticated, and complex materials than are their working-class counterparts."[43] Another aspect of the hidden curriculum concerns the social organization of the school and the classroom. Some hidden curriculum theorists suggest that tracking, ability grouping, and conventional teacher-centered classroom interactions contribute to the reproduction of the social relations of production at the workplace. This perspective derives from the work of Bowles and Gintis; their seminal work, *Schooling in Capitalist America,* proposes that there is a correspondence among the social relations of the workplace, the home, and the school.[44] Lower-track classrooms are disproportionately filled with working-class and minority students. Students in lower tracks are more likely than those in higher tracks to be assigned repetitive exercises at a very low level of cognitive challenge. Lower-track students are likely to work individually and to lack classroom experience with problem solving or other independent, creative activities.[45] Such activities are more conducive to preparing students for working-class jobs than for professional and managerial positions. Many proponents of the correspondence principle argue that educational experiences from preschool to high school differentially prepare students for their ultimate positions in the workforce, and a student's placement in various school programs is based primarily on her or his race and class origin.[46] The correspondence principle has sometimes been applied in too deterministic and mechanical a fashion.[47] Nonetheless, in certain cases, it is a compelling contribution to explanations of how and why school processes and outcomes are so markedly affected by the race, gender, and class of students. . . .

Conclusion

In this chapter we have argued that educational reforms cannot eliminate inequality. But education remains important to any struggle to reduce inequality. Moreover, it is more than a meal ticket; it is intrinsically worthwhile. Desegregation, compensatory education, Title IX, and bilingual education all facilitate cognitive growth and promote important nonsexist, nonracist attitudes and practices; they make schools a more humane place for adults and children. Furthermore, education, even reformist liberal education, contains the seeds of individual and social transformation. Those of us committed to the struggle against inequality cannot be paralyzed by the structural barriers that make it impossible for education to eliminate inequality. We must look upon the schools as areas of struggle. To do otherwise would be to concede what must be contested in every way.

NOTES

1. This essay draws on an article by Roslyn Arlin Mickelson that appeared as "Education and the Struggle against Race, Class, and Gender Inequality," *Humanity and Society* 11, no. 4 (1987): 440–64. The authors thank Kevin Hawk for his technical assistance in the preparation of the graphs.

2. R. H. deLone, *Small Futures* (New York: Harcourt Brace Jovanovich, 1979). Ascertaining whether a set of beliefs constitutes the dominant ideology in a particular society or social formation involves a host of difficult theoretical and empirical questions. For this reason we use the term *putative dominant ideology.* For discussions of these questions, see Nicholas Abercrombie et al., *The Dominant Ideology Thesis* (London: George Allen & Unwin, 1980); James C. Scott, *Weapons of the Weak* (New Haven: Yale University Press, 1985); Stephen Samuel Smith, "Political Acquiescence and Beliefs about State Coercion" (Ph.D. dissertation, Stanford University, 1990).

3. Whether racism and sexism are epiphenomena is too large an issue to address in this article. We take the position that the logic of capitalism breeds sexism and racism, but that both have a quasi-independent cultural history and are therefore important social phenomena in their own right (See C. A. Mackinnon, "Feminism, Marxism, Method, and the State: An Agenda for Theory," in N. O. Keohane et al. (eds.), *Feminist Theory* (Chicago: University of Chicago Press, 1981).

4. Kevin Dougherty, "After the Fall: Research on School Effects Since the Coleman Report," *Harvard Educational Review* 51, no. 2 (1981): 301–308.

5. Jennifer L. Hochschild, "The Double-Edged Sword of Equal Educational Opportunity." Paper presented at the meeting of the American Education Research Association, Washington, DC, April 22, 1987.

6. Douglas Rae, *Equalities* (Cambridge, MA: Harvard University Press, 1981), p. 64.

7. C. J. Hurn, *The Limits and Possibilities of Schooling* (Boston: Allyn & Bacon, 1978).

8. G. Myrdal, *An American Dilemma: The Negro Problem and Modern Democracy* (New York: Harper & Row, 1944).

9. R. Kluger, *Simple Justice* (New York: Knopf, 1975).

10. Ibid.

11. E. B. Fiske, "Integration Lags in Public Schools," *New York Times,* July 26, 1987, pp. 1, 24–25.

12. J. L. Hochschild, *The New American Dilemma* (New Haven: Yale University Press, 1984).

13. Ibid.

14. Jomills H. Braddock II, Robert L. Crain, and James M. McPartland, "A Long-Term View of School Desegregation: Some Recent Studies of Graduates as Adults," in Jeanne H. Ballantine (ed.), *Schools and Society* (Mountain View, CA: Mayfield, 1989), pp. 303-313; Robert L. Crain et al., *Making Desegregation Work* (Cambridge, MA: Ballinger, 1982); Hochschild, *New American Dilemma;* Charles V. Willie, *Desegregation Plans That Work* (Westport, CT: Greenwood Press, 1984).

15. Frye Gaillard, *The Dream Long Deferred* (Chapel Hill: University of North Carolina Press, 1989).

16. Fiske, "Integration Lags."

17. J. Karabel and A. H. Halsey, *Power and Ideology in Education* (New York: Oxford University Press, 1977), p. 20.

18. J. S. Coleman et al., *Equality of Educational Opportunity* (Washington, DC: U.S. Government Printing Office, 1966); Karabel and Halsey, *Power and Ideology.*

19. B. Heyns, "Educational Effects: Issues in Conceptualization and Measurement," in J. C. Richardson (ed.), *Handbook of Theory and Research for the Sociology of Education* (New York: Greenwood Press, 1986).

20. O. Lewis, "The Culture of Poverty," *Scientific American* (October 1966), pp. 19-25.

21. J. H. Ballantine, *The Sociology of Education* (Englewood Cliffs, NJ: Prentice-Hall, 1983).

22. A. F. Jensen, "How Much Can We Boost IQ and Scholastic Achievement?" *Harvard Educational Review* 39 (Winter 1969): 1–123. The genetic model of human intelligence Jensen used to substantiate his claims of African Americans' alleged lower levels of intelligence was the work of the late Sir Cyril Burt. In the mid-1970s, however, scientists exposed Burt's work as a major scientific fraud because he had fabricated his data on the IQs of separated identical twins as well as the existence of the two women who supposedly assisted him during his research. Stephen J. Gould's *The Mismeasure of Man* (New York: Norton, 1981) is a masterful exposé of Burt's fakery as well as the scientific and moral bankruptcy of the sexist, classist, and racist underpinnings of much of the intelligence testing movement.

23. J. F. Berrueta-Clement et al., *Changed Lives: The Effects of the Perry Preschool Project on Youths Through Age 19* (Ypsilanti, MI: The High/Scope Press, 1985); L. F. Carter, "The Sustaining Effects of Compensatory and Elementary Education," *Educational Researcher 13,* no. 7 (1984): 3–11.

24. Ronald Henkoff, "Now Everyone Loves Head Start," *Fortune,* Special Issue on Saving Our Schools (Spring 1990), pp. 35–43.

25. T. Schultz, "Investment in Human Capital," *American Economic Review* (March 1961), pp. 1–17; Karabel and Halsey, *Power and Ideology,* pp. 313–324.

26. Wilford Wilms, personal communication (1984); Paul Weckstein, personal interview (Washington, DC, March 8, 1990).

27. B. Bluestone, "Economic Policy and the Fate of the Poor," *Social Policy,* no. 2 (1972): 30–31.

28. Carol A. Ray and Roslyn A. Mickelson, "Corporate Leaders, Resistant Youth, and School Reform in Sunbelt City: The Political Economy of Education," *Social Problems 37,* no. 2 (1990): 178–190.

29. Ballantine, *Sociology of Education;* S. S. Klein, *Handbook for Achieving Sex Equity in Education* (Baltimore: Johns Hopkins University Press, 1985).

30. Klein, *Handbook,* pp. 94–95.

31. Title IX is not the only federal law attempting to achieve gender equity in education through legislative reforms. Other federal programs that target sexism in

education include Title IV of the 1964 Civil Rights Act, the Women's Educational Equity Act of 1974 and 1978, an amendment to the 1976 Vocational Education Act, the law authorizing the National Institute of Education, and the laws creating the National Science Foundation and the U.S. Commission on Civil Rights. Klein, *Handbook*; R. Salomone, *Equality of Education under the Law* (New York: St. Martin's Press, 1986).

32. Elizabeth Fennema and Gilah C. Leder, *Mathematics and Gender* (New York: Teachers College Press, 1990); Klein, *Handbook*; Cornelius Riordan, *Girls and Boys in School: Together or Separate* (New York: Teachers College Press, 1990).

33. L. McMillen, "Women Professors Pressing to Close Salary Gap: Some Colleges Adjust Pay, Others Face Lawsuits," *Chronicle of Higher Education* 33, (1987), p. 1.

34. To be sure, income does not measure class-based inequality, but there is a positive correlation between income and class. Income has the additional advantage of being easily quantifiable. Were we to use another measure of inequality—wealth—the disjuncture between it and increases in educational attainment would appear even larger. The distribution of wealth in U.S. society has remained fairly stable since the Depression, with the richest 10 percent of the population owning about 65 percent of the total wealth. Since the Reagan administration's regressive fiscal and monetary policies have been in effect, the wealth of this country has been further redistributed upward at the expense of the working and middle classes.

35. C. Jencks et al., *Inequality* (New York: Harper & Row, 1972), p. 11.

36. Ira Shor, *Culture Wars* (Boston: Routledge & Kegan Paul, 1986).

37. Lois Weis, *Working Class without Work: High School Students in a Deindustrialized Economy* (New York: Routledge, 1990); William J. Wilson, *The Truly Disadvantaged* (Chicago: University of Chicago Press, 1988).

38. Hochschild, *New American Dilemma*, pp. 14–16.

39. Reynolds Farley, *Blacks and Whites: Narrowing the Gap?* (Cambridge, MA: Harvard University Press, 1984).

40. R. Collins, *Credential Society* (New York: Academic Press, 1979); R. B. Freeman, *The Over-Educated American* (New York: Academic Press, 1976).

41. Jean Anyon, "Social Class and the Hidden Curriculum of Work," *Journal of Education* 162, no. 1 (1980): 67–92; Jean Anyon, "Social Class and School Knowledge," *Curriculum Inquiry*, no. 10 (1981): 3–42; Roslyn Mickelson, "The Secondary School's role in Social Stratification: A Comparison of Beverly Hills High School and Morningside High School," *Journal of Education* 162, no. 4 (1980): 83–112.

42. Robert Dreeben and Adam Gamoran, "Race, Instruction, and Learning," *American Sociological Review* 51, no. 5 (1986): 660–69.

43. Anyon, "Social Class and the Hidden Curriculum"; "Social Class and School Knowledge."

44. S. Bowles and H. Gintis, *Schooling in Capitalist America: Educational Reform and the Contradictions of Economic Life* (New York: Basic Books, 1976).

45. Jeannie Oakes, *Keeping Track* (New Haven, CT: Yale University Press, 1985).

46. Ibid.; S. Lubeck, *Sandbox Society* (Philadelphia: Falmer Press, 1985); Mickelson, "Secondary School's Role"; R. A. Mickelson, "The Case of the Missing Brackets: Teachers and Social Reproduction," *Journal of Education* 169, no. 2 (1987): 78–88.

47. M. Apple and L. Weis (eds.), *Ideology and Practice in Schooling* (Philadelphia: Temple University Press, 1983); H. Giroux, *Theory and Resistance in Education* (Boston: Bergin and Garvey, 1983).

38

THE MISEDUCATION OF BOYS
Changing the Script

MYRA SADKER AND DAVID SADKER

Boys confront frozen boundaries of the male role at every turn of school life. They grow up learning lines and practicing moves from a time-worn script: Be cool, don't show emotion, repress feelings, be aggressive, compete and win. As the script is internalized, boys learn to look down on girls and to distance themselves from any activity considered feminine. Dutifully they follow the lines of the script, but now changes are being made in the plot. Today's schoolboys are learning lines for a play that is closing. Consider these statistics:

- From elementary school through high school, boys receive lower report card grades. By middle school they are far more likely to be grade repeaters and dropouts.[1]
- Boys experience more difficulty adjusting to school. They are nine times more likely to suffer from hyperactivity and higher levels of academic stress.[2]
- The majority of students identified for special education programs are boys. They represent 58 percent of those in classes for the mentally retarded, 71 percent of the learning disabled, and 80 percent of those in programs for the emotionally disturbed.[3]
- In school, boys' misbehavior results in more frequent penalties, including corporal punishment. Boys comprise 71 percent of all school suspensions.[4]

Beyond academic problems, conforming to a stereotypic role takes a psychological toll:

- Boys are three times more likely to become alcohol dependent and 50 percent more likely to use illicit drugs. Men account for more than 90 percent of alcohol- and drug-related arrests.[5]
- Risk-taking behavior goes beyond drug and alcohol abuse. The leading cause of death among fifteen- to twenty-four-year-old white males is accidents. Teenage boys are more likely to die from gunshot wounds than from all natural causes combined.[6]

- Many boys are encouraged to pursue unrealistically high career goals. When these are not attained, males often feel like failures, and a life-long sense of frustration may follow.[7]
- Males commit suicide two to three times more frequently than females.[8]

The problems for minority males are more devastating:

- Approximately one in every three black male teenagers is unemployed, and those who are working take home paychecks with 30 percent less salary than white workers.[9] It is estimated that 25 percent of black youths' income results directly from crime and that one in every six African-American males is arrested by age nineteen.[10]
- The odds of a young white woman being a murder victim are one in 369; for a young white man, one in 131; for an African-American woman, one in 104; and for an African-American man, a shocking one in 21. Homicide is the leading cause of death for young black men.[11]

City by city, the statistics are even more alarming. In New York City, about three out of four black males never make it to graduation, and in Milwaukee, 94 percent of all expelled students are African-American boys.[12] Milwaukee, Detroit, and Chicago consider black males an "endangered academic species" and have resorted to some radical solutions.

Milwaukee was one of the first cities to create black male academies, public schools that serve only African-American boys. The idea spread to other metropolitan areas, along with the notion that the best teachers for black boys are black men. At Matthew Henson Elementary School in a poor, drug-infested section of Baltimore, Richard Boynton teaches a class of young black students. Most of them grew up without fathers, so Boynton's responsibilities go beyond the classroom. "There are three things I enforce," he said, "three things I want them to know in that room: responsibility, respect, and self-control. I feel that these three things will not only carry you through school, they'll carry you through life."[13] So Boynton checks to make sure that all the boys have library cards. On weekends he takes them to the Smithsonian or to play ball in the park. "It's almost as if I have twenty-seven sons," he said. Boynton tries to create a school that will turn each of his "sons" on to education. But not everyone is convinced that teaching black males separately is the best approach.

"I read these things, and I can't believe that we're actually regressing like this," said African-American psychologist Kenneth Clark. "Why are we talking about segregating and stigmatizing black males?"[14] Clark's stinging observations are particularly potent since his research paved the way for the 1954 *Brown* decision that desegregated America's schools. Other critics charge that black male academies are little more than a return to the cries of "woman peril," scapegoating female teachers, criticizing black mothers, and ignoring the needs of African-American girls. NOW, the ACLU, and several courts have found separate black male education to be an example of sex discrimination and a violation of the law.

Morningside Elementary School in Prince Georges County, Maryland, is not a black male academy, but its students take special pride in their school team, the Master Knights. Tuesdays and Thursdays are team days, and the members, wearing blue pants and white shirts, devote recess and afternoons to practice. But the Knights, the majority of whom are young black boys, differ from other school teams. Their practices take place in the school library, and the arena in which they compete is chess.

The idea for the team originated in the office of Beulah McManus, the guidance counselor. When children, most often African-American boys, were referred to her as behavior problems, she pulled out a worn chess set. Somehow the game got boys talking, and eventually they found out they enjoyed chess, with its emphasis on tactics and skill, and the chance to compete on a field where size and strength mattered less than brains. As Gregory Bridges, the twelve-year-old president of the Master Knights, said, "When you see someone who is big and bad on the streets, you hardly see anyone who plays chess . . . . You have to have patience and a cool head, and that patience carries outside the chess club."[15] While Morningside emphasizes the importance of getting African-American boys excited about education, girls are not excluded, says principal Elsie Neely. In fact, the school is trying to recruit more female players for next year.

While Morningside stresses extracurricular activities in order to involve boys, some teachers are bringing lessons that challenge the male sex role stereotype directly into the classroom. Often they use the growing number of children's books that show boys expanding their roles. In a fourth-grade class we watched a teacher encouraging boys to push the borders of the male stereotype. As we observed her lesson, we were struck by how much effort it took to stretch outmoded attitudes. She began by writing a letter on the board.

> Dear Adviser:
>
> My seven-year-old son wants me to buy him a doll. I don't know what to do. Should I go ahead and get it for him? Is this normal, or is my son sick? Please help!
>
> > Waiting for your answer,
> > Concerned

"Suppose you were an advice columnist, like Ann Landers," the teacher said to the class, "and you received a letter like this. What would you tell this parent? Write a letter answering 'Concerned,' and then we'll talk about your recommendations."

For the next twenty minutes she walked around the room and gave suggestions about format and spelling. When she invited the students to read their letters, Andy volunteered.

Dear Concerned:

You are in big trouble. Your son is sick, sick, sick! Get him to a psychiatrist fast. And if he keeps asking for a doll, get him bats and balls and guns and other toys boys should play with.

Hope this helps,
Andy

Several other students also read their letters, and most, like Andy, recommended that the son be denied a doll. Then the teacher read Charlotte Zolotow's *William's Doll*, the story of a boy who is ridiculed by other children when he says he wants a doll. Not until his grandmother visits does he get his wish so that, as the wise woman says, he can learn to be a father one day.

As the teacher was reading, several students began to fidget, laugh, and whisper to one another. When she asked the fourth graders how they liked the book, one group of boys, the most popular clique in the class, acted as if the story was a personal insult. Their reaction was so hostile, the teacher had trouble keeping order. We heard their comments:

"He's a fag."

"He'd better learn how boys are supposed to behave, or he'll never get to be a man."

"If I saw him playing with that baby doll, I'd take it away. Maybe a good kick in the pants would teach him."

"Dolls are dumb. It's a girly thing to do."

Next the teacher played the song "William Wants a Doll" from the *Free to Be You and Me* album. Several boys began to sing along in a mocking tone, dragging out the word *doll* until it became two syllables: "William wants a do-oll, William wants a do-oll." As they chanted, they pointed to Bill, the star athlete of the class. Both boys and girls whispered and laughed as Bill, slumped in his chair, looked ready to explode.

Belatedly the teacher realized the problem of the name coincidence; she assured the class that there was nothing wrong with playing with dolls, that it teaches both girls and boys how to become parents when they grow up. When the students began to settle down, she gave them her next instructions: "I'd like you to reread your letters and make any last-minute corrections. If you want to change your advice, you may, but you don't have to."

Later we read the students' letters. Most of them said a seven-year-old boy should not get a doll. But after listening to William's story, six modified their advice, having reached a similar conclusion: "Oh, all right. Give him a doll if you have to. But no baby dolls or girl dolls. Make sure it's a Turtle or a G. I. Joe."

For some nontraditional programs, reading *William's Doll* is just a first step. At Germantown Friends School in Philadelphia, parenting classes begin in elementary school where children learn to observe, study, and interact with infants. By the sixth grade both boys and girls are in charge of caring for babies at school. Programs that make child-rearing a central and required part of school life find that boys become more nurturant and caring in their relationships with others.

Schools in New York City and other communities are downplaying aggression and encouraging cooperation through programs in conflict resolution. In these courses students learn how to negotiate and compromise while they avoid attitudes and actions that lead to violence. Students learn techniques in how to control anger, to listen carefully to others, and to seek common ground.

These innovative courses are rare. Most schools are locked in a more traditional model, one that promotes competition over cooperation, aggression over nurturing, and sports victories rather than athletic participation. Some boys thrive on this traditional male menu, and most students derive some benefit. But the school program is far from balanced, and the education served to boys is not always healthy despite the extra portions they receive.

From their earliest days at school, boys learn a destructive form of division—how to separate themselves from girls. Once the school world is divided, boys can strive to climb to the top of the male domain, thinking that even if they fall short, they still are ahead of the game because they are not girls. Boys learn in the classroom that they can demean girls at will. Schools that do not permit racist, ethnic, or religious slights still tolerate sexism as a harmless bigotry.

In *American Manhood*, Anthony Rotundo writes that men need to regain "access to stigmatized parts of themselves—tenderness, nurturance, the desire for connection, the skills of cooperation—that are helpful in personal situations and needed for the social good."[16] Studies support Rotundo's contention: Males who can call on a range of qualities, tenderness as well as toughness, are viewed by others as more intelligent, likable, and mentally healthy than rigidly stereotyped men.[17] But boys cannot develop these repressed parts of themselves without abandoning attitudes that degrade girls. Until gender equity becomes a value promoted in every aspect of school, boys, as victims of their own miseducation, will grow up to be troubled men; they will be saddened by unmet expectations, unable to communicate with women as equals, and unprepared for modern life.

NOTES

1. Brophy, Jere, and Thomas Good. "Feminization of American Elementary Schools," *Phi Delta Kappan* 54 (1973), pp. 564–66.
   Sadker, Myra, and David Sadker. *Sex Equity Handbook for Schools*. New York: Longman, 1982.

2. Kessler, R., and J. McRae. "Trends in the Relationship Between Sex and Psychological Distress, 1957–76," *American Sociological Review* 46 (1981).
   McLanahan, S. S., and J. L. Glass. "A Note on the Trend in Sex Differences in Psychological Distress," *Journal of Health and Human Stress* 2 (1976).

3. Sadker, David, and Myra Sadker, updated by Mary Jo Strauss. "The Report Card # 1: The Cost of Sex Bias in Schools and Society." Distributed by the Mid-Atlantic Equity Center, Washington, D.C., and the New England Center for Equity Assistance, Andover, Massachusetts, 1989.

4. Duke, D. L. "Who Misbehaves? A High School Studies Its Discipline Problems," *Educational Administration Quarterly* 12 (1976), pp. 65–85.

    Office for Civil Rights. *1986 Elementary and Secondary Civil Rights Survey, State and National Summary of Projected Data.* Washington, DC: U.S. Department of Education, 1988.

5. Kimbrell, Andrew. "A Time for Men to Pull Together," *Utne Reader* (May–June 1991), pp. 66–75.

    Watts, W. David, and Loyd S. Wright. "The Relationship of Alcohol, Tobacco, Marijuana, and Other Illegal Drug Use to Delinquency Among Mexican-American, Black, and White Adolescent Males," *Adolescence* 25:97 (Spring 1990), pp. 171–81.

6. Unpublished data of the National Center for Health Statistics, Public Health Service, U.S. Department of Health and Human Services, 1986.

    "Death Rates from Accidents and Violence: 1970 to 1985," *Statistical Abstract of the United States,* 1988. Washington, DC: Bureau of the Census, U.S. Department of Commerce, 1988.

    Poinsett, Alvin. "Why Our Children Are Killing One Another," *Ebony* 43 (December 1987).

    Children's Defense Fund. *The State of America's Children: 1992.* Washington, DC: Children's Defense Fund, 1992.

7. Pleck, Joseph, and Robert Brannon (eds.). "Male Roles and the Male Experience," *Journal of Social Issues* 34 (1978), pp. 1–4.

    Komarovsky, M. *Dilemmas of Masculinity: A Study of College Youth.* New York: Norton, 1976.

    Sadker and Sadker, *Sex Equity Handbook for Schools.*

8. Lester, David. *Why People Kill Themselves: A 1990s Summary of Research Findings on Suicide Behavior,* third edition. Springfield, IL: Charles C. Thomas, 1992.

    Maris, R. W. *Pathways to Suicide: A Survey of Self-Destructive Behaviors.* Baltimore, MD: Johns Hopkins Press, 1981.

9. Dewart, J. (ed.) *The State of Black America, 1989.* Washington, DC: National Urban League, 1989.

    Garibaldi, Antoine M. *Educating Black Male Youth: A Moral and Civic Imperative.* New Orleans: Orleans Parish School Board, 1988.

    Collison, Michelle N.-K. "More Young Black Men Choosing Not to Go to College," *Chronicle of Higher Education* 34:15 (December 9, 1987), pp. A1, 26–27.

    Gibbs, Jewelle Taylor (ed.). *Young, Black, and Male in America: An Endangered Species.* Dover, MA: Auburn House, 1988.

10. Whitaker, Charles. "Do Black Males Need Special Schools?" *Ebony* (March 1991), pp. 17–18, 20.

11. Simons, Janet M., Belva Finlay, and Alice Yang. *The Adolescent Young Adult Fact Book.* Washington, DC: Children's Defense Fund, 1991.

    Children's Defense Fund. *The State of America's Children: 1992,* p. 52.

12. Lawton, Millicent. "Two Schools Aimed for Black Males Set in Milwaukee," *Education Week* X:6 (October 10, 1990), pp. 1, 8.

13. Dunkel, Tom. "Self-Segregated Schools Seek to Build Self-Esteem," *The Washington Times* (March 11, 1991), pp. E1–2.

14. Clark quoted in Whitaker, "Do Black Males Need Special Schools?" p. 18.

15. Leff, Lisa. "Maneuvering to Win Young Minds, P. G. School Chess Club Teaches Boys Self-Discipline, Self-Esteem," *The Washington Post* (May 17, 1993), pp. A1, A3.

16. Rotundo, E. Anthony. *American Manhood.* New York: Basic Books, 1993, p. 291.

17. Cramer, Robert Ervin, et al. "Motivating and Reinforcing Functions of the Male Sex Role: Social Analogues of Partial Reinforcement, Delay of Reinforcement, and Intermittent Shock," *Sex Roles* 20:9–10 (1989), pp. 551–73.

39

CONFLICT WITHIN THE IVORY TOWER

RUTH SIDEL

Either/or dichotomous thinking categorizes people, things, and ideas in terms of their difference from one another. . . . This emphasis on quantification and categorization occurs in conjunction with the belief that either/or categories must be ranked. The search for certainty of this sort requires that one side of a dichotomy be privileged while its other is denigrated. Privilege becomes defined in relationship to its other.[1]

PATRICIA HILL COLLINS,
*BLACK FEMINIST THOUGHT:
KNOWLEDGE, CONSCIOUSNESS, AND THE
POLITICS OF EMPOWERMENT*

Admission to college or university is, as has been noted, a first but crucial step in an individual's preparation for meaningful participation in the social, economic, and political life of postindustrial America. But admission is merely the first hurdle a student must clear in higher education. Financing college education, achieving academically, and maneuvering around the multitude of social, psychological, and political obstacles that impede the path to a bachelor's degree are often much higher hurdles than admission. Among the barriers that many students have had to face in recent years are virtually continuous clashes stemming from prejudice, ethnocentrism, and fear—fear of the unknown, of the stranger among us. At root these clashes are about entitlement and power, and about students' concerns with the precariousness of their position in the social structure.

Although colleges and universities have since the end of the Second World War been to a considerable extent transformed from elite bastions of privilege to increasingly open, heterogeneous communities, a wave of overt intolerance has recently swept over the academic community. There is little doubt that students today are more tolerant than their grandparents and their parents, yet clashes—some involving vocal or written assaults, some involving violence—continue to plague academic institutions and to shock observers. One of the reasons these so-called hate incidents are so shocking is the increasing unacceptability of overtly racist, sexist, anti-Semitic, and homophobic language and behavior in much of the wider society; another is the contrast between the violence of these incidents and the open expression of hatred and bigotry on the one hand, and the expectation of at least minimal civility in academic settings on the other.

Two relatively recent incidents that deal with the incendiary combination of race and gender point up the depth and pervasiveness of intergroup hostility on campuses all over the country. In the small rural town of Olivet, Michigan, at Olivet College, a school founded in 1844 by the abolitionist minister the Reverend John Shipherd as a "bastion of racial tolerance,"[2] a "racial brawl" involving approximately forty white students and twenty black students broke out one night in early April 1992. According to one report:

> Racial epithets were shouted at the black students as the two sides rumbled on the gray linoleum. Two students, one black, one white, were injured and briefly hospitalized.
>
> Afterward, blacks and whites who had crammed together for midterms and shared lunch money and dormitory rooms could not look each other in the face and were no longer on speaking terms.[2]

This incident was the culmination of increasing hostility among black and white students at Olivet. In the months prior to the incident, white male students had become more openly resentful of black men dating white women. Then, on April 1, a white female student claimed she had been attacked by four black students and left unconscious in a field near the campus. She was not hospitalized, and, despite a police investigation, no arrests were made. College officials were said to be skeptical about her accusations. Nonetheless, word spread, and later that night two trash cans were set on fire outside the dormitory rooms of black student leaders.

The specific incident that precipitated the brawl occurred the next night and again involved a white female student and black male students. Three male students, two black and one white, knocked on a female student's door to ask about a paper she was typing for one of the black students. The men later described the conversation as "civil." The woman, a sorority member, called her brother fraternity for help, saying she was being harassed by some male students. Within a few minutes, about fifteen members of the white fraternity Phi Alpha Pi arrived and confronted the two black men. More whites joined in, and black female students called more black males to even the numbers. Who threw the first punch is unclear; black students claim it was a white fraternity member. "What is clear," according to one report of the incident, "is that instead of seeing a roommate or a fellow sophomore, the students saw race."[2] Davonne Pierce, a dormitory resident assistant who is black, stated that his white friends shouted racial epithets at him as he was trying to break up the fight. He said to them, "How can you call me that when we were friends, when I let you borrow my notes?" But, he later recalled, "At that point, it was white against black. It was disgusting."[2]

After the incident, most of the fifty-five black students, who said they feared for their safety, left the college and went home. They made up 9 percent of the student body. Davonne Pierce stayed on campus but stated,

"Obviously they don't want us here."[2] Dave Cook, a white junior who was one of the fraternity members involved in the fight, later said, "There were a lot of bonds that were broken that didn't need to be broken." He talked about his friendship with a black female student: "We would high-five each other and study for tests. But I don't know what she thinks about me. I don't know whether she's hating me or what. I didn't say one word to her, and she didn't say one word to me. Now she's gone."[2]

Racist behavior on college campuses is, of course, not limited to students. An incident involving a campus in New York State reveals the deep-seated stereotyping and bigotry of some college administrators, police officers, and citizens in communities all over the country. In the early morning of September 4, 1992, a seventy-seven-year-old woman was attacked in the small town of Oneonta, New York. She told the state police that she thought her attacker was a black man who used a "stiletto-style" knife and that his hands and arms were cut when she fended him off.[3] In response to a request from the police, the State University of New York at Oneonta gave the police a list of all of the black and Hispanic males registered at the college. Armed with the list, state and city police, along with campus security, tracked down the students "in their dormitories, at their jobs and in the shower." Each student was asked his whereabouts at the time the attack occurred, and each had to show his hands and his arms.

Michael Christian, the second of five children from a family headed by a single mother, grew up in the Bronx. His mother encouraged him to go to Oneonta to get him away from the problems of the city. Shortly after the attack, two state-police officers and representatives of campus security went to his dormitory room and woke him at 10:00 A.M. After asking him where he was at the time of the attack and demanding to see his hands, they said they wanted to question him downtown, and then they left. His roommate, Hopeton Gordon, a Jamaican student who had gone to high school in the Bronx with Mr. Christian, was questioned in front of other students from their dormitory. When the police asked to see his hands and he demanded their reasons, they responded, "Why? Do you have something to hide?" He said that he had felt humiliated in front of his suite mates and in front of female students.

This is not the first time black students, faculty, and administrators have been humiliated and have seen their civil rights trampled in Oneonta. Edward I. (Bo) Whaley, who went to the small town in upstate New York in 1968 as a student, remained, and is currently an instructor and counselor in the school's Educational Opportunity Program for disadvantaged students, recalls being followed by salespeople in Oneonta shops because they feared he would shoplift. He remembers the two minority ball players—one of whom he was trying to recruit—who were picked up as suspects in a rape case and had to pay for DNA testing even though someone else was convicted for the crime.

An admissions coordinator, Sheryl Champen, who is also black, was herself stopped by the state police the night of the attack. They demanded to see her identification before she could board a bus to New York City. It is unclear why the police questioned her and three other black women traveling with children, who also had to show identification before boarding the bus, since the attacked woman had reported that the person who assaulted her was a man. Their only common characteristic was race. When she heard about the treatment of the students of color, Ms. Champen said, "I was devastated, ashamed of being an admissions coordinator. Am I setting them up?" She feels that the behavior of the police was not an example of overeagerness to solve a crime. After recounting thirteen years of incidents that had begun when she was a first-year student at SUNY/Oneonta, she stated, "I know what it was. It was a chance to humiliate niggers."[3]

The release of the names of the 125 black and Hispanic students not only violated their privacy (and their right to be presumed innocent until proven guilty) but also violated the Family Educational Rights and Privacy Act of 1974 (also known as the Buckley Amendment). Following the incident, the vice-president who authorized the release of the names was suspended for one month without pay and demoted. The president of SUNY/Oneonta called using the list in the investigation "an affront to individual dignity and human rights."[4]

Though each of these events is unique and a product of the particular social environment, demographics, personalities, and stresses at the particular institution, during the late 1980s and early 1990s campuses were rife with similar episodes. A Brown student describes one incident at her university:

> It was April 25, 1989, the end of spring term . . . . Students . . . were preparing for Spring Weekend, an annual fling before final exams. That day, found scrawled in large letters across an elevator door in Andrews dormitory were the words, NIGGERS GO HOME. Over the next 24 hours, similar racial epithets were found on the doors of several women of color living in that hall; on the bathroom doors WOMEN was crossed out and replaced with NIGGERS, MEN was crossed out, replaced with WHITE. And in that same women's bathroom, a computer-printed flyer was found a day later which read: "Once upon a time Brown was a place where a white man could go to class without having to look at little black faces or little yellow faces or little brown faces except when he went to take his meals. Things have been going downhill since the kitchen help moved into the classroom. Keep white supremcy [sic] alive! Join the Brown Chapter of the KKK."[5]

Seven years earlier, *The Dartmouth Review* had set the standard for racist denigration by publishing an article ridiculing black students. The article was entitled "Dis Sho' Ain't No Jive, Bro," and read in part: "Dese boys be saying that we be comin hee to Dartmut an' not takin' the classics . . . . We be culturally 'lightened, too. We be takin hard courses in many subjects, like Afro-Am studies . . . and who bee mouthin' bout us not bein' good read?"[5]

During the late 1980s, the University of Michigan experienced several racist incidents. One of the most infamous took place in 1988, when a poster mocking the slogan of the United Negro College Fund was hung in a classroom. It read "Support the K.K.K. College Fund. A mind is a terrible thing to waste—especially on a nigger."[6]

Violent behavior has also been part of the cultural climate over the past decade. In February 1991, two black students from the University of Maine were allegedly assaulted by nine white men. The two students, both twenty-one, were driving in downtown Orono when approximately a dozen white men attacked their car and shouted, "Nigger, get out of here." When they got out of the car to see what was going on, the two men were kicked and beaten. Three students from the university were among those who attacked the students.[7]

Incidents have not been limited to one kind of school, but have occurred at private as well as public, urban and rural, large and small, at Ivy League as well as less prestigious, little-known institutions. . . .

According to the Anti-Defamation League, anti-Semitic incidents on college campuses have risen sharply in recent years, from fifty-four in 1988 to over double that number, 114, in 1992.[8] In February 1990, at American University in Washington, D.C., anti-Semitic graffiti were spray-painted on the main gate and on a residence hall. On the gate were painted a Star of David, an equal sign, and a swastika. On the dormitory was sprayed an expletive followed by "Israel Zionist."[9] In 1991, at California State University at Northridge, a ceremonial hut used to celebrate the Jewish holiday of Sukkoth was vandalized with anti-Semitic writing. In addition to swastikas, "Hi' [sic] Hitler" and "Fuckin [sic] Jews" defaced the informative signs and flyers that decorated the hut.[10] Two months earlier, Dr. Leonard Jeffries, Jr., then chair of the African-American Studies department at the City College of New York, delivered a speech at a black cultural festival in which he spoke of "a conspiracy, planned and plotted and programmed out of Hollywood" by "people called Greenberg and Weisberg and Trigliani." He went on to say that "Russian Jewry had a particular control over the movies and their financial partners, the Mafia, put together a financial system of destruction of black people."[11]

Gay bashing has also been widely visible on college campuses. A Syracuse University fraternity, Alpha Chi Rho, was suspended by its national organization in 1991 for selling T-shirts with antihomosexual slogans, including one advocating violence against gays. On the front the shirts said "Homophobic and Proud of It!" and on the back, "Club Faggots Not Seals!" The picture illustrating the words was of a muscled crow, the fraternity's symbol, holding a club and standing over a faceless figure lying on the ground. Next to them is a seal hoisting a mug of beer.[12]

During the same year, *Peninsula,* a conservative campus magazine at Harvard, published an issue entirely devoted to the subject of homosexuality. The magazine called homosexuality a "bad alternative" to heterosexuality and stated in its introduction that "homosexuality is bad for society."[13] Within one hour of the magazine's distribution, the door of a gay student's room was defaced with antihomosexual words.

But, of course, discrimination does not need to be physical or perpetrated by students to wound, and to exclude some from mainstream college life. The football coach at the University of Colorado has called homosexuality "an abomination" and has supported a statewide group working to limit gay rights.[14] In 1992, the governor of Alabama signed legislation prohibiting gay student groups from receiving public money or using buildings at state universities.[15]

Sexual harassment and assault have been reported on campuses across the country. . . . Perhaps the most disturbing account of sexual harassment has been described by Carol Burke, currently an associate dean at Johns Hopkins University, about events at the U.S. Naval Academy, where she taught for seven years.[16] Marching chants—or "cadence calls," as they are called in the navy—provide a window into the macho male culture fostered at the academy, a culture that simultaneously celebrates the power of men and violence toward women. As Burke states:

> Cadence calls not only instill mutual solidarity but resurrect the Casey Jones of American ballad tradition as a brave pilot who survives the crash of his plane only to subdue women with greater ferocity:

> > Climbed all out with his dick in his hand.
> > Said, "Looky here, ladies, I'm a hell of a man."
> > Went to his room and lined up a hundred . . .
> > Swore up and down he'd fuck everyone.
> > Fucked ninety-eight till his balls turned blue.
> > Then he backed off, jacked off, and fucked the other two.

Members of the academy's Male Glee Club while away the hours on bus trips back from concerts by singing a particularly sadistic version of the song "The Candy Man":

> THE S&M MAN
> Who can take a chain saw,
> Cut the bitch in two,
> Fuck the bottom half
> and give the upper half to you. . . .
> The S&M Man, the S&M Man
> The S&M Man cause he mixes it with love
> and makes the hurt feel good!
> Who can take a bicycle,
> Then take off the seat,
> Set his girlfriend on it
> Ride her down a bumpy street. . . .
> Who can take an ice pick
> Ram it through her ear
> Ride her like a Harley,
> As you fuck her from the rear. . . .

Lest we think that such lyrics are sung only at the U.S. Naval Academy, the following incident took place at the Phi Kappa Psi fraternity at UCLA in 1992:

> A group of fraternity brothers waited outside the door. They sere-
> naded the rape victim inside, cheering a brother on as if it were a
> football game. To the tune of "The Candy Man," they sang, "Who
> can take his organ / Dip it in vaseline / Ram it up inside you till it
> tickles your spleen / The S and M man, the S and M man / The S
> and M man can / cause he mixes it with love and / makes the
> hurtin feel good."
>
> UCLA's administration looked the other way this spring as Phi
> Kappa Psi fraternity brothers distributed a songbook with lyrics glo-
> rifying necrophilia, rape and violent torture of women. Although a
> 1991 suspension for violation of alcohol and other policies forced the
> fraternity to implement pledge education programs and forums on
> sexism and homophobia, the recent songbook controversy reveals
> the inadequacies of such programs.[17]

In March 1992, *Together*, a feminist magazine at UCLA, "exposed" the songbook that was left anonymously in their office.[17] When asked about the songs, an assistant vice-chancellor of the university first responded, "What's the problem? They are just erotic lyrics." Later, when questioned by the media, he stated, "I was horrified, revolted, shocked and embarrassed. This book is sexist, homophobic and promoted violence." The president of Phi Kappa Psi claimed that the "lyrics are a joke [and] so exaggerated that it is . . . ridiculous to say these songs promote violence against women."

Nevertheless, it is clear that fraternities have been in the forefront of bias-related incidents. Among the most serious incidents occurred at a University of Rhode Island fraternity. An eighteen-year-old female first-year student claimed she was raped during a fraternity party while at least five other men watched. During the investigation a former student committed suicide just hours before he was to be questioned by the police. In this case, as in many others, not only had the fraternity members been drinking heav- ily but often the victims as well. . . .[18]

Over the past several years, an increasing number of rapes have been reported at campuses across the country. . . . Most studies indicate that alco- hol is involved, on the part of the victim as well as the perpetrator. A national study of women at thirty-two institutions of higher education in the U.S. found that 15 percent of college women said they had experienced attempted intercourse by the threat of force and 12 percent said they had experienced attempted intercourse by the use of alcohol or drugs.[19] Recent data plus in-depth studies of individual cases have made it clear that acquaintance rape is far more common than stranger rape in the United States. According to David Beatty, the public-policy director of the National Victim Center, a Washington-based advocacy group, "There is no question that acquaintance rape is more common than stranger rape. No one has the exact numbers, but the consensus is that probably in 80 to 85 percent of all rape cases, the victim knows the defendant."[20]

Many questions have been raised about acquaintance rape since the surge of reported cases has been noted across the country. Notorious cases such as the one involving William Kennedy Smith, in which rape was not proved, and the one involving Mike Tyson, in which the verdict was guilty, have also raised many questions: What is rape? Must physical force be used? When does "no" mean "no" and when is it part of a mating ritual? What about plying a woman with drugs or alcohol and then, when she is too inebriated or out of control to protest effectively, having sex with her? Is that rape?

An incident that came to be known as the "St. John's case" is a vivid and heart-wrenching example of the difficulties of establishing the parameters of acquaintance rape and of prosecuting the alleged perpetrators:

> As she recalled it, the evening of March 1, 1990, a Thursday, began ordinarily enough: the St. John's University student took target practice with another member of the school's rifle club and bantered with him and the coach about everything from the coach's shabby clothing to the other student's love life.
>
> But when the evening ended about seven hours later, as the 22-year-old woman later testified, she had been "forced" to drink nearly three cups of mixture of orange soda and vodka and had been disrobed, ogled, fondled, berated and sodomized by at least seven St. John's students, including her acquaintance from the rifle club. The debauchery began in a house near the Jamaica, Queens, campus; then she was transported, semiconscious and disheveled, to a second house where a party was underway and the assault continued.
>
> Later, she said, she heard the men debating what to do with her. One asked, "What if she talks?" Another replied: "So what? Remember Tawana Brawley? Nobody believed her. Nobody will believe this one."[21]

And, of course, he was partially right. After months of publicity and an extensive trial, after two students pleaded guilty to lesser charges while essentially corroborating the young woman's story, three of the defendants were found not guilty and the final defendant interrupted his trial to plead guilty to sharply reduced charges but, in so doing, admitted that he had done everything he had been accused of.

As newspaper accounts stressed, the case "rocked" the ten-thousand-student university, the country's largest Roman Catholic institution of higher education, and the surrounding community. Adding to the explosive nature of the accusations—that someone the female student knew took her back to a house where several of the accused lived and plied her with alcohol, and then, when she was on the couch with her eyes closed, appearing helpless, he and other male students fondled the woman and made her perform oral sex on them—all six defendants were white and the young woman was black. None of the six defendants were convicted of the original felony charges against them.

Perhaps the most disturbing analysis of rape on college campuses is anthropologist Peggy Reeves Sanday's shocking study of fraternity gang rape. Also known as "gang banging," the phenomenon of "pulling train" refers to a "group of men lining up like train cars to take turns having sex with the same woman."[22] Bernice Sandler, one of the authors of a report issued in 1985 by the American Association of American Colleges, has reported finding more than seventy-five documented cases of gang rape in recent years. These incidents, which occurred at all kinds of institutions—"public, private, religiously affiliated, Ivy League, large and small"—share a common pattern:

> A vulnerable young woman, one who is seeking acceptance or who is high on drugs or alcohol, is taken to a room. She may or may not agree to have sex with one man. She then passes out, or is too weak or scared to protest, and a train of men have sex with her. Sometimes the young woman's drinks are spiked without her knowledge, and when she is approached by several men in a locked room, she reacts with confusion and panic. Whether too weak to protest, frightened, or unconscious, as has been the case in quite a number of instances, anywhere from two to eleven or more men have sex with her.[23]

The specific case that is the centerpiece of Sanday's study involves a young woman, Laurel, who was known to have serious drinking and drug problems. The evening in question, she was drunk on beer and had taken "four hits of LSD" before going to a fraternity-house party. According to her account, she fell asleep after the party in a room on the first floor. When she awoke, she was undressed. One of the fraternity members dressed her and carried her upstairs, where she claimed she was raped by five or six "guys." She said, in Sanday's words, that she was "barely conscious and lacked the strength to push them off her."[24] This account was corroborated by another woman, a friend of the fraternity members, who felt that, because Laurel was incapable of consenting to sex, she had been raped. The fraternity brothers never publicly admitted to any wrongdoing; they claimed throughout the investigation that Laurel had "lured" them into a "gang bang," which they preferred to call an "express."

In this study, Sanday claims that "coercive sexual behavior" is prevalent on college campuses and that rape is "the means by which men programmed for violence and control use sexual aggression to display masculinity and to induct younger men into masculine roles."[25] Sanday continues her analysis:

> [The] male participants brag about their masculinity and . . . [the] female participants are degraded to the status of what the boys call "red meat" or "fish." The whole scenario joins men in a no-holds-barred orgy of togetherness. The woman whose body facilitates all of this is sloughed off at the end like a used condom. She may be called a "nympho" or the men may believe that they seduced her—a

practice known as "working a yes out"—through promises of becoming a little sister, by getting her drunk, by promising her love, or by some other means. Those men who object to this kind of behavior run the risk of being labeled "wimps" or, even worse in their eyes, "gays" or "faggots."26

As we have seen, a variety of groups have been perceived and treated as "the Other"—in Patricia Hill Collins' words, "viewed as an object to be manipulated and controlled"27—on college campuses over the past few years. Though many of the bias incidents have involved racial enmity and misunderstanding, anti-Semitism, homophobia, and blatant sexism have also been catalysts for hostile acts. Many academic institutions, concerned about overtly demeaning, sometimes violent behavior as well as the far more subtle denigration of women and other minority groups, have attempted to address these problems through a variety of measures: speech codes; orientation programs for entering students that stress respect for diversity and the importance of civility; curriculum changes that focus on multiculturalism; hiring policies whose goals are to increase the number of women and members of minority groups on the faculty and staff of the institution; and the recruitment of more students of color. These measures, often employed to counter the ignorance, ethnocentrism, and anger within the college community, have themselves become the subject of controversy and debate. Both academic and popular discourse have focused far more on political correctness, on affirmative action, and on changes in the curriculum than on the hate incidents and violence that continue to occur. Speech codes at the Universities of Wisconsin and Michigan became front-page news; discussions of what and who was p.c. seemed ubiquitous; and the pros and cons of a multicultural curriculum have been debated in university governing bodies and editorial meetings across the country.

NOTES

1. Patricia Hill Collins, *Black Feminist Thought: Knowledge, Consciousness, and the Politics of Empowerment* (Boston: Unwin Hyman, 1990), pp. 68, 225.
2. Isabel Wilkerson, "Racial Tension Erupts Tearing a College Apart," *New York Times,* April 13, 1992.
3. Diana Jean Schemo, "Anger over List Divides Blacks and College Town," *New York Times,* September 27, 1992.
4. "College Official Who Released List of Black Students Is Demoted," *New York Times,* September 18, 1992.
5. N'Tanya Lee, "Racism on College Campuses," *Focus* (monthly magazine of the Joint Center for Political Studies), Special Social Policy Issue, August/September 1989.
6. Michele Collison, "For Many Freshmen, Orientation Now Includes Efforts to Promote Racial Understanding," *Chronicle of Higher Education,* September 7, 1988.
7. Denise Goodman, "Racial Attack Jolts U. of Maine," *Boston Globe,* February 23, 1991.
8. "ADL 1992 Audit of Anti-Semitic Incidents: Overall Numbers Decrease but Campus Attacks Are Up," *On the Frontline* (monthly newsletter published by the Anti-Defamation League), March 1993.

9. "Anti-Semitic Slurs Are Painted: Campus Reacts," *New York Times*, February 11, 1990.

10. Sharon Kaplan, "Hillel Hut Vandalized with Anti-Semitic Graffiti," *Daily Sundial* (California State University, Northridge), September 26, 1991.

11. James Barron, "Professor Steps off a Plane into a Furor over His Words," *New York Times*, August 15, 1991.

12. "Anti-Gay Shirts Oust Syracuse Fraternity," *USA Today*, June 28, 1991.

13. "Magazine Issue on Homosexuality Leads to Rallies," *New York Times*, December 22, 1991.

14. Dirk Johnson, "Coach's Anti-Gay Stand Ignites Rage," *New York Times*, March 15, 1992.

15. "Alabama Denies Aid to Gay Student Groups," *New York Times*, May 16, 1992.

16. Carol Burke, "Dames at Sea," *New Republic*, August 17, 24, 1992, pp. 16–20.

17. Katrina Foley, "Terror on Campus: Fraternities Training Grounds for Rape and Misogyny," *New Directions for Women*, September/October 1992, pp. 15, 29.

18. William Celis, 3d, "After Rape Charge, 2 Lives Hurt and 1 Destroyed," *New York Times*, November 12, 1990.

19. Peggy Reeves Sanday, *Fraternity Gang Rape: Sex, Brotherhood, and Privilege on Campus* (New York: New York University Press, 1990), pp. 23–24.

20. Tamar Lewin, "Tougher Laws Mean More Cases Are Called Rape," *New York Times*, May 27, 1991.

21. E. R. Shipp, "St. John's Case Offers 2 Versions of Events," *New York Times*, July 6, 1991.

22. Sanday, *Fraternity Gang Rape*, p. 1.

23. Ibid., pp. 1–2.

24. Ibid., p. 6.

25. Ibid., pp. 8–9.

26. Ibid., p. 11.

27. Collins, *Black Feminist Thought*, p. 69.

40

BLACK AND FEMALE
Reflections on Graduate School

BELL HOOKS

Searching for material to read in a class about women and race, I found an essay in *Heresies: Racism is the Issue* that fascinated me. I realized that it was one of the first written discussions of the struggles black English majors (and particularly black women) face when we study at predominately white universities. The essay, "On Becoming A Feminist Writer," is by

From *Talking Back: Thinking Feminist, Thinking Black*, by bell hooks, 1989, pp. 55–61. Reprinted by permission of South End Press.

Carole Gregory. She begins by explaining that she has been raised in racially segregated neighborhoods but that no one had ever really explained "white racism or white male sexism." Psychically, she was not prepared to confront head-on these aspects of social reality, yet they were made visible as soon as she registered for classes:

> Chewing on a brown pipe, a white professor said, "English departments do not hire Negroes or women!" Like a guillotine, his voice sought to take my head off. Racism in my hometown was an economic code of etiquette which stifled Negroes and women.
>
> "If you are supposed to explain these courses, that's all I want," I answered. Yet I wanted to kill this man. Only my conditioning as a female kept me from striking his volcanic red face. My murderous impulses were raging.

Her essay chronicles her struggles to pursue a discipline which interests her without allowing racism or sexism to defeat and destroy her intellectual curiosity, her desire to teach. The words of this white male American Literature professor echo in her mind years later when she finds employment difficult, when she confronts the reality that black university teachers of English are rare. Although she is writing in 1982, she concludes her essay with the comment:

> Many years ago, an American Literature professor had cursed the destiny of "Negroes and women." There was truth in his ugly words. Have you ever had a Black woman for an English teacher in the North? Few of us are able to earn a living. For the past few years, I have worked as an adjunct in English. Teaching brings me great satisfaction; starving does not. . . . I still remember the red color of the face which said, "English departments do not hire Negroes or women." Can women change this indictment? These are the fragments I add to my journal.

Reading Carole Gregory's essay, I recalled that in all my years of studying in English department classes, I had never been taught by a black woman. In my years of teaching, I have encountered students both in English classes and other disciplines who have never been taught by black women. Raised in segregated schools until my sophomore year of high school, I had wonderful black women teachers as role models. It never occurred to me that I would not find them in university classrooms. Yet I studied at four universities—Stanford, University of Wisconsin, University of Southern California, and the University of California, Santa Cruz—and I did not once have the opportunity to study with a black woman English professor. They were never members of the faculty. I considered myself lucky to study with one black male professor at Stanford who was visiting and another at the University of Southern California even though both were reluctant to support and encourage black female students. Despite their sexism and internalized racism, I appreciated them as teachers and felt they affirmed that black scholars could teach literature, could work in English departments. They offered a degree of support and affirmation, however relative, that countered the intense racism and sexism of many white professors.

Changing hiring practices have meant that there are increasingly more black professors in predominately white universities, but their presence only mediates in a minor way the racism and sexism of white professors. During my graduate school years, I dreaded talking face-to-face with white professors, especially white males. I had not developed this dread as an undergraduate because there it was simply assumed that black students, and particularly black female students, were not bright enough to make it in graduate school. While these racist and sexist opinions were rarely directly stated, the message was conveyed through various humiliations that were aimed at shaming students, at breaking our spirit. We were terrorized. As an undergraduate, I carefully avoided those professors who made it clear that the presence of any black students in their classes was not desired. Unlike Carole Gregory's first encounter, they did not make direct racist statements. Instead, they communicated their message in subtle ways—forgetting to call your name when reading the roll, avoiding looking at you, pretending they do not hear you when you speak, and at times ignoring you altogether.

The first time this happened to me I was puzzled and frightened. It was clear to me and all the other white students that the professor, a white male, was directing aggressive mistreatment solely at me. These other students shared with me that it was not likely that I would pass the class no matter how good my work, that the professor would find something wrong with it. They never suggested that this treatment was informed by racism and sexism; it was just that the professor had for whatever "unapparent" reason decided to dislike me. Of course, there were rare occasions when taking a course meant so much to me that I tried to confront racism, to talk with the professor; and there were required courses. Whenever I tried to talk with professors about racism, they always denied any culpability. Often I was told, "I don't even notice that you are black."

In graduate school, it was especially hard to choose courses that would not be taught by professors who were quite racist. Even though one could resist by naming the problem and confronting the person, it was rarely possible to find anyone who could take such accusations seriously. Individual white professors were supported by white-supremacist institutions, by racist colleagues, by hierarchies that placed the word of the professor above that of the student. When I would tell the more supportive professors about racist comments that were said behind closed doors, during office hours, there would always be an expression of disbelief, surprise, and suspicion about the accuracy of what I was reporting. Mostly they listened because they felt it was their liberal duty to do so. Their disbelief, their refusal to take responsibility for white racism made it impossible for them to show authentic concern or help. One professor of 18th century literature by white writers invited me to his office to tell me that he would personally see to it that I would never receive a graduate degree. I, like many other students in the class, had written a paper in a style that he disapproved of, yet only I was given this response. It was often in the very areas of British and American literature where racism abounds in the texts studied that I would encounter racist individuals.

Gradually, I began to shift my interest in early American literature to more modern and contemporary works. This shift was influenced greatly by an encounter with a white male professor of American literature whose racism and sexism was unchecked. In his classes, I, as well as other students, was subjected to racist and sexist jokes. Any of us that he considered should not be in graduate school were the objects of particular scorn and ridicule. When we gave oral presentations, we were told our work was stupid, pathetic, and were not allowed to finish. If we resisted in any way, the situation worsened. When I went to speak with him about his attitude, I was told that I was not really graduate school material, that I should drop out. My anger surfaced and I began to shout, to cry. I remember yelling wildly, "Do you love me? And if you don't love me then how can you have any insight about my concerns and abilities? And who are you to make such suggestions on the basis of one class." He of course was not making a suggestion. His was a course one had to pass to graduate. He was telling me that I could avoid the systematic abuse by simply dropping out. I would not drop out. I continued to work even though it was clear that I would not succeed, even as the persecution became more intense. And even though I constantly resisted.

In time, my spirits were more and more depressed. I began to dream of entering the professor's office with a loaded gun. There I would demand that he listen, that he experience the fear, the humiliation. In my dreams I could hear his pleading voice begging me not to shoot, to remain calm. As soon as I put the gun down he would become his old self again. Ultimately in the dream the only answer was to shoot, to shoot to kill. When this dream became so consistently a part of my waking fantasies, I knew that it was time for me to take a break from graduate school. Even so I felt as though his terrorism had succeeded, that he had indeed broken my spirit. It was this feeling that led me to return to graduate school, to his classes, because I felt I had given him too much power over me and I needed to regain that sense of self and personal integrity that I allowed him to diminish. Through much of my graduate school career, I was told that "I did not have the proper demeanor of a graduate student." In one graduate program, the black woman before me, who was also subjected to racist and sexist aggression, would tell me that they would say she was not as smart as me but she knew her place. I did not know my place. Young white radicals began to use the phrase "student as nigger" precisely to call attention to the way in which hierarchies within universities encouraged domination of the powerless by the powerful. At many universities the proper demeanor of a graduate student is exemplary when that student is obedient, when he or she does not challenge or resist authority.

During graduate school, white students would tell me that it was important not to question, challenge, or resist. Their tolerance level seemed much higher than my own or that of other black students. Critically reflecting on the differences between us, it was apparent that many of the white students were from privileged class backgrounds. Tolerating the humiliations and degradations we were subjected to in graduate school did not radically call into question their integrity, their sense of self-worth. Those of us who were coming from underprivileged class backgrounds, who were black, often were able to attend college only because we had consistently defied those who had attempted to make us believe we were smart but not "smart enough"; guidance counselors who refused to tell us about certain colleges because they already knew we would not be accepted; parents who were not necessarily supportive of graduate work, etc. White students were not living daily in a world outside campus life where they also had to resist degradation, humiliation. To them, tolerating forms of exploitation and domination in graduate school did not evoke images of a lifetime spent tolerating abuse. They would endure certain forms of domination and abuse, accepting it as an initiation process that would conclude when they became the person in power. In some ways they regarded graduate school and its many humiliations as a game, and they submitted to playing the role of subordinate. I and many other students, especially non-white students from non-privileged backgrounds, were unable to accept and play this "game." Often we were ambivalent about the rewards promised. Many of us were not seeking to be in a position of power over others. Though we wished to teach, we did not want to exert coercive authoritarian rule over others. Clearly those students who played the game best were usually white males and they did not face discrimination, exploitation, and abuse in many other areas of their lives.

Many black graduate students I knew were concerned about whether we were striving to participate in structures of domination and were uncertain about whether we could assume positions of authority. We could not envision assuming oppressive roles. For some of us, failure, failing, being failed began to look like a positive alternative, a way out, a solution. This was especially true for those students who felt they were suffering mentally, who felt that they would never be able to recover a sense of wholeness or well-being. In recent years, campus awareness of the absence of support for international students who have many conflicts and dilemmas in an environment that does not acknowledge their cultural codes has led to the development of support networks. Yet there has been little recognition that there are black students and other non-white students who suffer similar problems, who come from backgrounds where we learned different cultural codes. For example, we may learn that it is important not to accept coercive authoritarian rule from someone who is not a family elder—hence we may have difficulties accepting strangers assuming such a role.

Not long ago, I was at a small party with faculty from a major liberal California university, which until recently had no black professors in the English department who were permanent staff, though they were sometimes visiting scholars. One non-white faculty member and myself began to talk about the problems facing black graduate students studying in English departments. We joked about the racism within English departments, commenting that other disciplines were slightly more willing to accept study of the lives and works of non-white people yet such work is rarely affirmed in English departments where the study of literature usually consists of many works by white men and a few by white women. We talked about how some departments were struggling to change. Speaking about his department, he commented that they have only a few black graduate students, sometimes none, that at one time two black students, one male and one female, had been accepted and both had serious mental health problems. At departmental meetings, white faculty suggested that this indicated that black students just did not have the wherewithal to succeed in this graduate program. For a time, no black students were admitted. His story revealed that part of the burden these students may have felt, which many of us have felt, is that our performance will have future implications for all black students and this knowledge heightens one's performance anxiety from the very beginning. Unfortunately, racist biases often lead departments to see the behavior of one black student as an indication of the way all black students will perform academically. Certainly, if individual white students have difficulty adjusting or succeeding within a graduate program, it is not seen as an indication that all other white students will fail.

The combined forces of racism and sexism often make the black female graduate experience differ in kind from that of the black male experience. While he may be subjected to racial biases, his maleness may serve to mediate the extent to which he will be attacked, dominated, etc. Often it is assumed that black males are better able to succeed at graduate school in English than black females. While many white scholars may be aware of a black male intellectual tradition, they rarely know about black female intellectuals. African-American intellectual traditions, like those of white people, have been male-dominated. People who know the names of W.E.B. Du Bois or Martin Delaney may have never heard of Mary Church Terrell or Anna Cooper. The small numbers of black women in permanent positions in academic institutions do not constitute a significant presence, one strong enough to challenge racist and sexist biases. Often the only black woman white professors have encountered is a domestic worker in their home. Yet there are no sociological studies that I know of which examine whether a group who has been seen as not having intellectual capability will automatically be accorded respect and recognition if they enter positions that suggest they are representative scholars. Often black women are such an "invisible presence" on campuses that many students may not be aware that any black women teach at the universities they attend.

Given the reality of racism and sexism, being awarded advanced degrees does not mean that black women will achieve equity with black men or other groups in the profession. Full-time, non-white women comprise less than 3 percent of the total faculty on most campuses. Racism and sexism, particularly on the graduate level, shape and influence both the academic performance and employment of black female academics. During my years of graduate work in English, I was often faced with the hostility of white students who felt that because I was black and female I would have no trouble finding a job. This was usually the response from professors as well if I expressed fear of not finding employment. Ironically, no one ever acknowledged that we were never taught by any of these black women who were taking all the jobs. No one wanted to see that perhaps racism and sexism militate against the hiring of black women even though we are seen as a group that will be given priority, preferential status. Such assumptions, which are usually rooted in the logic of affirmative action hiring, do not include recognition of the ways most universities do not strive to attain diversity of faculty and that often diversity means hiring one non-white person, one black person. When I and other black women graduate students surveyed English departments in the United States, we did not see masses of black women and rightly felt concerned about our futures.

Moving around often, I attended several graduate schools but finally finished my work at the University of California, Santa Cruz where I found support despite the prevalence of racism and sexism. Since I had much past experience, I was able to talk with white faculty members before entering the program about whether they would be receptive and supportive of my desire to focus on African-American writers. I was given positive reassurance that proved accurate. More and more, there are university settings where black female graduate students and black graduate students can study in supportive atmospheres. Racism and sexism are always present yet they do not necessarily shape all areas of graduate experience. When I talk with black female graduate students working in English departments, I hear that many of the problems have not changed, that they experience the same intense isolation and loneliness that characterized my experience. This is why I think it is important that black women in higher education write and talk about our experiences, about survival strategies. When I was having a very difficult time, I read *Working It Out*. Despite the fact that the academics who described the way in which sexism had shaped their academic experience in graduate school were white women, I was encouraged by their resistance, by their perseverance, by their success. Reading their stories helped me to feel less alone. I wrote this essay because of the many conversations I have had with black female graduate students who despair, who are frustrated, who are fearful that the experiences they are having are unique. I want them to know that they are not alone, that the problems that arise, the obstacles created by racism and sexism are real—that they do exist—they do hurt but they are not insurmountable. Perhaps these words will give solace, will intensify their courage, and renew their spirit.

41

TALES OUT OF MEDICAL SCHOOL

ADRIANE FUGH-BERMAN, M.D.

With the growth of the women's health movement and the influx of women into medical schools, there has been abundant talk of a new enlightenment among physicians. Last summer, many Americans were shocked when Frances Conley, a neurosurgeon on the faculty of Stanford University's medical school, resigned her position, citing "pervasive sexism." Conley's is a particularly elite and male-dominated subspecialty, but her story is not an isolated one. I graduated from the Georgetown University School of Medicine in 1988, and while medical training is a sexist process anywhere, Georgetown built disrespect for women into its curriculum.

A Jesuit school, most recently in the news as the alma mater of William Kennedy Smith, Georgetown has an overwhelmingly white, male and conservative faculty. At a time when women made up one-third of all medical students in the United States, and as many as one-half at some schools, my class was 73 percent male and more than 90 percent white.

The prevailing attitude toward women was demonstrated on the first day of classes by my anatomy instructor, who remarked that our elderly cadaver "must have been a Playboy bunny" before instructing us to cut off her large breasts and toss them into the thirty-gallon trash can marked "cadaver waste." Barely hours into our training, we were already being taught that there was nothing to be learned from examining breasts. Given the fact that one out of nine American women will develop breast cancer in her lifetime, to treat breasts as extraneous tissue seemed an appalling waste of an educational opportunity, as well as a not-so-subtle message about the relative importance of body parts. How many of my classmates now in practice, I wonder, regularly examine the breasts of their female patients?

My classmates learned their lesson of disrespect well. Later in the year one carved a tick-tack-toe on a female cadaver and challenged others to play. Another gave a languorous sigh after dissecting female genitalia, as if he had just had sex. "Guess I should have a cigarette now," he said.

Ghoulish humor is often regarded as a means by which med students overcome fear and anxiety. But it serves a darker purpose as well: Depersonalizing our cadaver was good preparation for depersonalizing our patients later. Further on in my training, an ophthalmologist would yell at me when I hesitated to place a small instrument meant to measure eye pressure

---

From the January 20, 1992 issue of *The Nation*. Reprinted with permission.

on a fellow student's cornea because I was afraid it would hurt. "You have to learn to treat patients as lab animals," he snarled at me.

On the first day of an emergency medicine rotation in our senior year, students were asked who had had experience placing a central line (an intravenous line placed into a major vein under the clavicle or in the neck). Most of the male students raised their hands. None of the women did. For me, it was graphic proof of inequity in teaching; the men had had the procedure taught to them, but the women had not. Teaching rounds were often, for women, a spectator sport. One friend told me how she craned her neck to watch a physician teach a minor surgical procedure to a male student; when they were done the physician handed her his dirty gloves to discard. I have seen a male attending physician demonstrate an exam on a patient and then wade through several female medical students to drag forth a male in order to teach it to him. This sort of discrimination was common and quite unconscious: The women just didn't register as medical students to some of the doctors. Female students, for their part, tended (like male ones) to gloss over issues that might divert attention, energy or focus from the all-important goal of getting through their training. "Oh, they're just of the old school," a female classmate remarked to me, as if being ignored by our teachers was really rather charming, like having one's hand kissed.

A woman resident was giving a radiology presentation and I felt mesmerized. Why did I feel so connected and involved? It suddenly occurred to me that the female physician was regularly meeting my eyes; most of the male residents and attendings made eye contact only with the men.

"Why are women's brains smaller than men's?" asked a surgeon of a group of male medical students in the doctors' lounge (I was in the room as well, but was apparently invisible). "Because they're missing logic!" Guffaws all around.

Such instances of casual sexism are hardly unique to Georgetown, or indeed to medical schools. But at Georgetown female students also had to contend with outright discrimination of a sort most Americans probably think no longer exists in education. There was one course women were not allowed to take. The elective in sexually transmitted diseases required an interview with the head of the urology department, who was teaching the course. Those applicants with the appropriate genitalia competed for invitations to join the course (a computer was supposed to assign us electives, which we had ranked in order of preference, but that process had been circumvented for this course). Three women who requested an interview were told that the predominantly gay male clinic where the elective was held did not allow women to work there. This was news to the clinic's executive director, who stated that women were employed in all capacities.

The women who wanted to take the course repeatedly tried to meet with the urologist, but he did not return our phone calls. (I had not applied for the course, but became involved as an advocate for the women who wanted to take it.) We figured out his schedule, waylaid him in the hall and insisted that a meeting be set up.

At this meeting, clinic representatives disclosed that a survey had been circulated years before to the clientele in order to ascertain whether women workers would be accepted; 95 percent of the clients voted to welcome women. They were also asked whether it was acceptable to have medical students working at the clinic; more than 90 percent approved. We were then told that these results could not be construed to indicate that clients did not mind women medical students; the clients would naturally have assumed that "medical student" meant "male medical student." Even if that were true, we asked, if 90 percent of clients did not mind medical students and 95 percent did not mind women, couldn't a reasonable person assume that female medical students would be acceptable? No, we were informed. Another study would have to be done.

We raised formal objections to the school. Meanwhile, however, the entire elective process had been postponed by the dispute, and the blame for the delay and confusion was placed on us. The hardest part of the struggle, indeed, was dealing with the indifference of most of our classmates——out of 206, maybe a dozen actively supported us——and with the intense anger of the ten men who had been promised places in the course.

"Just because you can't take this course," one of the men said to me, "why do you want to ruin it for the rest of us?" It seemed incredible to me that I had to argue that women should be allowed to take the same courses as men. The second or third time someone asked me the same question, I suggested that if women were not allowed to participate in the same curriculum as the men, then in the interest of fairness we should get a 50 percent break on our $22,500 annual tuition. My colleague thought that highly unreasonable.

Eventually someone in administration realized that not only were we going to sue the school for discrimination but that we had an open-and-shut case. The elective in sexually transmitted diseases was canceled, and from its ashes arose a new course, taught by the same man, titled "Introduction to Urology." Two women were admitted. When the urologist invited students to take turns working with him in his office, he scheduled the two female students for the same day——one on which only women patients were to be seen (a nifty feat in a urology practice).

The same professor who so valiantly tried to prevent women from learning anything unseemly about sexually transmitted diseases was also in charge of the required course in human sexuality (or, as I liked to call it, he-man sexuality). Only two of the eleven lectures focused on women; of the two lectures on homosexuality, neither mentioned lesbians. The psychiatrist who co-taught the class treated us to one lecture that amounted to an apology for rape: Aggression, even hostility, is normal in sexual relations between a man and a woman, he said, and inhibition of aggression in men can lead to impotence.

We were taught that women do not need orgasms for a satisfactory sex life, although men, of course, do; and that inability to reach orgasm is only a problem for women with "unrealistic expectations." I had heard that particular lecture before in the backseat of a car during high school. The urologist told us of couples who came to him for sex counseling because the woman was not having orgasms; he would reassure them that this is normal and the couple would be relieved. (I would gamble that the female half of the couple was anything but relieved.) We learned that oral sex is primarily a homosexual practice, and that sexual dysfunction in women is often caused by "working." In the women-as-idiots department, we learned that when impotent men are implanted with permanently rigid penile prostheses, four out of five wives can't tell that their husbands have had the surgery.

When dealing with sexually transmitted diseases in which both partners must be treated, we were advised to vary our notification strategy according to marital status. If the patient is a single man, the doctor should write the diagnosis down on a prescription for his partner to bring to her doctor. If the patient is a married man, however, the doctor should contact the wife's gynecologist and arrange to have her treated without knowledge of what she is being treated for. How to notify the male partner of a female patient, married or single, was never revealed.

To be fair, women were not the only subjects of outmoded concepts of sexuality. We also received anachronistic information about men. Premature ejaculation, defined as fewer than ten thrusts(!), was to be treated by having the man think about something unpleasant, or by having the woman painfully squeeze, prick or pinch the penis. Aversive therapies such as these have long been discredited.

Misinformation about sexuality and women's health peppered almost every course (I can't recall any egregious wrongs in biochemistry). Although vasectomy and abortion are among the safest of all surgical procedures, in our lectures vasectomy was presented as fraught with long-term complications and abortion was never mentioned without the words "peritonitis" and "death" in the same sentence. These distortions represented Georgetown's Catholic bent at its worst. (We were not allowed to perform, or even watch, abortion procedures in our affiliated hospitals.) On a lighter note, one obstetrician assisting us in the anatomy lab told us that women shouldn't lift heavy weights because their pelvic organs will fall out between their legs.

In our second year, several women in our class started a women's group, which held potlucks and offered presentations and performances: A former midwife talked about her profession, a student demonstrated belly dancing, another discussed dance therapy and one sang selections from *A Chorus Line*. This heavy radical feminist activity created great hostility among our male classmates. Announcements of our meetings were defaced and women in the group began receiving threatening calls at home from someone who claimed to be watching the listener and who would then accurately describe what she was wearing. One woman received obscene notes in her school mailbox, including one that contained a rape threat. I received insulting cards in typed envelopes at my home address; my mother received similar cards at hers.

We took the matter to the dean of student affairs, who told us it was "probably a dental student" and suggested we buy loud whistles to blow into the phone when we received unwanted calls. We demanded that the school attempt to find the perpetrator and expel him. We were told that the school would not expel the student but that counseling would be advised.

The women's group spread the word that we were collecting our own information on possible suspects and that any information on bizarre, aggressive, antisocial or misogynous behavior among the male medical students should be reported to our designated representative. She was inundated with a list of classmates who fit the bill. Finally, angered at the school's indifference, we solicited the help of a prominent woman faculty member. Although she shamed the dean into installing a hidden camera across from the school mailboxes to monitor unusual behavior, no one was ever apprehended.

Georgetown University School of Medicine churns out about 200 physicians a year. Some become good doctors despite their training, but many will pass on the misinformation and demeaning attitudes handed down to them. It is a shame that Georgetown chooses to perpetuate stereotypes and reinforce prejudices rather than help students acquire the up-to-date information and sensitivity that are vital in dealing with AIDS, breast cancer, teen pregnancy and other contemporary epidemics. Female medical students go through an ordeal, but at least it ends with graduation. It is the patients who ultimately suffer the effects of sexist medical education.

42

SCHOLARLY STUDIES OF MEN
The New Field Is an Essential Complement to Women's Studies

HARRY BROD

In something of a turn of the tables, scholars in women's studies are having to decide what to do about a new field that is emerging in academe. The new kid asking to enter the club is "men's studies."

For some feminist scholars, the phenomenon seems either preposterous or dangerous, or more likely both. After all, the traditional curriculum that women's studies sought to reform was, in essence, men's studies. Other feminists, however, believe that the new field of men's studies is really a welcome

Originally published in *Chronicle of Higher Education,* March 1990. Copyright © 1990 by Harry Brod. Reprinted by permission of the author.

extension of feminism's intellectual insights into hitherto male terrain. I believe that the field of men's studies is not only compatible with women's studies, but also an essential complement.

Men's studies begin by accepting as valid feminism's critique of traditional scholarship for its androcentric bias in generalizing from men to all human beings. The field adds the perspective that this bias not only excludes women and/or judges them to be deficient, but also ignores whatever may be specific to men *as men*, rather than as generic humans. The field also invokes feminist concepts that "gender" is not natural difference, but constructed power, to argue that the multiple forms of masculinities and femininities need to be re-examined.

The field of men's studies, for most of us anyway, thus is rooted in a feminist commitment to challenge existing concepts of gender. The debate within our still-nascent field over that commitment, however, has made some feminists skeptical about our entire enterprise. They see in the call for a new "gender studies" focused on both men and women the possibility that women's priorities and standpoints will again be subsumed and ignored under generic labels. Other feminists, though, find that the idea of a broadly conceived "gender studies," in which "gender" describes power and not just difference, does reflect the underlying conceptualization of their field. We should recognize, however, that the meaning of terms is still in flux. At my own institution, for example, our current solution is to develop a program in "Women's and Gender Studies."

Feminists' legitimate fear of once again having women's discourse subordinated to men's should not blind us to the very real and much-needed intellectual project that the field of men's studies is undertaking. To simplify a more extended argument, I believe the field is an essential complement to women's studies because neither gender ultimately can be studied in isolation. Gender is, itself, a relational concept: Masculinities and femininities are not isolated "roles," but contested relationships.

But it does not follow from my argument for men's studies as an intellectual enterprise that the field must be established in any particular form in academic institutions. Such decisions should be made by women in women's studies. And any efforts to divert resources from women's studies to men's studies must be resisted; funds for the new men's studies must come from the old.

The new field has important implications for scholarship. For example, many explanations of the "gender gap" in political voting patterns have failed to see that it takes two to make a gap. Having noted the appearance of a "gap," social scientists have rushed to explain the changes in women that have produced it. Yet some of the evidence shows that the gap was produced more by a shift in men's than in women's political identification and voting patterns. By trying to understand the mutability and diversity of masculinities, men's studies avoid the pitfall of associating change only with women while assuming male constancy—a sexist bias.

By pointedly taking up the question of power relations among men in addition to those between the sexes, the new field also allows for a more differentiated conception of patriarchy. For the power of the real and symbolic father is not simply that of male over female, but also that of heterosexual over homosexual, one generation over another, and other constellations of authority. The field forces us to ask, Why does society privilege some men over others, even as it gives all men power over women? Why do so many of our founding myths contain fathers willing to kill their sons—the violence committed and permitted by Abraham against Isaac, Laius against Oedipus, the Christian God the Father against Jesus?

Further, the field of men's studies is not simply calling for sensitivity to diversity, though it surely does that, but also tries to apply an understanding of difference gained from radical feminism to men, arguing that sexuality is as socially constructed as identity. The field therefore is also forging special links to gay studies.

Two current phenomena show the need for men's studies to transcend a white, middle-class origin and orientation: the large number of suicides among Vietnam-era veterans and the huge number of college-age black men in prison rather than in college. When we speak of men's issues, there really is more to consider than the existential anxieties of middle-aged, middle-class executives and fathers, popular media treatments notwithstanding.

A final example from my own experience highlights the way feminism has helped me to ask new questions about men. I have noticed in recent years that many of the female political activists I know have devoted increasing attention to women's issues, for example moving from the peace movement to the women's peace movement or from environmentalism to the fusion of ecological and feminist concerns called ecofeminism.

At first, I simply contrasted this to the conventional wisdom that people become more conservative, *i.e.,* more "mature," with age. But I also recalled that the women's movement has been said to differ from others precisely because its members tend to become more radical as they age; it took only brief reflection to identify the conventional dictum as a male norm. Accordingly, I then asked myself what it was about women's lives that made them different. As I was coming up with various plausible answers I suddenly caught myself. I realized that I was committing the usual error of looking only to women to explain difference. In fact, as I started to see, if one believes as I do that there is validity in various radical social critiques, then the women's pattern should be the norm, as life experiences increasingly validate early perceptions of biased treatment of certain groups. Thus the question should not be, "What happens to women to radicalize them?" but rather "What happens to men to deradicalize them?" That question, more for men's studies than for women's studies, can open up fruitful areas of inquiry.

Indeed, I believe that any strategy for fundamental feminist transformation requires a more informed understanding of men. By exposing and demystifying the culture of male dominance from the inside out, the field of men's studies offers both women and subordinated men the empowerment such knowledge brings.

By elucidating the many and varied prices of male power—the drawbacks and limitations of traditional roles—the field helps motivate men to make common cause with feminist struggles, though not, it must be said, on the basis of any simple cost-benefit analysis, since the price men pay still purchases more than it pays for.

The field of men's studies, then, emerges not as some counterweight or corrective to women's studies, but as the extension and radicalization of women's studies. For it is the adoption of thoroughly women-centered perspectives, taking women as norm rather than "other," that helps us ask new questions about men.

PART VIII
Paid Work and Unemployment

Nearly a quarter of all the children in the United States under the age of six live in poverty.

U.S. CENSUS BUREAU[1]

. . . women have been catching up with men in earnings at a rate of one-third of a percent a year. At this rate of progress, the sexes will receive equal pay in the year 2083.

BARBARA RESKIN AND IRENE PADAVIC[2]

The last chapter revealed that even if we have equality in education, this alone cannot produce equality in society. Once people enter or attempt to enter the workforce, they face two major obstacles: the economic structure blocks many people from finding any type of work at all; and discrimination in the workplace limits the progress of many. Our economic system privileges a small proportion of the population with large amounts of wealth and leaves a huge proportion with varying degrees of economic difficulty, including brutal poverty. For example, the richest fifth of the U.S. population holds 79 percent of household wealth (houses, cars, stocks, bonds, cash, and so on). At the other end of the spectrum, a fifth of U.S. children and 15 percent of the entire population live in poverty.[3]

Progressive economists debate ways to redistribute U.S. wealth more fairly, by creating a more socialistic economic structure, closing tax loopholes that benefit the rich, or redistributing some of the defense budget to social services and education. But politicians continue to support benefits for the rich and to cut social services. Many women on welfare struggle to provide basic needs for themselves and their children. Women and men face the effects of discrimination in the workplace on the basis of gender, race, sexual orientation, age, or ability. This discrimination includes sexual and other harassment, blocked access to promotion, and wage gaps that privilege the earnings of men over women and white people over people of color—occupations dominated by women or people of color generally have lower pay scales.[4]

As Mickelson and Smith state in Part VII, an economy in which the number of higher-paying industrial jobs is shrinking is a difficult place to earn a decent living. The dearth of well-paying jobs combined with systematic discrimination against many groups leaves large numbers of people without adequate income.[5] Even middle-class people are struggling to hold their own, no longer able to assume that they will do as well as their parents. In fact, many cannot afford to buy houses like the ones they grew up in, and others cannot buy houses at all.[6]

This chapter examines the experiences of some people who are trying to survive within the U.S. economic structure. We begin with an essay in which welfare activists Diane Dujon, Judy Gradford, and Dottie Stevens discuss the welfare system and its catch-22s. As they point out, many single women are struggling to hold families together at the margins of the economic order. One of the difficulties they face is low entry-level wages and salaries. For those without advanced education or training, entry-level jobs barely pay enough to keep a family fed, clothed, and housed, making the purchase of health insurance and day care impossible. Without a second income, poor families are trapped in an unsatisfactory, underfunded welfare system that is, itself, under siege by politicians who want to slash government subsidies to social programs.[7]

The next two articles address discrimination at work. Ben Fong-Torres talks about negative stereotypes of Asian men and how they interfere with upward mobility in the TV news industry. He asks, "Why are there no male Asian anchor*men* on TV?" Then sociologists Barbara Reskin and Irene Padavic address gender and race differences in promotion rates and in the ability to use authority in the workplace. They recommend how workers can improve this situation, and they discuss how current legislation can be used to discourage discrimination in the workplace. Legislation is effective only if people who experience discrimination are willing to use it and if enforcement agencies do their part. Reskin and Padavik compare women's promotions to men's, citing Christine Williams' metaphor of men in female-dominant careers who ride a "glass escalator" to the top. Meanwhile, women in male-dominant careers frequently hit glass ceilings—places beyond which they cannot go for reasons they sometimes cannot see.[8]

The next three authors discuss how they have resisted oppressive attitudes and discrimination at work. Barbara Trees, a union carpenter in New York City, talks of her ongoing battle to minimize the presence of insulting pornography at her work sites. Craig G. Harris, a Black gay man harassed for wearing an earring to work, successfully sues his employer for discrimination. This chapter concludes with a piece by Stan Gray, in which he describes his work as an ally to women workers who are about to join his shop in a factory. For anyone interested in establishing gender equality in the workplace, Gray's experience documents how difficult this challenge can be and how the participation of male allies is crucial to this effort.

This chapter examines the economic limits in many people's lives, identifies a few of the many groups who are subject to discrimination, and provides suggestions for empowerment at personal, group, and policy levels.

NOTES

1. Cited in Greg Mantsios, "Class in America: Myths and Realities," in Paula S. Rothenberg, ed., *Race, Class, and Gender in the United States: An Integrated Study*, 3rd ed. (New York: St. Martin's Press, 1995), p. 133.

2. Barbara Reskin and Irene Padavic, *Women and Men at Work* (Thousand Oaks, CA: Pine Forge Press, 1994), p. 126.

3. Mantsios, *Class in America*, p. 133.

4. Reskin and Padavik, *Women and Men at Work,* pp. 118–120.

5. For a comprehensive discussion of gender and the economy, see Reskin and Padavic, *Women and Men at Work,* especially pp. 101–126 and 143–164. For a discussion of discrimination against gay men in the workforce, see Martin P. Levine, "The Status of Gay Men in the Workplace," in Michael S. Kimmel and Michael A. Messner, eds., *Men's Lives*, 3rd ed. (Boston: Allyn & Bacon, 1995), pp. 212–224. Michelle Fine and Adrienne Asch report that it is estimated that between 65 and 76 percent of women with disabilities are unemployed: "Disabled Women: Sexism without the Pedestal," in Mary Jo Deegan and Nancy A. Brooks, eds., *Women and Disability: The Double Handicap* (New Brunswick, NJ: Transaction, 1985), pp. 6–22.

6. Katherine S. Newman, *Declining Fortunes: The Withering of the American Dream* (New York: Basic Books, 1993).

7. For more information about the economics of welfare, see Randy Albelda and Chris Tilly, *Glass Ceilings and Bottomless Pits: Women and Poverty in Massachusetts* (Boston: Women's Statewide Legislative Network, 1994).

8. For a more complete discussion of the glass escalator effect, see Christine Williams, "Riding the Glass Escalator," in *Still a Man's World: Men Who Do Women's Work* (Berkeley: University of California Press, 1995).

43

REPORTS FROM THE FRONT
Welfare Mothers Up in ARMS

DIANE DUJON, JUDY GRADFORD, AND DOTTIE STEVENS

Women on welfare know they are in constant battle to provide for themselves and their children. Their "enemies" are multiple, often including husbands, the welfare bureaucracy, and the attitudes of the general public. In this essay representatives from a group of welfare recipients in the Boston area who have organized into a welfare-rights group called ARMS (Advocacy for Resources for Modern Survival) describe some of the skirmishes they face every day.[1]

From *For Crying Out Loud: Women and Poverty in the U.S.,* Rochelle Lefkowitz and Ann Withorn, eds., 1986, pp. 211–19. Reprinted by permission of Pilgrim Press, Cleveland, Ohio.

Our Lives No Longer Belong To Us

One of my sons was diagnosed as having a high lead level in his blood. The Welfare Department placed my son under protective services and told me that I would have to find another place to live or they would put my son into a foster home. With six children on a welfare budget, it's not easy to find an apartment. And I had to find one within thirty days! To keep the state from taking my son, I was forced to move into the first available housing I could find.

Since I was an emergency case and eligible for a housing subsidy, my name was placed at the top of the list. I had to take the first available unit offered by the Housing Authority. The offer: a brand new town-house-type apartment *fifty miles away* in a white, middle-class suburb!

I knew this move would devastate my family because we would be so far away from our relatives and friends. When you're poor, you have to depend on your family and friends to help you through when you don't have the money to help yourself. At least two or three times every month I take my children to my mother's house to eat. How would we ever be able to get to her house from fifty miles away?

I also knew that my neighbors would not welcome me and my children: a black single woman with six children. I imagined the sneers of the merchants as I paid for my groceries with food stamps and the grunts of the doctors as I pulled out my Medicaid card.

I thought about the problems of transportation that were sure to crop up. How would I get my children to school? What if they got sick; how far was the nearest hospital? I envisioned the seven of us walking for miles with grocery bags. In short, I felt no relief at having found a nice clean apartment within the allotted time, but my back was against the wall. I could not refuse or my son would be put into foster care.

We now live in a totally hostile environment severed from our family and friends. And although we live in a physically beautiful development, life for us is hard. A poor family with no transportation is lost in the suburbs. We are as isolated as if we lived on a remote island in the Pacific.

Situations like the one described by this woman show how our lives no longer belong to us. We have, in effect, married the state. To comply with the conditions of our recipient status, we cannot make any personal decisions ourselves. We must consult the Welfare Department first, and the final decision is theirs. The state is a domineering, chauvinistic spouse.

Politicians often boast or complain about the many services and benefits welfare recipients receive. For us, these services and benefits are the bait that the predatory department uses to entrap us and our families. Like the wily fox, we are driven by hunger to the trap. We must carefully trip the trap, retrieve the bait, and escape, hopefully unscathed. Also similar to the fox, our incompetence can lead to starvation, disease, and death for ourselves and our families.

This may seem an unlikely analogy to some; but the Welfare Department, in its *eagerness* to help us constantly adopts policies that put us in catch-22 situations. We are continuously in a dilemma over whether we should seek the help we desperately need or not. The purportedly "free" social services that are available to us extort a usurer's fee in mental and physical anguish. So, although there are several services available, we are often unable or reluctant to receive them. Below we describe some of the catch-22's that constitute mental cruelty for us.

Catch-22: A Low Budget

The first catch-22 we encounter is living under the conditions set up by the state for recipients. Under penalty of law we are required adequately to house, clothe, feed, and otherwise care for our children on a budget that is two thirds of the amount considered to be at the poverty line. If we fail to fulfill our obligation in the opinion of friends, strangers, neighbors, relatives, enemies, or representatives of the Welfare Department, the state can and *will* take our children from our homes. Anyone can call the department anonymously and report that we are neglecting or abusing our children. With no further questions, the state initiates an investigation, which further jeopardizes our family stability. While it is necessary for the state to protect children from abuse and neglect, a large portion of the investigations are based on unfounded allegations for which no one can be held accountable. It is no easy task to fulfill the basic obligation of surviving on welfare, because we often pay as much as 85 to 95 percent of our income for rent and utilities.

On the other hand, there is no reward for a job well done. If we manage to clothe, feed, and house our children, the risk is the same: at the least, biting remarks from people in public, and at the most, an investigation of fraud.

We are constantly under public scrutiny. We are made to feel uncomfortable if we wear jewelry, or buy a nice blouse, or own a warm coat. It's as if we're not supposed to have families or friends who love us and might give us a birthday or Christmas present. Absolutely no thought is given to the fact that we may have had a life before welfare! Heaven forbid that anyone should honor the great job we must do as shoppers!

There are a few legal ways in which welfare mothers can supplement their monthly grant. Some of these supports are available upon eligibility for Aid to Families with Dependent Children (AFDC); others, termed "social services," have additional individual eligibility requirements. Each has its quota of catch-22's:

Catch-22: Emergency Assistance

I was $300 in arrears with my electric bill. The electric company sent me several reminders, but I didn't have the money to pay my bill. It made me very nervous. It was winter, and although I had oil, if my electricity were turned off, my pilot light would go out and my children would be cold.

I took my bill and the warning notices to my social worker at the Welfare Department. She told me that I could receive up to $500 of Emergency Assistance per year, but that only one such grant could be made in any twelve-month period. However, I could not receive any Emergency Assistance until I received a 'shut-off' notice. She further explained that I should wait because if I received the $300 EA grant, I could not get the additional $200 to which I was entitled that year. I would have to wait twelve months before I could be eligible for another grant. I really wasn't interested in getting all I could, I just wanted to be able to sleep at night; but since I didn't have a shut-off notice, I had no choice but to wait.

I received a shut-off notice when my bill was about $400. I applied for, and received, the EA grant.

The very next year, I was in a similar situation. I again attempted to wait for the shut-off notice. One day I received a notice from the electric company stating that I was scheduled for a "field collection." My social worker reminded me that EA can only be awarded upon my receipt of a shut-off notice. Even though the notice stated that my service would be "interrupted" if I failed to honor the collector, it did not have the specific words *shut off* and, therefore, I was ineligible for EA. I couldn't believe what she was telling me! To become eligible, I had to go to the electric company to ask them to stamp "shut off" on my bill. I was angry that I was being forced to humiliate myself by revealing my personal business to the electric company representative.

Catch-22: Medicaid

Medicaid is the most treasured benefit to families who must depend on AFDC, but it, too, falls short of the expectations of beneficiaries. Doctors, hospitals, druggists, and other health providers often refuse to accept Medicaid patients. The amount of paperwork that is required for each and every patient is tedious and time-consuming. Medicaid also sets limits on the type and amount of treatments it will cover.

Every trip to the doctor is a grueling, costly, and time-consuming event. First, we must search for a doctor or medical facility that will accept Medicaid. If we are lucky enough to have a neighborhood health center nearby, we will often go to the clinic. In either situation, we usually have to wait for hours to receive the medical attention we need. Doctors often remark about the amount of paperwork that is required by the state and the fact that they often have to wait six to eight months to obtain their fees from the state. It is exceedingly distressing to be sick and to have to hear about the doctor's problems.

> I had periodontal disease once. The dentist explained that an infection had settled under my gums and he would have to cut my gums and scrape the infection away. Since I was on Medicaid, I was required to wait until Medicaid approved the dental procedure.
>
> After several weeks, the approval arrived. My dentist informed me that although Medicaid approved the procedure, the amount approved was too low to allow him to use gas as was customary. I had a choice: either I could pay him the difference, and *enjoy* a painless procedure; or I could have the procedure done for the cost Medicaid allotted and he could use novocaine, which would be at least moderately painful.
>
> I didn't have the money to pay the difference, but I knew that if I delayed the operation I stood a good chance of losing my teeth. I decided to brave the novocaine.
>
> The dentist had to cut deep into my gums and the novocaine did nothing for the pain below the surface. I tried hard to be still and keep my mouth open wide, but I was in agony with the pain. The procedure took four hours and required sixty-four stitches and forty-seven injections of novocaine!

Catch-22: Food Stamps

Food Stamps are a symbol of the government's benevolence. Rather than increase the amount of the welfare budget so that we can afford to buy more food, the government *supplements* our budgets with food stamps. As the name suggests, food is all that can be purchased with them. And not much food at that. Households receiving the maximum amount of food stamps receive an average of forty cents per meal per person. All other commodities, such as soap, detergent, toilet paper, diapers, etc., must be separated at the time of purchase. Food, by anyone's definition, is a necessity for sustaining life. Why, then, do we feel as if food is a luxury?

Contrary to public opinion, we pay for these food stamps at a cost significantly higher than a cup of coffee per meal. We pay with the anguish of wondering how we are going to maintain healthy children on $1.20 per day.[2] Food stamps last an average of ten days, depending on the supply of staples (flour, sugar, cereal, salt, spaghetti, etc.) we have on hand; the rest of the month we struggle to keep up with the milk, eggs, juice, fruits, vegetables, and bread so vital to good health. The last two weeks we are challenged to use our imaginations to ensure that our children receive the best nutrition possible. For those of us who are lucky enough to be able to commit "fraud" through friends and relatives, it's a little easier; but for many of us it's often an impossible task!

> The way the food stamp budget is calculated, it's as if our diet is supposed to shrink in the summer. Our fuel costs are counted as an expense in the winter, so we receive more food stamps in the winter and less in the summer. This budget policy is ludicrous because most of our fuel costs in the winter are paid with Fuel Assistance.
>
> I had trouble one time receiving my food stamps. Every month I would have to commute to the next town where my welfare office was located to report that I had not received my food stamps. Each time I was interrogated by the food stamps worker about whether I had cashed my food stamps and was trying to get some more under false pretenses. I had to sign a sworn statement to the effect that I had not received my food stamps before they could issue replacement stamps.
>
> I finally decided that rather than go through the hassle and expense of picking up my food stamps from the welfare office each month, I would purchase a post office box. When I went to inform my worker of my box number, I was told that food stamps could not be sent to a post office box. This policy was supposed to deter fraud. I was forced to continue to pick up my stamps from the welfare office each month.

Food stamp redemption centers are generally located in areas that are virtually inaccessible to those of us without cars. Much of the money we are supposed to be saving with food stamps is spent on transportation to the centers.

> My food stamps usually come on the due date, but my welfare check is often late. This creates a problem for me because I always need the food, but with no cash money it is almost impossible to do the shopping I need to do the first time. I have to make at least two trips to the supermarket: the first trip for food only with the food stamps and the second, when my check comes, to buy soap, cleaning products, etc. Two trips to the store doubles the amount of transportation expenses, too.

Catch-22: Welfare Fraud

Fraud within the welfare system might also be called "devising a way to survive." The federal and state laws call it fraud if a welfare recipient uses up her allotment for any reason and seeks assistance from a friend, relative, or acquaintance (be it ten cents or $10). If she does not report this money to the welfare office, she is technically considered to be defrauding the Welfare Department. Such unrealistic definitions leave all of us vulnerable to fraud and make it difficult to separate honest need from intentional deception.

According to the narrow, unrealistic guidelines of the state and federal government, most or all welfare recipients could be accused of having committed fraud at some time during their ordeal with the welfare system, even though they would not have meant to defraud anyone. We are stuck in a system that inadequately provides for us and that even the social workers know, depends upon our having a "little help from our friends." However, if we are caught doing what we all have to do to survive, we may even be made into an "example" and used to discredit the difficulties faced by women on welfare.

We are poor because we do not receive enough money from the Welfare Department to live decently. If we lack family or friends, we may feel forced to find ways to get a little extra money for our families. Many who have been discovered working to buy Christmas presents, for example, have been brought to court by the Welfare Department and either fined, jailed, or made to pay back all monies received while working.

Although there seems to be large-scale vendor fraud among those who supply Medicaid services, it is seldom investigated or taken to court. While we are hounded for minor infractions, little is done to the unscrupulous doctors, dentists, druggists, nursing-home operators, and others in the health field who blatantly commit welfare fraud as a regular practice. Because of their "respectability" in the community, these providers are in a position to bill Medicaid for services never rendered, and they do so with some regularity. When these abuses are publicized, public outcry is minimal and fleeting at best. It is so much easier to blame "those people."

Even in the event of discovery by a Medicaid "fraud squad," the welfare recipient, rather than the health professional suspected of illegally using the system, often becomes the target of their investigation.

> I was ordered by our Medicaid fraud squad to appear at my local welfare office within the week. A dentist who had done surgery on my mouth for a periodontal disease was under suspicion of committing fraud.
>
> I arrived at the office not knowing what to expect. Two men who resembled G-Men arrived and hustled me into a cubicle and began interrogating me. Not being satisfied with my answers, they proceeded to look into my mouth at every tooth in my head to

prove I had fillings where they were not supposed to be, according to the computer printout they were studying. They also wanted me to account for every filling, extraction, check-up, and cleaning of my three children, which had been done by the same dentist. This took me another week.

I was treated as if I was guilty of something. When you are on welfare, no one cares about your feelings—they don't count.

The welfare system, in reality, has been set up to promote fraud as a means of survival. They *know* we can't live on budgets "below the poverty line." With a more reasonable system of providing financial assistance, there would be less "fraud" because people on welfare would be less desperate. But as it is, women are punished for being on welfare and pushed into impossible binds.

Enough Already

Families who must rely on the welfare system to survive are constantly torn to pieces by the bureaucratic policies that supply the services they need. Each benefit comes with its own rules and regulations, which must be followed if recipients are to remain eligible. The policies are designed separately, with little regard to policies of other agencies, so we are continuously in compromising positions.

Welfare policies are written in "still life." Like the prepackaged vegetables in the supermarkets, they look fine on the surface: but turn them over and look beneath the surface and you may see rotten spots. Living, breathing people need policies that allow for individuality and flexibility. No two families are alike or have the same needs. We should not be lumped together and threatened with extinction if we complain. Women who are already in crises do not need the added stress of conflicting policies among the services that are ours by right. We are strong, capable, and often wise beyond our years. We demand that we be allowed to have some control over our own lives. No governor, president, general, or legislator should be able to dictate to us where we live, what we eat, or where, or even, whether we should work outside the home when we are already taking care of our children.

NOTES

1. In addition to the three authors, several other members of the ARMS collective should be mentioned for their contributions to the larger unpublished paper from which this essay is taken, "Welfare Mothers up in ARMS." They are Angela Hannon, Marion Graham, Jeannie MacKenzie, Carolyn Turner, and Hope Habtemarian. The cited quotations in this essay are taken from interviews with various ARMS members.

2. Since this article was written, the allocation of food stamps has increased some-what while overall welfare support has dropped. Increases were calculated to offset higher rents and decreases in fuel assistance. The food stamps received still cover only about seven to ten days worth of food at current Massachusetts prices.

44

WHY ARE THERE NO MALE ASIAN ANCHOR*MEN* ON TV?

BEN FONG-TORRES

Connie Chung, the best-known Asian TV newswoman in the country, is a co-anchor of *1986*, a prime-time show on NBC. Ken Kashiwahara, the best-known Asian TV newsman, has been chief of ABC's San Francisco bureau for seven years; his reports pop up here and there on ABC's newscasts and other news-related programs.

Wendy Tokuda, the best-known Asian TV newswoman in the Bay Area, is a co-anchor of KPIX's evening news. David Louie, the most established Asian TV newsman, is a field reporter, covering the Peninsula for KGO.

And that's the way it is: among Asian American broadcasters, the glamour positions—the anchor chairs, whose occupants earn more then $500,000 a year in the major markets—go to the women; the men are left outside, in the field, getting by on reporters' wages that top out at about $80,000.

The four Bay Area television stations that present regular newscasts (Channels 2, 4, 5 and 7) employ more than 40 anchors. Only two are Asian Americans: Tokuda and Emerald Yeh, a KRON co-anchor on weekends. There is no Asian male in an anchor position, and there has never been one. (Other Asian women who have anchored locally are Linda Yu [KGO] and Kaity Tong [KPIX], now prime-time anchors in Chicago and New York.)

None of the two dozen broadcasters this reporter spoke to could name a male Asian news anchor working anywhere in the United States.

Don Fitzpatrick, a TV talent headhunter whose job it has been for four years to help television stations find anchors and reporters, maintains a video library in his San Francisco office of 9000 people on the air in the top 150 markets.

From *San Francisco Chronicle*, "Datebook," July 13, 1986. Reprinted with permission.

There are, in fact, several reasons proposed by broadcasters, station executives, talent agents and others.

- Asian men have been connected for generations with negative stereotypes. Asian women have also been saddled with false images, but, according to Tokuda, "In this profession, they work for women and against men."
- Asian women are perceived as attractive partners for the typical news anchor: a white male. "TV stations," says Henry Der, director of Chinese for Affirmative Action, "have discovered that having an Asian female with a white male is an attractive combination." And, adds Sam Chu Lin, a former reporter for both KRON and KPIX, "they like the winning formula. If an Asian woman works in one market, then another market duplicates it. So why test for an Asian male?"
- Asian women allow television stations to fulfill two equal-opportunity slots with one hiring. As Mario Machado, a Los Angeles-based reporter and producer puts it, "They get two minorities in one play of the cards. *They* hit the jackpot."
- Asian males are typically encouraged by parents toward careers in the sciences and away from communications.
- Because there are few Asian men on the air, younger Asian males have no racial peers as role models. With few men getting into the profession, news directors have a minuscule talent pool from which to hire.

And, according to Sumi Haru, a producer at KTLA in Los Angeles, the situation is worsening as stations are being purchased and taken over by large corporations. At KTTV, the ABC affiliate, "The affirmative action department was the first to go." At her own station, the public affairs department is being trimmed. "We're concerned with what little Asian representation we have on the air," said Haru, an officer of the Association of Asian-Pacific American Artists.

Honors Thesis

Helen Chang, a communications major at UC Berkeley now working in Washington, DC, made the missing Asian anchorman the subject of her honors thesis. Chang spoke with Asian anchorwomen in Los Angeles, Chicago and New York as well as locally. "To capsulize the thesis," she says, "it is an executive decision based on a perception of an Asian image. On an executive decision level, the image of the Asian woman is acceptable."

"It's such a white bread medium; it's the survival of the blandest," says a male Asian reporter who asked to remain anonymous. A native San Franciscan, this reporter once had ambitions to be an anchor, but after several static years at his station, "I've decided to face reality. I have a white man's credentials but it doesn't mean a thing. I'm not white. How can it not be racism?"

"Racism is a strong word that scares people," says Tokuda.

"But whatever's going on here is some ugly animal. It's not like segregation in the south. What it is is very subtle . . . bias."

To Mario Machado, it's not that subtle. Machado, who is half Chinese and half Portuguese, is a former daytime news anchor in Los Angeles who's had the most national television exposure after Kashiwahara. Being half-Chinese, he says, has given him no advantage in getting work. "It's had no bearing at all. There's a move on against Asians, period, whether part-Asian or full-Asian."

TV executives, he charges, "don't really want minority males to be totally successful. They don't want minority men perceived as strong, bright, and articulate. We can be cute second bananas, like Robert Ito on *Quincy*. But having an Asian woman—that's always been the feeling from World War II, I guess. You bring back an Asian bride, and she's cute and delicate. But a strong minority man with authority and conviction—I don't think people are ready for that."

War Image

Bruno Cohen, news director at KPIX, agrees that "for a lot of people, the World War II image of Japanese, unfortunately, is the operative image about what Asian males are all about."

That image, says Serena Chen, producer and host of *Asians Now!* on KTVU, was one of danger. "They may be small, but they're strong. So watch out, white women!"

The Vietnam war and recent movies like *Rambo*, Machado says, add to the historic negativity. "You never went to war against Asian women," he says. "You always went to war against Asian men."

Today, says Tokuda, Asian men are saddled with a twin set of stereotypes. "They're either wimpy—they have real thick glasses and they're small and they have an accent and they're carrying a lot of cameras—or they're a murderous gangster." "Or," says Les Kumagai, a former KPIX intern now working for a Reno TV station, "they're businessmen who are going to steal your jobs."

"The Asian woman is viewed as property, and the Asian male has been denied sexuality," says Chen. "Eldridge Cleaver created a theory of the black male being superglorified in the physical and superdecreased in the mental. It's very difficult for people to see a successful black male unless he's an athlete or a performer. If he's in a corporate situation, everyone says, 'Wow, he's the product of affirmative action.' That theory holds that in this society, people who have potential to have power have to be male, and have both mental and physical [strength] to be the superior male. In this society, they took away the black male's mental and gave him his physical. The Asian male has been denied the physical and given the mental."

Veteran KRON reporter Vic Lee listens to a tally of stereotypes and images associated with Asian men. "All those reasons limit where an Asian American can work. I've always said to my wife, if I'm fired here, there're only a couple of cities I can go to and get a job based on how well I do my work, not how I look or what color my skin is. There are cities with Asian American populations, and you can count them on one hand: Seattle, Los Angeles, New York, Boston, and possibly Washington.

"The rest of the country? You might as well forget Detroit. They *killed* a [Chinese] guy just 'cause he looked Japanese." Lee is referring to Vincent Chin, who was beaten to death by two white auto workers who mistook him for a Japanese and blamed him for their unemployment.

"Exotic" Females

In contrast to the threatening Asian male, says Les Kumagai, "Females are 'exotic.' They're not threatening to non-Asian females and they're attractive to non-Asian males. You're looking to draw the 18-to-45-year-old female demographic for advertising. You just won't get that draw from an Asian male."

To Tokuda, the Asian woman's persisting stereotype is more insidious than exotic. "It's the Singapore girl: not only deferential but submissive. It's right next to the geisha girl."

At KGO, says one newsroom employee, "somebody in management was talking about [recently hired reporter] Janet Yee and blurted out, 'Oh, she's so cute.' They don't care about her journalistic credentials. . . . That type of thinking still persists."

Aggressive

Janet Yee says she can take the comment as a compliment, but agrees that it is "a little dehumanizing." Yee, who is half Chinese and half Irish-Swedish, says she doesn't get the feeling, at KGO, that she was hired for her looks. Stereotypes "are the things I've fought all my life," she says, adding that she isn't at all submissive and deferential. "I'm assertive and outgoing, and I think that's what got me the job."

Emerald Yeh, who worked in Portland and at CNN (Cable News Network) in Atlanta before joining KRON, says she's asked constantly about the part being an Asian woman played in her landing a job. "The truth is that it's a factor, but at the same time, there is absolutely no way I can keep my job virtually by being Asian."

Despite the tough competition for jobs in television, Yeh, like Tokuda and several peers in Los Angeles, is vocal about the need to open doors to

Asian men. "People think Asians have done so well," he says, "but how can you say that if one entire gender group is hardly visible?"

George Lum, a director at KTVU who got into television work some 30 years ago at Channel 5, has a theory of his own. "The Asian male is not as aggressive as the Asian female. In this business you have to be more of an extrovert. Men are a little more passive."

Headhunter Don Fitzpatrick agrees. "Watching my tapes, women in general are much more aggressive than men. . . . My theory on that is that— say a boy and girl both want to get into television, and they have identical SATs and grade point averages. Speakers tell them, you'll go to Chico or Medford and start out making $17,000 to $18,000 a year. A guy will say, 'This is bull. If I stay in school and get into accounting or law . . . ' And they have a career change. A woman will go to Chico or Medford and will get into LA or New York."

"In Helen Chang's paper," recalls Tokuda, "she mentions the way Asian parents have channeled boys with a narrow kind of guidance."

"With Japanese kids," says Tokuda, "right after the war, there was a lot of pressure on kids to get into society, on being quiet and working our way back in." In Seattle, she says, "I grew up with a whole group of Asian American men who from the time they were in junior high knew that they were going to be doctors—or at least that they were gonna be successful. There was research that showed that they were very good in math and sciences and not good in verbal skills. With girls there's much less pressure to go into the hard sciences."

Most of the men who do make it in broadcasting describe serendipitous routes into the field, and all of them express contentment with being reporters. "Maybe I'm covering my butt by denying that I want to anchor," says Kumagai, "but I do get a bigger charge being out in the field."

Still, most Asian male reporters do think about the fame and fortune of an anchor slot. Those thoughts quickly meet up against reality.

David Louie realizes he has little chance of becoming the 6 o'clock anchor. "I don't have the matinee idol look that would be the most ideal image on TV. Being on the portly side and not having a full head of hair, I would be the antithesis of what an anchorman is supposed to look like."

Kind of like KPIX's Dave McElhatton? Louie laughs. "But he's white," he says, quickly adding that McElhatton also has 25 years of experience broadcasting in the Bay Area.

At least Louie is on the air. In Sacramento, Lonnie Wong was a reporter at KTXL (Channel 40), and Jan Minagawa reported and did part-time anchoring at KXTV (Channel 10). Both have been promoted into newsroom editing and production jobs. And neither is thrilled to be off the air.

Wong, who says he was made an assignment editor because, among reporters, he had "the most contacts in the community," says his new job is "good management experience. But I did have a reservation. I was the only minority on the air at the station; and I know that's valuable for a station."

Minagawa's station, KXTV, does have an Asian on the air: a Vietnamese woman reporter named Mai Pham. "That made the decision easier," says Minagawa, who had been a reporter and fill-in anchor for seven years. A new news director, he says, "had a different idea of what should be on the air" and asked him to become a producer. "I didn't like it, but there was nothing I could do."

Mitch Farris rejects any notion of a conspiracy by news directors against Asian American men. In fact, he says they are "desperate" for Asian male applicants. "Just about any news director would strive to get an Asian on the air and wouldn't mind a man."

To which Machado shouts, "We're here! We're here! We're looking for work."

45

SEX DIFFERENCES IN MOVING UP AND TAKING CHARGE

BARBARA RESKIN AND IRENE PADAVIC

Until 20 years ago, few employers even considered women for promotions that would take them outside the female clerical or assembly-line ghetto. Although more women have been promoted in recent years, women still have a long way to go. Now they may get some help from the legal system, however. For instance, the Supreme Court ruled in 1990 that Ann Hopkins should be promoted to partner status at the Big Six accounting firm of Price Waterhouse. The decision put other companies on notice that discriminating in promotions could be costly. Then in 1991 a jury awarded $6.3 million to a woman whom Texaco had twice passed over for promotion. On the legislative front, the Civil Rights Act of 1991 now allows employees to sue not merely for lost wages and litigation expenses but also for punitive damages. Similarly, the Glass Ceiling Act of 1991—designed to encourage employers to remove barriers to the progress of women and minorities—reflects increasing public concern with barriers to job mobility. But how effective this legislation will be remains to be seen.

As for access to authority, women have also made some strides. In 1940 many firms explicitly prohibited women from occupying managerial positions (Goldin 1990). By the 1970s, with women flooding the labor market and the number of managerial jobs expanding dramatically, unprecedented numbers of women were entering the ranks of management. Since then, American women have increased their representation in management ranks from 18 percent of all managers in 1970 to 30 percent in 1980 and 40 percent in 1990. These figures indisputably show that thousands of women are gaining access to jobs that usually confer organizational power. Whether women in these positions actually are able to act on the authority typical of managerial positions is a question we address in this chapter.

Women, Men, and Promotions

Television shows and movies offer a distorted image of women who have done well in the business and professional world. The successful woman is depicted as beautiful, white, and heterosexual. She has a spectacular wardrobe and plenty of money, and the people she works with take her seriously. She is sometimes ruthless in exerting her power. Few real women match this glamorous image.

The Promotion Gap

In the real world of work, just a handful of women reach the top of the corporate hierarchy. In 1990, only 19—or fewer than 0.5 percent—of the 4,012 highest-paid officers and directors in top companies were women (Fierman 1990). Within Fortune 500 companies, women and minorities held fewer than 5 percent of senior management posts (Fierman 1990), indicating snail-like progress from the early 1970s, when 1 to 3 percent of senior managers were women (Segal 1992).

A **glass ceiling** blocks the on-the-job mobility of women of all classes, as well as minorities of both sexes. Indeed, in some organizations the glass ceiling may be quite low; for many women of all races, the problem is the **sticky floor,** which keeps them trapped in low-wage, low-mobility jobs (Berheide 1992). Data from a study conducted in the early 1980s in Illinois found that the average man had 0.83 promotions and the average woman, 0.47 promotions (Spaeth 1989). National data for 1991 show a smaller but still significant promotion gap: 48 percent of men had been promoted by their current employer but only 34 percent of women (Reskin and Kalleberg 1993). Both these studies underestimate the promotion gap by failing to distinguish between small-step promotions (for example, clerk-typist 1 to clerk-typist 2) and larger ones (for example, sales representative to sales manager).

Historically, African-American women and men have fared worse in promotions than other groups have (Jones 1985).[1] In 1988, 72 percent of managers in companies employing more than 100 people were white men, 23 percent were white women, 3 percent were African-American men, and 2 percent were African-American women (Alexander 1990). Although some people believe that affirmative action programs give women of color an undue advantage over other groups, this is not the case (McGuire and Reskin 1993; Sokoloff 1992). Being a "twofer" (a term that personnel directors sometimes use for people who fill two Equal Employment Opportunity categories) may help some minority women get jobs, but it hurts them in promotions because it undermines their credibility. Many people assume that minorities—and especially minority women—are hired or promoted only to fill quotas. According to Ella Bell, an Organizational Behavior professor and consultant, "Being a twofer doesn't give you legitimization, doesn't give you a voice or power and doesn't move you up" (Alexander 1990).

Several studies have indicated that men do not confront blocked opportunities because of their sex; in fact, as one sociologist noted, men tend to "rise to the top like bubbles in wine bottles" (Grimm 1978). Christine Williams (1992) found that employers singled out male workers in traditionally female jobs—nurse, librarian, elementary school teacher, social worker, and the like—for an express ride to the top on a "glass escalator." Some of the men in Williams's study faced pressure to accept promotions, like the male children's librarian who received negative evaluations for not "shooting high enough."

The country's largest employer, the U.S. government, has a better record in promoting women and African Americans than private industry does. Historically, the government has been the only place outside the black community where African-American female managers, administrators, and professionals could find jobs in their fields (Higginbotham 1987). Even now, African-American women do better in government jobs than in private industry. In 1992 both black and white women were better represented in governor-appointed cabinet-level positions than in top jobs in private industry (Harlan 1992). In other nations as well, women tend to do better in the public sector than in the private sector (Antal and Izraeli 1993).

Even inside government, however, men have a substantial edge in access to top jobs. In this country, women accounted for 43.5 percent of the workforce in state and local governments but only 31.3 percent of high-level state and local government jobs (Harlan 1991). Minority women were 9.8 percent of jobholders but only 5.1 percent of top-level jobholders. Although women held half of all federal government jobs in 1992 and made up 86 percent of the government's clerical workers, they were only a quarter of supervisors and only a tenth of senior executives (U.S. Merit Systems Protection Board 1992). Minority women were fewer than 2 percent of senior executives and were promoted less often than white women with equivalent experience (U.S. Merit Systems Protection Board 1992).

What is striking about these disparities among government workers is that they exist 15 years after the 1978 Civil Service Reform Act. In fact, a government report declared that the 1980s had brought "a resurgence of discrimination" (U.S. Merit Systems Protection Board 1992). Ironically, senior-level women and minorities employed in the Department of Labor division that is charged with enforcing discrimination regulations recently filed a grievance, claiming that sex discrimination has prevented their advancement. Alluding to the glass ceiling, one worker told *The Wall Street Journal* (1992), "We need Windex and paper towels because we can't even see [it]!"

Although American women lag behind men in promotions, compared to women in most other countries, American women are doing relatively well. American women were four times more likely than French women to hold administrative and managerial jobs and six and a half times more likely to do so than British women (Crompton and Sanderson 1990:176). In no country, however, were women represented in top-level jobs on a par with their numbers in administrative and managerial positions (Farley 1993). In Denmark, women were 14.5 percent of administrators and managers in 1987 but only between 1 and 5 percent of top management; in Japan, women were 7.5 percent of administrators and managers but only 0.3 of a percent of top management in the private sector (Antal and Izraeli 1993:58; Steinhoff and Kazuko 1988). In all the countries for which information was available, women were vastly underrepresented in top-level jobs (Antal and Izraeli 1993).

Consequences of the Promotion Gap

Does it matter that women are locked out of the higher-level jobs? Yes. First of all, the practice is unfair. Americans of both sexes value promotions as a path to greater pay, authority, autonomy, and job satisfaction (Markham et al. 1987:227). And both sexes are ready to work hard for a promotion. In a recent survey of federal employees, 78 percent of the women and 74 percent of the men agreed that they were willing to devote whatever time was necessary in order to advance in their career (U.S. Merit Systems Protection Board 1992). Among minority women, 86 percent were willing to devote as much time as it takes (minority men's responses were not reported separately). Upward mobility is the heart of the American dream, and its denial to women reflects poorly on our society. A second reason to be concerned about the promotion gap is that it depresses women's wages. At a time when women's wages average only 70 percent of men's, this is a serious consideration. Third, promotion barriers reduce women's opportunities to exercise authority on the job (as we discuss later) and to have autonomy from close supervision. **Autonomy**—the freedom to design aspects of one's work, to

decide the pace and hours of work, and to not have others exercising authority over oneself (M. Adler 1993)—enhances job satisfaction. A fourth consequence of women's blocked mobility is that it often leads women to quit in
frustration.

Some women try to get around blocked mobility by starting their own
business. In 1990 women owned 30 percent of all small businesses, and the
Small Business Administration expects the number to rise to 40 percent by
the year 2000 (Shellenbarger 1993). Yet women are less successful than men
in these ventures; in 1982 the average business run by a woman grossed
only 35 percent of what the average man-run business grossed (U.S. Small
Business Administration 1988). A partial explanation is that women-run
businesses are usually economically marginal. Many women business owners have the legal status of entrepreneur but are **independent contractors:**
workers hired on a freelance basis to do work that regular employees otherwise would do in-house (Christensen 1989). Far fewer women own a
business that employs others. The median hourly wage for a full-time, self-
employed woman was $3.75 in 1987, compared to $8.08 for a full-time
female employee (Collins 1993). Often self-employed women provide services that help other employed women cope with domestic work, such as
catering, housecleaning, caring for children, and being a "mother's helper."

Explanations for the Promotion Gap

Many factors impede women's mobility. Although women are as committed
to their careers as men are, women have less of the education, experience,
and training that employers desire. Women also tend to be located in jobs
that do not offer the same diversity of experience or the same opportunities
for upward mobility as men's jobs. Finally, in making promotion decisions,
employers discriminate against women. These are the three basic explanations of why companies still promote more white men than women and
minorities.

Human-Capital Inequities and Promotion
Human-capital theorists claim
that sex differences in promotion rates are due to sex differences in commitment, education, and experience. These differences are presumed to make
women less productive than men.

The claim that men are more committed than women to their jobs is
based on the idea that women place family responsibilities ahead of career
commitment. According to this reasoning, family demands do not allow
women to devote as much time to their careers as men, and therefore women
are unable to do all the things necessary to get promoted rapidly. Although
employers act on this stereotype of women's lesser commitment, it is not
founded in reality. . . . Women's career commitment does not differ from
men's.

The second human-capital claim is that educational differences account for the promotion gap. Indeed, in 1992, women earned 47 percent of the bachelor's degrees in business administration but only 34 percent of the master's degrees. Thus educational differences do contribute to the sex disparity in promotion rates. However, they do not account for all of the disparity. Women with the same educational credentials as men are not attaining top-management jobs at the same rate. When told that women will slowly make their way to the top as more get advanced degrees, one woman manager countered, "My generation came out of graduate school 15 or 20 years ago. The men are now in line to run major corporations. The women are not. Period" (Fierman 1990).

As for the third human-capital claim, women do receive less training and have less experience both within a firm and within the labor force. It is implausible, however, that women voluntarily acquire less experience. In many settings, employers prevent women from acquiring the essential experiences needed for advancement. For example, military promotion to the rank of commissioned officer is usually reserved for people with combat experience, but Congress and the military have banned women from combat positions. In banking, managers who hope for a top spot need extensive experience in commercial lending. But until recently, most women bank managers were not given the chance to work in commercial lending, so few women could acquire the expertise needed to rise beyond middle management. In the same way, the sex segregation of blue-collar production jobs denies women the experience they need to rise to management positions in manufacturing firms.

Similarly, in an increasingly global economy, some corporations are requiring international experience for future executives. However, women are far less likely than men to receive international assignments. According to *The Wall Street Journal*, international experience is increasingly crucial for advancement, and researchers agree (N. Adler 1984; Antal and Izraeli 1993). A human-resources vice president admitted, "No one will be in general management [in this company] by the end of the decade who didn't have international exposure and experience" (Bennett 1993). This trend will benefit white men more than women and minorities (Antal and Izraeli 1993). Many companies think twice before posting a woman or an African American to a foreign assignment, partly because they fear that sexist or racist attitudes will hinder their employee's ability to get the job done. Among industrial and service companies that regularly post employees to international assignments, 36 percent post men exclusively (Moran, Stahl & Boyer, Inc. 1988). Employers' fears are often unfounded, however: Most women posted to foreign assignments have succeeded in them, and their employers subsequently have made women a large proportion of the employees sent on international missions (N. Adler 1988). Those women will be in a better position than many others to advance in their careers.

Segregation and Promotion The segregation explanation of the promotion gap focuses on differences between men and women's organizational locations. A key concept in this explanation is the **internal labor market** or a firm's system for filling jobs by promoting experienced employees. Internal labor markets are composed of related jobs (or job families) connected by **job ladders,** which are promotion or transfer paths that connect lower- and higher-level jobs. These ladders may have only two rungs (as in a take-out restaurant that promotes counter workers to delivery persons), or they may span an entire organization. Job ladders also differ in shape. Some are shaped like a ladder—for example, a company's sales division whose job ladder includes one stock clerk, one sales trainee, one sales representative, one assistant sales manager, and one sales manager. When the vice president in this division retires, everyone moves up one step. In contrast, other job ladders are shaped like a pyramid, with many entry-level jobs feeding into smaller and smaller numbers of jobs at progressively higher levels of the organization, so many workers compete for relatively few jobs. The broader the base of the pyramid, the smaller a worker's odds of being promoted.

The basic idea behind the segregation explanation is that women are promoted less often than men partly because access to internal labor markets is gendered. Women workers are more likely than men to be in jobs with short job ladders or to be in dead-end jobs. This sort of sex segregation begins with entry-level jobs. Men, but not women, are more often placed in jobs with long job ladders and chances at top jobs.

Many traditionally female jobs, such as switchboard operator or teacher, do not have job ladders (Tomaskovic-Devey 1993). Employers have often designed these sorts of jobs without job ladders because they were not interested in reducing turnover and in fact wanted to encourage turnover in order to keep wages low. (Job ladders discourage turnover by giving workers an incentive to stay.) Women in traditionally male occupations are also more likely than men to have dead-end jobs. Women faculty in law schools, for example, disproportionately work as clinical instructors or instructors of research and writing, where they teach professional skills; these jobs usually are not on the tenure ladder (Reskin and Merritt 1993).

For workers who are on job ladders, men tend to be found on longer ladders that reach higher in the organization. In contrast, women and minorities are concentrated on short ladders, with just one or two rungs above the entry level. Clerical work, for example, is usually part of a two-rung system. A typical word-processing office, for instance, consists of many word-processing workers and one supervisor; a travel agency employs many reservation agents and one supervisor (Gutek 1988:231).

An illustration of how internal labor markets can affect promotion comes from a grocery chain whose female employees sued for discrimination because it had promoted almost no women or minorities to store manager. A diagram of this chain's internal labor market (Figure 8.1) shows that women's underrepresentation in the top jobs stemmed largely from sex seg-

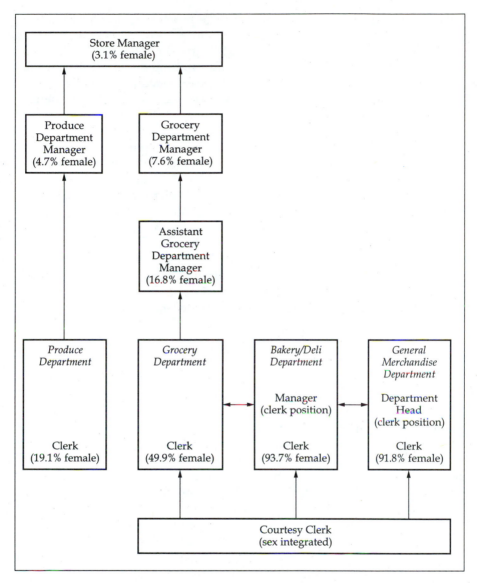

FIGURE 8.1   Internal Labor Market for Grocery Store Chain, 1981 to 1984

Source: Unpublished data from *Marshall et al. v. Alpha Beta.*

regation of lower-level jobs. Job ladders in the predominantly male produce departments led to top management. In contrast, the most heavily female department—bakery/deli and general merchandise—were on short job ladders not directly connected to the ladder to top management.

The different kinds of establishments that employ women and men explain much of the promotion gap. Large organizations are more likely to have the resources that allow them to create promotion ladders. Moreover, their sheer size lets them create more opportunities to promote deserving workers (Spaeth 1989). Therefore, women's greater concentration in small, entrepreneurial firms and nonprofit organizations and men's concentration in large corporations and for-profit companies also reduce women's odds of promotion relative to men. In one survey, corporations employed 47 percent of a random sample of men, compared to 34 percent of women (Reskin and Kalleberg 1993).

Segregation also contributes to the promotion gap by making women's accomplishments invisible. In prestigious Wall Street law firms, for example, senior partners have tended to assign women lawyers to research rather than litigation. Appearing in the courtroom less often than their male peers made women less visible, thus hampering their promotion to partner (Epstein 1993). In corporations, women managers are concentrated in staff positions, such as personnel or public relations, and men are concentrated in the more visible and important line positions, such as sales or production. Staff positions involve little risk and therefore provide few opportunities for workers to show senior management their full capabilities. When top executives are looking for people to promote to senior management, they seldom pick vice presidents of personnel management or public relations. They usually pick vice presidents in product management or sales, who more often than not are male.

Discrimination and Promotion Sex discrimination by employers is a third explanation for the promotion gap. In brief, it recognizes that employers reward men's qualifications more than women's. The case of Ann Hopkins illustrates blatant discrimination. Despite having brought more money into Price Waterhouse than any other contender for promotion had done, Hopkins was denied promotion to partner. According to the court that ruled in her favor, the senior partners based their evaluation on her personality and appearance and ignored her accomplishments. Her male mentor had advised Hopkins that her chances of promotion would improve if she would "walk more femininely, talk more femininely, wear makeup, have [her] hair styled, and wear jewelry" (White 1992:192).

Actually, appearing feminine does not help a woman get a promotion. In fact, the mere fact of being a woman may be an insurmountable barrier. A male personnel officer told a female bank manager that her career had stalled because

> *what the chairman and presidents want are people that they are comfortable with, and they are not . . . comfortable with women. It doesn't even get to the . . . level of you as an individual and [your] personality; it is the skirt that's the problem. (Reskin and Roos 1990:156).*

Top-level management is a male environment, and some men feel uncomfortable with women. The result is discrimination. The Federal Bureau of

Investigation (FBI), for example, refused to even hire women as agents until the death of Director J. Edgar Hoover in 1972 (Johnston 1993). The lingering effect of this discrimination is that the highest-ranking woman is the agent in charge of the FBI's smallest field office, in Anchorage, Alaska.

Statistical discrimination comes into play as well. Employers statistically discriminate against women when they stereotype them as disinterested in advancement or as lacking the attributes needed in higher-level jobs. According to Rosabeth Moss Kanter (1977), when managers are uncertain about the qualifications necessary to do a job, they prefer to promote people who have social characteristics like their own. Kanter called this practice **homosocial reproduction.** Presumably managers believe that similar people are likely to make the same decisions they would. Thus they seek to advance others who are the same sex, race, social class, and religion; who belong to the same clubs; who attended the same colleges; and who enjoy the same leisure activities. Homosocial reproduction is especially likely in risky ventures, like launching a new TV series. Denise Bielby and William Bielby (1992) argued that, because most studio and network executives are male, they view male writers and producers as "safer" than women with equally strong qualifications and are more likely to give men rather than women long-term deals and commitments for multiple series. The fear that someone who seems different—a woman, perhaps, or a Hispanic—will conform to executives' negative stereotypes results in a cadre of top managers who look alike and think alike.

Women, Men, and Authority

In addition to getting promoted less often than men, women are allowed to exercise less authority. Exercising **authority** means, broadly, having power: the capacity to mobilize people, to get their cooperation, to secure the resources to do the job (Kanter 1983). A person with job authority is someone who sets policy or makes decisions about organizational goals, budgets, production, and subordinates (for example, about hiring, firing, and pay).

Women's lack of authority in the workplace appears in two guises. First, women usually do not occupy the kinds of positions that offer opportunities to exert power. Second, when they are in such positions, they are not usually given as much power as men are. These barriers affect women at all levels, including managers, professionals, and blue-collar workers.

The belief that women should not have authority over men is embedded in employers' personnel practices. According to Barbara Bergmann (1986:114–6), many employers adhere to an informal segregation code that keeps women from supervising men and that reserves the training slots leading to higher-level jobs for men. Men rule over women and junior men, women rule over women, but women rarely if ever rule over men. This code applies to minorities as well: Minorities may give orders to one another but not to members of the dominant group.

Bergmann (1986:114–6) dubbed this set of principles the **segregation code.** In many lines of work, coworkers often help enforce the code. Many men resent women who are promoted above them, and they often make their resentment known. According to one male corporate manager, "It's okay for women to have these jobs, as long as they don't go zooming by *me"* (Kanter 1977:218). A woman pipe fitter recalled how,

> *when I first made [pipe]fitter, the helpers were really pissed and angry that they were going to have to work with me. There was a lot of talk about having to work for a woman, take orders from a woman. Some of them came right out in saying I didn't know what I was doing. . . . One man [was] marching around telling everybody that he was . . . too important to have to work for a woman. (Schroedel 1985:23)*

Similarly, male bus drivers found it difficult to take a female supervisor seriously. According to the female supervisor,

> *It was a blow to their ego to have a woman tell them what to do. . . . Some would not respond at all, and there was no way you could make them do it. . . . A lot of the drivers tell me now that they're glad I'm not in [supervision] any more. They couldn't handle a woman telling 'em what to do on the road. (Schroedel 1985:209–211)*

As one woman said, "Let's face it, how is an employer going to think a woman is manager material if he thinks her maternal instincts have primacy over business priorities?" (Kleiman 1993). Such deep-seated cultural stereotypes allow the segregation code to remain.

Remedies for the Promotion and Authority Gaps

The social forces that maintain sex differences in opportunities to move up and take charge are resistant to change. Yet employers can help increase women's access to promotion and authority in many ways. To improve advancement opportunities for clerical and service workers, for example, companies could create "bridge" positions that help workers to switch job ladders—for example, move from a clerical ladder to an administrative one—without penalty (Kanter 1976). Some large companies have already made such changes, usually in response to court decrees that they promote more women. USX (formerly U.S. Steel) changed its rules so that women in traditionally female jobs could transfer to more promising steelworker jobs without losing their seniority (Ullman and Deaux 1981). The plan was highly successful: In just four years, the number of women in production and maintenance jobs in two steel mills increased threefold (Reskin and Hartmann 1986:93). AT&T's modifications of its promotion and training policies brought similar results. In the early 1970s, the Equal Employment Opportunities Commission required the company to improve its record of promotions for minorities and women. The nondiscriminatory promotion policies that the company instituted yielded a 300 percent increase in the number of women in middle- and upper-management positions (Northrup and Larson 1979).

Another way that organizations can shrink the promotion and authority gaps is by replacing informal promotion practices with formal ones. In the absence of formal criteria for personnel decisions, managers' biases are more likely to come into play (Roos and Reskin 1984). Lucky Grocery Stores, for example, did not formally post announcements of promotion opportunities because male store managers thought they knew which employees were interested in promotion. The result was that few women were promoted, prompting a successful lawsuit by women who had been passed up (*Stender et al. v. Lucky* 1992). In general, formal recruitment methods and promotion procedures—such as job advertisements, objective hiring criteria, and open transfer policies—help ensure women's access to jobs that bring authority (Szafran 1982; Roos and Reskin 1984).

Raising the price that employers pay to discriminate would help eliminate several of the obstacles described in this chapter. Despite the wastefulness of excluding potentially productive people from top jobs on the basis of their sex and color, employers have done just that. Organizations have multiple goals, and they act on the ones that have the highest priority. Making a profit is usually the highest goal, so higher fines and other financial sanctions could raise equal opportunity on the agenda of priorities.

Another avenue that women and minorities can follow to increase their promotion opportunities is to pursue additional litigation and legislation. However, powerful remedies are necessary in the wake of the Reagan and Bush administrations, which severely undermined laws intended to protect women and minorities from discriminatory practices in the workplace. In addition, anti-affirmative action decisions of the Supreme Court have now trickled down into lower courts, slowing the pace of change (White 1992:201). Still, the courts and the legislature have provided some help in recent years. For example, a 1991 court case led Marriott Corporation to pay $3 million to women managers who had been denied promotions. At fault was the company's informal promotion policy and a work culture that "froze women out" (Goozner 1991). A legislative example is the Glass Ceiling Division within the U.S. Department of Labor, established by Congress in 1991, which is supposed to eliminate the barriers to women's and minorities' promotion to top posts. Although the division has little enforcement power, it works with the Office of Federal

Contract Compliance, which has the rarely used power to debar discriminating companies from receiving government contracts. It is too soon to tell if enforcement agencies will actively enforce the Glass Ceiling Act. Much depends on the political process that allocates budget resources and penalties. In addition, the 1992 Civil Rights Act, which allows for punitive damages, may also help increase promotion opportunities for excluded groups.

These are potentially powerful weapons because they impose a cost on employers. However, their ability to close the promotion and authority gaps still depends on two things: the willingness of aggrieved parties to press for change and the willingness of enforcement agencies to enforce.

Summary

In the past 20 years, women have made progress in closing the promotion and authority gaps, but they still have a long way to go. Will the outlook be better for the college students of today? We don't know. History shows that women's job options do not improve automatically. They improved during the 1970s through the efforts of federal agencies enforcing new laws, advocacy groups, and companies voluntarily establishing Equal Employment Opportunity programs (Reskin and Hartmann 1986:97). Further progress depends on similar efforts in the 1990s and beyond.

NOTE

1. A study in the late 1920s of a northern meat-packing plant found that African-American women were assigned to the worst departments—hog killing and beef casing—and had no access to the better jobs. They were denied promotion to jobs in the bacon room supposedly because the public did not want black hands to touch meat in the last stages of processing (Jones 1985:177).

REFERENCES

Adler, Marina A. 1993. "Gender Differences in Job Autonomy: The Consequences of Occupational Segregation and Authority Position." *Sociological Quarterly* 34:449–66.

Adler, Nancy J. 1984. "Women Do Not Want International Careers: And Other Myths About International Management." *Organizational Dynamics* 13:66–79.

——. 1988. "Pacific Basin Managers: A Gaijin, Not a Woman." Pp. 226–49 in Nancy J. Adler and Dafna N. Izraeli (eds.), Women in Management Worldwide. New York: M. E. Sharpe.

Alexander, Keith L. 1990. "Minority Women Feel Racism, Sexism are Blocking Path to Management." *Wall Street Journal.* (July 25):B1.

Antal, Ariane B. and Dafna N. Izraeli. 1993. "A Global Comparison of Women in Management: Women Managers in Their Homelands and as Expatriates." Pp. 52–96 in Ellen A. Fagenson (ed.), *Women in Management: Trends, Issues and Challenges in Managerial Diversity.* Newbury Park, CA: Sage.

Bennett, Amanda. 1993. "Path to Top Jobs Now Twists and Turns." *Wall Street Journal* (March 15):D1, D6.

Bergmann, Barbara R. 1986. *The Economic Emergence of Women.* New York: Basic Books.

Berheide, Catherine W. 1992. "Women Still 'Stuck' in Low-Level Jobs." *Women in Public Services: A Bulletin for the Center for Women in Government* 3 (Fall).

Bielby, Denise D. and William T. Bielby. 1992. "Cumulative Versus Continuous Disadvantage in an Unstructured Labor Market." *Work and Occupations* 19:366–87.

Christensen, Kathleen. 1989. "Flexible Staffing and Scheduling in U.S. Corporations." *Research Bulletin No. 240.* New York: The Conference Board.

Collins, Nancy. 1993. "Self-Employment Versus Wage and Salary Jobs: How Do Women Fare?" *Research-in-Brief.* Washington, DC: Institute for Women's Policy Research.

Crompton, Rosemary and Kay Sanderson. 1990. *Gendered Jobs and Social Change.* Boston: Unwyn Hyman.

Epstein, Cynthia F. 1993. *Women in Law.* Urbana: University of Illinois Press.

Farley, Jennie. 1993. "Commentary." Pp. 97–102 in Ellen A. Fagenson (ed.), *Women in Management: Trends, Issues and Challenges in Managerial Diversity.* Newbury Park, CA: Sage.

Fierman, Jaclyn. 1990. "Why Women Still Don't Hit the Top." *Fortune* (July 30):40,42,46,50,54,58,62.

Goldin, Claudia. 1990. *Understanding the Gender Gap.* New York: Oxford University Press.

Goozner, Merrill. 1991. "$3 Million Sex-Bias Accord at Marriott." *Chicago Tribune* (March 6):sec. 3, p. 3.

Grimm, James W. 1978. "Women in Female-Dominated Professions." Pp. 293–315 in Ann Stromberg and Shirley Harkess (eds.), *Women Working: Theories and Facts in Perspective.* Palo Alto, CA: Mayfield.

Gutek, Barbara. 1988. "Women in Clerical Work." Pp. 225–40 in Ann H. Stromberg and Shirley Harkess (ed.), *Women Working: Theory and Facts in Perspective.* Mountain View, CA: Mayfield.

Harlan, Sharon. 1991. "Number of Women in Government Increasing." *Women in Public Services: A Bulletin for the Center for Women in Government* 1 (Summer).

———. 1992. "Women Face Barriers in Top Management." *Women in Public Services: A Bulletin for the Center for Women in Government* 2 (Winter 1991/92).

Higginbotham, Elizabeth. 1987. "Employment for Professional Black Women in the Twentieth Century." Pp. 73–99 in Christine Bose and Glenna Spitze (eds.), *Ingredients for Women's Employment Policy.* Albany, NY: SUNY Press.

Johnston, David. 1993. "FBI Agent to Quit Over Her Treatment in Sexual Harassment Case." *New York Times* (October 11):A7.

Jones, Jacquelyn. 1985. *Labor of Love, Labor of Sorrow.* New York: Vintage.

Kanter, Rosabeth Moss. 1976. "The Policy Issues: Presentation VI." Pp. 282–91 in Martha Blaxall and Barbara Reagan (eds.), *Women and the Workplace.* Chicago: University of Chicago Press.

———. 1977. *Men and Women of the Corporation.* New York: Basic Books.

———. 1983. "Women Managers: Moving Up in a High Tech Society." pp. 21–36 in Jennie Farley (ed.), *The Woman in Management: Career and Family Issues.* Ithaca: New York State School of Industrial and Labor Relations, Cornell University.

Kleiman, Carol. 1993. "Women End Up Sacrificing Salary for Children." *Tallahassee Democrat* (March 3):D8.

Markham, William T., Sharon Harlan, and Edward J. Hackett. 1987. "Promotion Opportunity in Organizations." *Research in Personnel and Human Resource Management* 5:223–87.

McGuire, Gail M. and Barbara F. Reskin. 1993. "Authority Hierarchies at Work: The Impacts of Race and Sex." *Gender & Society* 7:487–506.

Moran, Stahl & Boyer, Inc. 1988. *Status of American Female Expatriate Employees: Survey Results.* Boulder, CO: International Division, Moran, Stahl & Boyer, Inc.

Northrup, Herbert R. and John A. Larson. 1979. *The Impact of the AT&T-EEO Consent Decrees.* Labor Relations and Public Policy Series, No. 20. Philadelphia: Industrial Research Unit, University of Pennsylvania.

Reskin, Barbara F. and Heidi Hartmann. 1986. *Women's Work, Men's Work: Sex Segregation on the Job.* Washington, DC: National Academy Press.

Reskin, Barbara F. and Arne L. Kalleberg. 1993. "Sex Differences in Promotion Experiences in the United States and Norway." R.C. No. 28, Presented at the International Sociological Association meeting, Durham, NC.

Reskin, Barbara F. and Deborah J. Merritt. 1993. "Sex Segregation Among Law Faculty Members." Unpublished paper.

Reskin, Barbara F. and Patricia A. Roos. 1990. *Job Queues, Gender Queues: Explaining Women's Inroads Into Male Occupations.* Philadelphia: Temple University Press.

Roos, Patricia A. and Barbara F. Reskin. 1984. "Institutionalized Barriers to Sex Integration in the Workplace." Pp. 235–60 in Barbara F. Reskin (ed.), *Sex Segregation in the Workplace.* Washington, DC: National Academy Press.

Schroedel, Jean Reith. 1985. *Alone in a Crowd: Women in the Trades Tell Their Stories.* Philadelphia: Temple University Press.

Segal, Amanda T. with Wendy Zellner. 1992. "Corporate Women." *Business Week* (June 8):74–8.

Shellenbarger, Sue. 1993. "Work and Family: Women Start Younger at Own Businesses." *Wall Street Journal* (March 15):B1.

Sokoloff, Natalie J. 1992. *Black Women and White Women in the Professions.* New York: Routledge.

Spaeth, Joe L. 1989. *Determinants of Promotion in Different Types of Organizations.* Unpublished manuscript. Urbana: University of Illinois.

Steinhoff, P.G. and T. Kazuko. 1988. "Woman Managers in Japan." Pp. 103–21 in Nancy J. Adler and Dafna N. Izraeli (eds.), *Women in Management Worldwide.* New York: M. E. Sharpe.

Stender et al. v. Lucky. 1992. "Findings of Fact and Conclusion of Law," *Federal Reporter,* vol. 803, Fed. Supplement, p. 259.

Szafran, Robert F. 1982. "What Kinds of Firms Hire and Promote Women and Blacks? A Review of the Literature." *Sociological Quarterly* 23:171–90.

Tomaskovic-Devey, Donald. 1993. *Gender and Racial Inequality at Work.* Ithaca: New York State School of Industrial and Labor Relations, Cornell University.

Ullman, Joseph P. and Kay Deaux. 1981. "Recent Efforts to Increase Female Participation in Apprenticeship in the Basic Steel Industry in the Midwest." Pp. 133–49 in Vernon M. Briggs, Jr., and Felician Foltman (eds.), *Apprenticeship Research: Emerging Findings and Future Trends.* Ithaca: New York State School of Industrial and Labor Relations, Cornell University.

U.S. Merit Systems Protection Board. 1992. *A Question of Equity: Women and the Glass Ceiling in the Federal Government. A Report to the President and Congress by the U.S. Merit Systems Protection Board.* Washington, DC: U.S. Merit Systems Protection Board.

U.S. Small Business Administration. 1988. *Small Business in the American Economy.* Washington, DC: U.S. Government Printing Office.

White, Jane. 1992. *A Few Good Women: Breaking the Barriers to Top Management.* Englewood Cliffs, NJ: Prentice-Hall.

Williams, Christine L. 1992. "The Glass Escalator: Hidden Advantages for Men in the 'Female' Professions." *Social Problems* 39:253–67.

46
_____

LIKE A SMACK IN THE FACE
Pornography in the Trades

BARBARA TREES

In 1990 the New York City Human Rights Commission held hearings on sex and race discrimination in the New York City building trades. Barbara Trees helped organize those hearings in the hope that they would lead to public acknowledgment of the plight of tradeswomen. Forty women and people of color testified about their treatment. A major point of the testimony was that pornography is used as a weapon to push women out of the trades.

I want to tell you a bit about myself and construction work because most people who don't work in construction have no idea what it's like. I am a carpenter in New York City. I applied to the Carpenters' Union in 1978 and began my four-year apprenticeship in 1980. I am college educated and was thirty years old at the time. There were maybe ten women—tops—and 20,000 men in the union at the time.

I wanted to be a carpenter because it was daring, well paid, and out of the mainstream. I thought women merely had to prove we could do the work and then many more women would join us.

It made perfect sense to see the building trades as a great opportunity for women to achieve equality with men. Jobs were available, and the apprenticeships were open to people with limited educations. But, in spite of the possibilities, this field has not really opened up for women. And the mistreatment of women in construction is a horror story which has not been adequately told.

A woman who is sent to a job at a construction site can usually expect to be the only one on a crew of hundreds of men. For the first five or six years I went through the motions of fitting in. I guess we all did, we "first women." It was so very important to get along. The job sites were dirty and dangerous and the work was hard; we all got the difficult jobs, not the "tit" jobs, as easy work is called. The men we were supposed to learn the trade from usually had no intention of teaching us. They thought it was the most preposterous thing that women actually wanted to do this work.

These men found ways to push us out, and they were *not* nice about it. They were scary and belligerent and did not want "girls" around (the lone woman on a job or crew is always called "the girl"). The atmosphere was and is horrible. There is filthy language. There is total contempt for women and wives. The men piss and shit out in the open and on the floor instead of in toilets. Women are given the worst jobs to do, made to work alone at a job two or three men would do, and laid off first without cause. There are no changing facilities or bathrooms with locks for women. The men use binoculars to look for women in nearby buildings, and when they spot one in a bathroom or undressed, they yell, "There's one, there's one!" In addition to all this harassment, physical violence is common. I know of several women who were hit or punched by fellow construction workers, and nothing was done about it.

Pornography is commonplace on construction jobs. You see it in the locker rooms; on drinking fountains, on and inside lunch boxes, on and inside toolboxes, on tools, on walls in management, union, and other offices. It is often posted on job sites or on half-constructed buildings. I found it humiliating. I began to avoid areas where I found it and tore it down when I saw it. After that, it had a funny way of showing up where I was working or walking—just one little dirty picture, like a smack in the face—and nobody around to take the credit. The men feel they have an absolute right to display these pictures. It is very risky to complain about pornography in the construction industry. You can get harassed. You can get hurt. You can get fired, and once fired, you have no recourse. The contractor does not have to say why you were fired. The union stewards don't want to hear about it. There is no grievance procedure. I was fired from a job after politely asking a foreman to remove a beaver shot from our shanty, but only found out a year later that that was why I was fired.[1] But losing your job is not the only threat. The mafia, some of whom deal in prostitution and pornography, lurk everywhere. Most of us who are activists have nightmares about construction workers chopping our doors down to get into our homes. We fear for our lives.

Many women in the trades try to ignore the pornography, but I could not do that and survive. I had listened to filthy woman-hating "jokes," had coworkers "accidentally" touch my breasts or ass, and put up with the idea of women as funny—the mere mention of breasts or anything about women's bodies bringing smirks. I just couldn't take it anymore.

So I got sick, quite seriously sick, and stayed out of work for two years. For women, this is not an uncommon reaction to these pressures in the nontraditional work world. But during the time I was ill, I thought about the situation, and when I went back I vowed that I would practice pro-woman self-defense. It worked. It gave me a sense of entitlement—to dignity, to the job, to fight for the women in my union as if we are the most important people on earth. It meant that I refused to listen to men bad-mouthing women, that I took these "jokes" and remarks for the insults they were, and that I responded accordingly.

In 1989, I founded New York Tradeswomen, a support group for women in the building trades. We formed a Women Carpenters Committee in the New York City District Council. I was appointed a shop steward in my local union in 1990, the first woman in my 2,000-member local to hold this position. As a steward, the union representative for the carpenters on a particular job site, I've battled pornography for the last three years. The union office gave me the protection to fight it and not be fired. But I still have problems. I've had long pornographic phone messages placed on my answering machine from men who boasted of being in my local. I've had a contractor tell me to go fuck myself when I asked him to remove the pornography from the trailer where, as a steward, I had to go to call my union. I told a teamster that I wouldn't hang a door in his shanty until he removed a nude picture. Later he chases me around waving a nude picture, yelling, "This is beautiful, this is good!" Once a pornographic picture showed up on the cooler. I saw it and took off my hard hat and bashed the closest guy to me over the head with it and said, "Is that yours?!" He may not even have put it there, but I didn't care, I was so mad. When I asked a tin knocker to simply turn his large toolbox, which was covered with beaver shots, away from the door so that I wouldn't have to see them, he accused me of being ridiculous and said that I should know better, that these pictures are everywhere, that this is the way it is in the construction industry, that I had to fit in, and that I would be to blame if he got fired over something so "minor." After I complained to union officials, this same guy followed me, glaring, to the subway.

I thought that women could change these job sites, but so far we haven't. There aren't enough of us, and the men are picking us off, one by one, both the weak and the strong. Using pornography and other forms of sexual harassment, men have successfully kept women out of construction in any significant numbers. Now that the recession has hit, we are devastated.

NOTES

1. See Dorchen Leidholdt, "Pornography in the Workplace," pp. 216–232 in Laura Lederer and Richard Delgado, eds., *The Price We Pay: The Case against Racist Speech, Hate Propaganda, and Pornography*, New York: Hill & Wang, 1995, for other stories about how men use pornography to harass and intimidate women in the workplace.

47

MAD AS HELL

CRAIG G. HARRIS

Discrimination in the workplace should come as no surprise. Caught in an economic web dominated by heterosexual white males, we know that our being black, or female, or gay is viewed as a demographic mutation, if not a handicap. We are unconsciously conditioned to equate success with an alabaster phallus and go to self-abasing extremes to

From *New Men, New Minds: Breaking Male Tradition*, Franklin Abbott, ed., 1987, Crossing Press. Reprinted with permission of the author.

attain that success. Blacks are reared to set super nigger goals for themselves—"to get over, you gotta be twice as good as the white man." Fashion
consultants tell women executives that tailored pinstripes will aid their success in a man's world. Second-rate career counselor/interior designers
advise gays to conform to the status quo by constructing revolving doors for
our closets.

When we make the choice to follow these instructions, we are in effect
slashing our own wrists and dressing our wounds with BandAids—praising
the American dream in acceptance of our alleged inferiority. Ostensibly, our
navigation through alien waters into a pseudo-Aryan, gender specific, male
supremacist territory is testimony to our crossover appeal. In reality, it is this
type of assimilation that feeds a malignant self-hatred which we use to
oppress ourselves and undermine our own efforts toward achieving our
individual and collective civil rights.

Subconsciously, we all know this. But we go on role playing, eating
crow, accepting our bi-weekly momentary insults until something, some
last-straw incident, triggers a response like that heard in the movie *Network*:
"I'm mad as hell, and I ain't gonna take it no more!"

For me the breaking point came last summer, when I entered my office
clad in a blue button-down oxford, white linen tie, baggy seersucker trousers
with multiple pleating and a tiny turquoise stud. Within the hour, the management consulting firm's business manager had deemed my sartorial presentation inappropriate, demanding: "Don't wear an earring into this office
again." When I questioned the logic behind the order, she responded, "Don't
push it, the pants are questionable as well."

Following her into her office to continue the conversation, I was told that
my immediate supervisor, an avowed racist and sexist, had problems working with a black male assistant. He had also intimated that several clients
had difficulty with the pitch of my telephone voice. The business manager's
response: "Craig, you gotta sound more butch on the phone."

I was hot, but I also had bills and no other source of income. I talked and
thought about it over the weekend, searching for a reason to tolerate the condition. Against the advice of family and friends, I phoned in my resignation
on Monday morning.

This situation is typical and more often than not goes unreported. So
many believe there is nothing that can be done, no way of fighting the system. Others fear "coming out" in an emotionally wrenching court case and
risking maltreatment from a homophobic legal system, or of gambling away
large sums of money and time in a precarious pursuit of justice. Few are willing to make the necessary waves to propel the advancement of civil rights in
our society.

It doesn't take much time, or money for that matter, and, considering the
stakes—self-respect, esteem, and possibly a favorable judgment ($$$)—the
challenge is worth it. And all it takes is a little research, careful preparation,
and some follow-up.

I took the advice of a co-worker, who had noticed the harassment I was continually subjected to, and met with her sister, an attorney for the Puerto Rican Legal Defense and Education Fund. She instructed me to file for unemployment insurance claiming "constructive discharge" (meaning an employee is essentially forced by harassment to quit), and to contact Lambda Legal Defense and Education Fund for further information.

According to a Lambda board member, my best course of action was to file a complaint with the Equal Employment Opportunities Commission charging discrimination on the basis of race and sex. The private firm which I had worked for had no contracts with the City of New York and so was exempt from the provisions outlined in Mayor Koch's Executive Order 50, prohibiting discrimination on the basis of "sexual orientation or affectional preference."

There is no filing fee for registering a claim with any of the three government agencies (EEOC, the State Division of Human Rights, and the NYC Bureau of Labor Services), and there is no need to retain a lawyer. The initial complaint is filed by an intake officer, who also explains the process—to the point of settlement, or if necessary, litigation.

Blatant discrimination is a rarity—no sane employer will call you a "nigger faggot" in the presence of witnesses. Subtle discrimination is not so easy to prove, and the burden of proof lies with the complainant. Documentation is essential and can come in the form of employee profiles, performance evaluations, detailed accounts of discriminatory incidents, and witnesses. Build a strong case and the opposition will be hard-pressed to produce a convincing denial.

An out-of-court settlement is the desirable solution for all parties involved. From the respondent's viewpoint, the legal fees incurred during a lengthy trial can cost more than a cash settlement. The complainant benefits by having equal power in negotiating the terms of a cash settlement. The entire process, from start to finish, can last as long as two years. As in my case, steady telephone follow-up can bring about an agreeable settlement within six months.

Employment is only one example of discrimination which can be addressed legally. Third world gays face all types of discrimination within both the gay and straight communities. Once my case was settled, I began to repay my debt to the various attorneys who counseled me by becoming a member of Lambda's Public Education Committee. With help from members of the staff and board of directors, I planned a conference to facilitate an exchange of information and to ensure that the legal needs of third world gays and lesbians were heard. As a result, Lambda is currently making program alterations based on the feedback from this initial meeting.

In order to achieve civil rights, get gay rights legislation passed, and assert our legitimacy, we must first accept that legitimacy as a given. It is time that we take a closer look at the political/legal implications of our position as gay people of color. By doing so, our intolerance of prejudices and role expectations will become second nature. Only then will we evolve into more self-loving, liberated individuals.

48

SHARING THE SHOP FLOOR

STAN GRAY

On an October evening in 1983, a group of women factory workers from Westinghouse came to the United Steelworkers hall in Hamilton, Ontario, to tell their story to a labor federation forum on affirmative action. The women told of decades of maltreatment by Westinghouse—they had been confined to job ghettoes with inferior conditions and pay, and later, when their "Switchgear" plant was shut down, they had fought to be transferred to the other Westinghouse plants in the city. They had to battle management and the resistance of some, though not all, of their brothers in the shops. They won the first round, but when the recession hit, many were laid off regardless of seniority and left with little or no income in their senior years.

By the night of the forum I had worked at Westinghouse for ten years and had gone through the various battles for equality in the workplace. As I listened to the women, I thought of how much their coming into our plant had changed me, my fellow workers, and my brother unionists.

The women were there to tell their own story because the male staff officials of their union, United Electrical Workers, had prevented the women's committee of the local labor council from presenting their brief. The union claimed it was inaccurate, the problems weren't that bad, and it didn't give union officials the credit for leading the fight for women's rights. The Westinghouse women gave their story and then the union delivered a brief of its own, presenting a historical discussion of male-female relations in the context of the global class struggle, without mentioning Westinghouse or Hamilton or any women that it represented.[1]

This kind of thing happens in other cities and in other unions. The unanimous convention resolutions in support of affirmative action tend to mask

---

Originally published in *Canadian Dimension*, 18 June 1984.

a male resistance within the unions and on the shop floor. Too many men pay lip service to women's rights but leave the real fighting to the women. They don't openly confront the chauvinism of their brothers on the shop floor and in the labor movement. Yet an open fight by men against sexism is an important part of the fight for sexual equality. It is also important because sexism is harmful for working men, in spite of whatever benefits they gain in the short term; it runs counter to their interests and undermines the quality of their trade unionism.

I was one of those unionists who for years sat on the fence in this area until sharp events at work pushed me off. I then had to try to deal with these issues in practice. The following account of the debates and struggles on the shop floor at Westinghouse concentrates on the men rather than on the women's battle; it focuses on the men's issues and tries to bring out concretely the interests of workingmen in the fight against sexism.

My Education Begins

My education in the problems of the Westinghouse women began in November 1978, when I was recalled to work following a bitter and unsuccessful five-month strike. The union represented eighteen hundred workers in three plants that produced turbines, motors, transformers, and switchgear equipment. When I was recalled to work it wasn't to my old Beach Road plant—where I had been a union steward and safety rep—but to an all-female department in the Switchgear plant and to a drastic drop in my labor grade. The plant was mostly segregated; in other words, jobs (and many departments) were either male or female. There were separate seniority lists and job descriptions. The dual-wage, dual-seniority system was enshrined in the collective agreement signed and enforced by both company and union.

At Switchgear I heard the complaints of the women, who worked the worst jobs in terms of monotony, speed, and work discipline but received lower pay, were denied chances for promotion, and were frequently laid off. They complained too of the union, accusing the male leadership of sanctioning and policing their inferior treatment. In cahoots with management, it swept the women's complaints under the carpet. From the first day it was obvious to me that the company enforced harsher standards for the women. They worked harder and faster, got less break time, and were allowed less leeway than the men. When I was later transferred to the all-male machine shop, the change was from night to day.

Meanwhile the men's club that ran the union made its views known to me early and clearly. The staff rep told me that he himself would never work with women. He boasted that he and his friends in the leadership drank in the one remaining all-male bar in the city. The local president was upset when he heard that I was seriously listening to the complaints of the women workers. He told me that he always just listened to their unfounded bitching, said "yes, yes, yes," and then completely ignored what he had been told. I ought to do the same, was his advice. Although I had just been elected to the executive in a rank-and-file rebellion against the old guard, he assumed that a common male bond would override our differences. When I persisted in taking the women's complaints seriously, the leadership started to ridicule me, calling me "the Ambassador" and saying they were now happy that I was saving them the distasteful task of listening to the women's bitching.

Then in 1979 the boom fell at Switchgear: the company announced it would close the plant. For the women, this was a serious threat. In the new contract the seniority and wage lists had been integrated, thanks to a new Ontario Human Rights Code. But would the women be able to exercise their seniority and bump or transfer to jobs in the other Hamilton plants, or would they find themselves out in the street after years at Switchgear?

Divide and Conquer

By this time I had been recalled to my old department at the Beach Road plant, thanks to shop-floor pressure by the guys. There was a lot of worry in the plants about the prospect of large-scale transfers of women from Switchgear. A few women who had already been transferred had met with harassment and open hostility from the men. Some of us tried to raise the matter in the stewards' council, but the leadership was in no mood to discuss and confront sexism openly. The union bully boys went after us, threatening, shouting, breast beating, and blaming the women for the problems.

Since the union structures weren't going to touch the problem, we were left to our own resources in the shop. I worked in the Transformer Division, which the management was determined to keep all male. As a steward I insisted that the Switchgear women had every right to jobs in our department, at least to training and a trial period as stipulated by seniority. Since this was a legal and contractual right, management developed a strategy of Divide and Rule: present the women as a threat to men's jobs; create splits and get the hourly men to do the bosses' dirty work for them. Management had a secondary objective here, which was to break our shop-floor union organization. Since the trauma of the strike and post-strike repression, a number of stewards and safety reps had patiently rebuilt the union in the plant, block by block—fighting every grievance, hazard, and injustice with a variety of tactics and constructing some shop-floor unity. We did so in the teeth of opposition from both company and union, whose officials were overly anxious to get along peacefully with each other. A war of the sexes would be a weapon in management's counteroffensive against us.

For months before the anticipated transfers, foremen and their assorted rumor mongers stirred up the pot with the specter of the Invasion of the Women. Two hundred Switchgear women would come and throw all Beach Road breadwinners out in the street; no one's job would be safe. Day after day, week after week, we were fed the tales: for example, that fourteen women with thirty years' seniority were coming to the department in eight days and no male would be protected. Better start thinking now about unemployment insurance.

In the department next to mine a few transfers of women were met with a vicious response from the men. Each side, including the militant steward, ended up ratting on the other to the boss. The men were furious and went all over the plant to warn others against allowing any "cunts" or "bitches" into their departments.

Meanwhile I had been fighting for the women to be called into new jobs opening up in the iron-stacking area of my department. The union's business agent had insisted that women couldn't physically handle those and other jobs. But I won the point with the company. The major influx of women would start here.

For weeks before their arrival, the department was hyper-alive, everyone keyed to the Invasion of the Women. I was approached by one of the guys, who said that a number of them had discussed the problem and wanted me, as their steward, to tell management the men didn't want the women in here and would fight to keep them out.

The moment was a personal watershed for me. As I listened to him, I knew that half measures would no longer do. I would now have to take the bull by the horns.

Over the years I had been dealing with male chauvinism in a limited fashion. As a health and safety rep, I had to battle constantly with men who would knowingly do dangerous work because it was "manly" to do so and because it affirmed their masculine superiority. The bosses certainly knew how to use guys like that to get jobs done quickly. With a mixture of sarcasm, force, and reason, I would argue, "It's stupidity not manliness to hurt yourself. Use your brains, don't be a hero and cripple yourself; you're harming all of us and helping the company by breaking the safety rules we fought so hard to establish, rules that protect all of us."

From this I was familiar with how irrational, self-destructive, and anti-collective the male ego could be. I also felt I had learned a great deal from the women's movement, including a never-ending struggle with my own sexism. Off and on I would have debates with my male co-workers about women's liberation. But all this only went so far. Now with the approaching invasion and the Great Fear gripping the department, I had to deal with an angry male sexism in high gear. I got off the fence.

I told this guy, "No. These women from Switchgear are our sisters, and we have fought for them to come into our department. They are our fellow workers with seniority rights, and we want them to work here rather than get laid off. If we deny them their seniority rights, it hurts us, for once that goes down the drain, none of us has any protection. It is our enemies, the bosses, who are trying to do them out of jobs here. There's enough work for everyone; even if there weren't, seniority has to rule. For us as well as for them. The guys should train the women when they come and make them feel welcome."

And with that reply, the battle was on. For the next few weeks the debate raged hot and heavy, touching on many basic questions, drawing in workers from all over the plant. Many men made the accusation that the women would be the bosses' fifth column and break our unity. They would side with the foremen, squeal on us, outproduce us, and thereby force speed-ups. The women were our enemy, or at least agents of the enemy, and would be used by *them* against *us*. Many of them pointed to the experience of the next department over, where, since the influx of a few women, the situation had been steadily worsening.

The reply was that if we treated the women as sisters and friends they'd side with us not the boss. Some of us had worked in Switchgear and knew it was the *men* there who got favored treatment. What's more, our own shop-floor unity left a lot to be desired and many of our male co-workers engaged in squealing and kowtowing to the boss. Some of us argued sarcastically that women could never equal some of our men in this area.

We argued that we had common class interests with our sisters against the company, particularly in protecting the seniority principle.

It was easy to tease guys with the contradictions that male double standards led them to. Although they were afraid the women would overproduce, at the same time they insisted that women wouldn't be physically strong enough to do our "man's work." Either they could or they couldn't was the answer to that one, and if they could, they deserved the jobs. It would be up to us to initiate them into the department norms. Many of the guys said that the women would never be able to do certain of the heavy and rotten jobs. As steward and safety rep I always jumped on that one: we shouldn't do those jobs either. Hadn't we been fighting to make them safer and easier for ourselves? 'Well, they answered, the women would still not be able to do all the jobs. Right, I would say, but how many guys here have we protected from doing certain jobs because of back or heart problems, or age, or simply personal distaste? If the women can't do certain jobs, we treat them the same way as men who can't. We don't victimize people who can't do everything the company wants them to. We protect them: as our brothers, and as our sisters.

By pointing out the irrationalities of the sexist double standards, we were pushing the guys to apply their class principles—universal standards of equal treatment. Treat the women just as we treat men regarding work tasks, seniority, illness, and so on.

Countering Sexism

Male sexist culture strives to degrade women to nothing but pieces of flesh, physical bodies, mindless animals . . . something less than fully human, which the men can then be superior to. Name-calling becomes a means of putting women in a different category from *us*, to justify different and inferior treatment.

Part of the fight to identify the women as co-workers was therefore the battle against calling them "cunts" or "bitches." It was important to set the public standard whereby the women were labeled as part of us, not *them*. I wouldn't be silent with anyone using these sexist labels and pushed the point very aggressively. Eventually everyone referred to "the women."

After a while most of the men in the department came to agree that having the women in and giving them a chance was the right thing to do by any standard of fairness, unionism, or solidarity, and was required by the basic human decency that separates *us* from *them*. But then the focus shifted to other areas. Many men came back with traditional arguments against women in the workforce. They belong at home with the kids, they're robbing male breadwinners of family income and so forth. But others disagreed: most of the guys' wives worked outside the home or had done so in the past; after all a family needed at least two wages these days. Some men answered that in bad times a family should have only one breadwinner so all would have an income. Fine, we told them, let's be really fair and square: you go home and clean the house and leave your wife at work. Alright, they countered, they could tolerate women working who supported a family, but not single women. And so I picked out four single men in our department and proposed they be immediately sacked.

Fairness and equality seemed to triumph here too. The guys understood that everyone who had a job at Westinghouse deserved equal protection. But then, some men found another objection. As one, Peter, put it, "I have no respect for any women who could come in to work here in these rotten conditions." The comeback was sharp: "What the hell are *you* putting up with this shit for? Why didn't you refuse to do that dirty job last month? Don't *you* deserve to be treated with respect?"[2]

As the Invasion Date approached I got worried. Reason and appeals to class solidarity had had a certain impact. Most of the guys were agreeing, grudgingly, to give the women a chance. But the campaign had been too short; fear and hostility were surfacing more and more. I was worried that there would be some ugly incident the first day or two that would set a pattern.

Much of the male hostility had been kept in check because I, as the union steward, had fought so aggressively on the issue. I decided to take this one step further and use some intimidation to enforce the basics of public behavior. In a tactic I later realized was a double-edged sword, I puffed myself up, assumed a cocky posture, and went for the jugular. I loudly challenged the masculinity of any worker who was opposed to the women. What kind of man is afraid of women? I asked. Only sissies and wimps are threatened by equality. A *real man* has nothing to be afraid of; he wants strong women. Any man worth his salt doesn't need the crutch of superiority over his sisters; he fears no female. A real man lives like an equal, doesn't step on women, doesn't degrade his sisters, doesn't have to rule the roost at home in order to affirm his manhood. Real men fight the boss, stand up with self-respect and dignity, rather than scapegoat our sisters.

I was sarcastic and cutting with my buddies. "This anti-woman crap of yours is a symbol of weakness. Stand up like a real man and behave and work as equals. The liberation of the women is the best thing that ever came along. . . . It's in *our* interests." To someone who boasted of how he made his wife cook his meals and clean his floors, I'd ask if she wiped his ass too? To the porno addicts I'd say, "You like that pervert shit? What's wrong with the real thing? Can you only get it up with those fantasies and cartoon women? Afraid of a real woman?" I'd outdo some of the worst guys in verbal intimidation and physical feats. Then I'd lecture them on women's equality and on welcoming our sisters the next week. I zeroed in on one or two of the sick types and physically threatened them if they pulled off anything with the women.

All of this worked, as I had hoped. It established an atmosphere of intimidation; no one was going to get smart with the women. Everyone would stand back for a while, some would cooperate, some would be neutral, and those I saw as "psycho-sexists" would keep out.

The tactic was effective because it spoke directly to a basic issue. But it was also effective because it took a leaf from the book of the psycho-sexists themselves.

At Westinghouse as elsewhere, some of the men were less chauvinistic and more sensible than others, but they often kept quiet in a group. They allowed the group pattern to be set by the most sexist bullies, whose style of woman baiting everyone at least gave in to. The psycho-sexists achieved this result because they challenged, directly or by implication, the masculinity of any male who didn't act the same way. All the men, whatever their real inclinations, are intimidated into acting or talking in a manner degrading to women. I had done the same thing, but in reverse. I had challenged the masculinity of any worker who would oppose the women. I had scared them off.

The Day the Women Arrived

The department crackled with tension the morning The Women arrived. There were only two of them to start with. The company was evidently scared by the volatile situation it had worked so hard to create. They backed off a direct confrontation by assigning my helper George and me to work with the women.

The two women were on their guard: Betty and Laura, in their late thirties, were expecting trouble. They were pleasantly shocked when I said matter-of-factly that we would train them on the job. They were overjoyed when I explained that the men had wanted them in our department and had fought the bosses to bring them here.

It was an unforgettable day. Men from all corners of the plant crept near the iron-stacking area to spy on us. I explained the work and we set about our tasks. We outproduced the standard rate by just a hair so that the company couldn't say the women weren't able to meet the normal requirements of the job.

My strategy was to get over the hump of the first few days. I knew that once the guys got used to the women being there, they'd begin to treat them as people, not as "women" and their hysteria would go away. It was essential to avoid incidents. Thus I forced the guys to interact with them. Calling over one of the male opponents, I introduced him as Bruce the Slinger who knew all the jobs and was an expert in lifts and would be happy to help them if asked and could always be called on to give a hand. This put him on the spot. Finally he flashed a big smile, and said, "Sure, just ask and I'd be pleased to show you anything, and to begin with, here's what to watch out for. . . ."

The morning went by. There were no incidents. From then on it was easy. More guys began to talk to the two women. They started to see them as Betty with four kids who lived on the mountain and knew wiring and was always cheerful; or Laura, who was a friend of John's uncle and was cranky early in the morning, who could easily operate the crane but had trouble with the impact gun, and who liked to heat up meat pies for lunch. After all, these men lived and worked with women all of their lives outside the plant— mothers, sisters, wives, in-laws, friends, daughters, and girlfriends. Having women at work was no big deal once they got over the trauma of the invasion of this male preserve. Just like helping your sister-in-law hang some wallpaper.

As the news spread, more and more women applied to transfer to our department. They were integrated with minimum fuss. The same thing happened in several adjoining departments. Quickly, men and women began to see each other as people and co-workers, not as enemies. Rather than man vs. woman it was John, Mary, Sue, Peter, Alice, George, and Laura. That Christmas we had a big party at someone's home—men and women of the department, drinking and dancing. The photos and various raucous tales of that night provided the basis for department storytelling for the next three months.

Was this, then, peace between the sexes? The integration of men and women as co-workers in the plant? Class solidarity triumphing over sex antagonism? Not quite. Although they were now together, it was not peace.

The result was more complicated, for now the war between the sexes was being extended from the community into the workplace.

Workplace Culture

As our struggle showed, sexism coexists and often is at war with class consciousness and with the trade union solidarity that develops among factory men. Our campaign was successful to the extent that it was able to sharply polarize and push the contradictions between these two tendencies in each individual. With most of the men, their sense of class solidarity triumphed over male chauvinism.

Many of the men had resisted the female invasion of the workplace because for them it was the last sanctum of male culture. It was somewhere they could get away from the world of women, away from responsibility and children and the civilized society's cultural restraints. In the plant they could revel in the rough and tumble of a masculine world of physical harshness, of constant swearing and rough behavior, of half-serious fighting and competition with each other and more serious fighting with the boss. It was eight hours full of filth and dirt and grease and grime and sweat—manual labor and a manly atmosphere. They could be vulgar and obscene, talk about football and car repairs, and let their hair down. Boys could be boys.

The male workplace culture functions as a form of rebellion against the discipline of their society. Outside the workplace, women are the guardians of the community. They raise the kids and enforce some degree of family and collective responsibility. They frequently have to force this upon men, who would rather go drinking or play baseball while the women mind the kids, wash the family's clothes, attend to problems with the neighbors and in-laws, and so on. Like rebellious teenage sons escaping mother's control, male wage earners enter the factory gates, where in their male culture they feel free of the restraints of these repressive standards.

Even if all factory men don't share these attitudes, a large proportion do, to a greater or lesser degree.

The manly factory culture becomes an outlet for accumulated anger and frustration. But this is a vicious circle because the tedious work and the subordination to the bosses is in large part the very cause of the male worker's dissatisfaction. He is bitter against a world that has kept him down, exploited his labor power, bent him to meet the needs of production and profit, cheated him of a better life, and made the daily grind so harsh. Working men are treated like dirt everywhere: at work they are at the bottom of the heap and under the thumb of the boss; outside they are scorned by polite society. But, the men can say, we are better than them all in certain ways; we're doing men's work; it's physically tough; women can't do it; neither can the bankers and politicians. Tough work gives a sense of masculine superiority that compensates for being stepped on and ridiculed. All that was threatened by the Women's Invasion.

However, this male workplace culture is not one-sided, for it contains a fundamentally positive sense of class value. The workingmen contrast themselves to other classes and take pride in having a concrete grasp of the physical world around them. The big shots can talk fancy and manipulate words, flout their elegance and manners. But we control the nuts and bolts of production, have our hands on the machines and gears and valves, the wires and lathes and pumps, the furnaces and spindles and batteries. We're the masters of the real and the concrete; we manipulate the steel and the lead, the wood, oil, and aluminum. What we know is genuine, the real and specific world of daily life. Workers are the wheels that make a society go round, the creators of social value and wealth. There would be no fancy society, no civilized conditions if it were not for our labor.

The male workers are contemptuous of the mild-mannered parasites and soft-spoken vultures who live off our daily sweat: the managers and directors, the judges and entertainers, the lawyers, the coupon clippers, the administrators, the insurance brokers, the legislators. . . all those who profit from the shop floor, who build careers for themselves with the wealth we create. All that social overhead depends upon our mechanical skills, our concrete knowledge, our calloused hands, our technical ingenuity, our strained muscles and backs.

The Dignity of Labor, but society treats us like a pack of dumb animals, mere bodies with no minds or culture. We're physical labor power; the intelligence belongs to the management class. Workers are sneeringly regarded as society's bodies, the middle class as society's mind. One is inferior; the other is superior and fully human. The workers are less than human, close to animals, society's beasts of burden.

The male workplace culture tends to worship this self-identity of vulgar physicalness. It is as if the men enjoy wallowing in a masculine filth. They brag of being the wild men of the factory. Say it loud: I'm a brute and I'm proud.

Sexism thus undermines and subverts the proud tradition of the dignity of labor. It turns a class consciousness upside down by accepting and then glorifying the middle-class view of manual labor and physical activity as inferior, animalistic, and crude. When workers identify with the savages that the bosses see them as, they develop contempt for themselves. It is self-contempt to accept the scornful labels, the negative definitions, the insulting dehumanized treatment, the cartoon stereotypes of class chauvinism: the super-masculine menials, the industrial sweat hogs.

Remember Peter, who couldn't respect a woman who would come to work in this hellhole. It was obviously a place where he felt he had lost his own self-respect. My reply to him was that he shouldn't put up with that rotten treatment, *that the men also deserved better*. We should be treated with dignity.

Respect yourself—fight back like a man, not a macho fool who glorifies that which degrades him.

Everything gets turned inside out. It is seen as manly to be treated as less than a man, as just a physical, instinctual creature. But this is precisely how sexist society treats women: as mindless bodies, pieces of flesh . . . "biology is destiny." You would think that male factory workers and the women's movement would be natural allies, that they'd speak the same language. They share a common experience of being used as objects, dehumanized by those on top. Men in the factory are treated not as persons, but as bodies, replaceable numbers, commodities, faceless factors of production. The struggles of workingmen and of women revolve around similar things. The right to choice on abortion, for example, revolves around the right for women to control their own bodies. Is this not what the fight for health and safety on the shop floor is all about? To have some control over our bodies, not to let the bastards do what they want with our lives and limbs, to wreck us in their search for higher profits.

But male chauvinism turns many workingmen away from their natural allies, away from a rational and collective solution to their problems, diverting them from class unity with their sisters into oppressors and degraders of their sisters. Robbed of their real manhood—their humanity as men—they get a false sense of manhood by lording over women.

Playing the Foreman at Home

Many men compensate for their wage-labor status in the workplace by becoming the boss at home. Treated terribly in the factory, he plays foreman after work and rules with authority over his wife and kids. He thus gains at home that independence he loses on the shop floor. He becomes a part-time boss himself with women as his servants. This becomes key to his identity and sense of self-esteem. Working-class patriarchs, rulers of the roost.

This sense of authority has an economic underpinning. The male worker's role as primary breadwinner gives him power over the family and status in society. It also makes him the beneficiary of the woman's unpaid labor in the household.

A wage laborer not only lacks independence, he also lacks property, having nothing but his labor power to sell. Sexism gives him the sense of property, as owner of the family. His wife or girlfriend is his sexual property. As Elvis sang, "You are my only possession, you are my everything." This domination and ownership of a woman are basic to how he sees himself.

These things are powerful pressures toward individualism, a trait of the business class: foreman of the family, man of property, possessiveness. They elevate the wage earner above the category of the downtrodden common laborer, and in doing so divert him from the collective struggle with his brothers and sisters to change their conditions. Capitalism is based on competitiveness and encourages everyone to be better than the next guy, to rise up on the backs of your neighbors. Similarly the male chauvinist seeks superiority over others, of both sexes. Men tend to be competitive, always putting one another down, constantly playing one-upmanship. Men even express appreciation and affection for each other through good-natured mutual insults.

Sexist culture thus undermines the working-class traditions of equality and solidarity and provides a recruiting ground for labor's adversaries. Over the years at Westinghouse I had noticed that a high proportion of workers who became foremen were extreme chauvinists—sexual braggarts, degraders of women, aggressive, individualistic, ambitious, ever willing to push other workers around. Male competition is counterproductive in the shop or union, where we ought to cooperate as equals and seek common solutions. The masculine ego makes for bad comradeship, bad brotherhood. It also makes it difficult for chauvinistic men to look at and deal objectively with many situations because their fragile egos are always on the line. They have to keep up a facade of superiority and are unable to handle criticism, no matter how constructive. Their chauvinistic crutches make them subjective, irrational, unreliable, and often self-destructive, as with men who want to work or drive dangerously.

Workingmen pay a high price for the limited material benefits they get from sexist structures. It is the bosses who make the big bucks and enjoy the real power from the inferior treatment of women.

The Next Round and a Peek Into the Women's World

Battles continued about the women getting a crack at the more skilled and high-paying assembly jobs up the floor. Next we won the fight against the company, which was trying to promote junior men. This time women were there to fight for themselves, and there were male stewards from other departments who backed them up. The shop floor was less hostile, many of the men being sympathetic or neutral.

But despite the general cooperation, most men still maintained that the women were inferior workers. The foremen did their best to foster sex divisions by spreading stories of all the mistakes the women supposedly made. They would reserve the worst jobs for the men, telling them the women couldn't do them. The men would thus feel superior while resenting the women's so-called privileges and the women would feel grateful for not having to do these jobs. The supervisors forged a common cause with some of the guys against the women. They fed their male egos and persuaded them to break safety rules, outproduce, and rat on other workers. The male bond often proved stronger than the union bond, and our collective strength suffered as a result.

As for myself, I was learning and changing a lot as a result of my experiences. I would often meet with the women at the lunch table to plan strategy. These sessions affected me in many ways. They were good talks, peaceful and constructive, with no fighting and argument, no competition, all of us talking sensibly about a common problem and figuring out how to handle it as a group. It was a relaxed and peaceful half hour, even when we had serious differences.

This was in marked contrast to the men's lunch tables, which were usually boisterous and raucous during those months. There was a lot of yelling and shouting, mutual insults, fists pounding, and throwing things at one another. When you ate at the women's table, you sat down to rest and relax. When you ate at the men's table, you sat down to fight.

I had read and heard a lot from my feminist friends about this so-called woman's world of warmth, cooperation, and friendship, as contrasted to men's norm of aggression, violence, and competition. Although I had always advocated women's liberation and respected the women's movement, I paid only lip service, if that, to this distinction, and was in fact more often scornful of this "women's world." Over the years I had become a more aggressive male, which I saw as distinct from being a chauvinist or sexist male. In the world of constant struggle, I thought, you had to be aggressive or go under. We'd have peace and love in the socialist future, some distant day.

As a unionist it became very clear to me that the women almost automatically acted like a collective. And in those months of going back and forth between the men's and women's tables, I took a long and serious look at this women's world. It was an unnerving but pleasant experience to sit down among friends, without competition and put-downs, not to have to watch out for flying objects, not to be on the alert for nerve-shattering noises, to be in a non-threatening atmosphere. There was obviously something genuine there and it seemed to offer a better way. It also became obvious to me that the gap between the sexes was enormous and that men and women were far from speaking a common language.

New Struggles and the Recession

In the months ahead there were new struggles. There was the fight to form a women's committee in the union in order to bring women's demands to the fore, to combat sexism among the male workers, and to give women a forum for developing their own outlook, strategy, and leadership. We launched that fight in the fall of 1981, with Mary, a militant woman in our rank-and-file group, in the lead. The old guard, led by the union's national president, fought us tooth and nail. The battle extended over a number of months and tumultuous membership meetings, and we eventually lost as the leadership railroaded through its chauvinistic policy. No women's committee was formed. In time, however, the leadership came to support women's rights formally, even though they did little to advance the cause in practice.

In the spring of 1982 the recession finally caught up with us at Westinghouse and there were continuous layoffs in every division. Our bargaining power shrank, everyone was afraid for his or her own job, and the contract became little more than a piece of paper as the company moved aggressively to roll back the clock on our hard-won traditions on seniority rules, health and safety regulations, and so on. Bitterness and frustration were everywhere.

The company went after the women. Their seniority rights were blatantly ignored as they were transferred to "chip and grind" duties—the least skilled, the heaviest, dirtiest, and most unpleasant jobs. The progress the men had made also seemed to vanish. From the first day of the layoff announcements, many rallied to the call of "Get the women out first." Those most hostile to women came back out in the open and campaigned full blast. They found many sympathetic responses on the shop floor: protect the breadwinners and, what's more, no women should be allowed to bump a male since they're not physically capable of doing the jobs anyway. It was the war of the sexes all over again, but far worse now because the situation allowed little leeway. There was some baiting of the women, and the plant became a tension-ridden, hateful place for all workers.

The bosses managed to seize back many of the powers the shop floor had wrenched away from them over the years, and even to create newer and deeper divisions within the workforce. But the recession was not all-powerful. We still managed to win all our battles on health and safety, and the shop floor continued to elect our militant shop stewards.

Some of the women gave in to the inevitable and were laid off despite their seniority. But others fought back and fought well. Some of them were even able to gain the sympathy of the male workers who had at first stood aside or resisted them. In some cases, the men joined in and helped the women retain their jobs.

Obviously, things had changed a great deal amongst the men since the first women began to come into the division. *When the chips were down, many men took their stand with their sisters against the company—despite the recession. . . .*

Workingmen share basic common interests with our sisters. When more of us recognize this, define and speak about these interests in our own way, and act in common with women, then we will be able to start moving the mountains that stand in our way.

NOTES

1. United Electrical Workers (UEW) is a union whose militant rhetoric is rarely matched by its actual behavior. For example, it has passed resolutions at its national conventions favoring the formation of women's committees at the national and local levels, but what is on paper often does not match daily reality. Some leaders have a habit of advocating a position that suits the political needs of

the moment rather than consistent principles. These limitations are not peculiar to UEW, which is much like the rest of the labor movement, despite its sometimes radical rhetoric. Like most of the labor movement, it has its good and its bad locals, its good and its bad leaders. Like a lot of other unions it has moved toward a better position on "women's" issues, although with a lot of sharp contradictions and see-saws in behavior along the way, given its authoritarian style.

2. The names of the plant workers in this article are not their real ones.

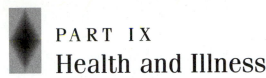

PART IX
Health and Illness

*As a middle-class, educated, bilingual Asian-American woman, I was aware of
the importance of having the choice to have an abortion. . . . I had been
unaware of how the right to have an abortion is also a right to survival in this
country if you are a poor, uneducated, non-English-speaking immigrant.*

CONNIE CHAN[1]

*A recent study . . . concluded that men in western countries today have sperm
counts less than half as high as their grandfathers had at the same age.*

PETER MONTAGUE[2]

Women and men face different challenges related to health and illness. Gender-
linked illnesses correlate with genetic/biological differences between women
and men (for example, women don't get testicular cancer) and with masculine and feminine behavior (the vast majority of lung cancer patients were
men before women earned the right to smoke).[3] The structure of sex-
segregated work and the widely shared assumption that men should engage
in risky physical behavior put many women and men at different risks for
various illnesses. These differences probably explain why women live longer
than men in the United States.[4] They probably also explain why women are
more likely than men to become addicted to prescription drugs and are more
likely to report feeling depressed.[5]

New research on the effects of environmental toxins on male and female
reproductive systems suggests that these toxins create different kinds of illnesses in men than in women. For instance, Janet Raloff examined the
impact of environmental toxins on men's reproductive health and concluded
that toxins are linked to such reproductive issues as low sperm counts, testicles that fail to descend, and male urinary tract defects.[6]

Other factors, such as sexual orientation and race, interact with gender
to put different groups at higher or lower risk for illness and injury. The
AIDS epidemic, for example, thus far has affected primarily men, in part
because the majority of early victims of this epidemic were gay men and IV
drug users. Few lesbians, on the other hand, have contracted AIDS.[7] The
faces of people with HIV infection and AIDS are changing, however, as the
epidemic spreads. Heterosexual women are now the fastest-growing group
with AIDS in the United States.[8] Teenage girls, especially girls of color, are at
particularly high risk; in some regions, they have higher rates of HIV infection than boys.[9]

Race interacts with gender to create vast disparities in the health of
Blacks and whites. African American women face higher rates of violence
and childbirth-related illness and death than do white women.[10] Both Black

399

and white men die from homicide at higher rates than Black and white women. Although both Black and white men die in automobile accidents at similar rates, Black men are more likely than white men to die in other kinds of accidents.[11] Among young men, Black men aged 15–24 are six times more likely than white men to die of homicide, and homicide is the principal cause of death for Black men in this age group.[12] Men are more likely than women to commit suicide, and among both women and men, whites are twice as likely as Blacks to do so.[13] White men are much more likely than men of color to contract testicular cancer.[14] Black men are twice as likely as white men to die of prostate cancer.[15]

Apart from differences in the kinds of health risks faced by various groups, the issue of access to health care is becoming increasingly serious in the United States. People who hold low-paying jobs without health insurance frequently cannot afford to buy it. Women are more likely than men to hold such jobs, and are more likely than men to be the primary caretakers of children who need coverage.[16] A recent estimate put the number of uninsured state residents in Massachusetts alone at 750,000.[17] Managed care is also interfering with health care in many cases, as doctors and patients must submit requests for treatment to third parties who do not know the individual patients involved. Without major structural reform of the health care system, this situation is very likely to worsen, since individual and small collective efforts at empowerment cannot really change the system.

Literature on health and illness explores the links between illness or death and gender socialization, including the ways that various women and men cope with illness.[18] The readings in this chapter address several aspects of this large and growing field of study.

In the first reading, nurse anthropologist Evelyn Barbee and medical geographer Marilyn Little present a wide range of issues related to the health of African American women. They first place African American women's health in the context of racism and then describe the particular health problems African American women face. Naming high rates of violence and sexual abuse, high risk for HIV infection, and high rates of childbirth-related illness and death, they discuss how African American women have mobilized themselves to address these crises (see also the article by Byllye Avery in Part XI). Barbee and Little also discuss reproductive freedom, as distinct from reproductive rights, which frequently centers only on the right to choose abortion. They point out some crucial rights, including the right to bear healthy, living children; the right to good health care for children; to live through childbirth; and to not be unwillingly sterilized.

The next article deals with abortion. Connie Chan argues that access to legal, inexpensive, and safe abortions is crucial to women of color. She bases her conclusion on her contact with many low-income Chinese women seeking abortion.

Environmental toxins and their effect on health is a growing concern in both the United States and other parts of the world. Professor and activist

Rita Arditti and activist writer Tatiana Schreiber argue for a causal link between breast cancer and toxins in the environment. They describe activist strategies to put the breast cancer epidemic on the national health agenda.

Next is a study of white, mostly white collar and professional men who have had testicular cancer. Sociologist David Frederick Gordon talked with men about their adjustments to this largely curable form of cancer, exploring how it affected their identities as men.

This chapter concludes with an excerpt from an essay by David Deitcher, in which he describes how ACT UP, the AIDS Coalition to Unleash Power, has battled the medical establishment to improve health care for people with HIV infection and AIDS.

The voices in this chapter make powerful pleas for decent health care for African American women, for a nontoxic world, for sensitive access to abortion, and for an adequate medical response to the AIDS epidemic.

NOTES

1. Connie S. Chan, "Reproductive Issues Are Essential Survival Issues for the Asian-American Communities," in Marlene Gerber Fried, ed., *From Abortion to Reproductive Freedom* (Boston: South End Press, 1990), p. 176.

2. Peter Montague, "Are Environmental Chemicals Causing Men to Lose Their Essential Masculinity?," *Rachel's Hazardous Waste News*, 343, June 23, 1993: 1.

3. Ingrid Waldron, "Contributions of Changing Gender Differences in Behavior and Social Roles to Changing Gender Differences in Mortality," in Donald Sabo and David Frederick Gordon, eds., *Men's Health and Illness: Gender, Power, and the Body* (Thousand Oaks, CA: Sage, 1995), p. 27.

4. Judith M. Stillion, "Premature Death among Males: Extending the Bottom Line of Men's Health," in Sabo and Gordon, *Men's Health and Illness*, pp. 46–67.

5. Regarding addictions, see "Addictive Behaviors from the Women's Health Data Book," reprinted in Nancy Worcester and Marianne Whatley, eds., *Women's Health: Readings on Social, Economic, and Political Issues*, 2nd ed., (Dubuque, IA: Kendall/Hunt, 1994), pp. 153–57. Regarding depression, see Marian Murphy, "Women and Mental Health," reprinted in Worcester and Whatley, eds., *Women's Health*, pp. 127–32.

6. Janet Raloff, "That Feminine Touch: Are Men Suffering from Prenatal or Childhood Exposures to 'Hormonal' Toxicants?," *Science News*, 145, January 22, 1994: pp. 56–58.

7. Ruth L. Schwartz, "New Alliances, Strange Bedfellows: Lesbians, Gay Men and AIDS," in Arlene Stein, ed., *Sisters, Sexperts, and Queers: Beyond the Lesbian Nation* (New York: Plume, 1993), pp. 230–244.

8. M. Wolfe, "Women and HIV/AIDS Education," paper prepared for the NEA Health Information Network, Atlanta, 1991. Cited in the American Association of University Women Educational Foundation, *How Schools Shortchange Girls* (New York: Marlowe, 1992), p. 137.

9. L. D'Angelo et al., "HIV Infection in Adolescents: Can We Predict Who Is at Risk?," poster presentation at the Fifth International Conference on AIDS, June 1989. Data from Washington D.C. was reported. Cited in the American Association of University Women Educational Foundation, *How Schools Shortchange Girls*, p. 137.

10. Evelyn L. Barbee and Marilyn Little, "Health, Social Class, and African-American Women," in Stanlie M. James and Abena P. A. Buscia, eds., *Theorizing Black Feminisms: The Visionary Pragmatism of Black Women* (New York: Routledge, 1993).

11. Stillion, "Premature Death among Males," p. 52.

12. Jewell Taylor Gibbs, "Anger in Young Black Males: Victims or Victimizers?," in Richard G. Majors and Jacob U. Gordon, eds., *The American Black Male: His Status and His Future* (Chicago: Nelson-Hall, 1994), p. 128.

13. Stillion, "Premature Death among Males," p. 53.

14. David Frederick Gordon, "Testicular Cancer and Masculinity," in Sabo and Gordon, *Men's Health and Illness*.

15. National Cancer Institute, *Cancer among Blacks and Other Minorities: Statistical Profiles* (Washington, D.C.: U.S. Department of Health and Human Services, NIH Publication #86-2785, 1986), p. 10.

16. I recently saw an advertisement in Boston offering health insurance for children. Parents had the option to insure their children when they could not afford to insure the whole family.

17. Boston Globe Dialogues, "What State N.E. Health Care?," *The Boston Sunday Globe,* March 10, 1996, p. 72.

18. For more information on women's and men's health, see Sabo and Gordon, *Men's Health and Illness,* Worcester and Whatley, eds., *Women's Health*; Evelyn C. White, ed., *The Black Women's Health Book* (Seattle: Seal Press, 1990).

49

HEALTH, SOCIAL CLASS AND AFRICAN-AMERICAN WOMEN

EVELYN L. BARBEE AND MARILYN LITTLE

The litany of health problems which plague African-American women at rates disproportionate to their percentage of the US population is familiar: hypertension, lupus, diabetes, maternal mortality, cervical cancer, etc. Of these problems, the success rate in terms of maintenance (in cases of chronic diseases) and cure (in cases of episodic illnesses) is affected by the constant circumscribing effect of being an African-American female in a white, patriarchal, racist society. This chapter asserts that being African-

From *Theorizing Black Feminisms: The Visionary Pragmatism of Black Women*, Stanlie M. James and Abena P. A. Buscia, eds., Routledge, 1993, pp. 182–199. Reprinted by permission of the publisher, Routledge: New York and London.

American and female constitutes a unique position in American society. The position of African-American women in American society is unique because the same ideology used during slavery to justify the roles of Black women underlies the external, controlling images of contemporary African-American women (Collins, 1990). As a result, the multiple jeopardies (King, 1988) and externally imposed images of African-American women interact in ways that serve to compromise their health status.

Consequently, the health needs of the African-American woman cannot be met by reformulation or "reform" of racist health policies or sexist health policies; rather her needs will only be addressed by looking at the point where the two sets of policies converge and form a barrier to her mental, emotional and physical well-being. Although we agree with King's (1988) conclusion that scholarly descriptions that concentrate on our multiple oppressions "have confounded our ability to discover and appreciate the ways in which African-American women are not victims," one area that has not been adequately explored, an area in which African-American women currently and historically have been victimized, is the "health care" arena.

In 1988 an estimated 30.3 million African-Americans represented more than 12 per cent of the population (US Bureau of the Census, 1989a). More than 52 per cent of these 30.3 million people were female. Within the African-American population the ratio of women to men is 110 to 100. The respective Euro-American sex ratio is 104 females for every 100 males. Although African-American males outnumber females up until the age of 20 years, after the age of 20 years the number of African-American women to men increases to the extent that the ratio at ages 65 years and over is 149:100 (US Bureau of the Census, 1989a).

In terms of family structure, 51 percent of African-American families were married couples; 43 percent female householders, no husband present; and 6 percent were male householders, no wife present (US Bureau of the Census, 1989b). The respective median incomes for these households were: $27,182, $9,710 and $17,455. Among families that included children under 18 years of age, those households headed by women were four times more likely to be poor than those of two-parent families (US Bureau of the Census, 1988).

The Position of African-American Women

Contemporary efforts to explain the position of African-American women in the USA were built upon the notion of "double jeopardy" (Beale, 1970). Beale's idea recognized that African-American women faced double discrimination because of their race and sex. Lewis's (1977) exploration of the structural position of African-American women was premised on "double jeopardy." "While inequality is *manifested* in the exclusion of a group from public life, it is actually *generated* in the group's unequal access to power and resources in a hierarchically arranged social order" (Lewis, 1977: 343). Because African-American women have membership in two subordinate groups, African-American and women, they lack access to authority and resources in society and are in structural opposition with the dominant racial/ethnic group (Euro-American) and the dominant sexual group (male) (Lewis, 1977).

In her critique of the concepts of double jeopardy and triple jeopardy (racism, sexism and classism), King (1988) noted that because each conceptualization presumes direct independent effect on status, neither was able to deal with the interactive effects of sexism, racism and classism. African-American women are subjected to several, simultaneous oppressions which involve multiplicative relationships. The importance of any one factor in explaining African-American women's circumstances varies and is dependent upon the particular aspect of life under consideration and the reference group to whom African-American women are being compared (King, 1988). In regard to health, the multifaceted influences of race, gender and often social class interact in ways that render African-American women less healthy and more vulnerable to sickness than Euro-American women. Furthermore, they have to contend with their illness at the same time that they seek care from the racist, sexist and class-based system of American medicine.

While African-American women may be invisible in many spheres of life (hooks, 1981), their visibility vis-à-vis the medical establishment appears to be dependent upon procedures that need to be practiced (e.g., hysterectomies) and drugs that need to be tested (e.g., birth control). Elsewhere Barbee (1992) argued that the externally produced images of African-American women profoundly influence how medical and social professionals treat African-American women when these women are victims of violence. Here it is argued that these same images influence the kind of medical care or treatment given or not given to African-American women.

Images of African-American Women

Because of the interactions among racism, sexism and often classism, African-American women occupy a structural position in which they are viewed as subordinate to all other women and men in this society. Beliefs, myths and stereotypes about African-American women have served to intensify their status as "other." This view of the African-American woman as an object encourages the deployment of externally applied images and makes it particularly difficult to be viewed as a person, let alone an individual, by medical practitioners. As Christensen (1988: 191) noted: "No other woman has suffered physical and mental abuse, degradation, and exploitation on North American shores comparable to that experienced by the Black female."

In pointing out that race, class and gender oppression depend on powerful ideological justification for their existence, Collins (1990) identifies four externally defined, socially constructed, controlling images that are applied to African-American women. These images are mammy, the faithful, obedient domestic servant; the matriarch; the welfare mother and the Jezebel. The prevailing images of mammy, matriarch, welfare mother and Jezebel provide the ideological justification for racial oppression, gender subordination and economic exploitation (Collins, 1990). Each of these images contributes to society's and consequently medicine's view of African-American women.

The mammy image, the faithful, obedient servant, was created to justify the economic exploitation of Black women during slavery. As a social construction, its persistence is due to a need to rationalize the long-standing restriction of Black women to domestic service (Collins, 1990). In general medical workers are not receptive to questions from clients and patients. Those who subscribe to the mammy image are even less receptive to questions from African-American women. An additional danger is that those African-American women who internalize the mammy image may consciously and unconsciously sustain gender and racial exploitation in a number of ways. One of the more dangerous consequences may be a tendency to agree voluntarily to medical procedures because they believe in obeying the doctor.

Matriarchs are considered to be overly aggressive, emasculating, strong, independent, unfeminine women. The matriarch image implies the actuality of a social order in which women exercise social and political power. This image is central to the interlocking systems of race, class and gender oppression. The matriarch image allows the dominant group to blame African-American women for the success or failure of their children (Collins, 1990). An additional effect of this image is that it allows "helping" professionals to ignore African-American women when they need assistance. It is difficult to acknowledge that an African-American woman needs medical assistance when she is constantly referred to as being "strong."

Equally damaging is the welfare mother image. This is essentially an updated version of the breeder image that was created during slavery (Collins, 1990). Welfare mothers are viewed as being too lazy to work and thus are content to sit around and collect their welfare checks. This current objectification of African-American women as welfare mothers serves to label their fertility as unnecessary and dangerous. The welfare mother image provides Euro-Americans (and some African-Americans who have embraced these images without understanding their underlying ideology) with ideological justification for restricting the fertility of some African-American women because they are producing too many economically non-productive children (Davis, 1983).

The Jezebel image is one of a whore or a sexually aggressive woman (Collins, 1990). As Collins (1990) notes, the whore image is a central link in the Euro-American elite male's images of African-American women because attempts to control African-American women's sexuality lie at the heart of African-American women's oppression. Historically, the sexually promiscuous stereotype was used to contrast African-American women with the "virtuous" Euro-American woman. It also provided the rationale that justified the sexual assaults on Black women by Euro-American men (Collins, 1990; hooks, 1981). In contemporary times the Jezebel image is used as reason both for the sexual denigration of African-American women and for ignoring or minimizing such sexual abuse. The repercussions of these images on African-American women are most clearly seen in health statistics. While these "facts" are in and of themselves tragic enough, the real tragedy lies in how they have been used in an attempt to undermine the self-esteem of African-American women.

Health Statistics and the Right to Privacy

One of the first things a poor person loses is the right to privacy. She must surrender information about her private life in exchange for a modicum of basic needs which the state grudgingly provides. The fact that the information extracted often goes beyond what is required for service is of little use to her. She is powerless and in need. *They* have the ability to determine her ineligible and consequently to affect her physical survival.

The vulnerability of the poor is ruthlessly exploited in the name of science. Countless graduate students in the health sciences have benefited from this vulnerability. Innumerable theses and dissertations have been written based on data collected from the poor. The informants were usually corralled at points of defenselessness: while waiting for WIC tickets (a nutritional supplement program for poor women and children), for emergency medical care, etc. Many of these women probably had no idea that it was unnecessary to submit to the questions. Some may have been given an option but believed compliance would improve their future service.

The data collected are never returned to the informants in a way that is useful. The original reports are written for the intellectual elite. The final dissemination of the data is through the mass media and only then if the results are newsworthy (i.e,. sensational). Results are deemed newsworthy when they support the prevailing myths of our system. The master myth relevant to health is the inherent (i.e., genetic) instability of African-Americans' minds, bodies and "culture."

The right to privacy is predicated by income and mediated by race. The vast numbers of poor whites have not been an issue of interest for the intellectual elite. There has been historically a conscious choice to analyze health data by race not by income. The impact of this decision is manifested by our present inability to relieve the health problems of any Americans as we remain the only industrialized society outside of South Africa not to have a national health insurance plan. It is unquestionable that the same obstacles as in South Africa exist in the USA: the unwillingness to provide adequate health care to all regardless of color or income.

Public health statistics support the resistance to a national health insurance as they imply an inequity in health problems. When they suggest that only certain segments of the population suffer from certain diseases, and then are used to promote interventions for another segment of the population, health statistics are used as instruments of oppression. For example, although health statistics clearly indicate that coronary heart disease (CHD) is and has been a very serious problem for African-American women, public intervention programs imply that it is primarily a problem for Euro-American males. African-American women's death rate from CHD exceeds that of Euro-American women (Myers, 1986). Although there are different types of heart disease, the different types share common risk factors. For African-American women these risk factors include cigarette smoking, hypertension, obesity and diabetes. The social and structural risk factors include higher life stresses (Harburg *et al.*, 1973), truncated medical care access and lower-quality care (Yellin *et al.*, 1983).

A comparison of other CHD impact variables attributable to smoking (deaths, related lost years of life, cases, related hospital days, related days of restricted activity and related medical expenditures) between African-American and Euro-American women concluded that there were no "racial" differences (Kumanyika and Savage, 1986: 243). However, these comparisons did not take into account the fact that a large number of African-American women are heads of households and often responsible for young children. The sociocultural impact of CHD on African-American women is much greater for them and their families than it is for Euro-American women.

The prevalence of hypertension in African-American women increases with age and is 1.7 to 3 times higher in African-American women than Euro-American women in every age group (Kumanyika and Savage, 1986). In addition to being a risk factor for heart disease and heart failure, hypertension leads to pathological changes which can cause kidney disease or stroke. Demographically the highest levels of blood pressure for African-American women are in the South and the West. A major structural risk factor for hypertension is stress. Urban women's blood pressures are lower than those of rural women (Kumanyika and Savage, 1986). The aetiology for these demographic differences is unknown. Hypertension is often associated with another health problem of African-American women, obesity.

Obesity, an excess of body fat, can range from mild (120 percent) to severe (more than 200 percent) of the desirable or ideal body weight (Moore, 1990). Overweight, a weight in excess of the desirable body weight (Moore, 1990), is often confused with obesity. Because the prevalence of overweight in African-American women is higher than that of comparable groups of Euro-American women (Gillum, 1987), fat is a feminist issue that affects large numbers of African-American women.

Research-identified variables that make it more difficult for African-American women to lose weight are: (1) education below college level, (2) marriage and (3) low family income (Kahn *et al.*, 1991). Narratives from African-American women reveal entirely different factors:

> *I work for General Electric making batteries, and from the stuff they suit me up in, I know it's killing me. My home life is not working. My old man is an alcoholic. My kids got babies. Things are not well with me. And the one thing I know I can do when I come home is to cook me a pot of food and sit down in front of the TV and eat it. And you can't take that away from me until you're ready to give me something in its place. (Avery, 1990: 7)*

What confounds the issue in regard to weight and African-American women are Eurocentric notions about attractiveness, biomedical determinations about health and African-American cultural ideas about beauty. Many of the negative traits associated with obesity, lack of control, unattractiveness and slovenliness, have long been associated with African-Americans as a "race." On the one hand, Eurocentric ideas about obesity tend to equate fat with unattractiveness. Consequently, those African-American women who subscribe to Euro-American standards of beauty are placed in a double bind in which one culturally evaluated trait (obesity) reinforces this society's negative view of their physical appearance. On the other hand, in African-American communities, a certain level of obesity is considered attractive. Historically, African-Americans have associated degrees of overweight with well-being. To be thin was to be "poor." The African-American community's preference for "healthy" women has resulted in much lower rates of anorexia and bulimia for African-American women. However, the close relationship between adult onset diabetes and obesity requires that African-American women closely monitor their weight.

Diabetes is a disease that has particularly severe consequences for African-American women. Data from the 1981 National Health Interviews demonstrated that African-American women's diabetes rate was 38.2 per 1,000. One of the ten leading causes of death in 1988 was diabetes mellitus and African-American women's death rate from this was 27.3 versus 17.6 for Euro-American women (National Center for Health Statistics, 1990). An additional problem for African-American women is that the associations among obesity, diabetes and hypertension increase the risk for heart disease.

Comparison health statistics between African-American and Euro-American women that illustrate less, little or no difference in incidence between them for a specific disease sometimes serve to mask the enormity of certain problems for African-American women. Breast cancer statistics are a case in point. For years the focus on the lower incidence of breast cancer in African-American versus Euro-American women effectively served to mask the fact that African-American women have a higher death rate from breast cancer than Euro-American women. Although the breast cancer rate for

African-American women is less than that for Euro-American women, their mortality rate for this disease exceeds that of any other group of women (National Center for Health Statistics, 1990). Some of the reasons given for this disparity in mortality rates are socioeconomic status (SES), later stage at diagnosis, delay in detection and treatment, treatment differences and biological/constitutional factors (Report of the Secretary's Task Force, 1986). Since biological/constitutional factors are neither defined nor discussed in the report, they can be dismissed as factors. SES, later stage at diagnosis, and delay in treatment are related to problems of access. Poverty is a major factor in both later diagnosis and delay in treatment. The poor have not benefited from the various advances in cancer prevention, detection and treatment (American Cancer Society, 1990). However, poverty is not the only factor. McWhorter and Mayer (1987) found that when age, stage of cancer and histology were adjusted, African-American women received less aggressive surgical treatment, were less likely to be treated surgically and were more likely to be treated nonsurgically than Euro-American women.

Human Immunodeficiency Virus (HIV)/Autoimmunodeficiency Disease (AIDS)

AIDS is a national problem that is wreaking devastation in the African-American community. It is one of the ten leading causes of death for the African-American population (National Center for Health Statistics, 1990). African-Americans accounted for 25 percent of the AIDS deaths in 1988 (National Center for Health Statistics, 1990). HIV affects African-American women in a number of ways. First, African-American women and their children are part of the fastest-growing population of AIDS victims. Second, if diagnosed with AIDS, in addition to being concerned about herself, the woman has to be concerned with the effect of her death on her children. Third, the case definition of AIDS is based upon a male profile. As a result the profile does not take into account gynecological manifestations of HIV. As Anastos and Marte note: "If women's disease manifests with the same infections as it does in men, it may be recognized and reported as AIDS; if the infections, still HIV related, are different, the women are not considered to have AIDS" (1989: 6). Since eligibility for Social Security Supplemental (SSI) is based upon a diagnosis of AIDS, many women with AIDS are deemed ineligible for SSI benefits. Fourth, if a woman is pregnant and HIV positive, she is concerned with transmitting the disease to her newborn. Fifth, if she is diagnosed as HIV positive, her chances of contracting AIDS are higher and she will die sooner than her Euro-American sister. This disparity is usually accounted for by the mode of transmission. Many African-American women are exposed to HIV through intravenous drug use. As a result, the virus reaches their bloodstream much faster than it does when the virus is transmitted through sexual contact. Sixth, if someone in a woman's family, i.e., her child or partner, contracts the disease, in all likelihood she will be responsible for taking care of them.

Mental Health

In 1979, African-American women reported a lower level of well-being than African-American males, white females and white males (Institute for Urban Affairs and Research, 1981). One third of the women surveyed reported a level of distress comparable with that of an independent sample of mental health patients (Institute for Urban Affairs and Research, 1981). Although the research on depression in African-American women reports high rates of depressive symptomatology and depression (Carrington, 1980; Dressler, 1987; Dressler and Badger, 1985; Gary *et al.*, 1985), African-American women are less likely to be medically diagnosed as depressive than Euro-American females (Smith, 1981).

Among African-Americans the highest rates of depression occur in women under 45 years of age; the lowest rates are in African-Americans aged 45 years and older. At all ages and income levels, women's depressive symptomatology is greater than men's (Gary *et al.*, 1985). Factors that increase the risk of depression in younger African-American women are: being poor, being between 18 and 45 years of age, being unemployed, high school education or less, the presence of minor children in the household, and being divorced or separated (Brown, 1990).

There is some evidence that suggests that support networks as traditionally viewed are not as useful to African-American women when they are depressed. In an examination of the relationships among economic stressors, extended kin support, active coping and depressive symptoms in a sample of 285 African-American households in a southern community, Dressler (1987) found a positive relationship between extended kin support and depressive symptoms. Women who reported higher active coping strategies reported fewer depressive symptoms. In addition to the previously discussed medical conditions two other conditions that disproportionally affect the health of African-American women are reproductive rights and violence.

Reproductive Rights Versus Reproductive Freedom

We take issue with the notion of reproductive rights, particularly as it concerns African-American women. The national debate on reproductive rights is one that almost totally eclipses the interest and needs of African-American women. The debate, from its intellectual framework to its proposed goals, does not address the serious health problems of marginalized groups. The philosophical boundaries of the debate are seriously compromised. To talk in terms of "reproductive rights" is an intellectual abdication to a legal system primarily concerned with property rights *not* human rights. The phrase is an oxymoron. Human reproduction is not a right; it is a biological possibility. The two major opponents in the debate have chosen or accepted the media terms of "pro choice" and "right to life." The right to life seems to presume the "right" begins with conception, is most vibrant during gestation and ends at birth. The success of neither of the two will significantly improve the plight of Black females who have historically suffered disproportionally from the institutionalized attack on the Black family and "Third World" rates of infant mortality.

Tervalon (1988) notes that there are three interconnected aspects of reproductive rights: access to abortion, infant mortality and forced sterilization. Rather than talking about reproductive rights, it would be more accurate to speak of reproductive freedom. Reproductive freedom is defined here as unrestrained access to the medical knowledge (information) available in one's society that is necessary for the optimum maintenance of one's reproductive health. In addition to the aspects referred to by Tervalon, reproductive freedom would include safe, effective, affordable forms of birth control, family planning, sexual education, freedom from forced sterilization (Ditzion and Golden, 1984), the right of consenting adults to conduct their sex lives as they choose, reduction in African-American infant and maternal mortality rates, and affordable access to diagnosis and treatment of sexually transmitted diseases (STDs).

The lack of reproductive freedom has resulted in disastrous consequences for African-American women. These consequences include being three times more likely than Euro-American women to die of causes associated with pregnancy, childbirth and the puerperium (the period during and immediately after childbirth), an infant mortality rate of 17.6 (National Center for Health Statistics, 1990) and sterilization. Sterilization of African-American women encompasses a broad range of issues: (1) the right of African-American women to give informed consent to surgical procedures; (2) the racism that underlies the actions of physicians and surgeons who treat African-American women; and (3) the need for African-American women to be informed about a broad range of gynecological problems which may lead to hysterectomies or other sterilizing procedures (Black Women's Community Development Foundation, 1974). Data on sterilization in the USA demonstrate that a higher percentage of African-American women are sterilized and that the rate of sterilization of African-American women is increasing (Mosher and Pratt, 1990). The respective figures for African-American and Euro-American women's sterilization in 1982 and 1988 were 38.1 percent versus 26.1 percent and 30 percent versus 22.1 percent (Mosher and Pratt, 1990).

This high rate of sterilization underscores African-American women's lack of basic human rights. It sends a clear message about the links between African-American women's sexuality, fertility and roles within the political economy (Collins, 1990). Under slavery Black women were reproducers of human capital; slave women who reproduced often were rewarded (Giddings, 1984). Over time, changes in the political economy have trans-formed African-American women's fertility from a necessity for an economy in need of cheap labor to a costly threat to political and economic stability (Collins, 1990). As a result, the fertility of African-American women, partic-ularly those who carry the image of welfare mothers, must be controlled. Additional issues of sterilization include: the relationship of African-American women to the pro- and anti-abortion movements, the role that African-American women should play in policy-making around these issues, the genocide issue, and the effort of African-American women to bal-ance their right not to have unwanted children with their fears of genocidal national and international policies (Black Women's Community Development Foundation, 1974).

The year 1990 was to have been the target date for the completion of the "second public health revolution" (US Department of Health, Education and Welfare, 1979: vii). Goals were set to improve the health conditions of all ages of the U.S. populace. A primary goal was to reduce the national infant mortality rate to 9 deaths per 1,000 live births. The ability of the USA as a nation to execute a second revolution was in doubt from the beginning. Joseph A. Califano in the foreword of the report which listed the goals wrote: "What is in doubt is whether we have the personal discipline and political will to solve these problems" (US Department of Health, Education and Welfare, 1979: viii). Some communities in the USA have reached the goal of "9 by 90." Other communities, poor, marginalized and dark in hue, have infant mortality rates exceeding 30 per 1,000. When the debate over repro-ductive rights is over, the debate that begins at the birth of each African-American child will still rage: can s/he survive? Will this child be allowed to thrive?

Violence

Although violence in African-American communities is disproportional in its effects upon women, the continued focus has been on the African-American male homicide rate. This exclusive focus on males serves to mask the violence to which African-American women are constantly exposed. For African-American women crime statistics are also health statistics. Homicide is one of the ten leading causes of death for African-American women. The reported rape rate for African-American women is almost three times that of Euro-American women (US Department of Justice, 1991). Once raped, African-American women have a harder time getting police and medical professionals to believe them.

In popular African-American magazines rape, a crime of violence usu-ally perpetrated against women, is explained by African-American male authorities as being caused by male frustration. Although one would like to believe that African-American male physicians might bring more sensitivity and awareness to the problems of African-American women, often male physicians are unwilling or unable to recognize either their own sexism or their own inability to understand that sexual violence transcends race. Thus in an article about rape in *Ebony* magazine, Alvin Poussaint, an African-American male psychiatrist, concluded that the high rate of rape of African-American women was due to the "feelings of rejection" of African-American males and to their need to bolster their self-esteem (Norment, 1991: 96).

Poussaint's apologist stance comes dangerously close to the rationale used historically by Euro-American males to justify their sexual abuse of African-American women. He joins the long line of African-American males who do not believe that Black males should be held responsible for their violence against African-American women (Lorde, 1990). Most rapes are planned (Amir, 1971) which suggests premeditation and hence responsibility. African-American male psychiatrists are not the only ones to beg the issue on the subject of rape in African-American communities. Ironically, Davis (1983) in an entire chapter on rape, in a book about women, while appropriately criticizing Euro-American women's treatises about the African-American male rapist, ignores the high rape rate of African-American women in African-American communities.

In addition to the high rape rate, there is also a high prevalence of sexual abuse. According to the empirical literature, African-American women are more frequently victims of sexual abuse than Euro-American women (Katz and Mazur, 1979). Furthermore, African-American women are at risk of rape and child sexual abuse across all age groups (Amir, 1971; Peters, 1976; Kercher and McShane, 1984). Wyatt (1985) found that African-American pre-teens were most likely to experience abuse in their homes from male nuclear or extended family members. African-American women reported more incidence of sexual abuse involving stepfathers, mothers' boyfriends, foster fathers, male cousins and other relatives than did Euro-American women (Wyatt, 1985).

Although battering is a strong concern of African-American women, Coley and Beckett (1988) in a twenty-year (1967-87) review of the empirical literature in counseling, psychology, social work and sociology, found only two sources on battering and African-American women. In addition to being physically battered, African-American women are also psychologically battered through music. The lyrics in some rap songs or hip hop music are especially violent toward and degrading of women. In an interesting combination of blaming the victim, transforming violence to sexism and holding women accountable for male behavior, a hip hop expert writes:

> *As I once told a sister, hip hop lyrics are, among other things, what a lot of Black men say about Black women when Black women aren't around. In this sense the music is no more or less sexist than your fathers, brothers, husbands, friends and lovers and in many cases more upfront. As an unerringly precise reflection of the*

community, hip hop's sexist thinking will change when the community changes.
Because women are the ones best able to define sexism, they will have to chal-
lenge the music—tell it how to change and make it change—if change is to come.

(Allen, 1989: 117)

If males are creating and perpetuating violent, sexist lyrics, why is it
women's responsibility to change them? Another question is why would
African-American women take part in such music? African-American
women who participate in and create women-abusing rap lyrics, have essentially embraced the external controlling images and are participating in their
own oppression.

Hospitals Are Dangerous

In addition to having to deal with the danger in the communities, African-
American women are exposed to added dangers when they seek medical
care. The vulnerability of African-American women is only too apparent. Dr.
Norma Goodwin (1990: 12) in her analysis of why African-Americans die six
to seven years earlier than their white counterparts listed two factors central
to the dilemma of black females: "the lack of culturally sensitive health information" and "decreased access to high quality care." These factors are
excruciatingly sensitive to the economic status of the individual. The African-
American woman all too often finds herself on Medicaid (health insurance
for the poor) not Medicare (health insurance for the elderly). The reluctance
of private physicians to accept Medicaid is not even apologetic. Even so,
those individuals are better off than the estimated 35 million Americans
without any form of health insurance (Edelman, 1987: x).

The absence of a national health insurance means that many African-
American women receive their basic health care from public health clinics
and county hospitals. The other historical source of health care is the university research hospital. Most of the major university hospitals in the country are located in economically distressed areas. For centuries marginalized
groups have served the medical establishment as disease models, guinea
pigs and cadavers. The ever present vulnerability of African-American
women was brought back to our memories with the exposé of medical
research at Cook County Hospital in Chicago in 1988.

More than 200 pregnant women were given a drug, Dilantin, without
their knowledge. Fortunately, to date, the drug, used normally to treat
epilepsy, has not caused damage to the resulting offspring or their mothers.
The fact that such blatant abuses of human rights can occur in a publicly
monitored setting only indicates the probability of what is occurring in private practices. According to the Public Citizen Health Research Group, the
trend is for clinical trials to be conducted in doctors' offices (1990b: 1). That
African-American women will continue to be guinea pigs sacrificed to the

US medical establishment is a foregone conclusion. In 1989, the Food and Drug Administration found that there were irregularities in the informed consent forms in 75 percent of the investigations of drug trials conducted in doctors' offices, outpatient clinics and hospitals (Public Citizen Health Research Group, 1990b: 1). Those same factors elucidated by Goodwin suggest who is most likely to participate in experimental drug trials.

Summary

Lewis suggested in 1977 that the structural position of African-American women would cause them to become more responsive to feminist issues. One area in which Lewis's prophecy has materialized is in the area of African-American women's health. One of the first conferences exclusively devoted to African-American women's health was sponsored by the Black Women's Community Development Foundation. As B. Smith pointed out: "The health of Black women is a subject of major importance for those of us who are committed to learning, teaching, and writing about our sisters" (1982: 103).

Although there is a greater awareness of African-American women's health problems, the massive budget cuts for social and health programs under the Reagan-Bush administrations have only served to undermine the progress of and place pressure on local African-American women's health initiatives. At the state level, redefinition of the eligibility requirements for Medicaid have reduced or eliminated medical coverage for large numbers of African-American women and their children. At a time when we should be concentrating on thriving, we are still concerned with survival. However, as Collins (1990: 92) noted: "Resisting by doing something that 'is not expected' could not have occurred without Black women's long-standing rejection of mammies, matriarchs, and other controlling images." The development of the National Black Women's Health Project and the organization of the First National Conference on Black Women's Health exemplifies doing the "unexpected." The Black Women's Health Project's first conference on Black women's health received an overwhelming response. In addition the Black Women's Health Project has developed regional networks that provide an environment that encourages African-American women to define and respond to their own health problems.

At the First National Conference on Black Women's Health Issues, Christmas, an African-American woman physician, made the following points about African American women's health: (1) we must not accept the blame for our condition; (2) we must be responsible for ourselves and at the same time hold the medical community and community agencies accountable, and (3) we must demand affordable, accessible, responsive facilities and medical providers (Butler, 1984). The life we want is one in which basic health care is assured. African-American women need and have a right to health. The state must try to provide safe living and workplace conditions, a safe environment, primary health care and adequate nutrition throughout life to its citizens. These rights which the state could guarantee are not on the table for debate.

REFERENCES

Allen, H. (1989) "Rap Is Our Music!" *Essence* 20 (12): 78-80, 114, 117, 119.

American Cancer Society (1990) *Cancer and the Poor: A Report to the Nation*, Atlanta, GA: American Cancer Society.

Amir, M. (1971) *Patterns of Forcible Rape*, Chicago: University of Chicago Press.

Anastos, K. and Marte, K. (1989) "Women—The Missing Persons in the AIDS Epidemic," *Health/PAC Bulletin* 19 (4): 6-11.

Avery, B. Y. (1990) "Breathing Life into Ourselves: The Evolution of the Black Women's Health Project," in E. White (ed.) *The Black Women's Health Book: Speaking for Ourselves*, Seattle: Seal Press: 4-10.

Barbee, E. L. (1992) "Ethnicity and Woman Abuse in the United States," in C. Sampselle (ed.) *Violence Against Women: Nursing Research, Practice and Education Issues*, Washington, DC: Hemisphere: 153-66.

Beale, F. (1970) "Double Jeopardy: To Be Black and Female," in T. Cade (ed.) *The Black Female*, New York: New American Library: 90-100.

Black Women's Community Development Foundation (1974) *Miniconsultation on the Mental and Physical Health Problem of Black Women*, Washington, DC: Black Women's Community Development Foundation.

Brown, D. R. (1990) "Depression Among Blacks," in D. S. Ruiz (ed.) *Handbook of Mental Health and Mental Disorder Among Black Americans*, New York: Greenwood Press: 71-93.

Butler, E. (1984) "The First National Conference on Black Women's Health Issues," in N. Worcester and M. H. Whatley (eds.) *Women's Health: Readings in Social, Economic & Political Issues*, Dubuque, IA: Kendall/Hunt: 37-42.

Carrington, C. H. (1980) "Depression in Black Women: A Theoretical Appraisal," in L. F. Rodgers-Rose (ed.) *The Black Woman*, Beverly Hills, CA: Sage: 265-71.

Christensen, C. P. (1988) "Issues in Sex Therapy with Ethnic and Racial Minority Women," *Women & Therapy* 7: 187-205.

Coley, S. M. and Beckett, J. O. (1988) "Black Battered Women: A Review of the Literature," *Journal of Counseling and Development* 66: 266-70.

Collins, P. H. (1990) *Black Feminist Thought: Knowledge, Consciousness, and the Politics of Empowerment*, Boston, Mass.: Unwin Hyman.

Davis, A. Y. (1983) *Women, Race and Class*, New York: Vintage Books.

Ditzion, J. and Golden, J. (1984) "Introduction," in Boston Women's Health Book Collective, *The New Our Bodies Ourselves*, New York: Simon & Schuster: 201-2.

Dressler, W. W. (1987) "The Stress Process in a Southern Black Community: Implications for Prevention Research," *Human Organization* 46: 211-20.

Dressler, W. W. and Badger, L. W. (1985) "Epidemiology of Depressive Symptoms in Black Communities," *Journal of Nervous and Mental Disease* 173: 212-20.

Edelman, M. W. (1987) *Families in Peril*, Cambridge, Mass.: Harvard University Press.

Gary, L. E., Brown, D. R., Milburn, N. G., Thomas, V. G. and Lockley, D. S. (1985) *Pathways: A Study of Black Informal Support Networks*, Washington, DC: Institute for Urban Affairs and Research, Howard University.

Giddings, P. (1984) *When and Where I Enter . . . : The Impact of Black Women on Race and Sex in America*, Toronto: Bantam Books.

Gillum, R. F. (1987) "Overweight and Obesity in Black Women: A Review of Published Data from the National Center for Health Statistics," *Journal of the National Medical Association* 79: 865-71.

Goodwin, N. J. (1990) "Health and the African-American Community," *Crisis* 97 (8): 12 and 50.

Harburg, E., Erfurt, J. C., Chape, L. S., Hauestein, L. S., Schull, W. J. and Schork, M. A. (1973) "Socioecological Stress Areas and Black-White Blood Pressure: Detroit," *Journal of Chronic Diseases* 26: 595-611.

hooks, bell (1981) *Ain't I a Woman: Black Women and Feminism*; Boston, Mass.: South End Press.

Institute for Urban Affairs and Research. (1981) *Statistical Profile of the Black Female*, Washington, DC: Howard University 7 (1): 1-4.

Kahn, H. S., Williamson, D. F. and Stevens, J. A. (1991) "Race and Weight Change in US Women: The Roles of Socioeconomic and Marital Status," *American Journal of Public Health* 81: 319-23.

Katz, S. and Mazur, M. (1979) *Understanding the Rape Victim: A Synthesis of Research Findings*, New York: Wiley.

Kercher, G. and McShane, M. (1984) "The Prevalence of Child Sexual Abuse Victimization in an Adult Sample of Texas Residents," *Child Abuse and Neglect* 8: 495-502.

King, D. K. (1988) "Multiple Jeopardy, Multiple Consciousness: The Context of a Black Feminist Ideology," *Signs: Journal of Women in Culture and Society* 14 (1) (August): 42-72.

Kumanyika, S. and Savage, D. D. (1986) "Ischemic Heart Disease Risk Factors in Black Americans," in Report of the Secretary's Task Force on Black & Minority Health, Vol. IV, *Cardiovascular and Cerebrovascular Disease, Part 2*, US Department of Health and Human Services, Washington, DC: US Government Printing Office: 229-90.

Lewis, D. (1977) "A Response to Inequality: Black Women, Racism and Sexism," *Signs: Journal of Women in Culture and Society* 3: 339-405.

Lorde, A. (1990) *Need: a Chorale for Black Woman Voices*, Latham, NY: Kitchen Table Press.

McAdoo, H. P. (1990) "A Portrait of African American Families in the United States," in S. E. Rix (ed.) *The American Woman, 1990-91: A Status Report*, New York: W. W. Norton: 71-93.

McWhorter, W. P. and Mayer, W. J. (1987) "Black/White Differences in Type of Initial Breast Cancer Treatment and Implications for Survival," *American Journal of Public Health* 77: 1515-17.

Moore, M. C. (1990) "Nutritional Alterations," in P. G. Beare and J. L. Myers (eds.) *Principles and Practices of Adult Health Nursing*, St Louis, MO: Mosby: 343-84.

Mosher, W. D. and Pratt, W. F. (1990) *Contraceptive Use in the United States, 1973-88*, Advance data from vital and health statistics; no. 182, Hyattsville, MD: National Center for Health Statistics.

Myers, H. F. (1986) "Coronary Heart Disease in Black Populations: Current Research, Treatment and Prevention Needs," in Report of the Secretary's Task Force on Black & Minority Health, Vol. IV, *Cardiovascular and Cerebrovascular Disease, Part 2*, US Department of Health and Human Services, Washington, DC: US Government Printing Office: 303-44.

National Center for Health Statistics (1990) *Advance Report of Final Mortality Statistics, 1988*, Monthly Vital Statistics report; Vol. 39, no. 7, supplement, Hyattsville, MD: Public Health Service.

Nieboer, H. J. (1971) *Slavery as an Industrial System*, 2nd edn, New York; Burt Franklin.

Norment, L. (1991) "What's Behind the Dramatic Rise in Rapes?" *Ebony* 46 (11) (September): 92, 94, 96-8.

Peters, J. J. (1976) "Children Who Are Victims of Sexual Assault and the Psychology of Offenders," *American Journal of Psychotherapy* 30: 393-421.

Public Citizen Health Research Group (1990a) *Health Letter* 6 (8).

——— (1990b) *Health Letter* 6 (11).

Report of the Secretary's Task Force on Black & Minority Health (1986) Vol. III, *Cancer* US Department of Health and Human Services, Washington, DC: US Government Printing Office.

Smith, B. (1982) "Black Women's Health: Notes for a Course," in G. T. Hull, P. Bell-Scott and B. Smith (eds.) *All the Women are White, All the Blacks are Men, But Some of Us are Brave,* Old Westbury, NY: Feminist Press: 103-14.

Smith, E. J. (1981) "Mental Health and Service Delivery Systems for Black Women," *Journal of Black Studies* 17: 126-41.

Tervalon, M. (1988) "Black Women's Reproductive Rights," in N. Worcester and M. H. Whatley (eds.) *Women's Health: Readings in Social, Economic & Political Issues,* Dubuque, IA: Kendall/Hunt: 136-7.

US Bureau of the Census Current Population Reports (1988) series P-60, no. 161, *Money, Income and Poverty Status in the United States: 1987,* Washington, DC: US Government Printing Office: August.

US Bureau of the Census Current Population Reports (1989a) series P-25, no. 1018, *Projection of the Population of the United States by Age, Sex and Race: 1988 to 2080,* Washington, DC: US Government Printing Office: January.

US Bureau of the Census Current Population Reports (1989b) series P-20, no. 433, *Marital Status and Living Arrangements: March, 1988,* Washington, DC: US Government Printing Office: January.

US Department of Health, Education and Welfare (1979) *Healthy People,* Washington, DC: US Government Printing Office.

US Department of Justice, Office of Justice Programs, Bureau of Justice Statistics (1991) *Criminal Victimization in the United States: 1973-88 Trends,* Washington, DC: US Government Printing Office: July.

Wyatt, G. E. (1985) "The Sexual Abuse of Afro-American and White Women in Childhood," *Child Abuse and Neglect* 9: 507-19.

Yellin, E. H., Kramer, I. S. and Epstein, W. V. (1983) "Is Health Care Use Equivalent Across Social Groups? A Diagnosis-Based Study," *American Journal of Public Health* 73: 563–71.

50

REPRODUCTIVE ISSUES ARE ESSENTIAL SURVIVAL ISSUES FOR THE ASIAN-AMERICAN COMMUNITIES

CONNIE S. CHAN

When the Asian-American communities in the United States list their priorities for political action and organizing, several issues concerning basic survival are usually included: access to bilingual education, housing, health care, and child care, among others. Yet the essential survival issue of access to reproductive counseling, education, and abortions is frequently missing from the agenda of Asian-American community

From *From Abortion to Reproductive Freedom,* Marlene Gerber Fried, ed., pp. 175–78, 1990. Reprinted by permission of South End Press.

organizations. Why is the reproductive issue perceived as unimportant to the Asian-American communities? I think there are several reasons—ignorance, classism, sexism, and language barriers. Of course, these issues are interrelated, and I'll try to make the connections between them.

First, let me state that I am not an "expert" on the topic of reproductive issues in the Asian-American communities, but I do have first-hand experiences which have given me some insight into the problems. Several years ago, I was a staff psychologist at a local community health center serving the greater Boston Asian population. Most of our patients were recent immigrants from China, Vietnam, Cambodia, Laos, and Hong Kong. Almost all of these new immigrants understood little or no English. With few resources (financial or otherwise), many newcomers struggled to make sense of life in the United States and to survive in whatever fashion they could.

At the health center, the staff tried to help by providing information and advocacy in getting through our confusing system. I thought we did a pretty good job until I found out that neither our health education department nor our ob-gyn department provided *any* counseling or information about birth control or abortion services. The medical department had interpreted our federal funding regulations as prohibiting not only the performance of abortions on-site, but also the dissemination of information which might lead to, or help patients to obtain, an abortion.

Needless to say, as a feminist and as an activist, I was horrified. When I found out that pregnant women who inquired about abortions were given only a name of a white, English-speaking ob-gyn doctor and sent out alone, it seemed a morally and ethically neglectful practice. One of the nurse-midwives agreed with me and suggested that I could serve as an interpreter/advocate for pregnant women who needed to have abortions, or at least wanted to discuss the option with the English-speaking ob-gyn doctor. The only catch was that I would have to do it on my own time, I could not claim any affiliation with the health center, and I could not suggest follow-up care at the health center.

Not fully knowing the nature of what I was volunteering for, I agreed to interpret and advocate for Cantonese-speaking pregnant women at their appointments with the obstetrician. It turned out that over the course of three years I interpreted during at least a hundred abortions for Asian immigrant women who spoke no English. After the first few abortions, the obstetrician realized how essential it was to have an interpreter present, and began to require that all non-English-speaking women have an interpreter during the abortion procedure.

As a middle-class, educated, bilingual Asian-American woman, I was aware of the importance of having the choice to have an abortion, and the necessity of fighting for the right to choose for myself. I had been unaware of how the right to have an abortion is also a right to survival in this country if you are a poor, uneducated, non-English-speaking immigrant.

The women I interpreted for were, for the most part, not young. Nor were they single. They ranged in age from 25 to 45, with a majority in their late twenties and early thirties. Almost all were married and had two or more children. Some had as many as five or six children. They needed to have abortions because they had been unlucky enough to have gotten pregnant after arriving in this country. Their families were barely surviving on the low wages that many new immigrant workers earned as restaurant workers, garment factory workers, or domestic help. Almost all of the women worked full-time: the ones who had young children left them with older, retired family members or did piece-work at home; those with older children worked in the factories or hotels. Without fail each woman would tell me that she needed to have an abortion because their family could not afford another mouth to feed, that the family could not afford to lose her salary contribution, not even for a few months, to care for an infant. In some ways, one could not even say that these women were choosing to have abortions. The choice had already been made for them, and it was a choice of basic survival.

Kai Ling was one of the women for whom I interpreted. A 35-year-old mother of four children, ages 2 to 7, she and her husband emigrated to the United States from Vietnam. They had no choice; in their emigration, they were refugees whose village had been destroyed and felt fortunate to escape with their lives and all four of their children. Life in the United States was difficult, but they were scraping by, living with another family in a small apartment where their entire family slept in one room. Their hope was that their children would receive an education and "make it" in American society; they lived with the deferred dream for the next generation.

When Kai Ling found out that she was pregnant, she felt desperate. Because she and her husband love children and live for their children, they wanted desperately to keep this child, this one who would be born in America and be an American citizen from birth. Yet they sadly realized that they could not afford another child, they could not survive on just one salary, they could not feed another one. Their commitment was to the children they already had, and to keeping their family together.

When I accompanied Kai Ling to her abortion, she was saddened but resigned to what she had to do. The $300 that she brought to the clinic represented almost a month of wages for her; she had borrowed the money from family and friends. She would pay it back, she said, by working weekends for the next ten weeks. Their major regret was that she would not be able to buy any new clothes for her children this year because of this unexpected expense.

Kai Ling spoke very little English. She did not understand why she had to go to a white American doctor for her abortion instead of receiving services from her Asian doctor at the health center. She had no real understanding of reproductive rights issues, of *Roe v. Wade*, or of why there were demonstrators waving pictures of fetuses and yelling at her as we entered the clinic. Mercifully, she did not understand the questions they shouted at her in English, and she did not ask me what they had said, remarking only that the protesters seemed very angry at someone. She felt sure, I think, that they were not angry at her. She had done nothing to provoke anyone's anger. She was merely trying to survive in this country under this country's rules.

It is a crime and an injustice that Kai Ling could not receive counseling in her language and services from her doctors at the Asian neighborhood health center. It is a crime that she had to borrow $300 to pay for her own abortion, that her Medicaid benefits did not pay for it. It is a grave injustice that she had to have me, a stranger, interpreting for her during her abortion because her own doctor could not perform the procedure at her clinic. It was not a matter of choice for her to abort her pregnancy, but a matter of basic survival.

Kai Ling speaks no English. Kai Ling will probably never attend a march or a rally for choice. She will not sign any petitions. She might not even vote. But it is for her and the countless thousands of immigrant women like her that we need to continue to struggle for reproductive rights. Within the Asian-American communities, the immigrant women who are most affected by the lack of access to abortions have the least power. They do not speak English; they do not demand equal access to health care; their needs are easily overlooked.

Thus, it is up to those of us who are bilingual, who can speak English, and who can speak to these issues, to do so. We need to ensure that the issue of reproductive rights is an essential item on the Asian-American political agenda. It is not a women's issue; it is a community issue.

We must speak for the Kai Lings, for their children, for their right to survive as a family. We must, as activists, make the connections between the issues of oppression based upon gender, race, national origin, sexual orientation, class, or language. We can and must lead the Asian-American communities to recognize the importance of the essential issue of reproductive rights for the survival of these communities.

51

BREAST CANCER
The Environmental Connection

RITA ARDITTI AND TATIANA SCHREIBER

Today in the United States, we live in the midst of a cancer epidemic. One out of every three people will get some form of cancer and one out of four will die from it. Cancer is currently the second leading cause of death; by the year 2000, it will likely have become the primary cause of death. It is now more than two decades since the National Cancer Act was

Reprinted by permission of *Sojourner: The Woman's Forum*, December 1992.

signed, yet the treatments offered to cancer patients are the same as those offered 50 years ago: surgery, radiation, and chemotherapy (or slash, burn, and poison, as they are called bitterly by both patients and increasingly disappointed professionals). And in spite of sporadic optimistic pronouncements from the cancer establishment, survival rates for the three main cancer killers—lung, breast, and colo-rectal cancer—have remained virtually unchanged.

In the '60s and '70s, environmental activists and a few scientists emphasized that cancer was linked to environmental contamination, and their concerns began to have an impact on public understanding of the disease. In the '80s and '90s, however, with an increasingly conservative political climate and concerted efforts on the part of industry to play down the importance of chemicals as a cause of cancer, we are presented with a new image of cancer. Now it is portrayed as an individual problem that can only be overcome with the help of experts and, then, only if one has the money and know-how to recruit them for one's personal survival efforts. This emphasis on personal responsibility and lifestyle factors has reached absurd proportions. People with cancer are asked why they "brought this disease on themselves" and why they don't work harder at "getting well."

While people with cancer should be encouraged not to fall into victim roles and to do everything possible to strengthen their immune systems (our primary line of defense against cancer), it seems that the sociopolitical and economic dimensions of cancer have been pushed completely out of the picture. "Blaming the victim" is a convenient way to avoid looking at the larger environmental and social issues that form individual experiences. Here we want to talk about environmental links to cancer in general and to breast cancer in particular, the kinds of research that should be going on, why they're not happening, and the political strategies needed to turn things around.

Extensive evidence exists to indicate that cancer *is* an environmental disease. Even the most conservative scientists agree that approximately 80 percent of all cancers are in some way related to environmental factors. Support for this view relies on four lines of evidence: (1) dramatic differences in the incidences of cancer between communities—incidences of cancer among people of a given age in different parts of the world can vary by a factor of ten to a hundred; (2) changes in the incidence of cancer (either lower or higher rates) in groups that migrate to a new country; (3) changes in the incidence of particular types of cancer with the passage of time; and (4) the actual identification of the specific causes of certain cancers (such as the case of beta-naphthylamine, responsible for an epidemic of bladder cancer among dye workers employed at Du Pont factories). Other well-known environmentally linked cancers are lung cancer, linked to asbestos, arsenic, chromium, bischloromethyl ether, mustard gas, ionizing radiation, nickel, polycyclic hydrocarbons in soot, tar, oil, and of course, smoking; endometrial cancer, linked to estrogen use; thyroid cancer, often the result of childhood irradiation; and liver cancer, linked to exposure to vinyl chloride.

The inescapable conclusion is that if cancer is largely environmental in origin, it is largely preventable.

Our Environment Is a Health Hazard

"Environment" as we use it here includes not only air, water, and soil, but also our diets, medical procedures, and living and working conditions. That means that the food we eat, the water we drink, the air we breathe, the radiation to which we are exposed, where we live, what kind of work we do, and the stress that we suffer—these are responsible for at least 80 percent of all cancers. For instance, under current EPA regulations as many as 60 cancer-causing pesticides can legally be used to grow the most commonly eaten foods. Some of these foods are allowed to contain 20 or more carcinogens, making it impossible to measure how much of each substance a person actually consumes. As Rachel Carson wrote in *Silent Spring* in 1962, "This piling up of chemicals from many different sources creates a total exposure that cannot be measured. It is meaningless, therefore, to talk about the 'safety' of any specific amount of residues. "In other words, our everyday food is an environmental hazard to our health.

Recently, a study on the trends in cancer mortality in industrialized countries has revealed that while stomach cancer has been steadily declining, brain and other central-nervous-system cancers, breast cancer, multiple myeloma, kidney cancer, non-Hodgkin's lymphoma, and melanoma have increased in persons aged 55 and older. Given this context, it is not extreme to suspect that breast cancer, which has reached epidemic proportions in the United States, may be linked to environmental ills. This year, estimates are that 180,000 women will develop breast cancer and 46,000 will die from it. In other words, in the coming year, nearly as many women will die from breast cancer as there were American lives lost in the entire Vietnam War. Cancer is the leading cause of death among women aged 35 to 54, with about a third of these deaths due to breast cancer. Breast cancer incidence data meet three of the four lines of reasoning linking it to the environment: (1) the incidence of breast cancer between communities can vary by a factor of seven; (2) the risk for breast cancer among populations that have migrated becomes that of their new residence within a generation, as is the case for Japanese women who have migrated to the United States; and (3) the incidence of breast cancer in the United States has swelled from one in twenty in 1940 to one in eight in the '90s.

A number of factors have been linked to breast cancer; a first blood relative with the disease, early onset of menstruation, late age at first full-term pregnancy, higher socioeconomic status, late menopause, being Jewish, etc. However, for the overwhelming majority (70 to 80 percent) of breast cancer patients, their illness is not clearly linked to any of these factors. Research suggests that the development of breast cancer probably depends on a complex interplay among environmental exposures, genetic predisposition to the disease, and hormonal activity.

Research on the actual identification of causal factors, however, is given low priority and proceeds at a snail's pace. We still don't know, for example, the effects of birth control pills and the hormone replacement therapy routinely offered to menopausal women. Hormonal treatments are fast becoming the method of choice for the treatment of infertility, while we know nothing about their long-range effects. And the standard addition of hormones in animal feed means that all women (and men) are exposed to hormone residues in meat. Since there is general consensus that estrogen somehow plays a role in the development of breast cancer, hormonal interventions (through food or drugs) are particularly worrisome.

A startling example of the lack of interest in the prevention of breast cancer is the saga of the proposed study on the supposed link between high-fat diets and breast cancer. The "Women's Health Trial," a fifteen-year study designed to provide conclusive data about the high fat-cancer link, was denied funding by the National Cancer Advisory Board despite having been revised to answer previous criticisms and despite feasibility studies indicating that a full-scale trial was worth launching. Fortunately, it now appears that the study will be part of the Women's Health Initiative, a $500-million effort that will look at women's health issues. This success story is a direct result of women's activism and pressures from women's health groups across the country.

But even if the high fat-breast cancer correlation is established, it is unlikely to fully explain how breast cancer develops. The breast is rich in adipose cells, and carcinogens that accumulate in these fat tissues may be responsible for inducing cancer rather than the fat itself or the fat alone. Environmental contamination of human breast milk with PCBs, PBBs and DDE (a metabolite of the pesticide DDT) is a widely acknowledged phenomenon. These fat-soluble substances are poorly metabolized and have a long half-life in human tissue. They may also interact with one another, creating an additive toxic effect, and they may carry what are called "incidental contaminants": compounds like dibenzofurans, dioxins, etc., each with its own toxic properties.

Among the established effects of these substances are: liver dysfunction, skin abnormalities, neurological and behavioral abnormalities, immunological aberrations, thyroid dysfunction, gastrointestinal disturbances, reproductive dysfunction, tumor growth, and enzyme induction. Serious concerns have been raised about the risks that this contamination entails for infants who are breast-fed. But what is outrageous in the discussion about human breast milk poisoning is that little or no mention is made of the possible effects on the women themselves, particularly since it is known that most of these substances have *estrogenic* properties (that is, they behave like estrogen in the body). It is as if the women, whose breasts contain these carcinogens, do not exist. We witness the paradox of women being made invisible, even while their toxic breasts are put under the microscope.

The Pesticide Studies

Very recently, some scientists have at last begun to look at the chemical-breast cancer connection. In 1990, two Israeli scientists from Hebrew University's Hadassah School of Medicine, Elihu Richter and Jerry Westin, reported a surprising statistic. They found that Israel was the only country among 28 countries surveyed that registered a real drop in breast cancer mortality in the decade 1976 to 1986. This happened in the face of a worsening of all known risk factors, such as fat intake and age at first pregnancy. As Westin noted, "All and all, we expected a rise in breast cancer mortality of approximately 20 percent overall, and what we found was that there was an 8 percent drop, and in the youngest age group, the drop was 34 percent, as opposed to an expected 20 percent rise, so, if we put those two together, we are talking about a difference of about 50 percent, which is enormous."

Westin and Richter could not account for the drop solely in terms of demographic changes or improved medical intervention. Instead, they suspected it might have been related to a 1978 ban on three carcinogenic pesticides (benzene hexachloride, lindane, and DDT) that heavily contaminated milk and milk products in Israel. Prior to 1978, Westin said, "at least one of them [the three pesticides] was found in the milk here at a rate 100 times greater than it was in the U.S. in the same period, and in the worst case, nearly a thousand times greater." This observation led Westin and Richter to hypothesize that there might be a connection between the decrease in exposure following the ban and the decrease in breast cancer mortality. They believed the pesticides could have promoted enzymes that in turn increased the virulence of breast cancer in women. When the pesticides were removed from the diet, Westin and Richter speculated, there was a situation of much less virulent cancer and the mortality from breast cancer fell.

Westin and Richter are convinced that there is a critical need to increase awareness about environmental conditions and cancer. Health care clinicians, for example, could play an important role in the detection of potential exposures to toxic chemicals that might be missed in large studies. This is a refreshing view since it encourages individual physicians to ask questions about work environments, living quarters, and diet, the answers to which could provide important clues about the cancer–environment connection.

In the United States, only one study we know of has directly measured chemical residues in women who have breast cancer compared to those who do not. Dr. Mary Wolff, a chemist at New York's Mount Sinai School of Medicine, recently conducted a pilot study with Dr. Frank Falck (then at

Hartford Hospital in Hartford, Connecticut) that was published in *The Archives of Environmental Health*. In this case-controlled study, Falck and Wolff found that several chemical residues from pesticides and PCBs were elevated in cases of malignant disease as compared to nonmalignant cases.

The study involved 25 women with breast cancer and the same number of women who had biopsies but did not have breast cancer. The results showed differences significant enough to interest the National Institute for Environmental Health Sciences, which will fund a larger study to look at the level of DDT and its metabolites in the blood samples of 15,000 women attending a breast cancer screening clinic in New York. A recent report just released by Greenpeace, entitled "Breast Cancer and the Environment: The Chlorine Connection," provides further evidence linking industrial chemicals to breast cancer.

In the United States, levels of pesticide residues in adipose tissue have been decreasing since the 1970s (following the banning of DDT and decreased use of other carcinogenic pesticides) while the breast cancer rate continues to rise. This observation would seem to contradict the pesticide hypothesis. However, it is important to remember that the chemicals could act differently at different exposure levels, they are unlikely to act alone, and the time of exposure may be important. For example, if a child is exposed during early adolescence, when breast tissue is growing rapidly, the result may be different than exposure later in life.

Radiation and Mammography

Another area that demands urgent investigation is the role of radiation in the development of breast cancer. It is widely accepted that ionizing radiation at high doses causes breast cancer, but low doses are generally regarded as safe. Questions remain, however, regarding the shape of the dose-response curve, the length of the latency period, and the importance of age at time of exposure. These questions are of great importance to women because of the emphasis on mammography for early detection. There is evidence that mammography screening reduces death from breast cancer in women aged 50 or older. However, Dr. Rosalie Bertell (director of the International Institute of Concern for Public Health, author of *No Immediate Danger: Prognosis for a Radioactive World* [1985] and well-known critic of the nuclear establishment) raises serious questions about mammography screening. In a paper entitled "Comments on Ontario Mammography Program," Bertell criticized a breast cancer screening program planned by the Ontario Health Minister in 1989. Bertell argued that the program, which would potentially screen 300,000 women, was a plan to "reduce breast cancer death by increasing breast cancer incidence."

Bertell's critique of mammography suggests that the majority of cancers that would have occurred in the group could have been detected by other means. A recent Canadian mammography study on 90,000 women looked at cancer rates between 1980 and 1988. Preliminary results show that for women aged 40 to 49, mammograms have no benefits and may indeed harm them: 44 deaths were found in the group that received mammograms and 29 in the control group. The study also suggests that for women aged 50 to 69, many of the benefits attributed to mammography in earlier studies "may have been provided by the manual breast exams that accompanied the procedure and not by the mammography," as Bertell noted in her paper. Not surprisingly, the study has been mired in controversy. As study director Dr. Anthony Miller remarked, "I've come up with an answer that people are not prepared to accept."

According to Bertell, the present breast cancer epidemic is a direct result of "above ground weapons testing" done in Nevada between 1951 and 1963, when 200 nuclear bombs were set off and the fallout dispersed across the country. Because the latency period for breast cancer peaks at about 40 years, this is an entirely reasonable hypothesis.

Other studies have looked at the effect of "low-level" radiation on cancer development. A study investigating the incidence of leukemia in southeastern Massachusetts found a positive association with radiation released from the Pilgrim nuclear power plant. (The study was limited to cases first diagnosed between 1978 and 1986.) In adult cases diagnosed before 1984, the risk of leukemia was almost four times higher for individuals with the greatest potential for exposure to the emissions of the plant. Other types of cancer take a greater number of years to develop, and there is no reason to assume that excessive radiation emission was limited to the 1978-to-1986 time frame. In other words, as follow-up studies continue, other cancers (including breast cancer) may also show higher rates.

The Surveillance Theory

Current theory supports the concept that cancerous mutations are a common phenomenon in the body of normal individuals and that the immune system intervenes before mutated cells can multiply. Known as the "surveillance" theory of cancer, the basic premise is that cancer can develop when the immune system fails to eliminate mutant cells. Carcinogenic mutations can be induced by radiation or chemicals, for instance, and if immunological competence is reduced at a critical time, the mutated cells can thrive and grow.

Given the apparent importance of the immune system in protecting us from cancer, we ought to be concerned not only with eliminating carcinogens in our environment but also with making certain that our immune systems are not under attack. Recent evidence that ultraviolet radiation depresses the immune system is therefore particularly ominous. At a hearing on "Global Change Research: Ozone Depletion and Its Impacts," held in

November 1991 by the Senate Committee on Commerce, Science, and Transportation, a panel of scientists reported that ozone depletion is even more serious than previously thought. According to the data, the ozone layer over the United States is thinning at a rate of 3 to 5 percent per decade, resulting in increased ultraviolet radiation that "will reduce the quantity and quality of crops, increase skin cancer, *suppress the immune system*, and disrupt marine ecosystems" [our emphasis]. (The report also states that a 10 percent decrease in ozone will lead to approximately 1.7 million additional cases of cataracts world-wide per year and at least 250,000 additional cases of skin cancer.) As the writers make chillingly clear, since this is happening literally over our heads, there is no place for us to run.

In addition, dioxin (an extremely toxic substance that has been building up steadily in the environment since the growth of the chlorinated-chemical industry following World War II) can produce alterations that disrupt the immune system. "Free radicals" created by exposure to low-level radiation can cause immune system abnormalities. In other words, our basic mechanisms of defense against cancer are being weakened by the chemical soup in which we are immersed.

It follows that an intelligent and long-range cancer-prevention strategy would make a clean environment its number one priority. Prevention, however, is given low priority in our national cancer agenda. In 1992, out of an almost $2 billion National Cancer Institute (NCI) budget, $132.7 million was spent on breast cancer research but only about 15 percent of that was for preventive research. Moreover, research on the cellular mechanism of cancer development, toward which much of the "prevention" effort goes, does not easily get translated into actual prevention strategies.

In his 1989 exposé of the cancer establishment, *The Cancer Industry*, Ralph Moss writes that until the late '60s, the cancer establishment presented the view that "cancer is . . . widely believed to consist of a hereditable, and therefore genetic," problem. That line of thinking is still with us but with added emphasis on the personal responsibility we each have for our cancers (smoking and diet) and little or no acknowledgement of the larger environmental context. In a chapter appropriately titled "Preventing Prevention," Moss provides an inkling of why this is so.

The close ties between industry and two of the most influential groups determining our national cancer agenda—the National Cancer Advisory Board and the President's Cancer Panel—are revealing. The chair of the President's Cancer Panel throughout most of the '80s, for example, was Armand Hammer, head of Occidental International Corporation. Among its subsidiaries is Hooker Chemical Company, implicated in the environmental disaster in Love Canal. In addition, Moss, formerly assistant director of public affairs at Memorial Sloan-Kettering Cancer Center (MSKCC), outlines the structure and affiliations of that institution's leadership. MSKCC is the world's largest private cancer center, and the picture that emerges borders on the surreal: in 1988, 32.7 percent of its board of overseers were tied to the oil, chemical and automobile industries; 34.6 percent were professional investors (bankers, stockbrokers, venture capitalists). Board members included top officials of drug companies—Squibb, Bristol-Myers, Merck— and influential members of the media—CBS, the *New York Times,* Warner's Communications, and *Reader's Digest*—as well as leaders of the $55-billion cigarette industry.

Moss's research leaves little doubt about the allegiances of the cancer establishment. Actual cancer prevention would require a massive reorganization of industry, hardly in the interest of the industrial and financial elites. Instead of preventing the generation of chemical and toxic waste, the strategy adopted by industry and government has been one of "management." But as Barry Commoner, director of the Center for the Biology of Natural Systems at Queens College in Brooklyn, New York, put it rather succinctly, "The best way to stop toxic chemicals from entering the environment is to not produce them."

Instead, the latest "prevention" strategy for breast cancer moves in a completely different direction. A trial has been approved that will test the effect of a breast cancer drug (an antiestrogen, tamoxifen) in a healthy population, with the hope that it will have a preventive effect. The trial will involve 16,000 women considered at high risk for breast cancer and will be divided into a control group and a tamoxifen group. The National Women's Health Network (a national public-interest organization dedicated solely to women and health) is unequivocal in its criticism of the trial. Adriane Fugh-Berman, a member of the Network board, wrote in its September/October 1991 newsletter, "In our view the trial is premature in its assumptions, weak in its hypothesis, questionable in its ethics and misguided in its public health ramifications." The criticisms center on the fact that tamoxifen causes liver cancer in rats and liver changes in all species tested and that a number of endometrial cancers have been reported among tamoxifen users. Fugh-Berman points out that approving the testing of a potent, hormonal drug in healthy women and calling that "prevention" sets a dangerous precedent. This drug-oriented trial symbolizes, in a nutshell, the paradoxes of short-sighted cancer-prevention strategies: more drugs are used to counteract the effect of previous exposures to drugs, chemicals or other carcinogenic agents. It is a vicious circle and one that will not be easily broken.

Cancer, Poverty, Politics

Though it is often said that affluent women are at higher risk for breast cancer, this disease is actually on the rise (both incidence and mortality) among African-American women, hardly an "affluent" population overall. The African-American Breast Cancer Alliance of Minnesota, organized in October 1990, has noted this steady increase and the limited efforts that have been made to reach African-Americans with information and prevention strategies. People of color often live in the most polluted areas of this country, where factories, incinerators, garbage, and toxic waste are part of the landscape. Native American nations are particularly targeted by waste-management companies that try to take advantage of the fact that "because of the sovereign relationship many reservations have with the federal government, they are not bound by the same environmental laws as the states around them."

Poverty and pollution go hand in hand. The 1988 Greenpeace report *Mortality and Toxics Along the Mississippi River* showed that the "total mortality rates and cancer mortality rates in the counties along the Mississippi River were significantly higher than in the rest of the nation's counties" and that "the areas of the river in which public health statistics are most troubling have populations which are disproportionately poor and black." These are also the areas that have the greatest number of toxic discharges. Louisiana has the dubious distinction of being the state with the most reported toxic releases—741.2 million pounds a year. Cancer rates in the Louisiana section of the "Chemical Corridor" (the highly industrialized stretch of river between Baton Rouge and New Orleans) are among the highest in the nation. Use of the Mississippi River as a drinking-water source has been linked to higher than average rates of cancer in Louisiana. The rates of cancer of the colon, bladder, kidney, rectum, and lung all exceed national averages. Louisiana Attorney General William J. Guste, Jr., has criticized state officials who claimed that people of color and the poor *naturally* have higher cancer rates. You can't "point out race and poverty as cancer factors," said Guste, "without asking if poor people or blacks . . . reside in less desirable areas more heavily impacted by industrial emissions."

It follows that African-American women, living in the most contaminated areas of this country, would indeed be showing a disproportionate increase in breast cancer incidence. However, widespread epidemiological studies to chart such a correlation have not been undertaken. For instance, given the evidence implicating pesticides in the development of breast cancer, studies of migrant (and other) farm workers who have been exposed to such chemicals would seem imperative.

Women's groups around the country have started organizing to fight the breast cancer epidemic. A National Breast Cancer Coalition was founded in 1991. Its agenda is threefold: to increase the funding for research, to organize, and to educate. All of the recently organized groups consider prevention a priority, and one of their tasks will undoubtedly entail defining what effective prevention really means. In Massachusetts, the Women's Community Cancer Project, which defines itself as a "grassroots organization created to facilitate changes in the current medical, social, and political approaches to cancer, particularly as they affect women," has developed a Women's Cancer Agenda to be presented to the federal government and the NCI. Several demands of the agenda address prevention and identification of the causes of cancer. The group has received endorsements of its agenda from over 50 organizations and individuals working in the areas of environmental health, women's rights, and health care reform and is continuing to gather support. This effort will provide a networking and organizing tool, bringing together different constituencies in an all-out effort to stop the cancer epidemic.

Cancer *is* and needs to be seen as a political issue. The women's health movement of the '70s made that strikingly clear and gave us a road map to the politics of women's health. In the '80s, AIDS activists have shown the power of direct action to influence research priorities and treatment deliveries. In the '90s, an effective cancer-prevention strategy demands that we challenge the present industrial practices of the corporate world, based solely on economic gains for the already powerful, and that we insist on an end to the toxic discharges that the government sanctions under the guise of "protecting our security." According to Lenny Siegel, research director of the Military Toxic Network, the Pentagon has produced more toxic waste in recent years—between 400,000 tons and 500,000 tons annually—than the five largest multinational chemical companies combined.

Indeed, if we want to stop not only breast cancer but all cancers, we need to think in global terms and to build a movement that will link together groups that previously worked at a respectful distance. At a worldwide level, the Women's World Congress for a Healthy Planet (attended by over 1500 women from 92 countries from many different backgrounds and perspectives) presented a position paper, Agenda 21, at the 1992 United Nations Earth Summit conference in Brazil. The paper articulates a women's position on the environment and sustainable development that stresses pollution prevention, economic justice, and an end to conflict resolution through war and weapons production, probably the greatest force in destroying the environment.

On February 4, 1992, a group of 65 scientists released a statement at a press conference in Washington, D.C., entitled "Losing the 'War against Cancer'—Need for Public Policy Reforms," which calls for an amendment to the National Cancer Act that would "re-orient the mission and priorities of the NCI to cancer causes and prevention." The seeds of this movement have been sown. It is now our challenge to nourish this movement with grassroots research, with demonstrations, and with demands that our society as a whole take responsibility for the environmental contamination that is killing us.

NOTE

Author's note: Many thanks to the women of the Women's Community Cancer Project in Cambridge, Massachusetts, for their help and support. A longer version of this article with complete footnotes and references appeared in the *Resist* newsletter (May/June 1992). Copies of the issue (which includes the Women's Cancer Agenda) are available from: Resist, One Summer St., Somerville, MA 02143. Send $1.00 for handling.

52

TESTICULAR CANCER AND MASCULINITY

DAVID FREDERICK GORDON

Testicular Cancer

When a testicular tumor is discovered, the affected testicle is removed in what is called an *orchiectomy.* If there is suspicion that the tumor has metastasized to the abdominal lymph nodes, an additional operation, called a *lymph node dissection,* is performed to remove these lymph nodes. This is a lengthy operation that leaves a large abdominal scar. It is also common for the nerves that control ejaculation to be damaged during this operation. If this occurs, the patient is left with a dry ejaculation. Ejaculation is normal except that no semen or fluid is ejaculated. This condition can reverse itself after several years if the nerves are able to regenerate. In many cases, though, the loss of an ejaculate is permanent. Depending on the type of cancer cell that was found in the testicular tumor, surgery can be followed by either radiation or chemotherapy to kill any stray cancer cells left in the body. A newer approach, used in some cases in which the tumor is in an early stage, is to forego therapy following surgery. Instead, the patient is monitored closely to watch for any further evidence of cancer (Pizzocaro et al., 1986; Sogani et al., 1984).

Testicular cancer is relatively rare in the general population, with approximately 6,800 new cases per year (American Cancer Society, 1994, p. 6). It is, however, the most common cancer in white men between the ages of 20 and 34 and the second most common between the ages of 35 and 39 (National Cancer Institute, 1987). This is a period when men typically are making commitments to careers, spouses, and families, and a life-threatening disease at this stage could have serious effects on these commitments. Testicular cancer is highly curable,[1] but surgery, chemotherapy, or radiation therapy can physically limit sexual functioning and fertility,[2] and the cultural meanings associated with sexual function, testicles, and potency, especially for young men, make this a potentially serious issue for masculine identity.

Studies of the psychosocial consequences of testicular cancer have found that most men who have had testicular cancer make positive long-term adjustments (Gorzynski & Holland, 1979; Rieker, Edbril, & Garnick, 1985; Tross, Holland, Bosl, & Geller, 1984). In her review of studies of psychological adjustment to testicular cancer, Tross (1989) states,

> There is general agreement that the cancer experience does not impair the major areas of function of the survivor's life, such as employment, marriage, or economic status. When explicit questions are asked about mood, especially depressed and anxious states, increased subjective distress is observed among these survivors, but it is subtle and nonimpairing (p. 242).

There is evidence that some men's outlook on life in general was improved by having experienced testicular cancer (Rieker et al., 1989). These findings are generally consistent with studies of the long-term quality of life of other cancer survivors (de Haes & Van Knippenberg, 1987).

The evidence related to sexuality and masculinity is mixed. Although some studies have found that testicular cancer threatens sexual potency and masculinity (Gorzynski & Holland, 1979), others have found no significant differences in sexuality between men who have received an orchiectomy and those who have not (Blakemore, 1988). There is evidence, however, that up to 30% of testicular cancer survivors experience problems with sexual functioning, body image, or infertility as a result of the treatments for testicular cancer (Gritz et al., 1989; Moynihan, 1991; Ricker et al., 1989; Schover, 1987; Schover, Gonzales, & Eschenbach, 1986). Those who experience ejaculatory impairment are also at greater risk for concern about sexual functioning, especially as the years since the treatment increase (Rieker et al., 1985).

Although these studies have produced important findings, they leave some important questions unanswered. First, they do not reveal *how* most men arrive at positive long-term adjustments to these physical changes in their bodies. Second, they do not reveal how men who experience physical problems deal with these problems. Third, even though some of the existing studies gathered responses from both survivors and their wives (Gritz et al., 1989), they did not investigate the gender-related processes by which men and their partners attempted to cope with the experience of cancer and its aftermath. As Fife, Kennedy, and Robinson (1994) point out, in studies of cancer,

> little research pertaining to the variable of gender has been done with respect to either the stress of the illness or an individual's adjustment to the crisis. Although many studies concerning the impact of cancer on individuals' psychosocial well-being have focused on women, few have focused predominantly or exclusively on men or on a comparison by gender (p. 2).

The present study was undertaken to investigate the ways in which men and those close to them attempt to adjust to and make sense of the experience of having testicular cancer, especially as it influences their thoughts about themselves as men. The study's most general finding is that testicular cancer created a transitional phase that encouraged men to reassess their priorities (Gordon, 1990). In the course of this reassessment, they drew on cultural meanings and engaged in social practices that in one way or another reaffirmed their masculine identities. The paradox is that although losing a testicle, and in some cases the ability to conceive children, they maintained or strengthened their sense of being men.

The Male Sex Role

One way in which to conceptualize masculinity is through sex roles. According to Pleck (1981), the sex role paradigm claims that

> the individual is preprogrammed to learn a traditional sex role as part of normal psychological development; thus culturally defined sex roles do not arbitrarily restrict individuals' potential—on the contrary, they are necessary external structures without which individuals could not develop normally (p. 4).

The central characteristics of the male sex role in American society were summarized by Brannon (1976) as follows:

1. No Sissy Stuff: the need to be different from women
2. The Big Wheel: the need to be superior to others
3. The Sturdy Oak: the need to be independent and self-reliant
4. Give 'Em Hell: the need to be more powerful than others, through violence if necessary

Earlier, Parsons and Bales (1953) formulated the distinction between male instrumental, technical roles and female expressive, supportive roles. Harrison, Chin, and Ficarrotto (1992) summarize the resulting socially prescribed male role as one that "requires men to be noncommunicative, competitive and nongiving, and inexpressive, and to evaluate life success in terms of external achievements rather than personal and interpersonal fulfillment" (p. 272). Although there is some debate over specific elements of this role, I will use the previous characteristics as an approximate description of what I will refer to as the traditional male sex role.

The concepts of sex roles in general and the male sex role in particular have been heavily criticized by men's studies. First, the use of the sex role paradigm in social science is seen as conceptually imprecise, too static, politically conservative, overly simplistic, and inconsistent with social reality (Carrigan, Connell, & Lee, 1987; Kimmel, 1987; Pleck, 1981). The second type of objection to this approach is that there are psychological and behavioral problems created when men use the idea of a masculine sex role to form their own identities or to evaluate themselves as men. This becomes a particularly serious problem when one set of masculine characteristics becomes dominant in the culture. On the one hand, this "hegemonic masculinity" is used by men to their advantage to legitimate their power in relation to women (Carrigan et al., 1987). On the other hand, because the hegemonic male sex role is based on stereotyping and an unrealistic conception of masculinity, few men are able to live up to its standards. This leads to feelings of inadequacy, attributions of deviance, and hypermasculine compensations such as rape and other forms of violence and aggression (Pleck, 1981). In addition, hegemonic masculinity fosters behaviors such as risk taking that are harmful to men's health (Harrison et al., 1992; Waldron, 1976). In sum, the men's studies critique of the male sex role argues that rather than furthering normal male development, using the standards of hegemonic masculinity as norms to guide one's behavior and to judge one's adequacy as a man leads to both psychological and physical problems for men.

The question in relation to testicular cancer is, to what extent and with what results do men who contract this disease employ the norms of hegemonic masculinity? Before addressing this question, I will describe the methods used to perform this study.

Methods

Twenty face-to-face intensive interviews were conducted with men who have had testicular cancer at some point in their lives.[3] This method was selected as a means of investigating the question of *how* men had adjusted to testicular cancer. The men were selected by several methods. Some were identified through a tumor registry at a cancer center. These men contacted me in response to a letter sent to them by the cancer center. Other men had participated in a support group for testicular cancer and were identified by the group's organizer. These men were contacted by phone, and all of them readily agreed to be interviewed. Others were found by word of mouth and referrals by acquaintances. These men also initially were contacted by phone. All but one of the interviews were conducted in the homes of the men. Five of the interviews were joint interviews, including both husband and wife together.[4] The interviews lasted approximately 1.5 hours each. In all except two cases, the interviews were tape-recorded and later were transcribed verbatim. Two of the interviews were reconstructed from jotted notes immediately after they were completed.

A semistructured, open-ended interview guide was used, and the men were encouraged to talk about what they considered important. Questions in the interview guide were organized into four general categories: (a) medical aspects, (b) social relationships, (c) self-concept, and (d) a general overview of the experience. The early interviews began with the general question, Has testicular cancer changed your life in any way? Later interviews began with the question, What was it like to have testicular cancer? The goal of the interviewing was to discover how testicular cancer patients interpreted various aspects of this experience rather than to discover how widely these interpretations were distributed among such patients (McCracken, 1988).

The research methods used in this study have particular strengths and weaknesses. I am a testicular cancer survivor myself, and in every case but one, the men I contacted were enthusiastic about discussing their experiences with me. In many cases, I was the *first* person with whom they had discussed their experiences with testicular cancer. My first-hand familiarity with the disease and its treatment combined with my ability to relate some of my own experiences to the men resulted in interviews that were very personal and candid. On the other hand, if there are psychological processes at work such as denial of fears and anxieties, my own personal involvement could have made it more difficult for me to recognize these or to probe effectively into some areas of the experience. In the final analysis, this study is based on what men were willing or able to tell me about their experiences and how they defined them.

Another crucial aspect of the methods resulted from the relative rarity of this disease in the population. This required the use of a convenience sample that was largely self-selected, thus making any generalizations extremely tentative. What I have attempted to do, instead, is to examine the processes by which these men successfully (as defined by them) coped with the disease and its various effects on their lives. Although these processes may not exhaust all of the possible ways in which this can be accomplished, they do provide insights into several types of strategies that are related to gender. I describe these strategies in the remainder of the chapter.

Focusing on Performance

Following their diagnosis for testicular cancer, the men went through three major stages of adjustment. The first, and usually the shortest stage, was intense fear. This included fear of death, fear of disfigurement, and fear of suffering. The second stage was the process of working through what this experience meant to them and to their lives. This stage generally began once they knew that their chances of survival were very high. The third stage was an (at least tentative) arrival at a set of meanings that allowed them to make sense of the experience. This stage was usually arrived at some time after treatment was completed. Although there was considerable overlap among these stages, they can be distinguished on the basis of the concern that was most prominent at a particular time.

One of the questions in the interview guide asked, Has this experience had any effect on the way you think about yourself? This was followed with probes asking, as a person, as a man, as a husband/lover/father? If the man did not specifically discuss masculinity in his response, I also asked, Do you feel any less masculine in any way?

None of the men who were interviewed for this study reported feeling uncertain or concerned about their masculinity by the time they reached stage three. One important reason for this is that once men have completed treatment for testicular cancer, they are almost always able to return to whatever activities they were involved in prior to the cancer. This enables them to leave the dependency of the sick role, and it enables them to construct a presentation of self that they and others typically use to impute masculinity. For example, none of the men lost their jobs or suffered from lost occupational status, all those who were married remained married, and most reported returning to what they considered a normal sex life. Furthermore, the physical traces of treatment, such as the loss of a testicle and surgical scars, are not visible when the men are dressed.

On the other hand, these traces *are* visible when men are undressed. In addition, treatment frequently leaves men with dry ejaculations, infertility, and feelings of decreased attractiveness (Gritz et al., 1989). If there is an effect of testicular cancer on masculinity, then one would expect it to arise from feelings related to sexual performance, fertility, and physical attractiveness.

It was not uncommon for men to report that they had felt less masculine immediately following surgery or chemotherapy, because at this point they were unable to function normally sexually. Once normal functioning was restored, however, these feelings disappeared. Often, the wife's supportive attitude helped men through this period, but even in cases of unmarried men, the return of sexual functioning was usually enough to allow them to feel "back to normal" and to overcome any doubts about their masculinity.

For some men, the second stage was more difficult than for others. A college administrator in his 40s described his struggle:

> The ejaculation is not there. That by itself bothered me initially, the
> sensation, the sexual side of it. I got some counseling on that
> because I didn't know how to handle it. Pretty dramatic, phew!

Even he reached what he considered a satisfactory adjustment eventually. A more typical response came from a 34-year-old computer programmer. He said,

> At the beginning, when I first lost my testicle, I thought, Oh my
> God, I'm only half a man now. But that really went away quickly.
> Once I had been through my surgery and stuff like that, and after I
> was feeling better, we went back to, you know, making love. It was
> easy. I didn't feel stifled. I was having a normal ejaculate, which I
> think made a difference.

Although the loss of a testicle was itself distressing to some men, in many cases it led them to a reassessment of their ideas about masculinity. The computer programmer continued,

> As a matter of fact, I think if I lost my other testicle and was not able
> to ejaculate or even have an erection, I don't even feel at this point
> that I would feel it was a threat to my masculinity because I realize
> there's so much more involved now than just the sexual.

One of the men had lost both testicles as the result of two unrelated testicular tumors. He reported feeling no less masculine than before he had cancer,
and his wife commented that the hormone injections he was taking actually
made him even "friskier" than he had been before. A 34-year-old electrician
pointed out that because you do not really need two testicles, he did not lose
something all that important. He went on, "The thing is, I had cancer. That's
what bothered me, not the testicular part. Who cares?" Only one man I interviewed bothered to get a prosthesis to replace the lost testicle. He was a single man in his 20s, and he said that he did it to look normal so that he could
tell women about the cancer when he wanted to rather than when he was
having sex. He did not, however, feel any less masculine as a result of the
experience.

Men who were married prior to their diagnosis commonly reported that
their wives' continued support and sexual interest in them made it easier for
them to adjust to the physical changes in their bodies. A 41-year-old techni-
cian described his appearance while he was undergoing chemotherapy. In
describing his wife's reaction, he said,

> And seeing that she could look at me when I could look in the mir-
> ror and I couldn't stand what I was seeing, and she could still hug
> me and make love to me. The whole ability to get through it, I think,
> was because of her support and that feeling of that nonchanging
> love regardless of physical condition.

Although focusing on performance worked as a strategy for maintaining
masculinity, there were also expressions of ambivalence toward this
approach. A high school teacher who had been divorced just prior to discovering the cancer said,

> I think what it's done is make me focus on what it means to be a
> man, and one of the men in the support group said it's who you are
> on the inside that makes you a man. That's true, but at the same
> time sometimes you think, well, that's a lot of bullshit. I'd like
> another testicle, you know. But at the same time you recognize that,
> hey, sexually I'm able to function as well as I could before.

The ability of the men to return to their precancer activities, including
sexual activities, as well as the support of their wives, made it possible for
them to minimize the effects of the disease on their definitions of themselves
as men. Beyond this general experience, men employed two different strategies in thinking about their masculinity. The first strategy was to define the

experience as reaffirming a traditional version of masculinity. The second strategy was to adopt a less traditional view of masculinity.

The Traditional Strategy

One criticism of the sex role paradigm is that it presents an image of normal masculinity that is unattainable by most men. In addition, if one does accept the traditional definition of masculinity, it is difficult to know when and if one has attained it. As Orrin Klapp (1969) points out,

> *Of course, modern man does not hanker for primitive initiation rites; but what many people seem to be striving for in strenuous and dangerous play—not to say sex and other things not usually thought of as sports—is some kind of ritual by which to prove themselves, some test which requires a person to extend his whole self, not merely play a role. . . . The majority of roles a man takes are "grown into" or contracted without his ever having a clear impression of himself as having "made it," or having been created, remade, reborn—without, in other words, a distinct experience: "I am a new man" (p. 34).*

The experience of surviving testicular cancer provided just such an opportunity for men to test themselves and to feel reborn.

The Good Fight

Arthur Frank (1991), a sociologist who has written about his own experience with testicular cancer, points out that people with other diseases are sick, but people with cancer "fight" it. This idea was prominent in the accounts given by the men I interviewed. Many of them defined the experience as a serious fight in which they displayed courage in the face of fear. When asked to characterize his experience with testicular cancer, a 39-year-old high school teacher said,

> Yeah, I mean scary. Just this frightening experience. . . . Yeah, being forced to stay in there, being forced into a situation where you had to assert yourself against it . . . basically that sense of being frightened and not running from the fear.

This feeling emerged even in men who had not feared for their lives. A 42-year-old man who owned his own store described how the experience had increased his confidence level even though

> I didn't feel my life was threatened in any way, so I didn't think that. I didn't really believe that I was going to die any younger than the average person. I just knew I wasn't guaranteed anything. Also, my confidence level went up. No question about it. [Just because you had gotten through the experience?] Yeah. Some of

the John Wayne attitude, you know. Tough it out and prove that you can do it.

Several of the men spoke of facing and conquering the fear of castration. A 32-year-old college professor said,

It's a kind of defiance. I mean it is very much Oedipal. It is very much that kind of defiance of castration. And I like that . . . I like being able to say to myself, You know, you've had cancer and you beat the son of a bitch. . . . So it was in a way a kind of test of courage and hanging together, and that I didn't just go all scrambled with it in one form or another.

This feeling of having been tested in a dangerous contest outweighed any challenges to masculinity that may have been created by the actual loss of a testicle or the loss of fertility. It is important to note that not only did these men feel victorious and self-confident but that they also felt they suc-ceeded by "toughing it out" and not going "all scrambled." In every case, the men I interviewed regarded keeping their emotions under control as very important.

The nature of the turning point that this experience created in men's lives was summarized by the high school teacher quoted above. He said,

But there's that sense, clearly it's a rite of passage. There are other rites of passage, but somehow this one seems to be a rite of passage which almost reveals itself as such, both because it involves one's masculinity, one's sense of masculine self-image, and because of the mortality and because it happens to younger men, primarily.

Body Image

Although the physical losses experienced by these men did not result in them feeling less masculine, the surgeries and treatments did have negative effects on their thoughts about their bodies. The aftereffects of treatment that were troubling to men included the loss of an ejaculate, the inability to father children, scars from surgery, the general loss of physical capacity, and the loss of a testicle. Survey studies of testicular cancer survivors have found that these effects are associated with elevated levels of psychological distress (Gritz et al., 1989; Rieker et al., 1989; Schover, 1987; Schover et al., 1986). A 33-year-old machinist who had several serious complications from surgery said,

I feel almost like an old man sometimes with my legs being the way they are. And that really bugs me the most because I was always an athletic person. I like playing sports. I like being competitive. And that was all taken away from me.

The electrician quoted above, who said that losing a testicle did not particularly bother him, gave up his weight lifting because any ache or pain that he developed frightened him that cancer was returning. Several of the men felt a shame for having had cancer. A salesman in his 20s said,

> I didn't want anybody to know that I had testicular cancer because a lot of people, my friends, guys and girls, they really don't know. When they hear testicular cancer they think maybe you had everything chopped off.

When the wife of a 27-year-old manager said that her husband was self-conscious about his abdominal scar, he replied,

> I don't know if it's as much the scar or that someone's going to ask you what's the scar from. And then you have to go and explain it to them and you talk to strangers or something like that. It's not something you just feel comfortable talking about.

Even though most of the men did not feel that their sense of masculinity was diminished because of the cancer, there were these lingering feelings of a less positive body image and some feelings of shame and stigma associated with the cancer.

Emotional Work and Gender

How did the men handle these and other negative feelings associated with having testicular cancer? The blunt answer is that in most cases they handled it like men. That is to say, they attempted to deny or hide their feelings. When I asked the machinist when he started feeling better mentally, he responded, "I haven't. I haven't yet. I mean I make the best out of situations, but I try to block out a lot of this." A 39-year-old college professor, who clearly was bothered by the loss of a testicle, said, "And you think about that. I don't let it bother me now as much, because you can't let it bother you. You can't, you know, you move on to other things."

A 30-year-old manager, who was married with one child, wanted additional children. He and his wife both attempted to downplay his infertility. He said,

> Occasionally you just start thinking about it, that you can't father children, and I just play some games with that. Other than that, I really don't think about it [the testicular cancer] that much any more. It's been six years and I've pretty much adjusted to it. It was hard for a little while but now it doesn't bother me.

His wife added, "Yeah, it's something that happened and it's over with. It could have been worse. That's our standard thing we say."

Joking was a common way for the men to cope with the loss of a testicle. A 42-year-old man said,

> I feel that it's probably helpful living here in New York, so if you get kicked in the nuts you probably won't miss half . . . you have a 50% chance of escaping [laughs].

Other men denied the seriousness of the event by returning to activities such as sports and work as soon as possible. According to a college administrator in his 40s,

> I remember I wanted to do every sport that I did before cancer. And I said I want to do it within 1 year. Not 2 years or 3 years or 4 years. One year! And that summer I did everything.

A 27-year-old father of three said, "Within a week I got out, did some snowmobiling and sledding . . . I went right back to work. I was back to work, in one week." His wife added, "Yeah, but he would go and do something and then end up in bed for 4 hours." Later in the interview he discussed how he felt about losing the testicle. He said,

> I joked about it for a while. I pretended I was lefty for a while. You pretend things don't bother you but losing a testicle is part of one's, to me, a male, I don't want to say ego, but, yeah in a sense, it's part of your manliness and so it's a big thing. But I usually get over it, getting out and snowmobiling the first week after surgery. I try to get things behind me very quickly. I'm not one to put a lot of thought into things.

As this statement suggests, the men may have been feeling more of a threat to their masculinity than they were willing to admit. This man's hesitations in these comments suggest that he was having difficulty making this admission. This was, however, the only such statement in the interviews.

Men avoided confronting their feelings by trying not to think about them, by joking, and by returning to previous activities as soon as possible. What happened to the feelings that many of these men were attempting to keep hidden? In many cases, the men's wives were left to do the emotional work for them. A common theme in the wives' comments was that they did not really know what their husbands were thinking or feeling as they went through the experience. The wife of the man who went snowmobiling said,

> I guess the hardest part was not knowing what I can do to make him feel better, to help him get through this. He's not a very open person with people around him because he's not very open with himself a lot of times. I think he could be the most open with me as he could with anybody else, but I don't think he would tell me his fears because he wouldn't want me to worry.

This man was maintaining the strong, silent approach for himself as well as for his wife. This leaves his wife, who is attempting to be supportive of him, to do whatever emotional work needs to be done. This aspect of the experience is evident in the comments of the wife of a 35-year-old plumber. She said,

> I can tell you I'm a worry wart, but I think of it all the time. Jim's much more casual than I am. I think he went through the whole thing, even though it was his body, much more easily than I did.

The men themselves were aware of this pattern and talked about it freely. When I asked the store owner, who referred to his "John Wayne" attitude, if he talked with his wife about the surgery and treatments as he was going through them, he said,

> Oh yeah. I'm sure we did. I'm more the quiet type. Betty is the questioning type, and she wants to know what's going on and how you feel. So I was used to that. So yeah, we did talk about it and her concerns.

Even when they did discuss the experience, then, it was at his wife's urging and over *her* concerns. Some of the men justified this pattern by saying that they were attempting to protect their wife's feelings. One of the single men attempted to protect his mother's feelings by not revealing the facts about his illness to her. He said,

> I didn't want to give her any more troubles, so I kind of kept things in. Just right in the hospital and stuff I only let her know certain things so that it wouldn't bother her so much.

In summary, the men who used this approach to make sense of their testicular cancer experiences interpreted their survival as a fight they had won by displaying courage and toughness. This John Wayne approach was often accompanied by displays of physical strength (returning to sports, snowmobiling) and inexpressiveness. In effect, they arrived at a secure sense of their masculinity by defining themselves through several of the key characteristics of the traditional male sex role. Their inexpressiveness also forced their wives, who were already trying to be supportive, to become more emotional, further polarizing their relationships with women into male instrumental behavior and female expressive behavior. This strategy enabled them to avoid feeling less masculine, but it also prevented them from working through the negative emotions that were created by the changes in their bodies. Fife, Kennedy, and Robinson (1994) found a very similar pattern in their study of over 300 cancer patients. Based on responses to a self-report questionnaire, they compared men's and women's coping strategies at various points following a cancer diagnosis. They found that the men used a more task-oriented approach and the women focused on altering their emotions and mobilizing family support. The authors argue that the outcome of this difference was that the men made a less positive psychosocial adjustment than did the women.

The Nontraditional Strategy

The existence of the traditional strategy does not mean, however, that men cannot cope in other ways. As we have seen, during the second stage of their adjustment to testicular cancer, men wrestled with the question of what it is that makes them masculine. Although one strategy was to draw upon elements of the traditional male sex role in answering this question, another strategy was to define masculinity in nontraditional terms. These two strategies do not necessarily correspond to different individuals, because in some cases individual men used elements of both strategies simultaneously.

Using the nontraditional strategy, men defined themselves as more emotionally expressive, more concerned about personal relationships, and more empathetic to others. A 35-year-old man, who works in research and development for a large corporation, talked about how he had always coped with problems by not talking about them. He said,

> And my wife has tried over the years to get me out of that, and up until the cancer I would still be that way with my own family. Whereas it's easier for me not to be that way with my own family since the cancer.

The most commonly expressed change in the men was the feeling that since the cancer experience, personal relationships had become more important to them. For example, the college administrator said,

> I think you start thinking more about yourself as to how you are as a person in your relationships to other people. It's not so much of a me attitude. It's us. And you know we all count in this world. I remember, I don't think I ever hugged anybody all that much. My father was never a hugger. But I'll tell you, since I've been through this, I've hugged more people in the past six years than I had in my entire life.

The man who worked in research and development pointed out that he now put his family first and his job second:

> Before the cancer I probably didn't have as much of an appreciation for my own family and for my own well-being, and I probably put my job up there at a little higher point. It [the cancer] certainly put that in perspective, and now myself and my family come first, and my job is second or third on the list.

Others limited this greater concern for others to those with cancer. Many of them became active in volunteer programs that involve talking with current cancer patients to help answer their questions and to offer support. A Ph.D recipient with two children took a job with a human service organization. Referring to his experience with testicular cancer, he said,

> It makes you appreciate other people's suffering more. I think in that sense it makes you feel like you can relate to others better, so you can relate to your children better.

Men who employed elements of this strategy reported feeling better about themselves and better about life in general. As the college administrator said, "Certainly as a result of all this I feel that I'm a better person than I was. I certainly have a much more sensitive feeling for people." The young salesman said, "I appreciate my health and just being alive and everything I do. That's the major thing, just being a better person toward other people."

Even though this second strategy moved away from traditional masculinity to some extent, for most of the men it was somewhat limited. First, men often used elements of both traditional and nontraditional masculinity simultaneously. Second, when these men's statements of greater sensitivity are examined closely, they reveal very few expressions of emotion, and only one of the men actually cried while being interviewed for this study. Many of the statements express a desire to offer practical (instrumental) help to others, such as the volunteer and service programs mentioned above. Frequently, this desire to help was seen as a form of repayment for having survived. A final indication of the limited nature of this movement away from traditional masculinity is that none of the men questioned the idea of gender identity or masculinity.

Conclusion

Testicular cancer is a disease that results in the loss of a testicle. In addition, it can lead to the loss of an ejaculate, sterility, and large abdominal scars. Despite the cultural association between testicles, fertility, and masculinity, none of the men who were interviewed in this study reported feeling less masculine by the time their physical recovery had been completed. These results can be understood by examining the meanings that the men used to interpret their cancer experiences and the resulting changes in their bodies.

One approach employed by almost all the men who were interviewed was for them to focus on their ability to perform their major roles following physical recovery from the cancer. This allowed them to interpret the cancer as an interruption to their lives (Charmaz, 1991). Beyond this approach, there were two different strategies that the men used.

The first strategy of interpretation was to draw upon elements of the traditional male sex role. One traditional element involved defining the testicular cancer as a fight in which the men had been required to exert themselves against a potentially deadly foe ("Give 'Em Hell"). This approach to dealing with cancer is reinforced by the cultural assumption that cancer is something that one fights against in a win or lose contest (competitiveness). Some men also used rapid returns to physical activities and to work as ways of proving their toughness.

Another element of the traditional approach was for the men to define themselves as stoical, unemotional, and protective toward their women ("The Sturdy Oak"). This casts the women in the expressive role of providing emotional support for their men as well as becoming emotionally agitated themselves.

A third element of the traditional strategy was for the men to focus on their sexual performance and to rely on their wives or lovers to treat them as still desirable sexual beings. Pleck (1981) refers to these latter two elements as powers that men have granted to women and that men have come to depend on: the power to express emotions and the power to validate masculinity.

Constructing a traditional masculine identity had both positive and negative effects for the men. Using the traditional model to interpret their cancer as a struggle that proved their courage and toughness enabled them to feel more self-confident and more masculine. Traditional masculinity can also help maintain advantaged positions within marriages (Sabo, 1990; Sattel, 1992). The most important negative effect evident in these interviews was difficulty in coping with a less desirable body image.

The second strategy the men used was to employ nontraditional masculine characteristics in defining themselves. The men who employed this strategy interpreted the testicular cancer experience as having changed them in one or more of three ways: becoming more emotionally expressive, becoming more relationship oriented, and becoming more concerned about the well-being of others. Men who employed elements of this strategy did not report feeling less masculine, but rather redefined masculinity to include these characteristics. They also reported feeling better about themselves, and there were no apparent negative effects from this strategy.

The findings of this study have several theoretical implications for the study of gender and men's health. First, when faced with a serious health crisis, creating a satisfactory self-definition became crucially important for these men. The potential threat to masculinity posed by testicular cancer led to attempts to define themselves as men, and having a clear-cut masculine identity of some kind became very important. Although most of the men were influenced by the traditional model of masculinity and focused on some of its features, this was not their only alternative.

The presence of the nontraditional strategy indicates that it is possible for men to choose to follow a different model. Not only was the nontraditional strategy effective in satisfying men's desire for a gender identity but it also enabled them to cope more effectively with the experience of testicular cancer.

Finally, men were able to exercise some individual control over the process of self-definition. Whether they used traditional, nontraditional, or a combination of both types of masculine characteristics, the men seemed to be attempting to create the most advantageous set of interpretations for themselves personally. This suggests that masculinity is not conferred by nature or biology and that it is not fixed. Rather, it is constructed by actors within a meaningful social context and in response to life experiences.

NOTES

Author's Note: My thanks to Don Sabo for his helpful comments on an earlier draft of this chapter. This research has been supported by the Geneseo Foundation.

1. The present rate of cure is approximately 93% (American Cancer Society, 1994, p. 17).
2. See Tross (1989) for a review of studies on the frequency of various types of sexual dysfunction among testicular cancer survivors.
3. The ages of the men at the time of interview ranged from 26 to 58 years (average 38). The ages at the time of diagnosis ranged from 24 to 40 years (average = 32). The time since treatment at the time of interview ranged from 1 to 24 years (average = 6.4). At the time of the interview 18 of the men were married and 14 of them had one or more children. All had received orchiectomies, 15 had received lymph node dissections, 9 had received chemotherapy, 2 had received radiation therapy, 3 had received both chemotherapy and radiation therapy, and 6 had received neither chemotherapy nor radiation therapy.

    Testicular cancer is rare in men of African descent. Increased risk for testicular cancer also is associated with higher occupational status (Haughey et al., 1989; Murphy, 1983). The men interviewed for this study all were white, and all but three were employed in white-collar and professional occupations. The three exceptions were skilled laborers.
4. The presence of the wives in these five interviews could have biased the men's descriptions. I had set up these joint interviews as an experiment to test whether the type or amount of information would, in fact, be different than that obtained from individual interviews. As far as I can tell, there was little difference except that the joint interviews tended to yield more detail concerning specific events. I am currently reinterviewing the men and their wives separately.

REFERENCES

American Cancer Society. (1994). *Cancer facts and figures—1994.* (Available from the American Cancer Society, 1599 Clifton Rd., NE, Atlanta, GA 30329-4251.)

Blakemore, C. (1988). The impact of orchidectomy upon the sexuality of the man with testicular cancer. *Cancer Nursing, 11*(1), 33–40.

Brannon, R. (1976). The male sex role: Our culture's blueprint of manhood, and what it's done for us lately. In D. David & R. Brannon (Eds.), *The forty-nine percent majority* (pp. 1–45). Reading, MA: Addison-Wesley.

Carrigan, T., Connell, B., & Lee, J. (1987). Toward a new sociology of masculinity. In H. Brod (Ed.), *The making of masculinities—The new men's studies* (pp. 63–100). Boston: Allen and Unwin.

Charmaz, K. (1991). *Good days, bad days: The self in chronic illness and time.* New Brunswick, NJ: Rutgers University Press.

de Haes, J., & Van Knippenberg, F. (1987). Quality of life of cancer patients: Review of the literature. In N. Aaronson & J. Beckmann (Eds.), *The quality of life of cancer patients* (pp. 167–182). New York: Raven.

Fife, B. L., Kennedy, V. N., & Robinson, L. (1994). Gender and adjustment to cancer: Clinical implications. *Journal of Psychosocial Oncology, 12*(1), 1–21.

Frank, A. (1991). *At the will of the body.* Boston: Houghton Mifflin.

Gordon, D. F. (1990). Testicular cancer: Passage to new priorities. In E. Clark, J. Fritz, & P. Rieker (Eds.), *Clinical sociological perspectives on illness & loss* (pp. 234–247). Philadelphia: Charles Press.

Gorzynski, J., & Holland, J. (1979). Psychological aspects of testicular cancer. *Seminars in Oncology, 6*(1), 125–129.

Gritz., E. R., Wellisch, D. K., Wang, H., Siau, J., Landsverk, J. A., & Cosgrove, M. D. (1989). Long-term effects of testicular cancer on sexual functioning in married couples. *Cancer, 64,* 1560–1567.

Harrison, J., Chin, J., & Ficarrotto, T. (1992). Warning: Masculinity may be dangerous to your health. In M. Kimmel & M. Messner (Eds.), *Men's lives* (2nd ed., pp. 271–285). New York: Macmillan.

Haughey, B. P., Graham, S., Brasure, J., Zielenzny, M., Sufrin, G. & Burnett. W. S. (1989). The epidemiology of testicular cancer in upstate New York. *American Journal of Epidemiology, 130*(1), 25–36.

Kimmel, M. (1987). The contemporary "crisis" of masculinity in historical perspective. In H. Brod (Ed.), *The making of masculinities—The new men's studies* (pp. 121–153). Boston: Allen and Unwin.

Klapp, O. (1969). *Collective search for identity.* New York: Holt, Rinehart & Winston.

McCracken, G. (1988). *The long interview.* Newbury Park, CA: Sage.

Moynihan, C. (1991). Testicular cancer. In M. Watson (Ed.), *Cancer patient care: Psychosocial treatment methods* (pp. 238–259). Cambridge, UK: British Psychological Society.

Murphy, G. P. (1983). Testicular cancer. *CA-A Cancer Journal for Clinicians, 33,* 100–104.

National Cancer Institute. (1987). *Testicular cancer-research report* (NIH Pub. No. 87-654). Washington, DC: Public Health Service.

Parsons, T. & Bales, R. F. (1953). *Family, socialization and interaction process.* London: Routledge & Kegan Paul.

Pizzocaro, G., Zanoni, F., Milani, A., Salvioni, R., Piva, L., Pilotti. S., Bombardieri, E., Tesoro-Tess, J., & Musumeci, R. (1986). Orchiectomy alone in clinical stage I nonseminomatous testis cancer: A critical appraisal. *Journal of Clinical Oncology, 4,* 35–40.

Pleck, J. (1981). *The myth of masculinity.* Cambridge: MIT Press.

Ricker, P., Edbril, S., & Garnick, M. (1985). Curative testis cancer therapy: Psychosocial sequelae. *Journal of Clinical Oncology, 3,* 1117–1126.

Rieker, P., Fitzgerald, E. M., Kalish, L. A., Richie, J. P., Lederman, G. S., Edbril, S. D., & Garnick, M. B. (1989). Psychosocial factors, curative therapies, and behavioral outcomes: A comparison of testis cancer survivors and a control group of healthy men. *Cancer, 64,* 2399–2407.

Sabo, D. (1990). Men, death anxiety, and denial: A radical feminist interpretation. In E. Clark, J. Fritz, & P. Rieker (Eds.), *Clinical sociological perspectives on illness & loss* (pp. 71–84). Philadelphia: Charles Press.

Sattel, J. (1992). The inexpressive male: Tragedy or sexual politics? In M. Kimmel & M. Messner (Eds.). *Men's lives* (2nd ed., pp. 350–358). New York: Macmillan.

Schover L. (1987). Sexuality and fertility in urologic cancer patients. *Cancer, 60,* 553–558.

Schover, L., Gonzales, M., & Eschenbach, A. C. (1986). Sexual and marital relationships after radiotherapy for seminoma. *Urology, 27,* 117–123.

Sogani, P., Whitmore Jr., W., Herr, H., Bosl, G., Golbey, R., Watson, R., & DeCosse, J. (1984). Orchiectomy alone in the treatment of clinical stage I nonseminomatous germ cell tumor of the testis. *Journal of Clinical Oncology, 2,* 267–270.

Tross, S. (1989). Psychological adjustment in testicular cancer. In J. C. Holland & J. H. Rowland (Eds.), *Handbook of psychooncology* (pp. 240–245). New York: Oxford University Press.

Tross, S., Holland, J., Bosl, G., & Geller, N. (1984, March). A controlled study of psychosocial sequelae in cured survivors of testicular neoplasms. *Proceedings of the
American Society of Clinical Oncology, 3*(74), Abstract C-287.

Waldron, I. (1976). Why do women live longer than men? *Social Science and Medicine,
10,* 349–362.

53

LAW AND DESIRE

DAVID DEITCHER

Contending in the conservative political climate of the Reagan era with an epidemic that has had no equal in twentieth-century American history, gay men and lesbians had been noticeably slow to anger—in the opinion of some, too slow. The first attempt to stimulate a less courteous, more forceful queer reaction to the AIDS epidemic occurred in 1983, when novelist and screenwriter Larry Kramer published "1,112 Deaths and Counting" in the *New York Native.* In that article, the future author of *The Normal Heart* and cofounder in 1981 of New York's Gay Men's Health Crisis (then a grassroots organization of volunteers that provided support services through its buddy program, as well as education, counseling, and legal services) demanded action not just on the part of government officials, scientists, medical insurers, and health-care providers, but also on the part of the gay community.

"Our continued existence," Kramer wrote, "depends on just how angry you can get." Four years later, after the number of officially reported cases of AIDS in the United States was surpassing thirty-two thousand, only ten months after the *Hardwick* decision,[1] a group of mostly gay men who had gathered at New York's Lesbian and Gay Community Services Center to hear Kramer speak were sufficiently enraged and terrified by the events of the previous several years to respond to his inflammatory speech by scheduling a meeting to form a new organization that would go beyond the service orientation and the conventional advocacy methods of GMHC. The roughly three hundred men and women who met on March 12, 1987, formed the AIDS Coalition to Unleash Power, "a diverse, nonpartisan group united in anger and committed to direct action to end the AIDS crisis." Gregg Bordowitz saw this development as an important indication of growing activist self-determination. "What was interesting about the turn from the early *Hardwick* protests to the early ACT UP meetings," he said, "was that we went from a defensive position to an offensive position. Instead of just protesting against repression, we built ourselves up and went forward with our own positive agenda."

As a crucial catalyst in what would become the international AIDS activist movement, ACT UP has played a highly significant role in helping to navigate a safer and more humane course through this crisis. Of course, in the eyes of most people, such as my family back in Canada, who have remained largely oblivious to the effects of this still-selective plague, ACT UP has been synonymous with hecklers, hyperbole, and all manner of ill-mannered theatrics. Without knowing in so many words that I was then a member of ACT UP (New York), my father once said, while we were watching a TV news broadcast together on one of my holiday visits, that such antics would get us precisely nowhere if we were trying to get sympathy from the disengaged or openly hostile "general population." I might have told him that sympathy was not high on ACT UP's agenda.

Through the activities of its general membership and specialized subcommittees, ACT UP has, on the other hand, helped to revolutionize the way that drug research is conducted, to redefine the syndrome more fairly and accurately so that women with AIDS are included in drug trials and receive disability benefits. ACT UP managed to cut through red tape at federal agencies such as the FDA and the NIH, bringing about the release of nonharmful, potentially promising, but federally unapproved experimental drug treatments in compassionate use programs. Theatrical confrontations have embarrassed more than one pharmaceutical giant into reducing the high cost of drugs that might extend people's lives. By risking arrest and criminal prosecution ACT UP members instituted needle-exchange programs that have since become widely accepted as an effective means of decreasing the rate of HIV infection among intravenous drug users and their sexual partners. A sadly depleted ACT UP struggles on against highly organized and ruthless conservative opponents in local school boards to ensure that safer-sex education is available for students in public high schools so they can make informed choices about how to conduct their sex lives. Subcommittees have been formed to fight for improved health care and living conditions of male and female prisoners with HIV and AIDS; to secure the release of Haitian refugees with HIV and AIDS from American refugee camps in Guantánamo Bay; to secure housing for homeless people with AIDS in some of this country's largest cities.

The rise of AIDS activism signaled other sea changes in the lesbian and gay movement as well. Since the mid- to late 1980s, queer men and women have been working together in significant numbers for the first time since gay liberation, arguably in more productive ways. Homophobia, AIDS, and other women's health-care issues supplied the initial common ground, but trying to work together in often anxious affiliations has produced a deepening insight into the possibility that political progress does not depend on the misguided belief that the differences dividing men and women either don't exist or should be made to disappear; any more than one can expect or even desire that the varied experiences of queer people from different racial, ethnic, and class backgrounds can be denied when denial may seem politically convenient. It is no longer necessary to aspire as a political movement to the conventionally monolithic exemplar of unity, which in any event, we've never been able to maintain. The key to maintaining a sense of common purpose in the face of so much difference is, of course, a challenge that confronts the burgeoning queer culture: to give meaningful symbolic shape to varied needs, aspirations, and experiences.

EDITOR'S NOTE

1. Michael Hardwick, who was arrested and charged with violating Georgia sodomy statute for having oral sex with another man in the privacy of his bedroom, challenged the statute on privacy grounds. The United States Supreme Court upheld the Georgia statute by a vote of five to four in *Bowers vs. Hardwick*, 1986. See David Deitcher, "Law and Desire," in David Deitcher, ed., *The Question of Equality: Lesbian and Gay Politics in America Since Stonewall* (New York: Scribner, 1995), pp. 144–49.

PART X
Violence

Terror is my link to a childhood filled with real-life haunted houses, where children were too petrified to move, too paralyzed to breathe. Terror was probably the most effective weapon of the child molester who got me. . . .

PAUL SEIDMAN[1]

Gangs are not alien powers. They begin as unstructured groupings, our children, who desire the same as any young person. Respect. A sense of belonging. Protection. The same thing that the YMCA, Little League or the Boy Scouts want. It wasn't any more than I wanted as a child. . . . Today, many young people will never know what it is to work. They can only satisfy their needs through collective strength—against the police, who hold the power of life and death, against poverty, against idleness, against their impotence in society.

LUIS RODRÍGUEZ[2]

. . . two Asian women were gang raped by fraternity brothers in two separate incidents. One of the rapes was part of a racially targeted game called the "Ethnic Sex Challenge," in which the fraternity men followed an ethnic checklist indicating what kind of women to gang rape.

HELEN ZIA[3]

Violence and abuse pervade U.S. society and put millions of people at risk for direct or indirect attack. When we combine the numbers of people who have been victims of violence with those whose loved ones have been victims and those who fear victimization, nearly everyone in this society is touched by violence. However, as with the other issues addressed in this book, one's position in the matrix of domination and privilege affects how much violence one person is likely to encounter. As Part IX reports, African American women and men are victims of violence more often than are white women and men. And people in urban neighborhoods run a much higher risk of being shot in cross fire than people in the suburbs.

It is difficult to deny the reality of violence in U.S. society. Many children are terrorized by adults, often by their parents or other family members, sometimes by pedophiles and kidnappers outside their families. Women are physically and sexually attacked and terrorized in many social contexts, especially in their own homes, primarily by men. Boys and men are frequently attacked and terrorized by other boys and men, starting with schoolyard fights, and continuing in violent sports, military training, street violence, gangs, war, and physically dangerous jobs. People and communities of color, Jewish communities, gay men, lesbians, bisexuals, and transgendered people are often victims of hate crimes.[4] Institutions and the people within them are victims of terrorism—some examples are attacks on

452

abortion clinics and the 1995 Oklahoma City bombing.[5] The daily crime reports in all urban areas and many suburban and rural ones suggest a country at war with itself. Many urban children are growing up in war zones, caught in the cross fire between warring teenagers and adults; many will, unfortunately, be pressed into gangs as their only option for a sense of meaning in life, and into violence as their only means of self-defense (see Luis Rodríguez, Part II).

The recent study of trauma has shed much light on violence and its effects on victims. Focusing on victims of war, torture, rape, incest, domestic violence, and other horrors, psychiatrist Judith Lewis Herman describes the process of abuse and identifies symptoms experienced by survivors, including post-traumatic stress, addictions, suicidal feelings, suicide attempts, and general life upheaval.[6] The rates of violence against women, for example, are even more upsetting when we consider the devastating pain, loss of time, and loss of quality of life that results from such violence. Most women who have been raped, for example, take at least a few months or, more frequently, several years to recover.[7] When I think about the profound waste of human potential and life due to violence, I often wonder how different the world would be without it. And it is not just the victims who suffer; their families and friends, as well as the families of the perpetrators of violence, are often forced to turn their attention to violence rather than to more productive concerns.

This chapter deals with several issues within the broader topic of violence. In the first reading, sociologist J. William Gibson takes a broad look at the United States since the Vietnam War and identifies several causes of increased media violence and paramilitary activity. He names the loss of the war, the shrinking economy, the women's movement, and increased immigration as factors contributing to the general insecurity of many white men. White men have turned, he argues, to heroes like Rambo and activities involving paramilitary activity and the use of guns. Next, Melanie Kaye/Kantrowitz documents a wide range of violence against women and describes the services women have established to address the violence, such as shelters and rape crisis centers. She then discusses self-defense for women and argues that learning to use a gun can be an effective response to violence.

Next, in a personal account, Paul B. Seidman describes the impact of being sexually abused in childhood, and he notes his ongoing sense of terror. He initially turns to pornography for escape. Later, he analyzes the structure of pornography, identifies with the women in the pornographic images, and redirects his anger toward male supremacy.

The next article addresses one aspect of learning to be violent. Edward Donnerstein and Daniel Linz review some of the research on how mass media sexual violence affects male viewers. They conclude, among other things, that media portrayals of violence against women—with or without a sexual component—create more negative attitudes toward women than does nonviolent pornography, and they call for intervention to lower the rates of violence against women. Other writers have critiqued the limitations of this kind of research, asking scholars to take a closer look at the effects of nonviolent pornography and sexual objectification on attitudes toward women.[8]

This chapter concludes with two strategies for responding to violence. Rus Ervin Funk issues a call to men to become anti-rape educators for other men. He argues that men are in a good position to do this, and he shares his vision of a world free of rape and other oppressions. Finally, Helen Zia proposes a legal strategy for dealing with violence against women of color. She suggests that when women are targeted for both their race and their gender, these crimes should be prosecuted as hate crimes as well as crimes of violence so that the legal system will respond to both aspects of the crime. Zia believes this strategy would provide a second avenue of prosecution for many cases, and lead to more appropriate punishment.

The authors in this chapter find violence unacceptable, and they advocate a world in which all people are safe from violence in their everyday lives.

NOTES

1. Paul B. Seidman, "A Personal Exploration into the Politics of Boyhood," in Franklin Abbott, ed., *Boyhood, Growing Up Male: A Multicultural Anthology* (Freedom, CA: Crossing Press, 1993) p. 40.
2. Luis J. Rodríguez, *Always Running* (New York: Simon & Schuster, 1993) p. 250.
3. Helen Zia, "Where Race and Gender Meet: Racism, Hate Crimes and Pornography," in Laura Lederer and Richard Delgado, eds., *The Price We Pay: The Case Against Racist Speech, Hate Propaganda, and Pornography* (New York: Hill & Wang, 1995) p. 234.
4. "Bias Incidents Reported During 1994," *Klanwatch Intelligence Report*, 77 March 1995: 14ff.
5. For a series of articles on clinic violence and the ongoing commitment to providing abortion to women who want one, see *Ms.*, May/June 1995, pp. 42–66. For a discussion of recent militia activity that threatens public officials, see "Extremists Pose Increasing Threat of Violence to Police, Other Public Officials," *Klanwatch Intelligence Report*, 80 October 1995: 1ff.
6. Judith Lewis Herman, *Trauma and Recovery* (New York, Basic Books, 1992).
7. Herman cites several studies of rape victims in *Trauma and Recovery*, pp. 47–48.
8. Gloria Cowan and Wendy Stock, "The Costs of Denial: Self-Censorship of Research on Degrading/Dehumanizing Pornography," in Lederer and Delgado, eds., *The Price We Pay*, pp. 104–108.

54

WARRIOR DREAMS
Violence and Manhood in Post-Vietnam America
J. WILLIAM GIBSON

W e couldn't see them, but we could hear their bugles sound the call. The Communist battalions were organizing for a predawn assault. Captain Kokalis smiled wickedly; he'd been through this before. A "human wave" assault composed of thousands of enemy soldiers was headed our way. The captain ordered the remaining soldiers in his command to check their .30- and .50-caliber machine guns. Earlier in the night, the demolitions squad attached to our unit had planted mines and explosive charges for hundreds of meters in front of our position.

And then it began. At a thousand meters, the soldiers emerged screaming from the gray-blue fog. "Fire!" yelled Captain Kokalis. The gun crews opened up with short bursts of three to seven rounds; their bullets struck meat. Everywhere I could see, clusters of Communist troops were falling by the second. But the wave still surged forward. At five hundred meters, Kokalis passed the word to his gunners to increase their rate of fire to longer strings of ten to twenty rounds. Sergeant Donovan, the demolitions squad leader, began to reap the harvest from the night's planting. Massive explosions ripped through the Communist troops. Fire and smoke blasted into the dawn sky. It was as if the human wave had hit a submerged reef; as the dying fell, wide gaps appeared in the line where casualties could no longer be replaced.

But still they kept coming, hundreds of men, each and every one bent on taking the American position and wiping us out. As the Communists reached one hundred meters, Kokalis gave one more command. Every machine gun in our platoon went to its maximum rate of sustained full-automatic frenzy, sounding like chain saws that just keep cutting and cutting.

And then it was over. The attack subsided into a flat sea of Communist dead. No Americans had been killed or wounded. We were happy to be alive, proud of our victory. We only wondered if our ears would ever stop ringing and if we would ever again smell anything other than the bitter-sweet aroma of burning gunpowder. . . .

Although an astonishing triumph was achieved that day, no historian will ever find a record of this battle in the hundreds of volumes and thousands of official reports written about the Korean or Vietnam war. Nor was the blood spilt part of a covert operation in Afghanistan or some unnamed country in Africa, Asia, or Latin America.

No, this battle was fought inside the United States, a few miles north of Las Vegas, in September 1986. It was a purely *imaginary* battle, a dream of victory staged as part of the *Soldier of Fortune* magazine's annual convention. The audience of several hundred men, women, and children, together with reporters and a camera crew from CBS News, sat in bleachers behind half a dozen medium and heavy machine guns owned by civilians. Peter G. Kokalis, *SOF*'s firearms editor, set the scene for the audience and asked them to imagine that the sandy brushland of the Desert Sportsman Rifle and Pistol Club was really a killing zone for incoming Communist troops. Kokalis was a seasoned storyteller; he'd given this performance before. When the fantasy battle was over, the fans went wild with applause. Kokalis picked up a microphone, praised Donovan (another *SOF* staff member)—"He was responsible for that whole damn Communist bunker that went up"—and told the parents in the audience to buy "claymores [antipersonnel land mines] and other good shit for the kids." A marvelous actor who knew what his audience wanted, Kokalis sneered, "Did you get that, CBS, on your videocam? Screw you knee-jerk liberals."[1]

The shoot-out and victory over Communist forces conducted at the Desert Sportsman Rifle and Pistol Club was but one battle in a cultural or imaginary "New War" that had been going on since the late 1960s and early 1970s. The bitter controversies surrounding the Vietnam War had discredited the old American ideal of the masculine warrior hero for much of the public. But in 1971, when Clint Eastwood made the transition from playing cowboys in old *Rawhide* reruns and spaghetti westerns to portraying San Francisco police detective Harry Callahan in *Dirty Harry,* the warrior hero returned in full force. His backup arrived in 1974 when Charles Bronson appeared in *Death Wish,* the story of a mild-mannered, middle-aged architect in New York City who, after his wife is murdered and his daughter is raped and driven insane, finds new meaning in life through an endless war of revenge against street punks.

In the 1980s, Rambo and his friends made their assault. The experience of John Rambo, a former Green Beret, was the paradigmatic story of the decade. In *First Blood* (1982), he burns down a small Oregon town while suffering hallucinatory flashbacks to his service in Vietnam. Three years later, in *Rambo: First Blood, Part 2.* he is taken off a prison chain gang by his former commanding officer in Vietnam and asked to perform a special reconnaissance mission to find suspected American POWs in Laos, in exchange for a Presidential pardon. His only question: "Do we get to win this time?" And indeed, Rambo does win. Betrayed by the CIA bureaucrat in charge of the mission, Rambo fights the Russians and Vietnamese by himself and brings the POWs back home.

Hundreds of similar films celebrating the victory of good men over bad through armed combat were made during the late 1970s and 1980s. Many were directed by major Hollywood directors and starred well-known actors. Elaborate special effects and exotic film locations added tens of millions to production costs. And for every large-budget film, there were scores of cheaper formula films employing lesser-known actors and production crews. Often these "action-adventure" films had only brief theatrical releases in major markets. Instead, they made their money in smaller cities and towns, in sales to Europe and the Third World, and most of all, in the sale of videocassettes to rental stores. Movie producers could even turn a profit on "video-only" releases; action-adventure films were the largest category of video rentals in the 1980s.

At the same time, Tom Clancy became a star in the publishing world. His book *The Hunt for Red October* (1984) told the story of the Soviet Navy's most erudite submarine commander, Captain Markus Ramius, and his effort to defect to the United States with the Soviets' premier missile-firing submarine. *Red Storm Rising* (1986) followed, an epic of World War III framed as a high-tech conventional war against the Soviet Union. Clancy's novels all featured Jack Ryan, Ph.D., a former Marine captain in Vietnam turned academic naval historian who returns to duty as a CIA analyst and repeatedly stumbles into life-and-death struggles in which the fate of the world rests on his prowess. All were bestsellers.

President Reagan, Secretary of the Navy John Lehman, and many other high officials applauded Clancy and his hero. Soon the author had a multimillion-dollar contract for a whole series of novels, movie deals with Paramount, and a new part-time job as a foreign-policy expert writing op-ed pieces for the *Washington Post,* the *Los Angeles Times,* and other influential newspapers around the country. His success motivated dozens of authors, mostly active-duty or retired military men, to take up the genre. The "techno-thriller" was born.

At a slightly lower level in the literary establishment, the same publishing houses that marketed women's romance novels on grocery and drugstore paperback racks rapidly expanded their collections of pulp fiction for men. Most were written like hard-core pornography, except that inch-by-inch descriptions of penises entering vaginas were replaced by equally graphic portrayals of bullets, grenade fragments, and knives shredding flesh: "He tried to grab the handle of the commando knife, but the terrorist pushed down on the butt, raised the point and yanked the knife upward through the muscle tissue and guts. It ripped intestines, spilling blood and gore."[2] A minimum of 20 but sometimes as many as 120 such graphically described killings occurred in each 200-to-250-page paperback. Most series came out four times a year with domestic print runs of 60,000 to 250,000 copies. More than a dozen different comic books with titles like *Punisher, Vigilante,* and *Scout* followed suit with clones of the novels.

Along with the novels and comics came a new kind of periodical which replaced the older adventure magazines for men, such as *True* and *Argosy*, that had folded in the 1960s. Robert K. Brown, a former captain in the U.S. Army Special Forces during the Vietnam War, founded *Soldier of Fortune: The Journal of Professional Adventurers* in the spring of 1975, just before the fall of Saigon. *SOF*'s position was explicit from the start: the independent warrior must step in to fill the dangerous void created by the American failure in Vietnam. By the mid-1980s *SOF* was reaching 35,000 subscribers, had news-stand sales of another 150,000, and was being passed around to at least twice as many readers.[3]

Half a dozen new warrior magazines soon entered the market. Some, like *Eagle, New Breed,* and *Gung-Ho,* tried to copy the *SOF* editorial package— a strategy that ultimately failed. But most developed their own particular pitch. *Combat Handguns* focused on pistols for would-be gunfighters. *American Survival Guide* advertised and reviewed everything needed for "the good life" after the end of civilization (except birth control devices—too many Mormon subscribers, the editor said), while *S.W.A.T.* found its way to men who idealized these elite police teams and who were worried about home defense against "multiple intruders."

During the same period, sales of military weapons took off. Colt offered two semiautomatic versions of the M16 used by U.S. soldiers in Vietnam (a full-size rifle and a shorter-barreled carbine with collapsible stock). Euro-pean armories exported their latest products, accompanied by sophisticated advertising campaigns in *SOF* and the more mainstream gun magazines. Israeli Defense Industries put a longer, 16-inch barrel on the Uzi submachine gun (to make it legal) and sold it as a semiautomatic carbine. And the Communist countries of Eastern Europe, together with the People's Republic of China, jumped into the market with the devil's own favorite hardware, the infamous AK47. The AK sold in the United States was the semiautomatic ver-sion of the assault rifle used by the victorious Communists in Vietnam and by all kinds of radical movements and terrorist organizations around the world. It retailed for $300 to $400, half the price of an Uzi or an AR-15; com-plete with three 30-round magazines, cleaning kit, and bayonet, it was truly a bargain.

To feed these hungry guns, munitions manufacturers packaged new "generic" brands of military ammo at discount prices, often selling them in cases of 500 or 1,000 rounds. New lines of aftermarket accessories offered parts for full-automatic conversions, improved flash-hiders, scopes, folding stocks, and scores of other goodies. In 1989, the U.S. Bureau of Alcohol, Tobacco and Firearms (ATF) estimated that two to three million military-style rifles had been sold in this country since the Vietnam War. The Bureau released these figures in response to the public outcry over a series of mass murders committed by psychotics armed with assault rifles.

But the Bureau's statistics tell only part of the story. In less than two decades, millions of American men had purchased combat rifles, pistols, and shotguns and begun training to fight their own personal wars. Elite combat shooting schools teaching the most modem techniques and often costing $500 to over $1,000 in tuition alone were attended not only by soldiers and police but by increasing numbers of civilians as well. Hundreds of new indoor pistol-shooting ranges opened for business in old warehouses and shopping malls around the country, locations ideal for city dwellers and suburbanites.

A new game of "tag" blurred the line between play and actual violence: men got the opportunity to hunt and shoot other men without killing them or risking death themselves. The National Survival Game was invented in 1981 by two old friends, one a screenwriter for the weight-lifting sagas that gave Arnold Schwarzenegger his first starring roles, and the other a former member of the Army's Long Range Reconnaissance Patrol (LRRP) in Vietnam.[4] Later called paintball because it utilized guns firing balls of watercolor paint, by 1987 the game was being played by at least fifty thousand people (mostly men) each weekend on both outdoor and indoor battlefields scattered across the nation. Players wore hard-plastic face masks intended to resemble those of ancient tribal warriors and dressed from head to toe in camouflage clothes imported by specialty stores from military outfitters around the world. The object of the game was to capture the opposing team's flag, inflicting the highest possible body count along the way.

One major park out in the Mojave Desert seventy miles southeast of Los Angeles was named Sat Cong Village. *Sat Cong* is a slang Vietnamese phrase meaning "Kill Communists" that had been popularized by the CIA as part of its psychological-warfare program. Sat Cong Village employed an attractive Asian woman to rent the guns, sell the paintballs, and collect the twenty-dollar entrance fee. Players had their choice of playing fields: Vietnam, Cambodia, or Nicaragua. On the Nicaragua field, the owner built a full-size facsimile of the crashed C-47 cargo plane contracted by Lieutenant Colonel Oliver North to supply the contras. The scene even had three parachutes hanging from trees; the only thing missing was the sole survivor of the crash, Eugene Hasenfus.

The 1980s, then, saw the emergence of a highly energized culture of war and the warrior. For all its varied manifestations, a few common features stood out. The New War culture was not so much military as paramilitary. The new warrior hero was only occasionally portrayed as a member of a conventional military or law enforcement unit; typically, he fought alone or with a small, elite group of fellow warriors. Moreover, by separating the warrior from his traditional state-sanctioned occupations—policeman or soldier—the New War culture presented the warrior role as the ideal identity for *all* men. Bankers, professors, factory workers, and postal clerks could all transcend their regular stations in life and prepare for heroic battle against the enemies of society.

To many people, this new fascination with warriors and weapons seemed a terribly bad joke. The major newspapers and magazines that arbitrate what is to be taken seriously in American society scoffed at the attempts to resurrect the warrior hero. Movie critics were particularly disdainful of Stallone's Rambo films. *Rambo: First Blood, Part 2* was called "narcissistic jingoism" by *The New Yorker* and "hare-brained" by the *Wall Street Journal*. The *Washington Post* even intoned that "Sly's body looks fine. Now can't you come up with a workout for his soul?"

But in dismissing Rambo so quickly and contemptuously, commentators failed to notice the true significance of the emerging paramilitary culture. They missed the fact that quite a few people were not writing Rambo off as a complete joke; behind the Indian bandanna, necklace, and bulging muscles, a new culture hero affirmed such traditional American values as self-reliance, honesty, courage, and concern for fellow citizens. Rambo was a worker and a former enlisted man, not a smooth-talking professional. That so many seemingly well-to-do, sophisticated liberals hated him for both his politics and his uncouthness only added to his glory. Further, in their emphasis on Stallone's clownishness the commentators failed to see not only how widespread paramilitary culture had become but also its relation to the historical moment in which it arose.

Indeed, paramilitary culture can be understood only when it is placed in relation to the Vietnam War. America's failure to win that war was a truly profound blow. The nation's long, proud tradition of military victories, from the Revolutionary War through the century-long battles against the Indians to World Wars I and II, had finally come to an end. Politically, the defeat in Vietnam meant that the post–World War II era of overwhelming American political and military power in international affairs, the era that in 1945 *Time* magazine publisher Henry Luce had prophesied would be the "American Century," was over after only thirty years. No longer could U.S. diplomacy wield the big stick of military intervention as a ready threat—a significant part of the American public would no longer support such interventions, and the rest of the world knew it.

Moreover, besides eroding U.S. influence internationally, the defeat had subtle but serious effects on the American psyche. America has always celebrated war and the warrior. Our long, unbroken record of military victories has been crucially important both to the national identity and to the personal identity of many Americans—particularly men. The historian Richard Slotkin locates a primary "cultural archetype" of the nation in the story of a heroic warrior whose victories over the enemy symbolically affirm the country's fundamental goodness and power; we win our wars because, morally, we deserve to win. Clearly, the archetypical pattern Slotkin calls "regeneration through violence" was broken with the defeat in Vietnam.[5] The result was a massive disjunction in American culture, a crisis of self-image: If Americans were no longer winners, then who were they?

This disruption of cultural identity was amplified by other social transformations. During the 1960s, the civil rights and ethnic pride movements
won many victories in their challenges to racial oppression. Also, during the
1970s and 1980s, the United States experienced massive waves of immigration from Mexico, Central America, Vietnam, Cambodia, Korea, and Taiwan.
Whites, no longer secure in their power abroad, also lost their unquestionable dominance at home; for the first time, many began to feel that they too
were just another hyphenated ethnic group, the Anglo-Americans.

Extraordinary economic changes also marked the 1970s and 1980s. U.S.
manufacturing strength declined substantially; staggering trade deficits
with other countries and the chronic federal budget deficits shifted the
United States from creditor to debtor nation. The post-World War II
American Dream—which promised a combination of technological progress
and social reforms, together with high employment rates, rising wages,
widespread home ownership, and ever-increasing consumer options—no
longer seemed a likely prospect for the great majority. At the same time, the
rise in crime rates, particularly because of drug abuse and its accompanying
violence, made people feel more powerless than ever.

While the public world dominated by men seemed to come apart, the
private world of family life also felt the shocks. The feminist movement challenged formerly exclusive male domains, not only in the labor market and in
many areas of political and social life but in the home as well. Customary
male behavior was no longer acceptable in either private relationships or
public policy. Feminism was widely experienced by men as a profound
threat to their identity. Men had to change, but to what? No one knew for
sure what a "good man" was anymore.

It is hardly surprising, then, that American men—lacking confidence in
the government and the economy, troubled by the changing relations
between the sexes, uncertain of their identity or their future—began to
dream, to fantasize about the powers and features of another kind of man
who could retake and reorder the world. And the hero of all these dreams
was the paramilitary warrior. In the New War he fights the battles of
Vietnam a thousand times, each time winning decisively. Terrorists and drug
dealers are blasted into oblivion. Illegal aliens inside the United States and
the hordes of nonwhites in the Third World are returned by force to their
proper place. Women are revealed as dangerous temptresses who have to be
mastered, avoided, or terminated.

Obviously these dreams represented a flight from the present and a
rejection and denial of events of the preceding twenty years. But they also
indicated a more profound and severe distress. The whole modern world
was damned as unacceptable. Unable to find a rational way to face the tasks
of rebuilding society and reinventing themselves, men instead sought refuge
in myths from both America's frontier past and ancient times. Indeed, the
fundamental narratives that shape paramilitary culture and its New War

fantasies are often nothing but reinterpretations or reworkings of archaic warrior myths.

In ancient societies, the most important stories a people told about themselves concerned how the physical universe came into existence, how their ancestors first came to live in this universe, and how the gods, the universe, and society were related to one another. These cosmogonic, or creation, myths frequently posit a violent conflict between the good forces of order and the evil forces dedicated to the perpetuation of primordial chaos.[6] After the war in which the gods defeat the evil ones, they establish the "sacred order," in which all of the society's most important values are fully embodied. Some creation myths focus primarily on the sacred order and on the deeds of the gods and goddesses in paradise. Other myths, however, focus on the battles between the heroes and villains that lead up to the founding.[7] In these myths it is war and the warrior that are most sacred. American paramilitary culture borrows from both kinds of stories, but mostly from this second, more violent, type.

In either case, the presence, if not the outright predominance, of archaic male myths at the moment of crisis indicates just how far American men jumped psychically when faced with the declining power of their identities and organizations. The always-precarious balance in modern society between secular institutions and ways of thinking on the one hand and older patterns of belief informed by myth and ritual on the other tilted decisively in the direction of myth. The crisis revealed that at some deep, unconscious level these ancient male creation myths live on in the psyche of many men and that the images and tales from this mythic world of warriors and war still shape men's fantasies about who they are as men, their commitments to each other and to women, and their relationships to society and the state.

————————

The imaginary New War that men created is a coherent mythical universe, formed by the repetition of key features in thousands of novels, magazines, films, and advertisements. As the sociologist Will Wright points out, the component elements of myth work to create a common "theoretical idea of a social order."[8] These New War stories about heroic warriors and their evil adversaries are ways of arguing about what is wrong with the modern world and what needs to be done to make society well again. . . .

War games took these fantasies one step further and allowed men to act on their desires in paramilitary games and theme parks that one would-be warrior described as "better than Disneyland." Here, away from the ordinary routines of world and family life, men could meet, mingle, and share their warrior dreams. Three major types of imaginary war zones developed: the National Survival Game, or paintball; the annual *Soldier of Fortune* convention in Las Vegas; and combat shooting schools and firing ranges. In these special environments, the gods of war could be summoned for games played along the edges of violence.

Finally, the imaginary New War turned into the real nightmares of "War Zone America." Since the 1970s, a number of racist groups, religious sects, mercenaries, and madmen have literally lived their own versions of the New War. At the same time, as hundreds of thousands of military-style rifles have entered the domestic gun market and become the weapon of choice for some killers, the gun-control debate has escalated to a new level. And not surprisingly, the myths of the New War have profoundly influenced several presidential administrations, affecting both those leaders who make military policy decisions and the lower-ranking personnel who carry out covert and overt operations.

Only at the surface level, then, has paramilitary culture been merely a matter of the "stupid" movies and novels consumed by the great unwashed lower-middle and working classes, or of the murderous actions of a few demented, "deviant" men. In truth, there is nothing superficial or marginal about the New War that has been fought in American popular culture since the 1970s. It is a war about basics: power, sex, race, and alienation. Contrary to the *Washington Post* review, Rambo was no shallow muscle man but the emblem of a movement that at the very least wanted to reverse the previous twenty years of American history and take back all the symbolic territory that had been lost. The vast proliferation of warrior fantasies represented an attempt to reaffirm the national identity. But it was also a larger volcanic upheaval of archaic myths, an outcropping whose entire structural formation plunges into deep historical, cultural, and psychological territories. These territories have kept us chained to war as a way of life; they have infused individual men, national political and military leaders, and society with a deep attraction to both imaginary and real violence. This terrain must be explored, mapped, and understood if it is ever to be transformed.

NOTES

1. Peter G. Kokalis, speaking at the *Soldier of Fortune* firepower demonstration at the Desert Sportsman Rifle and Pistol Club, Las Vegas, Nev., September 20, 1986.
2. Gar Wilson, *The Fury Bombs,* vol. 5 of *Phoenix Force* (Toronto: Worldwide Library, 1983), 30.
3. *SOF* regularly hired the firm of Starch, Inra, Hopper to study their readership. A condensed version of their 1986 report, from which these figures were taken, was made available to the press at the September 1986 *SOF* convention in Las Vegas.
4. Lionel Atwill, *Survival Game: Airgun National Manual* (New London, N.H.: The National Survival Game, Inc., 1987), 22–30.
5. Richard Slotkin, *Regeneration through Violence: The Mythology of the American Frontier, 1660–1860.* (Middletown, Conn.: Wesleyan University Press, 1973).
6. Mircea Eliade, *Myth and Reality,* trans. Willard R. Trask (New York: Harper and Row, 1963).
7. Richard Stivers, *Evil in Modern Myth and Ritual* (Athens: University of Georgia Press, 1982).

8. Will Wright, *Sixguns and Society: A Structural Study of the Western* (Berkeley: University of California Press, 1975), 20.

55

WOMEN, VIOLENCE, AND RESISTANCE[1]

MELANIE KAYE/KANTROWITZ

Prologue

March 17, 1992. I am working on final revisions of the essay on violence. I read in the *New York Times* about Shirley Lowery, stabbed to death by her ex-"lover." Shirley Lowery was 52, African American, divorced for almost 20 years. She'd earned money as a domestic worker to raise her five children, took care of her sick father until he died. Then she got a job as a bus driver, a huge step forward.

A man on the bus flirts with her. She has been alone for how long—17, 18 years? They become lovers. He moves in. Two years later her daughter finds out the man was raping, terrorizing, threatening to kill her mother. She helps her mother move out, hide, get a restraining order. And when Shirley Lowery shows up in court to apply for a two-year injunction, the man is waiting. He stabs her 19 times.

What haunts me is the bright smiling picture of Shirley Lowery with her round cheeks. It's her words quoted by her daughter, Vanessa Davis: "My mother was embarrassed about what was happening to her. But when we moved her out, she said she felt free for the first time in a year. She said, 'If he kills me tomorrow, at least I know what it's like to be free again. '"

What haunts me is the picture of Vanessa with her husband and infant son: Vanessa's face, bleak, staring away from the camera, the husband sweetly focused on the baby. It seems Shirley Lowery raised her daughter with a sense of options that her daughter then fed back to her to help her escape. But options weren't enough. He wouldn't let go.[2]

What haunts me also are the statistics. Millions of women beaten every year by male partners. At least 20% of all women seeking emergency hospital assistance are injured by domestic violence.[3]

From *The Issue Is Power: Essays on Women, Jews, Violence and Resistance,* by Melanie Kaye/Kantrowitz, 1992, pp. 7–28. Aunt Lute Books.

In 1990, of 4,399 women murdered in the U.S., 30% were killed by boyfriends or husbands.

Almost four women every single day. Each with her own story.

I. Men's War Against Women

Frances Thompson (colored) sworn and examined. By the Chairman: 2919. State what you know or saw of the rioting. [Witness] Between one and two-o'clock Tuesday night seven men, two of whom were policemen, came to my house. I know they were policemen by their stars. They were all Irishmen. They said they must have some eggs, and ham, and biscuit. I made them some biscuit and some strong coffee, and they all sat down and ate. A girl lives with me; her name is Lucy Smith; she is about 16 years old. When they had eaten supper, they said they wanted some women to sleep with. I said we were not that sort of women, and they must go. They said, "that didn't make a damned bit of difference." One of them then laid hold of me and hit me on the side of my face, and holding my throat, choked me. Lucy tried to get out of the window, when one of them knocked her down and choked her. They drew their pistols and said they would shoot us and fire the house if we did not let them have their way with us. All seven of the men violated us two. Four of them had to do with me, and the rest with Lucy.

2912. Were you injured? I was sick for two weeks. I lay for three days with a hot, burning fever.

from "Memphis Riot and Massacres,": Congressional Report, 1865–66[4]

I got his number from a friend as someone who might fix my furnace cheap. He came by early evening. He seemed nice enough. He checked out the furnace. Then he came into the living room where I was reading. I started to ask him about the furnace and he grabbed me. I pushed him away and the next thing I knew he was on top of me, tearing at my clothes, saying things. I know he punched me a couple of times. When it was over, he just got up, zipped his pants, said goodbye, and left. He actually said goodbye. And he sent me a bill for the furnace.

conversation, Portland, Oregon, 1978

Even though I hate it, if he needs it, then I feel I ought to do it. After all, I'm his wife.

I tell him I don't want to do it, but it doesn't do any good. If it's what he wants, that's what we do.

interviews with married women, 1976[5]

Naming It War

In 1977 I taught Feminist Theory and Practice at Portland State University, which pointed me in a direction for the next several years of my life. I had asked the class, all women, to look at our lives as the raw material for change, and to seek commonalities as bases for action. The unanimity that emerged from the fairly diverse group was striking.[6] Every one of us saw violence as a central issue in our lives. Every one of us lived in fear of rape; many of us had been raped. Some of us had been beaten by male partners. The more we talked, read, gathered information, from the then-few books and from other women, the more obvious it became: violence against women coiled at the heart of our oppression. We understood that trivializing and eroticizing rape and beatings suited the abusing male's experience of abuse, while our experience included terror, nightmares, injury, and even death, as well as interference with and destruction of our sense of integrity and capacity for sexual pleasure.

When the term ended, about a third of the class formed the core of an action group, and we helped plan the first Take Back the Night march in Portland. I and another group member were hired into CETA-funded positions at the Rape Relief Hotline. As I immersed myself in the issue, talking on a daily basis to women who'd been raped and beaten, learning the statistics, studying the legal remedies, I still was not prepared for what I found. Somewhere in the U.S. a woman was being raped every minute or two. Two or three women were being beaten every minute. Every minute. It was painful to look at a clock.

So much of what I learned then is now such common knowledge that it's hard to recreate the moment of discovery. Sexual harassment from bosses, teachers, landlords, etc., was a yet-unnamed concept, though virtually every one of us had come up against it. We hated it, just as we hated boring jobs, anxiety about money, and harsh weather. But not until then had any of us questioned the inevitability of dealing with male sexual demands in the course of trying to get an education, earn a living, find a place to live, get a cavity filled or an abortion performed.[7]

Information about rape, race and class was especially disturbing. Prior to women's liberation, rape was a political subject only in white racist circles, identified only as a crime committed by Black men against white women— or, really, against white male ownership of white women.[8] The response of liberal and radical men of all colors was to dismiss the subject as a function of sexual uptightness, or as a racist plot. What rape meant to women, including women of color, was barely addressed.

At Rape Relief Hotline, as we heard from woman after woman who'd been raped by doctors, teachers, ministers, bosses, from African American and Native American women who'd been raped by white men, I realized it was anyone's guess how many women are raped by men in positions of authority, how many professional men are sexually abusive, how many women of color are raped by white men.[9] Few of these women reported to the police. I learned that a great many rapes were committed not by strangers, but by dates, co-workers, repairmen, friends of the family.[10] Especially shocking was information about group and gang rape. Many women had been gang-raped at parties—a common initiation to college life or the hideous outcome to a barmaid or waitress job. I learned that rape by men working in pairs and groups was on the rise.

I learned that most rapists were not sex-starved, relationless psychopaths, but by all psychological profiles perfectly normal men with functioning sexual relationships.[11] That it was not a spontaneous crime of passion: three out of four rapes were planned. I grasped that our feminist definition of rape as a crime of violence describes women's experience of rape, but masks a sickening truth: many men consider rape "sex." Many can't tell rape apart from sex. Many can, but still find rape sexy. Later I'd come upon the words of an honest rapist: mocking the psychiatrists who call him troubled, fearful, sick, and hostile, he says the truth is, "I find rape enormously stimulating and very exciting. It's fun."[12]

I learned that just as rape was not "about" race, battering was not "about" class, though women's ability to leave violent relationships is of course connected to money and often to literacy—everything from "do I have cab fare?" to "can I support myself?" But batterers can't be typed by psychological or sociological profile any more than rapists. Most startling, higher education actually seems to increase acceptance and approval of marital violence.[13]

Incest was the biggest shock of all. At that time, the word still conjured up Oedipus, Tobacco Road, Egyptian royalty. To answer the Hotline phone and hear a young girl's voice, a child's voice, say, *um, um, my father keeps bothering me and I don't know what to do*; or, *he says if I tell he'll kill me*; or, *he says if I leave he'll do it to my little sister*; or, most painful, *my mother says I'm lying. . . .* I learned that daughter rape, far from being an aberration, was, in the words of Florence Rush,

> . . . an unspoken but prominent factor in socializing and preparing
> the females to accept a subordinate role; to feel guilty, ashamed, and
> to tolerate, through fear, the power exercised over her by men.[14]

And I learned the most insidious aspect of daughter rape: girls discover not only their own powerlessness, but also their mother's. This violation of trust between mother and daughter, woman and girl, undermines feminist unity at its most intimate level.[15]

When I looked at legal remedies, the picture was grim. Legislation about restraining orders was just being enacted, though of course there were problems with enforcement. Incest was barely addressed by the legal system.[16] And rape? I learned what happened to the one out of ten rapes that actually got reported to the police. 15% would be unfounded—that is, disbelieved or otherwise invalidated by police—and a decision made not to proceed. (When women police officers investigate rape charges, rates of unfounding drop to 3%, about the same as for other crimes.) In half the remaining cases, the rapist would be caught, and three-quarters of those arrested would be prosecuted. Between 3% and 53% of those prosecuted would end in conviction, often on a lesser charge. [17]

In other words, when 1000 women are raped (and in 1990, on an average *day* nearly twice that number got raped), at best less than seventeen rapists get convicted, often on a lesser charge; at worst, less than one gets convicted.

War or Massacre?   The jovial image of "the war between the sexes," suggesting as it does sexual bantering, cloaks an authentic war waged by men against women. The out-of-uniform army functions with implicit orders. Young men rape, making the world dangerous to women, warning women we need protection from other men. On dates, in fraternities, in thousands of "acquaintance" situations, men assert their right to have sex when they want it, and contribute to breaking women's will. The need for male protection, not to mention male access to money, locks many women into the nuclear family, where men can use the threat of violence to control; they can demand sex, from their wives/women, their daughters and sometimes sons. Sexual harassment acts it out in the workplace.

The war. Or, I thought then and think still, it would be more accurate to call it a massacre, because it is hard to find the injury we women are inflicting back on men.

And yet we have no name for this war. In writing I feel keenly this lack. Rape, battering, incest, sexual harassment—each word points toward a particular, often a legal, definition. Abuse, the generalized term, is vague and colorless. There is no word that includes all sexual violation and physical brutalization, the physical component of male domination of women.

You could say, if we had power to shape the language we would probably also have power to stop the acts.

But sexism was once a new word. So was consciousness raising. So was clitoris. We didn't need liberation to name our oppression or our experience, only a willingness to confront our oppression and claim our experience. That we have no word for the violence against us reflects some collective unwillingness or inability to grapple with the issue.

Changes and Limits

In the context of a vigorous movement for women's liberation, women began to change our consciousness about rape and other sexual violence so that we would no longer accept these things as natural events. From this different way of seeing the world, we acted: to create rape centers, hotlines, battered women's shelters, free taxi and escort services, self-defense training; to perform aggressive political action, in defense of these centers and shelters, against institutions, events, and individual men who perpetuated abuse; and to change the laws so that women who were raped or beaten had more options. As women blame ourselves less for the abuse that lands on us, we avail ourselves more of legal remedies. In many states, a woman's sexual history can no longer be dragged into court. A woman being beaten by a man, including her husband, can get a restraining order against him. Marital rape is now a crime in several states. The milk carton in my refrigerator carries an ad for the National Domestic Violence Hotline, with a toll-free number.

Women can sue men who abuse them, and victims of incest, especially, have been availing themselves of this remedy.[18] There has been massive public education about rape, battering, sexual abuse of children, and at least some children grow up being taught they have a right to control their own bodies, to trust and act on their feelings about good touch/bad touch.

In 1977, when I wrote "women & violence" and listed 56 names of women who had defended themselves,[19] hardly anyone knew these names or these stories. By now, feminist legal teams all over the country have defended women whose crime was self-defense, and women have organized support for these defenses, including community education about the "battered woman syndrome"—the psychological impact of continued violence on a woman's ability to make choices.[20] Information is at least available about what should be called the "battering man's syndrome"—his frequent refusal to accept the relationship's end, his pursuit, threats, increased violence. The collusion of police, clergy, and often therapists and family members to preserve the holy family, no matter what cost to the woman, has been exposed to feminist scrutiny, if not to common scrutiny. In this climate, created by feminists, governors in several states have granted clemency to formerly battered self-defenders who swell the ranks of women imprisoned across the country.

Popular culture reflects and re-enforces these changes too. Farrah Fawcett played Francine Hughes in *The Burning Bed* on network television. Greta Rideout's story, the first rape-in-marriage trial, was also a made-for-TV movie. Julia Roberts in *Sleeping With the Enemy* was the final glitz on the subject, and however glitzy, she escapes and kills her crazed, persecuting ex—and I don't believe a person in the movie theater ever objects. The success of *Thelma and Louise,* its leap into the culture, makes it clear that a vacuum had existed: women had been waiting for such a story. The male response, frantic about man-bashing, was likewise instructive.

But we should note the cultural rip-off. Among the first *known* self-defenders against rape or other male violence were Inez Garcia, Joan Little, and Yvonne Wanrow: all women of color, as are many self-defenders. Yet every treatment—docudrama or not—has depicted white women. Such erasure robs all of us of accurate history and role models, obscures the relation between self-defense and a strength perhaps derived from surviving oppression, from learning to fight for yourself because you can't depend on a cushion of privilege.[21] It reinforces a notion of "white feminism," by not acknowledging that some of our century's greatest feminist practitioners are women of color.[22]

The conflation of women's liberation and the contemporary health consciousness has created a generation of young women, especially but not exclusively middle and upper class, who stay in shape, work out, pursue athletics. And though this new feminine norm is exploited, in classic American fashion, as a money-making industry, and though it constitutes yet one more demand on the would-be perfect modern woman, the fact is young women can no longer be counted on to be unathletic or physically passive. What this often means, however, is that men up the ante. Partner and gang rape, rape with weapons, rape with brutal beatings are all on the rise. Men are responding to women's new strength with more violence.

Service and Ideology   In the late seventies a vital movement to stop violence against women came into existence, strongly tied to women's liberation. By the early eighties, the practice of the movement had split in two directions: service providers and anti-pornography activists.

Service providers took on the backbreaking labor of sustaining shelters, counselling centers, etc., including—once the Jimmy Carter-CETA funding which initially supported many of these projects was cut—the burden of raising funds to sustain the services. And fund-raising is an inherently conservatizing task.

I say "inherently conservatizing" as a fact, not a judgment. Few of us get paid, at least not for long, to make social change. So the fiery activists of the pre-funding days became an organizational liability. Women began to define our projects into forms which United Way et al. would sanction. Boards of directors were formed of community notables, often potential donors or those who have achieved their status through actions and views which don't threaten potential donors. Lesbians, who founded many of the shelters and anti-violence groups, were asked "to be cool"—that is, keep closeted. Executive directors were hired with MSWs and impeccable manners to lunch graciously with the moneyed, on whom the projects now depend.

Susan Schechter describes the tensions between service and activism, and speaks eloquently in favor of an activist battered women's movement where politics and service/advocacy are not separate, and where confronting homophobia and racism is an essential part of movement work.[23] Many shelter projects and anti-violence coalitions also offer community education, train police, sometimes work with abusive men to help them change. Many organize demonstrations, lobby for legislation, infiltrate and pressure in the public arena so that some services once provided on a volunteer or scantily funded basis are now part of city and state budgets.

But in many places, the work of service providers focuses, of necessity, on helping abused women get on with their lives, rather than on the political work of stopping the violence.

The anti-pornography activists raised a different set of issues. Kathleen Barry, Susan Brownmiller, Andrea Dworkin, Susan Griffin, and Diana Russell, five major theorists from the seventies about sexual violence against women—along with Catherine MacKinnon, who broke ground on sexual harassment—emerged in the eighties as theorists and activists against pornography.[24] Such concordance seemed to suggest anti-pornography activism as the natural next step for those who wish to stop violence against women. 'Pornography is the theory, rape is the practice,' went the short-form analysis, as the militant wing of the violence against women movement galvanized against pornography. Even the anthology published in 1980, which gathered feminist opinion against pornography, sports the title of the stop-violence-against-women marches, *Take Back the Night*[25]; as if pornography and violence were identical phenomena.

It's a good thing when women rise in outrage against degrading and violence-inspiring media, as it is a good thing when we rise in outrage against anything we find oppressive. And early feminist campaigns against violence-provoking media were feisty empowering protests.[26] They also represented one aspect of a then-diverse movement, which was experimenting with a broad range of strategies and tactics, at least some of which targeted individual abusive men. In the eighties and nineties, pornography as the lone target of this militant energy seems singularly narrow: a swerve towards ideology and away from practice.

True, pornography is also the practice. Women have been abused in production of pornography, some in horrible ways. But, a straightforward feminist approach would assume that sex workers, like any other women, deserve support to improve the conditions of their lives and work.[27] Instead, anti-pornographists sometimes seem motivated not by a concern for the women directly abused in the sex industries, but by a conviction that pornography causes sexual violence against *other* (decent?) women.[28]

The conviction that pornography causes sexual violence ascribes a great deal of power to pornography. Ann Jones, for example, tells the story of a brutal torturer and murderer of a young woman who explained, "Ever since I was a young boy I have wanted to torture a beautiful young girl." She concludes archly, "Now where do you suppose he got an idea like that?"[29] She expects us to answer "from pornography," though I can think of a hundred gothic, horror, and detective films and novels which might give him the same idea, albeit in less graphic sexual detail.

> The point is not: where did he get his idea?
> The point is: *where did he get the idea that he could act out his idea?*
> *Pornography is the theory, rape is the practice,* goes the saying. But isn't the point that men have the power to practice their theory?
> Isn't the point that we are not powerful enough to practice ours?

Although a movement against pornography inspired many women with anger and horror at incredibly cruel and disgusting images, this strategic twist also drained the potential of the violence-against-women movement. As an issue, anti-pornography has drawn mostly middle class women, often college students and church women. College is where people learn to identify ideas with reality; to overemphasize theory and undervalue experience.

Church is one locus of sexual repression, often equated with morality.[30] Middle class people are less apt than poor and working class people to regard capitalism as a brutal system; and whites are more likely than people of color to seek a quick patch-up to what they think is a basically sound society, as opposed to considering the possibility that the entire enterprise is rotten. These perspectives limit the vision of the anti-pornography movement.

Pornography, as an industry, garners millions and millions of dollars by exploiting and degrading women's sexuality. Anti-pornography activists often neglect to situate pornography as an aspect of capitalism, on a continuum—along with advertising, popular culture, many service and office jobs, etc., all of which also exploit women's bodies for profit. Instead, emphasis has often fallen on explicit depictions of sexuality, as if sex or women's sexuality were the problem, instead of *forced* sex and *exploited* sexuality.

Confusion between explicit sexuality and violence in pornography has obscured, to some extent, the horror perpetuated in art and in popular culture. Wandering through Western culture with a newly acquired feminist consciousness is disorienting, to say the least, from Leda and the Swan to Lolita, the Rape of the Sabine Women to Manet's Picnic on the Grass, with its fully clothed bourgeois men and fully naked women. Popular culture, too, teems with images of violence against women: both white and Black popular music, much of what passes for comic routines, and money-making sleazy soft-porn—from ads for skin-tight jeans to movies in which women are violated and killed in graphic detail, but the killer gets caught so it's not as if the movie is really pro-violence, right?[31] X-rated flicks have no edge on the following random (misogynist and racist) blip from AM radio: the DJ, after airing Shelly West's playful song about getting drunk on tequila, quips, "Thank you, Shelly—and Shelly, the whole Mexico City Soccer Team thanks you too."

The result has been a powerful movement split into false categories of pro-sex and anti-sex, privatizing and psychologizing a real honest-to-god war which rages happily, violently on, totally unconcerned with how any woman *feels* about sex.

Most significantly, as violence against women is an oppression, a terror, and an experience we share across lines of class, race, and culture, a movement might have been created to cross these lines. I do not ignore what *has* been created: the battered women's movement in particular and the anti-violence movement in general. But as the militant activist wing of the movement veered to focus on pornography, the potential for a movement to join us across lines of class, race and culture was undermined. It is this potential that must be actualized if we are to stop the violence.

We help the victims. We attack the theory.
Who is attacking the practice?

What we did was significant, and now I refer to the larger *we,* a huge sweep of feminist activity that has to some extent transformed the conditions of our lives. We ignore important victories if we don't register the impact of the women's liberation movement on this issue.

But What Has Really Changed?   Are women any safer walking down the street? Are women beaten less by their lovers and kin? Are girls, and boys, abused less by male family members? A recent study found that 683,000 adult women had been raped in 1990, more than one a minute. This doesn't even count those under 18—*and 61% of all women raped endured this rape before age 18; 29% before age 11.*[32] Another recent study found that perfectly ordinary men, when angry, become sexually aroused in response to descriptions of rape: "With the right combination of factors, most men can be aroused by violent sex," concluded the researcher.[33] Campus rape, including acquaintance rape, and sexual harassment in the workplace and in schools, are being exposed as so common that they practically constitute a norm—though exposure is also the first step towards change.[34]

The criminal justice system has improved somewhat, for the classic street rape situation, though, as I've discussed, the chances of a rapist being caught, prosecuted, and convicted remain minuscule. Beneath the iceberg tip of street violence looms the much larger structure of sexual violence that rests on male entitlement to sex from women, the valuing of male needs and priorities over female ones.

And while there is much more awareness, support, and some legal protection concerning incest, most of the discussion has shifted from political to psychological grounds: away from the deep structure of feminist insight into the danger, for girls and women, of the patriarchal family; and towards the psychological damage out of which the individual once-abused abuser continues the cycle of abuse: away from examining male power over women and children, towards exploring our shared genderless condition as victims. [Meanwhile the male power base, though challenged, goes along pretty much unchanged.]

———————

1991 will be remembered as a banner year, in which privileged men who sexually abuse women got exposed . . . and nothing happened to them. Clarence Thomas, William Kennedy Smith, and the St. Johns' rapists (white male students charged with gang-raping a Black female student) illustrate the immunity with which privileged men still sexually abuse women. These particular men may be more cautious from now on, but women, too, learn caution. We learn—if we didn't already know—that our charges will be met with disbelief. How many of us have pasts or presents that can stand up to scrutiny like Anita Hill's? "A Quickie for Willie" read the *New York Post's* headline, about Smith's acquittal. (The jury took just over an hour.) [35] A male friend of the St. Johns' rapists testified to witnessing them rape the woman whose testimony was nevertheless deemed by the jury "too contradictory" for conviction.

Most cases of course get neither publicity nor much legal attention. It's obvious that the legal system is inadequate against men of privilege; it was, after all, designed to protect their rights.[36] We face the virtual use-lessness of the criminal justice system, the civil courts, the legislature; the near-impermeability of these institutions to feminist impact.

Yet something *is* happening. Thomas, Smith, the St. Johns' rapists all escaped legal damage. But Anita Hill abruptly and irrevocably raised national consciousness and made visible the chasm between male and female experience.[37] Despite Hill's treatment by the Senate committee, she has enlarged the space in which women who have been sexually harassed can decide how to respond. As the 1992 election nears, women are seeking political office in record numbers; some, like Lynn Hardy Yeakel, specifically in response to the sexism made sickeningly visible in the Hill-Thomas hearings. Patricia Bowman, who charged "Willie" with rape, has become an ardent anti-rape activist. The most famous last words of all may be NOW President Patricia Ireland's: "When we get screwed, we multiply."

Refocusing the Issues

The Degendering of Male Violence   In the activist anti-pornography wing of the movement, sexism remains a clear focus, though the line between sex and violence often blurs. But more generally we have witnessed a depoliticization of the issue of male violence against women. Husband battering—a relatively rare phenomenon—receives a flurry of publicity. The same is true about the rape of men and boys—not at all a rare phenomenon, but what gets obscured in the attention lavished on male victims is that the agents of sexual violence are almost always men, and the act is usually designed to "womanize" the victim, to assert male power over him. As a man abused by his uncle at age ten remarked astutely: "I felt dirty, disgusting, and nasty. Just like a girl."[38] Homophobia only underscores the role of sexism and male dominance in male sexual violence. Faggots are hated because they don't act like real men; therefore they will be treated like women. Sexism needs to be reintegrated into our analysis of male sexual violence.

Rape and Race   At the same time, the connection with racism in particular and privilege in general needs to be more deeply understood. In a racist culture, with its history of slavery and lynching, its present of prisons disproportionately full of men of color, violence must be considered through a racial—and class—lens.[39]

What are the issues? First, media and police attention is skewed toward those cases where privileged white women are attacked by men of color (the rape and beating of the "Central Park Jogger," for example, was headlined for days, during a week when some twenty-eight other women in New York City also reported being raped). Second, black-on-black and color-on-color crime is generally treated as trivial, especially when these are instances of men abusing women. Third, what happens when white men or wealthy men commit crimes against women or less privileged men? Take the example of Jeffrey Dahmer, a white man charged with the sexual abuse and murder of seventeen men and boys. One of these, Kontarek Sinthasomphone, a young Cambodian, was reported by at least two women to the police as wandering naked and apparently hurt. The police looked at the hurt naked child, saw "a lover's quarrel," and returned Kontarek to Dahmer, who killed him. Perhaps their racist limited vision kept them from seeing that Kontarek was a child. Should we be pleased that the police "honored" what they saw as a homosexual relationship, as they would a heterosexual one, by condoning abuse?

Fourth, the extra vulnerability of poverty, which often intersects with color. Poor women have less choice about housing, less police patrol and less reason to believe in police protection, less money to drive cars or take taxis instead of using public transportation, less possibility of refusing night jobs, or jobs which include sexual harassment or generally expose us to unsafe conditions. Poverty keeps us from seeking paid counselling, and often prevents us from leaving abusive relationships. Women of color, frequently poor, are often exposed to abuse in dangerous neighborhoods and in demeaning jobs. Women surviving on women's wages—single women, lesbians—are frequently poor. Perceived as unprotected because "man-less," we are particularly vulnerable to abuse by men, especially if we live outside our own cultural or racial community: outsider women are marks, and visible lesbians are doubly outsiders.

A clear response from the left or from communities of color on the issue of violence against women has not been forthcoming. White men feel threatened because they fear either accusation or diminution of privilege. Men of color, in addition, fear the racist use of the rape charge. More recently, African American men have focused on the rape of African American women by white men. But the rape and other violence done to women of color by men from their own community has been addressed almost exclusively by women of color.[40] Many women of color, Jewish women, and other non-dominants have refrained from naming the abuse dealt them by "their" men, fearful of fueling bigotry. And no one can have failed to notice the difference in how even celebrities are treated by the courts when one is William Kennedy Smith and the other is Mike Tyson.

Meanwhile, as long as any woman fears how the issue of male violence against women will be used against her sons, brothers, and husbands—ntozake shange's "the suspect is always black and in his early 20s"[41]—we are all blocked from the very unity we need.[42]

Rape As Hate Crime   The connection between rape and racism has strategic implications. Legislation to classify bias or hate crimes and to treat them with special gravity has been considered in many cities and states and passed in some. There have been vigorous battles over whether to include or exclude lesbian and gay bashing. But battering and sexual violence against women has rarely been classified as they warrant: as bias/hate crimes against women.[43]

Yet rape is always a crime of woman hate: as performed against women, or as a "womanizing" act against boys and men.

Indeed, there are casual or occasional rapists, who rape almost as an afterthought, along with robbery—*might as well*—or as an evening activity. But this property-theft attitude on the part of rapists, or property-abuse on the part of batterers, implies deep contempt for women. It's risky, however, to focus too much on the feelings of the abuser: his anger, his hatred of women (which usually gets laid at the doorstep of his overbearing mother). There are many ways to express anger and even hatred. In our culture, rape and battering are relatively low-risk ways. This fact suggests profound societal apathy about the condition of women and children.

The point of classifying violence against women as a bias crime is to raise its priority on civic agendas. This classification would promote alliances between feminists and communities of color, Jews, lesbians and gays, and offer opportunities for mutual struggle against sexism, racism, homophobia, and anti-Semitism. It would force feminists to integrate a racial lens into anti-violence work, as it would force activists of color, Jews, and gay men to integrate a gender lens into anti-bias work.

II. Blocks To Resistance

Imagination: To Consider Violence

A woman raped by a landlord showing her an apartment remarks, "the only degrading thing I can recall about it is simply not being able to hit the guy. I just really wanted to sock him in the teeth."[44]

> Another woman, awakened and raped with a knife at her throat:
> . . . You never forget it and you're never the same. . . . It hits you where you're most vulnerable. . . . About six months to a year later some of the vulnerability disappeared. It was replaced by rage. Oh, I wish now I had hit him. Or killed him.[45]

Listen to women cheer at karate demonstrations simulating attack when the woman playing "victim" strikes back. Think about women's reaction to *Thelma and Louise*.[46] In response to violence, it's natural to consider violence.

Yet as a movement, we don't.

If a woman is abused and strikes back, we often work for her defense. We respond to her risk. But we do not ourselves shoulder it, even as a movement. Nor do we encourage women to avail ourselves of violence as a serious, perhaps effective option.

Why?

Obvious response #1: *Violence is wrong.*
Obvious response #2: *Violence won't work.*

What do we mean, *wrong?* What do we mean, *work?* When women are prepared to use violence, they are less likely to get raped, abused and murdered.

Listen.

> . . . all of a sudden he got this crazy look in his eye and he said to me, "Now I'm going to kill you." Then I started saying my prayers. I knew there was nothing I could do. He started to hit me—I still wasn't sure if he wanted to rape me at this point—or just to kill me. He was hurting me, but hadn't yet gotten me into a strangle-hold because he was still drunk and off balance. Somehow we pushed into the kitchen where I kept looking at this big knife. But I didn't pick it up. Somehow no matter how much I hated him at that moment, I still couldn't imagine putting the knife in his flesh, and then I was afraid he would grab it and stick it into me. . . .[47]

I couldn't imagine.
I was afraid.

I couldn't imagine corresponds to *it's wrong.* Sticking the knife into his flesh is unimaginable, too horrible.

This horror, this failure of imagination might have cost her life. Her life against his, and she chooses his.

> *I was afraid* corresponds to *it won't work.* Using the knife might make it worse. But how much worse could it get? He's already threatened to kill her.

Is this in women's interest?

If we avoid the question of using violence because it makes us uncomfortable, many men have no such compunctions. They continue to rape, mutilate, beat and kill us. So we are not avoiding violence, only the guilt we associate with using it. Something about innocence is dangerous here. We are innocent because helpless. As long as we insist on maintaining our innocence, we lock ourselves into helplessness. In this way we become complicit with our oppression.

A few feminists have touched on the question. Phyllis Chesler, M. F. Beal, Karen Haglund conclude similarly; in Chesler's words:

> Women, like men, must be capable of violence or self-defense before their refusal to use violence constitutes a free and moral choice rather than "making the best of a bad bargain."[48]

> But how do we become capable? What if we are already capable? And what if we don't refuse?

Let us begin to imagine putting the knife in his flesh. If we choose not to, let the reason *not* be that we couldn't imagine doing it. The women who wrote the excellent *Women's Gun Pamphlet* have an answer to the *violence is wrong* voice:

> The only way I've figured out to try and eliminate the all-nurturing masochist in each of us is to remember that the man or men who attack, rape, mutilate, and try to kill you, have done and will do the same to as many women as they can. While you defend yourself, bear in your mind all the women you love that you are fighting for, especially those you know who have been attacked.[49]

Violence and Power   Yes, I'm talking about violence. But the violence did not originate with us. If we submit, evade, fight back directly or indirectly—no matter what we do we are responding to a violence that already is. Janet Koenig has described how the oppressor's violence

> becomes routinized and ritualized. It becomes so part of the environment, of the school, factory, prison, and family that it is barely perceived consciously. Ideology distorts the perception of violence. The source of violence now appears to be not the system but those who rebel against it.[50]

And Assata Shakur succinctly remarks:

> Women have been raped throughout history, and now when we fight back, now that we have the consciousness to fight back—they call us violent.[51]

To avoid this conceptual error, Ti-Grace Atkinson would call responsive violence, the violence of rebellion, by another name:

> When "violence" appears *against* "oppression," it is a *negation of institutionalized* violence. "Violence," these opening blows are a positive humane act—under such circumstances. Such acts are *acts of bravery. . .* It is a betrayal of humanity, and of hope, to represent such acts as shameful, or regrettable.[52]

Not to deny the horror of violence. Or to invalidate or mock the part in us that does not want to harm. We have an honorable past on this subject. Often life has been preserved solely because of our efforts to feed, wash, clothe, and keep our families in health. We have been active in movements to stop slavery, wars, imperialism, lynching, and abuse of all kinds.

It's hard to transform such concerns into a willingness to cut down another woman's son.

Nor am I saying violence should be leapt to lightly. But the situation is hardly light. I am saying only that using violence should be thinkable. And that the grounds on which we decide whether or not to commit violence against men be *our* grounds: *is it in our interest?*

Violence is an aspect of power. In a conflictual society, where power imbalance exists, so does the possibility of physical force to meet physical threat. "Women," Karen Hagberg points out,

> are called violent (indeed, we actually consider ourselves violent) whenever we assert ourselves in the smallest ways. One woman recently described the verbal challenging of men on the streets as an act of violence.[53]

This is absurd or tragic. Yet the piece of embedded truth is that any woman's challenge to male power—from a calm "I'm not interested" to an assertive "please turn down your stereo"—may be perceived as aggressive and met with violence. Most of us know we risk danger in even a mild confrontation with a man. Every male-female interaction assumes: *in a physical fight he will win.* Every man assumes this about every woman. This is the assumption behind rape. As Ellen Willis remarked in 1968, *Men don't take us seriously because they're not physically afraid of us.*

An Analog: African American Liberation from Slavery   Recent scholarship about African Americans in the South during and after the Civil War sheds intriguing light on the relationship between violence and freedom. When the war began, the great abolitionist and former slave, Frederick Douglass,

> immediately called for the enlistment of slaves and free blacks into a "liberating army" that would carry the banner of emancipation through the South. Within thirty days, Douglass believed, 10,000 black soldiers could be assembled. "One black regiment alone would be, in such a war, the full equal of two white ones. The very fact of color in this case would be more terrible than powder and balls. The slaves would learn more as to the nature of the conflict from the presence of one such regiment, than from a thousand preachers."[54]

But Northern white men were not so sure. As they debated the question of arming Blacks—slaves or freedmen—three fears were repeated. They feared slave insurrections against slaveholders who, though the enemy, were, after all, white. They feared Black incompetence; no less a personage than President Lincoln speculated that, if Blacks were armed, "in a few weeks the arms would be in the hands of the rebels." But perhaps the deepest and most revealing fear was that Blacks would prove competent. As one Union congressman noted,

> If you make him the instrument by which your battles are fought, the means by which your victories are won, you must treat him as a victor is entitled to be treated, with all decent and becoming respect.[55]

In the South, the same debate was much more anxiety-laden: would armed slaves turn on their masters? (The transparency of the "happy slave" myth is evident in these musings.) What would happen if distinctions were levelled? "The day you make soldiers of them is the beginning of the end of the revolution," warned General Howell Cobb. "If slaves will make good soldiers, our whole theory of slavery is wrong."[56]

In fact, Black soldiers were crucial to the North, and their performance in the Union army, by all accounts courageous and impressive as Douglass had predicted, revealed that "the whole theory of slavery" was more resilient than General Cobb had imagined, surviving as it did the institution of slavery itself. But whether violence is a tool, a back-up to power, a psychological release or an inevitable response to oppression,[57] *being able* to use violence may be a critical aspect of freedom. Listen to Felix Haywood, a former slave in Texas:

> If everymother's son of a black had thrown 'way his hoe and took up a gun to fight for his own freedom along with the Yankees, the war'd been over before it began. But we didn't do it. We couldn't help stick to our masters. We couldn't no more shoot 'em than we could fly. My father and me used to talk 'bout it. We decided we was too soft and freedom wasn't goin' to be much to our good even if we had an education.[58]

Couldn't shoot them. Soft. The definition of manliness that depends on murder may be the saddest comment on patriarchy anyone can dredge up. As W.E.B. Du Bois remarked with some disgust,

> How extraordinary, and what a tribute to ignorance and religious hypocrisy, is that fact that in the minds of most people, even those of liberals, only murder makes men. The slave pleaded; he was humble; he protected the women of the South, and the world ignored him. The slave killed white men; and behold, he was a man.[59]

What about the women? Slave women were vulnerable to sexual abuse by white and Black men alike, though solidarity between enslaved women and men appears to have been very strong.[60] Many women resisted, sometimes with violence. Rose Williams tells of taking a poker to the man chosen by her master for her to marry (i.e., breed with), and of capitulating only after her owner threatened her with a whipping.[61] Cherry Loguen used a stick to knock out a man armed with a knife who tried to rape her. Two women attacked by an overseer waited till he undressed and "pounced upon him, wrestled him to the ground, and then ran away."[62] It's likely that women were able to resist assaults and unwanted attention more forcefully from other slaves than from their owners, though Linda Brent's excruciating narrative of resistance to her owner's sexual demands demonstrates the lengths to which some women went to preserve their sexual integrity.[63]

Did women resist enslavement? During the Middle Passage, women, unlike men, were not chained or confined to the hold. While this freedom left them vulnerable to sexual abuse by the ship's crews, it also left them freer to rebel, and there are several reported instances of women inciting or assisting insurrections at sea.[64] On the plantations,

Some murdered their masters, some were arsonists, and still others refused to be whipped. . . . Equipped with a whip and two healthy dogs, an Alabama overseer tied a woman named Crecie to a stump with intentions of beating her. To his pain and embarrassment, she jerked the stump out of the ground, grabbed the whip, and sent the overseer running.[65]

A Union official recorded several women entering the Union camp with marks of severe whipping. The whipper was caught and a male slave first lashed him twenty times, and then the women, one after another, gave him twenty lashes, according to the official, "to remind him that they were no longer his";[66] but maybe also because releasing rage where it belongs is one step towards healing.[67] There are also instances of women fighting against their men being taken away.[68]

The ability to defend oneself, one's people, one's dignity, to struggle for one's own liberation, is clearly a survival skill. As Robert Falls, former slave, summed it up: "If I had my life to live over, I would die fighting rather than be a slave again. . . ."[69]

Observations by Black and white, Southerners and Northerners indicate that the Black soldiery affected everyone strongly. Blacks felt pride. Whites felt fear. Both groups recognized that consciousness changed radically when the Black divisions marched through.

And not only consciousness. In New Orleans free Blacks formed two regiments for the Confederacy, in part to improve their status and esteem by learning firearms (though they were never called for combat duty).[70] We could argue the absurdity and tragedy of such a stance, not unlike the arguments that have swirled around Black police or military today. Yet Blacks understood that a Black soldiery might be fair, might protect them, would not automatically assume they were chattel and without rights. A Black soldiery gave Black—and white—people a vision of a differently ordered world: a hint that perhaps the whole theory of slavery was, indeed, wrong.

The analogy is suggestive. Women police officers, fire fighters, soldiers do challenge "the whole theory of slavery,"[71] as do women athletes and construction workers, as well as physicists. But particularly since physical domination so characterizes male-female relations under patriarchy, if women were to defend ourselves and other women, could avail ourselves of violence when needed; and if this potential for self-defense became an expectation, a norm, then patriarchal definitions of male and female would be shaken. Not only minds would change, but reality. Would men begin to wonder if *perhaps the whole theory of patriarchy is wrong?* Would women?

Fear of the Self/Fear of Our Power[72]

If in a patriarchal system violence is an aspect of power, if capacity for violence is a basis for resistance, it's obvious whose interests are served by *it won't work* and *it's wrong;* by the implied fear and horror.

Women often learn to see with the eyes of the dominant culture: male eyes. Especially middle-class heterosexual white women are taught to fear strong women, women with power, women with physical strength, angry women who express that anger forcefully. *It isn't ladylike. It isn't nice.* Even those of us who have long rejected these norms (or accepted our inability to live inside them) still may fear the explosiveness of anger—though this fear obscures the reason for our deep anger, which is our powerlessness. Instead of learning to cherish this rage and to direct it effectively, we often try to suppress it, in ourselves and in others. It's exactly as if we have an army we're afraid to mobilize, train, and use.

Yet we are not always victims. We can be violent. How have we managed to avoid noticing? The idea that men are inherently violent, women inherently non-violent, is dangerous, not only because it is a doctrine of biological superiority, and such doctrines have supported genocide.[73]

The idea that women are inherently non-violent is also dangerous because it's not true. Any doctrine that idealizes us as the non-violent sex idealizes our victimization and institutionalizes who men say we are: intrinsically nurturing, inherently gentle, intuitive, emotional. They think; we feel. They have power; we won't touch it with a ten-foot pole. Guns are for them; let's suffer in a special kind of womanly way.

Such an analysis dooms us to inappropriate kindness and passivity; overlooks both our capacity for and experience with violence; ignores in fact everything about us that we aren't sure we like, including how we sometimes abuse each other. Whatever we disapprove of, we call *theirs,* and then say, when women do these things—talk loud, use reason, fuck hard, act insensitive or competitive, ride motorcycles, carry weapons, explode with rage, fight—they are acting like men.[74]

But who defines "like men," "like women"? On what basis? Remember Sojourner Truth's challenge to restrictive definition: *ain't I a woman?* All women defined as deviant might well echo her words. We may be numerous enough to redefine the "norm." When we find many of us doing what only men are supposed to do, and nearly all of us expressing in some form what is supposed to be a male behavior, then maybe we need to enlarge our notion of who *we* are. The woman who is violent is not acting like a man. She may be announcing a host of contradictions: that her condition is intolerable; that she is or isn't afraid; that she feels entitled; that she has nothing to lose or something to protect; that she needs physical release; that she's a bully; that she has lost or given over or seeks control. But always, in addition, she announces that women are not who men say we are.

TO SEE WOMEN'S VIOLENCE AS A FIELD INCLUDING: SLASHING YOUR WRISTS STANDING UP TO A THREATENING LANDLORD KILLING A RAPIST ATTACKING A WOMAN AT THE BAR FIGHTING AN ABUSIVE HUSBAND PUNCHING YOUR LOVER PUNCHING A MAN WHO MOUTHS OFF AT YOU LEARNING KARATE KICKING A DOG SHOOTING UP WRESTLING FOR

MONEY DRINKING TOO MUCH ALCOHOL WRESTLING FOR
FUN BEATING YOUR CHILD KILLING ANOTHER WOMAN'S
RAPIST

To see women's violence as a wide range of behavior which can serve, protect, endanger, or violate women and children—or be neutral.[75] To expose the
taboo which clothes even our questions about violence. To admit that when we
don't fight back against men's violence, it's not because we're passive, not even
because we're good: but because we're afraid of what they'll do back.

And for good reason. Consider these words from two married women:

*Sometimes I get so mad I wish I could hit him. I did once, but he hit me
back, and he can hurt me more than I can hurt him.*

*When he's so much bigger and stronger, and you got four kids to take care
of, what's a woman supposed to do?*[76]

Consider the implications of the fact that in the late seventies a full 40%
of the women imprisoned for homicide in Chicago's Cook County jail had
killed men in response to physical abuse by these men.[77] Even though judges
in some states have ruled to release women serving time on such convictions, many women still remain in prison.

The fact is, fighting back, even supporting women who fight back, can
be dangerous. The wife who feigns sleep when her husband comes home
drunk; the child who lies to avoid getting beaten; these are tactics based on
experience. Sometimes evasion works better than confrontation. At least it
has sometimes kept us alive.

We worry about making things worse. "If you do what I say, I won't hurt
you," says the rapist, but the woman who trusts him forgets, in her desperation and terror, that he is, after all, a rapist: hardly a basis for trust. With the
husband or mate, while appeasement may be plausible, it's hardly desirable
as a way of life.

What happens to women who actively resist violence? The facts, especially about street violence, flatly contradict the usual police/male advice of
"don't fight it." When a woman resists a rape *in any way*—saying NO like she
means it, screaming, kicking, running, fighting—her chance of escaping
ranges from 60-80%.[78]

Whereas *if she doesn't resist her chance of getting raped is 100%*.

Women and Guns

From my journal, 1978:
*For three or four years I've dreamed about rape regularly. The can't run
dreams. The can't scream ones. Dreams where I'm being attacked and I
have a knife in my pocket but I can't get it, or I'm afraid to use it. The
dream that keeps extending into more complication, more danger, until
there he is again, "my" rapist. I even had a dream where I'm sitting by a
lake and a man swims up, sticks his head out of the water, and says: "I'm
your rapist."*

In many of these dreams, I don't recognize the danger early enough to respond.

Since I bought a gun and have learned to use it, my dreams have changed. Whatever the situation, whatever the form of attack, I simply whip out my gun. Sometimes I shoot. Sometimes I don't even need to shoot, I just aim and he is suddenly harmless. The man who called himself "my rapist " laughs at me when I draw my gun; he says, "The hospital can suck those bullets out in no time." But I know, and he doesn't, that it's a .38 I'm holding, and I shoot, confident that the bullets will do the job.

If resistance alleviates abuse and increases dramatically our chances of escape, how can we increase our ability to resist? The most certain way to refuse violation would be to keep a gun handy.

Many women immediately reject this option. Some call guns "masculine." Many are simply terrified of guns' murderous power. But aside from fears of legal repercussions or male retaliation, fears which are realistic and need to be addressed—is a gun really more dangerous than, for example, a car? Is owning a gun more dangerous than not owning one? Past the realistic fears is, I believe, a fear of our own selves.

I've talked with many women about getting a gun and learning to shoot.

R. tells me, "I'm afraid I'd kill my husband."

Not to dismiss killings that happen in rage because a gun is handy (though how many of these killings are committed by women?) But to recognize that in her mind she's protected against killing her husband only because she lacks the means.

K. says she's afraid she'd shoot the first man she saw acting like an asshole.

I ask what she means by "an asshole." She says, "Like some man beating up on some woman." Again, she is protected (from her best impulses) only by her inability to act.

N. says she's afraid she'd shoot her nose off.

As if a woman who has learned to cook, play the recorder, ride the subway, drive a car, and change a diaper couldn't learn to shoot.

H., B., C., E., many many women say, "I'm afraid if I have a gun it'll get used against me."

Of course this is exactly what men tell us. For example, in Boston in 1979, after the sixth Black woman in as many weeks had been killed, police still advised Black women against carrying weapons because they could be used against them. Yet what alternatives did the police offer?

In fact I've rarely heard of a real-life woman's weapon being used against her, though I've seen it happen over and over again on TV and in the movies. I've heard of a 14-year-old woman who shot her assailant with his gun; a 17-year-old who sliced her attacker's jugular vein with his knife; a mother who shot with his gun the policeman who threatened her child—she killed him and wounded his partner.[79] Maybe it's men who shouldn't carry weapons. But no one tells them that.

I also discover among my friends women who aren't afraid of guns. L., who teaches me to shoot, grew up around guns in rural Oregon. P. learned to shoot in the army. F.'s father hunted. M.'s grandfather was a gangster. Against the dominant experience of women—which is to have little acquaintance with deadly weapons—an alternative perspective emerges: that of women who were taught to shoot as girls; country women who'd as soon live without a knife in the kitchen as a gun in the bedroom; women who recognize a gun as a tool: useful, dangerous but controllable, like a book of matches.

The first time L. took me shooting with a handgun, I tried a .22 pistol for a while, practiced aiming again and again till it came easy. Then I tried the .38. Fire leaped from the barrel, my hand jumped. TV and movies lie about the sound of guns: it is unbelievably loud. The noise, even with earplugs, shook me. After the first round I sat down, took a deep breath, and said, "I feel like I can't control it."

"It feels like that," L. said, "you just have to get used to how it feels."

After a few minutes, I got up to try again. I started to hit the target.

A learning experience, like a million others in a woman's life. Yet so many of us consider ourselves tiny children when it comes to guns. We're afraid a gun—a source of possible protection—will be turned against us. This fear deprives us of strength, lest our strength benefit them, not us. We're afraid what we'd do *if we could*—which, again, keeps us powerless, lest we use our power badly.

To fear ourselves is to use them as model:

> *they abuse their power, therefore we would too*
> is to imagine only helplessness keeps us in line:
> *the more choices we have, the worse we'll be*
> is to insist in some hidden corner of the body:
> *we need oppression*
> Like, *you can't take the law into your own hands.*
> But what better hands to take the law into?

Our fear of ourselves then is fear of ourselves empowered. As we worry about what we'd do if we could, we are undermined in our attempts to end our oppression. We are partly afraid we can't be trusted with freedom.

NOTES

1. I want to acknowledge general indebtedness to the work that preceded or has accompanied the writing of this essay. The first feminist speak-out on rape, in New York City in 1971, was documented in Noreen Connell and Cassandra Wilson, *Rape: The First Sourcebook for Women* (1974). Susan Griffin, *Rape: The Power of Consciousness* (1979) includes her earlier essay, which is still one of the best discussions of the issue. Andrea Medea and Kathleen Thompson, *Against Rape* (1974) remains useful, as does Susan Brownmiller, *Against Our Will: Men, Women*

and Rape (1975)—the classic, limited but essential. Early work on battering includes Erin Pizzey, *Scream Quietly or the Neighbors Will Hear You* (1974), Betsy Warrior, *Battered Lives* (1974) and Del Martin, *Battered Wives* (1976). Susan Schechter, *Women and Male Violence: The Visions and Struggles of the Battered Women's Movement* (1982) remains the best single text on battering to combine service-provider and activist consciousness. On incest, Florence Rush's early work is included in the *Sourcebook* noted above, and her book *The Best Kept Secret: Sexual Abuse of Children* (1980) contains the earliest discussion of how Freud suppressed information and revised his theory, based on his women patients' experience of incestuous abuse by male relatives, in favor of his oedipal theory that women fantasized this abuse. Sandra Butler, *Conspiracy of Silence: The Trauma of Incest* (1978) remains one of the clearest treatments built from women's experience, compassionate and politically savvy. Also, Judith Lewis Herman, with Lisa Hirschman, *Father-Daughter Incest* (1981). General books on violence against women: Andrea Dworkin's *Woman Hating* (1974) and *Our Blood* (1976); Kathleen Barry's *Female Sexual Slavery* (1979); and Frederique Delacorte and Felice Newman, eds., *Fight Back! Feminist Resistance to Male Violence* (1981). Pauline B. Bart and Patricia H. O'Brien, *Stopping Rape: Successful Survival Strategies* (1985), and Evelyn C. White, *Chain Chain Change: For Black Women Dealing with Physical and Emotional Abuse* (1985) are extremely useful.

   I want also to acknowledge general indebtedness to numerous conversations in the late seventies with Paula King and Michaele Uccella, and to the many thinkers and activists with whom I worked in the Portland, Oregon movement to stop violence against women. Many women have read pieces of this essay over the years and shared their responses with me: Gloria Anzaldúa, Margaret Blanchard, Sandy Butler, Chrystos, Irena Klepfisz, Helena Lipstadt, Fabienne McPhail-Grant, Bernice Mennis, Maureen O'Neill, Linda Vance, and Judy Waterman, in addition, of course, to Joan Pinkvoss, my editor and publisher at Aunt Lute. I alone am responsible for its weaknesses.

2. According to psychiatrist Carole Warshaw, "The greatest risk of getting killed is when the woman attempts to leave. . . . The husband or the partner can't tolerate the idea of her leaving." Information drawn from the *New York Times* (3/15/92).

3. The term "domestic violence" may conceal some instances of women abused by women. Lesbians in the emergency room might well fabricate a male abuser or allow assumptions of heterosexuality to protect them from further exposure to scrutiny and humiliation. On the whole, though, one suspects that lesbians often pursue the same course as heterosexual women, blaming phantom doorknobs, stairs, etc., rather than acknowledge battering. With murder, it's another story; probably the gender of the killer is accurately ascertained. It does not appear that lesbians regularly kill their lovers or ex-lovers.

4. US Document 1274, 39th Congress, 1st Session, 1865–66. House Reports, Vol. 3, No. 101, in Gerda Lerner, ed., *Black Woman in White America* (1973), 174.

5. Lillian Rubin, *Worlds of Pain: Life in the Working Class Family* (1976) 139–40. These fairly ordinary quotes ought not to be construed to support the mistaken idea that working-class men rape their wives more than men of other classes, though of course the married woman's ability to assert her rights, leave the marriage, etc., is closely connected to independent resources.

6. Diverse in terms of age, class, sexual preference, ethnicity/religion, partnered and single, mothers and non-mothers; racially not diverse, 15–20 white and one Japanese American. While more immediate survival concerns may preoccupy poor women, including many women of color, I am still convinced that violence against women is a key issue for all but the most powerful, protected and inde-

pendent of women. As such, it still has the potential to unite women across differences, when we approach the issue informed by our differences.

7. Before abortions were legalized, seeking an abortion was like putting your body on the meat rack.

8. The myth of the Black rapist dates from Reconstruction, and was used to justify white terror against emerging Black freedom. See Frederick Douglass, "The Lesson of the Hour" (pamphlet, 1894), quoted in Angela Davis, *Women, Race and Class* (1981), 184. In the lexicon of patriarchy, rape by Black men of white women constitutes theft of white male property. (The myth, by sexualizing Blacks, disguises and justifies sexual abuse of Black women, and repression of Black men).

   Most of this myth-dashing material, except about race and class, comes from Menachem Amir's classic study, *Patterns in Forcible Rape* (1971). Amir's work is extremely useful for information on the police-blotter rapist, but his reliance on statistics from the criminal justice system excludes consideration of all those rapists who are protected by privilege from this system. Thus his conclusion, that rapists fit squarely within the subculture of violence, describes only those rapists who get caught and punished. A more accurate conclusion is that rapists fit squarely within the dominant culture of patriarchy.

9. Latinas rarely used the Hotline at that point; later two Chicanas were hired to translate Hotline literature, to do community outreach in Spanish, and to staff the phone line with Spanish speakers.

10. Statistics indicate that men tend to rape women of their own race and class. But statistics reflect only the small percentage, 10% by FBI estimates, that filters through the criminal justice system. Acquaintance rape, which tends to go unreported, usually reinforces the same-race, same-class category. But contradicting this category is the also seldom-reported category of privileged men who rape women of lower class or race status.

11. One study of thousands of men revealed "only one third [who] said there was no possibility that they could be sexually violent toward women"; Mary Kay Blakely, in "The New Bedford Gang Rape: Who Were the Men?," *Ms.* (July, 1983), 50 ff., citing the research of Neil Malmuth and Edward Donnerstein. This and other research on the subject is surveyed and critiqued in several articles in *Take Back the Night: Women on Pornography,* Laura Lederer, ed. (1980). Cf. Medea and Thompson, note 1, "from all data available it appears that normal men rape normal women," 134.

12. In *Heresies 6: Women and Violence* (1979), 52, from Nadia Telsey and Linda Maslanko, with the help of the Women's Martial Arts Union, Self-Defense for Women (1974). See also Catherine MacKinnon's discussion in *Sexual Harassment of Working Women* (1979), 218–221; Lilia Melani and Linda Fodaski, "The Psychology of the Rapist and His Victim," in *Sourcebook*, note 1, 84, and Irene Diamond, "Pornography and Repression: A Reconsideration," in Catherine Stimpson and Ethel Spector Person, eds., *Women, Sex and Sexuality* (1980), 129–44.

13. Martin, *Battered Wives*, note 1, 20.

14. Florence Rush, "The Sexual Abuse of Children: A Feminist Point of View," in *Sourcebook*, note 1, 73–74. It was startling during the Thomas hearings to see the incest pattern mirrored; the defense—that Thomas wasn't the sort who would do such a thing—is often heard about "upstanding members of the community" when girl children charge them with sexual abuse.

15. Butler, note 1, 97, 100; Herman, note 1, cites restoration of the mother-daughter bond as the major task of therapy for incest survivors, 144 ff.

16. In the most typical scenario, a girl victimized by incest can report to the police, or talk to a doctor, psychologist, teacher, social worker, etc., each of whom is legally

obligated to report to the police. Then, if the mother refuses to exclude the abusive man (very often the case and quite the challenge to visions of universal sisterhood), the girl is yanked out of her home and placed in foster care where the chance of further abuse runs very high. That is one option. The second: she can put up with it and wait to turn 18. Third: she can run away, often to support herself by prostitution. Margot St. James, organizer of COYOTE (the prostitute's union, Call Off Your Old Tired Ethics) estimates that 80% of girls under 18 who become prostitutes are incest victims (Diana Russell and Nicole Van de Ven, eds., *The Proceedings of the International Tribunal on Crimes Against Women*, 1976, 180) though I wonder if this huge figure simply means that incest is far more widespread than anyone imagines. (Similarly, Schecter, note 1, points out that the many battered women who were incestuously abused as girls may only indicate "that incest is much more widespread than anyone has previously recognized," 213.)

17. Statistics from Brownmiller, note 1, 175.

  Calculations: With a base of 1000 actual rapes, 100 women will go to the police, and 85 of them will be believed. In half the cases (42.5 rapes), a perpetrator will be arrested. Three quarters of them will be prosecuted (31.9 rapes). Of these anywhere between 53% ($31.9 \times 53\% = 16.9$ rapes) and 3% ($31.9 \times 3\% = .95$ rapes) will end in a conviction. (1000 rapes $\times$ 10% = 100 $\times$ 85% = 85 $\times$ 50% = 42.5 $\times$ 75% = 31.9 prosecuted; $31.9 \times 53\%$ =16.9 convictions; $31.9 \times 3\%$ = .95 convictions, often a lesser charge.) What may have changed in the past 15 years is the rate of reporting; some estimate as many as half the women raped will report to the police.

18. Legal battles to exempt such cases from statutes of limitations have been critical, since it may take many years for a woman to remember the sexual abuse she endured as a girl, or to learn that she has some legal recourse.

19. The idea of collecting these names was Paula King's.

20. Lenore E. Walker, *The Battered Woman* (1979).

21. Anita Bracy Brooks, discussing cultural differences about violence remarks,

  [the black woman] has been socialized to live with violence on an everyday basis. She may observe daily in the community one-to-one physical violence inflicted in states of anger, sexual exploitation, and accommodation for goods and services, as well as family violence, and be powerless to intervene. Or, she may find she must defend herself against aggression because she does not have any expectation of anyone coming to her rescue or protecting her from physical or emotional harm, even the police. Thusly, she learns to not only protect herself or avoid encounters, but to fight back if necessary. . . .

  The advocate must be aware of and examine her/his own threshold and attitude toward the tolerance of anger/violence because Black people experience anger and violence differently.

  Anita Bracy Brooks, "The Black Woman Within the Program and Service Delivery Systems for Battered Women: A Cultural Response," *Battered Women: An Effective Response*, Chapter 2, Minnesota Department of Corrections, June, 1980, 7, quoted in Schecter, note 1, 272.

22. A disproportionate number of sexual harassment charges have been filed by Black women (MacKinnon, note 12, 53), which may mean that Black women are disproportionately harassed on the job—given the way racism and racist myths about Black sexuality function, this should come as no shock (see Lerner, note 4, 150 ff. and *passim*)—and may also mean that Black women are choosing to fight sexual harassment more.

23. Schecter, note 1, alone among those who have written the major texts on the subject, comes from the service end of the spectrum, and her work remains the best combined practical/theoretical work on the subject.

24. See notes 1, 12.

25. See note 11.

26. Especially against Warner Brothers' record albums which depicted bruised and beaten women; Nikki Craft's work against pornography magazines; Marcia Womongold shooting into a porn theater, documented in Marcia Womongold, "Setting a 'Bad' Example," in *Fight Back,* note 1, 222–25.

27. The woman whose sexual—and domestic—slavery takes place in the family apartment is only more invisible, not freer, than the prostitute—like the file clerk, who may or may not be subject to sexual harassment and she performs the world's dreariest work. The servitude of any woman reinforces women's oppression, but feminists do not talk about forcing housewives and file clerks to stop what they're doing. We talk about creating options.

    Historian Judith Walkowitz points to the experience of nineteenth century middle-class women who tried to help prostitutes reform, only to discover that, while there were those who accepted the opportunity to earn "an honest day's pay," there were also quite a number who looked at the reformers like they were demented, offering backbreaking work for hardly any money. "The Politics of Prostitution," in *WSS,* eds., Stimpson & Person, note 11, 145–56. In another essay Walkowitz discusses the casual and occasional nature of prostitution for English working class women prior to the mid-nineteenth century (when the Contagious Disease Acts were introduced, 1864–1869). One result of the Acts was to isolate prostitutes, make of them a distinct class of women, and destroy their mobility. "The Making of an Outcast Group," in *A Widening Sphere, Changing Roles of Victorian Women,* ed., Martha Vicinus (1977), 82.

28. Brownmiller is one of the worst offenders, joining with repressive church groups to protest at Times Square. Kathleen Barry, on the other hand, is an exception to this; she alone of the theorists has devised some innovative practical suggestions for reducing female sexual slavery, including monitoring bus stations for young runaways (who are often escaping abusive homes and are marks for pimps), providing childcare to women who work as prostitutes and attempting to reach them through their concern for their children. She also suggests a source for funding: that portion of city budgets spent policing and prosecuting prostitution. Dworkin's rage and compassion on behalf of women victimized by sex work is unmistakable.

29. Ann Jones, "A Little Knowledge," in *TBtN,* note 10, 184.

30. Lesbians, whose sexuality is illegal in several states, may find this equation especially contradictory to our vision of feminism. See Lisa Orlando, "Bad Girls and 'Good' Politics," *Literary Supplement, Village Voice* (#13, December 1982), and Ellis Willis's classic "Feminism, Moralism and Pornography," in *Beginning to See the Light* (1981), 219–227.

31. Some activists criticize popular and high culture as well, like those who picketed the Broadway production of *Lolita* or *Miss Saigon* (the latter, picketed by The Heat is On Miss Saigon, a multiracial coalition of mostly lesbians and gays outraged by the play's racism as well as sexism). But most anti-pornography work has been directed at places like Times Square and hard-core low-class porn.

32. *New York Times* (4/24/92).

33. *New York Times* (12/10/91).

34. See Ann Russo on campus rape in the *Women's Review of Books* (Feb., 1992). At one small private New England college in 1990, for example, three charges of sexual harassment were reported in a single department. Now, sexual harassment charges are popping up all over in the wake of Anita Hill's consciousness-raising charges against Clarence Thomas.

35. About Smith, sympathetic newscasters commiserated that he had to spend his entire fortune, two million dollars, on his defense (poor thing, soon to become a doctor, he possessed a personal fortune of two million dollars, and he'll inherit millions more). Did anyone remark that the law, created by (and often for) lawyers, leaves unrestricted the amount of money that individuals may spend on defense?

36. Some of these rights (the right to bear arms, to free speech, etc.) are spelled out in the Constitution and Bill of Rights, because they're being asserted against kings, governments, and the like, while other rights (the right to beat wives and children; to obtain sex from wives by force; to own Black men, women and children) are not even articulated; they are simply assumed.

37. What if Hill had been white? Would she have waited ten years to speak? Would the Senate have dared to disbelieve publicly a privileged professional white woman charging a Black man, even a privileged Black man, with a sex crime? Might they have voted not to confirm—not because women have the right to a work environment free of sexual harassment but because white men have exclusive rights over the bodies of white women? This is the public stance I would predict, though privately some of these enlightened spirits might well have responded as white officials at Notre Dame reacted to a white woman who charged with rape several Black members of the football team. "We believed the boys," they said—these boys being, presumably, the kind of Blacks up-to-date college officials would adopt as "best friends." In that same incident, the more old-fashioned, also white police ranked race over gender and believed the woman. From Dworkin, "The Rape Atrocity and the Boy Next Door," *Blood,* note 1, 38–42.

38. Butler, note 1, 32. On incestuous abuse of children, Butler notes 87% girls, 13% boys, 3.

39. This means recognizing, honoring, but not depending on the resistance skills of those women most burdened by sexism. Working class women and butches often have developed their ability to physically fight. Single women and lesbians often do not depend on male money.

    A poll following the Hill-Thomas hearings showed that working class women (not identified by race) tended not to believe Anita Hill because they'd all had to cope with sexual harassment and they didn't see why she hadn't told the fucker off. At the same time, see note 22, on the disproportionate number of sexual harassment charges filed by Black women. Women who are less tied into the system also may have the clearest vision.

40. Alice Walker's depiction of Black male violence against Black women in *The Color Purple* was roundly condemned by some Black men as "white feminist."

41. ntozake shange, *nappy edges* (1978).

42. See, for example, Anne Braden, "A Second Open Letter to Southern White Women," *Southern Exposure* IV.4 (1977), 50–53. Braden, a white Southern anti-racist activist, recalls attending a lecture by Susan Brownmiller where a Black woman asked, "What you are saying may help me protect myself, but how can I protect my son?" Feminists need to throw our collective weight behind the abuse of those women least empowered by the system. This also means respecting the concerns of women of color about the random and unequal persecution of their men.

43. In Brooklyn, in January, 1992, a fifteen-year-old white girl was raped by two Black men. This was labelled a bias crime, because of two mentions of race, one of which was reported as: she asked, "Why are you doing this to me?" and one rapist answered, "Because you're white and perfect." Does the "white and perfect" remark make this a bias crime? Is retaliatory rage the same as racist hate? I

don't excuse rape of any sort. But I'd hate to see hate crime labelling used most frequently for crimes against whites, christians, men and heterosexuals.

44. *Sourcebook,* note 1, 49.

45. Brownmiller, note 1, 363.

46. Interesting that in patriarchal western culture, revenge is considered practically a sacred duty for men, Hamlet and Orestes being only two of the more obvious examples (both sons avenging their fathers in part against their mothers). But women are not even supposed to entertain vengeful feelings.

47. Griffin, *Consciousness,* note 1, 21.

48. Phyllis Chesler, *Women and Madness* (1973), 292; see also M.F. Beal, *S.A.F.E. House* (1976) and Karen Hagberg, "Why the Women's Movement Cannot Be Non-Violent," *Heresies 6,* note 12, 44.

49. *The Women's Gun Pamphlet by and for Women* (1975), 3.

50. Janet Koenig, "The Social Meaning of Violence," *Heresies 6,* note 12, 91.

51. Assata Shakur, from an interview in *Plexus* by Women Against Prison, quoted in Beal, note 49, 111.

52. Ti-Grace Atkinson, *Amazon Odyssey* (1974), ccxlix. The term *violence* she reserves to represent "a class function," available as a *tactic* only to the oppressor class (200).

53. Hagberg, note 49, 44.

54. Leon Litwack, *Been in the Storm So Long: The Aftermath of Slavery* (1980), 65-66.

55. Litwack, note 55, 66.

56. Litwack, note 55, 43. What is being said here? First, the "whole theory of slavery" boiled down to an assumption of African inferiority, less-than-humanness. Second, military prowess dominated patriarchal notions of humanness: only competent soldiers, i.e., men who could act like "real men," were equal human beings. Consider that slaves were not an unknown people but the very people who not only performed necessary physical labor, but also raised white Southern children and tended the white Southern sick; obviously, tenderness, intelligence, caring, etc. did not challenge "the whole theory of slavery." See Deborah Gray White, *Ar'n't I a Woman: Female Slaves in the Plantation South* (1985).

57. Frantz Fanon, *The Wretched of the Earth* (1963), discusses the political implications of the oppressed's psychological need to release rage.

58. Litwack, note 55, 46.

59. W.E.B. Du Bois, *Black Reconstruction* (1935), quoted in Litwack, note 55, 64.

60. See Angela Davis, "The Legacy of Slavery: Standards for a New Womanhood," in *WRC,* note 8, 3–29, and Linda Brent, *Incidents in the Life of a Slave Girl* (1973; 1st pub. 1861), which depicts extreme sexual harassment and abuse suffered by enslaved Black women from white men, and solidarity among Black women and men, both enslaved and free. Of course Brent was writing an abolitionist document.

    It appears that women employed all the forms of resistance used by men, direct and indirect. But unlike the men, the women had no access to the military, no institutional focus through which to transform capacity for violence into organized strength. And if "manliness," as Du Bois caustically remarked, meant murder, "womanliness" translated into what Black women were deprived of, the right to be protected by their men, and to raise their own babies.

61. White, *Ar'n't I a Woman,* note 57, 102–03, citing B.A. Botkin, ed., *Lay My Burden Down: A Folk History of Slavery* (1945), 160–62.

62. White, note 57, 78.

63. Brent, note 61.

64. White, note 57, 63–64.

65. White, note 57, 77–78.

66. Litwack, note 55, 65.

67. Toni Morrison's *Beloved* (1987) and Sherley Anne William's *Dessa Rose* (1986) both imagine permutations of violence from enslaved women.

68. Litwack, note 55, 76, 114.

69. Litwack, note 55, 46.

70. Litwack, note 55, 42.

71. Susan Brownmiller argued in *Against Our Will* for the critical importance of integrating by gender the military and the police. Though we have seen some signal changes as some gender integration occurs, and though women police and soldiers may improve their individual status, challenge stereotypes, and offer better service or protection to women, it's no more an adequate solution to rape than Black soldiers were an adequate solution to racist violence. The missing link in Brownmiller's argument is the role of the army and police in the U.S., which is to safeguard the interests of the powerful at home and abroad. This means men. Until or unless male institutions truly serve our interest, we can't adequately fight for women through them. During the Civil War and Reconstruction the interests of northern capitalists uniquely coincided with the interests of the slaves.

72. An earlier version of part of this chapter appeared in *Fight Back*, note 1, co-authored by me and Michaele Uccella. The ideas emerged in our discussions; the actual writing was done by me.

73. Andrea Dworkin argued this in "Biological Superiority: The World's Most Dangerous and Deadly Idea," *Heresies 6*, note 12, 46.

74. "The belief that violence is somehow gender-linked is amazingly prevalent throughout all literature, even feminist literature. . . . Obviously it would be stupid and cruel to say that women are not brutally victimized, systematically, institutionally, across all age, class, and race barriers. Quite the contrary. But the assumption that women are inherently incapable of violence is something else. My own inquiry into the matter has shown me that this assumption is simply not true." Michalele Uccella, *Lesbian Violence,* presented at Goddard College and at the Montpelier (Vermont) Women's Center, September, 1978.

75. The theory that a woman's capacity for doing violence (however covert or unacceptable the expression) is also a capacity for resistance was developed by Michaele Uccella in *Lesbian Violence.*

76. Two women quoted in Rubin, note 5, 117, 42.

77. C. McCormick, "Battered Women" (1977), cited by Schneider, Jordan, and Arguedas, "Representation of Women Who Defend Themselves," in *Heresies 6,* note 12, 100 ff.

78. Police statistics from Portland, Oregon, 1976, indicated a 60% rate of escape for women who use some form of resistance. Considering that many women who get away don't bother to report to the police, the higher rate of 80% indicated by other studies seems plausible. (Of course many many women who don't escape also refuse to report to the police, perhaps as many as 90% of all women who get raped.) Bart, note 1, has compiled resistance strategies from women who escaped.

79. The first escape was recorded in the Portland Oregonian sometime in 1979; the second came from the New York Post, 1/31/79. Neither of these women was charged. Also note the following divine judgment: "An axwielding Portland

youth was killed early Friday when he accidentally struck himself in the side of the neck while allegedly threatening two girls in the parking lot of a convenience market." Oregon Journal, 7/19/78.

56

A PERSONAL EXPLORATION INTO THE POLITICS OF BOYHOOD

PAUL B. SEIDMAN

I

As I write this, I am thirty-one years old and just over 5'11". But when the sibling sensations of terror and vulnerability hit, I am young and small, returned in a fear flash to my childhood of daily survival in men's war against women and children. Some incest survivors call these flashbacks post-traumatic stress disorder, or P.T.S.D., which is what the Vietnamese have—the boys who saw their families shot and burned, the girls and women who were prostituted and raped by U.S. troops. We have trouble, at times, separating what's happening now from what happened then. The past bleeds into my present with little or no warning.

Terror is not an easy state to describe to someone who has not visited it since childhood. Terror is an unwelcome companion, following me everywhere, taking me over from time to time, trapping me in my past, in locked rooms with feelings too intense and annihilating to let out. Terror is my link to a childhood filled with real-life haunted houses, where children were too petrified to move, too paralyzed to breathe. There are times when my breathing is faint and shallow, not noticeable to the people around me. It is then I remember to unwrap the terror that binds my ribs like a corset, and pull air down into my lungs. You mustn't move, I learned as a child. You must keep very, very still. Then maybe he won't hurt you again. Terror was probably the most effective weapon of the child molester who got me and many other kids in the early 1970s. The fear that he would find me if I spoke about what he had done kept me silent for many years. Terror keeps me silent still, making writing this a very difficult task. But unlike some of the women I know, I have some control over terror. Men learn to control terror by seeking it out and conquering it, first as

From *Boyhood, Growing Up Male: A Multicultural Anthology*, Franklin Abbott, ed., 1993. Crossing Press. Reprinted with permission.

boys—by telling ghost stories in dark tents, by riding roller coasters without holding on, by going to see scary movies and not covering their eyes—then as men, by terrorizing women and children. My control over terror is not yet perfect. When I went to see *The Silence of the Lambs* (no woman I know would go to see it with me: most women aren't taught mastery of terror is possible, and daily experience reminds them they are supposed to be its victims), I displaced my terror onto an older white man sitting behind me. The entire time I was in the dark theater I thought he was going to stab me. I would have changed my seat, but that was already the fifth seat I had occupied in the first half-hour of the movie. I kept moving to get away from men who seemed unsafe. (If I could hear them breathing, they were unsafe to me.) Never mind the cannibal/serial killer staring at me from the movie screen; I was freaked out by the sixty-year-old man with emphysema.

Feeling terror when I am not, in fact, in danger is just one of the many effects of the childhood abuse. I have begun to list these effects, the events and feelings and beliefs that plague my daily life, in order to piece them together with the specific abuses I remember. Feeling vulnerable sleeping on my back, fear of making someone next to me in bed angry if I move, being afraid of men who are larger than me, all trace back to my childhood traumas. Not knowing appropriate sexual limits, not being able to distinguish love from sex from affection from use, are some of the effects of the incest. The longer the list gets, the more sure I am that I have been abused, and that there are still plenty of wounds which need to be healed.

Abuse causes damage, but in a society that normalizes certain forms of damage—submissiveness, for example—it is often difficult to take seriously what has happened, and to accurately name the damage. Sexual abuse inhibits identity and selfhood in ways that have been socially recognized as harmful only when exhibited by those who are not supposed to be victimized. Depression, eating disorders, and self-mutilation are only now understood as responses to the pain and trauma of abuse, often sexual. As I hear other survivors of child sexual abuse talk about their daily struggles, I am reminded of other effects, other facets of damage. We recognize our pain in each other's stories. Some of us have survived family incest, child molestation, Satanic ritual abuse, sexual torture, fondling, profound emotional abuse and neglect, or sexual violation from trusted adults such as clergy or doctors. The damage varies but is remarkably similar. Sexual abuse, whatever the degree, teaches many of the same things. We learn we are worthless, invisible, contaminated, bad, ugly, stupid, incompetent, out of control, dirty, crazy, wrong, unlovable, unsafe, and alone. We find ourselves in situations which reinforce these beliefs. We carry terror, vulnerability, isolation, shame, guilt, remorse, grief, sadness, loneliness, confusion, anguish, disgust, distrust, desperation, despair, betrayal, contempt, and rage. We find ourselves in situations which elicit these feelings. The situations we find ourselves in, and the directions our feelings go (inward or outward), depends partly on what we have learned is acceptable self-expression. Generally, men learn to rage out; women learn to rage in. Men hate women; women hate themselves. Men cut up women; women cut themselves. Men learn to express anger when hurt or sad; women learn to express sadness when hurt or angry. Men learn to be destructive; women learn to be self-destructive. This system isn't perfect; some men are anorexic, some women do hate men, but, by and large, feelings and actions follow the proper political channels, keeping socially subordinated people down and socially dominant people up (figuratively and sexually speaking).

Incest and other childhood abuse cause pain, rage, and injury to the body and soul. A healthy society would support the constructive release of that pain and rage, but, under male supremacy, boys are systematically shamed for their vulnerability. Those compressed and thunderous feelings are carried into adulthood. Male supremacy directs their paths and points of destination. Child sexual abuse doesn't cause men to be rapists or child molesters; the political system which divides humanity in two, with men on top and women and children on the bottom, causes rape and incest. This male supremacist gender system causes children with penises to be boys and later men, and gives men permission and the emotional/sexual training to act violently against women and children. It is not accurate, therefore, to say that men rape because they were raped. Men rape because they have learned that being a rapist is an acceptable way to express rage. If men who were abused as children were not socially dominant they would probably have eating disorders and self-mutilation compulsions just like women. If women were not socially subordinated their male abusers would probably have to watch out.

II

> "Not last night but the night before
> Twenty-four robbers came knocking at my door
> I asked them what they wanted
> And this is what they said
> Lady, lady show your slip
> Lady, lady do the split
> Lady, lady turn around
> Lady, lady touch the ground."

So went one of the many jump-rope songs I skipped to with several girls in elementary school. Some of the deepest lessons about life came to us outside the classroom, on the playground, as segregation by sex was enforced with rules and codes that had no textbook. I broke the rules by preferring to play with the girls. The punishments girls and women receive for being female under male supremacy made several appearances in my little boy life because I aligned myself with them, rejecting the ways of boys. I was to be systematically abused—verbally and physically—for the next eight years. The names given to boys who liked girls as friends (who saw girls as equals, not subordinates) reveal the misogyny implicit in the tyranny of male socialization—"sissy," "pansy," "fairy," were terms that linked me to females, to white femininity, in my case. These were the terms that carried the stigma of the female, that brought my superior status as a male down to the lowly and contemptuous status of the female. To be female, as the jump-rope song goes, is to be victimized and violated, by one male or twenty-four. And what they rob is not the silverware, but the self-esteem, integrity and dignity of the female. Inside the threat of their forty-eight fists and twenty-four cocks, the female is forced to submit to their whims, their humiliations and degradations. Inside a system which wanted and needed all males on one side, the side opposing the females, I was coerced into playing the boys' games, and, fortunately for the girls in 1970 in Staten Island, N.Y., the game at the time was softball, not gang rape. Even the male principal of the school came out onto the asphalt diamond to show me how to swing a bat. Leaning over me, his hands engulfing mine, he moved my body the way he wanted it to go, the way a boy's body should go, so that I wouldn't be perceived as a girl. I buried my shame, but not my contempt for the rules of conduct.

III

In childhood, emotional worlds are formed and set in motion. Youth is not so much a time of innocence as a time when terrors and traumas are repressed, so that the child can move out of the neighborhood of devastating neglect, excruciating invisibility, scalding vulnerability, and haunting violation while thinking things "weren't so bad, really." Virtually everything a child ever needs to know about abuse is learned by the time puberty strikes. But the lessons are buried quickly, so one's actions beyond childhood appear mysterious, seemingly without cause or context.

So it was for me. The psychosis, feuding, secret touching and the constant, instant editing and revising (read: "forgetting") of the ten thousand violations and humiliations of life called "my wonderful childhood" left me, at thirteen, quite ready for drugs.

A single volume of literary pornography on the living room bookshelf disappeared into my bedroom often. Masturbating to a world in which self-alienation and violation were both worshipped and eroticized was my ticket to oblivion, emotional numbness, and the world of male supremacist sex in which pain is not pain but pleasure. I rejected other drugs because I associated them with the groups of boys who hurt me. Pornography seemed to be enough to keep the torment of my emotionally and sexually land-mined childhood at bay.

My longest sexual relationship began with some magazines a junior high school friend and I bought at a used bookstore. The owner pimped the images of women and men to us, two thirteen-year-olds, for 25 cents an issue. We were his customers for months. He kept us supplied with a steady stream of objectified, fetishized bodies. We kept his change-purse full. He even led us through the dusty aisles in the front of the store to the musty, dimly lit back room, where the dirtier stuff was kept. We pawed through it all, picking and choosing the magazines that most fit our newly cultivated taste for porn. The magazines that worked best at home were the ones I'd come back for. The pictures that most effectively anaesthetized my pain and gave me a sense of power over myself were the images I pursued repeatedly in the front and back of that store. And among those chosen images were letters, cartoons and stories about incest. So distant was my recent past that I read these as if they were not about me at all. And they weren't, really. In these stories the children wanted it to happen; the whole family was in on the act—no secrets, no shame. The incest I read about was as emotionally and politically truthful as the smile painted across a Playboy model's face.

Pornography is the travel brochure of the world of sexual violence. It maps out who should be targeted for destruction, and how and where and why. Childhood abuse caused me pain. Male supremacy choreographed that abuse and its resulting pain, the limitations of its healthy expression, the directions for its abusive display, against myself and others. Male supremacy supplied me with the drug I found most effective for anaesthetizing the pain. That drug—pornography—was also a textbook, and a document, the lesson plan and recording of male supremacist sex. If everything male supremacist had been extracted from the pornography I used, I would have been left with piles of blank paper.

Fantasyland was the world I most needed to inhabit. I could pretend, as the pornographers wished, that what I was seeing was not the atrocious destruction of human life. I could pretend that what I had just lived through, and would live through for another couple of years, was also not the destruction of human life.

I needed to escape my pain because I lived in a culture which could not bear its honest expression. Pornography deadened my pain and my capacity to understand anything about the ethics and meaning of abuse. Male supremacy thrives on this emotional and ethical numbness. To break through the walls of terror and vulnerability and pain, to understand what happened to me and to those people in pornography, to understand the connections between what happened to me and what is happening to them, is what has saved my emotional and ethical life, and directed my rage away from myself and women, and focused it instead on male supremacy.

Unfortunately for girls, growing up does not bring freedom from sexual violence and violation. Fortunately for me, as I scrambled out of the wreckage of my childhood, I found sanctuary in adulthood. Though old terrors still haunt me, my future will not resemble my past.

57

MASS MEDIA, SEXUAL VIOLENCE, AND MALE VIEWERS
Current Theory and Research

EDWARD DONNERSTEIN AND DANIEL LINZ

The influence of pornography on male viewers has been a topic of concern for behavioral scientists for many years, as well as a recent volatile political and legal question. Often research on pornography and its effects on behavior or attitudes are concerned with sexual explicitness. But it is not an issue of sexual explicitness; rather, it is an issue of violence against women and the role of women in "pornography" that is of concern to us here. Research over the last decade has demonstrated that sexual images per se do not facilitate aggressive behavior, change rape-related attitudes, or influence other forms of antisocial behaviors or perceptions. It is the violent images in pornography that account for the various research effects. This will become clearer as the research on the effects of sexual violence in the media is discussed. It is for these and other reasons that the terms *aggressive pornography* and *sexually violent mass media images* are preferred. We will occasionally use the term *pornography* in this article for communication and convenience.

In this essay we will examine both the research on aggressive pornography and the research that examines nonpornographic media images of violence against women—the major focus of recent research and the material that provokes negative reactions. Our final section will examine the research on nonviolent pornography. We will also refer to various ways in which this research has been applied to the current political debate on pornography

From *American Behavioral Scientist*, 29(5), May/June 1986, pp. 601–18. Copyright © 1986 Sage Publications, Inc. Reprinted by permission of Sage Publications, Inc.

and offer suggestions to mitigate the negative effects from exposure to certain forms of pornography and sexually violent mass media.

Research on the Effects of Aggressive Pornography

Aggressive pornography, as used here, refers to X-rated images of sexual coercion in which force is used or implied against a woman in order to obtain certain sexual acts, as in scenes of rape and other forms of sexual assault. One unique feature of these images is their reliance upon "positive victim outcomes," in which rape and other sexual assaults are depicted as pleasurable, sexually arousing, and beneficial to the female victim. In contrast to other forms of media violence in which victims suffer, die, and do not enjoy their victimization, aggressive pornography paints a rosy picture of aggression. The myths regarding violence against women are central to the various influences this material has upon the viewer. This does not imply that there are not images of suffering, mutilation, and death—there are. The large majority of images, however, show violence against women as justified, positive, and sexually liberating. Even these more "realistic" images, however, can influence certain viewers under specific conditions. We will address this research later.

There is some evidence that these images increased through the 1970s (Malamuth & Spinner, 1980). However, more recent content analysis suggests that the increase has abated in the 1980s (Scott, 1985). The Presidential Commission on Obscenity and Pornography of 1970 did not examine the influence of aggressive pornography, mainly because of its low frequency. This is important to note, as it highlights differences between the commission and the position outlined in this chapter. The major difference is not in the findings but in the type of material being examined. (The Commission on Obscenity and Pornography was interested only in sexually explicit media images.)

In many aggressive pornographic depictions, as noted, the victim is portrayed as secretly desiring the assault and as eventually deriving sexual pleasure from it (Donnerstein & Berkowitz, 1982; Malamuth, Heim, & Feshbach, 1980). From a cognitive perspective, such information suggests to the viewer that even if a woman seems repelled by a pursuer, eventually she will respond favorably to forceful advances, aggression, and overpowering by a male assailant (Brownmiller, 1975). The victim's pleasure could further heighten the aggressor's. Viewers might then come to think, at least for a short while, that their own sexual aggression would also be profitable, thus reducing restraints or inhibitions against aggression (Bandura, 1977). These views diminish the moral reprehensibility of any witnessed assault on a woman and, indeed, suggest that the sexual attack may have a highly desirable outcome for both victim and aggressor. Men having such beliefs might therefore be more likely to attack a woman after they see a supposedly

"pleasurable" rape. Furthermore, as there is a substantial aggressive component in the sexual assault, it could be argued that the favorable outcome low-
ers the observers restraints against aggression toward women. Empirical
research in the last few years, which is examined below, as well as such cases
as the New Bedford rape, in which onlookers are reported to have cheered
the rape of a woman by several men, suggests that the above concerns may
be warranted.

Aggressive Pornography and Sexual Arousal

Although it was once believed that only rapists show sexual arousal to
depictions of rape and other forms of aggression against women (Abel,
Barlow, Blanchard, & Guild, 1977), research by Malamuth and his colleagues (Malamuth, 1981b, 1984; Malamuth & Check, 1983; Malamuth &
Donnerstein, 1982; Malamuth, Haber, & Feshbach, 1980; Malamuth, Heim,
& Feshbach, 1980) indicates that a nonrapist population will show evidence
of increased sexual arousal to media-presented images of rape. This
increased arousal primarily occurs when the female victim shows signs of
pleasure and arousal, the theme most commonly presented in aggressive
pornography. In addition, male subjects who indicate that there is some
likelihood that they themselves would rape display increased sexual
arousal to all forms of rape depictions, similar to the reactions of known
rapists (Malamuth, 1981a, 1981b; Malamuth & Donnerstein, 1982).
Researchers have suggested that this sexual arousal measure serves as an
objective index of a proclivity to rape. Using this index, an individual
whose sexual arousal to rape themes was found to be similar to or greater
than his arousal to nonaggressive depictions would be considered to have
an inclination to rape (Abel et al., 1977; Malamuth, 1981a; Malamuth &
Donnerstein, 1982).

Aggressive Pornography and Attitudes toward Rape

There are now considerable data indicating that exposure to aggressive
pornography may alter the observer's perception of rape and the rape victim. For example, exposure to a sexually explicit rape scene in which the victim shows a "positive" reaction tends to produce a lessened sensitivity to
rape (Malamuth & Check, 1983), increased acceptance of rape myths and
interpersonal violence against women (Malamuth & Check, 1981), and
increases in the self-reported possibility of raping (Malamuth, 1981a). This
self-reported possibility of committing rape is highly correlated with (a) sexual arousal to rape stimuli, (b) aggressive behavior and a desire to hurt
women, and (c) a belief that rape would be a sexually arousing experience
for the rapist (see Malamuth, 1981a; Malamuth & Donnerstein, 1982).

Exposure to aggressive pornography may also lead to self-generated rape fantasies (Malamuth, 1981b).

Aggressive Pornography and Aggression against Women

Recent research (Donnerstein, 1980a, 1980b, 1983, 1984; Donnerstein & Berkowitz, 1982) has found that exposure to aggressive pornography increases aggression against women in a laboratory context. The same exposure does not seem to influence aggression against other men. This increased aggression is most pronounced when the aggression is seen as positive for the victim and occurs for both angered and nonangered individuals.

Although this research suggests that aggressive pornography can influence the male viewer, the relative contribution of the sexual and the aggressive components of the material remains unclear. Is it the sexual nature of the material or the messages about violence that are crucial? This is an extremely important question. In many discussions of this research the fact that the material is aggressive is forgotten and it is assumed that the effects occur owing to the sexual nature of the material. As we noted earlier the sexual nature of the material is not the major issue. Recent empirical studies shed some light on this issue.

The Influence of Nonpornographic Depictions of Violence against Women

It has been alleged that images of violence against women have increased not only in pornographic materials but also in more readily accessible mass media materials ("War Against Pornography," 1985). Scenes of rape and violence have appeared in daytime TV soap operas and R-rated movies shown on cable television. These images are sometimes accompanied by the theme, common in aggressive pornography, that women enjoy or benefit from sexual violence. For example, several episodes of the daytime drama *General Hospital* were devoted to a rape of one of the well known female characters by an equally popular male character. At first the victim was humiliated; later the two characters were married. A similar theme was expressed in the popular film, *The Getaway*. In this film, described by Malamuth and Check (1981):

> Violence against women is carried out both by the hero and the antagonist. The hero, played by Steve McQueen, is portrayed in a very "macho" image. At one point, he slaps his wife several times causing her to cry from the pain. The wife, played by Ali McGraw, is portrayed as deserving this beating. As well, the antagonist in the movie kidnaps a woman (Sally Struthers) and her husband. He

rapes the woman but the assault is portrayed in a manner such that the woman is depicted as a willing participant. She becomes the antagonist's girlfriend and they both taunt her husband until he commits suicide. The woman then willingly continues with the assailant and at one point frantically searches for him. (p. 439)

In a field experiment, Malamuth and Check (1981) attempted to determine whether or not the depiction of sexual violence contained in *The Getaway* and in another film with similar content influenced the viewers' perceptions of attitudes toward women. A total of 271 male and female students participated in a study that they were led to believe focused on movie ratings. One group watched, on two different evenings, *The Getaway* and *Swept Away* (which also shows women as victims of aggression within erotic contexts). A group of control subjects watched neutral, feature-length movies. These movies were viewed in campus theaters as part of the Campus Film Program. The results of a "Sexual Attitudes Survey," conducted several days after the screenings, indicated that viewing the sexually aggressive films significantly increased male but not female acceptance of interpersonal violence and tended to increase rape myth acceptance. These effects occurred not with X-rated materials but with more "prime-time" materials.

A recent study by Donnerstein and Berkowitz (1985) sought to examine more systematically the relative contributions of aggressive and sexual components of aggressive pornography. In a series of studies, male subjects were shown one of four different films: (1) the standard aggressive pornography used in studies discussed earlier, (2) an X-rated film that contained no forms of aggression or coercion and was rated by subjects to be as sexual as the first; (3) a film that contained scenes of aggression against a woman but without any sexual content and was considered less sexual and also less arousing (physiologically) than were the previous two films; and (4) a neutral film. Although the aggressive pornographic film led to the highest aggression against women, the aggression-only film produced more aggressive behavior than did the sex-only film. In fact, the sex-only film produced no different results than did the neutral film. Subjects were also examined for their attitudes about rape and their willingness to say they might commit a rape. The most callous attitudes and the highest percentage indicating some likelihood to rape were found in the aggression-only conditions; the X-rated sex-only film was the lowest.

This research suggests that violence against women need not occur in pornographic or sexually explicit context in order for the depictions to have an impact on both attitudes and behavior. Angered individuals became more aggressive toward a female target after exposure to films judged not to be sexually arousing but that depict a woman as a victim of aggression. This supports the claim by Malamuth and Check (1983) that sexual violence against women need not be portrayed in a pornographic fashion for greater acceptance of interpersonal violence and rape myths.

In the Malamuth and Check study the victim's reaction to sexual violence was always, in the end, a positive one. Presumably the individual viewer of nonsexually explicit rape depictions with a positive outcome comes to accept the view that aggression against women is permissible because women enjoy sexual violence. In the studies by Donnerstein and Berkowitz, however, several other processes may have been at work. Exposure to nonpornographic aggression against women resulted in the highest levels of aggressive behavior when subjects were first angered by a female confederate of the experimenter or when the victim of aggression in the film and the female confederate were linked by the same name. Presumably, subjects did not come to perceive violence as acceptable because victims enjoy violence from this material. Instead, the cue value or association of women with the characters in the film (Berkowitz, 1974) and the possibility that the pain cues stimulated aggression in angry individuals might better account for the findings. When the individual is placed in a situation in which cues associated with aggressive responses are salient (for example, a situation involving a female victim) or one in which he is predisposed to aggression because he is angered, he will be more likely to respond aggressively both because of the stimulus-response connection previously built up through exposure to the films and/or because the pain and suffering of the victim reinforce already established aggressive tendencies.

An important element in the effects of exposure to aggressive pornography is violence against women. Because much commercially available media contain such images, researchers have begun to examine the impact of more popular film depictions of violence against women. Of particular interest have been R-rated "slasher" films, which combine graphic and brutal violence against women within a sexual context. These types of materials do not fit the general definition of pornography, but we believe their impact is stronger.

The Effects of Exposure to R-rated Sexualized Violence

In a recent address before the International Conference on Film Classification and Regulation, Lord Harlech of the British Film Board noted the increase in R-rated sexually violent films and their "eroticizing" and "glorification" of rape and other forms of sexual violence. According to Harlech:

> Everyone knows that murder is wrong, but a strange myth has grown up, and been seized on by filmmakers, that rape is really not so bad, that it may even be a form of liberation for the victim, who may be acting out what she secretly desires—and perhaps needs—with no harm done. . . . Filmmakers in recent years have used rape as an exciting and

titillating spectacle in pornographic films, which are always designed to appeal to men.

As depictions of sex and violence become increasingly graphic, especially in feature-length movies shown in theaters, officials at the National Institute of Mental Health are becoming concerned:

> Films had to be made more and more powerful in their arousal effects. Initially, strong excitatory reactions [may grow] weak or vanish entirely with repeated exposure to stimuli of a certain kind. This is known as "habituation." The possibility of habituation to sex and violence has significant social consequences. For one, it makes pointless the search for stronger and stronger arousers. But more important is its potential impact on real life behavior. If people become inured to violence from seeing much of it, they may be less likely to respond to real violence.

This loss of sensitivity to real violence after repeated exposure to films with sex and violence, or "the dilemma of the detached bystander in the presence of violence," is currently a concern of our research program. Although initial exposure to a violent rape scene may act to create anxiety and inhibitions about such behavior, researchers have suggested that repeated exposure to such material could counter these effects. The effects of long-term exposure to R-rated sexually violent mass media portrayals are the major focus of our ongoing research program investigating how massive exposure to commercially released violent and sexually violent films influence (1) viewer perceptions of violence, (2) judgments about rape and rape victims, (3) general physiological desensitization to violence, and (4) aggressive behavior.

This research presents a new approach to the study of mass media violence. First, unlike many previous studies in which individuals may have seen only 10–30 minutes of material, the current studies examine 10 hours of exposure. Second, we are able to monitor the process of subject's desensitization over a longer period of time than in previous experiments. Third, we examine perceptual and judgmental changes regarding violence, particularly violence against women.

In the program's first study, Linz, Donnerstein, and Penrod (1984) monitored desensitization of males to filmed violence against women to determine whether this desensitization "spilled over" into other kinds of decision making about victims. Male subjects watched nearly 10 hours (five commercially released feature-length films, one a day for five days) of R-rated or X-rated fare—either R-rated sexually violent films such as *Tool Box Murders, Vice Squad, I Spit on Your Grave, Texas Chainsaw Massacre*; X-rated movies that depicted sexual assault; or X-rated movies that depicted only consensual sex (nonviolent). The R-rated films were much more explicit with regard to violence than they were with regard to sexual content. After each movie the men completed a mood questionnaire and evaluated the films on several dimensions. The films were counterbalanced so that comparisons could be made of the same films being shown on the first and last day of viewing. Before participation in the study, subjects were screened for levels of hostility, and only those with low hostility scores were included to help guard against the possibility of an overly hostile individual imitating the filmed violence during the week of the films. This is also theoretically important because it suggests that any effects we found would occur with a normal population. (It has been suggested by critics of media violence research that only those who are already predisposed toward violence are influenced by exposure to media violence. In this study, those individuals have been eliminated.) After the week of viewing the men watched yet another film. This time, however, they saw a videotaped reenactment of an actual rape trial. After the trial they were asked to render judgments about how responsible the victim was for her own rape and how much injury she had suffered.

Most interesting were the results from the men who had watched the R-rated films such as *Texas Chainsaw Massacre* or *Maniac*. Initially, after the first day of viewing, the men rated themselves significantly above the norm for depression, anxiety, and annoyance on a mood adjective checklist. After each subsequent day of viewing, these scores dropped until, on the fourth day of viewing, the males' levels of anxiety, depression, and annoyance were indistinguishable from baseline norms.

What happened to the viewers as they watched more and more violence? We believe they were becoming desensitized to violence, particularly against women, which entailed more than a simple lowering of arousal to the movie violence. The men actually began to perceive the films differently as time went on. On Day 1, for example, on the average, the men estimated that they had seen four "offensive scenes." By the fifth day, however, subjects reported only half as many offensive scenes (even though exactly the same movies, but in reverse order, were shown). Likewise, their ratings of the violence within the films receded from Day 1 to Day 5. By the last day the men rated the movies less graphic and less gory and estimated fewer violent scenes than they did on the first day of viewing. Most startling, by the last day of viewing graphic violence against women the men were rating the material as significantly less debasing and degrading to women, more humorous, and more enjoyable, and they claimed a greater willingness to see this type of film again. This change in perception due to repeated exposure was particularly evident in comparisons of reactions to two specific films—*I Spit on Your Grave* and *Vice Squad*. Both films contain sexual assault; however, rape is portrayed more graphically in *I Spit on Your Grave* and more ambiguously in *Vice Squad*. Men who were exposed first to *Vice Squad* and then to *I Spit on Your Grave* gave nearly identical ratings of sexual violence. However, subjects who had seen the more graphic movie first saw much less sexual violence (rape) in the more ambiguous film.

The subjects' evaluations of a rape victim after viewing a reenacted rape trial were also affected by the constant exposure to brutality against women. The victim of rape was rated as more worthless and her injury as significantly less severe by those exposed to filmed violence when compared to a control group of men who saw only the rape trial and did not view films. Desensitization to filmed violence on the last day was also significantly correlated with assignment of greater blame to the victim of her own rape. (These types of effects were not observed for subjects who were exposed to sexually explicit but nonviolent films.)

Mitigating the Effects of Exposure to Sexual Violence

This research strongly suggests a potential harmful effect from exposure to certain forms of aggressive pornography and other forms of sexualized violence. There is now, however, some evidence that these negative changes in attitudes and perceptions regarding rape and violence against women not only can be eliminated but can be positively changed. Malamuth and Check (1983) found that if male subjects who had participated in such an experiment were later administered a carefully constructed debriefing, they actually would be less accepting of certain rape myths than were control subjects exposed to depictions of intercourse (without a debriefing). Donnerstein and Berkowitz (1982) showed that not only are the negative effects of previous exposure eliminated, but even up to four months later, debriefed subjects have more "sensitive" attitudes toward rape than do control subjects. These debriefings consisted of (1) cautioning subjects that the portrayal of the rape they had been exposed to is completely fictitious in nature, (2) educating subjects about the violent nature of rape, (3) pointing out to subjects that rape is illegal and punishable by imprisonment, and (4) dispelling the many rape myths that are perpetrated in the portrayal (e.g., in the majority of rapes, the victim is promiscuous or has a bad reputation, or that many women have an unconscious desire to be raped).

Surveys of the effectiveness of debriefings for male subjects with R-rated sexual violence have yielded similar positive results. Subjects who participated in the week-long film exposure study that was followed by a certain type of debriefing changed their attitudes in a positive direction. The debriefings emphasized the fallacious nature of movie portrayals that suggests that women deserve to be physically violated and emphasized that processes of desensitization may have occurred because of long-term exposure to violence. The results indicated an immediate effect for debriefing, with subjects scoring lower on rape myth acceptance after participation than they scored before participation in the film viewing sessions. These effects remained, for the most part, six weeks later. The effectiveness of the debriefing for the subjects who participated in two later experiments (one involving two weeks of exposure to R-rated violent films) indicated that even after seven months, subjects' attitudes about sexual violence showed significant positive change compared to the preparticipation levels.

This research suggests that if the callous attitudes about rape and violence presented in aggressive pornography and other media representations of violence against women are learned, they can likewise be "unlearned." Furthermore, if effective debriefings eliminate these negative effects, it would seem possible to develop effective "prebriefings" that would also counter the impact of such materials. Such programs could become part of sex education curricula for young males. Given the easy access and availability of many forms of sexual violence to young males today, such programs would go a long way toward countering the impact of such images.

The Impact of Nonaggressive Pornography

An examination of early research and reports in the area of nonaggressive pornography would have suggested that effects of exposure to erotica were, if anything, nonharmful. For instance:

> It is concluded that pornography is an innocuous stimulus which leads quickly to satiation and that the public concern over it is misplaced. (Howard, Liptzin, and Reifler, 1973, p. 133)

> Results . . . fail to support the position that viewing erotic films produces harmful social consequences. (Mann, Sidman, & Starr, 1971, p. 113)

> If a case is to be made against "pornography" in 1970, it will have to be made on grounds other than demonstrated effects of a damaging personal or social nature. (President's Commission on Obscenity and Pornography, 1970, p. 139)

A number of criticisms of these findings, however (such as Cline, 1974; Dienstbier, 1977; Wills, 1977), led to reexamination of the issue of exposure to pornography and subsequent aggressive behavior. Some—for example, Cline (1974)—saw major methodological and interpretive problems with the Pornography Commission report; others (for example, Liebert & Schwartzberg, 1977) believed that the observations were premature. Certainly the relationship between exposure to pornography and subsequent aggressive behavior was more complex than first believed. For the most part, recent research has shown that exposure to nonaggressive pornography can have one of two effects.

A number of studies in which individuals have been predisposed to aggression and were later exposed to nonaggressive pornography have revealed increases in aggressive behavior (such as Baron & Bell, 1977; Donnerstein, Donnerstein, & Evans, 1975; Malamuth, Feshbach, & Jaffe, 1977; Meyer, 1972; Zillmann, 1971, 1979). Such findings have been interpreted in terms of a general arousal model, which states that under conditions in which aggression is a dominant response, any source of emotional arousal will tend to increase aggressive behavior in disinhibited subjects (for example, Bandura, 1977; Donnerstein, 1983). A second group of studies (Baron, 1977; Baron & Bell, 1977; Donnerstein et al., 1975; Frodi, 1977; Zillmann & Sapolsky, 1977) reports the opposite—that exposure to pornography of a nonaggressive nature can actually reduce subsequent aggressive behavior.

These results appear contradictory, but recent research (Baron, 1977; Donnerstein, 1983; Donnerstein et al., 1975; Zillmann, 1979) has begun to reconcile seeming inconsistencies. It is now believed that as pornographic stimuli become more arousing, they give rise to increases in aggression. At a low level of arousal, however, the stimuli distract individuals, and attention is directed away from previous anger. Acting in an aggressive manner toward a target is incompatible with the pleasant feelings associated with low-level arousal (see Baron, 1977; Donnerstein, 1983). There is also evidence that individuals who find the materials "displeasing or pornographic" will also increase their aggression after exposure, whereas those who have more positive reactions to the material will not increase their aggression even to highly arousing materials (Zillmann, 1979).

The research noted above was primarily concerned with same-sex aggression. The influence of nonaggressive pornography on aggression against women tends to produce mixed effects. Donnerstein and Barrett (1978) and Donnerstein and Hallam (1978) found that nonaggressive pornography had no effect on subsequent aggression unless constraints against aggressing were reduced. This was accomplished by both angering male subjects by women and giving subjects multiple chances to aggress. Donnerstein (1983) tried to reduce aggressive inhibitions through the use of an aggressive model but found no increase in aggression after exposure to an X-rated nonviolent film. It seems, therefore, that nonaggressive sexual material does not lead to aggression against women except under specific conditions (for example when inhibitions against aggression are lowered deliberately by the experimenter).

Almost without exception, studies reporting the effects of nonviolent pornography have relied on short-term exposure; most subjects have been exposed to only a few minutes of pornographic material. More recently, Zillmann and Bryant (1982, 1984) demonstrated that long-term exposure (4 hours and 48 minutes over a six-week period) to pornography that does not contain overt aggressiveness may cause male and female subjects to (1) become more tolerant of bizarre and violent forms of pornography, (2) become less supportive of statements about sexual equality, and (3) become more lenient in assigning punishment to a rapist whose crime is described in a newspaper account. Furthermore, extensive exposure to the nonaggressive pornography significantly increased males' sexual callousness toward women. This latter finding was evidenced by increased acceptance of statements such as "A man should find them, fool them, fuck them, and forget them," "A woman doesn't mean 'no' until she slaps you," and "If they are old enough to bleed, they are old enough to butcher." Zillmann and others (such as Berkowitz, 1984) have offered several possible explanations for this effect, suggesting that certain viewer attitudes are strengthened through long-term exposure to nonviolent pornographic material.

A common scenario of the material used in the Zillmann research is that women are sexually insatiable by nature. Even though the films shown do not feature the infliction of pain or suffering, women are portrayed as extremely permissive and promiscuous, willing to accommodate any male sexual urge. Short-term exposure to this view of women (characteristic of early studies of nonviolent pornography) may not be sufficient to engender changes in viewers' attitudes congruent with these portrayals. However, attitudinal changes might be expected under conditions of long-term exposure. Continued exposure to the idea that women will do practically anything sexually may prime or encourage other thoughts regarding female promiscuity (Berkowitz, 1984). This increase in the availability of thoughts about female promiscuity or the ease with which viewers can imagine instances in which a female has been sexually insatiable may lead viewers to inflate their estimates of how willingly and frequently women engage in sexual behavior. The availability of thoughts about female insatiability may also affect judgments about sexual behavior such as rape, bestiality, and sadomasochistic sex. Further, these ideas may endure. Zillmann and Bryant (1982), for example, found that male subjects still had a propensity to trivialize rape three weeks after exposure to nonviolent pornography. It is important to point out, however, that in these studies long-term exposure did not increase aggressive behavior but in fact decreased subsequent aggression.

Unfortunately, the role that images of female promiscuity and insatiability play in fostering callous perceptions of women can only be speculated upon at this point because no research has systematically manipulated film content in an experiment designed to facilitate or inhibit viewer cognitions. One cannot rule out the possibility, for example, that simple exposure to many sexually explicit depictions (regardless of their "insatiability" theme) accounts for the attitudinal changes found in their study. Sexual explicitness and themes of insatiability are experimentally confounded in this work.

Another emerging concern among political activists about pornography is its alleged tendency to degrade women (Dworkin, 1985; MacKinnon, 1985). This concern has been expressed recently in the form of municipal ordinances against pornography originally drafted by Catherine MacKinnon and Andrea Dworkin that have been introduced in a variety of communities, including Minneapolis and Indianapolis. One central feature of these ordinances is that pornography is the graphic "sexually explicit subordination of women" that also includes "women presented in scenarios of degradation, injury, abasement, torture, shown as filthy or inferior, bleeding, bruised, or hurt in a context that makes these conditions sexual" (City County general ordinance No. 35, City of Indianapolis,1984). These ordinances have engendered a great deal of controversy, as some individuals have maintained that they are a broad form of censorship. A critique of these ordinances can be found in a number of publications (for example, Burstyn, 1985; Russ, 1985).

The framers of the ordinance suggest that after viewing such material, "a general pattern of discriminatory attitudes and behavior, both violent and nonviolent, that has the capacity to stimulate various negative reactions against women will be found" (Defendants' memorandum, U.S. District Court for the Southern District of Indiana, Indianapolis Division, 1984, p. 8). Experimental evidence is clear with respect to the effects of pornography showing injury, torture, bleeding, bruised, or hurt women in sexual contexts. What has not been investigated is the effect of material showing women in scenarios of degradation, as inferior and abased.

No research has separated the effect of sexual explicitness from degradation, as was done with aggressive pornography, to determine whether the two interact to foster negative evaluations of women. Nearly all experiments conducted to date have confounded sexual explicitness with the presentation of women as a subordinate, objectified class. Only one investigation (Donnerstein, 1984) has attempted to disentangle sexual explicitness and violence. The results of this short-term exposure investigation, discussed above, revealed that although the combination of sexual explicitness and violence against a woman (the violent pornographic condition) resulted in the highest levels of subsequent aggression against a female target, the nonexplicit depiction that showed only violence resulted in aggression levels nearly as high and attitudes that were more callous than those that resulted from the combined exposure. The implication of this research is that long-term exposure to material that may not be explicitly sexual but that depicts women in scenes of degradation and subordination may have a negative impact on viewer attitudes. This is one area in which research is still needed.

Conclusion

Does pornography influence behaviors and attitudes toward women? The answer is difficult and centers on the definition of pornography. There is no evidence for any "harm"-related effects from sexually explicit materials. But research may support potential harmful effects from aggressive materials. Aggressive images are the issue, not sexual images. The message about violence and the sexualized nature of violence is crucial. Although these messages may be part of some forms of pornography, they are also pervasive media messages in general, from prime-time TV to popular films. Men in our society have callous attitudes about rape. But where do these attitudes come from? Are the media, and in particular pornography, the cause? We would be reluctant to place the blame on the media. If anything, the media act to reinforce already existing attitudes and values regarding women and violence. They do contribute, but are only part of the problem.

As social scientists we have devoted a great deal of time to searching for causes of violence against women. Perhaps it is time to look for ways to reduce this violence. This chapter has noted several studies that report techniques to mitigate the influence of exposure to sexual violence in the media, which involves changing attitudes about violence. The issue of pornography and its relationship to violence will continue for years, perhaps without any definitive answers. We may never know if there is any real causal influence. We do know, however, that rape and other forms of violence against women are pervasive. How we change this situation is of crucial importance, and our efforts need to be directed to this end.

Authors' Note: This research was partially funded by National Science Foundation Grant BNS-8216772 to the first author and Steven Penrod.

REFERENCES

Abel, G., Barlow, D., Blanchard, E., & Guild, D. (1977). The components of rapists' sexual arousal. *Archives of General Psychiatry, 34,* 395–403, 895–903.

Bandura, A. (1977). *Social learning theory.* Englewood Cliffs, NJ: Prentice-Hall.

Baron, R. A. (1977). *Human aggression.* New York: Plenum.

Baron, R. A., & Bell, P. A. (1977). Sexual arousal and aggression by males: Effects of type of erotic stimuli and prior provocation. *Journal of Personality and Social Psychology, 35,* 79–87.

Berkowitz, L. (1974). Some determinants of impulsive aggression: Role of mediated associations with reinforcements for aggression. *Psychological Review, 81,* 165–179.

Berkowitz, L. (1984). Some effects of thoughts on anti- and prosocial influences of media events: A cognitive-neoassociation analysis. *Psychological Bulletin, 95,* 410–427.

Brownmiller, S. (1975). *Against our will: Men, women and rape.* New York: Simon & Schuster.

Burstyn, V. (1985). *Women against censorship.* Manchester, NH: Salem House.

Cline, V. B. (Ed.). (1974). *Where do you draw the line?* Salt Lake City: Brigham Young University Press.

Dienstbier, R. A. (1977). Sex and violence: Can research have it both ways? *Journal of Communication, 27,* 176–188.

Donnerstein, E. (1980a). Pornography and violence against women. *Annals of the New York Academy of Sciences, 347,* 277–288.

Donnerstein, E. (1980b). Aggressive-erotica and violence against women. *Journal of Personality and Social Psychology, 39,* 269–277.

Donnerstein, E. (1983). Erotica and human aggression. In R. Geen & E. Donnerstein (Eds.). *Aggression: Theoretical and empirical reviews.* New York: Academic Press.

Donnerstein, E. (1984). Pornography: Its effect on violence against women. In N. Malamuth & E. Donnerstein (Eds.) *Pornography and sexual aggression.* Orlando, FL: Academic Press.

Donnerstein, E., & Barrett, G. (1978). The effects of erotic stimuli on male aggression toward females. *Journal of Personality and Social Psychology, 36,* 180–188.

Donnerstein, E., & Berkowitz, L. (1982). Victim reactions in aggressive-erotic films as a factor in violence against women. *Journal of Personality and Social Psychology, 41,* 710–724.

Donnerstein, E., & Berkowitz, L. (1985). *Role of aggressive and sexual images in violent pornography.* Manuscript submitted for publication.

Donnerstein, E., & Hallam, J. (1978). Facilitating effects of erotica on aggression against women. *Journal of Personality and Social Psychology, 36,* 1270–1277.

Donnerstein, E., Donnerstein, M., & Evans, R. (1975). Erotic stimuli and aggression: Facilitation or inhibition. *Journal of Personality and Social Psychology, 32,* 237–244.

Dworkin, A. (1985). Against the male flood: Censorship, pornography, and equality. *Harvard Women's Law Journal, 8.*

Frodi, A. (1977). Sexual arousal, situational restrictiveness, and aggressive behavior. *Journal of Research in Personality, 11,* 48–58.

Howard, J. L., Liptzin, M. B., & Reifler, C. B. (1973). Is pornography a problem? *Journal of Social Issues, 29,* 133–145.

Liebert, R. M. & Schwartzberg, N. S. (1977). Effects of mass media. *Annual Review of Psychology, 28,* 141–173.

Linz, D., Donnerstein, E., & Penrod, S. (1984). The effects of long-term exposure to filmed violence against women. *Journal of Communication, 34,* 130–147.

MacKinnon, C. A. (1985). Pornography, civil rights, and speech. *Harvard Civil Rights-Civil Liberty Law Review,* 20(l).

Malamuth, N. (1981a). Rape proclivity among males. *Journal of Social Issues, 37,* 138–157.

Malamuth, N. (1981b). Rape fantasies as a function of exposure to violent-sexual stimuli. *Archives of Sexual Behavior, 10,* 33–47.

Malamuth, N. (I984). Aggression against women: Cultural, and individual causes. In N. Malamuth & F. Donnerstein (Eds.) *Pornography and sexual aggression.* Orlando, FL: Academic Press.

Malamuth N., Feshbach, S., & Jaffe, Y. (1977). Sexual arousal and aggression: Recent experiments and theoretical issues. *Journal of Social Issues, 33,* 110–133.

Malamuth, N. M., & Spinner, B. (1980). A longitudinal content analysis of sexual violence in the best-selling erotic magazines. *Journal of Sex Research,* 16(3), 16–237.

Malamuth, N., & Check, J. V. P. (1981). The effects of mass media exposure on acceptance of violence against women: A field experiment. *Journal of Research in Personality, 15,* 436–446.

Malamuth, N., & Check, J. V. P (1983). Sexual arousal to rape depictions: Individual differences. *Journal of Abnormal Psychology, 92,* 55–67.

Malamuth, N., & Donnerstein, E. (1982). The effects of aggressive pornographic mass media stimuli. In L. Berkowitz (Ed.), *Advances in experimental social psychology (vol.15).* New York: Academic Press.

Malamuth, N., Haber, S., & Feshbach, S. (1980). The sexual responsiveness of college students to rape depictions: Inhibitory and disinhibitory effects. *Journal of Research in Personality, 14,* 399–408.

Malamuth, N., Heim, M., & Feshbach, S. (1980). The sexual responsiveness of college students to rape depictions: Inhibitory and disinhibitory effects. *Journal of Personality and Social Psychology, 38,* 399–408.

Mann, J., Sidman, J., & Starr, S. (1971). Effects of erotic films on sexual behavior of married couples. In *Technical Report of the Commission on Obscenity and Pornography* (vol. 8). Washington, DC: Government Printing Office.

Meyer, T. (1972). The effects of viewing justified and unjustified real film violence on aggressive behavior. *Journal of Personality and Social Psychology, 23,* 21–29.

President's Commission on Obscenity and Pornography. (1970). (vol. 8). Washington, DC: Government Printing Office.

Russ, J. (1985). *Magic mommas, trembling sisters, puritans and perverts.* New York: Crossing.

Scott, J. (1985). *Sexual violence in* Playboy *magazine: Longitudinal analysis.* Paper presented at the meeting of the American Society of Criminology.

The war against pornography. (1985, March 18). Newsweek, pp. 58–62, 65–67.

Wills, G. (1977, November). Measuring the impact of erotica. *Psychology Today,* pp. 30–34.

Zillmann, D. (1971). Excitation transfer in communication-mediated aggressive behavior. *Journal of Experimental Social Psychology, 7*, 419–433.

Zillmann, D. (1979). *Hostility and aggression.* Hillsdale, NJ: Erlbaum.

Zillmann, D., & Bryant, J. (1982). Pornography, sexual callousness, and the trivialization of rape. *Journal of Communication, 32*, 10–21.

Zillmann, D., & Bryant, J. (1984). Effects of massive exposure to pornography. In N. Malamuth & E. Donnerstein (Eds.), *Pornography and sexual aggression.* New York: Academic Press.

Zillmann, D., & Sapolsky, B. S. (1977). What mediates the effect of mild erotica on annoyance and hostile behavior in males? *Journal of Personality and Social Psychology, 35*, 587–596.

58

EMPOWERMENT
Men Taking Action

RUS ERVIN FUNK

Every man *must decide whether he will walk in the fight of creative altruism or the darkness of destructive selfishness. This is the judgment. Life's most persistent and urgent question is* what are you doing for others?
—Martin Luther King, Jr., 1962 (emphasis added)

Reading and writing about issues of men's sexism and sexist violence, supporting and challenging ourselves and each other in a respectful environment, offering support for survivors, and exposing the connections between rape and other forms of oppression are all necessary, but that is not enough. Men must begin taking action, in whatever form that may take. Men can do much in our personal lives. But my main goal is to encourage more men to organize and become active in their communities to stop rape.

Men have access to the boardrooms, the classrooms, the locker rooms, the bars, to any and all of the places where men congregate. We can use those opportunities creatively to educate. Men tend to listen more and better to men than we do to women. If you are supportive of women and are committed to ending men's violent behaviors, then it is incumbent on you to

---

From *Stopping Rape: A Challenge for Men*, by Rus Ervin Funk, 1993, pp. 113–18, 151–53. Reprinted by permission of New Society Publishers, Philadelphia, PA.

"break the silence to end men's violence" (the slogan of BrotherPeace, a project of the Ending Men's Violence Network)—it's incumbent upon you to ACT! The only way that men will begin responding appropriately to issues of men's violence and begin working towards a more peaceful world is by men putting action on our agendas. As men, we must band together and publicly call for an end to male violence, adequate support for programs providing services for survivors, appropriate educational programming, safer streets, and better child care. We must tear the pornographic pictures off the locker doors, from the hallways, and from our minds. We must interrupt men's sexism and confront harassment by other men. When men create peer pressure to interrupt rape-supporting behaviors on a consistent and ongoing basis, then we will begin to see a reduction in rape. The only way to get there from here is one step at a time. Men need to start taking steps—and making tracks—towards a rape-free world.

Nonviolence

A commitment to nonviolence is an absolute necessity for any man doing work against men's violence and oppression. When we act, it is essential that we be grounded in a solid understanding of nonviolence. Nonviolence is more than just the absence of violence—nonviolence is the presence of justice. Men acting without a commitment to nonviolence is no different than men acting in any other form. And, as is true with most issues but particularly in ending men's violence, the end cannot be separated from the means. In order to get to a rape-free world, we must begin acting rape-free lives. That *requires* a commitment to nonviolence.

Nonviolence begins with an understanding, an acceptance, and a recognition of each person's inherent humanity and, thus, each person's inherent right to be treated with complete dignity and respect. *Each person!* At the core of violence is a process of stripping a layer of a person's humanity away. It's part of the militaristic mindset that is so much a part of all of us. You learn to define the "enemy," dehumanize them, and hold rigidly to the concept of "them" as "enemy." As a result, it becomes easier to live with yourself when you try to kill them (in fact, it is impossible to kill them without going through a similar process). Using slurs to describe people is a part of the process of stripping their humanity from them, so that they no longer deserve the dignity and respect that all human beings are due. For example, think of a time when you're driving and you get cut off. If you're anything like me, and a majority of drivers, you scream something like "YOU *&%$#@*%*# PIG!!!"—which separates him (say it's a him) from his humanity. From there, you use the fact that he is now a "*$%*^&&*# PIG" to justify further fueling your anger, and gun your engine to go "get him"—flipping him off or cutting him off in return. Since you have successfully dissociated (both him and yourself) from your respective humanity, you can justify doing to him what he did to you.

That's a simple example, but the process is the same. When we think of men who harass, use pornography, are sexist, or who rape as inhuman, "monsters" or "animals," we successfully cut them off from their humanity and not only justify murdering them but also separate them from us. We're not like them, after all, so obviously we're not sexist, or the "sexism we do isn't as bad as what they did."

Barbara Deming pointed out the virtues of nonviolence this way:

> Nonviolent confrontation is the only confrontation that allows us to respond realistically to such complexity. In this form of struggle, we address ourselves both to that which we refuse to accept from others, and that which we have in common with them—however much or little that may be. (From McAllister, *Reweaving the Web of Life: Feminism and Nonviolence*, p. 12)

By using nonviolence, we are able to identify the ways that we are like the men who are overtly abusive while at the same time confronting their behavior. This is the only hope of effectively reaching out to them so that they might change.

When doing any action, it is important to stay grounded in these principles. When doing public events, people will respond in many different ways. As long as we stay committed to "reaching one hand out in justice" we increase our ability to actually touch that person. At one event in Washington, DC, an enraged (and probably intoxicated) man began approaching the podium, making abusive comments and asking the speaker to "meet him later." I went over to talk with him, and as he saw me approach, he squared off to meet me, assuming I was coming over to fight him. I backed off a bit, explaining that I just came over to talk—that he seemed angry and agitated and that I didn't want him to continue to interrupt the program. He then directed his anger toward me, but he immediately dropped his hands and unclenched his fists. As he continued to talk, he became less agitated and angry. Had I not allowed him to have his humanity by either ignoring him or attempting to "shut him up!" I would have only been successful at increasing his agitation. By responding in a nonviolent manner that recognized his humanity (by entering into a dialogue even when confronting his interruption), we (he and I—after all, he actually did most of the work) were able to reduce the tension and abusiveness of the situation.

Does a commitment to nonviolence necessarily mean that we are opposed to violence at all times? Frankly, that depends on which nonviolent theorist or activist you agree with. I don't think so; Mahatma Gandhi said that it is "better to resist violently than to submit but it is best of all to resist nonviolently." Violence may always have to be considered an option, for instance when violence has been an ongoing weapon of systematic oppression. For example, my commitment to nonviolence does not mean that I would oppose Blacks in South Africa fighting back against their oppression, or that I condemn battered women who kill the men who abuse them, or that I oppose women or children learning to shoot and get guns in order to protect themselves from men who rape. All of those situations concern and scare me, and I hope they don't have to occur, but it is not my place, coming from a position of privilege, to limit the options that abused or oppressed people have for fighting back.

As men, we are not a dispossessed or oppressed people. Gay and bisexual men are oppressed for being gay or bi; men of color are oppressed for being of color; but men are not oppressed. As such, our use of violence is coming from a very different context than the violence of people who have been oppressed. While I would never limit the already-too-few options of liberation that oppressed peoples have at their disposal, I will always limit the use of violence by men who *do* have other tools at our disposal. Men don't have to use violence to stop rape.

More than a behavior, nonviolence is a state of mind and being that is incorporated into every aspect of your life. If you choose to get more active, then nonviolence can be utilized in an ongoing way—regardless of the kind of activism you choose. Nonviolence can be used when lobbying Congress or your county council; it can be used during educational programs at a high school or at a training at a local business, in a men's reading and discussion group or in any other setting. Coming to whatever form of activism you choose from a perspective of nonviolence simply means *always* recognizing and celebrating the humanity of the people with whom you interact. As such, it means thinking about every encounter as an interaction—the point of which is not to "win" but to engage. It means remembering that you may have as much to learn from the other person as they have to learn from you. It means disengaging from the competitive mindset so common in our thinking, and reengaging from a place of mutual respect. Even when you walk into a hostile environment, you can enter respecting the people you are interacting with, and yourself; they can't help but respect you as well. Nonviolence also reminds us that there is always more than one way to confront rape-supporting behaviors and to encourage a rape-free environment. Nonviolence encourages creativity.

Nonviolence gives us a channel through which to direct our energies, an outlet for our anger. Most of us feel deeply and profoundly angry. We're angry that so many women are victimized, that so many women in our lives have been victimized, that men continue to be so hard to reach, that rape and violence continue to increase despite our efforts, and that we've been set up to be abusive and seen as a threat. This anger can feel overwhelming and can exacerbate burnout unless we provide opportunities to release that anger. Nonviolent activism gives us those opportunities. By taking direct action to confront the situation in a way that is loud, proud, humane, and nonthreatening we create an opportunity to release a part of that anger.

Activism too is a mindset more than a behavior. Being "active" simply means *thinking* actively about the situation and the issues. An activist is simply a person who examines and dissects what is happening, looks at various ways to interrupt the process, and engages in the way that seems most appropriate. An activist is someone who responds. By reading right now, you are being active—particularly if you are actively engaged in thinking about what you're reading. Activism is recognizing that you have an ability to respond to a situation, and acting based on that ability. Activism, in short, is acting out empowerment. It isn't necessarily organizing marches or demonstrations or risking arrest in civil disobedience. Activism just means responding actively.

Educational Activism

Education is an invaluable tool for creating change. By publicly breaking the silence, we express our support of women, disenfranchised men, and the work that has been done for centuries by feminists as well as for men in general. We also publicly support an end to men's violence and join our voices to the chorus of women who have been shouting for lifetimes. Finally, education offers information, and an example of how people can take action in their own lives.

Education is a process of learning new skills and new ways of looking at the world: bell hooks teaches us, "Education as the practice of freedom." Education teaches the critical-thinking skills men need in order to reevaluate the world and begin to change it. Educating men about rape consists of offering the thoughts that are offered here, and creating an opportunity for them to integrate this thinking into their very souls. Paulo Freire writes about the "integrated person as subject. . . [where] integration results from the capacity to adapt oneself to reality plus the critical capacity to make choices and transform that reality." As men we can critically examine and transform the world we live in, the definition of masculinity, and the ways that we all support rape culture. That is a first step in personal empowerment and political liberation.

Education can take any number of forms . . . doing verbal educating in workshops with small groups, while out with friends, and when confronting rape-supporting behaviors or attitudes. One mind shift that may help in doing anti-rape educating is to think of every interaction as an educational opportunity for both the other person(s), and for you. When we are on the subway and someone asks us about a button that we're wearing, that becomes an educational program—for the person we're talking with, as well as for the handful of people who are in our immediate vicinity. Educational opportunities do not have to be formal programs. The only difference between an informal educational program and a formal one is the level of structure. The information and skills are basically the same.

———

The Year 2000 and Beyond

What will the world be like when we are finally successful in our efforts to eliminate men's violence? What will it be like when women and men, children and adults, white people and people of color, heterosexuals, homosexuals, and bisexuals will be able to work, play, live, love, and laugh together in a caring, loving, and mutually respectful way? What will it be like for women to walk down the street free of fear, and for men to walk down a street free from being feared?

Imagine, those of you who are male, walking into a playground full of children and not having the children fear you, and their parents wary of you. Imagine, you who are white men, walking into a community of color and not being seen as a threat for being a member of an oppressor class. Imagine, if you will, being able to walk down any street you care to, holding hands with your same-sex friend and not fear being attacked because of heterosexism. Consider what it will be like when we will be able to have children, and the men are able to stay home without having to worry about financial survival.

All of this is truly possible. Radical feminism has offered a glimpse of such a world. All of us, all of everything takes up space in the universe. The clouds, the rocks, the plants, time, objects, animals, people; all of everything takes up space and is interconnected. What has been known for centuries by certain cultures, and what physicists are beginning to realize, is that just as it is true that we all take up space in the universe, so it is true that we have a direct and profound impact on the ways that the universe continues to function. That is true for all entities. What makes humans unique is that we are apparently the only entity that can *choose* what our impact on the universe will be.

We can choose to live our lives in keeping with the grandest vision we create. So begin thinking about it. Find someplace to be quiet and still. Relax your body, and uncross your feet and your arms. Breathe consciously and in a relaxed way—deeply and rhythmically. Close your eyes and create a picture in your mind of what a rape-free world would look like—with the most expansive definition of "rape-free" that you can come up with. Think about a world where women are not afraid to go out at night, where your housemate or friend or lover can dash out to the corner store at 3 A.M. to get some milk without being afraid. Imagine a world where no child is at risk for any kind of violence, and where gay people are free to express their partnership in any way and in any place—just like heterosexual couples.

Picture in your mind a place where men aren't feared, where you can leave a movie theater at midnight, walk back to your car and not see women afraid of you. Imagine never again having to hear a friend of yours tell you that they were victimized as a child, a young adult, or earlier that year. Imagine being at work and having a deeply felt and intense argument with a woman of a different race—a deep-down, in-your-face kind of argument that isn't muddled by racial or gender politics. Develop this picture of a world free of men's violence as fully and completely in your mind as you are able and hold onto it. (The only way we'll ever get there is to begin envisioning it.)

Now, *feel* that world—feel it in your heart, and feel it in your soul. Feel what it would be like to live in that kind of world. Notice the feelings that are coming up for you—not the feelings that arise as a result of us not being there yet, but the feelings that come up as a result of experiencing such a world. A world where we don't need to prove ourselves and our masculinity. A world where we aren't expected to be the "protector" all the time and a world where we are able to be in touch with children and in touch with the child inside of us; that playful, fun-loving, spirited, curious being that exists in each of us, but which we lose touch with in the process of "becoming men." Imagine living in a world where men and women have true friendships all the time, and one in which no woman ever again looks at you with some level of dread. Feel this world as deep in yourself as you can feel.

To make it just a bit more difficult, imagine that world being this world—tomorrow! Imagine walking down your street tomorrow evening as you come home from work, or school; living in your neighborhood; driving in your town that is now rape-free. Think about it—*feel* about it.

My vision involves all that I've described. I envision myself working at home so that I can care for my children and be an active part of their growing up. I see my partner as an active part of my life, and the children's; I see an active reciprocal participation in each other's lives—we clean together, we play together, we travel, we do different things together, we spend time away from each other. My vision is a world without gender roles—where people are allowed and encouraged to live their life however they see fit, and we see no need to add the caveat, "so long as it brings no harm to another person." I see a place where I'm able to hold my child who skins his or her knee and cry with him or her rather than telling him or her (as I was told) to "be a big boy" or "girl." I see a place where lovemaking is a positive experience for *everyone*, and sex isn't something feared or despised but celebrated and encouraged in healthful and fun ways. I see people being encouraged to experience their full creativity and to live their lives as completely as possible—with respect, dignity, and integrity.

I see a world where men are free. Where men are involved in day care and men organize the bake sales for the day care center. A world where not only do men and women work together, but where men and men work together—sharing hugs, massages, and child care. A world where we look to Congress and see a body that is truly representational, one that puts the needs of children and people first. A world where value is placed on how good we have become at supporting ourselves and each other, as communities and as a nation. We will also strive to support our neighbors all over the globe—not for our own betterment, but because we're good neighbors.

We can, you know. We deserve this kind of world. Creating a rape-free world is the best of what we can offer—and in the process we can create a new image of what "being a man" means. We have the ability to respond proactively and effectively to the issues of rape and men's violence.

We can create this kind of world—a world free of rape! It's up to you, it's up to us. It's time we began!

59

WHERE RACE AND GENDER MEET
Racism, Hate Crimes, and Pornography

HELEN ZIA

There is a specific area where racism, hate crimes, and pornography intersect, and where current civil rights law fails: racially motivated, gender-based crimes against women of color. This area of bias-motivated sexual assault has been called "ethnorape"; I refer to it as "hate rape."

I started looking into this issue after years of organizing against hate killings of Asian Americans. After a while, I noticed that all the cases I could name concerned male victims. I wondered why. Perhaps it was because Asian-American men came into contact with perpetrator types more often or because they are more hated and therefore more often attacked by racists. But the subordination and vulnerability of Asian-American women, who are thought to be sexually exotic, subservient, and passive, argued against that interpretation. So where were the Asian-American women hate-crime victims?

Once I began looking, I found them, in random news clippings, in footnotes in books, through word of mouth. Let me share with you some example I unearthed of bias-motivated attacks and sexual assaults:

- In February 1984, Ly Yung Cheung, a nineteen-year-old Chinese woman who was seven months pregnant, was pushed in front of a New York City subway train and decapitated. Her attacker, a white male high school teacher, claimed he suffered from "a phobia of Asian people" and was overcome with the urge to kill this woman. He successfully pleaded insanity. If this case had been investigated as a hate crime, there might have been more information about his so-called phobia and whether it was part of a pattern of racism. But it was not.

- On December 7, 1984, fifty-two-year-old Japanese-American Helen Fukui disappeared in Denver, Colorado. Her decomposed body was found weeks later. Her disappearance on Pearl Harbor Day, when anti-Asian speech and incidents increase dramatically, was considered significant in the community. But the case was not investigated as a hate crime and no suspects were ever apprehended.

- In 1985 an eight-year-old Chinese girl named Jean Har-Kaw Fewel was found raped and lynched in Chapel Hill, North Carolina—two months after *Penthouse* featured pictures of Asian women in various poses of bondage and torture, including hanging bound from trees. Were epithets or pornography used during the attack? No one knows—her rape and killing were not investigated as a possible hate crime.

- Recently a serial rapist was convicted of kidnapping and raping a Japanese exchange student in Oregon. He had also assaulted a Japanese woman in Arizona, and another in San Francisco. He was sentenced to jail for these crimes, but they were never pursued as hate crimes, even though California has a hate statute. Was hate speech or race-specific pornography used? No one knows.

- At Ohio State University, two Asian women were gang raped by fraternity brothers in two separate incidents. One of the rapes was part of a racially targeted game called the "Ethnic Sex Challenge," in which the fraternity men followed an ethnic checklist indicating what kind of women to gang rape. Because the women feared humiliation and ostracism by their communities, neither reported the rapes. However, campus officials found out about the attacks, but did not take them up as hate crimes, or as anything else.

All of these incidents could have been investigated and prosecuted either as state hate crimes or as federal civil rights cases. But they were not. To have done so would have required one of two things: awareness and interest on the part of police investigators and prosecutors—who generally have a poor track record on race and gender issues—or awareness and support for civil rights charges by the Asian-American community—which is generally lacking on issues surrounding women, gender, sex, and sexual assault. The result is a double-silencing effect on the assaults and deaths of these women, who become invisible because of their gender and their race.

Although my research centers on hate crimes and Asian women, this silence and this failure to provide equal protection have parallels in all of the other classes protected by federal civil rights and hate statutes. That is, all other communities of color have a similar prosecution rate for hate crimes against the women in their communities—namely, zero. This dismal record is almost as bad in lesbian and gay antiviolence projects: the vast preponderance of hate crimes reported, tracked, and prosecuted concern gay men— very few concern lesbians. So where are all the women?

The answer to this question lies in the way our justice system was designed, and the way women are mere shadows in the existing civil rights framework. But in spite of this history, federal and state law do offer legal avenues for women to be heard. Federal civil rights prosecutions, for example, can be excellent platforms for high-visibility community education on the harmful impact of hate speech and behavior. When on June 19, 1982, two white auto workers in Detroit screamed racial epithets at Chinese-American Vincent Chin and said, "It's because of you motherfuckers that we're out of work," a public furor followed, raising the level of national discourse on what constitutes racism toward Asian Americans. Constitutional law professors, and members of the American Civil Liberties Union and the National Lawyers Guild had acted as if Asian Americans were not covered by civil rights law. Asian Americans emphatically corrected that misconception.

Hate crimes remedies can be used to force the criminal justice bureaucracy to adopt new attitudes. Patrick Purdy went to an elementary school in Stockton, California, in which 85 percent of the students came from Southeast Asia. When he selected that school as the place to open fire with his automatic weapon and killed five eight-year-olds and wounded thirty other children, the police and the media did not think it was a bias-motivated crime. Their denial reminds me of the response by the Montreal officials to the anti-feminist killings of fourteen women students there. But an outraged Asian-American community forced a state investigation into the Purdy incident and uncovered hate literature in the killer's effects. As a result, the community was validated, and, in addition, the criminal justice system and the media acquired a new level of understanding.

Imagine if a federal civil rights investigation had been launched in the case of the African-American student at St. John's University who was raped and sodomized by white members of the school lacrosse team, who were later acquitted. Investigators could have raised issues of those white men's attitudes toward the victim as a black woman, found out whether hate speech or race-specific pornography was present, investigated the overall racial climate on campus, and brought all of the silenced aspects of the incident to the public eye. Community discourse could have been raised to a high level.

Making these investigations happen will not be an easy road. Hate crimes efforts are generally expended on blatant cases, with high community consensus, not ones that bring up hard issues like gender-based violence. Yet these intersections of race and gender hatred are the very issues we must give voice to.

There is a serious difficulty with pushing for use of federal and state hate remedies. Some state statutes have been used against men of color: specifically, on behalf of white rape victims against African-American men. We know that the system, if left unchecked, will try to use antihate laws to enforce unequal justice. On the other hand, state hate statutes could be used to prosecute men of color who are believed to have assaulted women of color of another race—interminority assaults are increasing. Also, if violence against women generally were made into a hate crime, women of color could seek prosecutions against men in their own community for their gender-based violence—even if this would make it harder to win the support of men in communities of color, and of women in those communities who would not want to be accused of dividing the community.

But at least within the Asian-American antiviolence community, this discourse is taking place now. Asian-American feminists in San Francisco have prepared a critique of the Asian movement against hate crimes and the men of that movement are listening. Other communities of color should also examine the nexus between race and gender for women of color, and by extension, for all women.

The legal system must expand the boundaries of existing law to include the most invisible women. There are hundreds of cases involving women of color waiting to be filed. Activists in the violence-against-women movement must reexamine current views on gender-based violence. Not all sexual assaults are the same. Racism in a sexual assault adds another dimension to the pain and harm inflicted. By taking women of color out of the legal shadows, out of invisibility, all women make gains toward full human dignity and human rights.

PART XI
A World that Is Truly Human

I am inseparably committed to the empowerment of both people with disabilities and women. Therefore, my pro-choice stance must lie somewhere in the common ground between feminism and disability rights.

LAURA HERSHEY[1]

We must create an environment, not only in the workplace but in our communities generally, in which harassment, abuse, and violence are no longer tolerated because men and women understand the damage such behavior does to all of us.

ROBERT L. ALLEN[2]

. . . while both [white feminist and black feminist] movements spurred us to organize, neither included our culturally specific agendas—about battering of immigrant women, the ghettoization of the South Asian community, cultural discrimination, bicultural history and identity, and other issues specific to our lives.

SONIA SHAH[3]

The introduction to this book quotes Gerda Lerner calling for " . . . a world free of dominance and hierarchy, a world that is truly human." A democratic society depends on equal access to the rights and benefits of the social order. It requires a system in which people born tied down by ropes of oppression are given the means to untie themselves and are offered equal opportunities once they are free. In a truly human world, the ropes would not exist. Our social, political, and economic systems do not provide such opportunities, so individuals, groups, and communities are left on their own to devise empowerment strategies.

As Part I discusses, altering the gender system, entrenched as it is in many structural arrangements, requires change at many levels—in individuals, in relationships, in families, in communities, in national alliances, through legal reform, and through global policy and action. Recall Elizabeth Janeway's conclusion, reported in the introduction to this book, that disempowered people can become empowered only after we question the truth of the ideas of those in power. Janeway argues that disbelief, the first stage, needs to be followed by action, both individual and collective.

In the preceding chapters of this book, we have heard from many people working for change in specific areas. In this final chapter, we hear from several people working toward a more human world across various differences and at various levels, ranging from individual efforts to community organizing to national strategies to global strategies. Also included are three writers who discuss the complex work of bridging cultures without losing one's identity.

First, Roberta Praeger reveals her struggle as a parent, a woman on welfare, and a survivor of sexual abuse. She describes her path to empowerment and healing as she works with others to organize tenants and fight for welfare rights. The second article is by Byllye Avery, who tells how she helped to organize the National Black Women's Health Project—an organization that has become the major resource in the United States for the health concerns of Black women.

Next, Edward Broadbent, a Canadian public official, argues for global policy changes that would acknowledge women as human and include women's rights as human rights. Broadbent is part of a long-term effort to establish women as people on both global and national levels.[4]

The next three articles ask us to consider the complexities of crossing cultures and building coalitions. First, Sonia Shah explores ways of being a bicultural, Asian-American feminist. Then Laura Hershey discusses some of the difficult issues surrounding disability rights and the right to choose abortion, pointing out that the feminist pro-choice movement has not taken a proactive stand for the rights of people with disabilities. As a pro-choice woman with a disability, Hershey makes a series of policy recommendations related to health care, choice, and the construction of a social order in which people with disabilities are considered fully human. Next, anti-Klan activist and writer Mab Segrest describes a process by which a coalition of people in North Carolina successfully fought Klan activity in various ways. The coalition included people of different races, genders, and sexual orientations.

Finally, Robert L. Allen describes some of the work that he and his colleagues do at the Oakland Men's Project (OMP). By looking at issues of power and inequality, boys and men in OMP workshops are encouraged to examine their socialization and consider other ways of being male, focusing especially on learning to use power *with* others for social change, rather than power *over* others for control. This message—using power with others for change—has recurred throughout this book. Allen and the other authors in this final chapter are some of the many activists who are working to help create a world that is truly human.

NOTES

1. Laura Hershey, "Choosing Disability" *Ms.*, July/August, 1994: 27.
2. Robert L. Allen, "Stopping Sexual Harassment: A Challenge for Community Education," in Anita Faye Hill and Emma Coleman Jordan, eds., *Race, Gender, and Power in America: The Legacy of the Hill-Thomas Hearings* (New York: Oxford, 1995) p. 130.
3. Sonia Shah, "Presenting the Blue Goddess: Toward a Bicultural Asian-American Feminist Agenda," in Karen Kahn, ed., *Frontline Feminism* (San Francisco: Aunt Lute, 1995) p. 56.

4. See work by Charlotte Bunch, for example, "Women's Rights as Human Rights: Toward a Re-Vision of Human Rights," in Charlotte Bunch and Roxanna Carrillo, *Gender Violence: A Development and Human Rights Issue* (New Brunswick, NJ: Rutgers University Center for Women's Global Leadership, 1991) p. 4.

60

A WORLD WORTH LIVING IN

ROBERTA PRAEGER

As an impoverished woman I live with the exhaustion, the frustration, the deprivation of poverty. As a survivor of incest I struggle to overcome the emotional burden. One thing has led to another in my life as the causes of poverty, of incest, of so many issues have become increasingly clear. My need to personalize has given way to a realization of social injustice and a commitment to struggle for social change.

Living on Welfare

I live alone with my four-year-old child, Jamie. This state (Massachusetts) allocates $328 a month to a family of two living on Aid to Families with Dependent Children (AFDC). This sum places us, along with other social service recipients, at an income 40 percent below the federal poverty line. In today's economy, out of this sum of money, we are expected to pay for rent, utilities, clothing for two, child-care expenses, food not covered by food stamps, and any other expenses we may incur.

My food stamps have been cut to the point where they barely buy food for half the month. I have difficulty keeping up with the utility bills, and my furniture is falling apart. Furniture breaks, and there is no money to replace it. Things that others take for granted, such as sheets and towels, become irreplaceable luxuries.

Chaos exists around everything, even the most important issues, like keeping a roof over one's head. How are people expected to pay rent for their families on the shameful amount of income provided by the Welfare Department? The answer, in many cases, is reflected in the living conditions of welfare recipients. Some of us live in apartments that should be considered uninhabitable. We live with roaches, mice, sometimes rats, and floors about to cave in. I live in subsidized housing. It's that or the street. My rent without the subsidy is $400 a month, $72 more than my entire monthly income. It took over a year of red tape between the time of my first application to the time of final acceptance into the program, all the while watching the amount of my rent climb higher and higher. What becomes of the more than 80 percent of AFDC recipients who are not subsidized because there isn't enough of this housing available?

Emergencies are dealt with in the best way possible. One cold winter day, Jamie broke his ankle in the day-care center. It was the day my food stamps were due to arrive. With no food in the house, I had to take him, on public transportation, to the hospital emergency room and then walk to the supermarket with my shopping cart in a foot of snow. This was not an unusual event in my life. All AFDC mothers get caught up in situations like this, because we are alone, because we have few resources and little money.

Ronald Reagan's war on the poor has exacerbated an already intolerable situation. Human service programs have been slashed to the bone. Regulations governing the fuel assistance program have been changed in ways that now make many of the impoverished ineligible. Energy assistance no longer pays my utility bills. For some these changes have meant going without needed fuel, thereby forcing people to endure freezing temperatures.

The food stamp situation has gone from bad to worse. The amount of money allocated for the program has been drastically reduced. My situation reflects that of most welfare recipients. Last year, my food stamps were cut back from $108 to $76 a month, barely enough to buy food for two weeks. Reagan doesn't even allow us to work to supplement our meager income. His reforms resulted in a law, the Omnibus Budget Reconciliation Act, that, in one fell swoop, instituted a number of repressive work-related changes. Its main impact came when it considerably lowered the amount of money a recipient can earn before the termination of benefits. Under this new law even a low-paying, part-time job can make a person no longer eligible for assistance.

The complexity of our lives reaches beyond economic issues. Monday through Friday, I work as an undergraduate student at the University of Massachusetts. On weekends, when in two-parent families, one parent can sometimes shift the responsibility to the other, I provide the entertainment for my child. All the household chores are my responsibility, for I have no one to share them with. When Jamie is sick I spend nights awake with him. When I am sick, I have no one to help me. I can't do things others take for granted, such as spend an evening out at the movies, because I don't have enough money to pay both the admission fee and for child care. Even if I did, I would be too exhausted to get out the front door. Often I wind up caught in a circle of isolation.

What kind of recognition do I and other welfare mothers get for all this hard work? One popular image of welfare recipients pictures us as lazy, irresponsible women, sitting at home, having babies, and living off the government. Much of society treats us like lepers, degrading and humiliating us at every turn, treating us as if we were getting something for nothing. One day I walked into a small grocery store wearing a button that read "Stop Reagan's War on the Poor." The proprietor of the store looked at my button and said to me, "You know, all those people on welfare are rich." Most welfare recipients would say anything rather than admit to being on welfare because of the image it creates. My brother-in-law had the audacity to say to me in conversation one day, "People are poor because they're lazy. They don't want to work."

And the Welfare Department shares this image of the recipient with the general public. From the first moment of contact with the department, the client is treated with rudeness, impatience, mistrust, and scorn. She is intimidated by constant redeterminations, reviews, and threats of being cut off. Her life is controlled by a system wracked with ineptness and callous indifference. Two years ago, unable to pay my electric bill, I applied for emergency assistance. It took the Welfare Department so long to pay the bill that the electric company turned the power off. We lived for two days without electricity before my constant badgering of the Welfare Department and the utility company produced results.

The department gives out information that is misleading and/or incomplete. The recipient is made to feel stupid, guilty, and worthless, a "problem" rather than a person. When I first applied I had to answer all sorts of questions about my personal life time and again. Many of my replies were met with disbelief. I sat there for hours at a time, nine months pregnant, waiting to be interviewed. And that was just the beginning of hours and hours of waiting, of filling in forms for the programs that keep us and our children alive.

The Personal Is Political

For most women in this situation, suffering is nothing new. Poverty is seldom an isolated issue. It's part of a whole picture. Other issues complicate our lives. For myself, as for many of us, suffering is complicated by memories, the results of trauma brought forward from childhood. Under frilly pink dresses and little blue sailor suits lay horror stories shared by many. The memories I bring with me from my childhood are not very pretty.

I was born in a Boston neighborhood in 1945. My father was a linoleum installer, my mother a homemaker. I want to say that my childhood was colored by the fact that I was an abused child. It's still difficult for me to talk about some things to this day.

My mother didn't give me a life of my own. When I was an infant she force-fed me. At age nine, she was still spoon-feeding me. Much of the time she didn't let me out of her sight. She must have seen school as a threat to her control, for she kept me home half the time. In me she saw not a separate person but an extension of herself. She felt free to do as she wished with my body. Her attempts to control my elimination process have had a lasting impact on my sexuality. The methods she used have been documented for their use in cases of mother-daughter incest. She had an obsessive-compulsive desire to control what went into me, to control elimination, to control everything about me. I had no control over anything. I couldn't get out from under what was happening to me psychologically. Powerlessness, frustration, and emotional insecurity breed a chain of abuse as men abuse women and children and women abuse children.

In the face of all the adverse, perverted attention received from my mother, I turned to my father for love and affection. We became close. In time, though, it became clear he knew as little about child rearing as my mother. His own deprived childhood had taught him only bitterness.

Throughout the years I knew him, he had gambled literally thousands of dollars away at the horse track. He left me alone outside the track gate at age five or six when the sign read "No children allowed." When I was twelve, he set fire to our house. He had run out of money for gambling purposes, and the house was insured against fire. When the insurance money arrived, my mother somehow managed to intercept it and bought new furniture. When my father found out what she had done, he went on a rampage. I had a knickknack shelf, charred from the fire. He threw it across the room, splinters of glass flying everywhere, and then he hit my mother. This was not an uncommon scene in my childhood.

By the time I reached eleven, my father was beginning to see me in a different light. At this point, the closeness that had developed between him and me still existed. And he proceeded to take advantage of it.

My mother belonged to a poker club, and once a week she would leave the house to go to these sessions. On these occasions my father would come over to me and remove both my clothes and his. He would then use my body to masturbate until he reached orgasm. He attempted to justify these actions by saying, "A man has to have sex and your mother won't." This occurred a number of times when I was between the ages of eleven and thirteen. I cried the last time he did this and he stopped molesting me sexually. In incestuous situations there doesn't have to be any threat; very often there isn't, because parents are in a position of trust, because parents are in a position of power, and because the child needs love. Children are in a developmental stage where they have no choice.

I went to public school and did very well. When I was sixteen, the school authorities told me that no matter how well I did, no matter how high my grades were, they could not keep me in school if I appeared only half the time. So I dropped out. I just spent the whole time sitting in front of the television until my mother died.

I didn't understand the extent of my mother's sickness in her treatment of me. Fear that if my mother knew what my father was doing she would kill him seemed realistic to me at the time. And so, I kept silent. I looked at my parents, as all children do, as authority figures. Longing for a way out of the situation, I felt trapped. In the face of all this I felt overwhelmed, afraid, and isolated. I retreated from reality into a world of fantasy. For only through my imagination could I find any peace of mind or semblance of happiness. The abuse I had taken all these years began to manifest itself in psychosomatic symptoms. Periodically, I started suffering intense abdominal pain. Once I fainted and fell on the bathroom floor. There were three visits to the hospital emergency room. My doctor had misdiagnosed the symptoms as appendicitis.

When I was seventeen, my father, after a major argument with my mother, moved out. Without money to pay the rent, with no job training or other resources, we rented out a room. Ann, the young woman renting the room, was appalled at the situation she discovered. She began to teach me some basic skills such as how to wash my own clothes. For the first time in my life I related positively to someone. My father moved back two months later. For two years this is how the situation remained, my mother, father, Ann, and I all living together.

In 1965 my mother was diagnosed as having lung cancer. Three months later she was dead. I felt nothing, no sorrow, no anger, no emotion. I had long ago learned how to bury my emotions deep down inside of me. I packed my belongings and moved out with Ann, in the midst of my father's ranting and raving.

Living in an apartment with Ann made things seem to improve on the surface. My life was quieter. I held a steady job for the first time. There was a little money to spend. I could come and go as I pleased. It felt good, and I guess, at that point I thought my life had really changed. It took me a long time to realize what an adult who has had this kind of childhood must still go through. I had nightmares constantly. There were times when I went into deep depressions. I didn't know what was going on, what was happening to me, or why.

After holding my first job for three years, I went through a series of jobs in different fields: sales, hairdressing, and, after a period of training, nursing. It seemed I was not functioning well in any area. I fell apart in any situation where demands were made of me. I had no tolerance for hierarchy. I discovered that I performed best when I was acting as charge nurse. Unfortunately, in my role as a Licensed Practical Nurse, I usually wound up low person on the totem pole, generally having to answer to someone else. In time, it became clear to me, that control was a major factor in a variety of situations that I encountered.

My self-confidence and self-esteem were abysmally low. Every time something went wrong my first thought was, "There must be something wrong with me." I didn't know then, what I know now. Children never blame their parents for the wrong that is done. They blame themselves. This feeling carries on into adulthood until it is difficult not to blame oneself for everything that does not go right.

I was depressed, suicidal, frightened out of my wits, and completely overwhelmed by life. After a series of failed relationships and a broken marriage, I wound up alone, with a small child, living on welfare. The emotional burden I carried became complicated by the misery and exhaustion of poverty.

Why have I survived? Why am I not dead? Because I'm a survivor. Because I have Jamie and I love him more than words can say. In him I see the future, not the past.

A Major Change

I survived because in the midst of all this something happened, something that was to turn out to be the major guiding force in my life. In 1972 the owner of my building sent out notices threatening eviction if the tenants did not pay a huge rent increase. Everyone in the building was aghast at the prospect and so formed a tenant union to discuss alternatives. Through my activities with the union, I learned of an organization that did community work throughout the city. Cambridge Tenants Organizing Committee (CTOC) was a multifaceted organization involved in work around issues such as tenants' rights, welfare advocacy, antiracist work, and education concerning sexism in society. I began working with a group of people unlike any that I had been exposed to in the past. They treated me as a person capable of assuming responsibility and doing any job well. My work with CTOC included organizing tenant unions throughout the city, counseling unemployed workers, and attending countless demonstrations, marches, picketings, and hearings. As a group we organized and/or supported eviction blocking, we helped defend people against physical racist attacks, and we demonstrated at the state house for continuation of rent control. I wasn't paid for my work. What I earned was far more important than money. I learned respect for myself as a woman. I learned the joys and pitfalls of working collectively and began assimilating more information than I had at any other time of my life.

And I flourished. I went to meeting after meeting until they consumed almost all of my nonwork time. Over the years I joined other groups. One of my major commitments was to a group that presented political films. My politics became the center of my life.

Through counseling and therapy groups with therapists who shared my political perspective, the guilt I had shouldered all these years began to lessen. Within a period of three years, through groups and conventions, I listened to and/or spoke with more than three hundred other survivors of incest. I heard stories that would make your hair stand on end. New learning led to making connections. Although the true extent of incest is not known, owing to the fact that sexual abuse within families usually goes unreported, various statistics estimate that 100,000 to 250,000 children are sexually molested each year in the United States. Other studies show that one out of every three to four women in this country is a victim of sexual abuse as a child. Incest Resources, my primary resource for group counseling, believes these statistics heavily underestimate the extent of actual abuse. So do I. Although the guilt for the abuse lies with the abuser, the context of the problem reaches far beyond, beyond me or my parents, into society itself as power and inequality surround us.

Connections with other people have become part and parcel of my life as my life situation has led me into work surrounding the issue of poverty. Although I had known for years of the existence of the Coalition for Basic Human Needs (CBHN)—a progressive group composed almost totally of welfare recipients—my political work, reflecting my life situation, had led me in other directions. Now I found myself alone with a toddler, living on AFDC. When Jamie was two, I returned to school to acquire additional skills. My academic work led me into issues concerning poverty as I became involved in months of activity, along with students and faculty and a variety of progressive women's groups, constructing a conference on the issue of women and poverty. Members of CBHN were involved in work on the conference, and we connected.

Social change through welfare-rights struggles became a major focus in my life as I began working with CBHN. Collectively, we sponsored legislative bills that would improve our lives financially while, at the same time, we taught others how we actually live. Public education became intertwined with legislative work as I spoke at hearings on the reality of living on AFDC. Political support became intertwined with public education as I spoke on the work of CBHN to progressive groups and their constituencies, indicting this country's political system for the impoverishment of its people.

CBHN is composed of chapters representing various cities and towns across Massachusetts. Grass-roots organizing of welfare recipients takes place within local chapters, while the organization as a whole works on statewide issues. We mail out newsletters, hold press conferences, and initiate campaigns. We are currently involved in our most ambitious effort. Whereas in the past our work has been directed toward winning small goals such as a clothing allowance or a small increase in benefits, this time we have set about to bring welfare benefits up to the poverty level, a massive effort involving all of our past strategies and more. We have filed a bill with the state legislature. Public education has become concentrated in the campaign as we plan actions involving the work of welfare-rights groups and individuals throughout the state.

The courage we share as impoverished women has been mirrored throughout this effort. At a press conference to announce the campaign a number of us gave truth to the statement that we and our children go without the basic necessities of life. One woman spoke of sending her child to school without lunch because there was no food in the house. Others had no money for winter jackets or shoes for their children. Sharing the reality of living at 40 percent below the poverty level brings mutual support as well as frustration and anger. In mid-April hundreds of welfare recipients—women carrying infants, the disabled, and the homeless—came from all over Massachusetts to rally in front of the state house along with our supporters and testify to the legislature in behalf of our "Up to the Poverty Level" bill. Courage and determination rang out in statements such as this:

> Take the cost of implementing this program and weigh it, if it must be weighed at all; then weigh it against the anguish suffered by the six-month-old twins who starved to death in a Springfield housing project.
>
> The day that the state legislature has to scrape the gilt off the dome of the state house and sell it for revenue is the day that this state can answer to us that there is not the means to do this.

The complexity of the situation comes home to me again and again as I sit in the CBHN office answering the telephone and doing welfare advocacy work. I've spoken with women on AFDC who have been battered to within an inch of their lives, some who are, like myself, survivors of child abuse, and others who are reeling from the effects of racism as well as poverty.

In this society so many of us internalize oppression. We internalize the guilt that belongs to the system that creates the conditions people live in. When we realize this and turn our anger outward in an effort to change society, then we begin to create a world worth living in.

The work isn't easy. Many of us become overwhelmed as well as overextended. It takes courage and fortitude to survive. For we live in a society laden with myths and an inequality that leads to human suffering. In order to alleviate the suffering and provide the equality each and every one of us deserves, we must effect social change. If we are to effect social change, then we must recognize social injustice and destroy the myths it creates. Little did I realize, years ago, when I first began this work how far it reached beyond my own survival. For those of us involved in creating a new society are doing the most important work that exists.

61

BREATHING LIFE INTO OURSELVES
The Evolution of the National Black Women's Health Project

BYLLYE Y. AVERY

I got involved in women's health in the 1970s around the issue of abortion. There were three of us at the University of Florida, in Gainesville, who just seemed to get picked out by women who needed abortions. They came to us. I didn't know anything about abortions. In my life that word couldn't even be mentioned without having somebody look at you crazy. Then someone's talking to me about abortion. It seemed unreal. But as more women came (and at first they were mostly white women), we found out this New York number we could give them, and they could catch a plane and go there for their abortions. But then a black woman came and we gave her the number, and she looked at us in awe: "I can't get to New York. . . . " We realized we needed a different plan of action, so in May 1974 we opened up the Gainesville Women's Health Center.

As we learned more about abortions and gynecological care, we immediately started to look at birth, and to realize that we are women with a total reproductive cycle. We might have to make different decisions about our lives, but whatever the decision, we deserved the best services available. So, in 1978, we opened up Birthplace, an alternative birthing center. It was exhilarating work; I assisted in probably around two hundred births. I understood life, and working in birth, I understood death, too. I certainly learned what's missing in prenatal care and why so many of our babies die.

Through my work at Birthplace, I learned the importance of being involved in our own health. We have to create environments that say "yes." Birthplace was a wonderful space. It was a big, old turn-of-the-century house that we decorated with antiques. We went to people's houses and, if we liked something, we begged for it—things off their walls, furniture, rugs. We fixed the place so that when women walked in, they would say, "Byllye, I was excited when I got up today because this was my day to come to Birthplace." That's how prenatal care needs to be given—so that people are excited when they come. It's about eight and a half or nine months that a woman comes on a continuous basis. That is the time to start affecting her life so that she can start making meaningful lifestyle changes. So you see, health provides us with all sorts of opportunities for empowerment.

Reprinted by permission of *Sojourner: The Woman's Forum*, 1990.

Through Birthplace, I came to understand the importance of our attitudes about birthing. Many women don't get the exquisite care they deserve. They go to these large facilities, and they don't understand the importance of prenatal care. They ask, "Why is it so important for me to get in here and go through all this hassle?" We have to work around that.

Through the work of Birthplace, we have created a prenatal caring program that provides each woman who comes for care with a support group. She enters the group when she arrives, leaves the group to go for her physical checkup, and then returns to the group when she is finished. She doesn't sit in a waiting room for two hours. Most of these women have nobody to talk to. No one listens to them; no one helps them plan. They're asking: "Who's going to get me to the hospital if I go into labor in the middle of the night, or the middle of the day, for that matter? Who's going to help me get out of this abusive relationship? Who's going to make sure I have the food I need to eat?" Infant mortality is not a medical problem; it's a social problem.

One of the things that black women have started talking about regarding infant mortality is that many of us are like empty wells; we give a lot, but we don't get much back. We're asked to be strong. I have said, "If one more person says to me that black women are strong I'm going to scream in their face." I am so tired of that stuff. What are you going to do—just lay down and die? We have to do what's necessary to survive. It's just a part of living. But most of us are empty wells that never really get replenished. Most of us are dead inside. We are walking around dead. That's why we end up in relationships that reinforce that particular thought. So you're talking about a baby being alive inside of a dead person; it just won't work.

We need to stop letting doctors get away with piling up all this money, buying all these little machines. They can keep the tiniest little piece of protoplasm alive, and then it goes home and dies. All this foolishness with putting all this money back into their pockets on that end of the care and not on the other end has to stop. When are we going to wake up?

The National Black Women's Health Project

I left the birthing center around 1980 or '81, mostly because we needed more midwives and I wasn't willing to go to nursing school. But an important thing had happened for me in 1979. I began looking at myself as a black woman. Before that I had been looking at myself as a woman. When I left the birthing center, I went to work in a Comprehensive Employment Training Program (CETA) job at a community college and it brought me face-to-face with my sisters and face-to-face with myself. Just by the nature of the program and the population that I worked with, I had, for the first time in my life, a chance to ask a nineteen-year-old why—please give me the reason why—you have four babies and you're only nineteen years old. And I was able to listen, and bring these sisters together to talk about their lives. It was there that I started to understand the lives of black women and to realize that we live in a conspiracy of silence. It was hearing these women's stories that led me to start conceptualizing the National Black Women's Health Project.

First I wanted to do an hour-long presentation on black women's health issues, so I started doing research. I got all the books, and I was shocked at what I saw. I was angry—angry that the people who wrote these books didn't put it into a format that made sense to us, angry that nobody was saying anything to black women or to black men. I was so angry I threw one book across the room and it stayed there for three or four days, because I knew I had just seen the tip of the iceberg, but I also knew enough to know that I couldn't go back. I had opened my eyes, and I had to go on and look.

Instead of an hour-long presentation we had a conference. It didn't happen until 1983, but when it did, 2,000 women came. But I knew we couldn't just have a conference. From the health statistics I saw, I knew that there was a deeper problem. People needed to be able to work individually, and on a daily basis. So we got the idea of self-help groups. The first group we formed was in a rural area outside of Gainesville, with twenty-one women who were severely obese. I thought, "Oh this is a piece of cake. Obviously these sisters don't have any information. I'll go in there and talk to them about losing weight, talk to them about high blood pressure, talk to them about diabetes—it'll be easy."

Little did I know that when I got there, they would be able to tell me everything that went into a 1200-calorie-a-day diet. They all had been to Weight Watchers at least five or six times; they all had blood-pressure-reading machines in their homes as well as medications they were on. And when we sat down to talk, they said, "We know all that information, but what we also know is that living in the world that we are in, we feel like we are absolutely nothing." One woman said to me, "I work for General Electric making batteries, and, from the stuff they suit me up in, I know it's killing me." She said, "My home life is not working. My old man is an alcoholic. My kids got babies. Things are not well with me. And the one thing I know I can do when I come home is cook me a pot of food and sit down in front of the TV and eat it. And you can't take that away from me until you're ready to give me something in its place."

So that made me start to think that there was some other piece to this health puzzle that had been missing, that it's not just about giving information; people need something else. We just spent a lot of time talking. And while we were talking, we were planning the 1983 conference, so I took the information back to the planning committee. Lillie Allen (a trainer who works with NBWHP) was there. We worked with her to understand that we are dying inside. That unless we are able to go inside of ourselves and touch and breathe fire, breathe life into ourselves, that, of course, we couldn't be healthy. Lillie started working on a workshop that we named "Black and Female: What is the Reality?" This is a workshop that terrifies us all. And we are also terrified not to have it, because the conspiracy of silence is killing us.

Stopping Violence

As we started to talk, I looked at those health statistics in a new way. Now, I'm not saying that we are not suffering from the things we die from—that's what the statistics give us. But what causes all this sickness? Like cardiovascular disease—it's the number one killer. What causes all that heart pain? When sisters take their shoes off and start talking about what's happening, the first thing we cry about is violence. The violence in our lives. And if you look in statistics books, they mention violence in one paragraph. They don't even give numbers, because they can't count it: the violence is too pervasive.

The number one issue for most of our sisters is violence—battering, sexual abuse. Same thing for their daughters, whether they are twelve or four. We have to look at how violence is used, how violence and sexism go hand in hand, and how it affects the sexual response of females. We have to stop it, because violence is the training ground for us.

When you talk to young people about being pregnant, you find out a lot of things. Number one is that most of these girls did not get pregnant by teenage boys; most of them got pregnant by their mother's boyfriends or their brothers or their daddies. We've been sitting on that. We can't just tell our daughters, "just say no." What do they do about all those feelings running around their bodies? And we need to talk to our brothers. We need to tell them, the incest makes us crazy. It's something that stays on our minds all the time. We need the men to know that. And they need to know that when they hurt us, they hurt themselves. Because we are their mothers, their sisters, their wives; we are their allies on this planet. They can't just damage one part of it without damaging themselves. We need men to stop giving consent, by their silence, to rape, to sexual abuse, to violence. You need to talk to your boyfriends, your husbands, your sons, whatever males you have around you—talk to them about talking to other men. When they are sitting around womanizing, talking bad about women, make sure you have somebody stand up and be your ally and help stop this. For future generations, this has got to stop somewhere.

Mothers and Daughters

If violence is the number one thing women talk about, the next is being mothers too early and too long. We've developed a documentary called "On Becoming a Woman: Mothers and Daughters Talking Together." It's eight mothers and eight daughters—sixteen ordinary people talking about extraordinary things.

The idea of the film came out of my own experience with my daughter. When Sonja turned eleven, I started bemoaning that there were no rituals left; there was nothing to let a girl know that once you get your period your life can totally change, nothing to celebrate that something wonderful is happening. So I got a cake that said, "Happy Birthday! Happy Menstruation!" It had white icing with red writing. I talked about the importance of becoming a woman, and, out of that, I developed a workshop for mothers and daughters for the public schools. I did the workshops in Gainesville, and, when we came to Atlanta, I started doing them there. The film took ten years, from the first glimmer of an idea to completion.

The film is in three parts. In the first part all the mothers talk about when we got our periods. Then the daughters who have their periods talk about getting theirs, and the ones who are still waiting talk about that. The second part of the film deals with contraception, birth control, anatomy and physiology. This part of the film is animated, so it keeps the kids' attention. It's funny. It shows all the anxiety: passing around condoms, hating it, saying, "Oh no, we don't want to do this."

The third part of the film is the hardest. We worked on communication with the mothers and daughters. We feel that the key to birth control and to controlling reproduction is the nature of the relationship between the parents and their young people. And what's happening is that everybody is willing to beat up on the young kids, asking, "Why did you get pregnant? Why did you do this?" No one is saying to the parents, "Do you need some help with learning how to talk to your young person? Do you want someone to sit with you? Do you want to see what it feels like?" We don't have all the answers. In this film, you see us struggling.

What we created, which was hard for the parents, is a safe space where everybody can say anything they need to say. And if you think about that, as parents, we have that relationship with our kids: we can ask them anything. But when we talk about sex, it's special to be in a space where the kids can ask *us*, "Mama, what do you do when you start feeling funny all in your body?" What the kids want to know is, what about lust? What do we do about it? And that's the very information that we don't want to give up. That's "our business." But they want to hear it from us, because they can trust us. And we have to struggle with how we do that: How do we share that information? How do we deal with our feelings?

Realizing the Dream

The National Black Women's Health Project has ninety-six self-help groups in twenty-two states, six groups in Kenya, and a group in Barbados and in Belize. In addition, we were just funded by the W.K. Kellogg Foundation to do some work in three housing projects in Atlanta. We received $1,032,000 for a three-year period to set up three community centers. Our plan is to do health screening and referral for adolescents and women, and in addition to hook them up with whatever social services they need—to help cut through the red tape. There will be computerized learning programs and individualized tutorial programs to help young women get their General Equivalency Degrees (GED), along with a panel from the community who will be working on job readiness skills. And we'll be doing our self-help groups—talking about who we are, examining, looking at ourselves.

We hope this will be a model program that can be duplicated anywhere. And we're excited about it. Folks in Atlanta thought it was a big deal for a group of black women to get a million dollars. We thought it was pretty good, too. Our time is coming.

62

GETTING RID OF MALE BIAS

EDWARD BROADBENT

It is a sad truth that people who would never scoff at or belittle human rights do not treat women's rights with the same seriousness. In 1992 a woman from Saudi Arabia landed at Mirabel Airport, in Quebec, and asked for refugee status saying she was persecuted in her country as a woman who refused to accept second-class status. She had been stoned for revealing her hair. She reported that she was laughed at by immigration officials who dismissed such claims as cause for refugee status.

In addition to the violations of human rights that we readily condemn, women face a series of abuses that are normally ignored, overlooked and forgotten by the human rights community: forced childbirth, sexual slavery, rape, genital mutilation, discrimination in education and employment, female infanticide, domestic violence, sexual harassment. This depressing and only partial list describes a global phenomenon which has reached epidemic proportions.

The truth is that the international community has done precious little to correct these abuses. We have yet to see effective mobilization of international public opinion against states enacting discriminatory laws and repressing activists for women's rights. While cultural relativism and the principle of state sovereignty are no longer acceptable justifications for extrajudicial killings or torture, they are still being used as lame excuses to prevent the international community from speaking out on behalf of women whose fundamental human rights are denied in law and in practice.

From *Ours By Right,* Joanna Kerr, ed., 1993, pp. 10–12. Reprinted by permission of Zed Books.

There are at least some signs of change. Human rights organizations around the world are beginning to recognize that they cannot ignore 52 percent of the population. Getting rid of that male bias means looking at human rights from a perspective that can account for both the female and male experience. I do not know whether it means re-writing the Universal Declaration of Human Rights, but it certainly means re-reading it. On one level, the increasingly popular slogan 'Women's rights are human rights' is simply stating the obvious. Yet it requires a concerted effort, both political and intellectual, to make this statement a reality.

'Women's rights are human rights' suggests a profound change in the way most people see international human rights. It means that, just as I have the right to 'life, liberty and security of the person,' so do all women have the right to be free from violence in the street and the home, because that is what life, liberty and security means from a woman's point of view. It means that, just as I have the right not to be subjected to cruel, inhuman or degrading treatment, so should women be freed from forced childbirth, forced prostitution, clandestine abortions and genital mutilation—all of which are cruel, inhuman and degrading. It means that, just as I have the right to an education, so do the women who live in rural Nepal; yet only two per cent of them are functionally literate. The right to equality before the law means that, as human rights advocates, we must stand up not simply for the rule of law but simultaneously against all laws which discriminate against women.

The world will not change just because we put new lenses in our glasses. It will only change if we act and if we are given the means to act. As the President of the International Centre for Human Rights and Democratic Development, a body that is accountable to the Parliament of Canada, I take the funds at our disposal—limited as they are—as a most serious matter. A good portion of that money goes to the protection and promotion of women's rights, to the growing number of groups in all areas of the world that are fighting the poverty and disenfranchisement of women, and the violence against them. These groups often face tremendous hostility from their governments, and from the male-dominated societies in which they live. They require our solidarity, our collaboration and, last but not least, our financial support.

Governments must be made to understand that human rights include women's rights and that any international forum that claims to discuss human rights must look at the situation of women and the specific abuses they confront. Women need to meet among themselves to determine priorities and strategies for change. The Convention on the Elimination of All Forms of Discrimination Against Women has now been signed by 119 countries, but not a single one of them has accomplished its paramount objective and raison d'être: the elimination of all forms of discrimination against women. There is a great deal of work to be done.

I urge other foundations and donors to support the women who are fighting to get their concerns on the agenda of the World Conference on

Human Rights. We cannot condemn states which torture political prisoners without condemning those who condone domestic violence by failing to prosecute offenders. We cannot decry those states which forbid citizens their freedom of movement without decrying those states who refuse passports to women, prohibit women from driving, or prevent them from obtaining a legal medical procedure in a neighboring country. We cannot claim to defend the international human rights treaties, if we do not examine them clause by clause and see what each means for women.

The language of human rights is powerful. It carries great moral authority, and is having an increasing impact on the peoples and the states of the world. If it is, however, to aspire to true universality, it must deal not only with the different experiences and realities of North and South, East and West, but also the different experiences of women and men. We must make the language of human rights relevant to women's lives.

63

PRESENTING THE BLUE GODDESS
Toward a Bicultural Asian-American Feminist Agenda

SONIA SHAH

We all laughed sheepishly about how we used to dismiss the South Asian women in our lives as doormats irrelevant to our cultural location. For most of us in that fledgling South Asian-American women's group in Boston, either white feminists or Black feminists had inspired us to try to find our feminist heritage. Yet neither movement had really prepared us for actually finding anything. The way feminism was defined by either group did not, could not, define our South Asian feminist heritages, which for most of us consisted of stuff like feisty immigrant mothers, ball-breaking grandmothers, Kali-worship (Kali is the blue goddess who sprung whole from another woman and who symbolizes "shakti"—Hindi for woman-power), social activist aunts, and freedom-

Reprinted by permission of *Sojourner: The Women's Forum,* May 1994. A longer version of this article appears in *The State of Asian America: Activism and Resistance,* edited by Karin Aguilar-San Juan (South End Press, 1994).

fighting/Gandhian great-aunts. In many ways, white feminism, with its "personal is political" maxim and its emphasis on building sisterhood and consciousness raising, had brought us together. Black feminism, on the other hand, had taught us that we could expect more—that a feminism incorporating a race analysis was possible. Yet, while both movements spurred us to organize, neither included our culturally specific agendas— about battering of immigrant women, the ghettoization of the South Asian community, cultural discrimination, bicultural history and identity, and other issues specific to our lives.

Today, our numbers are exploding in our immigrant communities and the communities of their progeny, and subsequently, in our activist communities. Our writers, poets, artists, and filmmakers are coming of age. Our activism, against anti-Asian violence, battery, and racism, is becoming more and more inspired and entrenched. Yet our movement for Asian-American feminism faces crucial internal challenges. Long-time Asian-American feminist activists such as Helen Zia, a contributing editor to *Ms.* magazine, wonder, "What makes us different from white feminists or Black feminists? What can we bring to the table?" And they complain that "these questions haven't really been developed yet."

Our needs, our liberation, and our pan-Asian feminist agenda have been obscured by a Black/white dichotomy that permeates both activist movements and the mainstream. This racialist essentialism has divided us, stripping us of the tools we need to articulate an Asian-American feminism. Our movement, in all of its different forms, has been forced to smash itself into definitions, assumptions, and activist protocols that simply don't work for us. So, while we have been able to get a lot of good work done, and will continue to do so, we haven't been able to show each other, tell each other, or teach each other, about what Asian-American feminism really means.

The movements of the '60s, out of which the first wave of Asian women's organizing sprung, collided with the mainstream in defining racism in Black and white terms; racism is still defined as discrimination based on skin color. These earlier activists also, to some extent, elevated discrimination based on skin color to the top layer of oppression. According to these assumptions, an assault on an Indian because she "dresses weird" is not racist; the harassment of a Chinese shopkeeper because she has a "funny accent" is not racist. Neither are as disturbing, unacceptable, or even downright "evil" as, for example, an attack on a Black person because of her skin color. Racism is seen as a problem between people of different skin colors, between Black people and white people, and one must be in either the Black or the white camp to even speak about it. Those of us who are neither Black nor white are expected to forget ourselves. Whites try to convince us we are really *more like them*; depending upon our degree of sensitivity toward racist injustice, we try to persuade Blacks that we are similar to them. This narrow definition has distorted mainstream perceptions of anti-Asian racism and has distorted even our perception of ourselves—we either don't see our-selves as victims of racism or we see ourselves as victims of racism based on skin color.

For example, many Asian-American women have described Asian women's experience of racism as a result of stereotypes about "exotica" and "china dolls," two stereotypes based on the fact that we look different from white people. Of course, we do encounter racism that emanates from these stereotypes. But there are many more layers of oppression just as unaccept-able and pernicious as this discrimination based on skin color. By focusing solely on "racial" differences, however, we fail to see them for what they are, and we fail to name the reality of our experiences.

For our experiences of oppression are in *many* ways qualitatively differ-ent from those of Black and white people. For me, the experience of "other-ness," the formative discrimination in my life, has been a result of culturally different (not necessarily racially different) people thinking they were cul-turally central: thinking that *my* house smelled funny, that *my* mother talked weird, that *my* habits were strange. They were normal; I wasn't.

The Black/white paradigms of both feminist and civil rights struggles create false divisions and false choices for Asian-American women. Not long ago, a group of South Asian women organizing against battery held a conference on South Asian women. Recent emigrees, the conference orga-nizers tended to hail from greater class privilege than the parents of second-generation South Asian Americans. This difference led second-generation South Asian American activists, born and bred in the United States, to boy-cott the conference, charging that the organizers, because of their class priv-ilege and because of their relative newness to the Asian-American community, sidelined issues of U.S.-based racism and discrimination.

This is a false division, especially dangerous in such a relatively small activist community. When first faced with U.S. racism and its Black/white constructs, immigrants with class privilege, even activist ones, are apt to dis-miss racism as "not their problem." (As it has been defined by the main-stream, strictly speaking, it isn't.) Efforts by second-generation (and beyond) activists, to convince our sisters at other locations on the culture/class con-tinuum that what we suffer is similar to what the Black community suffers are fraught with difficulty precisely because we have been confined to the Black/white paradigm. We need to use an accurate portrayal of our own experiences of racism, defined on *our* terms, to create alliances with our sis-ters across generation, class, and culture gaps. As long as we don't, false dichotomies will continue to divide us.

As Asian-American women, Asian women in America, American women of Asian descent, or however we choose to think of ourselves, we all grapple with conflicting signals and oppressions in our lives because we are all situated, to differing degrees, in both Asian and American cultural milieus. We suffer not only cultural discrimination (as men do as well) but our own form of cultural schizophrenia, as we receive mixed and often contradictory signals about priorities, values, duty, and meaning from our families and greater communities. We encounter sexist Asian tradition; racist and sexist white culture; antiracist nonfeminist women heroes; racist feminist heroes; strong proud Asian women who told us not to make waves; strong proud non-Asian women who told us *to* make waves, and on and on.

We all reconcile these tensions and oppressions in different ways: by acting out a model minority myth, for some; by suffering silently, for others; by being activist, for still others. These conflicts, born of cultural duality, along with the experience of cultural discrimination, are what unite us as Asian-American women across our differences. But this commonality has been obscured; there is no room for cultural duality in a world where one is automatically relegated to one racial camp or the other based on biological fact. But as we grapple with conflicting signals and oppressions in our lives, we can reimagine and reinvent ourselves and our priorities. The cultural schizophrenia, the feeling of not belonging to either or any culture, is not necessarily a burden; it is also an opportunity for us to recreate ourselves. We do it every time we encounter a conflict anyway; why not politicize this process of cultural reconciliation, and tag it for feminism and liberation?

We need to reclaim our cultural duality as our commonality and, also, as our greatest strength: for the good of our movement and to save ourselves. When the poor immigrant Asian woman who follows an abusive husband to the United States, who doesn't speak English and is cut off from the women who supported her in her home country, is beaten nearly to death by her one contact to the outside world, she needs a bicultural feminism. Not one that helps her go back to Asia, nor one that suggests she become a typical liberated "American" woman. She needs an activism that recognizes the cultural discrimination she will encounter in this society, while still empowering her to liberate herself in this country (with money, legal services, shelter, and support). She needs a bicultural feminism that will recognize and politicize the cultural reconciliation she must undergo to liberate herself: for example, by reimagining her duty as an Asian wife as a duty to herself.

When my little sister, who is just beginning to see herself as a sexual person, thinks she is a "slut" for wearing tight jeans, she needs this bicultural feminism. Not a mainstream white feminism, which might suggest she throw away her tight jeans because she is objectifying herself, nor one that simply suggests she revert to the dress of her "homeland" and wear a revealing sari—but one that would affirm that she doesn't have to abandon Indian values of filial respect or whatever it is that makes her fear appearing "slutty." It is possible that my parents, first-generation Indian immigrants, reject the trappings of American sexuality, such as tight jeans, as culturally alien. My sister's subsequent interpretation, however, that Indians are antisexual stems from her assumption—promulgated by mainstream society—that there is but one culture, not many. If you don't appreciate the trappings of sexuality, you don't appreciate sexuality. The fact that tight jeans are a particular, cultural expression of sexuality is obscured. An Asian-American feminism that emphasized cultural duality and reconciliation would subvert such narrow-mindedness. There are many cultures, many sexualities. My sister needs to name the cultural conflicts she is involved in for what they are and to reconcile her visions of sexuality and empowerment within the cultural confines of white patriarchy and Indian patriarchy. A bicultural feminism would ensure that she does this in a feminist, liberatory way.

As bicultural feminists with multiple identities, we are empowered to enter the broader discussion and struggles around us with something more substantial than identity politics and a slightly different take on the Black/white dichotomy. The concept and practice of the extended family, for example, might lead us to apply our critical reinventions to the struggle for accessible child care, where we can shift the turgid debate away from paid care to building cooperative care centers and encouraging work-sharing. Understanding social and linguistic difference within Asian-American families, we can apply our insights to the current debates about gay parents raising potentially straight children, or to white families raising children of color, by advocating for the fitness of the child's cultural community rather than for the fitness of the parent. Remembering our histories as Asian women, we can apply our sense of outrage over issues such as the Japanese internment during World War II, "brain drain" immigration to the United States that has robbed the Third World of its professional class, and past and present treatment of refugees to the struggle for just immigration policies. We can reinterpret Asian paradigms of filial and familial duty as social responsibility. We can use antimaterialism as a basis for building an ecological society.

I remember, in that South Asian American women's group, we were all looking forward to Mira Nair's film, *Mississippi Masala*. We took Nair as a kind of model—a seemingly progressive Indian woman filmmaker who had gained the financial backing necessary for reaching wide sectors of the South Asian community. *Masala* was the first film we knew of that would portray an Indian-American woman in her cultural milieu as the protagonist.

I don't know what Nair's intentions were, but her Indian-American protagonist was little more than a standard Western-defined beauty, her biculturalism little more than occasional bare feet and a chureedar thrown over her shoulder. Although a refugee from Uganda living in Mississippi with Indian parents, she was phenomenally unconcerned with issues of race, history, culture, and gender. Given the dearth of accessible activist commentary on biculturalism and feminism beyond the Black/white divide, even a sympathetic "opinion maker" like Nair can hurt our movement, by portraying us as little more than exotic, browner versions of white women who by virtue of a little color can bridge the gap between Black and white (not through activism, of course, just romantic love). If Asian-American women's movements can effectively unite within bicultural feminist agendas, we can snatch that power away from those willing to trivialize us, and *Masala* and our less sympathetic foes beware.

64
_____

CHOOSING DISABILITY

LAURA HERSHEY

In 1983, when I was in college, local antiabortion protesters commemorated the tenth anniversary of *Roe v. Wade* with a rally. Our student feminist organization held a small counterdemonstration. Frantic in their zeal, anti-choice protesters assailed us with epithets like "slut" and "bitch." But the most hostile remark was directed at me. I was confronted by an angry nun whose "Abortion Is Murder" sign hung tiredly at her side. She stopped in front of me and aimed a pugnacious finger. "You see?" she announced. "God even let you be born!"

I'm not sure the sister realized that I had been part of the pro-choice demonstration. All she saw in me was a poster child for her holy crusade. I must have seemed to her an obvious mistake of nature: a severely disabled person, who, through a combination of divine intervention and legal restrictions, had been born anyway.

That was my first inkling of how attitudes about disability function in the volatile debate over reproductive rights. I understood that the nun and her co-crusaders were no friends of mine. To her, I was a former fetus who had escaped the abortionists. No room in that view for my identity as an adult woman; no room for the choices I might make. Now, more than a decade later, antiabortion groups are courting the disability community. The approach has become less clumsy, emphasizing respect for the lives of people with disabilities, and some activists have accepted the anti-choice message because they find it consistent with the goals of the disability rights movement. As a feminist, however, I recoil at the "pro-life" movement's disregard for the lives and freedom of women.

But I cannot overlook the fact that when a prenatal test reveals the possibility of a "major defect," as the medical profession puts it, the pregnancy almost always ends in "therapeutic abortion." The prospect of bearing a child with disabilities causes such anxiety that abortion has become the accepted outcome—even among people who oppose abortion rights in general.

_____

Indeed, fear of disability played a key role in the legalization of abortion in the United States in the 1960s. When thousands of pregnant women who had taken thalidomide (a drug used in tranquilizers) or had contracted rubella (German measles) gave birth to children with "defects," doctors called for easing abortion laws.

Today, despite three decades of activism by the disability community, and substantial disability rights legislation, avoiding disability is an important factor in the use and regulation of abortion. In a 1992 Time/CNN survey, for example, 70 percent of respondents favored abortion if a fetus was likely to be born deformed.

This is the quandary we face: the choices we all seek to defend—choices individual women make about childbirth—can conflict with efforts to promote acceptance, equality, and respect for people with disabilities. I am inseparably committed to the empowerment of both people with disabilities and women. Therefore, my pro-choice stance must lie somewhere in the common ground between feminism and disability rights. I want to analyze social and scientific trends, and to vocalize my troubled feelings about where all of this may lead. I want to defy patriarchy's attempts to control women, and also to challenge an age-old bias against people with disabilities. I want to discuss the ethics of choice—without advocating restrictions on choice. To draw a parallel, feminists have no problem attacking sex-selective abortion used to guarantee giving birth to a child of the "right" sex (most often male), but we try to educate against the practice, rather than seek legislation.

In an effort to clarify my own thinking about these complex, interlocking issues, I have been reading and listening to the words of other disabled women. Diane Coleman, a Nashville-based disability rights organizer, is deeply concerned about the number of abortions based on fetal disability. Coleman sees this as "a way that society expresses its complete rejection of people with disabilities, and the conviction that it would be better if we were dead." I find myself sharing her indignation.

Julie Reiskin, a social worker in Denver who is active in both disability rights and abortion rights, tells me, "I live with a disability, and I have a hard time saying, 'This is great.' I think that the goal should be to eliminate disabilities." It jars me to hear this, but Reiskin makes a further point that I find helpful. "Most abortions are not because there's something wrong with the fetus," she says. "Most abortions are because we don't have decent birth control." In other words, we should never have to use fetal disability as a reason to keep abortion legal: "It should be because women have the right to do what we want with our bodies, period," says Reiskin.

We are a diverse community, and it's no surprise to find divergent opinions on as difficult an issue as abortion. Our personal histories and hopes, viewed through the lens of current circumstances, shape our values and politics. Like all the women I interviewed, I must be guided by my own experiences of living with disability. At two years old, I still could not walk. Once I was diagnosed—I have a rare neuromuscular condition—doctors told my parents that I would live only another year or two. Don't bother about school, they advised; just buy her a few toys and make her comfortable until the end.

My parents ignored the doctors' advice. Instead of giving up on me, they taught me to read. They made sure I had a child-size wheelchair and a tricycle. My father built a sled for me, and when the neighborhood kids went to the park to fly downhill in fresh snow, he pulled me along. My mother performed much of my physical care, but was determined not to do all of it; college students helped out in exchange for housing. She knew that her own wholeness and my future depended on being able to utilize resources outside our home.

Now my life is my own. I have a house, a career, a partner, and a community of friends with and without disabilities. I rely on a motorized wheelchair for mobility, a voice-activated computer for my writing, and the assistance of Medicaid-funded attendants for daily needs—dressing, bathing, eating, going to the bathroom. I manage it all according to my own goals and needs.

My life contradicts society's stereotypes about how people with disabilities live. Across the country, thousands of other severely disabled people are working, loving, and agitating for change. I don't mean to paint a simplistic picture. Most of us work very hard to attain independence, against real physical and/or financial obstacles. Too many people are denied the kind of daily in-home assistance that makes my life possible. Guaranteeing such services has become a top priority for the disability rights movement.

Changes like these, amounting to a small revolution, are slow to reach the public consciousness. Science, on the other hand, puts progress into practice relatively quickly. Prenatal screening seems to give pregnant women more power—but is it actually asking women to ratify social prejudices through their reproductive "choices"? I cannot help thinking that in most cases, when a woman terminates a previously wanted pregnancy expressly to avoid giving birth to a disabled child, she is buying into obsolete assumptions about that child's future. And she is making a statement about the desirability or the relative worth of such a child. Abortion based on disability results from, and in turn strengthens, certain beliefs: children with disabilities (and by implication adults with disabliities) are a burden to family and society; life with a disability is scarcely worth living; preventing the birth is an act of kindness; women who bear disabled children have failed.

Language reinforces the negativity. Terms like "fetal deformity" and "defective fetus" are deeply stigmatizing, carrying connotations of inadequacy and shame. Many of us have been called "abnormal" by medical personnel, who view us primarily as "patients," subject to the definitions and control of the medical profession. "Medical professionals often have countless incorrect assumptions about our lives," says Diane Coleman. "Maybe they see us as failures on their part." As a result, doctors who diagnose fetuses with disabilities often recommend either abortion or institutionalization. "I really haven't heard very many say, 'It's O.K. to have a disability, your family's going to be fine," Coleman says.

The independent living movement, which is the disabled community's civil rights movement, challenges this medical model. Instead of locating our difficulties within ourselves, we identify our oppression within a society that refuses to accommodate our disabilities. The real solution is to change society—to ensure full accessibility, equal opportunity, and a range of community support services—not to attempt to eliminate disabilities.

The idea that disability might someday be permanently eradicated— whether through prenatal screening and abortion or through medical research leading to "cures"—has strong appeal for a society wary of spending resources on human needs. Maybe there lurks, in the back of society's mind, the belief—the hope?—that one day there will be no people with disabilities. That attitude works against the goals of civil rights and independent living. We struggle for integration, access, and support services, yet our existence remains an unresolved question. Under the circumstances, we cannot expect society to guarantee and fund our full citizenship.

My life of disability has not been easy or carefree. But in measuring the quality of my life, other factors—education, friends, and meaningful work, for example—have been decisive. If I were asked for an opinion on whether to bring a child into the world, knowing she would have the same limitations and opportunities I have had, I would not hesitate to say, "Yes."

I know that many women do not have the resources my parents had. Many lack education, are poor, or are without the support of friends and family. The problems created by these circumstances are intensified with a child who is disabled. No woman should have a child she can't handle or doesn't want. Having said that, I must also say that all kinds of women raise healthy, self-respecting children with disabilities, without unduly compromising their own lives. Raising a child with disabilities is difficult, but raising any child is difficult; just as you expect any other child to enrich your life, you can expect the same from a child with disabilities. But the media often portray raising a child with disabilities as a personal martyrdom. Disabled children, disabled *people*, are viewed as misfortunes.

I believe the choice to abort a disabled fetus represents a rejection of children who have disabilities. Human beings have a deep-seated fear of confronting the physical vulnerability that is part of being human. This terror has been dubbed "disabiliphobia" by some activists. I confront disabiliphobia every day: the usher who gripes that I take up too much room in a theater lobby; the store owner who insists that a ramp is expensive and unnecessary because people in wheelchairs never come in; the talk-show host who resents the money spent to educate students with disabilities. These are the voices of an age-old belief that disability compromises our humanity and requires us to be kept apart and ignored.

Disabiliphobia affects health care reform too. In the proposed Clinton health plan only people disabled through injury or illness—not those of us with congenital disabilities—will be covered. Is this exclusion premised on the assumption that those of us born with disabilities have lesser value and that our needs are too costly?

People with severe disabilities do sometimes require additional resources for medical and support services. But disabiliphobia runs deeper than a cost-benefit analysis. Witness the ordeal of Bree Walker, a Los Angeles newscaster with a mild physical disability affecting her hands and feet. In 1990, when Walker became pregnant with her second child, she knew the fetus might inherit her condition, as had the first. She chose to continue the pregnancy, which led talk-show hosts and listeners to feel they had the right to spend hours debating whether Walker should have the child (most said no). Walker received numerous hostile letters. The callers and letter writers seemed to be questioning her right to exist, as well as her child's.

Walker's experience also pointed out how easily disabiliphobia slips from decisions about fetuses with disabilities to decisions about people with disabilities. That's why abortion is an area where we fear that the devaluation of our lives could become enshrined in public policy. Pro-choice groups must work to ensure that they do not support legislation that sets different standards based on disability.

A case in point is Utah's restrictive 1991 antiabortion law (which has since been declared unconstitutional). The law allowed abortions only in cases of rape, incest, endangerment of the woman's life, a profound health risk to the woman—or "fetal defect." According to Susanne Millsaps, director of Utah's NARAL affiliate, some disability rights activists wanted NARAL and other pro-choice groups to join in opposing the "fetal defect" exemption. The groups did not specifically take a stand on the exemption; instead they opposed the entire law. I would agree that the whole statute had to be opposed on constitutional and feminist grounds. But I would also agree that there should have been a stronger response to the fetal disability exemption.

To group "fetal defect" together with rape, incest, and life-endangering complications is to reveal deep fears about disability. As Barbara Faye Waxman, an expert on the reproductive rights of women with disabilities, says: "In this culture, disability, in and of itself, is perceived as a threat to the welfare of the mother. I find that to be troublesome and offensive."

There is more at stake here than my feelings, or anyone else's, about a woman's decision. Rapidly changing reproductive technologies, combined with socially constructed prejudices, weigh heavily on any decision affecting a fetus with possible disabilities. While some women lack basic prenatal and infant care, huge amounts of money are poured into prenatal screening and genetic research. Approximately 450 disorders can now be predicted before birth. In most cases the tests reveal only the propensity for a condition, not the condition itself. The Human Genome Project aims to complete the DNA map, and to locate hundreds more physical and developmental attributes. There is little public debate about the worth or ultimate uses of this federally funded multibillion-dollar program. But there are issues with regard to abortion that we can no longer afford to ignore:

- Does prenatal screening provide more data for women's informed choices, or does it promote the idea that no woman should risk having a disabled child?
- Who decides whether a woman should undergo prenatal screening, and what she should do with the results?
- Are expensive, government-funded genetic research projects initiated primarily for the benefit of a society unwilling to support disability-related needs?
- Is society attempting to eradicate certain disabilities? Should this ever be a goal? If so, should all women be expected to cooperate in it?

The January/February 1994 issue of *Disability Rag & Resource*, a publication of the disability rights movement, devoted several articles to genetic screening. In one, feminist lawyer Lisa Blumberg argues that women are being coerced into accepting prenatal tests, and then pressured to terminate their pregnancies when disabling conditions appear likely. "Prenatal testing has largely become the decision of the doctor," Blumberg writes, and "the social purpose of these tests is to reduce the incidence of live births of people with disabilities."

A woman faced with this choice usually feels pressure from many directions. Family, friends, doctors, and the media predict all kinds of negative results should her child be disabled. At the same time, she is unlikely to be given information about community resources; nor is she encouraged to meet individuals who have the condition her child might be born with. This lack of exposure to real-life, nonmedical facts about living with a disability should make us wonder whether women are really making "informed" choices about bearing children with disabilities.

Few outside the disability community have dealt with these issues in any depth. "We are all aware of the potential for abuses in reproductive technology and in genetic testing," says Marcy Wilder, legal director for NARAL's national office in Washington, D.C. "I don't see that there have been widespread abuses—but we're certainly concerned." That concern has not led to any coalition-building with disability rights groups, however.

Many feminist disability rights activists report chilly responses when they attempt to network with pro-choice groups. Too often, when we object to positions that implicitly doubt the humanity of children born disabled, we are accused of being anti-choice. One activist I know recently told me about her experience speaking at a meeting of a National Organization for Women chapter. She mentioned feeling discomfort about the widespread abortion of disabled fetuses—and was startled by the members' reactions. "They said, 'How could you claim to be a feminist and pro-choice and even begin to think that there should be any limitations?' I tried to tell them I don't think there should be limitations, but that our issues need to be included."

On both sides, the fears are genuine, rational, and terrifying—if not always articulated. For the pro-choice movement, the fear is that questioning the motives and assumptions behind any reproductive decision could give ammunition to antiabortionists. Defenders of disability rights fear that the widespread use of prenatal testing and abortion for the purpose of eliminating disability could inaugurate a new eugenics movement. If we cannot unite and find ways to address issues of reproductive screening and manipulation, we all face the prospect that what is supposed to be a private decision—the termination of a pregnancy—might become the first step in a campaign to eliminate people with disabilities.

I am accusing the pro-choice movement not of spurring these trends, but of failing to address them. Most pro-choice organizations do not favor the use of abortion to eliminate disabilities, but their silence leaves a vacuum in which fear of disability flourishes.

Disabiliphobia and the "genetics enterprise," as activist Adrienne Asch calls it, have also had legal implications for the reproductive rights of all women. The tendency to blame social problems such as poverty and discrimination on individuals with disabilities and their mothers has made women vulnerable to the charge that they are undermining progress toward human "perfectibility"—because they insist on a genuine choice. Some legal and medical experts have developed a concept called "fetal rights," in which mothers can be held responsible for the condition of their unborn or newborn children. According to Lisa Blumberg, "fetal rights" could more accurately be called "fetal quality control." For women with hereditary disabilities who decide to have children this concept is nothing new. Society and medical professionals have often tried to prevent us from bearing and raising children. Disabled women know, as well as anyone, what it means to be deprived of reproductive choice. More broadly, decisions involving our health care, sexuality, and parenting have been made by others based on assumptions about our inabilities and/or our asexuality.

The right to control one's body begins with good gynecological care. Low income, and dependence on disability "systems," restrict access to that care. Like many women of disability, my health care choices are limited by the accessibility of medical facilities, and by providers' attitudes toward disability and their willingness to accept the low reimbursement of Medicaid. And Medicaid will not cover most abortions, a policy that discriminates against poor women and many women with disabilities.

Paradoxically, policy is often undermined by practice. Although public funding rarely pays for abortions, many women with disabilities are encouraged to have them—even when they would prefer to have a child. Doctors try to convince us an abortion would be best for "health reasons"—in which case, Medicaid will pay for it after all. "Abortions are easier for disabled women to get," says Nancy Moulton, a health care advocate in Atlanta, "because the medical establishment sees us as not being fit parents." Most women grow up amid strong if subtle pressures to become mothers. For those of us with disabilities, there is an equal or greater pressure to forgo motherhood. This pressure has taken the form of forced sterilization, lost custody battles, and forced abortion.

Consequently, for women with disabilities, reproductive freedom means more than being able to get an abortion. It is hard for many of us to relate to those in the reproductive rights movement whose primary concern is keeping abortions legal and available. But I believe our different perspectives on reproductive freedom are fundamentally compatible, like variations on a single theme.

Whatever the reason, feminist organizations seem inclined to overlook disability concerns. Feminist speakers might add "ableism" to their standard list of offensive "isms," but they do little to challenge it. Now more than ever, women with disabilities need the feminist movement's vigorous support. We need you to defend our rights as if they were your own—which they are. Here are a few suggestions:

- Recognize women with disabilities' equal stake in the pro-choice movement's goals. That means accepting us as women, not dismissing us as "other," or infirm, or genderless. Recognize us as a community of diverse individuals whose health needs, lifestyles, and choices vary.

- Defend all our reproductive rights: the right to appropriate education about sexuality and reproduction; to gynecological care, family planning services, and birth control; the right to be sexually active; to have children and to keep and raise those children, with assistance if necessary; and the right to abortion in accessible facilities, with practitioners who are sensitive to our needs.

- Remove the barriers that restrict the access of women with disabilities to services. Help to improve physical accessibility, arrange disability awareness training for staff and volunteers, and conduct outreach activities to reach women with disabilities.

- Continue struggling to build coalitions around reproductive rights and disability issues. There is plenty of common ground, although we may have to tiptoe through dangerous, mine-filled territory to get to it.

- Question the assumptions that seem to make bearing children with disabilities unacceptable.

Despite our rhetoric, abortion is not strictly a private decision. Individual choices are made in a context of social values; I want us to unearth, sort out, and appraise those values. I wouldn't deny any woman the right to choose abortion. But I would issue a challenge to all women making a decision whether to give birth to a child who may have disabilities.

The challenge is this: consider all relevant information, not just the medical facts. More important than a particular diagnosis are the conditions awaiting a child—community acceptance, access to buildings and transportation, civil rights protection, and opportunities for education and employment. Where these things are lacking or inadequate, consider joining the movement to change them. In many communities, adults with disabilities and parents of disabled children have developed powerful advocacy coalitions. I recognize that, having weighed all the factors, some women will decide they cannot give birth to a child with disabilities. It pains me, but I acknowledge their right and their choice.

Meanwhile, there is much work still to be done.

65

FEAR TO JOY
Fighting the Klan

MAB SEGREST

I am proud to be speaking today as a lesbian on this panel, "Spinning Threads of Women's Movement." We have been asked to address problems identified with our "societies" as well as solutions, strategies, and visions arising from the struggle with those problems.

As a lesbian, of course, my "society" is different from that of others represented here; it is not based on racial, ethnic, or tribal identity, or a heritage passed through each generation by kinship ties. We lesbians are a people who must always reconstitute ourselves, who must find our own identities, and then go in search of our sisters each generation. In the process we are often cast out by our families and by institutions in the home cultures (such as the church) that other peoples rely on for protection and strength and continuity of struggle.

Reprinted by permission of *Sojourner: The Women's Forum*, November 1987. Originally presented at the National Women's Studies Association Convention, Spelman College, June 1987.

You may have detected that I also speak as a Southerner. Like Angela Davis [who also spoke at NWSA] I was growing up in Alabama when four Black girls, three of them my age, were blown up in a church in Birmingham. And that experience, as well as many others like it in Alabama during those years, informs what I have to say.

Meeting here in Atlanta, lesbians don't have to look far for a problem encountered by our culture. Last summer, in *Hardwick v. Bowers,* the U.S. Supreme Court upheld the constitutionality of sodomy statutes used to oppress homosexuals in half of the states. The case originated with the arrest of Michael Hardwick, a gay man, in his own home here in Atlanta. Mr. Bowers is the attorney general of the State of Georgia. The majority decision of the justices made it clear that the right of lesbians and gay men to physical, passionate expressions of love is not included in the "concept of ordered liberty upon which this country's history and traditions are based." As Chief Justice Burger explained: "Decisions of individuals relating to homosexual conduct have been subject to state intervention throughout the history of Western civilization." Our mere "personal preferences," according to the justices, have little weight against a "millennia of moral teaching" and the "legislative authority of the state." In other words, I speak to you today as a felon in the state of Georgia, and in the state of North Carolina, which is my home. I consider that a problem.

And it is a problem—this antipathy of Western civilization to my "society"—that I share with every other woman on this panel: being on the death list in the United States. It is one of the common threads with which we are spinning movement. The same Constitution that protected slavery (counting Africans as three-fifths human for the purpose of determining propertied white male votes) protects the institution of heterosexual marriage. The same country whose slave codes once prohibited marriage between slaves and broke up and sold down the river the families of Africans, last year upheld the sodomy laws that give lesbians in this room no right to "family relationships, marriage, or procreation." The same Western tradition that arrived on this shore with guns and armor and began decimating native peoples finds lesbians anathema as well. Let me make it clear that I am not saying anything else was like slavery in our history. I am saying that conquerors employ similar tactics on populations they want to control or destroy: they go for the heart.

The Klan/Nazi Movement

In 1983, I saw this repressive climate working itself out in North Carolina in deadly ways. Organizers from the National Anti-Klan Network and Klanwatch reported that North Carolina has the worst Klan/Nazi problem in the United States. Nazi paramilitary troops were marching through Carolina towns to the strains of "Dixie" and Wagner; Klan/Nazi leaders

were running for public office, using free television to purvey the rawest bigotries and legitimize deadly ideologies; they were amassing legal and illegal
weapons, openly working for an Aryan revolution that would eliminate
every non-Aryan person from the face of the globe. All of this was happening within a vacuum of official response. In fact, when concerned citizens
presented the governor's representative with evidence of this resurgence
and a crisis in racist violence, he looked them in the face and said, "It's not
the responsibility of the state to uphold the law." The racism, homophobia,
anti-Semitism, antifeminism, and antilabor bigotries of the Klan/Nazi
movement found resonances with a North Carolina political culture that
elected Jesse Helms and helped create Jerry Falwell. And this Nazi/Klan
resurgence is not just happening in North Carolina or in the South. It's happening all over the country. It's not where you are. It's what you see.

The situation presented an opportunity for strong coalition work,
because Nazis do not make the subtle distinctions about differences between
us that we sometimes make. Their motto, in the words of a song sung by
Tom Metzger's White Aryan Resistance in California:

> Gas 'em all, gas 'em all, we're coming to power
> Gas a Jew every hour
> What the hell, gas 'em all.

I had this interchangeability of target groups pointed out to me when I
got a phone call from our number one Nazi in North Carolina. I had just
gone on TV to say, "Arrest this man."

He said, "Ms. Segrest, I am writing an article on you for my newspaper,
and I want to know more about your background. Is your Jewish origin from
New York or Miami?"

I hung up on him. Now I was raised Methodist, but I was proud to be
mistaken for a Jew—especially in that situation. I mainly thought: "No, you
sorry shit, I'm a lesbian. And boy, do you have bad intelligence!"

Beyond Consciousness

When I went to my first anti-Klan meeting in 1983, I was chiefly concerned
with being included as a lesbian in the efforts. I did not imagine then that I
would end up one of the people leading the charge. In 1985, I became a paid
organizer, coordinating an organization we put in place to deal with this
resurgence.

I had found myself both inspired by and frustrated with the lesbian-
feminist movement within which I had been working. I had heard Barbara
Smith say too often, "I don't live in the women's movement. I live on the
streets of North America." I had sat in many rooms and participated in
many conversations between lesbians about painful differences of race and

class, about anti-Semitism and ageism and able-bodiedism. They had been hard discussions, but they had given me some glimpse of the possibility of spinning a wider lesbian movement, a women's movement that truly incorporates diversity as strength. But in all those discussions, difficult as many of them were, we had never been out to kill each other. In the faces of Klan and Nazi men—and women—in North Carolina I saw people who would kill us all. I felt I needed to shift from perfecting consciousness to putting consciousness to the continual test of action. I wanted to answer a question that had resonated through the lesbian writing I had taken most to heart: "What will you undertake?"

At this point, none of my old buttons would do. I had a friend make me new ones. The first said, "Race Traitor." The second, "Pre-Mature Anti-Fascist." I also added another question to "What will you undertake?" and that is, "What will you accomplish?" I have had to learn to think in terms of goals and the strategies to achieve them.

So we wanted to stop the Klan in North Carolina. First we had to prove the extent of the problem through monitoring and research. Then we had to raise public consciousness through the media, and through going anywhere that any group asked us to speak. Then we had to try to focus that public consciousness on public officials—on law enforcement to actively seek convictions where there is clear lawbreaking; on the governor to take a stand as the highest elected official in the state. At the same time, we worked with victims and communities to ensure that those who had been attacked did not remain vulnerable and isolated.

I have been surprised, frankly, how much we have been able to accomplish in four years: today over 25 Klanspeople/Nazis have been convicted or pled guilty to crimes ranging from civil rights violations to paramilitary organizing to perjury. The governor has appointed a task force to deal with racial and ethnic violence. And we have models of how to work to deal with victim/communities "when the Klan comes to town."

The additional problem that I set for myself was: how much of this organizing could I do openly as a lesbian, and one, *stay alive,* and two, not be kicked out by the straight people I worked with. I felt that more models were needed of out lesbians doing work on progressive issues. I also didn't want the larger movement to have it both ways: homophobia is not important, but if you come out it will destroy our work.

In the past three years, I have often resisted my impulse to screech up to the phone booth in front of the Gulf pumps at dusk at the country grocery store full of stale moon-pies and no-telling-who-else, to call Barbara Smith and say: "Well, here I am girl. What do I do next?" But I would generally go inside and buy a moon-pie and a Coca-Cola, and my head would clear immediately so I'd know what to do.

In working with heterosexuals I wasn't sure I would have allies who would understand my vulnerability as a lesbian. It was a leap of faith that was entirely justified. I learned that when the chips were down the best het-erosexuals came through. When I was hired by a board of ten straight peo-ple, eight of whom were Black, two of those preachers, I explained how I was a homosexual felon with a "profile as an activist" and got hired any-way. My employment came with the organization's commitment to work on homophobic issues, something no other organization that works on Klan/Nazi issues, state or national, has yet done. The real test came when opposition from "my side" finally crystallized, as I pushed an affiliate orga-nization to deal with gay/lesbian issues. Its director (now its former direc-tor, a white woman) sat across a kitchen table at the home of a Klan victim and explained how she had dragged her feet about the organization's tak-ing a stand on antigay violence because she didn't want to "encourage homosexuality." And my friend whose home it was, a white woman in her fifties who had bought the house out of weekly savings from her salary as a waitress, stayed in the room when everyone else split. I said, "It's not about heroin, it's about the right of people not to be hurt and killed because of who they love," and my friend—whose life had been threatened because of her love for a Black man, but who often was afraid to speak because she had been beaten by the white men in her family—said, "That's right." I got back to Durham and reported the conversation to a Black woman friend also involved in the work. She said: "This homophobia is like racism. It's got to be opposed." And she helped me to raise the issue within the affili-ate organization.

Then, in 1986, the fundamentalist preachers of Durham launched an attack on the gay/lesbian community and on our progressive mayor be-cause he had signed a pro-gay proclamation. The campaign was fronted by two Black fundamentalist churches, although the impetus for it was com-ing from the Congressional Club and the Right. The Black women with whom I had worked for two years against racist violence came to me urg-ing, "We need to work on this issue now"—not only to oppose homopho-bia, but because they knew that they couldn't let the Black church become a front for fascism.

And when my lover, Barbara, and I found out she was pregnant through artificial insemination, the successful culmination of both of our longings for a child, I wrote to another friend, a Black minister and long-time freedom fighter, about my happiness and fears. I explained that the culture's concepts of family were as destructive as its concepts of race, as riddled with ownership. "But I feel very fierce, and hopeful, and deter-mined to take our happiness," I wrote him. "Because you are my friend, I wanted you to know." I mailed the letter, a bit apprehensive about whether he would prefer Leviticus and Paul to me. The very next time I saw him, he said immediately: "How's your family?" It took organizing against the Klan and Nazis to show me that lesbian space is, ultimately, the world.[1]

From Fear to Joy

Finally, I want to talk about fear and joy, since they are the emotions that have moved me most strongly over the past several years. First the fear. I am a person who, for much of my life, has been guided by fear. This philosophy brought me to my fear of Nazis. Since I was a little girl, I have had a fear of men in packs. One of my recurring nightmares is being chased by groups of men with weapons from hiding place to hiding place, none of which was ever safe. With the Greensboro Klan murders in 1979, followed by the Reagan administration, the pack took on a definite identity: storm troopers who busted down doors in the middle of the night to take people away. Within three years, there was a Nazi paramilitary organization within two hours of my home. What else could I do? I went into the task afraid that the work would increase my nightmares. I found it has diminished them. My experience was echoed in the experience of another white woman friend, at whose home a cross was burned because of an interracial relationship. After the first attack, she explained to me, sometimes she and her lover would wake up in the middle of the night, imagining flames at the window. But when a group of interracial couples who had all been attacked came together for support, her life changed. "After that," she said, "I began to believe that there are other people, real people, who felt like me. So the Klan—they might kill me—but they could never scare me like that again."

Organizing against the Klan and Nazis helped to open up a world beyond the fear of death: to turn me from fear to joy. The phrase came back to me like a boomerang I had thrown. "Go toward what you fear," I had told a friend who was still figuring if she could be a writer, in a long walk through the Chapel Hill campus. And a year or so later, in a poem by Jean Swallow in a journal, it came back: Yes, Mab, but what about the joy? So I put on my list: *fear of joy.*

And it was pure joy I felt as I talked with Annie through Barbara's stomach, and she kicked against my hand. Pure joy watching a body I had loved for years grow large with a little one we would love together for years to come. Pure joy—and tremendous relief—watching her head poke out into the immense new space as her birth team (two dykes and two faggots) at Durham County General Hospital wept and cheered; pure joy now as she rides my hip into Woolworths and we pick out a new rattle and diapers and pins.

And it was joy mixed with grief when the three of us returned home for my mother's funeral, at the saddest moment, to carry my lesbian family back into the old kinship circles—friends from the neighborhood, Sunday school teachers, cousins, sister and brother and their children—and find that finally, I had it all as home.

It is this finding our many ways home, this circling back with lesbian selves intact, to family or race or tribe or region, and carrying those selves into an increasingly rich lesbian culture, and an increasingly powerful women's movement and people's justice movement, that is our final answer to the death wish that the Klan and Nazis, and corporate boardrooms, and the Supreme Court, wish on us all.

NOTE

1. After I gave this talk, a Black lesbian shared with me her anger at these remarks. I had not acknowledged the fact that I could get this Black minister's approval as a white lesbian much sooner than she could as a Black lesbian.

66

STOPPING SEXUAL HARASSMENT
A Challenge for Community Education

ROBERT L. ALLEN

There can be little doubt that an important outcome of the 1991 Senate Judiciary Committee hearings has been growing public recognition of sexual harassment as a major social problem. Virtually the entire nation has engaged in the public discourse around this issue, and this engagement is to be welcomed.

Like many men in the aftermath of Anita Hill's testimony, I found myself hearing harrowing reports of sexual harassment from women relatives and friends who had previously felt constrained to remain silent. They told me of awful things that had been said or done to them, on the job or in the streets, sometimes recently and sometimes years ago. They spoke of their anger and humiliation, of their shame and feelings of self-blame, of their fear of the consequences of speaking out or rebuking their harassers. They experienced sexual harassment—the imposition of unwanted sexual attention—as a violation of their human dignity.

I listened and shared their outrage—but I also found myself recalling things I had said or done to women in the recent or distant past, and the recollections were sometimes distinctly discomforting. I think an important value of these exchanges was the opportunity for men to learn from the personal testimony of women they love and respect how widespread sexual harassment is. At the same time, the self-reflection and discussions among men that were sometimes provoked by the women's stories offered an opportunity for men to recognize that harassing behavior is not simply an aberration, nor is it exclusively the province of macho males; on the contrary, harassing behavior is something that many of us men have engaged in at some point, if not on the job, then on the streets or on campus or even in our homes. We knew what we were doing, because we knew the women involved were made to feel uncomfortable or humiliated by our words or actions.

Why did we do it? Why do men harass women? Why, until recently, was such behavior generally acceptable in our culture—that is, acceptable to men? Aside from punishment, what can be done to stop harassing behavior?

In this essay I want to raise two points for consideration as part of the discourse on sexual harassment.

First, sexual harassment should not be dismissed as aberrant behavior, as the macho mentality gone wild, or as the result of male biology or uncontrollable sexual desire. Sexual harassment, like child abuse and domestic violence, is an outgrowth of socialization into male and female gender roles in a sexist society. It is learned behavior.

Second, if harassment, abuse, and violence are forms of learned behavior, they can also be unlearned. I therefore argue that in addition to legal or punitive approaches to sexual harassment, it is imperative to adopt a preventive approach through community education. We must create an environment, not only in the workplace but in our communities generally, in which harassment, abuse, and violence are no longer tolerated because men and women understand the damage such behavior does to all of us. That means adopting a social change perspective critical of the values of the dominant culture, a culture that is premised on inequality.

Gender roles are not foreordained by our biology or our genes. We learn gender roles as part of our socialization into the culture. When a child is born, the first question inevitably asked is "Boy or girl?" Our response to the child is then mediated by our knowledge of its genitals, and it is *our* actions that tell the child its gender identity and the behavior appropriate to that identity.

In California I work with an organization called the Oakland Men's Project (OMP). Formed in 1979, OMP is a nonprofit multiracial organization of men and women devoted to community education around issues of male violence, sexism, racism, and homophobia. Over the years we have worked with thousands of boys and men (and girls and women) in high schools, church groups, colleges, prisons, community groups, and rehabilitation programs. We conduct workshops that involve interactive role playing and discussions that allow men and women to examine gender roles and the social training we get in this culture.

In our workshops we ask young people what they think it means to be a man or a woman. It is remarkable how consistently they express the same set of expectations about appropriate male and female behavior. Men are expected to be in control, tough, aggressive, independent, competitive, and emotionally unexpressive (with the exception of anger and sexual desire, which are allowable emotions for men). Women, on the other hand, are expected to be polite, dependent, emotional, and sexy, to take care of others, and not to be too smart or pushy. In recent years we have noticed that sometimes girls will challenge these role expectations and occasionally even a boy will object, but for the most part they remain widely accepted. Paul Kivel, who has summed up the experience of the Oakland Men's Project in his *Men's Work: How to Stop the Violence That Tears Our Lives Apart,* refers to these as "core expectations" that we all have, especially men, regarding appropriate male and female behavior.

How do young men learn these expectations? At OMP, to illustrate the socialization process, we use what we call role plays that dramatize common situations most boys and men have experienced. One of these involves an interaction between a father and his ten-year-old son, both played by facilitators. The son is sitting at home watching television when the father comes in from work, orders the boy to turn off the TV, and berates him for the messiness of the room. When the boy tries to explain that he was going to clean up later, the father tells him to shut up and stop making excuses. Then he shoves the son's report card in his face and demands to know why he got a D in math. The boy says he did the best he could. The father shames the son, telling him that he is stupid and that D stands for "dummy." The boy says that's not fair and begins to stand up. The father shoves him down, saying, "Don't you dare get up in my face, I didn't say you could go anyplace!" The boy is visibly upset and begins to cry. The father gets even more angry: "Now what? You're crying? You little mama's boy! You sissy! You make me sick. When are you going to grow up and start acting like a man?" The father storms out of the room.

When we do this role play, it gets the undivided attention of everyone in the room, especially the boys. Almost every young person has had the experience of being scolded and shamed by an adult. Most boys have had the experience of being humiliated by an older male and being told that they are not acting like men.

When we stop the role play, we ask the boys how it made them feel to witness this scene between the father and son. There may be a moment of embarrassed silence, but then the boys speak up and say it made them mad, upset, sad, etc. Often this is the first time they have articulated the feelings brought up by such an encounter, which sadly often replicates their own experience. Indeed, the power of this role play is that it is so familiar.

We ask the boys what messages such encounters send. They say things like, "A man is tough. A man is in control. A man doesn't cry. It's okay for a man to yell at someone. A man can take it. A man is responsible. A man is competent. A man doesn't take crap from anyone else." As they speak, we write their comments on a blackboard. Then we draw a box around the comments and label it the "Act Like a Man" box. Most males in this culture are socialized to stay in the box. We learn this from our fathers, older brothers, guys on the street, television, sports, movies, and so on. We may also learn it from our mothers and grandmothers, or from the reactions of girls in school. The fact is that this notion of manhood is so pervasive in our culture that everyone knows the role and anyone can teach it to a boy.

We ask the boys what happens if you step out of the box, if you stop acting tough enough or man enough. They reply that you get called names: sissy, wimp, nerd, fag, queer, mama's boy, punk, girl, loser, fairy. And what is the point of the name calling? The boys say that it is a challenge and you're expected to fight to prove that you're not what they called you. In other words, if challenged, boys are expected to fight to prove that they're in the box—that they're tough and not gay or effeminate. Homophobia and fear of being identified with women in any way are strong messages boys receive from an early age.

We also ask about expectations of female behavior. The young people say things like, "A girl should be polite and clean, she shouldn't argue, she's pretty, she doesn't fight or act too smart, she helps others, she's emotional." We ask what happens when a girl refuses to be submissive and dependent, when she's assertive and smart and doesn't kowtow to the boys. Again the reply is that she will be called names: bitch, tomboy, dyke, whore, ball-breaker, cunt. And what is the point of the name calling? To tell the girl she'd better start "acting right." In other words, the name calling is like a slap in the face, reducing the girl to a despised sexual object, with the purpose of humiliating her and intimidating her into resuming "acceptable" behavior. If a girl fights when called names, she may emerge the victor, but her very success raises questions about her femininity.

Though our forays into junior highs and high schools hardly constitute systematic research, again and again we find the same core expectations of acceptable male and female behavior among young people. As I have said, there is a growing tendency to question these expectations, especially among young women, but the grip of traditional roles remains very strong.

Our work at OMP involves challenging role expectations by showing that male and female behaviors are neither biologically determined nor a function of "human nature" but are learned from our interactions with significant others and from the culture at large. Our workshops and role plays give boys and girls and men and women a way of analyzing social roles, not abstractly, but by drawing insights from their own experiences. Moreover, we show that social interactions involve making choices, and that we can break free of old roles by supporting each other in changing our choices.

An important component of our work is to look at structural relationships of power and inequality in our society. We ask workshop participants to think about their experiences with different social groups and to tell us which groups they think are more powerful and which are less powerful. Most often this elicits statements to the effect that men as a group are more powerful than women as a group, whites more powerful than people of color, parents more powerful than children, teachers more powerful than pupils, the rich more powerful than the poor, straights more powerful than gays, bosses more powerful than workers, and so on. If we ask how these inequalities are maintained, we are told that it is done through laws, through rules and regulations, through discrimination and stereotypes, and ultimately through force and violence. Thus, despite our country's rhetoric of equality, experience teaches us that people are not treated equally, that we all have assigned places in the social hierarchy, and that violence is used to keep less powerful groups "in their place."

This violence takes many forms and is often legitimized through the process of blaming the victim. Consider the Rodney King case, in which the jury was told that the police officers thought he was dangerous because he was high on drugs and "out of control," and at the same time was persuaded that he was actually "in control," deliberately taunting and manipulating the officers. Either way, the message of this incredible argument was that Rodney King "deserved" the brutal beating he received and the policemen could be acquitted. Blaming victims for their own victimization is a widely employed means of justifying abuse and violence of all kinds.

Sexual harassment plays a part in reinforcing the power differential between men and women in our society, and that distinguishes it from flirtation or a simple mistake in judgment. For example, a man may harass a woman when she steps out of the role he expects her to play. In the workplace, "uppity" women who hold jobs traditionally held by men, or who are regarded as "too" assertive, competent, competitive, or emotionally reserved, are likely targets of harassment. Men may also harass women who are not "uppity" as a kind of ritual that confirms male dominance and female submissiveness. Thus, the female secretary or domestic worker may be "teased" or pinched or subjected to sexual remarks that serve to remind her of her low status and her vulnerability to men. She is expected to acquiesce in this treatment by laughing or otherwise acting as if the harassment is okay, thereby reaffirming the male's superior status and power. A woman worker may also be harassed by a male worker who is angry at the boss but fearful of the boss's power, and seeks to regain a sense of his own power by humiliating her.

Whether in the workplace or on the street, the purpose of sexual harassment is to reduce women to objects sexually vulnerable to men, and to reestablish the traditional power relationship between men and women. Indeed, women's sexual vulnerability to men is a key locus of male power, something men learn to expect. As boys we learn it from stories of sexual "conquest" we hear from older males; we learn it from films, magazines, pornography, advertising. We live in a capitalist culture that promises women's sexual availability as a reward to the male consumer of everything from cars to cigarettes. It is not surprising, then, that men come to believe that every woman should be sexually available to any man. Sexual harassment is both a manifestation and a reinforcement of an exploitive system in which men are socialized collectively and individually to expect to have power over women collectively and individually.

Moreover, of the thousands of women who experience sexual harassment every day, a great many of them are women of color and poor women employed in the jobs that racist and sexist discrimination forces them to take—as domestics, clerical workers, farm workers, sweatshop and factory workers. Not only are these women especially vulnerable to sexual harassment, they also have less access to the levers of power needed to seek redress. Often they do not report harassment because they fear revenge from their employers or know their complaints will be dismissed. They are doubly oppressed: subjected to abuse and then constrained to remain silent about it.

The nature of sexual harassment is such that it is particularly easy to blame the victims. Often there is a suggestion that the woman somehow provoked or invited the objectionable behavior by something she said or did, or simply the way she was dressed. And if she did not protest the behavior immediately, it is insinuated that she must have enjoyed it, and any subsequent protests are suspect. In any case, the female victim's character is called into question and the male harasser is conveniently let off the hook, again reinforcing male dominance.

Of course, all men don't engage in sexual harassment, but we must ask why men who witness it often fail to intervene. One reason is obvious: male bonding to maintain male dominance. Men who would not engage in harassing behavior themselves may condone it in others because they agree that women must be "kept in their place." A second reason is more hidden: men's fear of being shamed or even attacked by other men.

As boys, most men learn that other men are dangerous. How many of us were called names or beaten up by other males when we were young? How many of us were ridiculed and humiliated by fathers or older brothers or coaches or teachers? How many were sexually assaulted by another male? We protected ourselves in various ways. Some of us withdrew into the private world of our fantasies. Some of us became bullies. Some of us became alcoholics and addicts so we wouldn't have to feel the pain and fear. Most of us learned to camouflage ourselves: we took on the coloration of the men we feared, and we hoped that no one would challenge us. We never talked about our fear because that in itself was dangerous and could mark us as targets of ridicule or violence from other men.

Instead we learned to keep our fear inside, a secret. In fact, we learned to keep most of our emotions bottled up inside because any sincere expression of emotion in front of other men was risky business that set you up to be put down. Only one emotion was considered manly: anger. Some of us learned to take other feelings—pain, grief, sadness, shame, loneliness, depression, jealousy, helplessness, fearfulness—and translate them into anger, and then pass them on to someone weaker in the form of physical or psychological violence. The humiliation we experienced at work, the fear we experienced when hassled by cops, the grief we felt when a relationship ended, the helplessness we felt when we lost a job—we learned to take these feelings, roll them into a heavy fist of rage, and slam it into our wives, our children, our lovers, women on the job or on the streets, less powerful men.

Thus, women and children often live in fear of men, and men frequently live in fear of each other. Most of us men won't admit this, but deep inside we recognize that harassment, abuse, rape, and violence are not simply "women's issues"—they're our issues as well. We know, but seldom admit, that if we didn't constantly protect ourselves, other men would do to us what we all too often do to women and children—as men who have been imprisoned can attest. So those of us who are not abusers or harassers some-times wear the camouflage suits; we try to be "one of the boys." We present a front of manly power and control no matter what we may be feeling inside. We jostle and joke and push and shove, we make cracks about women and boast of our conquests, and we haze any guy who is different. We go along with harassers so as not to expose our own vulnerability, our fear of being shamed by other men—the weak point in our male armor.

Nevertheless, men have a stake in challenging sexual harassment, abuse, violence, and the sexist role training that underpins these behaviors. In the first place, men are not unconnected to women. We form a community of men and women—and children—together. A woman who suffers harass-ment might be my mother, my sister, my niece. She might be your daughter or your sister or your wife. A woman who is harassed, abused, or raped is part of a community that includes male relatives, lovers, and friends who are also hurt by the injury done to her. Men have a stake in stopping the abuse because it is directed against women we love and cherish.

I would argue that men have a further stake in challenging sexual abuse and the sexism on which it is based. Men are also damaged by sexism. A sys-tem that requires us to act as though we are always in control and to repress our emotions takes a heavy toll. It undermines our sense of authenticity. It results in a loss of intimacy with women and children. It conceals but does not change our fear of other men. It produces stress that is hazardous to our health and shortens our life spans. It makes us sick in our souls and bodies, and it turns us into enemies of those we love and of ourselves.

Historically, Black men and women in America have been victims of especially brutal and systematic violence. In the past our community has been terrorized by the lynching (and castration) of thousands of Black men by white men, and the rape (and lynching) of thousands of Black women by white men. Today white mob violence and police brutality continue unabated. African American men know intimately the violent capabilities of other men. It is a tragedy that many of us have internalized the violence of this oppressive system and brought it into our communities and our homes. The injuries done by racism to Black men's self-esteem are sometimes dev-astating, but the expectations of manhood we have learned block us from revealing or acknowledging our pain. Instead, we too often transform it into rage and violence against those we love. This must stop. African American men, as frequent victims of white male violence, have a particular stake in standing with women and children against all forms of violence.

How can men of all races be brought into the struggle against harassment, abuse, and violence? That is the question we have been seeking to answer through our work at the Oakland Men's Project. We have learned that it is extremely important for men to begin talking with each other about these issues. In our experience we have seen that there are growing numbers of men who are critical of sexism. All too often, however, these men as individuals are isolated and fearful of raising their concerns with other men. It is time for men who want to stop the violence to reach out to other men and break through the barrier of fear that has silenced us.

This is not an easy task, but as we have learned at OMP, it can be done. The male sex role, with its insistence on emotional "coolness" and reserve, makes open and honest communication from the heart difficult between men. We can begin to break through this isolation by sharing the often painful and humiliating ways we were socialized into the male role as young boys. At OMP we have found that workshops using interactive role plays, like the father-son encounter described earlier, are an effective method of opening up communication between men. Such techniques enable us to examine how the male sex role often sets men up to be dominating, controlling, and abusive. In another role play we watch a bully harassing the new boy at school. We discuss what the bully gains or fails to gain by bullying. For example, the bully may be seeking to compel respect from the victim, but what the victim often feels is contempt. At the same time, the bully models abusive behavior for the victim. He fails to get what he wants, but he may teach the victim how to bully someone else.

Through role plays like these, we look at how men are trained to take the hurt that has been done to them, translate it into anger, and direct the anger at a weaker person in the form of violence. This is the cycle of violence. We see it, for example, in the fact that the great majority of child abusers were themselves abused as children.

Another role play we use recreates a high school dating scene in which a boy and his girlfriend are sitting in his car in a secluded spot at night. We recruit two students from the audience to play the roles. We tell them that the boy wants to have sex that night but the girl, although she likes him, does not. Then we ask them to play out the scene. Sometimes the two actors work out a resolution acceptable to both. Sometimes the girl gets out of the car and walks away. But often the tension simply builds as the boy attempts to dominate and get his way while the girl tries to be responsive without giving in to his demands. We stop the role play and talk with the actors about the pressures they felt to behave as they did in the situation. We relate these pressures to the male and female role expectations discussed earlier. We also talk about the risk of the situation escalating into violence and rape, and the need to recognize danger signs to prevent this from happening. (For other examples of role plays and antiviolence exercises for teens, see *Helping Teens Stop Violence,* by Allan Creighton and Paul Kivel.)

Interrupting the cycle of violence requires that we unlearn sex roles that set us up to be perpetrators and victims of abuse. I am not talking only about men who are harassers or batterers, or women who have been abused. I believe that in this culture most of us are at risk for abusive behavior because most of us have been socialized into traditional sex roles. The cycle of abuse and violence can be broken at its root by challenging those roles and the institutions that support them—that is, through a process of community education and social change.

It is important for men of all races to become involved in this process. Men can take responsibility for stopping the cycle of violence and offering alternatives to violence. Men working with boys can model supportive ways of interacting and constructive methods of using anger to bring about change. All of us constantly make choices about how we relate to others, and in the power of choice is the power of change, for we are not simply passive victims of our socialization. For African American men there is a special urgency to this work. Our sons are dying in record numbers, often at each other's hands in angry acts of violence whose goal is to prove their manhood. We need to be clear that anger itself is not the problem. In a racist society Black people and other people of color have good reason to be angry. The problem lies in how the anger is expressed. Turning the anger against ourselves or others in acts of abuse and violence is self-destructive. Using righteous anger to challenge racist and oppressive institutions empowers individuals and communities, creates the possibility of real change, and builds self-esteem. Black men's organizations such as Simba, the Omega Boys' Club, and 100 Black Men of America are helping to develop new models of manhood among teenage Black males. We need organizations like these in every city.

Equally important, men working together can model a new version of power—*power with* others to make change, as opposed to *power over* others to perpetuate domination. In our society power generally means the ability to control others directly, with violence as the ultimate means of control. Men are socialized to exercise this form of power in all their relationships. Women sometimes learn to do the same. But this kind of power necessarily sets up conflicts with others—those we seek to control—and is alienating and isolating for the individual power holder. Power *with* others breaks down the isolation we feel and makes it possible to relate as allies rather than as competitors or opponents. It allows us to recognize that we are a community of people—men, women, and children—who are interdependent.

All of us have had the experience of powerlessness, for all of us have been children. As children we learned what it meant to be controlled by others, and often we learned what it meant to be humiliated and shamed by others. Such experiences are painful, and we may prefer to forget them, but ironically, by "owning" them, we create the possibility of empowerment through establishing our connection with others who have had similar experiences. In this way it becomes possible for men to become allies of women and children, not out of guilt, but through insight into their own lives.

Harassment, abuse, and violence arise from a system of sexual and racial inequality. To stop them we must challenge the gender roles, institutions, and power structures upon which sexism and racism stand. This is a big task, but it is one each of us can undertake in small ways—in our homes, in our schools, in our communities. We can educate ourselves and offer our children new models of male and female behavior. We can support each other in finding healing responses to the pain and hurt we have suffered. We can insist that the schools educate young people about empowering ways to counter sexism and racism. We can confront institutionalized oppression and violence. We can support movements and organizations that work for progressive social change. In sum, working together with others as allies, we can build community responses to the system of inequality and the cycle of violence that blight our lives.

REFERENCES

Beneke, Timothy. *Men on Rape: What They Have to Say about Sexual Violence.* New York: St. Martin's Press, 1982.

Bravo, Ellen, and Ellen Cassedy. *The 9 to 5 Guide to Combatting Sexual Harassment.* New York: John Wiley and Sons, 1992.

Chrisman, Robert, and Robert L. Allen, eds. *Court of Appeal: The Black Community Speaks Out on the Racial and Sexual Politics of Thomas vs. Hill.* New York: Ballantine Books, 1992.

Creighton, Allan, with Paul Kivel. *Helping Teens Stop Violence: A Practical Guide for Parents, Counselors, and Educators.* Alameda, Calif.: Hunter House, 1992.

Hagan, Kay Leigh, ed. *Women Respond to the Men's Movement.* San Francisco: HarperCollins, 1992.

Hemphill, Essex, ed. *Brother to Brother: New Writings by Black Gay Men.* Boston: Alyson Publications, 1991.

Jackson, Walter H. *Sporting the Right Attitude: Surviving Family Violence.* Los Angeles: Self Expansion, 1992.

Kaufman, Michael, ed. *Beyond Patriarchy: Essays by Men on Pleasure, Power, and Change.* New York: Oxford University Press, 1987.

Kimmel, Michael S., ed. *Men Confront Pornography.* New York: Meridian, 1990.

Kivel, Paul. *Men's Work: How to Stop the Violence That Tears Our Lives Apart.* Center City, Minn.: Hazelden, 1992.

Kunjufu, Jawanza. *Countering the Conspiracy to Destroy Black Boys.* Chicago: African American Images, 1985.

Lewis, Michael. *Shame: The Exposed Self.* New York: Free Press, 1992.

Madhubuti, Haki. *Black Men: Obsolete, Single, Dangerous?* Chicago: Third World Press, 1990.

Majors, Richard, and Janet Mancini Billson. *Cool Pose: The Dilemmas of Black Manhood in America.* New York: Lexington Books, 1992.

McGill, Michael E. *The McGill Report on Male Intimacy.* New York: Harper and Row, 1985.

Miedzian, Myriam. *Boys Will Be Boys: Breaking the Link between Masculinity and Violence.* New York: Doubleday, 1991.

Staples, Robert, ed. *The Black Family: Essays and Studies.* 4th ed. Belmont, Calif. Wadsworth, 1991.

Strauss, Susan, with Pamela Espeland. *Sexual Harassment and Teens: A Program for Positive Change.* Minneapolis: Free Spirit Publishing, 1992.

Wilkinson, Doris Y., and Ronald L. Taylor, eds. *The Black Male in America: Perspectives on His Status in Contemporary Society.* Chicago: Nelson-Hall, 1977.

Name Index

Subject Index